fifth edition

GLOBAL POLITICS

ORIGINS | CURRENTS | DIRECTIONS

ALLEN SENS
University of British Columbia

PETER STOETT
Concordia University

NELSON / EDUCATION

NELSON / EDUCATION

Global Politics: Origins, Currents, and Directions, Fifth Edition
by Allen Sens and Peter Stoett

Vice President, Editorial Higher Education:
Anne Williams

Executive Editor:
Anne-Marie Taylor

Marketing Manager:
Ann Byford

Developmental Editor:
Linda Sparks

Photo Researcher:
Melody Tolson

Permissions Coordinator:
Melody Tolson

Content Production Manager:
Hedy Sellers

Production Service:
Cenveo Publisher Services

Copy Editor:
Maria Jelinek

Proofreader:
Kavitha Ashok

Indexer:
BIM Indexing Services

Design Director:
Ken Phipps

Managing Designer:
Franca Amore

Interior Design:
Nelson Gonzalez

Cover Design:
Peter Papayanakis

Part Opener and Cover Image:
Willard Clay/Getty Images

Compositor:
Cenveo Publisher Services

Library and Archives Canada Cataloguing in Publication

Stoett, Peter John, 1965-, author

Global politics : origins, currents,
directions / Allen Sens,

Peter Stoett.—Fifth edition.

Includes bibliographical references
and index.
ISBN 978-0-17-650947-7 (pbk.)

1. World politics—1989–. 2.
Geopolitics. 3. International
economic relations. I. Sens, Allen
G. (Allen Gregory), 1964– author
II. Title.

D860.S45 2013
909.82'9   C2013-905698-X

ISBN-13: 978-0-17-650947-7
ISBN-10: 0-17-650947-X

For Pam and Cristina

Brief Contents

Detailed Contents

Preface

If teaching global politics is a challenging occupation, learning about global politics for the first time must be even more daunting. Few subjects are so interdisciplinary, requiring the level of command over history, geography, science, psychology, and politics that college and university courses demand of teachers and students alike. Many continuities and enduring concepts require careful historical exploration and theoretical elaboration, while current events and new research findings must be explained and understood in context. To make matters even more challenging for teachers and students, global politics is anything but a static subject, and the past 30 years have been particularly tumultuous. The collapse of the communist regimes in Eastern Europe and the disintegration of the Soviet Union brought a remarkably swift and dramatic end to an ideological, geopolitical, and military struggle that defined the post–World War II era. In the first decade of the 21st century, major events such as the terrorist attacks of September 11, 2001, the Iraq War of 2003, and the onset of a global recession in 2008 challenged us to grasp the complexities of a subject that displayed features of dramatic change as well as continuity, and trends of divergence as well as convergence.

The pace of developments has certainly not slowed in recent years. The global economy has been rocked by numerous crises, especially in Europe. Revolutions and uprisings in many Arab countries swept away or threatened established political orders in the Middle East and North Africa. A devastating tsunami in Japan precipitated the world's most serious nuclear accident since the Chernobyl disaster in 1986, leading to a global discussion of the future of nuclear power. Concern over the nuclear weapons ambitions of North Korea and Iran intensified. The growing economies of Brazil, Russia, India, and China (and others) inspired predictions of a global shift in political and economic power. A growing chorus of scientific warnings about the future of the environment failed to motivate countries to agree on concrete climate change mitigation efforts, despite a series of high-profile international conferences. All this, and so much more, makes the study of global politics exciting—and sometimes bewildering.

The word *globalization* is often used to define the new era that has emerged after the end of the Cold War, and although the word has its detractors, it does capture a sense of momentous change and uncertainty, and continues to resonate with a generation of students grappling with the reality that their lives are increasingly affected by world events and global trends. Students today have a heightened awareness of the threats to human society presented by militarism, poverty, intolerance, climate change, food insecurity, pandemics, and economic instability (to name a few global problems). They also share increased anxiety levels over the scale and scope of environmental degradation, and its growing impact on humans and ecosystems around the world. As a result, students do not want their comprehension of global issues stymied by traditional disciplinary barriers between the study of politics, economics, history, and culture, or between the social sciences and humanities and the physical and life sciences. Interdisciplinary (or even transdisciplinary) knowledge is more necessary than ever if we are to understand and address the global challenges of our time.

An additional challenge facing Canadian teachers and students of global politics is the scarcity of textbooks that are Canadian in orientation. Most international relations textbooks are American, and their examples focus almost exclusively on American foreign policy issues. One crucial function of the first four editions of this text was to relate the academic study of global politics to the lives of students who reside outside the United States. The fifth edition retains this basic philosophy, and the rationale for this new edition is largely practical: things change. It was necessary to update significant portions of the book, and although it is impossible to cover everything, our intent was to make the book as comprehensive and contemporary as possible, while retaining our appreciation of the necessity for a solid grounding in theory and history.

It is important to remind both teachers and students how the study and teaching of global politics was conducted in Canada a little over two decades ago. The Cold War between East and West dominated international politics and the attention of policymakers for more than 45 years. Scholars and their students focused on issues such as the strategic nuclear and military balance, nuclear arms control, the shifting tides of superpower diplomacy, the politics of alliances including NATO and the Warsaw Pact, and the extension of the Cold War rivalry into regional conflicts. The politics of the bipolar world also engaged many members of the public, as the superpower arms race sparked the development of a large peace and disarmament movement. It would be a mistake to argue that such Cold War issues excluded other global phenomena, since they occurred in a changing international context that included a growing and ever more integrated global economy; an increasing interdependence between societies and states; a growing divide between rich and poor societies, and between rich and poor within societies; the increased activity of non-state actors such as multinational corporations and non-governmental organizations; rapid technological advances; and a growing concern over environmental degradation. However, the politics of the superpower rivalry, attended by the threat of global nuclear war, was the primary subject of study for Canadian teachers and students.

Today, the focus of global politics has been reoriented toward a much broader set of issues. Beyond the end of the Cold War, the contextual shift that has occurred between 1997, when the first edition of this text was printed, and today (with nearly 30 000 copies sold in that time span) is tremendous. Perhaps the most visible shift that has occurred in the lives of students has been the electronic and information revolution, which has fundamentally changed the way communication and networking take place. Even in 1997 the Internet was dismissed as a fad by some prognosticators, and email was just beginning to dominate day-to-day communication (email is now being replaced by much more immediate messaging and social media tools). This has had a profound effect on the learning (and teaching) environment, as well as how global politics get done. We expand on this in Chapter 12.

But some of the dominant themes of our time are in fact much older issues that have been reconfigured by events and sea changes such as the communications revolution. These include efforts (often the object of vociferous protest) to manage the global economy, a vital subject to a trade-dependent state such as Canada. Of course, over 70 percent of Canadian trade is with the United States, so this relationship continues to dominate foreign policy discussions in Canada. But other issues of great concern to Canadians—armed conflicts, human rights violations, democratization, gender discrimination, the proliferation of conventional weapons and weapons of mass destruction, poverty and income inequality, threats to the global commons, refugee and population movements, and terrorism—all predate the end of the Cold War or the events of September 11, 2001. And so, in this text we have tried to situate the immense change occurring around us within an understanding of these elements of continuity.

The central aim of *Global Politics: Origins, Currents, and Directions* is to introduce readers to the rich and diverse experience that is the study of contemporary international relations, encouraging an appreciation of the theoretical roots of divergent perspectives on how the international system operates. The text also establishes the vital historical context in which the modern world is embedded, and intends to stimulate thoughtful analysis and critical thinking while promoting a healthy skepticism for established wisdom and prevailing assumptions. *Global Politics* also reveals the human element of international relations by providing insights and biographies of individuals who have made an impact on the world in which we live. Finally, this text was conceived from the beginning to reflect the contemporary global environment and the issues faced by today's scholars, policymakers, students, and citizens. To this end, *Global Politics* gives equal attention to the theoretical developments and historical events of the past, the key issues facing us today, and the emerging agenda that confronts us all. As the full title indicates, this book looks to the future as much as it looks to the past and the present. The book does not claim to be a crystal ball but it does identify trends and themes, and challenges the reader to think about the issues and theoretical approaches that loom on the horizon.

THE STRUCTURE OF THE BOOK

As our subtitle suggests, *Global Politics* is organized into three parts: *Origins*, *Currents*, and *Directions*. Part One, "Origins," examines the theoretical perspectives fundamental to any understanding of the debates and controversies in the discipline, and the historical evolution of the international system up to the end of the Cold War. The development of the key contending perspectives in international relations theory is discussed in historical context. Part One reveals how these contending perspectives tend to focus on different types of historical events or have different interpretations of history. For example, realists emphasize the history of empires, great powers, and wars, while liberals emphasize economic history and the development of interdependence. Critical theorists emphasize historical patterns of hierarchy and dominance and the processes that perpetuate poverty and disempowerment. In short, Part One looks at the history of war, the state, the Cold War, international political economy, international institutions, and law, and it gives us the theoretical background necessary to understand it.

In Part Two, "Currents," readers are introduced to some of the key issues on the contemporary security, economic, and ethical agendas. We look at today's varied conflict management efforts, the divisive impact of globalization on the world economy, and some principal human rights and human security questions. Part Two is designed to give the reader a snapshot of the contemporary international situation and an improved understanding of the issues that confront today's world. Key themes include armed conflict, weapons proliferation, terrorism, arms control, organized crime, humanitarian intervention, poverty and marginalization, relativist versus universalist conceptions of human rights, international criminal law, and many others.

In Part Three, "Directions," items of growing importance on the international agenda are explored. We begin with a discussion of contemporary global environmental problems and the long-term threats to human survival they pose. Next, we look at population growth and movements, global health issues, and the impact of the information revolution, looking toward possible future trends in all of these areas of study. These admittedly selective subjects are discussed because, in the view of the authors, they will dominate the future agenda of global politics over the long term, and presumably have a direct impact upon the lives of many, if not all, readers. Of course, all these issues are interlinked not only with each other but with the security, economy, and human rights contexts established in Part Two. Not all of them will affect Canadians directly, but the connections between Canada's future and the complex trends outside the country are genuine.

An overarching theme knits the subject matter of the book together. The past, present, and future of global politics can be characterized in terms of political *convergence* and *divergence*. Trends of convergence, or what some prefer to label *integration*, can be identified in economic globalization and interdependence; the development of international organizations and the expansion of international law; the growing volume of international communication and travel; the development of a global civil society of non-governmental organizations; efforts to promote and strengthen democratization; and reduced friction between the great powers. Trends of divergence, often termed *fragmentation*, can be identified in the divide between rich and poor and the information haves and have-nots; the disintegration of states; interstate and intrastate conflict; ethnic, religious, and factional tension and violence; the development of regional trading blocs; friction between world cultures; and the impact of environmental degradation as a cause of social tension or conflict. The convergence/divergence theme is revisited throughout the book.

NEW TO THE FIFTH EDITION

This edition continues to demonstrate our commitment to clarity and balance, two characteristics that are often lost in the conceptual fog of international relations and the emotive battleground of ideas. While we have retained what many readers have termed the helpful thematic/chronological structure of previous texts, the book has been thoroughly updated. This includes new treatments and references to theoretical material, as well as empirical updates on diplomatic relations, transnational movements, international organizations, peacekeeping operations, civil conflicts, and many other contemporary issues.

It is always a difficult decision: which major world events have most affected global politics since the previous edition? Many of these events were emerging when the fourth edition surfaced, but have become more pronounced since then. The global economic recession spread like wildfire, and the crises in Greece, Portugal, Spain, Ireland, and Italy have certainly reshaped how many view the prospects of the European Union. We've included a new section on human trafficking, one of the greatest human rights and women's rights issues today. Our discussion of information technology and global politics has deepened with continued advances in wireless and networking, with Wikileaks and other revelations about electronic surveillance. We've also deepened our discussions of global health governance, climate change science and diplomacy, refugee crises (for example, related to Syria), and many other burning issues of our time.

TO THE STUDENT

It is an exciting, and no doubt anxious, time to be studying global politics. You are part of a growing generation of students who have been exposed to a global political environment quite different from that faced by students of international relations during the Cold War, or even the pre-September 11 era. However, as you look to the future of the world in which you live, it would be wrong to ignore the past. Despite significant changes in the global political scene and heady advancements in technology and communications, in some respects little has changed. Many of the issues and problems that have plagued the world for decades and even centuries persist today. Discovering that a hot topic today was also a hot topic several generations ago can be humbling, but much can be understood from past events and from how current issues are both similar to and different from those events.

We began this preface by noting that the study of global politics is a demanding undertaking, for the subject matter is broad, deep, and multidimensional, and many points of dispute and controversy exist. It is tempting for students to focus on certain issues (the environment, war, or technology, for example) to the exclusion of others. However, this is a mistake, for virtually all subjects in global politics are closely related, and it is impossible to understand any one issue in isolation. Furthermore, an appreciation of different perspectives is an absolute must. Part of the challenge of any scholarly pursuit is to understand perspectives that differ from your own. When you do this, you gain in two ways: first, you improve your understanding of the basis for disagreements between individuals, groups, and states; and, second, you are forced to re-evaluate your own personal perspectives and beliefs. In some cases this process will cause you to change your mind, and in other cases it will not; but in any event, you will have gained a critical understanding of different views and ideas about the world and strengthened your own perspective.

This book is best treated as a guide through the interrelated subfields of global politics. It introduces the specialized terms and jargon international relations scholars use for different phenomena and contending perspectives. In each chapter we have put the significant terms, which are defined in the Glossary at the end of the book, in **bold** type. Of course, a large and rich literature exists on every subject discussed, and you may want to learn more about a certain topic or find materials for research papers. On the book's website, at http://www.nelson .com/site/globalpolitics5e, we supply a list of Suggested Readings and Internet Resources to assist you in this task. Further, take care to read the Endnotes section at the end of each chapter, for they include some of the better-known and valuable sources, and we do not list them all again in the online Suggested Readings.

Since it is intended as a guide, *Global Politics* is only an introduction to the vast field of international relations. Your instructor may cover other issues, and you may find that you or your instructor do not agree with many of the points made in this book. However, we have tried to be as inclusive and balanced as possible in presenting the subject matter. As individual authors, we differ on many aspects of our discipline and agree on many more. While it may be impossible to be completely balanced in such an undertaking (as we learned from preliminary reviews of the several editions), we have tried to incorporate as many diverse perspectives as possible while retaining the content traditionally expected in an international relations textbook. Ultimately, it is up to you to develop your own informed opinions and ideas. We would both be very interested in any comments regarding the present edition, and invite readers to email us with them at

peter.stoett@concordia.ca

asens@mail.ubc.ca

Since we completed our bachelor's and master's degrees in the late 1980s and obtained our doctorates in the early to mid-1990s at Canadian universities, our careers as students and professionals straddle the Cold War and post-Cold War eras. Our studies have taken us to Western and Eastern Europe, Africa, northern and southern Asia, Central and South America, and of course the United States. We have made our homes in Vancouver and Montreal. Our experience is one of change and flux, and we, like you, look to the future with excitement and deep concern. We hope this experience and dedication gives us ample qualifications for authorship of a text on global politics, and we hope you are inspired to pursue similar paths of discovery and engagement after reading *Global Politics: Origins, Currents, and Directions*.

ACKNOWLEDGMENTS

Many friends, colleagues, and scholars have contributed to the development, writing, and editing of this book. It would be impossible to list all those who have touched our lives and work in meaningful ways over the years, so any attempt that follows is necessarily partial.

We would like to thank the following colleagues whose expertise and assistance have been invaluable: Abbie Bakan, Robert Boardman, Max Cameron, Katharina Coleman, Andrew Cooper, David Cox, Simon Dalby, Gerald Dirks, Bill Graf, David Haglund, Kal Holsti, Horst Hutter, Rosalind Irwin, Bob Jackson, Brian Job, Eric Laferrière, Jayent Lele, Jorge Nef, Kim Richard Nossal, Kwasi Obu-Fari, Charles Pentland, Richard Price, Norrin Ripsman, Patricia Romano, Heather Smith, Lisa Sundstrom, Yves Tiberghien, Claire Turenne Sjolander, Henry Wiseman, and Mark Zacher. Our apologies to the many we have left off our list.

We owe special thanks to the many reviewers commissioned by Nelson Education, including Amanda Burgess, University of Windsor; Glenn Goshulak, York University; Annette Isaac, Carleton University; Arnd Jürgensen, University of Toronto–Mississauga Campus; Geoffrey Whitehall, Acadia University; and Russell Alan Williams, Memorial University. Their comments not only enriched the text and filled gaping holes but also gave us a sense of the current state of the discipline across Canada. We would also like to thank the invaluable administrative assistance provided by staff in the Political Science departments at the University of British Columbia and Concordia University. Anna Vartanyan provided valuable research assistance in Montreal.

For the exhaustive editorial, production, and marketing effort at Nelson Education, we thank all those who worked on the fifth edition, including, but not limited to, Anne-Marie Taylor, Linda Sparks, and Hedy Sellers. Special thanks go to Maria Jelinek and Kavitha Ashok for their comprehensive copyediting and proofreading, respectively.

Most importantly of all, we would also like to express our appreciation for the comments offered by our students over the years. Students are the lifeblood of any scholarly enterprise, and ours have provided a wealth of critical insights and suggestions.

A NOTE ON MAPS AND NAMES

In global politics, conflicts (especially territorial conflicts) are often symbolized by disputes over the name of a country or territory. For example, Macedonia is called "the Former Yugoslavian Republic of Macedonia" (FYROM), because the Greek government objects to the use of a name that distinguishes an area within Greece. In addition, the names of many countries change over time, often because of a change in government. For example, the Khmer Rouge changed the name of Cambodia to Kampuchea (today, Cambodia is the common usage once again); Burma was renamed Myanmar by the military regime while in power (although it was and is still commonly referred to as Burma); and following a revolution in 1997 the African country of Zaire was renamed the Democratic Republic of Congo. Furthermore, separatist or nationalist movements that want to create or recreate their own states often refer to an arca of land as their own. For example, the representatives of the Kurdish people claim parts of Turkey, Syria, and Iran as the territory of Kurdistan, while the Palestinian people want to re-establish an independent state of Palestine. The politically sensitive nature of names is compounded by the fact that the use of one name over another is often taken as an indication of political support for one cause or another. This book seeks to make the student aware of such disputes and changes, although space considerations often make this impractical. We have strived to be as balanced and respectful as possible.

PART ONE

ORIGINS

This section of the book lays the foundation for subsequent discussions of contemporary and emerging themes in global politics. It begins with an introduction to the academic field of inquiry widely known as *international relations,* and the prevalent theoretical perspectives that guide researchers in the discipline. In Chapter 2, we turn to a brief history of the evolution of the international political system, including the rise and fall of empires, the prominent role of the state in the Westphalian system, and the widespread, often transformative impact of major wars. The next chapter discusses the Cold War, which dominated global politics for over four decades, and helped motivate the study of foreign policy decision making. Chapter 4 discusses the evolution of the world economy, with emphasis on liberal economic theory and the origins of what is often called *globalization.* Finally, Chapter 5 examines the complex and interrelated evolution of international law and international institutions, including the United Nations. This foundation will allow us to pursue more contemporary topics in Part Two.

Global Politics: The Discipline and Its Theoretical Foundations

Let us not imitate the historians who believe that the past has always been inevitable, and thus suppress the human dimension of events.

—Raymond Aron

If everyone's strategy depends upon everyone else's, then the Hitlers determine in part the action, or better, reaction, of those whose ends are worthy and whose means are fastidious.

—Kenneth Waltz

Breaking with the powerful bond among men, states and war in international relations theory ... feminist approaches [offer] a normative standpoint from which to construct alternative world orders.

—Jacqui True[1]

ON THE MENU: COMPLEXITY, INSECURITY, CONVERGENCE, AND DIVERGENCE

For those of us interested in war and peace, **globalization**, **climate change**, poverty and inequality, human rights, gender discrimination, racial and religious divides, criminal acts, and criminal inaction, the study of global politics has it all—and more! Global politics is engaged with enduring debates over the essence of human nature, the origins and development of societies, the interaction between economics, politics, and culture, and the causes and impacts of change. It is a subject replete with frustrating constraints and sobering limitations, as well as examples of breathtaking progress and unexpected opportunities. It is also a subject enriched with human stories of tragedy, despair, compassion, and hope. This textbook is designed to introduce you to this inherently broad and complex field of study. And because all students of global politics make key decisions about how to proceed in their quest for greater understanding, we hope this textbook will help you make these decisions with a full awareness of the range of issues involved. This first chapter is intended to introduce you to the discipline, and provide the theoretical foundations necessary for the further pursuit of the subjects we highlight in subsequent chapters.

As individuals, our relationship with global politics is an interactive one. At the most basic level, it is unlikely you would be alive and reading this text if we had experienced a full-scale nuclear war. At the height of the Cold War such a fate seemed entirely plausible to many experts in the field, and it is possible that nuclear war could become a predominant threat in the future. For example, there are concerns that deteriorating relations between Russia and the United States are leading to a new Cold War. Tensions between India and Pakistan could result in war between these two nuclear-armed states. And the rise of Chinese military power and the possibility of an increasingly antagonistic relationship between Beijing and Washington could raise the profile of nuclear weapons in the strategic and military balance between these two powers. Finally, international crises over North Korean and Iranian nuclear weapons development could lead to military action against these countries.

All of these possibilities remind us that nuclear weapons are far from irrelevant in global politics. Nevertheless, today we are more immediately concerned with the threats posed by economic crises and destabilization, wars between and within states, climate change and environmental deterioration, the spread of infectious diseases, terrorist acts (and military responses to them), access to safe food and water, and many other global issues that threaten lives on a daily basis. Of course, the impact of these issues is felt differently depending on who we are and where we live. For example, changes in world oil or food prices will have a different impact on a wealthy person in Alberta than an impoverished person in Haiti. On the other hand, some threats to **human security** strike people regardless of income or location. Pandemics like HIV/AIDS and infectious diseases such as Severe Acute Respiratory Syndrome (SARS) can attack without discrimination, though some people have access to better health care than others (and billions lack adequate access at all).

Of course, you need not be a professional diplomat, corporate executive, or social activist to interact with global politics: even our mundane, everyday decisions impact the world economy, environment, and political landscape. This statement is as true for someone living in Canada as it is for someone living in Germany, Pakistan, Uganda, Peru, or Micronesia, although within and among these countries the range of choice available to any given individual (and the relative impact that choice may have) is remarkably varied. Furthermore, we are constantly absorbing impressions and images of global politics, and James Der Derian reminds us that many of these come "wrapped in representations, bundled in ideology, edited by the media, warped by official stories."[2] Anyone who boarded an airplane after the September 11, 2001, terrorist attacks on the United States experienced a much higher level of airport security than existed previously. However, for people of Arab origin the attacks have often also meant an increase in discrimination, ethnic stereotyping, and racial profiling. In short, we are all a part of global politics, although our lived experiences are unique.

Though some observers lament the passing of the good old bad days of the **Cold War** (or the "bipolar" era—see Chapter 2), things were hardly simple then either, as Chapter 3 indicates. However, there is no doubt that the sheer volume of contemporary issues and concerns makes the discipline a particularly challenging one today. Studying global politics can seem overwhelming because there is so much to learn, and so many issues to address. This places a great deal of importance on the theories, frameworks, and models used to analyze and understand developments and trends in global politics. We argue that two simultaneous trends have emerged as one of the central paradoxes of the last several decades: *convergence* and *divergence*. While political, economic, technological, and communications integration (labelled *globalization* by many) is taking place, so is political fragmentation in the form of separatist movements, competition for scarce resources, religious animosity, and other sources of conflict. This concept is not a novel one, and many other authors have touched on these apparently contradictory trends.[3] While it would be simpler for all of us if either convergence or divergence clearly prevailed, we have to deal with the confusing fact that the two are happening simultaneously. While it is obvious that there are military conflicts under way in many parts of the world, the effort to encourage trade and expand telecommunications systems continues unabated. The horrors of genocide during World War II provided the impetus for the establishment of a universal human rights regime to protect individuals from persecution conducted by the state, yet massive crimes against humanity continue. To varying degrees, ethnic minorities within many states continue to feel insecure in political systems dominated by others, whether it be the Québécois in Canada (and anglophones in Quebec) or the Kurds in Turkey, Iraq, and Syria. Efforts by minorities to protect their culture and gain political influence (and even formal independence) can spark confrontation and conflict. For example, indigenous peoples around the world continue to struggle for political and economic equality and recognition, often encountering political resistance or outright repression from governments. As you read this text and follow world events, you might look for evidence of convergence and divergence, in order to decide which, if either, is prevailing.

STUDYING GLOBAL POLITICS

Global politics is a complex, and often surreal, congruence of physical and intellectual power, geography and natural resources, political structures, formal institutions, transnational networks, and competing ideas. It is populated by personalities as varied as spiritual leaders such as the Dalai Lama, business leaders such as Bill Gates, and politicians such as Stephen Harper and Barack Obama. Behind the personalities, large numbers of foreign ministry officials toil in relative obscurity on a broad range of international issues, and activists and specialists working for a variety of non-state actors seek to influence policy and implement change around the world. Commonly, the study of international relations, or "IR," has been considered part of the larger field of political science, and most political science departments have international relations specialists. However, many universities have moved toward a much more explicitly interdisciplinary approach by granting degrees in *international studies* or *international relations*. Students of business, medicine, law, geography, history, economics, and many other disciplines need a solid background in international relations to better understand their own disciplines. It is not necessary to label them political scientists to achieve this, though most of the theories advanced to explain the complex phenomena of IR are derived from political philosophy and political science. A basic education in IR can also reveal the extent to which global politics impacts on a wide range of occupations and human activities. Most large-scale businesses are engaged in some form of international activity. Many foreign firms hire domestic nationals to work in their branch companies. Increasingly, many young people are travelling across continents to work or study abroad, and are finding opportunities to learn (and teach) languages and establish **transnational** careers. Still others are working with **non-governmental organizations (NGOs)** such as humanitarian aid agencies, or as journalists or international lawyers. Regardless of one's eventual career path, it will likely involve contact with people in other countries. Learning about your own country's foreign relations is a great place to start (see Profile 1.1).

Beyond the impact on employment opportunities and careers, there are other reasons for today's student to study global politics, not least of which—and here we reflect our personal bias without apology—is the sheer excitement of studying politics at the international level

PROFILE 1.1 Canada and Global Politics

In 2011, Canada had a population of 33 476 688 (according to the national Census), the second-largest territory in the world (Russia has the largest), and the tenth-largest economy (according to the International Monetary Fund). Canada is in an enviable position in global politics. It faces no traditional military threats to its territory or political independence, possesses a virtually unequalled standard of living, and is largely free of the violent conflict that characterizes many states. However, this position is no excuse for complacency. Canada depends on a generally peaceful and stable international order for its physical security and its economic health. The Canadian economy is heavily dependent on trade (in particular, trade with the United States, the destination for approximately 70 percent of all Canadian **exports**), and Canada, along with the United States and Mexico, is a member of the **North American Free Trade Agreement (NAFTA)**. Beyond trade, Canada's foreign policy emphasizes the maintenance of international peace and security and making contributions to international institutions, select multilateral military operations (such as in Libya in 2011), democracy promotion, human rights and human security, arms control, and development. The terrorist attacks of September 11, 2001, had a considerable impact on the security of Canadian borders, coastal zones, and airspace, and led to a major Canadian military commitment in

Afghanistan for many years. Canada is a significant diplomatic actor, and it belongs to many major international forums and institutions, including the **Group of Eight (G8)**, the Group of Twenty (G20), the **North Atlantic Treaty Organization (NATO)**, the **Commonwealth**, **La Francophonie**, and the United Nations, to name only a few. Successive Canadian governments have been strong supporters of **multilateralism**, because within international organizations and coalitions Canada can at least have a voice and some expectation of influence. And yet Canada's close proximity to the United States often overshadows all other concerns. In 2003, Canada's decision not to play an active role in the Iraq War presented a serious challenge to Canadian–American relations. While changes in government do lead to changes in Canada's position on international issues, for the most part Canadian foreign policy has remained remarkably consistent.

For further reading on Canada's role in global politics, see B. Bow and P. Lennox, *An Independent Foreign Policy for Canada? Challenges and Choices for the Future* (Toronto: University of Toronto Press, 2008); M. Byers, *Intent for a Nation: What Is Canada For?* (Vancouver: Douglas And McIntyre, 2007); A. Cohen, *While Canada Slept: How We Lost Our Place in the World* (Toronto: McClelland And Stewart, 2003); S.K. Holloway, *Canadian Foreign Policy: Defining the National Interest* (Peterborough, ON: Broadview Press, 2006); T. Keating, *Canada and World Order: The Multilateralist Tradition in Canadian Foreign Policy*, 2nd ed. (Don Mills: Oxford University Press, 2002); C.S. Sjolander, H.A. Smith, and D. Stienstra, eds., *Feminist Perspectives on Canadian Foreign Policy* (Don Mills: Oxford University Press, 2003); and J. Welsh, *At Home in the World: Canada's Global Vision for the 21st Century* (Toronto: HarperCollins, 2004).

and learning more about how it affects a wide range of human activities. Every day, newspapers, television, and various online sources carry news items, documentary features, and discussions on a bewildering array of events happening around the world. Indeed, knowledge may be power, but it must make sense to be of any use. Many Canadians are from immigrant families, and they are concerned about the life circumstances of family and friends in other parts of the world. Many travel to far-flung destinations, and need to have a solid educational foundation to help them adapt to new environments. While studying IR is no substitute for direct experience, it does advance one's understanding of the context in which other states and peoples exist.

To some extent, all academic disciplines suffer from what we call the *irrelevancy disease*. In many cases, academics prefer to rely on highly abstract theoretical thinking, which many

The U.S. presidency and global politics. Barack and Michelle Obama, with daughters Sasha and Malia, wave during celebrations of Obama's election to a second term in office in 2012. The election of Obama was an important symbolic moment in American history, but it raised the question of how much of a difference even the president of the United States can make in global politics. (Barry Brecheisen/WireImage)

students find difficult to relate to their daily lives. While some of the theories found in the discipline seem rather abstract at first glance, they can reveal patterns of historical behaviour, raise interesting questions about current events, propose solutions to serious problems, and even challenge prevailing assumptions about the nature of global politics. Ideas and knowledge generated from theoretical thinking enable us to critically evaluate the position and rationales of governments, political leaders, and orthodox explanations of events. It helps that the application of IR theory has become more diverse than ever, as the study of the discipline itself has become increasingly global and scholars outside Europe and North America add their voices and perspectives to the literature.

Furthermore, ours is a dangerous world filled with a great deal of human suffering, and many people want to make a difference (see Profile 1.2), perhaps by working with intergovernmental organizations (IGOs) or non-governmental organizations (NGOs). In many locales, civil wars, famines, harsh structural adjustment policies, chronic **malnutrition**, epidemics, pollution and environmental degradation, illiteracy, and many other hardships make life especially challenging. Though working on the ground in these areas can be very fulfilling, it comes with unique dangers, as we learned from the experience of Nancy Malloy, a Canadian Red Cross nurse and a specialist in hospital administration. A resident of Vancouver, she joined the Red Cross in 1987 and took her first international assignment in 1990, motivated by a personal desire to help alleviate suffering in war-torn areas. She worked in five war zones over the next six years, in Ethiopia (1990), Kuwait (1991), the former Yugoslavia (1993), Zaire (1995), and Chechnya (1996). But on the night of December 17, 1996, gunmen broke into a Chechen hospital complex and killed six Red Cross workers, including Ms. Malloy. A person need not be a ruling politician to be a hero in world politics, nor to be a victim of its vicissitudes.

PROFILE 1.2 Individual Actors on the Stage of World Politics

Members of the Brazilian Air Force, left, salute as Sérgio Vieira de Mello's coffin is loaded aboard a Brazilian presidential plane by UN officials at Baghdad International Airport, Iraq, August 22, 2003. Vieira de Mello, the top UN official in Iraq, was killed in a suicide truck bombing attack on UN headquarters on August 19, 2003, which killed at least 22 other people and left more than 100 injured. (AP Photo/Manish Swarup)

SERGIO VIEIRA DE MELLO

Sérgio Vieira de Mello was born in Rio de Janeiro in 1948. He joined the United Nations in 1969 while studying at the University of Paris. In the course of his impressive career, Vieira de Mello served as UN Assistant High Commissioner for Refugees, Under-Secretary-General for Humanitarian Affairs, and Emergency Relief Coordinator. For a short time he was the Special Representative of the Secretary-General in Kosovo, and he also served as UN Transitional Administrator in East Timor. On September 12, 2002, Vieira de Mello was appointed the UN High Commissioner for Human Rights.

In May 2003, he was asked by Secretary-General Kofi Annan to take a four-month leave of absence from his position as High Commissioner to serve in Iraq as his Special Representative. It was there that Sergio Vieira de Mello was tragically killed on August 19, 2003, when the UN headquarters in Iraq fell victim to a terrorist attack. Following the tragedy, Kofi Annan appointed an Independent Panel on the Safety and Security of UN personnel in Iraq, and work continues to assure that UN personnel are protected in such circumstances.

See S. Power, *Chasing the Flame: Sérgio Vieira de Mello and the Fight to Save the World* (New York: Penguin, 2007).

THE INTERDISCIPLINARY, YET DIVIDED, DISCIPLINE

Formally, and according to academic convention, the field of IR is divided into several subfields, or what some prefer to term *subdisciplines*. In this way, IR scholars can break an enormous amount of material and topics down into more digestible sections for investigation and analysis. For the sake of brevity, we will assume that the study of IR has four major subfields.

International relations theory is a body of literature that seeks to define and explain the nature of the international system and the behaviour of the actors within it.[4] *International security* has traditionally involved the study of conflict and war and attempts to prevent or control it. Recently, many international security specialists have adopted a broader agenda, examining topics such as ethnic and religious conflicts, the proliferation of weapons, and the link between the environment and security.[5] The study of *international political economy* has grown as issues such as trade, finance, debt, poverty, and economic crises became increasingly prominent in international affairs.[6] Finally, the subfield that examines institutions such as the United Nations is generally referred to as *international organization*, and focuses on instruments of cooperation such as the establishment of institutions, regimes, and agreements among states, groups, or individuals, and the development of international law.[7] This division of the field into subfields is admittedly arbitrary. Some would argue that other subfields exist, such as gender studies in IR, foreign policy analysis, international ethics, development studies, or global ecopolitics. Yet others would argue that such a large overlap exists between the subfields that to separate them is parochial at best and misleading at worst. Provided that we are aware of these objections, however, the divisions allow us to conceptualize the overall project of the study of global politics.

Moreover—and this will become increasingly obvious as you read this text—those engaged in this project benefit from the collaboration of a large number of specialists from other well-established fields in the social sciences and humanities, including experts in comparative and domestic politics, world and local history, economics, geography, psychology, sociology, and anthropology. When we move beyond the descriptive and analytical into more prescriptive areas, we engage in normative work, in which writers are as interested in putting forth their vision of how the world should be as they are in telling us how it is. Normative projects reflect moral and ethical judgments, and often seek to demonstrate how ethics inform the actions of world leaders and diplomats.[8] Some scholars argue that it is misleading to separate the analytic from the normative, since all investigators have their own biases, and all theories have their value-laden assumptions. Explicitly normative work borrows heavily from the vast literature on ethics and philosophy and ventures into questions concerning the just causes of war, the true meaning of human rights, religious differences, and environmental values. Finally, in this technological age, scholars and students also borrow knowledge and insights from the applied and natural sciences, such as physics, earth and ocean science, chemistry, biology, computer science, robotics, and genetics. In short, students of global politics must be interdisciplinary in their approach to issues, but also capable of practising the **synthesis** of ideas and information.

The discipline is divided further by differences over what primary level of analysis should demand our attention. Three main levels of analysis exist—the *individual* level, the **state** or *group* level, and the *systemic* level—although this rough division is open to dispute.[9] The *individual* level of analysis focuses on the decisions of individuals, and the perceptions, values, and experiences that motivate those decisions. Generally, it emphasizes the role of political leaders, for it is often assumed (perhaps erroneously) that those individuals most influence the trajectory of world events.[10] While it is clear that powerful leaders such as Napoleon and Hitler changed the course of history, they could hardly have done so alone, or without the right conditions to aid them. The *state* or *group* level of analysis focuses on the behaviour of individual states, which is often attributed to the form of government one finds at a particular time. We will return to the debate over democratic peace theory later, but the argument here is that liberal democracies do not fight wars against each other, and thus the explanation for war may be found through analyzing different political modes of governance at the state level. Of course, it is also necessary to look within states to determine which groups are influencing foreign policy. For example, **free trade** agreements are supported by the industrial sectors within states that will benefit most from lowering restrictions on trade in their products, and opposed by labour groups and others fearful of the impact on jobs and competitiveness.

At the *systemic* level of analysis, the actions of states are seen as the result of external influences and pressures on them in relation to their attributes or position in world politics. In other words, the nature of the environment, or system, in which actors find themselves largely explains their behaviour, and the capabilities and resources the actors have at their disposal establish the range of options they might have in any given situation. This leads us to an age-old debate within the social sciences concerning the relative causal weight assigned to systems and actors, otherwise known as structures and agents. Does the structure of the system predetermine the actions of actors? Or do humans shape events of their own accord? Many people today view this dichotomy as a false one, forcing us to reduce complex interactions to two essential forces. Rather, one can argue that continual interaction occurs between the individual and group or state units of action and the structures within which they operate. In the political world, each influences the other, although limitations exist as to how much influence can be projected by units into their environment, and by the environment onto units. For example, a state such as Canada cannot expect to be a dominant influence in the current international system, since it has a limited amount of power and is effectively overshadowed by the influence of its southern neighbour, the United States. However, in certain areas, such as peacekeeping and humanitarian assistance, notable Canadians have made extraordinary contributions to multilateral efforts. Though the modern state's extensive ties to the international system limit its ability to take autonomous action, they also provide opportunities for individuals to exert influence beyond their own country (see Profile 1.3).

When we examine the behaviour of actors within a system, as political scientists we are often most interested in discerning their relative influence; we seek to identify the dominant actors, be they states, socio-economic classes, organizations, corporations, or individuals. However, this identification is but half the story, for every form of dominance or control generates opposition. Thus, we seek also to identify and explain the motivations of counter-dominant actors, which could include the Ogoni resisting oppression by the Nigerian government, anti-globalization activists protesting the World Trade Organization, the people and social groups involved in the "Arab Spring" uprisings that began in 2010, the ambitious entrepreneurs introducing innovative products to the global market, or environmentalists opposing large-scale energy development and the destruction of habitat. However, it is too simple to say that dominant actors are conservative and support the status quo and counter-dominant actors are progressive and support positive change. After all, neo-Nazi groups in Europe and elsewhere would certainly consider themselves counter-dominant actors, as would the National Rifle Association when it opposes anti–small arms regulation at the international level.[11] Each sphere of human activity differs, and since the political playing field is neither level nor stable, the question of just who is dominant and who is counter-dominant is not amenable to an eternal formula. To further confuse the issue, it might be argued that the influence of some actors will be greater than that of others in times of social upheaval, and thus power relations reflect not only deep-seated structures of influence but also the unique social circumstances at specific moments in history.[12]

We also have to be careful regarding our use of the terms *power* and *influence*. The concept of power is central to the study of political science, but it is also one of the most contested concepts in the discipline. Power has both hard and soft dimensions.[13] *Hard power* refers to material capabilities and the ability to achieve desired outcomes through the use of military force or economic resources. Hard power is still frequently used today, as demonstrated in the American-led military assaults on Afghanistan and Iraq, the multilateral military intervention in Libya, and the sanctions imposed on North Korea and Iran. In contrast, *soft power* refers

Canadian Political Leadership: Pierre Elliott Trudeau, 1919–2000

Searching for peace. Canadian Prime Minister Pierre Trudeau meets with China's Chairman Deng Xiaoping in the Great Hall of the People in Beijing in 1983. Trudeau met with Deng to discuss his peace proposals. (CP Photo/Andy Clark)

Pierre Elliott Trudeau was Canada's prime minister from 1968 to 1979, and again from 1980 to 1984. While he was always occupied with matters of national importance such as the separatist movement in Quebec and constitutional questions, he was also very visible on the international stage. Early in his term as prime minister, Trudeau halved Canada's commitment of troops to NATO. He became a friend of Fidel Castro, despite the American embargo on Cuba. His government recognized the People's Republic of China in 1970. At one point, and against widespread public opposition, Trudeau allowed the United States to test **cruise missiles** over Canadian soil; yet he later undertook an international peace mission that saw him meet with world leaders to discuss disarmament. Although he was often controversial and his initiatives were frequently criticized, Trudeau was respected for his intellect and his commitment to peace and social justice. Abroad, Trudeau was known as a charming and novel statesman. He famously described Canada's relationship with the United States as "sleeping next to an elephant" and often worried about the threat America posed to Canadian sovereignty and independence. Thousands of Canadians paid tribute after his death in 2000 during a last train ride home, and at a large public funeral in Montreal.

See J.L. Granatstein and R. Bothwell, *Pirouette: Pierre Trudeau and Canadian Foreign Policy* (University of Toronto Press, 1991).

to social influence and the ability to persuade others through the creation of sound policy proposals, moral and ethical leadership, compelling cultural ideas and symbols, and innovation and creativity. Neither hard nor soft power is distributed equally in the world, and this inequality has had an important, if not decisive, role in the history of human social relations. However, the possession of superior material or social power does not guarantee a preferred outcome for those that wield it. The United States did not win the Vietnam War, nor has it been able to resolve the ongoing conflict between Israel and the Palestinian people. But the agent–structure debate noted above continues: should we focus on the power of states per se or on the power of a larger structure, or system, such as the capitalist world economic system, where the soft power of prevailing ideas becomes even more important? Some scholars argue that hegemony is not just about military or economic power but also the gradual acceptance of orthodoxy in the realm of ideas. For example, globalization is often described as an inevitable force with no alternative. Is this true, or have most governments and populations simply accepted it as such? Ultimately, this is one of the many analytic questions students need to answer for themselves.

Below we discuss some of the more prevalent basic perspectives that have been generated by international relations theorists. However, keep firmly in mind the interdisciplinary contributions, and methodological divisions, discussed above. Some have even suggested that we have moved into a world of "post-international" politics, an age characterized by the "decline of long-standing patterns" leaving us uncertain about "where the changes may be leading."[14] However, an unmistakable continuity exists: the international system remains fundamentally competitive, as different states, economic players, and ideas battle to secure or advance their interests or their dominance. Convergence and divergence continue their long dance. To gain even a cursory understanding of all this, we need to impose clarity, and this is done by referring to the various theoretical perspectives we have outlined below.

IR THEORY: A BRIEF SURVEY

Charles Lindblom, in the introduction to his book on the purpose and effects of contemporary social science, readily admits that "classical nineteenth-century liberalism is my prison. It is not the most inhumane of prisons; its cells are by far larger than those of any other prison I know. Indeed, its construction is such that inmates often succeed in persuading themselves that they are wholly free."[15] This admission acknowledges an important point: we are all, to some degree, trapped within our own particular way of seeing and making sense of the world. As Kenneth Boulding warned us back in 1959, "It is what we think the world is like, not what it is really like, that determines our behaviour."[16] Textbook writers are hardly free of this circumstance; our own origins, assumptions, and opinions—in short, our own perspectives—have inevitably become part of this book, though we have made every effort to be as inclusive as possible. However, we must keep in mind that human perspectives are best viewed as fluid conceptions, subject to change, reinterpretation, and manipulation. Further, none of these theories emerged from an intellectual vacuum: they took shape in a historical context that informed their development. As the historian Arthur Schlesinger Jr. has observed, traumatic events (such as war, acts of terror, and environmental disasters) often lead to "skeptical reassessments of supposedly sacred assumptions."[17] We might ask ourselves whether events such as the attacks on September 11, 2001, the Iraq War, the global economic crisis of 2008 to 2009, or the Arab Spring uprisings have forced us to rethink things yet again.

IDEALISM

The death and destruction caused by World War I resulted in a condemnation of how international politics had been conducted in the past. The epic confrontation also created a reaction against power politics, secret diplomacy, arms races, and what was seen as the abuse of unchecked power by the monarchs who led the Central Powers into war. For many, the horrors of World War I served as the final exhibit of the folly of war in human history. A change was required, a change that would alter the international environment in a way that would prevent future wars and eliminate the practices and policies that had made the history of humanity a tale of conflict and war. This sentiment prompted the search for a theory of international politics that provided an explanation for all wars and offered directions and policies for preventing them in the future. What emerged from this search was the theoretical framework known as political **idealism**. An idealist perspective assumes the best of human nature: we are essentially cooperative beings, but we are occasionally led astray by evil influences into war and conflict, and we have a natural affinity toward the communal, as opposed to the individual, good. When people behave violently, or when states go to war, it is because of the institutional or structural setting in which they exist, not an inherent human predisposition for armed conflict.

Political idealism has its origins in the philosophical tradition of **liberalism**, which emerged in Europe in the 16th century, although many of the moral principles of liberalism and idealism can be found in earlier works. This philosophical tradition emphasizes the liberty of the individual and the need to protect this liberty from the state or any form of tyranny. Liberalism, with its focus on individuals as the centre of moral virtue, regards the pursuit of power, authoritarian governance, and intolerance as obstacles to human progress. Some liberal philosophers place emphasis on building a tolerant, liberal society as the only humane response to pluralism and diversity. Others put more emphasis on the development of capitalism, free trade, and republican democracy as the answer to global problems and the absence of global order. Liberal philosophers include John Locke, Immanuel Kant, Benjamin Constant, John Stuart Mill, Montesquieu, David Hume, Adam Smith, T.H. Green, L.T. Hobhouse, and Thomas Jefferson.

Postwar idealists such as G. Lowes Dickinson, Alfred Zimmern, **Norman Angell**, James T. Shotwell, and U.S. President **Woodrow Wilson** drew on the liberal philosophical tradition. Although idealists differed on many issues, they all shared a number of assumptions about the nature of humanity, the nature of world politics, the experience of World War I, and the road to a better future. To varying degrees, idealists assumed the following:

- *Human nature is essentially good.* As a result, assistance and cooperation are possible and natural, motivated by the human qualities of altruism, philanthropy, and humanitarianism.

- *Evil is not innate to humanity.* Evil activity or harmful behaviour is the result of bad institutions, states, and structures that motivate individuals to act in a self-interested, distrustful, or aggressive fashion.

- *Social progress is possible.* Human society has developed and improved and will continue to do so: progress is the main narrative of history.

- *The main problem in international relations is war.* International society must reform itself with the aim of preventing future wars.

- *War can be prevented.* Eliminating bad institutions, states, and structures will eliminate the root causes of war.

- *International cooperation will promote peace.* International organizations and international law, based on enlightened self-interest, will help prevent war.

The policy program of the idealists—their proposed solutions to the problem of war and the issues facing the international system—was expansive and ambitious. Idealists regarded the structure of international relations as a war-making imposition that promoted distrust, hostility, conflict, and confrontation. The history of international relations, idealists believed, proved their argument that war was endemic because of the nature of the international system. Idealists believed that by changing the latter it would be possible to reduce or eliminate war. Their answer was the **collective security** system. Within such a system, all states would agree that in the case of aggression by any state against any other state in the system, all other states would respond to defend the attacked state. In effect, a collective security system sought to make any aggression against any member of the system an act of aggression against all members. As a result, any potential aggressor, faced with the prospect of having so many enemies, would not engage in aggression in the first place. In this way, peace would be preserved. Idealists also believed that international peace could be encouraged through the development of international organizations, international law, and arms control.

The principles and hopes of political idealism did serve as a guide for postwar efforts to remake the international system, most famously in the creation of the **League of Nations** and in U.S. President Woodrow Wilson's famous **Fourteen Points**, which influenced the post–World War I settlement. The Covenant of the League of Nations was drafted at the Paris Peace Conference in 1919. The League comprised an assembly and a council of permanent members, which included Great Britain, France, Italy, and Japan, and later Germany (1926) and the Soviet Union (1934). We discuss the operations of the League in more detail in Chapter 5. Between 1920 and 1939, the League considered 66 disputes between states and contributed to peaceful outcomes in 35 of them. The League reflected the idealist perspective's assumption that international organizations would serve to maintain peace and promote cooperation among states on a wide variety of international issues and problems. Peace would be strengthened by the development of international law, including efforts to make war illegal, such as the 1928 **Kellogg–Briand Pact**. Peace would also be strengthened through **arms control**, such as the 1922 Washington Naval Treaty, which restricted the number and armament of battleships in the fleets of the great powers. However, the treaty is also an example of how states pursue their own interests in arms control negotiations: under the treaty some states could have more battleships than others, and naval competition continued in the aircraft carrier and cruiser classes of ships.

The principles of political idealism were neither universally shared nor admired, and the immediate postwar period was characterized by "power politics" as much as by idealist behaviour. The events of the interwar period and the erosion or failure of many of the key elements of the idealists' reform program eroded much of the enthusiasm for idealist assumptions and solutions, though political idealism did not vanish. As we will see in later chapters, many of the key elements of this theoretical framework remained in place and were actively pursued long after idealism's golden years had faded. Today, the legacy of political idealism lives on in the principles that form the foundation for arms control, international organizations, and international law.

REALISM

Not surprisingly, the realist perspective developed within the IR discipline following World War II, which many felt provided clear evidence that idealist claims about the progressive inclination of human nature were hopelessly naive. *Classical realism*, as it has come to be called, is less generous regarding human nature. People are generally viewed as self-interested creatures, and political power merely reinforces this predisposition. Political relations between human groups revolve around conflict; they constitute unitary, rational actors seeking to protect or advance their own collective self-interest. In global politics, the most relevant human groups, and the primary actors in the system, are states. States seek their national interest at all times in an anarchic international environment lacking a world government or police force capable of enforcing order or peace. Military power is the most important expression and guarantor of survival, and the most important issue area in the field is the threat or actual use of physical force (everything else is considered "low politics"). When it comes to foreign policy and security, states have to choose what to do in certain situations purely on the basis of their own self-interest, and we should not be surprised when they choose to go to war. The only way to change this situation would be to make the world system non-anarchic; but this would require a world government, and realists reject that prospect as a virtual impossibility.

The intellectual roots of realism lay in early writings about war and statecraft in the analysis of the ancient Greek historian Thucydides, the opinions of Kautilya, the military instructions of Sun Tzu, the pragmatic advice of Niccolo Machiavelli, and the broader reflections of the English theoretician Thomas Hobbes (see Chapter 2). These and other writings emphasized the importance of power and self-interest above all other considerations. The realist perspective was thus built on the intellectual heritage of **realpolitik**. As writes David Boucher, in his excellent exposition on classical political philosophy and international relations, "Hobbes does not believe that there is any higher law ordained by a force outside of human will ... morality is equated with expediency. ... In the international sphere, in the absence of a sovereign, there is no justice or injustice, but there are principles relating to honourable and dishonourable acts which serve to restrain excessive acts of cruelty or recklessness."[18]

Early exponents of political realism in IR include E.H. Carr, Hans J. Morgenthau (see Profile 1.5), Kenneth W. Thompson, and Reinhold Niebuhr. As a group, realists made several assumptions about the character of international politics. States were the principal actors in international politics, since no secular authority superseded the authority of the state. States were also assumed to be rational, unitary actors, interested above all else in their security and in maximizing their power. It followed logically that the pursuit of power—the ability to make other actors do what they would not otherwise do—was the core aim of international politics. Although most realists would find these tenets to be an oversimplification of their worldview, to varying degrees, they presume the following:

- People are essentially selfish and acquisitive by nature and view others accordingly: insecurity is their natural state of being.

- The desire for power is instinctive to all individuals and cannot be eliminated.

- International politics is a *zero-sum* (see Chapter 2) struggle for power, where relative gains in power by one state or group necessarily mean a relative loss in power for other states or groups.

- The international system is anarchic in nature as no central authority or world government exists that is capable of enforcing rules.

- In such an environment, the primary objective of all states (i.e., their governments) is to follow the national interest, defined in terms of maximizing and maintaining power.

- In such an environment, states must ultimately rely on their own efforts to ensure their own security: self-help is the best approach to survival and progress.

- Military power and preparedness is the most important factor in determining state power and security.

- Alliances can increase the security of a state, but the loyalty and reliability of allies should never be taken for granted.

- International organizations and international law cannot be relied on to guarantee security, as state actions are not bound by enforceable rules.

- Order can be achieved only by the **balance of power** system in which stability is maintained by flexible alliance systems.

Profile 1.4 compares the realist and idealist perspectives.

If power is as important as realists suggest, we need to know how to measure it. This task is not easy, conceptually or empirically, since much emphasis has been placed on the tangible, measurable capabilities of states. Such factors include the base assets of a state, such as its territory, population, geography, natural resources, and **gross domestic product (GDP)**. These elements of power are long-term attributes that generally change slowly over time. They represent the foundation of state power, or what Canadian foreign policy analyst Kim Richard Nossal has termed "relative invariates."[19] Some states are more endowed with these elements than others by virtue of location or historical factors, such as conquest. Frequently, though not exclusively, these states become great powers. Other states stand little or no chance of attaining such status.

For realists, the most important kind of power is **hard power**, which emphasizes material measures such as military capabilities, economic size, and resource endowment. Military power is especially important, because it is the principal means through which states defend and promote their interests. Estimating the power—especially the military power—of others is a crucial element of international politics. As Sun Tzu wrote, "Know the enemy and know yourself; in a hundred battles you will never be in peril." However, even realists acknowledge that measurable hard power factors are not the only considerations in power politics. Power also encompasses intangibles, elements that are not easily measured or compared. And a state must be able to deploy hard-power capabilities in an effective fashion. This ability depends on the unity of purpose within the state, which can be influenced by public opinion, religion,

PROFILE 1.4	**The Idealist Perspective and the Realist Perspective Compared**	
ISSUE	**IDEALISM**	**REALISM**
Human nature	Communal, altruistic	Self-serving
Central problem	The establishment of peace	War
Key actors	States, international law, and individuals	States; governments
Motives of actors	Pursuit of security through mutual assistance and collaboration	Pursuit of power as reflected by the national interest
Nature of international system	A potentially cooperative, integrated community	Anarchy
Outlook on future	Optimism; human progress	Pessimism; stability at best
Policy prescriptions and solutions	Reform the system; develop institutions and international law	Enhance state power; protect national interests

PROFILE 1.5 Hans J. Morgenthau (1904–1980)

Hans J. Morgenthau was born in Germany and practised law in Frankfurt before moving to the United States in 1937, where he was appointed to the University of Chicago in 1943. His most famous work was entitled *Politics among Nations*, first published in 1948. Morgenthau presented a theory of international politics in the book, and his "six principles of political realism" became one of the foundations of the realist perspective:

1. Politics is governed by objective laws that have their roots in human nature, which has not changed since the time of classical China, India, and Greece.

2. States, and their leaders, think and act in terms of interest defined as power, and to understand their actions observers of international politics must think the same way.

3. The idea of interest is the essence of politics and is unaffected by time and place; efforts to transform politics without considering this basic law will fail.

4. Tension exists between moral command and the requirements of successful political action. Morality cannot be applied universally in the abstract but must be filtered through the circumstances of time and place.

5. The moral aspirations of a particular nation are not to be confused with the moral laws that govern the universe.

6. Intellectually, realism maintains the autonomy of the political sphere, as economists, lawyers, or doctors maintain theirs.

Morgenthau, then, argued that international relations is characterized by states pursuing their national interests defined in terms of power. The world is the result of forces inherent in human nature, and is characterized by opposing interests and conflicts among them. For Morgenthau, international politics was governed by universal principles or laws based on the pursuit of the national interest.

SOURCE: HANS J. MORGENTHAU (ED.), *POLITICS AMONG NATIONS*, 4TH ED. (NEW YORK: ALFRED A. KNOPF, 1967).

ideology, or nationalism (the conscription crisis in Canada during World War I is an example of such a difficulty, as was the American war effort in Vietnam). Nevertheless, for realists hard power is the most important currency in global politics.

Realism is not a monolithic theory, and has evolved considerably from its early origins. Classical realists such as Morgenthau and Niebuhr emphasize the role of human nature. **Structural realists** (often referred to as "**neorealists**") such as Kenneth Waltz emphasize the anarchic nature of the system as a determinant of state behaviour. The term *anarchy* implies not complete chaos or absence of law but rather the lack of a central authority or government capable of enforcing rules. Within states, governments can deter participants from breaking legal restrictions, enforce contracts, and employ their monopoly on the use of coercion to compel citizens to obey the law. In contrast, no central authority exists to enforce and ensure state compliance with international rules or norms. Consequently, states must become self-reliant if they are to survive. All states must, therefore, be prepared to use force in their own defence, for in an anarchic environment, a state may use coercion or force at any time if the benefits to be gained outweigh potential costs (see the discussion of the stag hunt in Profile 1.6). So, in the absence of an effective security system, states arm themselves for protection against such an eventuality, following the advice of the Latin phrase *Si vis pacem, parabellum*— "If you want peace, prepare for war."

PROFILE 1.6 The Trouble with Cooperation: The Stag Hunt

Jean-Jacques Rousseau. (© Bettman/CORBIS)

The stag hunt is an allegory that originated in the writings of the Geneva-born 18th-century philosopher *Jean-Jacques Rousseau*. Although Rousseau is best known for his enormous contributions to Western political thought that influenced conservative, liberal, and socialist theory and the idealism of the French Revolution, realists have borrowed and adapted his stag-hunt example to illustrate the power of self-interested motives in anarchic environments. In this allegory, five individual hunters exist in a state of nature, with no government or social structure to determine their behaviour. The hunters have a choice of cooperating to attain a mutually desired goal or defecting from such cooperation if their own individual short-term interests can be satisfied. They can collaborate to encircle and subsequently capture a stag, which will satisfy the food needs of all five hunters if they share it. However, in doing so, it is possible that one of the hunters will encounter a tempting hare, which will satisfy that individual hunter's food needs. That hunter then faces a choice: let the hare go and serve the common interest by continuing the effort to capture the stag, or take the hare and defect from the group, thus ruining the hunt for the other four hunters, who will not have their food needs satisfied.

The allegory raises several questions about incentives and disincentives for cooperation. If a hunter prefers to cooperate to capture the stag, can the other hunters be trusted to do the same? Is it not in the rational self-interest of a hunter to take the hare? If this is the case, how can the hunters trust each other to cooperate on a hunt for the stag? And if they cannot trust each other, is it not in their interests to take the hare before any of the other hunters do? Indeed, what is the incentive to cooperate at all? The allegory illustrates the difficulty of establishing cooperation in an anarchic environment and the corrosive effect short-term self-interest can have on collaborative efforts.

On Rousseau see S. Hoffman and D. Fidler, eds., *Rousseau on International Relations* (Oxford: Clarendon, 1991) and the famous treatment in K. Waltz, *Man, the State and War: A Theoretical Analysis* (New York: Columbia University Press, 1954).

In doing so, however, states can find themselves in what scholars have called the **security dilemma**. In this situation, when states take **unilateral** measures to ensure their own security (such as increasing the capabilities of their military forces), they decrease the security of neighbouring states, which will perceive these measures as threatening and will take countermeasures (increasing the capabilities of their own armed forces) to promote their own security. These military enhancements will provoke insecurity in other states, which will increase their military capabilities as well. This action–reaction cycle occurs when states increasingly spend resources on military capabilities but make no real gains in the way of security. This dynamic is the basis of the many arms races that have occurred between states. Characterized by periods of high tension and the rapid escalation of military capabilities and preparedness, security dilemmas increase hostility, deepen mistrust, and create the conditions in which a crisis could easily lead to misunderstanding, miscalculation, and war. In Chapter 3, we will examine in detail the evolution of what was, arguably, the greatest security dilemma of all time, the Cold War.

For realists, the existence of an anarchic self-help system does not mean that the international system lacks order or cooperation. In fact many **English School realists** (or **liberal realists**) such as Hedley Bull argue that the international system is far from chaotic.[20] In an anarchic system, states can cooperate and do so all the time. For example, states reach trade agreements, create and join international institutions, and form alliances. However, realists argue that this cooperation occurs, not for altruistic reasons, but because it is in the interests of states to cooperate. Cooperation is simply another reflection of self-help. Nevertheless, when states interact they follow international **norms** and conventions most of the time. Norms are shared expectations about what constitutes appropriate behaviour in the international system. An example of such a norm is the concept of sovereignty, the principle that a state has control over affairs within its own territory, free from external interference by other states. In principle, states are therefore autonomous in that they answer to no higher authority in the international system. Another prominent norm is respect for internationally recognized borders. Despite the fact that most borders in the world today are the result of past wars and international agreements or the legacy of colonial occupation, the territorial integrity of states is regarded as one of the foundations of international stability. Attempts to revise these borders—through conquest or intimidation—are generally regarded as dangerous or destabilizing events, because a challenge to an existing border is in principle a challenge to borders everywhere. Other norms regulate the conduct of diplomatic relations between states. For example, embassies are considered to be the territory of their home states, rather than that of the host country, and are therefore not subject to interference or the laws of the host country. As we will see, governments obey a wide variety of international norms, procedures, regulations, and laws every day.

English school realists argue that since cooperation and norms do provide the basis for some order in the international system, anarchy does not mean the complete absence of order in global politics. As a result, an international society does exist, based on these shared norms and agreements that regulate relations between states. However, all realists emphasize that when it comes to security issues, or so-called high politics concerns, states rely on hard power to manage relations between them. This reliance has led to the development of the concept of the balance of power, discussed in greater detail in Chapter 2.

Other recent developments in Realist theory suggest not all realists believe global politics is necessarily a constant, predatory struggle for power among chronically insecure states. While English School realists point to the existence of an international society of norms and practices that encourage cooperation rather than warfare, **Defensive Realism** suggests that achieving one's objectives through war is actually quite difficult, even in an anarchic environment. Conquest is not easy, particularly if an opponent is unified and committed to their defence, and if they have geographic and/or technological strengths that enable them to put up the prospect of robust resistance. Therefore, many states can achieve a measure of security from threats by adopting a defensive posture, without necessarily threatening the security of others. A more peaceful world could be the result. On the other hand, **Offensive Realism** maintains a firm belief in the relationship between anarchy and insecurity, and argues that most states will always be wary of the threat of conquest or a loss of power. Therefore, states will continue to seek to expand their own power and weaken the power of others. The offensive/defensive realism debate is another illustration of the diversity of realist thought, and the continued relevance and vitality of the theory.

LIBERALISM

As mentioned in our description of idealism, liberalism has deep intellectual roots. Liberals emphasize the importance of values such as liberty, private property, the rule of law, free markets, democracy, and justice in the governance of domestic society, and seek to project these values onto global politics. The aim is to remake the international system into a liberal society of states, governed by the same values that govern individuals in liberal democratic societies. Liberals are therefore champions of international trade, international law, the promotion of democracy around the world, and the development of international institutions to manage the affairs of states and regulate global politics. Liberals argue that individuals and states will rationally cooperate if given the opportunity to do so. They believe that cooperation is mutually beneficial, that what is good for one may be good for another (in contrast to a zero-sum world perspective in which a gain for one is a loss for another). Liberals place a great deal of importance on economic growth, both domestically and internationally, assuming prosperity will mean peace, and peace will mean prosperity. International trade is to be encouraged, because it will lead to greater wealth and human well-being, as well as fewer wars since trade promotes cooperation, trust, and mutual interest. In addition, so-called transnational avenues for international cooperation, such as the creation of international organizations, advocacy groups, and cultural exchanges, can reduce the chances of war through dialogue and understanding. In general, liberals assume the following about global politics:

- States are not the only important actors in global politics. Non-state actors such as multinational corporations and advocacy groups are also significant sources of agency and change.
- The state is in decline. Borders are increasingly permeable and governments have less control over economic activity, information, and social activity.
- Global politics is characterized by interdependence, not by anarchy. Interdependence is growing, reflected in increased trade, financial, social, and communications flows around the world.
- International institutions matter. Institutions bind states into mutual commitments and obligations that are costly to break.
- Domestic politics matter. The nature and interests of key domestic political actors decisively determine decisions made by states.
- War and failed efforts at cooperation are the result of flawed, often irrational decision making by leaders and governments.

Liberals do not share the realist view of the primacy of hard power. For liberals, the effective deployment of power also depends on **soft power**. Soft power includes the support a state has obtained in the international system, which may in turn depend on the moral legitimacy of its cause, the loyalty of its allies, and the diplomatic and political skills available to the state. Power can also be found in the ability of an actor to set agendas, establish norms of behaviour, and gain wider agreements on rules and regulations that others agree to obey. The less tangible elements of soft power reflect the appeal or attraction of ideas and values. If the ideas and values linked to a particular state are seen as attractive, they will provide that state with opportunities to exert influence and leadership. For example, some have argued that the United States leads the world in terms of soft power because of its position as the world's leading capitalist marketplace and liberal democracy. Many have also argued that American soft power was damaged by the unpopular Iraq War, the conduct of the so-called War on Terror, and other policies of the George W. Bush administration. Repairing that damage became a stated goal, only partially realized, of the Obama administration. Some Canadians (such as former Foreign Affairs Minister Lloyd Axworthy) have suggested that Canada often carried influence beyond its capabilities (especially its military capabilities) because of its emphasis on international cooperation and institutions over the use of military force and coercion. In this view, soft power has enabled Canada to provide leadership on issues such as peacekeeping, the movement to ban land mines, and sanctions against South Africa during the **apartheid** era. On the other hand, Canada's failure to obtain one of the non-permanent seats on the Security Council in 2010 could be interpreted as an indication of the erosion of Canada's soft power and a change in how the country is perceived abroad.

Arguably, the three most popular variants of liberalism in circulation today are complex interdependence, liberal institutionalism, and democratic peace theory. If we blend realism's concern with power and state conflict with liberalism's optimism and emphasis on transnational phenomena, we get what Robert Keohane and Joseph Nye Jr. called **complex interdependence**.[21] In a prelude to contemporary concerns about globalization, they argued that economic factors were fast becoming as important as military matters, and that non-state actors such as **multinational corporations (MNCs)** and **non-governmental organizations (NGOs)** play important roles alongside states. Further, states are not always rational, coherent, unitary actors, since they respond to internal discord. Keohane and Nye intended their theory to be a modification, not a refutation, of realism, but much of what they argued has been subsumed under the liberal banner.

Idealists and liberals have much in common, including the desire for stronger institutions to facilitate global cooperation. **Liberal institutionalism** focuses on the impact of formal international organizations in global politics. Other forms of cooperation, such as informal agreements or associations, are often called **regimes**, which can be defined as sets of principles, norms, rules, and decision-making procedures around which actors' expectations converge.[22] According to liberals, institutions and regimes increase cooperation and understanding and reduce uncertainty and conflict, facilitating the efforts of governments and individuals to engage in trade, investment, communication, travel, and activism efforts such as strengthening protection for human rights. The essential argument is that the anarchy so instrumental in a structural realist understanding of global politics need not prevent states and individuals from achieving a more harmonious world. This compliments neo-functionalist theory, exemplified by the evolution of the European Union, a supranational institution that has substantial impact on the daily lives of citizens in states as diverse as Belgium and Greece. Of course, not all citizens in the European Union are happy with the impact of Union policies, believing them to be an infringement on sovereignty by largely unaccountable European institutions. We return to these themes in Chapter 5.

Finally, democratic peace theory asserts that historically, liberal democracies rarely if ever go to war against each other. This view was an important component of the work of Immanuel Kant (see Profile 1.7). The key to global stability is not necessarily a balance of power, or even increased trade, but rather the spread of Western-style liberal democracies, whose executives are constrained in their autonomy and cannot get away with the hazardous act of starting

PROFILE 1.7   Immanuel Kant (1724–1804)

Immanuel Kant. (© Corbis Canada/Public Domain)

IMMANUEL KANT

Immanuel Kant was a German philosopher who wrote as the Enlightenment was sweeping through Germany in the 18th century. He wrote his most famous work, *Perpetual Peace*, in 1795. Based on the experience of the wars of the French Revolution, Kant argued that there were two possible futures for humanity: the end of all hostilities through international agreements, or the perpetual peace of the cemetery of humankind after an annihilating war. *Perpetual Peace* is written as a contract similar to the diplomatic documents of the day; in this sense, it is a model for the establishment of international peace through international agreements between states. In it Kant proposes the following: the establishment of a system of conduct among states, including the principles of sovereignty, non-interference, and eventual disarmament; the conversion of authoritative states into republican states (which are less likely to go to war than the former); the development of an international federation of free states with a republican constitution that respects the sovereignty of its members; and the creation of conditions for universal hospitality and growing commerce across state borders. Kant believed that these measures would lead to peace among all peoples, a peace that would be reinforced by the natural tendency of states to engage in commerce rather than war with one another:

> In connection with the life of the agriculturalist, salt and iron were discovered which were perhaps the first articles that were sought far and near, and which entered into the commercial intercourse of different peoples. Thereby they would be first brought into a peaceful relation to one another; and thus the most distant of them would come to mutual understanding, sociability and pacific intercourse.

SOURCE: "IMMANUEL KANT," IN M. FORSYTH ET AL., EDS., *THE THEORY OF INTERNATIONAL RELATIONS: SELECTED TEXTS FROM GENTILI TO TREITSCHKE* (LONDON: GEORGE ALLEN AND UNWIN, 1970), 220.

wars against other democracies. People will throw expansionist politicians out of office if their designs on international power exceed the willingness of the population to sacrifice. More to the point, there is little incentive for one liberal democracy to attack another, as neither will regard the other as a threat to its way of life. Democratic peace theory has come under considerable scrutiny for several reasons: it is based on a Western or Eurocentric definition of democracy, there are methodological problems with the measurement of war, and the fact that republics such as the United States are obviously quite willing to wage war is undeniable. The theory leads some to suggest the key to peace is the spread of not only democracy per se but also the market institutions that often accompany it. More nuanced explorations of the theory ask questions about the relative autonomy of the executive decision-making units in democratic states, and take into account the abilities of even democratically elected leaders to deceive civilians into accepting the need for warfare.[23] Again, we return to this theory in later chapters.

Liberalism offers explanations about war and peace, state behaviour, trade and globalization, and international institutions that are very different from those provided by realists. Liberals suggest that they are better able to explain state decision making because liberalism accounts for the domestic politics of states as a factor in foreign policy. While realists emphasize continuity in global politics and see history as cyclical in nature, liberals emphasize the impact long-term economic and social changes have had on state behaviour. Societies and states are different in character and structure than in the past, and are more grounded in consensual government, rule of law, and more inclusive social participation. Liberals are therefore optimistic about the future: progress has occurred and will continue to occur, as long as the liberal project is the guide to practice.

CRITICAL PERSPECTIVES

There are two central ways critical theories challenge the more mainstream variations of realism and liberalism described above. The first involves a rejection of the core philosophies and values posited by the realist and liberal frameworks. Critical theories feature counter-dominant thinking, especially on themes related to social justice, that neither realist nor liberal approaches fully embrace. The second is an epistemological rejection of the orthodoxy of positivism, or the belief that we can take adequate stock of the world through empirical observation and the testing of hypotheses. This does not mean critical theorists are on a different page altogether: if Christian Reus-Smit is correct, the main debate animating IR theory in the past two decades "revolves around the nature of social agency, the relative importance of normative versus material forces, the balance between continuity and transformation in world politics, and a range of other empirical–theoretical questions."[24] These same questions inspire theorists of all stripes; however, the different strands of critical theory discussed below are united by their common rejection of realism or liberalism as ideological justifications for an unjust status quo. Global politics is not only about relations among states; non-state actors and social forces, such as entrenched classes and popular movements, are also agents of change. History can be seen as a narrative of the domination, exploitation, and marginalization of one group by another: of the Southern Hemisphere by the northern European imperialist powers, of women by men, and of some races by others. See Profile 1.9 (p. 29) for a comparison of key aspects of realist, liberalist, and critical perspectives.

MARXISM

The origins of Marxism lie in the writings of **Karl Marx** (1818 to 1883), who studied law and philosophy and wrote about history. In league with Friedrich Engels (1820 to 1895), Marx campaigned for a socialist Germany. Marxism itself is a branch of thought emerging from the French Revolution, the British Industrial Revolution, and German philosophy. Marx insisted on a materialist worldview, asserting that throughout history the political nature of society was determined by its economic structure. For Marx, the economic structure of society in his time was characterized by capitalism. As a result, society was divided into classes, on the basis of their relationship to the means of production in a capitalist system. The **bourgeoisie** owned the factories and the land, and governed society in their own interests. This class controlled technology, natural resources, and property; and dominated religious, philosophical, governmental, legal, and moral values. In contrast, the **proletariat** did not own any means of production and were forced to sell their labour to the bourgeoisie in return for payment. For Marx, this social structure was inherently exploitative and unjust, and he envisioned a revolution of the proletariat, which would overthrow the bourgeoisie and usher in a classless communist society.

According to Marxism, classes are the social engines of history. The state is merely a vehicle of the ruling economic class; it exists primarily to serve their interests and not those of society as a whole. Although Marx did not write extensively on international affairs, Marxist thinkers such as **John Hobson**, **Rosa Luxemburg**, and **Vladimir Lenin** wrote about the international impact of capitalism, which they considered to be the primary cause of **imperialism** (see Profile 1.8). Luxemburg is a very significant figure, since she was a prototypical Marxist feminist intellectual. As the domestic economies of the European powers ran out of markets, it

---

PROFILE 1.8 **Lenin and Monopoly Capitalism**

Revolutionary leader Vladimir Ilyich Lenin, St. Petersburg, February 1897. Russians listed Lenin as their number one choice for "man of the century" in their country, followed by dictator Josef Stalin, the Interfax news agency reported December 26, 2000. Lenin (1870 to 1924) founded Bolshevism and was the Soviet leader from 1917 until his death in 1924. (AP Photo/CP Images)

Though Lenin's place in history is well known, his role in the formation of an intellectual perspective on international political economy is less celebrated. In a treatise published at the end of World War I ("Imperialism: The Highest Stage of Capitalism"), Lenin argued that the war had resulted from competition among the major capitalist powers, which had reached the target of monopoly capitalism, "in which the division of all territories of the globe among the great capitalist powers has been completed." Imperialism resulted from the concentration of production in combines, cartels, syndicates, and trusts; the competitive quest for sources of raw materials; and the development of banking oligarchies. Under these conditions, imperialism was inevitable and not a matter of choice. The principal exporters of capital were also the dominant powers in the international system. Critics argue that this essentially economic explanation does not take into account other causes of imperialism, such as the search for glory and recognition. However, Lenin did explain nationalism as part of the false consciousness that guided the working classes to the battlefield and perpetuated their mutual slaughter; the sentiment of futility that eventually characterized participation in World War I worked in the Bolshevik's favour immediately prior to the Russian Revolution in 1917. Lenin's ultimate creation, the Soviet Union, is dead, but for many concerned with the plight of the Southern Hemisphere, his ideas still form the core of their thinking.

For an engaging biography of Lenin, see R. Payne, *The Life and Death of Lenin* (New York: Simon and Schuster, 1964).

became necessary to expand into the colonial areas to find new markets, natural resources, and a place to export capital. This in turn brought about conflict between the capitalist empires over territory and resources, which ultimately (from a Marxist perspective) led to World War 1.

In global politics today, the central assumption behind what are known as **neo-Marxist** perspectives is that economic classes are the primary units of analysis in world affairs and the economic growth experienced by the rich world has come at the expense of others, namely those on the periphery of the world economy. Economic relations are determined by geography and colonial history. Thus, states rich in natural resources, such as Canada, have gained from exporting them abroad and in particular to large markets such as the United States. At the same time, however, this traps states such as Kenya, Argentina, Zambia, and Peru into dependencies based on staple exports such as tea, bauxite, coffee, tobacco, and wood. Reliance on staple products is exacerbated by relative political weakness. Within underdeveloped states, the upper classes participate in the North–South exploitative relationship, not only reinforcing global inequality but also benefiting from it. Thus, most neo-Marxist analysis in IR has focused on how global capitalism has created a world divided between a few rich and many poor, and how the contemporary form of globalization extolled by many liberals is merely imperialism and colonialism in another guise.

Neo-Marxist theorists share several additional assumptions and views regarding global politics:

- The most important actors in global politics are dominant economic interests or socio-economic classes.

- Both the state and war are largely (though not exclusively) instruments of the ruling economic classes.

- States (and their ruling elites) are bound into a hierarchical structural relationship characterized by patterns of dominance and dependence.

- A wide differential in power exists between the rich and the poor, and this is attributed largely to their relationship to the means of production in national and global economies.

- For the marginalized and dependent states and peoples everywhere, revolution and the overthrow of the world capitalist system are the only hope for change. However, since this prescription of "delinking" from the world economy has proven elusive, and stunted efforts have produced unwanted violence, many advocate major reform in both domestic and international systems instead.

International thinking along neo-Marxist lines has taken many paths. One of the more influential modern variants has been **World Systems Theory**, which argues that poor states and peoples have become trapped in a global system of exploitation, one that forces them to be dependent on rich countries for capital markets, and imprisons them in an unfair trading relationship. At the heart of world systems theory is the proposition that capitalism has expanded worldwide to become a global system that transfers wealth from poor countries and peoples (the periphery) to rich countries and peoples (the core). The wealth of the rich is therefore derived in whole or in part from the poverty of the poor. The governments of poor states are usually complicit, because the ruling classes in the periphery countries also benefit from this system. An important international network thus exists involving local political elites and capitalists (often one and the same), the state apparatus in poor countries, multinational corporations (or, put another way, transnational capital), and political elites and capitalists in rich countries. As a result, the world is not interdependent, as liberals claim. Instead, it is hierarchical and exploitative. A variant of world systems theory known as **Dependency Theory** suggests that Central and South American politics and economics evolved in the context of European imperialism and then American hegemony, largely to the disadvantage of peoples living in Latin America. We will explore world systems theory and dependency theory in more depth in Chapter 4.

Finally, many neo-Marxist scholars today are inspired by the work of the Italian Marxist scholar Antonio Gramsci. An influential form of neo-Marxist thought comes in the form of "neo-Gramscian" international political economy. Gramsci argued that a form of socio-economic hegemony exists within states and societies that serves to reinforce the capitalist order controlled by rich elites. While the realist concept of hegemony focuses on material or hard power, neo-Gramscian scholars such as Robert Cox emphasized the influence of hegemonic ideas and institutions in a global hegemonic system.[25] The instruments of this hegemony include liberal economic theory and practice, the media, social organizations, and government propaganda designed to socialize the masses to convince them that their lives are better off under capitalism than could be otherwise, and that they should aspire to imitate the upper classes in order to live the good life—a life most will never achieve. Dominant states and elite capitalist centres of the world economy have ensured that the development of global politics protects their wealth not only with guns and warships but also with the spread of capitalist ideology and aspirations, reflected perhaps most visibly in the idea that globalization will be good for all, and not just a select few. The neo-Marxist project calls for sustained attention to a critical reading of such ideology, and reform of the system that allows its perpetuation.[26]

FEMINISM

Feminism is a broad intellectual, political, and social movement that cuts across a wide variety of academic disciplines and social discourse. The primary focus of feminism is how gender matters. Feminists assert that gender has largely been ignored due to the false assumption that a universal human experience exists, when in fact the grand narratives of history have been based almost exclusively on the male experience, and have been written from the male perspective. In particular, feminists seek to expose the ways in which power, inequality, and injustice are gendered, and seek to describe the nature of the patriarchal (male-dominated) systems that perpetuate the marginalization and oppression of women. Feminist scholarship is also directed toward the advancement of women, in the form of legal and political equality and economic and social inclusion.

Feminists who study global politics argue that a patriarchal system exists at the international level. They point to the relative lack of women in senior government positions, on the boards of major multinational corporations, and in the leadership of major international institutions as evidence. In addition, they observe that women own very little land worldwide, have lower pay and incomes, and possess a very small share of societal private wealth. Systematic discrimination against women is common in many countries. Women also face high levels of sexual violence worldwide and often form a disproportionate share of **refugee** populations. In making these and many other observations, feminists reveal the gendered nature of global politics and the need for policy responses that must serve the specific needs of women as well as men if they are to be successful. Further, as J. Ann Tickner argues, dominant academic perspectives have served to reinforce patriarchy not only in research but in policy debates and decisions as well. In particular, realism has been criticized by feminists for its gender-specific language and the cult of masculinity surrounding realist concepts like sovereignty, militarism, and anarchy. Realism has also served to diminish the importance of issues of special relevance to women, such as human rights, health care, family planning, education, and development.[27] Furthermore, all feminists share a belief that the state has had an instrumental role in enforcing and perpetuating patriarchy. As Jean Bethke Elshtain writes, "Received notions of sovereignty incorporated in their absolutist heart of hearts a demand for blood-sacrifice: *pro patria mori.* This sacrificial demand got encoded into modern identities, male and female, with the triumph—the very bloody triumph—of the modern nation-state."[28]

However, quite distinct versions of feminism exist. **Liberal feminists** argue that women's participation in world affairs has been silenced or marginalized and that this situation must be corrected. By bringing women into the halls of political and economic power, female experiences and perspectives will be included and contribute to more effective decisions and policies. **Radical feminists** submit that merely bringing women into existing institutions and structures would be insufficient and deeper changes are therefore necessary. There is a large divide here: while liberal feminists argue the central injustice is the lack of women in positions of authority, for radical feminists the entire state and international apparatus is based on patriarchal ideologies that perpetuate cycles of violence and environmental destruction. **Socialist or Marxist feminists** (recall the mention of Rosa Luxemburg, above) assert that the capitalist system is patriarchal in character and privileges men and marginalizes women. The solution is to alter the character of the economic system of society toward socialist theories emphasizing equality and redistributive justice. **Postcolonial feminists** offer perspectives based on the unique experiences of women in the developing or postcolonial world, experiences grounded in racism, class discrimination, and cultural exclusion. Postcolonial feminists often criticize liberal feminists for assuming a universality to the female experience and ignoring the unique characteristics and issues confronting women of different backgrounds, particularly in the non-Western world. **Ecofeminists** link violence against women with violence against nature, and argue we need to transcend both to achieve a more just and sustainable world.

The feminist perspective operates at two levels: First, the argument is made that the role women play in global politics and economics is essential and must be recognized in any salient analysis, whether the researcher is looking at structural adjustment programs, the international sex trade, the microelectronics production industry, the generation of intellectual capital, armed conflict, or any other topic. Similarly, the role women have played in historical developments should not be overlooked simply because masculine histories have not valued or included them. Second, there is a rejection of many of the dominant theories and priorities in the study of global politics and an emphasis on community health, sexual and reproductive rights, violence against women, cooperation, peace and disarmament movements, and sustainable development. In this respect, there is often a disconnect between feminism and the study of global politics: feminism is oriented (at least in part) to issues that were not traditionally seen as part of the core subject matter of international relations, at least until recently. There can be little doubt that the feminist critique of traditional international relations theory has had a profound impact on the thinking of a new generation of scholars and on policy debates in government and international institutions such as the UN. The larger question may well be whether, in a political and economic world still dominated by males and masculine discourse, feminist perspectives can have a serious impact on actual policy decisions. As feminists themselves argue, as gendered approaches have become incorporated into policy language and practice in governments and international institutions, gender has become depoliticized: it has become detached from the fundamental feminist concern with power and inequity.[29] Feminism and gender have been made "safe" in the policy world and in translation from theory to practice have lost their transformative, revolutionary, and liberating motives. Feminists remind us that forms of gendered marginalization, inequity, and injustice persist and reproduce themselves in many forms. Even where progress has been made, it is important to be vigilant about the limitations of that progress, and the work that still needs to be done. We return to feminist approaches in specific issue areas throughout this book.

GLOBAL ECOPOLITICAL THEORY

Although environmental approaches are not unified in any coherent body of theory, environmentalists do agree that liberal economic theories do not adequately account for the ecological costs of global economic growth, while realism ignores the role played by the state in perpetuating environmental exploitation. The multitude of ecological crises afflicting the world at present did not appear without warning: the misuse of agricultural land, for example, has long been known to have dire consequences, and pollution was a prevalent theme in the 1960s in North America and Europe. The historic connection between industrial development and environmental decay has become for many the overwhelming theme of human history. In contemporary global politics the trend looks as problematic as ever. Although there have been improvements in certain areas, such as protection of the ozone layer, there remains great uncertainty about the ability of humanity to respond effectively to the challenges of climate change, declining biodiversity, the oceans crisis, toxic waste, desertification, and many other issues.

Many varieties of global ecopolitical theories exist, some of which stress dealing with overpopulation, overconsumption, pollution, or the threat to endangered species with an institutional, regime management approach. This line of thinking, with its liberal pedigree, dominates the policy process and much of mainstream political science. More radical approaches advocate reconceptualizing capitalism or redefining human relations. Again, ecofeminists link patriarchy with **ecocide**. Non-state actors are often seen as the most important agents of change, and some radical environmentalists believe in direct action through protest or even acts of violence. Others argue that stronger states are necessary to preserve what is left of the natural world, even if it means limiting human personal freedoms in the process. We address this issue in greater detail in Chapter 10. In general, one can argue that all the forms of theory discussed here, including realism and liberalism, begin with certain premises about the relationship between humans and nature, though it is evident that radical ecological thought has the most in common with critical approaches.[30]

Some commentators suggest that increasing energy prices resulting from a decline in reserves of easily accessible oil, and a string of economic crises that began in 2008 to 2009, will force those in high-consumption societies to rethink our priorities and re-examine the impact of our own behaviour on the environment and on global politics. It is possible that steadily rising oil prices will make many forms of renewable energy more viable. For years, analysts and many politicians (including U.S. President Obama) have emphasized the importance of developing alternative energy sources and more energy-efficient products and processes. However, higher energy prices also make previously unprofitable oil reserves economically viable. An excellent example of this is Canada's own oil sands reserves. Canada now finds itself at the centre of a global debate on energy and the environment. Exploitation of Canada's bituminous sands reserves will bring economic profit for some but at a considerable

PROFILE 1.9	**Realism, Liberalism, and Critical Theories Compared**		
ISSUE	**REALISM**	**LIBERALISM**	**CRITICAL THEORIES**
Human nature	Selfish, immutable	Cooperative, seeking mutual gain, mutable	Variable; largely progressive
Central problem	War and security	Encouraging cooperation on global issues	Marginalization and imperialism; gender inequality; ecocide
Key actors	States; governments and military apparatus	Individuals; MNCs; "penetrated" states; international institutions; NGOs	Classes; groups; MNCs; NGOs; governments
Motives of actors	Power; national interest; security	Rational self-interest; justice; peace; prosperity	Power; greed; liberation; justice
Nature of international politics	Anarchy; economic growth will not overcome state conflicts	Interdependent; economic growth will promote peace	Hierarchy; dominance; exploitation; resistance to physical/intellectual hegemony
Outlook on future	Pessimism; perhaps stability; states will pursue neomercantilist policies	Optimism; progress is possible; economic growth is good for all; institutions will help	Pessimism unless paradigmatic change is achieved
Policy prescriptions and solutions	Enhance power; protect national interests	Develop institutions and regimes to encourage cooperation	Engender revolution, transformation, and social change

environmental cost, including the release of more greenhouse gasses into the atmosphere, localized pollution and destruction of habitat, and the risk (some would say inevitability) of pipeline and tanker spills. The desire for energy also affects global politics in other ways, especially the dependence of the industrialized world on foreign oil supplies. This dependence has nurtured the rise and survival of many "petro-tyrannies," which are undemocratic and repressive. For decades, Western support for such governments has resulted in a muted response to human rights violations conducted by autocratic regimes, and a consequent growth of anti-Western sentiment among many peoples in those countries. Furthermore, those taking a critical international political economy perspective would stress the relationship between oil dependence and American and Western efforts to secure oil access in the Middle East and elsewhere through diplomacy, coercion, reward, and even war. Today, increasing dependence on foreign energy supplies by countries like China and India promise to add new layers to the international politics of energy and the environment. In these and many other ways, ecopolitical theory reminds us of the vital, and growing, relationship between global politics and ecology. In Chapter 10 we return to this theme, which is highly relevant for people living in a resource-dependent state such as Canada.

THE POSITIVIST/POSTPOSITIVIST DISTINCTION AND CONSTRUCTIVISM

As mentioned above, critical theories are separated not only by more explicit concerns with social justice issues but also by their tendency to reject the positivist foundations of liberalism and realism. (We need to be cautious here, since many Marxists, for example, base their analyses in historical materialism, which claims empirical validity, and it would be improper to label all feminists or environmentalists postpositivist.) Postmodernists are primarily concerned with how people interpret the world around them and how they act on this understanding; they are critical of the positivist aspirations of the traditional theories. Postmodernists reject the idea that realists, liberals, or Marxists (all positivist and materialist theories) can ever really know anything concrete about global politics (or build objective knowledge about the world), since their personal biases will invariably influence their conclusions. For postmodernists, we cannot truly understand reality because how we see the world is socially constructed by subjective images that have their origins in our formative experiences, our cultures, our educations, our languages, and our political perspectives. "Reality" is, therefore, inherently intangible and subjective and is dependent on the nature of the viewer, not on the existence of an objective world. Furthermore, all viewers are embedded in social contexts and in power relations previously socially constructed by others: "reality" is, therefore, also dependent on the ideas shared by groups of people and how these ideas form their identities.

The more critically inclined postmodernists argue that individuals who have inherited the Western tradition have performed the bulk of research work in the sciences and humanities. This hegemonic intellectual tradition serves to marginalize other perspectives and non-Western thought. At the heart of the postmodern research agenda is an investigation into how power distribution in a relationship affects policy and scholarship. Every analysis, or policy, is constructed in such a way as to perpetuate or enhance a power relationship; the traditional approaches contribute to the present social injustice brought about by the development of modernity and the scientific revolution of the West. Postmodernist thought has many strands as well: deconstructionists emphasize the importance of breaking down popular texts or discourses to understand the power relations they perpetuate, while feminist postmodernists look for gender bias in traditional discourse. It is not fruitful to contrast these more interpretive approaches with the positivist orientations, since they are analytically incommensurable: neither can claim to actually be "better" than the other. Their sets of assumptions and aims are fundamentally different. Where they do converge, however, is in the effort to contribute to the intellectual debate over the imperative and possibility of avoiding mass violence.

Another approach, broadly labelled **constructivism**, depicts global politics (or any social subject, for that matter) as intersubjective. That is, "material resources only acquire meaning for human action through the structure of shared knowledge in which they are embedded."[31] For constructivists, meaning is derived from collective understandings of the material world: it is on the basis of such collective understandings that human action, group action, and social action is based. Stefano Guzzini described the "common ground" of constructivist theory as the social construction of knowledge and the construction of social reality.[32] In other words, what we attempt to understand in global politics is not independent, or separate, from our interpretation of global politics and the language we use to describe it. Constructivism stresses the impact of intersubjective understandings among political actors on constituting their own identities. This social construction of the self, be it by national leaders ("I am the leader of the free world"), members of international organizations ("I am a neutral international civil servant"), environmental scientists ("I am a citizen of the world"), or others, determines the normative acceptability of practices and discourses within issue areas. Some or all of the practices and discourses considered acceptable and even normatively positive in one social context ("I will lead the free world in a war against terrorism") will be less positive in another ("I believe only the UN can legitimize a war on terrorism") or unacceptable in others ("I reject a war on terrorism as short-sighted and counterproductive"). In short, "it is collective meanings that constitute the structures which organize our actions."[33] Constructivism builds on the work of theorists such as Michel Foucault and Anthony Giddens. As Emanuel Adler suggests,

> unlike positivism and materialism, which take the world as it is, constructivism sees the world as a project under construction, as becoming rather than being. Unlike idealism ... and post-modernism, which take the world *only* as it can be imagined or talked about, constructivism accepts that not all statements have the same ... value and that there is consequently some foundation for knowledge.[34]

Constructivists argue that there is much more room for actors to effect change in global politics than is generally accepted by neorealists and structural materialists. They are skeptical of the idea that enduring realities or continuities or structures determine the behaviour of actors. For example, according to realists, the reality of international anarchy exerts pressure on decision makers to act in a certain way. For constructivists, anarchy is not a material condition or assumed reality of global politics, but a widely accepted idea, a social construct. As one iconic essay suggests, anarchy does not make states act the way they do: anarchy is what states make of it.[35]

We hesitate to include constructivism as a distinct theory since it is in essence a way of understanding change that borrows from postmodernism and can be applied by a wide range of analysts with roots in all the perspectives outlined above. In particular, constructivism can be applied by those interested in studying international institutions, many of whom come from the liberal institutional school.[36]

THE HISTORICAL PERSPECTIVE

Historians who study global politics approach the discipline from a different perspective, arguing that IR scholarship has emphasized the development of theories and abstract models, while de-emphasizing the importance of historical research and knowledge. This has led to the development of theory based on historical generalizations that are at the very least highly contentious and at worse completely inaccurate: only a deeper, careful understanding of history can enable us to truly comprehend the subject matter of IR. Furthermore, in-depth examination of historical cases can yield new information and insights that can challenge prevailing historical "truths" and "lessons" that inform not only theory but also policy practice. In other words, hindsight is seldom perfect and historical understanding is seldom static. Historians also remind students of IR that much of what seems new may not be that novel after historical reflection. For example, globalization is often described as a new phenomenon, one that has changed our world in ways never before experienced. However, many of the patterns we associate with globalization are actually quite old, and previous eras experienced some of the same angst and wonder about the dawning of a new age as we do today. Globalization is a contested term and idea in the study of global politics, and historians have often been at the centre of the debate over whether it even exists and whether its supposed qualities and impacts are as new or profound as they have been portrayed. IR scholars are certainly indebted to the painstaking work conducted by historians, without which it would be impossible to present any sort of contextual understanding of contemporary issues (we borrow quite widely from history in the next chapter to do just that).

EMBRACING THEORETICAL DIVERSITY

At this point it would be inaccurate to say that any one perspective dominates the study of global politics. Realism certainly held sway in the United States for much of the Cold War era, and neorealism was a popular perspective in recent decades, but liberal perspectives are at least as prominent today and have often been so in the United Kingdom, Australia, and Canada. Critical perspectives are as popular as ever, especially among graduate students and scholars in the Americas, Africa, and Asia. There has certainly been a growing interest in constructivism in the past two decades. While the debates between theoreticians can be fascinating, and often quite overwhelming, we will not devote significant sections of this text to them, but attempt to integrate various perspectives in our own treatment of the subject matter. It will be clear to most readers, for example, that the next chapter, focusing mostly on historical conflicts and empire-building, has a realist context. Subsequent chapters will also demonstrate the relevance of liberal, Marxist, feminist, postmodern, and historical and environmentalist perspectives. They will also reaffirm our initial premise that convergence and divergence are occurring simultaneously today, a fact that would encourage all of the theoretical perspectives presented here in different ways.

There may be very good reasons to insist on your own perspective being the right one. At the same time, however, we would encourage you to proceed in this complex field with an open mind, and try to arrive at new conclusions regarding which perspective best explains global politics to you. There is no need to impose a rigid orthodoxy on the field; one of its attractions is the eclectic nature of the work it has inspired among generations of scholars and practitioners.

ONWARD!

This book intends to introduce students to the discipline of IR in the 21st century, and from a distinctly non-American viewpoint. Put bluntly, most IR textbooks are written by Americans, from an American perspective, for American students. The key examples and foreign policy dilemmas offered are American ones, reflecting that state's obviously unique position in world affairs. However, students living in **middle powers** such as Canada appreciate an approach that takes the circumstances of their country (as well as their own values and interests) into account. The task before citizens of countries such as Canada, Norway, Australia, Brazil, South Africa, Thailand, and many others is to better understand the global political environment and all that it entails, rather than to maintain national pre-eminence within it. Some may think of themselves not as citizens of states at all, but as global citizens. None of this denies the significance of the question of American power and influence in today's global political theatre. Nevertheless, there are issues in the world beyond those that most immediately concern the United States, Russia, China, or other military giants, and these are central to both everyday life and the bigger picture of global politics but are often neglected or given peripheral treatment in other texts.

Though the older concepts that have shaped the field—such as state, war, and diplomacy—have retained their significance, we face an era when environmental issues and non-state actors are often as important, when market forces are changing millions of lives on a daily basis, and when people are attempting to overthrow unjust political orders and forge new definitions of human rights and dignity. This idea generates a lengthy set of questions—an *agenda for study*—that requires looking into both traditional and unconventional areas. A partial list of such questions includes the following:

1. Which theoretical perspective best describes and explains the world? Different theoretical perspectives provide very different explanations of events and have commensurate implications for policymakers. Does a postpositivist approach add to our understanding? Is constructivism a unifying approach? Is the feminist critique of realism reasonable? Is a Marxist understanding of the evolution of world order more or less relevant today?

2. Is there a historical tendency toward the spread of democracy, and what impact will this have on global politics? Are the "Arab Spring" and democratization in Burma an indication of a trend? Would the existence of more formal liberal democracies reduce global tensions?

3. Is the international system diverging or converging? Two phenomena seem to exist side by side in the international system: the breakup and collapse of empires and states, and increasing interdependence and political and economic amalgamation. Is there a discernable trend in one direction or another?

4. Are states becoming obsolete? One trend in international affairs has been the increased permeability and penetrability of state borders. Has the **sovereignty** of the state eroded to the point where we may speak of its imminent demise in global politics? Or has sovereignty survived, but in a reconceptualized form?

5. What are the implications of terrorism and responses to terrorism for the international system and our understanding of it, including our conceptions of national security and individual liberty?

6. What are the causes of war, and how can conflicts be managed or prevented? This enduring question in IR is also highly relevant for the problem of wars within states, as well as the protection of civilians during armed conflict and the so-called Responsibility to Protect doctrine described in later chapters.

7. How can the proliferation of conventional weapons and weapons of mass destruction be stopped? The flow of weapons of mass destruction, sophisticated conventional weapons, and small arms to areas of tension and conflict are pressing international concerns. What does history teach us about the pursuit of arms control and disarmament? Will concerns over nuclear weapons proliferation (especially in Iran and North Korea) lead to increased tension and violence in the near future?

8. Are we heading toward an increasingly liberalized world economy characterized by global free trade, or toward the development of regional trading blocs or increased protectionism? Will the global economy be characterized by growth and stability or by crisis and recession? Will the European Union, once the iconic example for regional integration, survive its own financial crisis?

9. Are international organizations getting stronger or weaker? Some analysts argue that they serve to enhance and reinforce cooperation, but they remain perpetually underfunded and even disrespected by many. The invasion of Iraq in 2003, and the bombing of Serbia in 1999, proceeded without United Nations approval, while military actions against the Libyan government in 2011 had Security Council clearance.

10. How will environmental issues, especially climate change, affect global politics? Will the political pressures from climate change, resource scarcity, and the oceans crisis contribute to convergence or divergence among states and peoples? Can international institutions contribute to sustainable solutions? Do we need stronger central techno-cratic governance, or a more decentralized approach to environmental policymaking?

11. What impact has the information revolution had on global politics? Are we witnessing the evolution of a promised world of improved communication and sharing of knowledge leading to a global community, or a world of the information-rich and the information-poor, surveillance and censorship, cyberwarfare, and the spread of malicious spyware?

12. How will the continued migration of people affect global politics? People are on the move around the world, in the form of emigrants, refugees, and migrant workers. Economic and environmental displacement patterns suggest that even larger popu-lation movements will occur in the future, posing hard questions for those forging immigration and refugee policy. Meanwhile, human smuggling and trafficking has become a staple activity of organized crime.

13. What will be the future impact of inequalities in wealth? Both within and between states, the gap between high- and low-income groups continues to rise, adding fuel to protest movements such as the widespread "Wall Street Occupation" of 2011, and protests against austerity measures in Greece, Spain, and elsewhere in 2012. Meanwhile the Davos Summit and G8 meetings continue to debate policy at the elite level. Is the divide between rich and poor a threat to the future of global capitalism?

14. What are the best strategies for development and aid? This issue has been a pressing one since the 1960s, and as the divide between the world's rich and the world's poor continues to widen, the debate over development strategies has taken on a new urgency. Placing more priority on the role of women in development has led to oppor-tunities and new challenges.

15. What will future great power rivalry entail as Russia struggles to retain its former glory amidst widespread corruption, China copes with its enormous economic and resource needs, and the United States faces a new world order in which its own economic woes threaten its pre-eminence? What type of foreign policy responses from non-nuclear weapon states such as Canada can we expect?

Arguably, all these issues are linked by the pursuit of various forms of security. And, if global politics is largely about the pursuit of security (or the freedom from harm), security must be understood in terms of individual, community, national, and even global survival. Responding to this broad agenda is the greatest challenge we face in global politics, and it will certainly require multilateral responses, if not formal forms of global governance. As one major study argued, "Diverse kinds of new or revitalised international institutions will be key to meeting strategic challenges as varied as limiting climate change, countering terrorism, pro-viding effective responses to humanitarian catastrophes, managing changing power dynamics in Asia, and preventing further nuclear proliferation."[37]

These are but a few of the many questions challenging students of global politics today as they embark on a journey of overwhelming complexity, frustration, and discovery. Above all, this text is designed to provide interested readers with a rough guide for that journey, one that encompasses origins, currents, and directions. Some aspects of the study of global politics are timeless. As one author contends, "Diplomacy, in the sense of the ordered conduct of relations between one group of human beings and another group alien to themselves, is far older than history."[38] Some theorists argue that human nature has always been with us and will not change; others insist it can change for the better, or worse, according to circumstances. While we have witnessed incredible changes over the centuries in governance, technology, and scholarship, as our historical discussions in Part One of this book suggest, war and trade—two primary modes of human interaction—have both been around a very long time. Arguably, they have forged much of the present political context in which we function today, and we turn now to a historical account of that immensely complex but endlessly fascinating system.

Endnotes

1. Raymond Aron, *Peace and War: A Theory of International Relations* (Garden City, NY: Anchor, 1966/1973), 9; Kenneth Waltz, *Man, the State and War: A Theoretical Analysis* (New York: Columbia University Press, 1959), 238; Jacqui True, "Feminism," in S. Burchill et al., *Theories of International Relations*, 2nd ed. (London: Palgrave, 1996), 231.

2. J. Der Derian, "A Reinterpretation of Realism: Genealogy, Semiology and Dromology," in Der Derian, ed., *International Theory: Critical Investigations* (New York: New York University Press, 1995), 363–96, 366.

3. One of the most cited examples is Kal Holsti's article "Change in the International System: Interdependence, Integration, and Fragmentation," in O. Holsti, R. Siverson, and A. George, eds., *Change in the International System* (Boulder, CO: Westview Press, 1980), 23–53; more popularly, see B. Barber, "Jihad vs. McWorld," *Atlantic* 269 (March 1992), 53–63.

4. See, for example, J. Dougherty and R. Pfaltzgraff Jr., *Contending Theories of International Relations: A Comprehensive Survey*, 5th ed. (New York: Harper & Row, 2000); R. Keohane, ed., *Neorealism and Its Critics* (New York: Columbia University Press, 1986); O. Holsti, "Models of International Relations and Foreign Policy," *Diplomatic History* 13 (1989), 15–43; K.J. Holsti, *The Dividing Discipline: Hegemony and Diversity in International Theory* (Boston: Allen and Unwin, 1985); J. Der Derian, "Reinterpretation of Realism"; J. Sterling-Folker, ed., *Making Sense of IR Theory* (Boulder, CO: Lynne Rienner, 2005); C. Weber, *IR Theory: A Critical Introduction*, 2nd ed. (London: Routledge, 2005); and R. Jackson and G. Sorensen, *Introduction to IR: Theories and Approaches* (New York: Oxford, 2007).

5. See D. Dewitt and D. Leyton-Brown, eds., *Canada's International Security Policy* (Scarborough, ON: Prentice Hall, 1995). A classic text on conflict management is R. Matthews, A. Rubinoff, and J. G. Stein, eds., *International Conflict and Conflict Management: Readings in World Politics* (Scarborough, ON: Prentice Hall, 1984). Another subfield, known formally as *peace studies*, has focused on theories related to cooperation. In fact, the study of peace has a technical name: *irenology*. See J. Starke, *An Introduction to the Study of Peace (Irenology)* (Leyden, Holland: A.W. Sijthoff, 1968).

6. See K. Stiles and T. Akaha, eds., *International Political Economy: A Reader* (New York: HarperCollins, 1991); and R. Stubbs and G. Underhill, eds., *Political Economy and the Changing Global Order*, 3rd ed. (Toronto: University of Oxford Press, 2005); for a Canadian perspective, see D. Drache and M. Gertler, eds., *The New Era of Global Competition: State Policy and Market Power* (Montreal/Kingston: McGill-Queen's University Press, 1991). See also K. Narinzny, *The Political Economy of Grand Strategy* (Ithaca: Cornell University Press, 2007).

7. See R. Riggs and J. Plano, *The United Nations: International Organization and World Politics* (Chicago: Dorsey Press, 1994); J. Ruggie and H. Milner, eds., *Multilateralism Matters: New Directions in World Politics* (New York: Columbia University Press, 1993); S. Krasner, ed., *International Regimes* (Ithaca, NY: Cornell University Press, 1983); and A. Cassese, *International Law* (Oxford: Oxford University Press, 2001). This subfield has been overtaken by the formal study of global governance: see Chapter 5, and the flagship journal *Global Governance: A Review of Multilateralism and International Organizations*; and S. Bernstein and L. Pauly, eds., *Global Governance: Towards a New Grand Compromise?* (Albany: State University of New York Press, 2007).

8. For example, see M. Walzer, *Just and Unjust Wars* (New York: Basic Books, 1992); F. Kratchvil, *Rules, Norms, and Decisions: On the Conditions of Practical and Legal Reasoning in International Relations and Domestic Affairs* (Cambridge, UK: Cambridge University Press, 1989); R. Jackson, *The Global Covenant: Human Conduct*

in a World of States (Oxford: Oxford University Press, 2000); T. Pogge, ed., *Global Justice* (Oxford: Blackwell, 2001); and R. Friman, ed., *Challenges and Paths to Global Justice* (New York: Palgrave Macmillan, 2007).

9. See J.D. Singer, "The Level of Analysis Problem in International Relations," *World Politics* 14 (1961), 77–92; K. Waltz, *Man, the State and War*; and R.C. North, *War, Peace, Survival: Global Politics and Conceptual Synthesis* (Boulder, CO: Westview Press, 1990).

10. In fact, much of this work is termed *diplomatic history*, and continues today; for example, the Society for Historians of American Foreign Relations continues to publish its flagship journal, *Diplomatic History*.

11. See C. Bob, *The Global Right Wing and the Clash of World Politics* (Cambridge University Press, 2012).

12. For example, John Naisbitt argues that the larger the system, the more powerful and important its smaller parts. See his *Global Paradox: The Bigger the World Economy the More Powerful Its Smallest Players* (New York: William Morrow, 1994).

13. These two dimensions are outlined in more detail in J.S. Nye Jr., *Bound to Lead: The Changing Nature of American Power* (New York: Basic Books, 1990).

14. J. Rosenau, *Turbulence in World Politics: A Theory of Change and Continuity* (Princeton: Princeton University Press, 1990), 6.

15. C. Lindblom, *Inquiry and Change: The Troubled Attempt to Understand and Shape Society* (New Haven: Yale University Press, 1990), x.

16. K. Boulding, "National Images and International Systems," *Journal of Conflict Resolution* 3 (June 1959), 120–31.

17. See A. Schlesinger Jr., *The Cycles of American History* (Boston: Houghton Mifflin, 1986).

18. D. Boucher, *Political Theories of International Relations: From Thucydides to the Present* (Oxford: University Press, 1998), 162–3.

19. See K.R. Nossal, *The Politics of Canadian Foreign Policy*, 2nd ed. (Scarborough, ON: Prentice-Hall, 1989).

20. See H. Bull, *The Anarchical Society: A Study of Order in World Politics* (London: The Macmillan Press, 1977).

21. For the most recent edition of this work, see *Power and Interdependence*, 3rd ed. (New York: Longman, 2001).

22. For a classic article see S.D. Krasner, "Structural Causes and Regime Consequences: Regimes as Intervening Variables," *International Organization* 36 (1982), 185–205.

23. A wealth of literature has emerged on this theoretical proposition; for an excellent overview and sophisticated application, see N. Ripsman, *Peacemaking by Democracies: The Effect of State Autonomy on the Post–World War Settlements* (University Park, PA: Pennsylvania State University Press, 2002). See also J. Owen, "How Liberalism Produces Democratic Peace," *International Security* 19, no. 2 (1994), 87–125.

24. C. Reus-Smit, "Constructivism," in S. Burchill et al., *Theories of International Relations* (London: Palgrave, 2000), 209–30, 221–2.

25. R. Cox, *Production, Power, and World Order: Social Forces in the Making of History* (New York: Columbia University Press, 1987).

26. See M. Rupert and H. Smith, eds., *Historical Materialism and Globalization* (London: Routledge, 2002), for a series of sophisticated essays; and S. Gill, and J. Mittelman, eds., *Innovation and Transformation in International Studies* (Cambridge University Press, 1997). For a critical take on the "appropriation" of Gramsci for these purposes see J. Femia, "Gramsci, Machiavelli and International Relations," *The Political Quarterly* 76, no. 3 (2005), 341–9.

27. For a review of feminist approaches to IR, see J. Ann Tickner, "Feminist Perspectives on International Relations," in W. Carlsnaes, T. Risse, and B. Simmons, eds., *Handbook of International Relations* (London: Sage, 2002), 275–91. See also J. Steans, *Gender and International Relations: An Introduction* (New Brunswick, NJ: Rutgers University Press, 1998), C. Sylvester, *Feminist International Relations: An Unfinished Journey* (Cambridge, UK: Cambridge University Press, 2002); J. Goldstein, *War and Gender: How Gender Shapes the War System and Vice Versa* (Cambridge: Cambridge University Press, 2001); and J. Joachim, *Agenda Setting, the UN and NGOs: Gender Violence and Reproductive Rights* (Washington: Georgetown University Press, 2007).

28. "Feminist Themes and International Relations," in J. Der Derian, "Reinterpretation of Realism," 340–62, 353. On Luxemburg, see R. Dunayevskaya, *Rosa Luxemburg, Women's Liberation, and Marx's Philosophy of Revolution*, 2nd ed. (Chicago: University of Illinois Press, 1991).

29. See S. Whitworth, "Feminism," in D. Snidal and C. Reus-Smit, eds., *The Oxford Handbook of International Relations* (Oxford: Oxford Handbooks Online, 2008), 391–404, www.oxfordhandbooks.com/oso/public/content/oho_politics/9780199219322/toc.html (accessed June 30, 2012).

30. See E. Laferrière and P. Stoett, *International Relations Theory and Ecological Thought: Towards a Synthesis* (London: Routledge, 1999); E. Laferrière and P. Stoett, eds., *International Ecopolitical Theory: Critical Approaches* (Vancouver: UBC Press, 2007); and R. Saunier and R. Meganck, *Dictionary and Introduction to Global Environmental Governance* (London: Earthscan, 2007).

31. A. Wendt, "Constructing International Politics," *International Security* 20 (Spring 1995), 73.

32. S. Guzzini, "A Reconstruction of Constructivism in International Relations," *European Journal of International Relations* 6 (Summer 2000), 149.

33. A. Wendt, "Anarchy Is What States Make of It: The Social Construction of Power Politics," *International Organization* 46, no. 2 (1992), 391–425.

34. E. Adler, "Constructivism and International Relations," in W. Carlsnaes, T. Risse, and B.A. Simmons, eds., *Handbook of International Relations*, 95.

35. Hence the title of Wendt's seminal article; see note 33.

36. For a spirited discussion and defence of this broad yet emergent thinking, see especially J. Der Derian, "Post-Theory: The Eternal Return of Ethics in International Relations," in M. Doyle and J. Ikenberry, eds., *New Thinking in International Relations Theory* (Boulder, CO: Westview, 1997), 54–76. For a general treatment of constructivism, see I. Hacking, *The Social Construction of What?* (Cambridge, MA: Harvard University Press, 1999); and see also P. Katzenstein, *The Culture of National Security: Norms and Identity in World Politics* (New York: Columbia University Press, 1996).

37. A. Nicoll and T. Huxley, "Introduction," in A. Nicol and T. Huxley, eds., *Perspectives on International Security*, Adelphi Paper 400–401 (London: International Institute of Strategic Studies, 2008), 27.

38. Sir Harold Nicolson, *Diplomacy*, 3rd ed. (London: Oxford University Press, 1963), 5.

History and Global Politics: War and Peace

Even the ordinary, the "impartial" historiographer, who believes and professes that he maintains a simply receptive attitude; surrendering himself only to the data supplied him—is by no means passive as regards the existence of his thinking powers. He brings his categories with him, and sees the phenomena presented to his mental vision, exclusively through those media.

—*Georg Wilhelm Friederich Hegel[1]*

The twentieth century is hardly behind us but already its quarrels and its achievements, its ideals and its fears are slipping into the obscurity of mis-memory.

—*Tony Judt[2]*

AN INTRODUCTION TO THE ROLE OF HISTORY

History is crucial to our understanding of contemporary global politics, because we need to understand the past in order to even begin to comprehend the present. The study of history can help us identify examples of continuity and change, and patterns of divergence and convergence. History can provide case studies for research into a limitless array of topics, such as the origins of war, revolution, international law, terrorism, and political tensions within states. For example, any attempt to understand or address the conflict in Afghanistan requires an awareness of the cultural evolution of the country as well as its past experiences with foreign occupation. The division of the Korean peninsula must be understood with reference to World War II, the Cold War, and the **Korean War**. An understanding of the September 11, 2001, terrorist attacks against the United States of America is impossible without an awareness of the history of the Middle East or American foreign policy. It is impossible to understand the persistent national unity question or First Nations issues in Canada without some knowledge of the colonial legacy in North America. In short, history is all around us, and both scholars and decision makers ignore it at their peril.

As our opening quotes suggest, rarely is the importance of perspective more evident than when examining history, since many different interpretations of past events exist and compete for validity. Constructivists remind us that states tend to have official versions of historical events, often glorifying the importance and righteousness of their actions, or perhaps minimizing the harm caused in their name. For example, Japanese textbooks still omit many of the facts about Japanese foreign policy during World War II (see Profile 2.1). Many states have suffered collective amnesia after particularly traumatic events, including war-related atrocities.[3] Groups of individuals unified by race, religion, or clan ties also have their own interpretations of history, which are frequently at odds with the interpretations of other groups or governments. Scholars of IR (international relations) also have divergent views of history, depending on their educational and social background, as well as their theoretical orientation. Furthermore, as feminists and postmodernists often argue, historical perspectives are inherently exclusionary. Many groups—including women and ethnic and religious minorities—make the accurate observation that they have been underrepresented in mainstream histories. Others insist that the legacy of human interaction with nature, or environmental history, is of fundamental importance.[4] Finally, history is vulnerable to radical revisions for political ends. For example, those who deny that the Holocaust ever took place are not interpreting history; they are trying to rewrite it for their own purposes. Vigilance against this sort of manipulation is as important as respect for different perspectives (see Profile 2.1).

In this chapter, we will briefly examine world history with a view to highlighting four key themes in the relationship between history and global politics. First, history is most often presented, as it is here, as the history of war and conflict and the rise and fall of civilizations, states, and empires. This is most consistent with the interpretation of the realist perspective, which emphasizes the historical continuity of balance of power politics, the importance of alliances, and the inevitability of war. Although this view of history is not necessarily inaccurate, as we will see in future chapters, it is incomplete. Second, developments in history have had a defining impact on the development of theories of war and peace. The two are inseparable, and the changing nature of global politics has stimulated the development of new theories and the adaptation of old ones; the theories we discussed in Chapter 1 are all grounded in differing interpretations of historical developments. Third, history reveals the central importance of ideas as driving forces of change and conflict. Religious faiths and political ideologies have had an enormous impact on the evolution of human societies and how they interact. Finally, historical interpretations are always undergoing revision, often by theories that seek to challenge prevailing assumptions. As a discipline, IR has been accused of relying on Eurocentric views of history that present the rest of the world as a mere appendage to European imperial power. As Philip Darby observes, "International relations remains wedded to a colonial world-view that both distorts its understanding of what is happening in the South and skews its normative horizons."[5] Hindsight is seldom 20/20, and the lessons of history are always subject to critical reassessment.

THE ANCIENT LEGACY: THE RISE AND FALL OF CIVILIZATIONS AND EMPIRES

In the Middle East, civilization first developed around 3500 BCE, in the basins of three great river systems. The river basin of the Tigris and Euphrates was the cradle for the early Mesopotamian city-states and the Assyrian (1244 to 605 BCE) and Persian (550 to 331 BCE) empires. The Nile River basin sustained the great Egyptian empires of the Pharaohs, which rose to the heights of the age of the pyramids (c. 2590 BCE) and the XII (1991 to 1786 BCE)

PROFILE 2.1　Abusing History

CONTENT OMISSION IN JAPANESE SCHOOL TEXTBOOKS

In 1997, a Japanese historian named Saburo Ienaga won a landmark case before the Japanese Supreme Court. The court ruled that the Japanese Education Ministry broke the law when it removed certain material from a high school textbook written by Ienaga. Since the 1950s, the Education Ministry has screened Japanese textbooks, removing references to the numerous atrocities committed by the Japanese military in World War II. As a result, generations of Japanese schoolchildren have experienced school with only a general or highly sanitized account of Japan's war record. One of the more egregious references removed from Ienaga's textbook concerned biological warfare experiments conducted by the Japanese military on Chinese subjects during the war. Support for state censorship comes from nationalists (who regard such references as an attack on Japanese pride) and relies on widespread ignorance of Japan's war record (itself largely a result of the education policy). Today's Japanese textbooks now include more uncomfortable facts concerning Japan's role in the war. For example, most textbooks now mention the "comfort women" who were infamously forced into prostitution to serve the soldiers of the Japanese military. However, references to Japan's share of the responsibility for World War II, and the extent of atrocities committed by the Japanese military, remain brief and incomplete. This provides an important example of how states and governments can abuse history through censorship and the suppression of unpopular ideas or facts. Because of the Court's decision, the material on biological warfare experiments was restored to Ienaga's textbook. However, other references in his book remain omitted. The selective coverage of Japan's war record remains a controversial subject inside and outside the country, leading to protests in China and Korea in 2005 and on the Japanese island of Okinawa in 2007.

SOURCE: G. HICKS, *JAPAN'S WAR MEMORIES: AMNESIA OR CONCEALMENT?* (ALDERSHOT: ASHGATE, 1997).

JIM KEEGSTRA AND HOLOCAUST DENIAL

In 1985, an Alberta schoolteacher and town mayor named Jim Keegstra went on trial in Red Deer, Alberta. Keegstra was charged with willfully promoting hatred against an identifiable group—Jewish people—from 1978 to 1982, while teaching social studies at Eckville High School in Alberta. Keegstra taught his students that Judaism was an evil religion that perverted the laws of God and condoned the harsh treatment of non-Jewish peoples. He implicitly taught his students that the Holocaust was a hoax and that an international Jewish conspiracy—called the *hidden hand*—was working behind the scenes with the support of Jewish financiers to establish a new order in which there would be a world government. According to Keegstra, Jews had infiltrated every institution of society, and this demanded that non-Jews be aware and watchful. Keegstra told his students that conventional history books were full of pro-Jewish lies, and he assigned readings from his own books and pamphlets instead. Class exams and essays were based on these readings and class notes. In most respects, Keegstra's teachings were typical of anti-Semitic views, full of conspiracy theories based on historical distortions and outright inaccuracies, suppression and denial of evidence, and barely concealed hatred. He passed these views on to students in a high school social studies class as factual, one example among many of the abuse of history by individuals or groups. Jim Keegstra was found guilty, fined $5000, and prohibited from teaching high school. The Supreme Court upheld this decision, although the Alberta Court of Appeal reduced his sentence.

SOURCE: SEE W. HARE, "LIMITING THE FREEDOM OF EXPRESSION: THE KEEGSTRA CASE," *CANADIAN JOURNAL OF EDUCATION*, VOL. 15, NO. 4, PG. 375–389, 1990.

and XVIII (1570 to 1320 BCE) dynasties. The Indus River basin and the plain of Ganges were the cradle of India's early Harappa and Mohenjo-Daro civilizations (c. 2550 to 1550 BCE). These city-states, empires, and civilizations developed complex instruments of diplomacy and trade. However, they also developed complex, effective systems for waging war.

Although hunter–gatherer societies certainly engaged in organized violent conflict, civilization and war have a powerfully symbiotic relationship. Given the conflictive nature of the past, it is difficult to avoid the conclusion that once individuals settle in a given area, and their survival becomes tied to the land around them, the idea of territorial ownership and the protective instinct become very strong. John Keegan bluntly suggests that "pastoralism, and agriculture even more so, make for war."[6] Furthermore, large-scale warfare can be conducted only by systems of governance that possess the organizational capacity to marshal the requisite surplus resources. In ancient civilizations, revenues from taxes, tributes, and rents were expended on war, worship, or welfare—usually in that order.[7]

Civilization in the Mediterranean was dominated by successive waves of Greek peoples, who established control over much of the region (c. 1150 to 550 BCE). In Asia Minor (present-day Turkey) the Greek advance clashed with the Persian Empire of Darius and Xerxes. Although Greece resisted conquest, the unity of the Greek city-states collapsed and the resulting Peloponnesian War (431 to 404 BCE) between Athens and Sparta enabled Macedon, under Philip, to dominate the Greek peninsula. The Peloponnesian War is regarded as one of the most important case studies in global politics, especially by realists (see Profile 2.2). Philip's son, **Alexander the Great**, conquered a dominion that stretched from Macedon to the Indus River, but his empire collapsed after his death. A new power centre developed around Rome in central Italy, and soon expanded over the entire Italian peninsula (510 to 264 BCE). Bolstered by an extremely effective military and administrative system, Roman rule (first as a republic and then as an empire) eventually stretched from present-day Spain to Mesopotamia. However, the Roman Empire declined due to internal decay, civil war, and "barbarian" invasions. Peter Heather suggests the fall of Rome was attributable to its thirst for conquest: "By virtue of its unbounded aggression, Roman imperialism was ultimately responsible for its own destruction."[8] The Roman Empire was divided in 330 CE when the eastern Byzantine Empire was created under the control of Constantinople (Byzantium). The western half of the

---

PROFILE 2.2 Thucydides (460–400 BCE)

Thucydides is regarded as the greatest of the classical Greek historians, mainly because of his unfinished account of the Peloponnesian War between Athens and Sparta (Lacedaemon). Thucydides himself was an exiled Athenian general who decided to record events for posterity; his exhaustive and dramatic account can be read as a Greek tragedy, a story of virtue and deceit, and an early exploration of the origins of war. Many contemporary scholars of global politics maintain that the themes in the book are applicable across time, culture, and place. Thucydides sought to draw themes and generalizations about the origin of all wars and to offer historical lessons for those who might read his work in the future. For Thucydides, "the growth in the power of Athens, and the alarm this inspired in Lacedaemon, made war inevitable." He thus identified the cause of war in the fear provoked by shifts in the distribution of power across the Greek city-states. His focus on the importance of power is most graphically illustrated in the famous Melian Dialogue, in which the powerful Athenians say to the less powerful Melians, "For you know as well as we do that right ... is in question only between equals in power, while the strong do what they can and the weak suffer what they must." Thucydides also reflected on the role of prominent individuals in the course of events, and he is considered one of the intellectual founders of political realism.

SOURCES: THUCYDIDES, *THE PELOPONNESIAN WAR*, THE CRAWLEY TRANSLATION (NEW YORK: THE MODERN LIBRARY, 1982), 14, 351. SEE ALSO J. MONTEN, "THUCYDIDES AND MODERN REALISM," *INTERNATIONAL STUDIES QUARTERLY* 50 (2006), 3–25.

Remembering Rome. Will tourists of the future learn about the decline and fall of the American empire, just as these tourists are learning about the decline and fall of the Roman Empire today? (AP Photo/Plinio Lepri)

empire fell to invasion in the fifth century, but the Byzantine Empire survived another 1000 years until Constantinople (today called Istanbul) was conquered by the Ottoman Empire in 1453 CE. When the power of Rome collapsed, most of the infrastructure, knowledge, and security its rule had provided disappeared as a Dark Age enveloped much of Europe and the Mediterranean. Many observers of our own time have argued that the United States exerts a greater hegemonic influence today than Rome at the height of its power: the rise, decline, and fall of Rome is therefore studied with great interest. Is American power failing, as did Rome's, and if so what will be the consequences?

In northern Europe, distinct cultural groups had developed by 800 BCE, but by 450 BCE it was largely under Celtic domination. Meanwhile, the Slavic peoples established a centre of civilization in what is today central Russia. The decline and fall of the Western Roman Empire in the fourth and fifth centuries exposed Europe to numerous invasions from nomadic peoples living in northern and southern Europe (Goths, Vikings, Vandals, and Magyars), and from larger incursions that originated in central Asia (Huns, Avars, and, later, Mongols). These nomadic peoples also invaded Mediterranean Europe, China, India, and Persia, throwing all of these centres of civilization into ruin or near-collapse. In the aftermath of the fall of Rome, power in Europe devolved to local nobles, ushering in the era of European feudalism and the Middle Ages. Political and economic life was highly localized and controlled by small numbers of nobles and knights who exerted a measure of political independence derived largely from their dominance over military affairs and the defensive strongholds of their castles. In feudal societies, concepts like nationalism and citizenship did not exist, and authority and loyalty were invested in lord, religion, town, and guild. For Karl Marx, the development of feudalism was an important step in the evolution of society toward capitalism, which in turn was a step toward communism. Feudal Europe continued to experience nomadic invasions: from 1206 to 1696 CE the Mongol empire launched repeated invasions into Europe, the Middle East, and Asia under Genghis Khan and his sons and grandsons. However, the unity of the Mongol empire broke down, and Mongol power receded in the face of expanding Russia and China.[9]

Larger kingdoms ruled by dynastic monarchies began to establish themselves in Europe between the 10th and 13th centuries in what are today the British Isles, Germany, France, and eastern Europe. Wealth from trade and gunpowder facilitated this process of political consolidation: cannon could destroy castle or city walls, and this diminished the ability of land-owning knights and fortified towns to resist a monarch with the wealth to purchase the new weapons. Indeed, the combination of commerce and cannon helped to make many a king. Yet this process of political consolidation, as well as agricultural, industrial, and intellectual development, was slowed by famine, plague, and war (in particular, the Hundred Years' War between England and France). European recovery from these events began in 1450, as the empires of France, the **Hapsburgs**, Muscovy/Russia, Sweden, and Lithuania all grew through the 15th and 16th centuries. However, resistance to amalgamation was widespread. For example, the Scots and Irish resisted the expansion of English rule. This resistance left an enduring legacy in the independence movements of Scotland and the violence in Northern Ireland. Italy remained divided into city-states, and this period is often regarded as a case study in power politics (see Profile 2.3). Finally, the religious wars of the Reformation, culminating in the devastating **Thirty Years' War** (1618 to 1648), dominated political, intellectual, and religious affairs (see Profile 2.4).

Despite this instability, this era was one of European exploration and expansion. European exploration by Portugal and Spain, and then by France, England, and Holland, was originally motivated by a desire to circumvent the controlling influence of the commercial cities (primarily Venice and Genoa) that dominated the medieval trade routes to central Asia and the Middle East. This brought a European presence to virtually all the inhabited continents. These events produced several lasting outcomes. The focus of political and commercial activity shifted from the Mediterranean to the trading empires of Western Europe. Trade and commerce became truly global in scope. The political and economic life of Europe was extended throughout the world, particularly in the form of growing rivalries between the trading empires, and the colonization of millions. Trade and political violence became inseparable. As Jeremy Black argues, "Violence was employed in order to influence or even dictate the terms of trade, in particular by excluding rivals, rather than to gain territory."[10] Slowly but steadily, the age of European empire was beginning.

In the Middle East, the spectacular rise and expansion of Islam dominated the period after the fall of Rome. Established by the prophet Muhammad (c. 570 to 632 CE), Islam expanded within a century from the Arabian Peninsula to include North Africa and southern Spain, and the western reaches of China and India. This extraordinary success was due to the weakness of the post-Roman world, military supremacy, and the vitality of the new religion of Islam.[11] After a period of great prosperity and cultural and intellectual development, internal dissension weakened the empire, which lost some of its territories in southern Europe and the Mediterranean to crusading Christians from Europe in the 10th century.[12] The Crusades remain a powerful source of resentment in the Arab world, and are often invoked (along with the colonial period of the 19th and 20th centuries) to contextualize and explain Western actions in the region. Islam experienced a significant

PROFILE 2.3 Niccolo Machiavelli (1469–1527)

Niccolo Machiavelli. (© Bettmann/CORBIS)

Machiavelli was a civil servant and diplomat in the republic of Florence during the 15th and 16th centuries, when city-states vied for power and influence across what is now Italy. Advising the rulers of Florence during this struggle was Machiavelli's profession. When Florence fell in 1512, Machiavelli was without a job, and he spent the final years of his life writing books, including his most famous works, *The Prince* and *The Discourses*. Drawing heavily on his examination of Greek and Roman writings as well as his own experience as a diplomat, he wrote of power, alliances, and the causes of conflict in the Italian city-state system. Much of what he wrote was aimed at the leaders—or princes—of states, advising them on the principles of statecraft, the conduct of their affairs with other princes, the importance of military force, and the lessons of historical experience. For Machiavelli, the security and survival of the state was the paramount concern of the prince; all other concerns were subordinated to this objective. The ends—the security of the state—justified the means necessary to achieve that objective. This Machiavellian approach to politics has often been criticized as amoral. However, Machiavelli argued that rulers must do what is in the best interests of the state; to do otherwise would in fact be immoral. Machiavelli also stressed that his advice to princes was based not on ethical principles or visions of the world as it should be or ought to be, but rather on the way the world was, according to historical and contemporary evidence. To act based on how one felt the world ought to be, as opposed to how the world really was, would be a recipe for disaster. In the study of IR, Machiavelli's emphasis on interests, power, and the conduct of statecraft is inseparable from the realpolitik tradition of political realism; he also engaged in the formal study of military strategy, and would have a lasting effect on strategic studies as well.

SOURCE: NICCOLO MACHIAVELLI, *THE PRINCE AND THE DISCOURSES* (NEW YORK: THE MODERN LIBRARY, 1950); F. GILBERT, "MACHIAVELLI: THE RENAISSANCE OF THE ART OF WAR," IN P. PARET, ED., *MAKERS OF MODERN STRATEGY: FROM MACHIAVELLI TO THE NUCLEAR AGE* (NEW JERSEY: PRINCETON UNIVERSITY PRESS, 1986), PG.11–31.

resurgence between 1300 and 1639, led by the Ottoman Empire. By 1354 the Ottoman Empire expanded through the Balkans east of the Adriatic and south of the Danube, and all around the Black sea. By the time of Suleiman the Magnificent (1520 to 1566), the Ottoman Empire was one of the great empires of the world. In the East, Islam spread through Persia, expanding to central Asia, southern Asia, and the outlying provinces of China, as well as present-day Indonesia (see Map 2.1). However, the Islamic world began to fracture politically (as the Mughal Empire in India and Safavid Persia clashed with each other and the Ottoman Empire) and religiously (as the **Sunni** and **Shiite** branches of Islam came into conflict). Although increasingly referred to as the "sick man of Europe," the Ottoman Empire remained a world power until World War I.[13]

PROFILE 2.4 Thomas Hobbes (1588–1679)

Thomas Hobbes. (Corbis Canada/Public Domain)

Hobbes was an English political philosopher who wrote in the turbulent years of the early 17th century, which were dominated by the Thirty Years' War in Europe. In England, Parliament was asserting its power against the monarchy, which would eventually lead to the English Civil War, and Hobbes, a royalist, was compelled to flee to France for eight years. In his writings,

Hobbes's primary focus was politics within the state. In his most famous work, *Leviathan*, he depicted the condition of humanity in a hypothetical "state of nature" that would exist in the absence of governmental authority. This condition, he argued, would be characterized by anarchy, "a war of every one against every one," in which there would be "continual fear and danger of violent death; and the life of man, solitary, poor, nasty, brutish, and short." This condition could be avoided only by the creation of the *Leviathan*, a state or ruler who would establish and maintain order. Without order, there could be no civilization. Realists often describe international relations as a Hobbesian state of nature that lacks a Leviathan in the form of a world government or a dominant power to impose order. Like individuals in a state of nature, states exist in an anarchic environment, in a war of everyone against everyone in which suspicion, distrust, conflict, and war are inevitable. In such a "self-help" world, states must pursue their individual self-interests.

SOURCE: THOMAS HOBBES, *LEVITHAN*, MICHAEL OAKESHOTT, ED. (NEW YORK: COLLIER MACMILLAN, 1974). SUGGESTED READING: FOR A CONTRARY VIEW ON HOBBES AND IR, SEE M. WILLIAMS, "HOBBES AND INTERNATIONAL RELATIONS: A RECONSIDERATION," *INTERNATIONAL ORGANIZATION*, VOL. 50, ISSUE 2, PG. 213–236, 1996.

In Asia, civilization began with the development of the first agricultural, hunting, and fishing communities around 4000 BCE, in what are today northern China, Southeast Asia, and India. The Shang Dynasty (1700 to 1100 BCE) was the first historical dynasty in China, but like the enormous Harappa and Mohenjo–Daro civilizations of India (c. 2550 to 1550 BCE), it succumbed to foreign invasion. A period of consolidation and fragmentation of political units in both China and India followed. In India, Chandra-Gupta and his dynasty (297 BCE to 236 CE) succeeded in unifying most of the Indian peninsula under one ruler (see Profile 2.5). Invasion from the north fragmented the empire, which was reestablished under the Gupta empires (320 to 410 CE). In China, the Chou Dynasty (1122 to 221 BCE) replaced the Shang Dynasty. Between 1122 and 771 BCE, this empire maintained stability and order based on a feudal system. However, after 771 BCE the empire increasingly fragmented into independent kingdoms engaged in almost continual conflict, culminating in the Warring States period of 403 to 221 BCE (see Profile 2.6 and Map 2.2). This period in Chinese history is often used to illustrate the themes of power politics, in much the same way as the Italian city-state period. The victorious Ch'in Empire in turn collapsed and was replaced by the Han Dynasty (206 BCE to 220 CE), which established a prosperous and well-administered empire.

Map 2.1 The Extent of the Islamic World in 1500

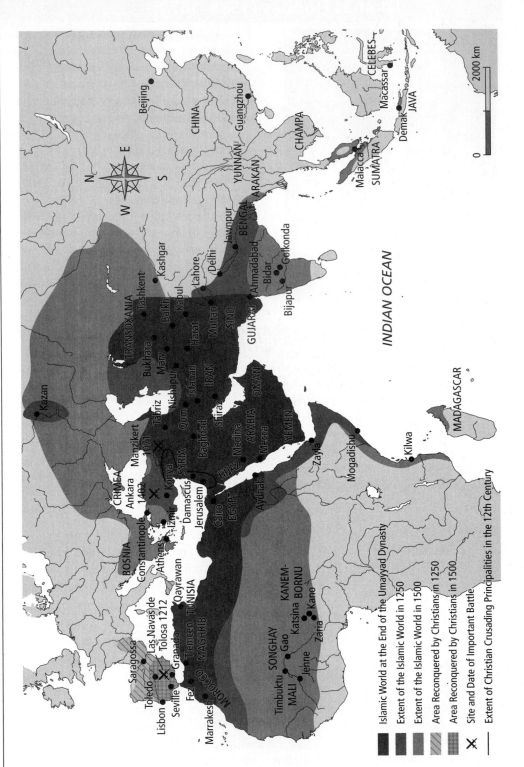

CELEBES

CHINA

Beijing

Guangzhou

YUNNAN

CHAMPA

ARAKAN

Macassar

Malacca

SUMATRA

Demak

JAVA

2000 km

0

INDIAN OCEAN

Jawnpur

BENGAL

Golkonda

Kashgar

Lahore

Ahmadabad

Bidar

Delhi

Bijapur

TRANSOXANIA

Tashkent

Balkh

Kabul

MADAGASCAR

Bukhara

Merv

Herat

Multan

SIND

GUJARAT

Kazan

Nishapur

Isfahan

IRAN

OMAN

Tabriz

Qum

Shiraz

Manzikert
1071

Baghdad

Medina

ARABIA

YEMEN

Kilwa

CRIMEA

Ankara
1402

Konya

SYRIA

HIJAZ

Mecca

Zayla

Mogadishu

Damascus

Cairo

EGYPT

Aydhab

Jerusalem

BOSNIA

Constantinople

Izmir

Athens

Qayrawan

TUNISIA

KANEM-
BORNU

Saragossa

Las Navas de
Tolosa 1212

Granada

Tlemcen

MAGHRIB

SONGHAY

Gao

Katsina

Kano

Toledo

Seville

Fez

MOROCCO

Timbuktu

MALI

Jenne

Zaria

Lisbon

Marrakesh

Islamic World at the End of the Umayyad Dynasty

Extent of the Islamic World in 1250

Extent of the Islamic World in 1500

Area Reconquered by Christians in 1250

Area Reconquered by Christians in 1500

Site and Date of Important Battle

Extent of Christian Crusading Principalities in the 12th Century

N E S W

PROFILE 2.5 Kautilya (350–275 BCE)

Also known as Chanakya or Vishnugupta, Kautilya was councillor and chief minister to Chandra-Gupta, the founder of the Mauryan Empire. His views survive in the form of the *Arthasastra (The Book of the State)*, a treatise on the science of politics, which is summarized in 6000 verses. Written primarily for rulers, the *Arthasastra* is essentially a compendium of reflections on human nature and the conduct of political activity. The Arthasastra contains advice to rulers on the conduct of war, foreign policy, and empire building. Kautilya argued that war must serve political objectives; its purpose is to strengthen an empire, not merely to destroy an enemy. Weakening an enemy before fighting was the key to success in battle and was more important than the actual force of arms. He advised that rulers should fight weaker states and ally with stronger ones, and warned them that their natural enemies were the rulers of bordering empires. However, the rulers of the empires that bordered one's neighbours were natural friends, a piece of advice more commonly captured by the dictum "The enemy of my enemy is my friend." Kautilya also commented on the qualities of the ideal ruler, who, he argued, had to possess good character and a willingness to listen to advisors (such as Kautilya himself, of course). The character of the ruler affected the character of the ruled. Kautilya warned about the corrosive effects of injustice and advised the ruler that it was his responsibility to keep the people content if rebellion, chaos, and violence were to be avoided. Kautilya is sometimes called the *Indian Machiavelli*, but it would be more accurate, or at least chronologically correct, to call Machiavelli the Italian Kautilya. Many of the themes familiar to the power politics approach can be found in the *Arthasastra*, far removed from the time and context of Machiavelli's Italy.

SOURCE: ARADHANA PALMAR, *TECHNIQUES OF STATECRAFT: A STUDY OF KAUTILYA'S ARTHASASTRA* (DELHI: ATMA RAM AND SONS, 1987).

PROFILE 2.6 Sun Tzu

Sun Tzu was a warrior philosopher in fourth-century (BCE) China. His classic text, *Art of War*, is one of the most influential books on strategy ever written. *The Art of War* was evidently composed during the Warring States period in ancient China, characterized by competition, shifting alliances, and warfare between the kings who struggled for power in the latter years of the Chou Dynasty. Sun Tzu drew heavily on Chinese philosophy—in particular, the Taoist works *I Ching (Book of Changes)* and *Tao Te Ching (The Way and Its Power)*—and Chinese military practices in writing what is in essence a study of the conduct of competition and conflict on any level, from the interpersonal to the international. Most popularly known for its general advice that to win without fighting is best, *The Art of War* emphasizes shunning battle except when victory is assured, avoiding risk, dominating an opponent through psychological means, and using time rather than force to wear an enemy down. The book also includes advice on preparations for war, battle tactics, sieges, manoeuvres, and the use of terrain. Much of the advice emphasizes the importance of achieving advantage over one's enemy before any military engagement. Today, military leaders, politicians, and business executives study *The Art of War* as a window on the political and business approaches of Asian countries and firms. For IR scholars, and realists in particular, the themes in sun Tzu's work reflect the nature of politics and power in anarchic environments. Along with Kautilya, sun Tzu offers evidence of the existence of power politics themes across time, place, and culture.

SOURCE: SUN TZU, *THE ART OF WAR*, TRANSLATED BY THOMAS CLEARY (BOSTON: SHAMBALA, 1988).

Map 2.2 China and the Warring States Period (300 BCE)

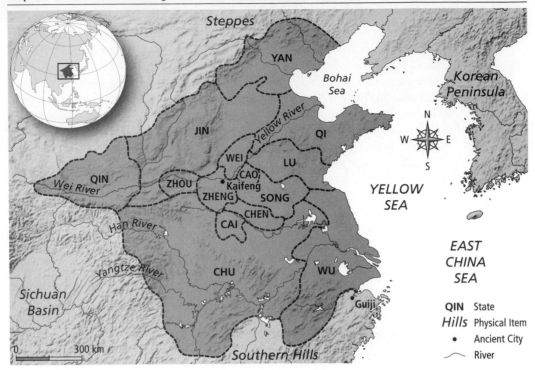

Invasions of nomadic peoples prompted both the Ch'in Empire and the Han dynasty to build the Great Wall of China. However, the Great Wall could not protect the Han Empire from internal disintegration, and nomadic invaders breached the wall in 304. Recovery was slow, but under the Sui (581 to 617 CE), T'ang (618 to 907 CE), and Sung (960 to 1279 CE) dynasties, China expanded and became prosperous, stable, and intellectually and scientifically advanced beyond any other civilization. Mongol invasion brought a period of decline, but under the Ming dynasty (1386 to 1644) Chinese power and prosperity were restored. In Japan, feudal warlords dominated politics until the Tokugawa shogunate unified Japan for 250 years before the forced opening of Japan by the European powers.

In Africa, civilization developed in the Nile tributaries and in eastern Africa, where the Kingdom of Kush dominated from c. 900 BCE to 400 CE. Settlers moved through present-day Ethiopia into southern Africa, and **Iron Age** civilizations developed in central and southern Africa by 100 CE. Great trading empires developed in Africa over the next 1000 years in what are today Ethiopia, Zimbabwe, the Democratic Republic of the Congo, and Ghana. The influence of Islamic expansion into North Africa contributed to the wealth of the Mali, Songhay, and the Kanem Borno empires, as Arab merchant colonies spread along Africa's north and east coasts (see Map 2.3). By the arrival of the first Europeans (the Portuguese in 1448), Africa had a thriving trading system based on gold, ivory, copper, and slaves. Portuguese, and later British and Dutch, trading stations spread rapidly in Africa. Trade with Europeans, at first based on gold, shifted to slaves, who were in demand for the colonial sugar plantations in South America and the West Indies and the tobacco and rice plantations of North America. Between 1450 and

Map 2.3 African Empires in History

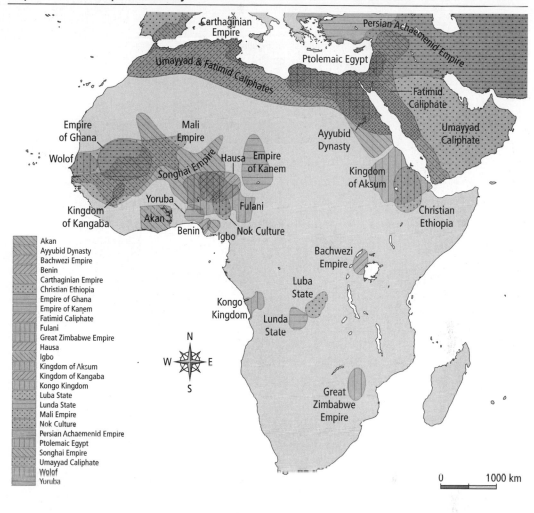

Legend:
- Akan
- Ayyubid Dynasty
- Bachwezi Empire
- Benin
- Carthaginian Empire
- Christian Ethiopia
- Empire of Ghana
- Empire of Kanem
- Fatimid Caliphate
- Fulani
- Great Zimbabwe Empire
- Hausa
- Igbo
- Kingdom of Aksum
- Kingdom of Kangaba
- Kongo Kingdom
- Luba State
- Lunda State
- Mali Empire
- Nok Culture
- Persian Achaemenid Empire
- Ptolemaic Egypt
- Songhai Empire
- Umayyad Caliphate
- Wolof
- Yoruba

1870, some 15 million Africans were shipped across the Atlantic, 90 percent of them to South America and the Caribbean. Many Africans suffered terribly from this trade; a few profited. In 1800, most of Africa (except the northern areas held by the Ottoman Empire) remained independent.

In the Americas, the first large civilizations emerged in Mesoamerica (present-day southern Mexico) in the form of the Olmecs and Zapotecs and in the central Andes around 1000 BCE. In the fifth century CE, the Olmecs and Zapotecs were conquered by the invading Maya (300 to 900 CE). In North America, large trading and agricultural centres emerged in Hopewell territory (300 BCE to 550 CE) around the southern Great Lakes. In Central America, Mayan civilization was followed first by the Toltecs in the 11th century, and then the Aztecs in the 13th century. Aztec expansion, conducted through a combination of alliance and conquest, reached its zenith under Montezuma II (1502 to 1520). In South America, several diverse civilizations developed in the Andes and were unified under the Huari and Tiahuanaco empires (600 to 800 CE). These empires collapsed, and unity in the Andes was not achieved until the Inca civilization of the 15th century. The Inca Empire

Map 2.4 The Peoples and Civilizations of Central and South America

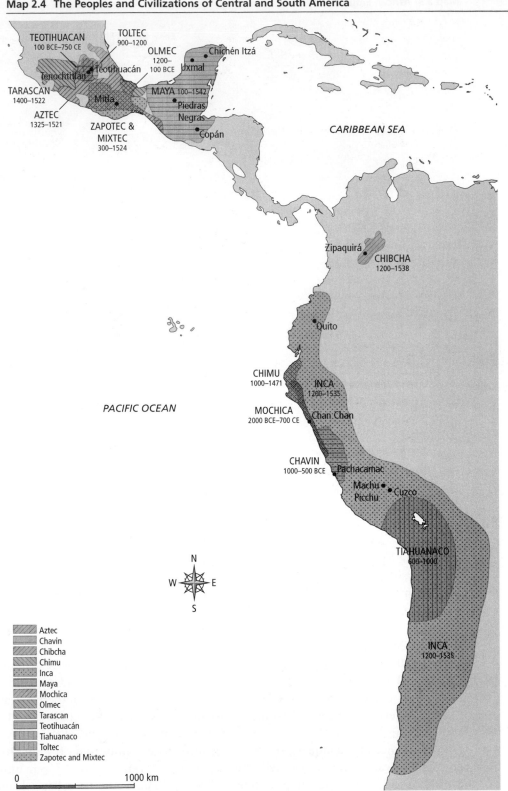

TEOTIHUACAN
100 BCE–750 CE

TOLTEC
900–1200

OLMEC
1200–
100 BCE

Chichén Itzá

Uxmal

Teotihuacán

Tenochtitlán

TARASCAN
1400–1522

MAYA 100–1542

Mitla

Piedras
Negras

AZTEC
1325–1521

ZAPOTEC &
MIXTEC
300–1524

Copán

CARIBBEAN SEA

Zipaquirá

CHIBCHA
1200–1538

Quito

CHIMU
1000–1471

INCA
1200–1535

PACIFIC OCEAN

MOCHICA
2000 BCE–700 CE

Chan Chan

CHAVIN
1000–500 BCE

Pachacamac

Machu
Picchu

Cuzco

TIAHUANACO
600–1000

INCA
1200–1535

N
W   E
S

- Aztec
- Chavin
- Chibcha
- Chimu
- Inca
- Maya
- Mochica
- Olmec
- Tarascan
- Teotihuacán
- Tiahuanaco
- Toltec
- Zapotec and Mixtec

0   1000 km

expanded between 1438 and 1525 to an area 4000 kilometres long and more than 300 kilo-metres wide, with a hereditary dynasty and an advanced bureaucracy and infrastructure (see Map 2.4). However, the Spanish on their arrival in the beginning of the 16th century overthrew the Aztec and Inca civilizations. The defeat of such large, established empires by small bands of Spanish soldiers has been explained by a combination of superior military technology, different cultural approaches to war, the introduction of disease, the assistance of native allies, and Aztec and Incan political weakness.[14] Elsewhere, the Portuguese slowly expanded into Brazil, establishing an extensive sugar industry worked by slaves. In North America, economic and political activity was conducted among a wide range of indigenous societies and linguistic communities (see Map 2.5).

So far, the principal actors in this narrative have been the mighty civilizations and empires. The fate of less powerful actors in the evolution of human society is often rather stark. In a history defined by power politics, the less powerful (whether groups, city-states, or small empires) have been at a disadvantage. The weak have indeed suffered what they must. The least powerful have often disappeared from history altogether, having been assimilated into larger political units, forced to accept humiliating terms of surrender or tributary status, or had their populations killed, scattered, or sold into slavery. For realists,

Map 2.5 The Peoples of North America (c. 1500)

SOURCE: "NATIVE AMERICAN PEOPLES" FROM *ATLAS OF THE HISTORY OF THE WORLD*, EDITED BY PATRICK K. O'BRIEN. REPRINTED WITH PERMISSION OF OCTOPUS PUBLISHING GROUP LTD.

this history confirms the centrality of power in the world, and the importance of those who wield the greater share of it. Across time and place, say realists, history is "made" by the powerful. The other, weaker actors, far more numerous though they may be, are largely irrelevant to the course of history. However, many cultural groups survived, maintaining their language and traditions, only to re-emerge later to find independence or some measure of autonomy. Furthermore, as critical theorists insist, weaker actors have made an impact in history, and even shaken empires and mighty civilizations through resistance and revolution.

At this point in history, the rise and fall of civilizations and empires came to be dominated by the slow but steady ascent of Europe to a position of global dominance. The legacy of this historical development (also referred to as the *rise of the West*) remains with us in many forms today, including the nature of the modern state, many of the formalities of diplomacy, the imposition of many Western customs and legal principles, and the impact of colonialism on the economies, social structures, and institutions of post-colonial states. The military and commercial power of Europe was to leave an indelible imprint on the rest of the world.

THE MODERN STATE AND THE PEACE OF WESTPHALIA

The modern international system is often called the *Westphalian state system*. The Peace of Westphalia ended the Thirty Years' War in Europe in 1648 (see Map 2.6) and established a new European order, which subsequently spread through the expansion of the European empires. With the virtual collapse of the European empires in the second half of the 20th century, what was left behind was a world of sovereign states that inherited the territorial, legal, and administrative structures and practices of the European tradition. However, this interpretation of the significance of the Peace of Westphalia is contested. It is important to recognize that the global expansion of the European order does not provide a complete picture of the evolution of the modern international system. After all, civilization flourished in other regions of the world long before it existed in Europe, and these historical and cultural traditions exerted, and continue to exert, a profound influence on contemporary international relations.[15] Furthermore, the states of Europe were hardly "modern" in any contemporary sense of that term, characterized as they were by the rule of monarchs and pre-capitalist economic structures. Nevertheless, the Peace of Westphalia endures as a significant benchmark, for it established the foundations of the modern state and much of international law. Although the principles behind the sovereign state had begun to emerge before 1648, this date is a useful, if limited, point of differentiation between medieval Europe and modern Europe, and "kingly states" and "territorial states."[16] In much of medieval Europe, kingly states were not fully autonomous or sovereign; they were under the authority (in spirit if not always in practice) of the Pope or the Holy Roman Emperor. Interference in the domestic politics of these states was commonplace, primarily in the form of efforts to convert the rulers or the people to one or another Christian denomination (a cause of the devastating Thirty Years' War). The Peace of Westphalia established the constitutional, legal status of states as territorial entities. The territorial state was sovereign, free to determine and practise its domestic affairs (meaning the religious denomination followed by the ruler and the people), and free from external interference. The year 1648 thus marked the beginning of the supremacy of the state in European affairs.

Map 2.6 Westphalian Europe, 1648

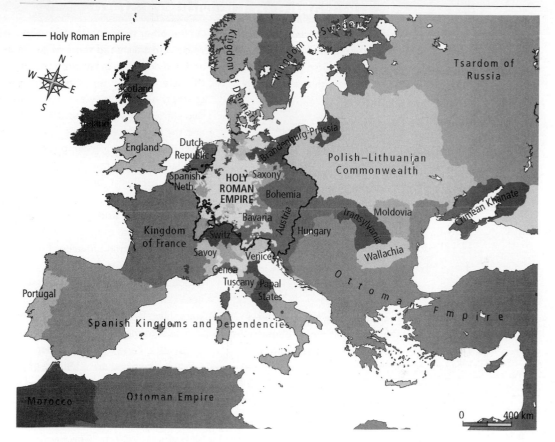

This change occurred for a number of reasons. First, the power of the church had been weakened by the splits in Christendom, in particular during the Reformation. The horrors of the Thirty Years' War (in what is today Germany, two-thirds of the population was killed or displaced) revealed the fragility of Christian Europe. The answer was the establishment of the sovereign state, which in principle was to be free from foreign interference in its domestic affairs. The hope was that devastating religious conflicts such as the Thirty Years' War might be prevented if the domestic affairs of territorial units were recognized as the exclusive reserve of the rulers of states. Second, some of the monarchs of medieval Europe had been slowly acquiring increased economic and military power, which enabled them to expand their territories through the amalgamation and conquest of less powerful political units. Furthermore, the establishment of hereditary monarchies promised increased stability with respect to inevitable transitions in leadership. The expansion of administrative and legal systems, with their power derived from the monarch, improved the capacity of rulers to exert control over their territories and subjects. For these reasons, the state emerged as the dominant political actor in international affairs and took on the distinctive characteristics that we recognize today (see Profile 2.7). As these developments occurred, European monarchies were embarking on the first period of European exploration and empire building. The world was entering the age of the European empires.

PROFILE 2.7 The Nature of the Modern State

Different theories abound in social science regarding the formation and present role of the state, but in typical IR discourse, the term *state* refers to political entities with the following qualities:

- They occupy a defined territory.
- They possess a permanent population.
- They are sovereign with respect to other states (that is, they are, in principle, free from interference in their internal affairs).
- They are diplomatically recognized by other states.
- They possess a monopoly on the legitimate use of force within their territories.

The terms *nation* and *state* are often used interchangeably in discussions of global politics. However, they are not quite equivalent. *State* refers to an autonomous institutional and legal structure that governs a defined territory; it is a political and legal concept.

On the other hand, *nation* refers to a people who possess a shared sense of common descent and unifying ethnic, religious, or linguistic characteristics; it is an ethnic and cultural concept. A nation may exist without a state: two contemporary examples are the Kurdish and the Palestinian nations. A state that has essentially one nation living within its borders is called a *nation-state*. In this sense, very few nation–states exist, because most states in the world comprise many nations within their borders. Canada and the United States are examples of such multi-nation-states.

The distinction between states and nations is becoming increasingly important in international politics, as in many cases disputes between the nations living within multi-nation-states have led to domestic instability, turmoil, and, in extreme cases, violence. The formalities of statehood and the complex legal and ethical questions involved are a feature of contemporary controversies over the status of Kosovo and Taiwan, among other examples.

THE RISE OF THE EUROPEAN EMPIRES

One of the defining features of the 17th and 18th centuries was European imperialism, particularly the overseas expansion of the Spanish, Portuguese, Dutch, English, and French empires. Under Louis XIV, France was the most powerful state in Europe in the mid- to late 1600s, but Louis's territorial ambitions provoked repeated alliances against France, which soon became weakened by almost continual warfare. Although formally in existence until 1806, the **Holy Roman Empire** had fragmented into some 300 small principalities and city-states, which were vulnerable to conquest. Prussia (largely through the conquests of Frederick the Great) and Austria under the Hapsburgs (largely through the conquests of Prince Eugene of Savoy) emerged as the dominant states in central Europe. Great Britain, protected from continental wars by the English Channel, carved out a global empire that was the envy of the rest of Europe. The Russian Empire (especially under **Peter the Great** and **Catherine the Great**) expanded to the borders of the Prussian and Austrian Empires in the west, the Ottoman Empire to the south, and China and the Pacific Ocean to the east.

However, revolts rocked the European empires in the second half of the 18th century. While the character of the revolts varied—from peasant unrest to a desire for independence in some regions—their origins lay in the spread of the Enlightenment, with its emphasis on the rights of individuals and its rejection of traditional authority. Aristocrats and rulers in provinces such as the Austrian Netherlands and Hungary rebelled against the centralization and reform policies imposed by enlightened monarchs. Overseas colonies, such as those in Spanish America and Haiti, rebelled against imperial rule and demanded more autonomy or outright independence. The most significant revolution occurred in the Thirteen Colonies in America, and the independence of the United States of America would later be recognized as one of the most important developments in world history. Many European regions, such as Corsica, Sardinia, Ireland, Serbia, and Tyrol, also sought independence. However, the most significant revolution in Europe occurred in France.

The French Revolution (1789 to 1794) changed the face of Europe. The revolution began as a middle-class or bourgeoisie phenomenon but spread to worker and peasant uprisings. When Austria and Prussia threatened invasion, combining external threat with internal chaos, the monarchy collapsed. A republic was established that ruthlessly suppressed its enemies at home and defeated its enemies abroad. The ideals of the French Revolution spread across Europe: equality before the law, the abolition of feudalism, and the "rights of man." The French Revolution sparked the beginning of the development of modern **nationalism**. While nationalism was initially resisted by monarchs (and unknown to the poor) it was to become one of the driving forces behind events in Europe and the idea would spread throughout the international system. In the 1830s Greece, Belgium, and Norway obtained independence. Italy was unified in 1861 and Germany (as the German Empire) in 1871. In both cases, political unification was accomplished through a combination of war and the use of nationalism as a political instrument. Nationalism would be a motive force for soldiers in battle, would enable the establishment of the first true national armies of citizen soldiers, would prove to be the main inspiration for several revolutions, and would become inextricably linked with the institutional and legal apparatus of the emerging nation-state.

However, the French Republic did not survive. In 1799 a 30-year-old general named **Napoleon Bonaparte** seized power. During the subsequent **Napoleonic Wars**, Napoleon was practically unbeatable, defeating the armies of Austria and Prussia (see Profile 2.8). By 1810 most of Europe was controlled by France. However, Napoleon could not subdue England, nor could he completely conquer the Iberian Peninsula. His invasion of Russia (1812) was a disaster, destroying most of the best formations in the Grand Army. Napoleon's final defeat at Waterloo in 1815 ended French dominance in Europe. The subsequent **Congress of Vienna** and the formation of the **Concert of Europe** were an attempt by the great powers to manage their relations and prevent a recurrence of the Napoleonic Wars. For almost 100 years, no continent-wide war occurred between the European great powers. The Concert of Europe is often studied by contemporary scholars interested in how great powers can successfully manage their affairs without resorting to major wars. However, it is inaccurate to say that peace prevailed, for several wars between states and empires took place in this period, including the Wars of Italian Unification, the **Crimean War**, and the Franco-Prussian War.

In addition, colonial wars were frequently waged against indigenous peoples, with what some would describe as genocidal motives, as the European empires continued to expand abroad. However, by the 19th century the nature of European imperialism was beginning to change. As the Industrial Revolution took hold in Europe, imperial expansion was driven less by the search for trade routes, precious metals, and slaves, and more by the search for raw materials, markets for products (emphasized by the neo-Marxist perspective), and territorial competition between the imperial powers. Between 1880 and 1914 the European empires added more than 13.6 million square kilometres (approximately one-fifth of the world's surface) to their colonial possessions (see Profile 2.9). Much of this was acquired in the so-called scramble for Africa, which began in earnest in 1882; by 1914, only Ethiopia and Liberia were

PROFILE 2.8 Karl von Clausewitz (1780–1831)

Karl von Clausewitz was a Prussian military officer, instructor, and strategist who rose to the rank of general in the Prussian army and served on the Prussian general staff during the Napoleonic Wars. His famous work, *On War*, was written after the Napoleonic Wars and his recall to duty in East Prussia in 1830 (he died of cholera in 1831, leaving *On War* unfinished, although his wife completed the manuscript). Virtually unknown when he was alive, Clausewitz had a major influence on all subsequent intellectual thought on war. He viewed war as a timeless phenomenon with its own elements and dynamics. Written in the dialectical and comparative style associated with German idealist philosophy, *On War* is often misunderstood or misinterpreted. For Clausewitz, war is distinguished from other social activity by its large-scale violence, which tends toward absolute war—the highest degree of violence. However, wars usually fall short of this level, because they are mitigated by political goals and the characteristics of societies and their economies and governments. Clausewitz believed that even military force had to be subordinate to the political aims and objectives of the state. War, Clausewitz argued, should not be regarded as separate and distinct from peacetime politics among states. Rather, war should be seen as "a continuation of political activity by other means." In IR theory, realists regard *On War* as an illuminating treatise of the prominence of the military instrument in the conduct of statecraft.

SOURCE: KARL VON CLAUSEWITZ, *ON WAR*, EDITED AND TRANSLATED BY MICHAEL HOWARD AND PETER PARET (PRINCETON: PRINCETON UNIVERSITY PRESS, 1976), PG. 87.

independent of colonial rule. For peoples across the world, colonial rule meant the imposition of arbitrary political boundaries, a profound dislocation in local patterns of commerce, and the dominance of colonial administrations. These administrations ruled through a combination of political and economic coercion and reward, often co-opting local elites into the colonial system of governance. This period was the beginning of the expansion of capitalism, both in Europe and across the European empires around the world. For Marx, this was another key development in the social history of human society.

Because of the worldwide expansion of the European empires, wars in Europe quickly became global in scope as early as the 16th and 17th centuries. Such wars had a profound impact on the history of North America. Wars between France, England, and Spain broke out in 1744 and 1754, and the supremacy of British naval power resulted in the loss of the French colonial empire in North America and the weakening of the Spanish empire. However, the rebellion of the 13 colonies in 1776 (aided by France) and the American War of Independence compelled Great Britain to recognize American independence in 1783. American expansion proceeded rapidly after independence (largely through the Louisiana Purchase, war with Mexico, the annexation of Texas, and war against indigenous peoples). The **American Civil War** interrupted the territorial expansion of the United States. After the war, the United States continued to expand with the purchase of Alaska from Russia, and territorial gains through annexation or conquest in the Pacific (Hawaii, Samoa, Midway, and the Philippines) and in Latin America (Cuba and Puerto Rico). The hope of some in the United States for expansion into British North America had been thwarted in the War of 1812, and subsequently with the formation of Canada in 1867 and its expansion to include western territories. Nevertheless, by 1914 the United States was one of the world's leading powers.

PROFILE 2.9 The Colonial Legacy

Many of the states that we consider independent today were at one point colonized by imperial powers or listed as protectorates. Here we list just some of them. Note that some were colonized by more than one empire over time. For example, the Philippines, a Spanish colony from 1565, became a U.S. possession after 1898 (it was occupied by the Japanese during World War II, and then achieved independence in 1946). Note also that many names have changed over time. For example, what is now known as Zimbabwe was once called Rhodesia, and while under British control Sri Lanka was known as Ceylon. What follows is a partial list of the imperial powers and some of their possessions over the course of the past few hundred years.

GREAT BRITAIN

Anguilla, Antigua and Barbuda, Australia, Bahamas, Bahrain, Botswana, Brunei, Canada, Ceylon, Dominica, Fiji, Gambia, Ghana, Grenada, Hong Kong, India, Ireland, Kenya, Malawi, Malaysia, Maldives, Malta, Nigeria, Papua New Guinea, Sierra Leone, South Africa, Uganda, Zambia, Zimbabwe

FRANCE

Algeria, Benin, Burkina Faso, Cambodia, Chad, Comoros, Dakar, Djibouti, French Cameroon, French Congo, Gabon, Haiti, Ivory Coast, Laos, Madagascar, Mali, Mauritania, Morocco, Niger, Senegal, Vietnam

THE OTTOMAN EMPIRE

Albania, Algeria, Anatolia (Turkey), Armenia, Bosnia-Herzegovina, Bulgaria, Cyprus, Egypt, Iraq, Jordan, Lebanon, Libya, Qatar, Yemen

SPAIN

Argentina, Bolivia, Chile, Colombia, Cuba, Ecuador, El Salvador, Equatorial Guinea, Guam, Guatemala, Honduras, Mexico, Nicaragua, Paraguay, Peru, Philippines, Puerto Rico, Venezuela

PORTUGAL

Angola, Azores, Brazil, East Timor, Equatorial Guinea, Guinea-Bissau, parts of India, Macao, Mozambique

GERMANY

Burundi, Cameroon, Namibia, Rwanda, Tanganyika (Tanzania), Togo, Western Samoa, other occupations during World War II

ITALY

Ethiopia, Libya, Somalia

THE NETHERLANDS

Dutch Borneo, Dutch East Indies, Dutch West Indies, Suriname

BELGIUM

Burundi, Rwanda, Zaire

DENMARK

Faroe Islands, north Germany, Greenland, Iceland, parts of Norway, Sweden

JAPAN

Bonin Island, Korea, other occupations during World War II

THE UNITED STATES

Guam, Hawaii, Midway, Panama, Philippines, Puerto Rico, Samoa, Cuba

In South America, Napoleon's invasion of the Iberian Peninsula enabled the Spanish and Portuguese colonies to attain independence. These revolutions were carried out by a colonial aristocracy that sought independence, but with minimal social change. For the most part, colonial administrations were replaced by military dictatorships, which were to become an enduring feature of political life in Central and South America. In 1823, revolution created the Republic of Mexico. In South America, Spanish power was broken by revolt and military defeat at the hands of the followers of Simón Bolívar. Portugal agreed to Brazilian independence in

1822. In post-revolutionary Central and South America, territorial disputes between the newly independent countries were frequent and violent, and efforts to unite South America into a union failed at the Congress of Panama (1826). Export-driven economic growth and control of land increased the wealth of elites, but the bulk of the population lived in poverty (and still does).

In China, dominated by the Ch'ing (or Manchu) dynasty since 1644, trade with Europe—primarily in textiles, tea, porcelain, and opium—had flourished, although the empire was beset with rebellions and internal unrest. By the 1830s, China was the world's largest and most populous empire, but economic and political decay left China vulnerable to the Western powers, which sought to open the Chinese market to their products. The British exerted their power in China through the Opium War (1839 to 1842), seized Hong Kong as an imperial possession, and opened five (later many more) treaty ports where foreigners enjoyed exemption from Chinese law and rule. Other powers—especially Russia, France, and Japan—then expanded their authority in China, seizing territory and opening more treaty ports. The failure of the Manchu leadership to institute reform and resentment of foreign influence in China led to the Taiping Rebellion (1850 to 1864), one of the third-bloodiest wars in human history. In 1900, the so-called Boxer Rebellion was inspired by growing anti-foreigner and anti-imperial sentiment in China. On the eve of World War I, China remained unstable and dominated by foreign colonial powers.

PATTERNS IN THE HISTORY OF WAR AND PEACE

As noted earlier, this conventional account of global history leading up to the world wars of the 20th century is obviously incomplete, emphasizing war and great power diplomacy over economic and social developments, and presenting history largely as a narrative about the development and expansion of European power. Nevertheless, this conventional approach to history has value, because many insightful themes and generalizations have been drawn from it. These themes and generalizations have formed the foundation of the realist approach to IR:

- *The recurrence of war and conflict between civilizations, peoples, and empires.* Political history is animated primarily by armed struggle. When cooperation does occur, it is in the form of alliances based on short-term need or convenience, or short-term trade and commercial interests. War is a historical inevitability, and the prudent are prepared for it, even in times of peace. The price for those who are not able or willing to prepare for war is to suffer political domination or outright conquest.

- *The rise and fall of civilizations and empires.* The explanations for the rise and fall of the great world civilizations and empires are many and varied. The fate of empires is often linked to the emergence and the decline of a single great ruler. Empires have repeatedly been subject to conquest, either at the hands of other empires or from invasion by "barbarian" peoples. Many empires suffer from internal decline due to a combination of economic failure, social decay, and the costs associated with protecting a growing territory. The fortunes of civilizations, empires, and great powers are, therefore, historically fleeting; all eventually decline, to be superseded by others.[17]

- *The recorded political history of the world is primarily the history of the activities of great civilizations, empires, and states.* History is made by the powerful. For some, history can be described in terms of the machinations of hegemonic powers, civilizations, great powers, or empires that dominated all others. As a result, smaller or weaker civilizations, empires, and states have not been considered significant in history except as allies or pawns of the powerful.

- *The development of an intellectual tradition on statecraft, drawn from historical experience.* Advice to leaders—monarchs or emperors—was the privilege of only a very few individuals, but these individuals represent the beginning of thought on international relations, offering insights into the perspectives of those who lived hundreds and even thousands of years ago. What is revealing about these writings is the extent to which they display common themes about the nature of the conduct of international politics. Writers such as sun Tzu, Kautilya, Thucydides, and Machiavelli established the intellectual foundation of the realist perspective in IR.

- *The rise of political geography and geopolitics.* Before World War II, diplomatic historians conducted most of the research on international affairs, with one notable exception. A small group of geographers developed theories that promoted the decisive influence of geography on state power in general and the calculations of decision makers in particular. The use of geographic explanations or arguments to characterize political decisions or advocate certain policies became known as political geography or geopolitics (see Profile 2.10). Geopolitical thought has had a profound influence on the conduct of many states and has served as the cornerstone for many national security strategies, including those of the European imperial powers, Nazi Germany, and the United States during the Cold War.[18]

The beginning of the 20th century was a time of general peace—with a few exceptions, most notably the Russo–Japanese War (1904 to 1905)—and growing prosperity. Long-term peace appeared to be in the offing: no major war had occurred in Europe since 1870, and international law on armaments and war had been strengthened at the Hague Peace Conferences of 1899 and 1907. The prevailing sentiment was that increasing trade and industrialization was making war more costly and less likely (an argument often made today). However, this sense of optimism began to erode as disputes between the European great powers and their alliances increased. Nationalist rhetoric intensified, an arms race ensued, and war flared in the Balkans (1912 to 1913). Nevertheless, few sensed the impending disaster that would soon befall Europe.

WORLD WAR I

The beginning of World War I is generally marked by the assassination of the heir to the throne of the Austro-Hungarian Empire, Austrian Archduke Franz Ferdinand, in Sarajevo, on June 28, 1914. The assassination of the Archduke set in motion a series of actions and reactions that led the European powers to war. However, while this event may indeed have been the spark that set Europe ablaze, the fuel for the conflict had been accumulating for years. Europe had divided into two hostile alliances: the Triple Alliance of Germany, Austro-Hungary, and Italy; and the Triple Entente of Great Britain, France, and Russia. The latter was wary of the increasing power of Germany and its desire for a place in the sun with the other established imperial powers. The Triple Alliance feared encirclement and the expansion of Russian power in the Balkans. Commercial rivalry, disputes over colonial possessions, and a naval arms race between Great Britain and Germany intensified the antagonism between these two countries. The naval arms race would later become one of the most studied arms races in history, as analysts sought to learn lessons that could be applied to the nuclear arms race between the superpowers during the Cold War. In all countries, enormous national armies could be created rapidly through the mobilization of the citizenry, and trained for war through **conscription**. Most European military establishments believed that success in a future war would go to the country that mobilized most rapidly and launched its offensive first. This "cult of the offensive" existed in most European countries.[19] In particular, German planning sought to avoid a two-front war by attacking and quickly defeating France before turning against Russia. The mood in most societies was one of extreme nationalism (which was often explicitly racist) and faith in the superiority of one's own country and people.

PROFILE 2.10 Geopolitical Thought: Sir Halford Mackinder and Alfred Thayer Mahan

SIR HALFORD MACKINDER (1861–1957)

Sir Halford Mackinder was a British geographer who wrote a famous paper on "the geographical pivot of history," which he presented to the Royal Geographical Society in 1904. Mackinder argued that the world could be divided into three regions: the Heartland (at the centre of Eurasia); the Interior or Marginal Ring (Europe, the Middle East, and southern and northern Asia); and the Ring of Islands or Outer Continents (North and South America, Africa, and Australia). For Mackinder, the geographic pivot in world politics was the Heartland. From this view he derived the following geopolitical calculation: whoever controls the Heartland controls the World Island (Europe, Asia, and Africa); whoever controls the World Island controls the world. He concluded that Russia must not be permitted to expand into the lands of the Interior Ring, as this would lead to Russian world domination. His theory was influential in Europe, particularly in Germany, where it contributed to the geopolitical views of Karl Hausofer, who advocated *Lebensraum,* German territorial expansion eastward. Mackinder's theory also influenced U.S. strategy to contain the Soviet Union, which already dominated the Heartland, during the Cold War. However, Mackinder's many critics have pointed out that his theory could not explain why tsarist Russia and the Soviet Union had not dominated the world despite controlling the Heartland. Nor could his theory explain the dominance of the United States for most of the 20th century. Others criticize his view as a thinly veiled rationale for the maintenance of the British Empire, which controlled territories in the Middle East and southern Asia and so served as the guardian of the Interior Ring against aggression from the Heartland.

ALFRED THAYER MAHAN (1840–1914)

Alfred Thayer Mahan was an American naval strategist. His most famous work, *The Influence of Sea Power on History 1660–1783,* influenced the naval doctrines of the United States and the European imperial powers. His central conclusion was that naval powers, rather than land powers, were dominant in history. For Mahan, the principles of naval strategy and naval warfare remained constant, and these principles pointed to one historical theme. Contrary to land power explanations of world politics, the key to state power lay in powerful naval forces supported by a network of overseas possessions and naval bases. From these possessions and bases, naval forces could dominate the seas, and that dominance would lead to control of the merchant traffic of the world. The influence of Mahan's views was felt in Europe in the struggle for naval mastery between Great Britain and Germany, and in the United States, where it provided a rationale for American imperial expansion during and after the Spanish–American War.

Map 2.7 The World According to Mackinder

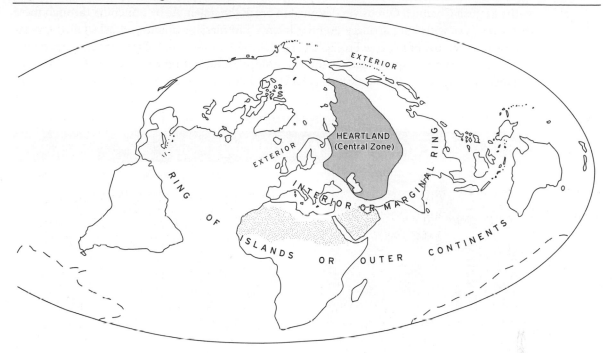

SOURCE: FROM *STRATEGIC ATLAS: A COMPARATIVE GEOPOLITICS OF THE WORLD'S POWERS*, 3RD ED. BY GERARD CHALIAND AND JEAN-PIERRE RAGEAU. PG. 21. COPYRIGHT © 1993 BY GERARD CHALIAND AND JEAN-PIERRE RAGEAU. REPRINTED BY PERMISSION OF HARPERCOLLINS PUBLISHERS, INC.

After the assassination of the Archduke, Europe began its slide toward war. The assassination, planned in Belgrade by Serbian nationalists, intensified Austro–Hungarian concerns about the threat Serbia posed to Austro–Hungarian power in the Balkans. Germany, hoping to deter Russian intervention in the Balkans in support of its Serbian ally, issued its famous "blank cheque" of support to Austria. Austria then delivered an ultimatum to Belgrade and declared war on July 28, 1914. Russia, fearing Austrian hegemony in the Balkans, mobilized to support Serbia, a fellow Slavic country. Germany then mobilized and, as called for in prewar planning, attacked France through neutral Belgium. Germany's violation of Belgian neutrality brought Great Britain into the war. The war assumed a global aspect with Japan's declaration of war on Germany, the outbreak of fighting between British and German colonial forces in Africa, and the entry into the war of the Ottoman Empire. For many, war was welcome, and nationalist fervour brought cheering crowds into the streets and long lines at recruiting stations. Throughout Europe, the war was expected to be short, with the recently mobilized soldiers expected home by Christmas. Some had more sombre thoughts. On August 3, following a speech to Parliament in which he confirmed British intentions to enter the war, British Foreign Minister Sir Edward Grey remarked, "The lamps are going out all over Europe; we shall not see them lit again in our lifetime."[20]

The German offensive into France was conducted according to the carefully crafted **Schlieffen Plan**, which saw Germany's armies in the west move through Belgium and northern France toward Paris. In doing so, Germany violated Belgian neutrality, another testament to the fate of weaker powers in great-power politics. However, Germany failed to defeat France quickly. The firepower of modern weapons soon created a stalemate, and by October 1914 a front line of trenches, barbed wire, machine guns, and artillery extended from the Swiss border to the English Channel. Offensives designed to break the stalemate by punching through these defensive lines with long artillery bombardments and massive infantry attacks failed repeatedly, with great loss of life (see Profile 2.11 for Canada's experience). Germany embarked on a submarine warfare campaign against merchant ships at sea. With the exception of the Battle of Jutland, the massive battleship fleets that had been built during the Anglo–German naval arms

PROFILE 2.11   Canada and World War I

We will always remember. Lance Corporal Iden Herbert Baldwin when he was 22 years old and waiting to return to Canada after fighting in World War I. Iden Baldwin died on January 31, 2003, at the age of 105. (CP PHOTO/Globe and Mail)

Canada entered World War I when Great Britain declared war on August 4, 1914. Canadian Prime Minister Robert Borden had promised Canadian support for the Empire's war effort. Little dissent existed in Parliament as the Liberals under Wilfrid Laurier supported Canada's entry into the war. However, dissent was expressed in French Canada, where many French Canadians opposed Canada's involvement in the war and the increasing sacrifices the war effort entailed. The First Canadian Division entered the battle lines in France in February 1915, although most of the senior commanders were British. Canadian troops performed admirably in the field during the Battle of Ypres

in April 1915. The Canadian contingent in Europe grew rapidly, and a Canadian Corps (composed of three divisions) was established in mid-1915. However, the war had settled into a costly stalemate, and losses at the front made conscription an issue in 1917. The conscription crisis was very divisive, generating strong opposition in French Canada and among workers and farmers. In April 1917, Canadian troops seized Vimy Ridge—at a cost of 3598 lives—after repeated Allied efforts had failed. This success was followed by the Passchendaele offensive, a sobering experience in which the Canadian Corps occupied a few square kilometres of mud- and water-filled craters at a cost of 8134 lives. By this time Canadian officers under General Arthur Currie commanded the Canadians. By the end of the war, 56 634 Canadians had been killed and more than 150 000 wounded.

Some maintain that Canadian nationalism (or, at least, a new Canadian identity) was born at Vimy Ridge in 1917—that Canada's service and sacrifice developed a sense of Canadian independence. Prior to the war, Canadian foreign policy was basically British foreign policy. Prime Minister Borden argued that the war had made Canada an international personality, entitled to a certain independent status. Canada was a signatory to the **Versailles Treaty**, and it received a seat in the League of Nations. The political and workplace advances of Canadian women during the war years can also be seen as transformative developments in the evolution of modern Canada. Others, however, caution that the conscription crisis and labour disputes divided the country and that, for many, the war meant little more than lost loved ones and shattered lives.

race saw little action. (The British battle fleet did impose a naval blockade against Germany, blocking German access to products and materials from abroad.) The German decision to expand the submarine campaign also brought the United States into the war against Germany on April 6, 1917.

In the east, military defeat and economic chaos had led to the collapse of the Russian war effort and opened the window of opportunity for the Bolshevik Revolution of October 1917. The Romanov dynasty was overthrown, and the new **Bolshevik** government sued for peace. With the eastern front secured, Germany transferred its forces west for a final great offensive aimed at defeating Britain and France before the United States could mobilize. The offensive, launched on March 21, 1918, failed with heavy losses, and in July the French, British, and Americans began their counter-offensive, which was to be the decisive turning point of the war. By September, Germany was near defeat. Its armies were exhausted, and its economy was in shambles from the war effort and the British naval blockade. Austria was near collapse. Fearful of domestic unrest and the possibility of a Bolshevik revolution in Germany, the German government sued for an **armistice**, which went into effect on November 11, 1918. Seven months later, on June 28, 1919, Germany signed the Treaty of Versailles. Under its terms, Germany was prevented from possessing a large army or modern military equipment, the province of Alsace-Lorraine was returned to France, Germany's colonies were distributed to the victors, East Prussia was separated from the rest of Germany by the new Poland, the German government was forced to pay reparations, and war guilt was assigned to Germany. The legacy of Versailles would cause much bitterness in Germany, bitterness that would be deftly exploited by Adolf Hitler and the Nazi Party.

The consequences of World War I were enormous. More than 13 million people had died, and millions more were wounded (as many died in an influenza pandemic—named the "Spanish flu"—made possible by the flow of refugees and military demobilization). The state, nationalism, and the Industrial Revolution had combined to create a lethal mix. Large, conscripted armies, motivated by nationalism and equipped, transported, and supplied by the technologies of the Industrial Revolution, were guided by the unparalleled strategic planning capacities of the modern state into organized slaughter by the killing machines of modern war. Entire societies, and not just military units, became targets in total war. As Richard Overy has remarked, "To be able to wage total war states would have to mobilize all the material, intellectual, and moral energies of their people; by implication the enemy community as a whole—its scientists, workers and farmers—became legitimate objects of war."[21] Four empires had collapsed—the German, Austro-Hungarian, Russian, and Ottoman—and new, independent nations emerged in Czechoslovakia, Poland, Yugoslavia, Finland, Estonia, Latvia, and Lithuania (see Map 2.8). The Russian Revolution had brought a change in government and ideology to Russia that would shape international politics in the years to come. Fear of the Russian Revolution was widespread, as was concern over the emergence of **fascism** as a major political movement. Nationalism remained a potent force, and the peace settlement left dissatisfied minorities across Europe seeking their own state and national independence. The United States emerged as a global power but slowly turned to **isolationism** with respect to European affairs. Finally, dissatisfied revisionist powers such as Germany, Japan, and Italy emerged from the ashes of the World War. The ambitions of these revisionist countries and their authoritarian ideologies would clash with democratic, anti-revisionist countries that favoured the status quo. Ultimately, the "war to end all wars," as it had been optimistically dubbed by H.G. Wells and American President Woodrow Wilson, among others, had merely set the stage for World War II.

Map 2.8 Territorial Changes in Europe after World War I

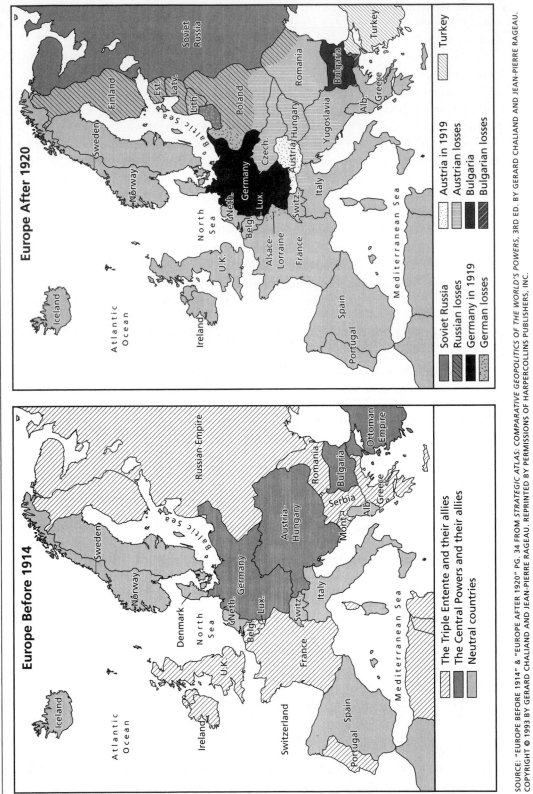

SOURCE: "EUROPE BEFORE 1914" & "EUROPE AFTER 1920" PG. 34 FROM *STRATEGIC ATLAS: COMPARATIVE GEOPOLITICS OF THE WORLD'S POWERS*, 3RD ED. BY GERARD CHALIAND AND JEAN-PIERRE RAGEAU. COPYRIGHT © 1993 BY GERARD CHALIAND AND JEAN-PIERRE RAGEAU. REPRINTED BY PERMISSIONS OF HARPERCOLLINS PUBLISHERS, INC.

THE INTERWAR PERIOD

The horrors of World War I inspired efforts to ensure it was a singular event. Pacifist sentiments were widespread, and peace movements were led by NGOs such as War Resisters' International and the Women's International League for Peace and Freedom (WILPF); both are still in operation today, almost a century later (WILPF gained consultative status at the UN in 1948). As we discussed in Chapter 1, idealism gained credence as an alternative to the realpolitik behaviour, balance of power machinations, and secret alliances that had led the world to such a disaster. For idealists, such as U.S. President Woodrow Wilson, the hope was to establish a new order, based on the League of Nations, collective security, the rule of law, and arms control. However, behind the outward unity displayed by the victorious powers after World War I were serious disagreements, particularly among Great Britain, France, and the United States, over the treatment of Germany. France was the most uncompromising. It had been devastated during the war: 1 355 800 French citizens had been killed and 4 260 000 wounded; almost 300 000 homes had been destroyed; and the country was heavily in debt due to the financial costs of the war effort.[22] The French were not willing to place their faith in Wilson's collective security concept (see Chapter 1), deciding instead that a system of alliances built against Germany would be the best guarantee of peace. Another matter of dispute was the issue of reparations. France and Great Britain wanted Germany to pay for the entire cost of the war, and Germany began to default on reparations payments as early as 1920. In response, the French government acted unilaterally and occupied the Ruhr Valley in 1923. Within Germany, popular resentment against the Versailles Treaty increased.

In the interwar period, Russia went through the throes of revolution to resurface as a major actor in Europe. Increased economic hardship, growing hunger, and the clear incompetence of the Russian political and military leadership in the war led to the overthrow of the Tsar in February 1917. The Duma, or Parliament, assumed power, but its decision to continue the war alienated the people, leaving it vulnerable to revolutionary organizations of workers, called *soviets*, and the return from exile of Vladimir Lenin, a charismatic Marxist who promised peace, land, bread, and all power to the Soviets (see Chapter 1). The provisional government collapsed, and Lenin's Bolsheviks seized power in the October Revolution. Lenin's first task was to obtain peace, and despite opposition he accepted unfavourable terms from Germany in return for peace in the Treaty of Brest–Litovsk (1918). After a civil war in which the Bolsheviks prevailed against a pro-monarchist White Russian movement supported by Britain, France, and the United States, the Union of Soviet Socialist Republics (U.S.S.R.), more commonly called the Soviet Union, was established in December 1922. Initially, many Marxists had seen the war as the culmination of the failures of the capitalist system and the beginning of the proletarian revolution that would sweep across the world. But as Marxist movements in other countries failed to attain power, there was a shift toward securing the revolution in Russia. By 1925 the Soviet Union had recovered economically and was reaching out internationally, even obtaining diplomatic recognition from France, Great Britain, and other European countries. Lenin's death in 1924 eventually brought Josef Stalin to power. With his doctrine of "socialism in one country," Stalin embarked on a massive program of industrialization and agricultural collectivization, leaving millions dead and displaced by famine, as well as brutal purges of the Communist Party and the Red Army. However, the Soviet Union was firmly established as a great power.

In the Middle East and Asia, the interwar period saw the fall of an empire, chaos in another, and the rise of a new great power. As one of the defeated powers, the Ottoman Empire was partitioned by the victorious states. These humiliations sparked a nationalist uprising led by Mustapha Kemal (Ataturk) that marked the beginning of a secular Turkish state, the heir to the Ottoman legacy. China experienced a period of chaos, instability, and invasion in the interwar period. Central rule broke down, and provincial warlords assumed local power. Under the leadership of Sun Yat-sen and then Chiang Kai-shek, the Nationalist (Koumintang) Party, allied with the Chinese Communists, attempted to suppress the warlords, end foreign power in China, and reunify the country. After initial success in the north of the country, the alliance between the Koumintang and the Communists collapsed. However, after the Japanese invasion of Manchuria in 1931, Chiang now had to meet two threats simultaneously: the Japanese, and the Communist movement in the countryside, led by Mao Tse-tung. Chiang's efforts to crush Mao's Communists forced Mao and his supporters into the famous long March of 1934 to 1935, and the nationalist and Communist forces were to battle the Japanese until the end of World War II.

The interwar period saw the rise of a new power in Asia: Japan. The Meiji Restoration of 1868 reopened Japan to the world after 200 years of isolation. Japan embarked on a period of rapid industrialization and began to expand its empire in Asia. Japan was recognized as a victorious power at the Paris Peace Conference with great-power status, and obtained a permanent seat on the Council of the League of Nations. However, the Great Depression hit hard as the rise of trade barriers around the world hurt the trade-dependent Japanese economy, which was also strained by a notable surge in the population. Militarists would launch several attacks on the government and eventually attain strong influence over Japanese foreign policy. These changes, coupled with China's efforts to recover Manchuria (an important source of raw materials and industrial production) from Japan, led to the Japanese fabrication of an attack on a Japanese railway line, which provided the pretext for a military invasion of Manchuria in 1931. The League of Nations failed to respond forcefully, issuing a report in 1933 calling for Chinese control of Manchuria with protection of Japanese interests. The collective security provisions of the League were not invoked. In response to its report, Japan walked out of the League of Nations. In 1937, Japan invaded China, and tensions between Japan and the United States escalated over the invasion and trade issues.

The League also failed to respond effectively to European aggression. The fascist leader Benito Mussolini came to power in Italy in 1922. In 1935 Italy invaded and conquered Ethiopia. The League responded with an arms **embargo**, but all other products (including oil, coal, and steel) could still be traded to Italy, and the enforcement of the embargo was never effective. Again, the collective security provisions of the League were not activated. In 1937, Italy withdrew from the League of Nations and annexed Albania in 1939.

The League would also prove unable to stop German expansionism. The onset of the **Great Depression** in Europe devastated the German economy and inflation spiralled out of control, plunging most Germans into misery. It was in this economic and political context that the Nazi Party rose to prominence in Germany on a platform of resentment toward the Versailles Treaty, renewed German nationalism, and **anti-Semitism**. Under Hitler's "Third Reich" Germany began to rearm at a rapid pace. It intervened in the Spanish civil war of 1936 to 1939, sending troops and weapons to support fascist dictator Franco. And in 1938 Germany annexed a largely welcoming Austria while also demanding a "solution" for the Sudetenland Germans, who lived in Czechoslovakia. At Munich, the British and French governments sought to appease Hitler and accepted the incorporation of the Sudetenland into the Third Reich. This region was also Czechoslovakia's main line of defence; the annexation left the Czechs unable to effectively resist any further German expansion. This was not lost on Hitler, of course, and in April 1939, Germany occupied the rest of Czechoslovakia; once again a small state had fallen victim to the power politics of the great powers, despite the collective security architecture of the League of Nations. Subsequent German demands for territory in the Danzig region from Poland prompted the British and the French into a temporary alliance, but Hitler's campaign to dominate Europe was well underway.

In the face of increasing international diplomatic and economic tensions, the League was increasingly unable to act effectively. For most of its history, the League counted only four of the seven great powers among its membership, and as a result it could not serve as the universal organization it was intended to be. The league was further damaged when it could not take effective action against Italian aggression in Ethiopia, Japanese aggression in Manchuria, and later German and Soviet Union aggression in Europe. The aims of the revisionist powers of the 1930s were fundamentally at odds with the principles of the Covenant. Although some League committees continued to operate during the war, the organization was irrelevant as an instrument of peace and security. In April 1946, it was formally disbanded. Its shortcomings would play an important role in the subsequent design of the United Nations Charter.

The revisionist powers of the interwar period—Germany, Italy, and Japan—encountered limited resistance to their territorial gains and aggressive acts. Why? The experience of World War I was clearly a factor; no one wanted to risk another world war. The neutralist position of the United States also weakened the strength of non-revisionist states. Without U.S. support and active involvement in world affairs, countries such as Great Britain and France lacked the power to decisively respond to aggression, or so they believed. In addition, governments everywhere were grappling with enormous domestic economic problems, especially after the stock market crash of 1929. In the face of huge domestic economic hardships, military aggression in Manchuria and Ethiopia seemed very far away. Countries had turned inward: the United States had retreated into isolationism, the British behind the English Channel, and the French behind the supposedly impregnable fortifications of the Maginot Line. As a result, the policy toward revisionist countries, in particular toward Germany, became known as **appeasement**: giving in to the demands of revisionist states in the hope that they would soon be satisfied with their gains. Munich, and appeasement, would later be vilified as a naive and idealistic failure. However, appeasement was not a policy of blind subjection to threats. The publics in Great Britain, France, and the United States and Canada were opposed to war, and their governments unprepared for it. Appeasement might satisfy Hitler and Mussolini, and if not it would at least buy time to rearm.

WORLD WAR II: TOTAL WAR

In August 1939, Nazi Germany and the Soviet Union signed the Nazi–Soviet Nonaggression Pact. The pact was a surprise, since German National Socialism and Soviet Communism were self-declared ideological enemies. A month later, the motivation for the pact would become clear. Hitler invaded Poland on September 1, 1939, and would later split the gains with the Soviet Union, which would invade Poland and the Baltic states only a few weeks later, and Finland in late November. By then, Britain and France had honoured their pledge to Poland by declaring war on Germany on September 3, 1939. World War II had begun.

Utilizing the new tactics of the *blitzkrieg* (lightning war), and seizing command of the air, German forces invaded and conquered Denmark, Norway, the Netherlands, and Belgium.

France succumbed as German forces swept around the Maginot Line, circumventing forti-fications that had been built at great effort and cost. Paris fell in June 1940, and the long occupation of France, governed by the puppet Vichy regime, began. The Battle of Britain then commenced, an air campaign in which the German Luftwaffe (air force) unsuccess-fully attempted to bomb Britain into submission. In World War II, the use of air power to attack cities and terrorize civilian populations became an accepted tactic in modern warfare. In the Mediterranean, Mussolini's Italy had invaded Greece, but the failure of the campaign brought Germany into the conflict, and Germany conquered Yugoslavia and Greece in early 1941. German and Italian troops in Africa moved toward Egypt, with the aim of wresting the Suez Canal from British control. And, in what we might in retrospect label the most mon-umental strategic blunder of all time, in June 1941 Hitler betrayed the Nonaggression Pact and invaded the Soviet Union. Having achieved total surprise, German forces swept through Russia, destroying much of the Red Army in the process. By December, German troops had advanced to within a few kilometres of Moscow. However, the German advance was halted by the Russian winter, lack of supplies, and stiffening resistance around Moscow and Leningrad as Stalin's totalitarian government began to mobilize the Soviet Union's citizens and resources in an epic and costly effort to reverse German advances.

In another notable strategic blunder, on December 7, 1941, Japan launched a surprise attack on the United States at Pearl Harbor, home of the American Pacific Fleet. Japan also mounted a swift campaign of conquest in the western Pacific, seizing the Philippines, French Indochina, the Dutch East Indies, Singapore, much of New Guinea, and the Bismarck and Solomon Islands in the South Pacific in the course of a few months. American isolationist sentiment collapsed in the face of the Pearl Harbor attack, and American President Franklin Roosevelt delivered his famous "day of infamy" speech to Congress, and subsequently obtained a Declaration of War against Japan, on December 8. Though the U.S. had been involved in the European war though a "lend and lease" program that sent materials to aid in the fight against Hitler, the Japanese attack gave Roosevelt political space to involve the U.S. directly in the European theatre of war. Thus the liberal democratic United States and Great Britain forged an unlikely alliance with the communist Soviet Union—a group labelled the ***Allied powers***—to oppose Nazi Germany, fascist Italy, and Imperial Japan—known as the ***Axis powers***. Allied powers also collaborated with resistance movements in the occupied European states, such as France, the Netherlands, and Czechoslovakia, and the American economy was converted to war production, churning out the weapons necessary to fight a two-front air, land, and sea war in Asia and Europe. Canada, which had declared war along with Great Britain and was already sending troops to Europe (see Profile 2.12 on page 72), vastly increased its military production as well, further integrating the American and Canadian economies in the process.

In 1942 and 1943, the fortunes of war began to turn against the Axis powers. German and Italian forces were repulsed from Egypt. The 1942 German offensive in southern Russia ended in bitter German defeat at Stalingrad. In the Atlantic, after heavy losses to German submarines, more and more merchant ships carrying supplies from Canada and the United States began to get through to Britain. In the Pacific, the Japanese Imperial navy was defeated at the Battle of Midway and at the Battle of the Coral Sea. The United States then began to embark on a series of campaigns to retake the south Pacific from the Japanese. In May 1943, German and Italian forces in North Africa were defeated. At the decisive battle of Kursk in July 1943, the Soviet Red Army was victorious, forcing the Germans onto the defensive on the entire eastern front. American and British strategic bombing raids against Germany began, damaging German industry and transportation, killing many civilians, and complicating the German war effort.

The decisive blows of the war were struck against the Axis powers in 1944; Allied resolve was reinforced as news spread of German and Japanese atrocities, such as the Holocaust, forced labour, and the mistreatment of prisoners of war. On June 6, 1944—commonly referred to as D-Day—British, Canadian, and U.S. troops landed in the Normandy region of northern France, broke through German defences, and went on to liberate France, Belgium, and the Netherlands. The Soviet Union launched an offensive on the eastern front a few weeks later and by late 1944 had pushed German forces back into Eastern Europe. In 1945, after an unsuccessful German counteroffensive in the west, British and American forces advanced into Germany (see Map 2.9). In January 1945, the Red Army launched a final offensive aimed at Berlin.

Adolf Hitler committed suicide in his Berlin bunker on April 30, and on May 7 Germany surrendered unconditionally. Thus would end the career of one of the most influential and darkly troubling politicians in modern history. Indeed, one might argue that World War II would not have occurred without the existence of this single man, lending credence to the value of the individual level of analysis discussed in Chapter 1. Before his death he had ordered German troops to engage in a "scorched earth" policy, demanding they destroy all remaining German infrastructure and agriculture to deny the Allied forces any spoils of war. Such a policy (largely disobeyed) was indicative of the megalomaniac personality of a dictator accustomed to absolute obedience upon pain of death and who had a firm belief in his own providence as leader of a superior race. By far the darkest policy of Hitler and the Nazi Party was the mass murder of Jews and other targeted groups during the war. This planned and systematic campaign of extermination has left many enduring legacies that continue to influence global politics today. One of those legacies is the concept of *genocide*, a term we will return to in Chapter 9.

In the Pacific, American forces began the reconquest of the Philippines, and the Imperial Japanese Navy was eliminated as an effective fighting force at the Battle of Leyte. British and Indian troops retook Burma. Japan came under air attack from American bases in China and the Marianas Islands; a single two-day "firebombing" of Tokyo by high-flying American B-29s killed an estimated 100 000 people as the city was engulfed in flames. In 1945, the American capture of Iwo Jima and Okinawa secured air bases closer to Japan, enabling the air offensive to be accelerated. Despite the devastation of most Japanese cities and Japan's industrial capacity, the Japanese still resisted, and preparations were made to invade the home islands of Japan (see Map 2.10). However, the war did not end in such a conventional manner.

Throughout the war the United States had been engaged in top-secret research to develop an atomic weapon. Such a device had been successfully tested near Alamogordo, New Mexico, in the spring of 1945. In a controversial decision, President Truman authorized the first military use of the **atomic bomb**, which was dropped on Hiroshima on August 6, 1945. A second bomb was dropped on Nagasaki on August 9. On September 2, 1945, facing the grim prospect of total obliteration, Japan capitulated, and the war was over.

The use of the atomic bomb in 1945 remains controversial even today. Was it necessary? Defenders of the decision cite the enormous casualties that American service personnel would have suffered in any invasion of Japan. Others suggest the atomic bomb was dropped primarily to demonstrate American military might to the Soviet Union. Many argue that the decision to

Map 2.9   The War in Europe

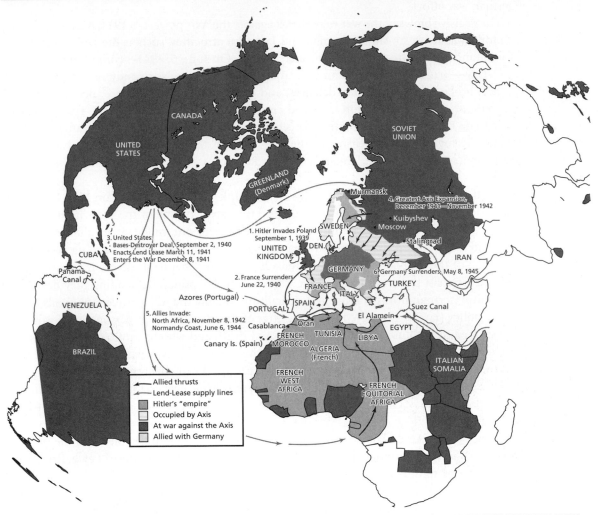

SOURCE: R. PALMER & J. COLTON, *A HISTORY OF THE MODERN WORLD*, 8TH ED. (NEW YORK: MCGRAW-HILL, 1995). REPRINTED WITH PERMISSION OF THE MCGRAW-HILL COMPANIES.

use the bombs against densely populated civilian targets was inhumane, and strategically questionable. However, the saturation bombing of cities had long been practised by both sides during the war. London, Rotterdam, Dresden, Hamburg, and many other cities suffered extensive bombing; the firebombing of Tokyo caused more casualties than those suffered at Hiroshima and Nagasaki. In this context, the atomic bomb did not seem very different. Nevertheless, to this day the bombings of Hiroshima and Nagasaki retain special symbolic importance, since the atomic era and the fear of a future nuclear war began with the destruction of those cities.

World War II was the most destructive conflict in history. Approximately 15 million combatants and 35 million civilians were killed. The Soviet Union alone suffered 20 million casualties—more than the entire population of Canada at the time (for Canada's role in the war, see Profile 2.12). Six million Jews and more than five million others were murdered in the concentration camps of Nazi-occupied Europe (see Chapter 9 on human rights for a discussion of genocide, the Holocaust, and the important **Nuremberg war crimes trials**). Cities and industries across Europe and Asia had been reduced to rubble. A massive rebuilding task faced the

Map 2.10 The War in the Pacific

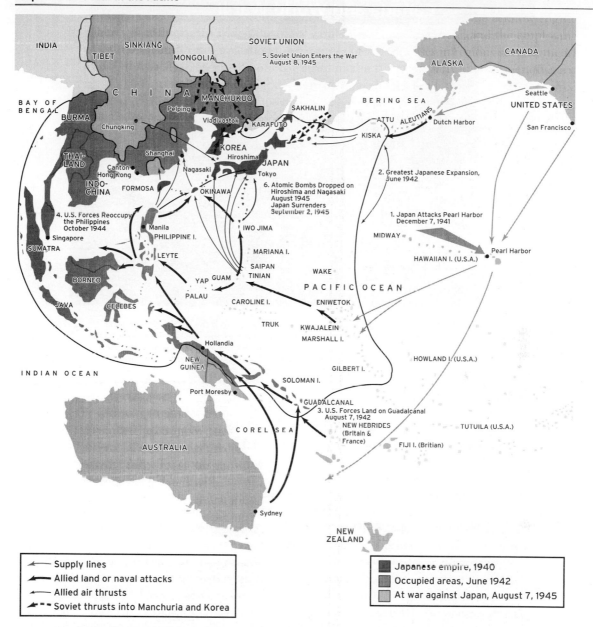

Legend:
- Supply lines
- Allied land or naval attacks
- Allied air thrusts
- Soviet thrusts into Manchuria and Korea

- Japanese empire, 1940
- Occupied areas, June 1942
- At war against Japan, August 7, 1945

SOURCE: R. PALMER & J. COLTON, *A HISTORY OF THE MODERN WORLD*, 8TH ED. (NEW YORK: MCGRAW-HILL, 1995). REPRINTED WITH PERMISSION OF THE MCGRAW-HILL COMPANIES.

survivors. Never before had war so fundamentally affected the lives of civilians. To an unprecedented degree, they had become targets of bombing campaigns and had participated in war production.[23] The concept of total war had reached its apogee: industrialization, nationalism, and the power of the state had combined with the increased firepower of new technologies to truly devastate whole societies.[24] World War II was the ultimate war of attrition: the societies that could bring the greatest human and material resources to bear were victorious, but at a terrible price.

PROFILE 2.12 | **Canada and World War II**

Finally laid to rest. The coffin of Private Ralph Tupper Ferns is carried during a funeral ceremony at the Canadian war cemetery at Bretteville-sur-laize, 2008. Private Ferns went missing during the Normandy campaign in 1944 and his remains were discovered in 2005. Family members, World War II veterans, youth representatives, and parliamentarians attended his funeral. (AP Photo/David Vincent/CP Photo)

Canada declared war on Nazi Germany on September 10, 1939, seven days after Great Britain. The government of Mackenzie King had envisioned a limited overseas commitment when it entered the war. Opinion in Canada was not as deeply divided as it had been in World War I, and although conscription was once again an issue in 1944 due to battlefield losses, the divisive debates of 1917 were not repeated (liberating occupied France was not an unpopular prospect in Quebec). By June 1940 only Great Britain, Canada, and the other Commonwealth countries stood against the Axis. Canada was now committed to a total war and produced vast amounts of ammunition and military equipment in cities such as Hamilton, Toronto, and Montreal. The Royal Canadian Navy bore most of the convoy escort duty early in the war, providing security for the vital merchant shipping lanes to Great Britain. More than 1 100 000 Canadians served during the war, and at its peak, the Canadian Army fielded nearly 500 000 soldiers; most students are surprised to learn that, at this time, the Canadian Air Force and the Navy were among the largest in the world after those of the great powers.

Canadians first fought together in large numbers in the disastrous Dieppe raid in August 1942. The circumstances of the raid are a subject of controversy to this day, since some suggest Allied commanders sent the Canadians to their slaughter. Canadians first saw mass service in the Italian campaign in 1943. Canada was later assigned its own landing beach (along with the United States and Great Britain) in the Normandy invasion, and Canadian troops went on to liberate much of the Netherlands. (To this day, the people of the Netherlands have a deep respect for the sacrifice made by Canadians in liberating their country in the war and for hosting the Dutch royal family during the Nazi occupation.)

More than 42 000 Canadians died in World War II. It may seem surprising now, but Canada ended the war as one of the most powerful countries in the world. This position was the foundation of Canada's postwar middle-power status and the basis for Canada's postwar internationalism.

See D. Bercuson, *Maple Leaf Against the Axis: Canada's Second World War* (Toronto: Stoddart, 1995).

World War II also had enormous political consequences. Most obviously, the victory of the Allied powers over the Axis powers altered the global distribution of power, and ushered in the nuclear era. Borders in Europe changed in accordance with agreements made between **Winston Churchill** and Josef Stalin in 1944 and at the "big three" conference of Roosevelt, Stalin, and Churchill at Yalta in February 1945. The Soviet Union absorbed some 600 square kilometres of territory, which included the Baltic states and land from Poland, Finland, Czechoslovakia, and Romania, recovering what had been lost under the Treaty of Brest–Litovsk. Poland was compensated with land from Germany, which was divided into four occupation zones. Austria was separated from Germany. In the Far East, Japan lost control over Manchuria, Taiwan, and Korea (which was divided into Soviet and U.S. zones) and suffered the loss of the Kurile Islands, which were seized by the Soviet Union. The European colonial powers were weakened, and a great wave of decolonization swept the world in the following decades, leading to an explosion in the number of independent states. Finally, the end of World War II saw the emergence of two powers—the United States and the Soviet Union— that possessed capabilities far greater than those of any other country. The emergence of these superpowers would define international politics in the postwar era, and suspicion and distrust between them grew rapidly. World War II had ended, but the Cold War, to which we will turn in Chapter 3, had just begun.

HISTORY, ALLIANCES, AND THE BALANCE OF POWER CONCEPT

For realists, war and the rise and fall of states and empires are a universal experience, and the writings of thinkers from Clausewitz to Kautilya confirm that political responses are common across time and culture. In essence, these responses champion the importance of military power and the utility of **alliances**. Military power and alliances are at the core of what realists argue has been the ordering mechanism of global politics since the ancient world: the **balance of power**.

The term *balance of power* can be used in several ways. It can be used as a descriptive term to denote the state of the power balance between certain states or groups of states in a geographic region. (It was not until the 20th century and the superpower confrontation that the concern with a global balance of power gained widespread currency.) The term can be used to describe a particular policy of states that may be actively seeking to balance the power of others. Most commonly, it refers to a historical phenomenon in which empires and states have repeatedly formed alliances against other states or groups of states. The balance of power is a system of order in an anarchic international system in which states act to ensure that no one state or group of states can come to dominate the system or conquer all other states in the system. This balancing behaviour preserves the system of sovereign states because no one state or group of states can acquire the power to control the entire region (or the world). This balancing behaviour can also preserve peace, by redistributing power in an effort to maintain an equilibrium, or balance, in the system. However, the balance of power does not necessarily mean the preservation of peace. In fact, the balance of power does not exist to ensure peace, but rather to ensure the survival of states. The preservation of the balance of power system often requires war to defeat the efforts of certain states to dominate or significantly alter the system.

States can balance in one of two ways. They can increase their own power (generally through military spending) or they can engage in alliances with other states. Alliances are formal agreements between states that commit them to a common purpose, such as military security against a common threat. Alliances are often referred to as **collective defence** arrangements.

Arrangements that are not formalized in treaties and that tend to be of shorter duration are often called *coalitions*. Alliances are a quick and relatively cheap method of supplementing one's own power with the power of another. Therefore, alliances are a form of self-interested cooperation (a "marriage of convenience"). Realists argue that the historical frequency of alliances reveals the universality of the balance of power concept.

Generally, alliances form when two or more states share a perceived threat and agree to coordinate their efforts to meet that threat.[25] This agreement may take the form of treaty obligations to assist the other state if it is attacked. In other cases, agreements may extend to high levels of cooperation on political and military issues, including the formation of joint institutions and joint military forces. Alliances are notoriously fluid and changing, and alliance commitments are often broken. However, a state might be reluctant to defect from an alliance relationship because of concerns that it would acquire a reputation as an unreliable ally. When the threat common to alliance members disappears, alliances tend to collapse, although as our discussion of the North Atlantic Treaty Organization (NATO) in subsequent chapters suggests, some alliances have endured after the threat that led to their formation has disappeared. In such cases, alliances might survive because of the emergence of a new threat or because self-interested states want to maintain the advantages of the cooperative relationship they have built. On the other hand, constructivists and liberals would argue that alliances are conducive to community formation, and can generate important institutions in their own right. Alliances vary with respect to the commitment of their members and their internal unity, often called **alliance cohesion**. Cohesive alliances (such as NATO) have a high degree of shared interests and coordination among their members, and tend to be formally institutionalized. Alliances that are less cohesive have lower levels of coordination and have more widely divergent interests among their membership. Cohesion is important because the ability to form a strong united effort against a threat is the key to a credible alliance.

For realists, because states will act to balance the power of other states, the distribution of power in the international system or in regional systems is extremely important. The distribution of power is defined by concentrations of power in a region or in the entire international system and by how many of these concentrations exist. These concentrations of power are called *poles*, and the distribution of power is often described in terms of **polarity** (a term borrowed from physics), which describes the number of independent centres or concentrations of power in the system. These poles of power, and the relations between them, determine the polarity of the system. Other actors may exist, but they are not decisive in determining system polarity. Changes in the distribution of power may take place slowly, the result of different economic growth rates and technological innovation among states. Some changes in the distribution of power may be very dramatic, the result of a sudden shift in alliances across the states or the sudden weakening of one or more of the poles through internal collapse or defeat in war. When this happens, the polarity of the system may change, and a different kind of system may emerge. For the purposes of study, realist scholars have identified three different kinds of polarity in the history of international relations: multipolar systems, bipolar systems, and unipolar systems. Each system type has a certain distribution of power (polarity), and each is the subject of debate as to its relative advantages and disadvantages.

Multipolar systems consist of three or more independent centres, or poles, that are relatively equal in power. These systems can be global in scope (the global balance of power), regional (such as the historical European balance of power systems), or localized (such as the Warring States period in China). The stability of multipolar systems is a major issue of debate among realists. Morgenthau argued that such a system is stable (and therefore more peaceful) because enough centres of power always exist to prevent a single power or group of powers from domi-nating. However, some neorealists, such as Kenneth Waltz, warn that multipolar systems are inherently unstable, precisely because they are so flexible.[26] In such a system, the actions of one centre of power (such as an attack on another centre of power or a decision to expand its military) can reverberate throughout the system and have unintended consequences (such as system-wide war or an arms race). A special kind of multipolar system is the tripolar system in which three centres of power exist. Tripolar systems are very unstable, as there is a tendency for two of the power centres to ally against the third, with no prospect of achieving a power bal-ance to deter war. Historical examples of such power distributions are rare, although some of the characteristics of such systems can be found in the "strategic triangle" between the United States, the Soviet Union, and China during the Cold War.[27]

In **bipolar** systems, two centres of power, in the form of either two predominant states or two great rival alliance blocs, dominate the international system, such as in Greece during the height of the Athenian and Spartan empires, and during the early Cold War between the superpowers and their respective allies. As the Cold War wore on, however, other countries attained more flexibility, largely because of their recovery from the devastation of World War II. As a result, while the superpowers remained militarily and economically predominant, other states increasingly embarked on their own foreign policy agendas and relationships, although these rarely challenged the policy of the superpowers. (In practice, the major allies of the United States maintained more freedom of manoeuvre than the allies of the Soviet Union did.) This system is sometimes referred to as **bipolycentrism**. Realists also disagree on the stability of bipolar systems. Some, such as Waltz, argue that bipolar systems are stable because the two centres of power deter each other from rash actions, and they can develop a familiarity that will reduce the chances of miscalculation. Others argue that such a system is inflexible because of the lack of balancing potential and because each state sees its position with respect to the other as a **zero-sum game**.[28] As a result, even small changes in the distribution of power between the two poles can have destabilizing effects that might lead to war. As we shall see in the next chapter, this became particularly dangerous in the nuclear age, when an all-out war between the two poles could have resulted in the destruction of most life on the planet.

The third configuration is a **unipolar** system, characterized by a single centre of power: a state or a powerful state and its allies dominate the forums, rules, and arrangements governing political and economic relations in the system. Such actors are often called *hegemons*. Most often, **hegemony** is a reflection of one state's preponderant power in traditional economic and military terms. However, as we saw in Chapter 1, hegemony can also refer to the dominance of ideas, including political perspectives and cultural norms.[29] The theory of **hegemonic stability** holds that a hegemon can have a stabilizing or ordering influence on a regional system or the international system by performing some of the functions a central government would perform. It can deter aggression or use political and economic pressure to prevent or stop wars between smaller countries. It can provide hard currency for use as a world standard. Two prominent examples of hegemonies in history are Great Britain in the 19th century and the United States in the 20th century. Great Britain's period of dominance occurred after the defeat of France in the Napoleonic Wars. The United States' period of hegemony began with the defeat of Nazi Germany and Imperial Japan at the end of World War II, and, arguably, persists to this day.

It is important to note that scholars of IR do not always agree on which states have achieved hegemonic status in the past and how long this position lasted. Some scholars would include 17th-century Netherlands and 16th-century Spain as examples of hegemons. It is also important to note that in practice a hegemon may exist in a multipolar setting (as did Great Britain in the 19th century) and in a bipolycentric setting (as did the United States during the Cold War). In such cases, the term *hegemony* merely describes the existence of a state that is more powerful than all others in the system but not so powerful that one can speak with empirical confidence of a unipolar system. For example, the Cold War is described as a period of bipolarity, as there were two clearly pre-eminent centres of power in the system. However, it was also clear that the United States was the more powerful in terms of the influence it exerted over international institutions, rules, and the world economy. As a result, the American role was often described as hegemonic, despite the broader bipolar context.

States that achieve hegemonic status do not retain this status indefinitely. Hegemonic decline will eventually occur over decades or centuries. A combination of domestic internal decay and costly military overextension weakens the hegemonic state. The hegemon will then face the efforts of a challenger to overthrow the hegemon's pre-eminent position. The transition from one hegemon to another may take the form of a hegemonic war or a peaceful transition in which the first hegemon will be compelled to pass on its status to a rising power.[30] Alternatively, the challenger may fail and the hegemon survive. As we shall see in Chapter 4, the status of the United States today is a point of debate among scholars, who disagree on whether the United States is a hegemon in decline.[31]

Realist concepts such as the balance of power and polarity have had an enduring impact on the study of global politics. However, other theoretical perspectives have challenged these concepts and their explanatory prowess. Liberals argue that focusing on a supposed quest for the balance of power de-emphasizes the importance of economic interdependence and other forms of cooperation between states, as well as the influence exerted by international institutions, regimes, norms, and law. Constructivists suggest the balance of power concept serves to reinforce and perpetuate ways of thinking about global politics that create crisis and conflict. In other words, these concepts are part of the problem, not just descriptions of historical "patterns" or "truths." Feminists point out that the balance of power and polarity are inherently masculine frameworks, serving to marginalize issues such as economic development, social justice, human rights, and a variety of other concerns of import to people in general and women in particular. These perspectives remind us that much of what we know (or think we know) about history is reflective of a certain perspective, one that is contestable and subject to challenge in many different ways.

HISTORY AND ASYMMETRIES IN POWER

The historical record also reveals that across time and place most political units (whether they be groups or states) do not possess anything like the power wielded by the strongest political units. Realists tend to focus on the most powerful actors, or **great powers**, because these actors define the character of the system (the distribution of power and the polarity of the system), and therefore their actions are deemed the most important. Of course, there is no question that great powers are tremendously influential. Few of them exist at any given point in history, and yet they possess most of the world's power resources at that time. Great powers possess the strongest military forces and the largest economies. Often these capabilities are based on natural endowments of large populations and plentiful resources, as in the case of the United States, Russia, and China. In other cases, these resources might be acquired through expansion, as was the case with the British Empire, or through economic growth and trade, as is the case with Japan. As a result, great powers tend to endure. Only great powers (or alliances of great powers) can decisively defeat other great powers militarily. They also tend to have global interests and commitments, and have a disproportionate influence on the spread of ideas, the rules and laws governing diplomatic affairs, and the regulations governing international trade and finance. And on occasion, great powers are formally recognized as such by international structures such as the Concert of Europe or the UN Security Council.

However, the bulk of state actors in the history of global politics have not been great powers. For the most part, historical systems have been composed of a small number of large (powerful) states and a large number of smaller (less powerful) states. The latter states vary widely in terms of their characteristics, resources, and capabilities, and, as a result, classifying them has been very difficult. The term *middle power* has been used to refer to a group of states that rank below the great powers in terms of power resources and influence in global politics. These states may exert influence within their respective regions, or they may have an international profile on certain specific issues, but for the most part their ability to influence the larger global setting is limited. Some middle powers may be geographically large, such as Canada or Australia, while others may be quite small, such as South Korea or Sweden. Small powers, or **small states** as they are more generally known, are countries that have less power capabilities than middle powers and little or no influence on global politics. They generally have smaller populations, less geographic territory, smaller economies (although many are very wealthy on a per capita basis), and limited military power capabilities. Small states are generally considered significant only to the extent that they become important in the schemes of the great powers. For example, Belgium has been a small state in Europe since its creation, but it has been important because of its status as a buffer state between Germany and France. Vietnam might be far less well known today but for the engagement of the United States in the Vietnam War and its historical conflicts with China. In addition, regional context is an important factor in judging the importance of states. Some small states in Europe or Asia would be among the most powerful states if they were relocated in different regions of the world. And Brazil, South Africa, and India all have a claim to great-power status in their respective regions.

Canada provides a good example of the difficulty inherent in classifying states according to an assessment of their overall power. The country has been described variously as a small state, a satellite of the United States, a middle power, and even a "principal power."[32] Canada has one of the leading economies of the world but has a very small military. The country is rich in resources but has a relatively small population, certainly in proportion to its extensive geographic territory. And yet, Canada consistently is ranked among the top 10 countries in the world in which to live, has one of the 15 largest economies in the world, and is a member of the G8 group of countries. Classifying states according to their material power therefore raises the question of how power is measured. For realists, military and economic indicators (hard power) best determine a state's power and its associated diplomatic status. However, power can also be measured in terms of the power to persuade without coercion, the power of ideas and values, and the power of social stability and a high quality of life (soft power). In this sense, small states can be significant actors in global politics, often serving as a source of ideas, as mediators, and as contributors to multilateral institutions. Furthermore, in an increasingly interdependent world, classifying states may become increasingly problematic in the face of the permeability of borders, the significance of multinational corporations, and the evident limitations on the use of superpower force as experienced by the United States in Vietnam and the Soviet Union and U.S. in Afghanistan.

Nevertheless, the classification of states continues. After the end of the Cold War and the demise of the U.S.S.R., the United States was often described as the world's only superpower.

The United Kingdom, France, China, Russia, and sometimes Germany and Japan are frequently referred to as great powers. Some countries are described as *regional powers*, such as India, Israel, Indonesia, Australia, and Brazil. Almost all other states are called small states. And some states are so small (often literally) they are called *micro-states*. The symbolism of state equality is maintained in the principles of diplomatic formality (see Chapter 7) and in organizations such as the UN General Assembly (see Chapter 5), in which the United States has the same number of votes (one) as Nauru. However, that is where the equality ends, and the reality of power asymmetry begins.

CONCLUSIONS

In this chapter we have provided a necessarily brief (and of course incomplete) history of global politics, focusing on the rise and fall of civilizations and empires, the formation of the modern state system, and the enduring problem of war. This historical experience reminds us of the need to be aware of both continuities and changes in the course of human affairs, and to be careful when proclaiming the dawning of a new era or a transformation in the nature of world politics. We also explored some of the core themes related to war and peace up to 1945, and noted the seminal impact they had on the development of related ideas and theories, such as geopolitics, realism, collective security, and the balance of power. All of these ideas, derived from historical developments and interpretations of those developments, maintained their relevance into the Cold War period. The next chapter examines in detail the most protracted power struggle in recent history, one that affected all states, small and large: the epic confrontation between the West and the East during the Cold War.

Endnotes

1. G.W.F. Hegel, "An Introduction to the Philosophy of History," in J. Loewenburg, ed., *Hegel Selections* (New York: Scribner's, 1929).
2. T. Judt, "What Have We Learned, If Anything?" *New York Review of Books*, May 1, 2008, 16.
3. P. Darby, "A Disabling Discipline?" in D. Snidal and C. Reus-Smit, eds., *The Oxford Handbook of International Relations* (Oxford: Oxford Handbooks Online, 2008), 391–404, www.oxfordhandbooks.com/oso/public/content/oho_politics/9780199219322/toc.html (accessed June 30, 2012).
4. For an engaging read on this topic, see E. Paris, *Long Shadows: Truth, Lies and History* (Toronto: Vintage Canada, 2001).
5. See, for example, J.R. McNeill, *Something New under the Sun: An Environmental History of the Twentieth Century World* (New York: Norton, 2001); J.F. Richards, *The Unending Frontier: An Environmental History of the Early Modern World* (Berkeley: University of California Press, 2003); and B. Fagan, *The Great Warming: Climate Change and the Rise and Fall of Civilizations* (New York: Bloomsbury Press, 2008).
6. J. Keegan, A *History of Warfare* (New York: Alfred A. Knopf, 1993), 122.
7. See W.H. McNeill, *The Pursuit of Power: Technology, Armed Force, and Society since AD 1000* (Chicago: University of Chicago Press, 1982), 5.
8. P. Heather, *The Fall of the Roman Empire: A New History of Rome and the Barbarians* (Oxford: Oxford University Press, 2006), 458.
9. For a history of Mongol power, see R. Marshall, *Storm from the East: From Genghis Khan to Kublai Khan* (Berkeley: University of California Press, 1993).
10. J. Black, *War and the World: Military Power and the Fate of Continents, 1450–2000* (New Haven: Yale University Press, 1998), 32.
11. H. Kennedy, *The Great Arab Conquests: How the Spread of Islam Changed the World We Live In* (London: Phoenix, 2007), 376.
12. For an excellent account of the impact of Islamic expansion on Europe, see D.L. Lewis, *God's Crucible: Islam and the Making of Europe, 570–1215* (New York: W. W. Norton, 2008).

13. See A. Hourani, *A History of the Arab Peoples* (Cambridge, MA: Belknap Press, 1991).

14. See V.D. Hanson, Carnage and Culture: Landmark Battles in the Rise of Western Power (New York: Anchor Books, 2001), esp. 193–232; and M. Cocker, Rivers of Blood, Rivers of Gold: Europe's Conquest of Indigenous Peoples (New York: Grove Press, 1998).

15. See A.B. Bozeman, *Politics and Culture in International History* (Princeton University Press, 1960).

16. P. Bobbitt, The Shield of Achilles: War, Peace, and the Course of History (New York: Alfred A. Knopf, 2002), 118–43.

17. Meanwhile, contemporary political geography is more likely to fall within the constructivist and/or critical theory camp than assume the realist approach; see, for example, the work of Simon Dalby on environmental security, such as "Environmental Security: Ecology or International Relations?" in E. Lafferiére and P. Stoett, eds., *International Ecopolitical Theory: Critical Approaches* (Vancouver: UBC Press, 2006), 17–33.

18. On the theme of the overextension and decline of empires, see the popular text by P. Kennedy, *The Rise and Fall of the Great Powers: Economic Change and Military Conflict from 1500 to 2000* (London: Unwin Hyman, 1988).

19. See S. Van Evera, "The Cult of the Offensive and the Origins of the First World War," *International Security* 9 (1984), 58–107; and J.L. Snyder, *The Ideology of the Offensive: Military Decision Making and the Disasters of 1914* (Ithaca, NY: Cornell University Press, 1984).

20. Quoted in B.W. Tuchman, *The Guns of August* (New York: Bantam Books, 1962), 146.

21. R. Overy, "Total War II: The Second World War," in C. Townshend, ed., *The Oxford History of Modern War* (Oxford: Oxford University Press, 2000), 139.

22. See W.L. Shirer, *The Collapse of the Third Republic* (New York: Simon and Schuster, 1969).

23. It is important to note that as Canadian and American men fought abroad, women were recruited into wartime production at home, continuing a fundamental shift in the economic role played by women in advanced capitalist economies that began under similar circumstances during World War I.

24. See G. Kolko, *Century of War: Politics, Conflicts, and Society since 1914* (New York: New Press, 1994).

25. See S. Walt, *The Origins of Alliances* (Ithaca, NY: Cornell University Press, 1987).

26. See K. Waltz, "The Stability of a Bipolar World," in D. Edwards, ed., *International Political Analysis* (New York: Rinehart and Winston, 1970), 340. See also J. Mearsheimer, "Why We Will Soon Miss the Cold War," *Atlantic Monthly*, August 1990, 37.

27. See A.N. Sabrosky, ed., *Polarity and War: The Changing Nature of International Conflict* (Boulder, CO: Westview Press, 1985).

28. See K.W. Deutsch and J.D. Singer, "Multipolar Power Systems and International Stability," in J. Rosenau, ed., *International Politics and Foreign Policy*, rev. ed. (New York: Free Press, 1969), 315–24. In a zero-sum game, one state's gain is automatically perceived as another's loss. Therefore, the outcome of the game is still zero (+1 for the winner, −1 for the loser = 0).

29. The Marxist (Gramscian) tradition in international political economy refers to hegemony as ideational domination by transnational class interests. See S. Gill, *American Hegemony and the Trilateral Commission* (Cambridge, UK: Cambridge University Press, 1990).

30. The most famous treatment of this theory of hegemonic stability and transformation is probably R. Gilpin's *War and Change in World Politics* (Cambridge, UK: Cambridge University Press, 1981). For a more liberal interpretation see R. Keohane, *After Hegemony: Cooperation and Discord in the World Political Economy* (Princeton University Press, 1984).

31. This debate is crystallized in two popular works: P. Kennedy, *The Rise and Fall of the Great Powers*; and J.S. Nye Jr., *Bound to Lead: The Changing Nature of American Power* (New York: Basic Books, 1990). A recent book by a prominent analyst argues that the liberal world order created by American hegemony will survive, even if American power is no longer as evident as it once was (and that American foreign policy designers should take this into account): J. Ikenberry, *Liberal Leviathan: The Origins, Crisis, and Transformation of the American World Order* (Princeton University Press, 2012).

32. See D. Dewitt and J. Kirton, *Canada as a Principal Power: A Study in Foreign Policy and International Relations* (Toronto: John Wiley and Sons, 1983). For further discussion, see K.R. Nossal, The *Politics of Canadian Foreign Policy*, 3rd ed. (Scarborough, ON: Prentice-Hall, 1997), 52–68; and A. Cooper, *Canadian Foreign Policy: Old Habits and New Directions* (Scarborough, ON: Prentice-Hall, 1997), 9–21.

The Cold War and Foreign Policy Analysis

> *To the extent that the nuclear threat has deterrent value, it is because it in fact increases the risk of nuclear war.*
>
> *—Robert S. McNamara[1]*

> *Restraint? Why are you so concerned with saving their damn lives? The whole idea is to kill the bastards. At the end of the war if there are two Americans and one Russian left alive, we win.*
>
> *—General Thomas Power, Commander of U.S. Strategic Air Command in the 1960s[2]*

THE COLD WAR: POWER POLITICS ASCENDANT

The Cold War dominated global politics for over 40 years.[3] Citizens of every state on earth were put at risk by the nuclear arms race. Canadians would have been caught in a horrific crossfire if nuclear war had occurred. A high level of animosity existed between the ideologies of the communist command economies (the so-called East or Second World) and democratic liberal capitalism (the so-called West or First World), between the Red Scare and the American imperialists, between the "commies" and the "Yankees," between the "pinkos" and the "fascists"—the list of quaint phrases depicting the evils of each side seemed endless. The Cold War was a comprehensive ideological, geopolitical, military, and international rivalry between the two **superpowers** (and their respective allies and **client states**) that became increasingly global in scope as the postwar era evolved. Thankfully, the Cold War never became a global hot war. The vast military capabilities of the superpowers never directly fought each other. Instead, the Cold War was fought in the international arena through diplomacy, ideological rhetoric, arms races, regional **proxy wars** and interventions, and the competition for allies and military bases around the world. Although the Cold War was sometimes called the *long peace*, this somewhat misleading label only applies to the absence of great-power war between 1946 and 1991.[4] Millions of people died in the regional wars and related human rights outrages of this period. The Cold War may have been a long peace for some, but it was certainly not so for all.

The Cold War was not the only issue in post–World War II international relations. Decolonization greatly increased the official number of states, and development became a major international issue. There was growing interest in the protection and promotion of human rights. The global economy grew dramatically. Non-state actors, especially multinational corporations and non-governmental organizations, became more prominent. Nevertheless, the dominant characteristic of this era was the superpower rivalry; the global politics of this period cannot be addressed or examined in isolation from this fact. The history of the relationship between the superpowers reveals several themes that persisted until the collapse of the Soviet Union:

- *A cyclical pattern of confrontation and cooperation.* The Cold War was characterized by periods of high tension and crisis between the superpowers, alternating with periods of a relative relaxation of tensions and increased levels of cooperation. Good relations reached a high point between 1968 and 1978, a period sometimes called **détente**, in which both countries sought restraint and increased cooperation.

- *The nuclear stalemate.* For most of the Cold War, especially after the late 1960s, each superpower was vulnerable to complete destruction by the nuclear arsenal of the other. Nuclear deterrence was the dominant military strategy of the Cold War.

- *The development of informal rules and mutual understandings.* Over time, the superpowers established formal and informal understandings and agreements that often guided relations between them. For example, it was generally understood that both sides possessed spheres of influence (such as Eastern Europe and Central America) within which the other side would not overtly interfere. When these agreements or understandings were violated in the view of one of the superpowers, tensions between the countries increased.

- *Political pragmatism versus ideological rhetoric.* During the Cold War, both superpowers professed the superiority of their respective ideologies. However, they also sacrificed ideological principles if geopolitical considerations demanded it, supporting allies with political systems antithetical to their own.

- *Superpower involvement in regional wars.* Although the two superpowers avoided direct warfare, both used or supported allies and client states in wars directed against their opponent's allies and clients. These wars are referred to as *proxy wars*. For example, Cuba's involvement in the Angolan Civil War was a proxy for direct Soviet involvement.

For other countries in the international system, the Cold War was the context for much of their foreign policy decision making. Many countries voluntarily sought security arrangements and alliances with the superpowers. Most of the countries of Western Europe joined the United States and Canada in the North Atlantic Treaty Organization (NATO), which bound its members to come to the assistance of any member should it be attacked. This alliance was built against the threat posed by the Soviet Union. The Warsaw Treaty Organization (WTO), more commonly called the **Warsaw Pact**, joined the countries of Eastern Europe with the Soviet Union in an alliance against NATO. However, the Warsaw Pact countries were much more tightly controlled from Moscow than NATO countries were by Washington. Indeed, the Soviet Union used force to keep puppet governments in power in Hungary in 1956 and Czechoslovakia in 1968.

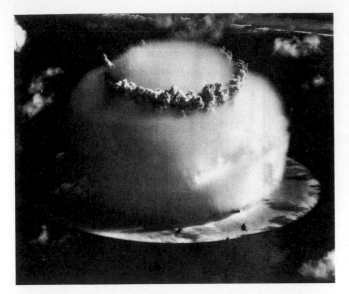

We can destroy you. The testing of nuclear weapons by the United States and the Soviet Union was the most visible expression of Cold War animosity. This was the U.S. test at the Bikini Atoll in the Marshall Islands on July 24, 1946. The dark spots in the foreground are old naval vessels placed near the blast to test the effects of nuclear explosions on ships. Such technology introduced a new possibility: omnicide. (AP Photo/CP Archive)

Around the world, states established relationships with the superpowers based on a combination of ideological affinity and pure self-interest. Both superpowers established a network of client states. The United States gave large amounts of assistance to countries such as Israel, Iran (before the Iranian Revolution), Pakistan, and South Korea. The Soviet Union supported North Korea, Cuba, Vietnam, and Syria. A few countries succeeded in following a neutral path, such as Switzerland, Austria, and Sweden. Some countries such as India, Indonesia, and Egypt sought to distance themselves from the Cold War by forming the **Nonaligned Movement (NAM)**, but never succeeded in becoming a major political force, since few if any countries could escape the fact that international issues were invariably affected by the behaviour of one or both superpowers. To varying degrees, all countries had to accommodate this fact when making foreign policy decisions.

The aim of this chapter is to explore the origins, character, and collapse of the Cold War. This task is a crucial one because our own time is often defined as the "post–Cold War era." The chapter also examines the formal study of decision making, or *foreign policy analysis*, which developed dramatically during the Cold War because the consequences of intentional or accidental nuclear war were such great threats to our collective survival. Today, decision-making theories are valuable tools in our search to understand how the decisions that shape global politics are made.

THE ORIGINS OF THE BIPOLAR ERA

The seeds of the Cold War were planted in the latter half of World War II, when distrust and friction began to develop between the Western allies (primarily the United States and Great Britain) and the Soviet Union. Each side was suspicious of the other's ultimate intentions, although distrust was held in check by the larger interest in continued cooperation to defeat Nazi Germany and Imperial Japan. Was the Cold War inevitable? The Western allies and the Soviet Union had cooperated during World War II despite their differences, and both had expressed a desire to maintain that cooperation in the postwar period. The membership of the U.S. and the U.S.S.R. in the newly created United Nations (UN), which was mandated to preserve world peace, offered hope that cooperation would continue. However, relations between "the West" and "the East" deteriorated into open hostility and a rivalry that largely paralyzed the UN Security Council. This structural tension had at least four interrelated dimensions: ideological, geopolitical, strategic, and international.

THE IDEOLOGICAL DIMENSION

The Cold War was a rivalry between two antagonistic political, economic, and social systems. It was a confrontation between two different ways of life, and a competition to determine which system performed best and could build a better society. On the one hand, the majority of Western countries and their peoples perceived Marxism–Leninism as a fundamentally authoritarian political ideology that stifled the political and economic freedom of the individual. Communism threatened the overthrow of Western liberal democracy and the free market economic system. The imposition of communist rule in Eastern Europe after World War II was seen as evidence of the intentions of the Soviet leadership. On the other hand, the ideological pronouncements of the Soviet Union characterized the West as a bastion of capitalist interests that controlled the world economy and was bent on surrounding and then destroying the Marxist–Leninist revolution in Russia. Capitalism and communism could not coexist, and the Soviet Union had to do what it could to accelerate the historical inevitability of communist revolutions around the world. The efforts of Western states to overthrow the communist revolution in the Russian Civil War and the delay in the opening of a second front in Europe until 1944 were seen as evidence of the hostile intent of the West. More broadly, U.S. secretary of state James Byrnes once argued, "There is too much difference in the ideologies of the U.S. and Russia to work out a long term program of cooperation."[5] These ideological differences, reinforced by historical experiences, served to create a climate of suspicion and outright animosity between the Western allies and the communist bloc.

During the Cold War, a persistent and intense debate raged in government and academic circles (as well as in the general public) about whether the U.S.S.R. was an expansionist power. For many, particularly early in the Cold War, the answer to this question was yes: the Soviet Union was a messianic state bent on expanding its power and influence through direct aggression and the support of communist national liberation movements abroad. For these **hawks**, Marxist–Leninist ideology was a blueprint, a guide, for Soviet actions. Just as Hitler's book *Mein Kampf* had outlined the plans and world view of that dictator, the ideological writings of Lenin and Stalin and the pronouncements of Soviet leaders outlined the plans and worldview of the Soviet leadership. However, many argued otherwise. These **doves** argued that the foreign policy of the Soviet Union was essentially defensive, concerned primarily with preserving and protecting the Soviet state. While the Soviet Union would take advantage of opportunities to increase its power or expand its influence, it would not take undue risks in the pursuit of such opportunities. Doves argued that ideology was not a guide to Soviet policy. At best, it was a perceptual lens through which the Soviet leaders saw the world. Soviet behaviour actually had more in common with the policies of Russia's Tsars. It was power politics that drove Soviet policy, not ideology.

As the Cold War dragged on, the ideological intensity of the superpower competition receded, as did the hostility of the rhetoric between the two countries. However, ideology remained the cornerstone of the confrontation between the United States and the Soviet Union. The competition between the two systems manifested in extreme nationalism (or patriotism) in both countries. Even in periods of détente, it surfaced in sports, the arts, scientific achievement, and space travel. In the 1980s, the ideological rhetoric of the Cold War intensified when Ronald Reagan became president of the United States. He took a firmly hawkish view of the U.S.S.R., believing it was the root of all evil in the world. The ideological animosity of the Cold War also existed between allies of the United States and other communist countries; however, the ideological rivalry of the Cold War was not uniform. Canada, for example, had better relations with Romania and Cuba than did the United States. In fact, Canada's relatively friendly relations with (and financial investment in) Cuba remain a point of contention in Canada–U.S. relations today.

THE GEOPOLITICAL DIMENSION

Ideological rivalry does not provide a complete characterization or explanation for the events of the Cold War. Just as important was the geopolitical rivalry between the superpowers. The pre-eminence of the United States and the Soviet Union at the end of World War II led them naturally to regard each other with suspicion. As Robert Tucker has observed, "The principal cause of the Cold War was the essential duopoly of power left by World War II."[6] In other words, the structure of the international system at the end of World War II led each super-power to regard the other as a rival. The ideological differences between the two countries only exacerbated this situation. As the Cold War intensified, geography played an important role in the strategic and foreign policy decisions of Washington and Moscow.

In the United States, the Soviet threat was cast in the geopolitical context of Halford Mackinder and his view of the world (see Chapter 2). The Soviet Union, after all, seemed to occupy the "heartland," and was poised to expand along the "interior ring" to dominate the "world island"—and thereafter the world. From this position, the Soviet Union had the tremendous geopolitical advantage of the interior lines of transport and was thus poised to expand anywhere along a wide perimeter (see Map 3.1). To contain the U.S.S.R., the United States and its allies were forced to defend this wide perimeter around the heartland of Eurasia. This prompted the U.S. to form multilateral and bilateral alliances with countries around the perimeter of Eurasia, and it found many willing partners. The governments of Western Europe saw the Soviet Union as a direct (and geographically close) threat. Common threat perceptions shared by most Western European countries and the United States led to the creation of **NATO** in 1949. Japan, occupied by the U.S. from 1945 to 1952, also felt threatened, not least because the U.S.S.R. had occupied several Japanese territories at the end of World War II. Japan and the U.S. would sign a bilateral security treaty in 1951. In Canada, concern arose about the threat the Soviet Union represented to the postwar order.[7] This would prompt the Canadian government to join NATO as a founding country and to establish a wide array of security agreements with the United States, most notably the **North American Air Defence Agreement** (**NORAD**) in 1958.

However, in its search for allies the United States also found willing partners that capitalized on the anti-communist passions of U.S. foreign policy by accepting American aid and using it for their own purposes. In its desire to geographically contain the Soviet Union and prevent the spread of communism, the United States would assist not only democratic countries that felt threatened by the U.S.S.R., but also dictatorial and military regimes that maintained their power through repressive and systematic human rights violations. Realists would proclaim that such alliances were natural if unfortunate manifestations of power politics. For successive U.S. governments, the enemies of communism and the U.S.S.R. were automatically perceived as friends. However, for liberals, Marxists, and feminists, U.S. support for regimes in Chile, Guatemala, South Africa, Indonesia, Iran (and later Iraq), and the Philippines were perversions of American principles and values. By supporting such regimes diplomatically, financially, and militarily while ignoring the brutal treatment that many citizens of these countries endured at the hands of their governments, the United States was complicit in some of the worst human rights abuses perpetrated during the Cold War.

In the Soviet Union, the geopolitical position of the country was regarded in a rather different fashion. When we simulate a Soviet geopolitical view by using a polar projection of the world (see Map 3.2), the difference is striking. No longer does the Soviet Union seem poised to strike out in any direction with the advantage of the interior lines.

Map 3.1 The Western Geopolitical View of the World during the Cold War

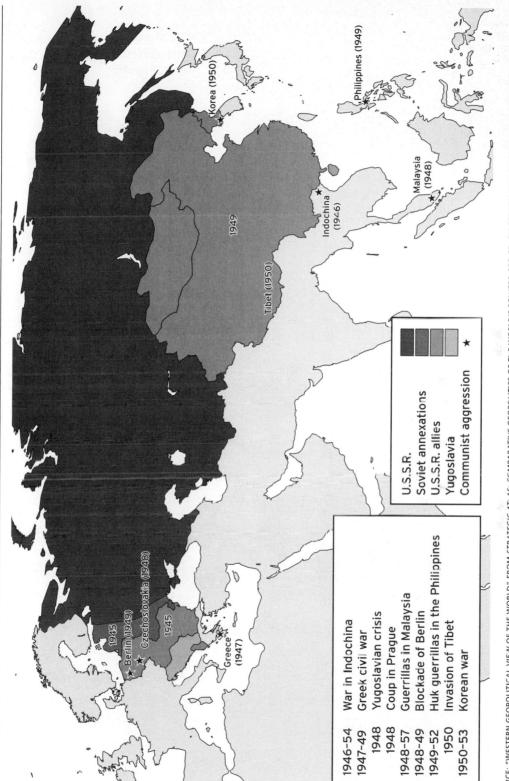

Korea (1950)

Philippines (1949)

1949

Malaysia (1948)

Indochina (1946)

Tibet (1950)

Berlin (1949)

Czechoslovakia (1948)

1945

1945

Greece (1947)

				★
U.S.S.R.	Soviet annexations	U.S.S.R. allies	Yugoslavia	Communist aggression

1946–54	War in Indochina
1947–49	Greek civil war
1948	Yugoslavian crisis
1948	Coup in Prague
1948–57	Guerrillas in Malaysia
1948–49	Blockade of Berlin
1949–52	Huk guerrillas in the Philippines
1950	Invasion of Tibet
1950–53	Korean war

SOURCE: "WESTERN GEOPOLITICAL VIEW OF THE WORLD" FROM STRATEGIC ATLAS: COMPARATIVE GEOPOLITICS OF THE WORLD'S POWERS, 3RD ED. BY GERARD CHALIAND AND JEAN-PIERRE RAGEAU. COPYRIGHT © 1993 BY GERARD CHALIAND AND JEAN-PIERRE RAGEAU. REPRINTED BY PERMISSIONS OF HARPERCOLLINS PUBLISHERS, INC. PG. 69.

Map 3.2 The Soviet Geopolitical View of the World during the Cold War

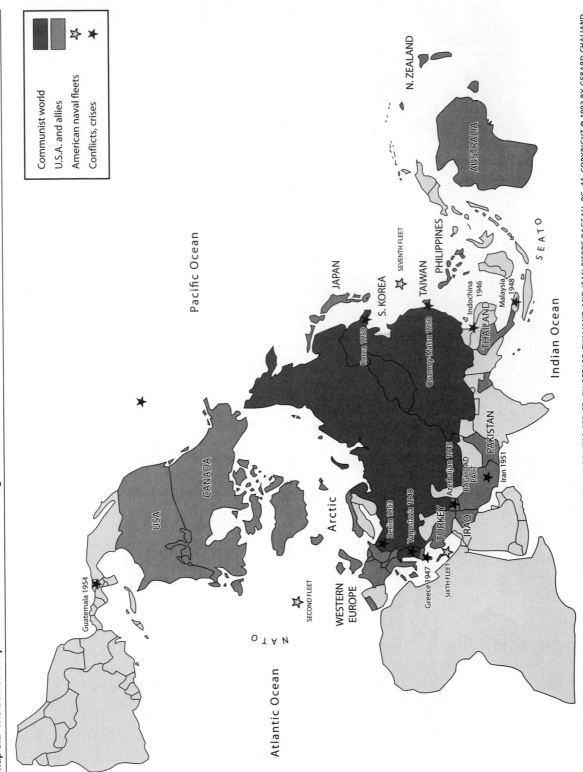

Legend:
- Communist world
- U.S.A. and allies
- American naval fleets
- Conflicts, crises

N. ZEALAND

AUSTRALIA

SEATO

Pacific Ocean

JAPAN

SEVENTH FLEET

S. KOREA

TAIWAN

PHILIPPINES

Indochina 1946

Malaysia 1948

THAILAND

Indian Ocean

Korea 1950

Quemoy-Matsu 1950

PAKISTAN

Iran 1951

Azerbaijan 1945

BAGHDAD PACT

Arctic

CANADA

USA

Berlin 1953

Yugoslavia 1948

TURKEY

IRAQ

Greece 1947

SIXTH FLEET

SECOND FLEET

WESTERN EUROPE

NATO

Guatemala 1954

Atlantic Ocean

SOURCE: FROM *STRATEGIC ATLAS: COMPARATIVE GEOPOLITICS OF THE WORLD'S POWERS*, 3RD ED. BY GERARD CHALIAND AND JEAN-PIERRE RAGEAU. PG. 44. COPYRIGHT © 1993 BY GERARD CHALIAND AND JEAN-PIERRE RAGEAU. PREVIOUSLY REPRINTED BY PERMISSION OF HARPERCOLLINS PUBLISHERS, INC.

Instead, the Soviet Union is encircled, and the long border of the Soviet Union is threatened by enemies and security concerns. Any potential effort to break out of this encirclement or to conduct military operations from the U.S.S.R. would encounter some of these enemies or threats. In Europe are the NATO countries, backed by the power of the United States. In southern Europe are the NATO countries of Greece and Turkey, which dominate the straits between the Black Sea and the Mediterranean. In the Middle East lies the Muslim world, a security concern because of the fear that this region might have an influence in the Islamic republics of the Soviet Union. To the east is China, a great ideological competitor by the second half of the Cold War, and Japan, a close ally of the United States. From the perspective of Soviet planners, the geopolitical position of the U.S.S.R. was not an enviable one.

THE STRATEGIC DIMENSION

Both superpowers and their respective allies maintained large conventional military forces throughout the Cold War. An immense amount of time, money, and effort was devoted to the maintenance of these forces and their training, equipment modernization, and deployment around the world. By the late 1980s the size of these conventional military forces was immense. In particular, Europe was host to the large armies of NATO and the even larger armies of the Warsaw Pact. However, the strategic character of the Cold War was defined by nuclear weapons and the nuclear arms race between the United States and the Soviet Union. The nuclear weapon was a revolutionary development in the history of warfare, a fact dramatically punctuated by the two bombs dropped on Japan at the end of World War II.[8] Ironically, the weapons were so destructive, and the consequences of their use so enormous, that their real military value came under question. But if nuclear weapons could not be usefully employed on the battlefield, what could they be used for? In short, they were useful only for preventing their use by others. In other words, nuclear weapons were instruments of **deterrence**, not war-fighting.

Deterrence is a policy of preventing or discouraging an action by confronting an opponent or opponents with risks they are unwilling to take. The actor doing the deterring is a *deterrer*, and the actor being deterred is a *deterree*. A potential aggressor will likely be deterred when the probability of victory is low or the costs of a war (whatever the outcome) are high. There are two broad types of deterrence strategies:

- *Deterrence by denial.* A deterree will not start a war because it is convinced it cannot achieve its objectives. Deterrence by denial was a pre–nuclear era phenomenon, based on the view that powerful military forces and high levels of military preparedness could discourage an attack by one country against another.

- *Deterrence by punishment.* A deterree will not start a war because of the threat that it will receive unacceptable damage in return. The enormous destructive power of nuclear weapons, coupled with advanced delivery systems, made deterrence by punishment feasible.

Nuclear deterrence defined the military relationship between the superpowers during the Cold War. Though the nuclear arsenal of the United States remained superior to that of the U.S.S.R. at least until the mid-1960s, the explosion of the Soviet atomic bomb in 1949 had ended America's nuclear monopoly, forcing both leaderships to contemplate the consequences of a nuclear war between them. By the mid-1960s, a rough parity, or equivalence, existed between the arsenals of the two superpowers, with each capable of inflicting **unacceptable damage** on the military forces and civilian populations of the other in the event of a nuclear war. The logic of deterrence by punishment suggested that if the two superpowers could inflict unacceptable damage on each other in a nuclear war, neither would start such a war by launching an attack, or **first strike**. The ability of both sides to essentially destroy the other was a signature feature of Cold War politics and came to be called **mutual assured destruction (MAD).** During the Cold War both superpowers devoted massive resources to the development and maintenance of enormous nuclear forces so there could be no doubt that they were capable of devastating the other under any possible set of circumstances. The result was a nuclear arms race (see Figure 3.1).[9]

As the Cold War progressed, the size and destructive potential of the nuclear arsenals of both superpowers led to a growing realization that all-out nuclear war between the two countries would be devastating on a global level. Indeed, the known effects of nuclear radiation and the possibility of nuclear winter (the cooling of the global climate from the ejection of dust and debris into the atmosphere) raised the question of whether humanity itself would survive a nuclear war. This fear of **omnicide**, coupled with the enormous expenses of the nuclear arms race, fostered the development of large peace and anti-nuclear movements dedicated to stopping the nuclear arms race and promoting arms control and disarmament (see Chapter 7). The signing of arms control agreements often accompanied larger efforts to improve the relationship between the United States and the Soviet Union in periods of détente. In addition, some arrangements were made in an informal manner: U.S. President Jimmy Carter and Soviet Foreign Minister Andrei Gromyko promised each other that their countries would never be the first to use nuclear weapons. This pledge was never made formal in an agreement, despite the efforts of "no-first-use declaration" advocates.

Profile 3.1 lists the bilateral arms control agreements signed between the United States and the Soviet Union/Russia. (The list includes agreements signed after the end of the Cold

Figure 3.1 Nuclear Warhead Stockpiles of Permanent Security Council Members, 1945–2012

YEAR	UNITED STATES	U.S.S.R./RUSSIA (1949)	UNITED KINGDOM (1953)	FRANCE (1964)	CHINA (1964)	TOTAL
1945	6	—	—	—	—	6
1950	369	5	—	—	—	374
1955	3 057	200	14	—	—	3 271
1960	20 434	1 605	42	—	—	22 081
1965	31 982	6 129	436	32	5	38 584
1970	26 662	11 643	394	36	75	38 810
1975	27 826	19 055	492	188	180	47 741
1980	24 304	30 062	492	250	205	55 313
1985	24 237	39 197	422	360	243	64 459
1990	23 270	37 000	422	505	232	61 429
1995	15 527	27 000	422	500	234	43 683
2000	11 423	21 500	281	470	232	33 906
2005	10 714	17 000	281	350	235	28 580
2010	9 400	12 000	225	300	240	22 165
2012	8 500	12 000	225	300	240	21 265

Note: Date in brackets is year of acquisition. In 2010, Israel was believed to have a stockpile of at least 80 warheads, the first of which may have been assembled as early as 1967. India is believed to have approximately 80 nuclear warheads, and Pakistan about 70.

SOURCES: ROBERT S. NORRIS AND HANS M. KRISTENSEN, "GLOBAL NUCLEAR WEAPONS INVENTORIES, 1945–2010," *BULLETIN OF THE ATOMIC SCIENTISTS* 66 (JULY/AUGUST 2010), 81–2. DATA FOR 2012 FROM ROBERT S. NORRIS AND HANS M. KRISTENSEN, "NUCLEAR PURSUITS, 2012," *BULLETIN OF THE ATOMIC SCIENTISTS* 68 (JANUARY 2012), 96.

PROFILE 3.1 — Major Bilateral Arms Control Agreements between the United States and the Soviet Union/Russia

DATE	AGREEMENT	PRINCIPAL AIMS
1963	Hotline Agreement	Establishes a direct radio and telegraph communications link between Moscow and Washington (updated with a satellite communications link in 1971).
1971	Nuclear Accidents Agreement	Creates a procedure for notification of a nuclear weapons–related accident or unauthorized detonation and establishes safeguards to prevent accidents.
1972	SALT I Interim Agreement	Limits number of ICBMs and SLBMs allowed by each side.
1972	Anti-Ballistic Missile Treaty	Limits deployment of anti-ballistic missile systems to two sites (later reduced to one in a protocol in 1974) and prohibits development of space-based ABM systems.
1973	Agreement on the Prevention of Nuclear War	Commits superpowers to consult in the event of an imminent threat of nuclear war.
1974	Threshold Test Ban	Restricts underground testing of nuclear weapons over the yield of 150 kilotonnes; broadened in 1976.
1977	Convention of the Prohibition of Military or Any Other Hostile Use of Environmental Modification Techniques	Bans the use of weapons that threaten alteration or modification of the environment under certain conditions.
1979	SALT II (not ratified)	Restricts number of strategic delivery vehicles permitted by both sides.
1987	Nuclear Risk Reduction Centers Agreement	Establishes facilities in both capitals to manage nuclear crisis.
1987	Intermediate-Range Nuclear Force Treaty (INF Treaty)	Eliminates U.S. and Soviet ground-launched intermediate-range nuclear weapons in Europe.
1990	Chemical Weapons Destruction Agreement	Bans further production of chemical weapons and calls for reduction in weapons stockpiles to 5000 tonnes each by 2002.
1991	START (Strategic Arms Reduction Treaty)	Reduces nuclear arsenals by approximately 30 percent.
1992	START I Protocol	Commits Russia, Belarus, Ukraine, and Kazakhstan to strategic weapons reductions specified in START I.
1993	START II	Reduces strategic nuclear arsenals to 3000 (Russia) and 3500 (United States) by 2003; bans multiple-warhead land-based missiles.
2002	SORT	Reduces strategic nuclear arsenals of both Russia and U.S. to no more than 1700 to 2200 by 2012.
2010	**New START**	Reduces strategic nuclear arsenals of both Russia and U.S. to no more than 1550 warheads, and reduces the ballistic missile and heavy bomber arsenals of both countries to 700, by 2018.

War, when Russia assumed the U.S.S.R.'s treaty obligations.) Among the most important treaties signed during the Cold War were the **Strategic Arms Limitation Treaty (SALT)** and the **Strategic Arms Reduction Treaty (START)**. Signed in 1972, SALT I placed limits on the number of **intercontinental ballistic missiles (ICBMs)** and **submarine-launched ballistic missiles (SLBMs)** deployable by both sides for five years. SALT I also placed limits on the deployment of **anti-ballistic missiles (ABMs)** in the so-called ABM Treaty. In 1979, the more comprehensive SALT II agreement established a ceiling of 2250 on the number of ICBMs, SLBMs, heavy bombers, and air-to-surface ballistic missiles (ASBMs) permitted for each side. In retaliation for the 1979 Soviet invasion of Afghanistan, the U.S. Senate never ratified SALT II, although both countries continued to abide by the basic provisions of the treaty. The criticism of both SALT I and SALT II was that neither agreement actually reduced the number of weapons held by the superpowers, simply introducing restrictions on the numbers of weapons that could be deployed in the future.

However, progress on nuclear arms control was quickly overshadowed when the Reagan administration embarked on a new course. In a speech on March 23, 1983, President Reagan announced a program to develop a defence against ballistic missiles. The idea was not a new one: by the 1960s both the United States and the U.S.S.R. had developed anti-ballistic missile systems. However, these systems were of doubtful reliability and effectiveness, and in a world of nuclear deterrence, defences could threaten the logic of MAD. Indeed, the 1972 ABM Treaty ensured the dominance of deterrence by banning the development and deployment of missile defences (with the exception of two installations of 100 interceptors). President Reagan proposed a much more ambitious scheme. His Strategic Defense Initiative (SDI) envisioned the deployment of ground and space-based missile and directed-energy weapons of sufficient capability to shoot down incoming missiles and nuclear warheads. SDI would completely protect the United States and would render nuclear weapons, as Reagan put it, "impotent and obsolete."[10] Due to the high-technology aspects of the program, SDI became known popularly as "Star Wars" after the famous 1977 science fiction movie.

SDI had many supporters. As hard as it is to believe today, some analysts in the United States believed that the U.S.S.R. was surpassing the Americans in military power, and missile defences promised to restore U.S. dominance. Others hoped to escape the immorality of MAD and the prospect of a devastating nuclear war. U.S. defence contractors, and many scientific researchers, were naturally supportive of SDI and the billions of dollars in contracts the program promised. Others argued that SDI would strengthen deterrence: faced by both assured destruction and U.S. strategic defences, the U.S.S.R. would never contemplate war. However, there were also many critics of the program, who argued that SDI was technically infeasible, could never be 100 percent effective, was too costly, would start an arms race in space, and would violate the 1972 ABM Treaty.[11] Critics also argued that SDI was destabilizing and could increase the risk of nuclear war. If a U.S. shield were only partially effective (as it certainly would be) then both the United States and the U.S.S.R. would have an incentive to strike first in a crisis. The U.S.S.R. could strike first, firm in the knowledge that a U.S. shield could not stop a massive first attack. However, if the United States were to strike first and damage the Soviet nuclear arsenal, weakening its striking power, SDI might be able to protect the United States from this smaller, less coordinated retaliatory attack. The United States could thus "win" a nuclear war, unless the U.S.S.R. struck first! SDI would thus undermine the logic of MAD and make nuclear war more likely.

By the mid-1980s, political developments began to undermine the SDI program. The possibility of a nuclear war receded as the diplomatic relationship between the Reagan administration and the new Soviet government of Mikhail Gorbachev steadily improved. Arms control once again became a focus of bilateral relations, and in 1987 the superpowers signed the Intermediate-Range Nuclear Forces (INF) agreement, eliminating all U.S. and Soviet medium-range nuclear missile systems in Europe. SDI was quietly shelved, but some research continued, and as we shall see the debate over ballistic missile defences would re-emerge in the late 1990s. In July 1991 the superpowers signed the START treaty, which committed both sides to reducing their nuclear arsenals by one-third. This dramatic agreement was made possible largely by the changing climate in the last years of the Cold War. Critics charged that the agreement would reduce the nuclear arsenals of the superpowers only to the levels that existed in 1982, the year the START negotiations began. However, as we shall see in Chapter 7, by 1989 to 1991 events were in motion that would dramatically alter the entire context of nuclear arms control.

THE INTERNATIONAL DIMENSION

The Cold War rapidly became a fixture of international politics, and it had a visible impact in Latin America, Europe, Africa, the Middle East, and in South and East Asia (for the impact of the Cold War on Canada, see Profile 3.2). Indeed, no region was uninfluenced by the super-power rivalry, and crises occurred with startling frequency. In the early years of the Cold War, tensions were high and confrontations were numerous, including the Soviet refusal to pull out of Iran in 1946 and reports of Soviet involvement in the Greek Civil War. These events prompted U.S. President Harry S. Truman to adopt the policy suggestions put forward by **George Kennan**. Kennan, a junior official in the American embassy in Moscow, decisively influenced postwar U.S. attitudes toward the Soviet Union. Instructed to analyze the postwar intentions of the Soviet Union, Kennan responded with a famous "long telegram," in which he argued that the U.S.S.R. regarded the United States as its foremost international opponent, and that as long as the U.S. remained strong, Soviet power could not be secure. In an anony-mous published statement of his beliefs in the influential journal *Foreign Affairs* in 1947—the famous "X" article—Kennan argued that the Soviet Union represented a dangerous blend of an autocratic ruler (Stalin), a revisionist and messianic ideology (Marxism–Leninism), and a violent and expansionist history. Kennan recommended the political containment of the Soviet Union until the internal nature of the Soviet Union changed, and, along with it, its foreign policy.[12]

Truman soon declared "that it must be the policy of the United States to support free peo-ples who are resisting attempted subjugation by armed minorities or outside pressures."[13] This commitment came to be called the **Truman Doctrine**, and was the first articulation of what was to become America's grand strategy during the Cold War: the **containment** of the per-ceived expansionist and revisionist power of the Soviet Union. The aim of containment was to prevent the spread of communist ideology around the world, to prevent any direct aggres-sion by the U.S.S.R., and to prevent the Soviet Union from expanding its influence in the world. Virtually all U.S. foreign policy action, from foreign assistance to military intervention to diplomacy, was directly related to or influenced by the objectives of containment. Kennan, however, did not support the emphasis placed on military containment. He felt that the Soviet threat was primarily political and that it could not be met entirely by military means.[14] As tensions between the United States and the Soviet Union escalated, further crises followed, including the American decision to establish the Federal Republic of Germany, a commu-nist coup in Czechoslovakia in 1948, the Soviet blockade of West Berlin of June 1948, the

PROFILE 3.2   Canada and the Cold War

Canadian Prime Minister Lester Pearson and American President Lyndon Johnson. Though they had some differences over American foreign policy, particularly with regard to the war in Vietnam, Canada was for the most part a firm ally during the Cold War. (CP PHOTO)

Canada was a close ally of the United States and a member of the "Western club" of countries. Some have argued that Canada was a close American ally because it was largely controlled by American interests and capital; essentially, a satellite economy with little real foreign policy autonomy. However, although the flexibility of Canadian governments was limited, Canada shaped its foreign policy largely on the basis of an appraisal of Canadian interests in the Cold War world. The reality was that Canada was strategic territory, and any attack on the continental United States would devastate Canada as well. As a result, Canada joined in efforts to deter or prevent war by participating in NATO and the North American Air Defence (later Aerospace) Agreement. Canada's economy was heavily dependent on a stable, American-led international trading system and on direct trade with the U.S. itself. Since Canada was a democratic country with a firmly entrenched capitalist economy, Canadian governments and the majority of the Canadian people were suspicious and even hostile to communism as a political and economic system. In other words, Canada was a status quo state, comfortable with its position in the world under the *Pax Americana* and interested in the prevention of instability or war.

However, this comfort did not mean that Canada did not exert an independent foreign policy. Canada was a strong supporter of the United Nations throughout the Cold War and was a key contributor to UN peacekeeping, which contributed to efforts to prevent regional wars from becoming larger conflagrations that might draw in the superpowers. It has been suggested that Canada was a major contributor to peacekeeping because the U.S. could not participate directly in such operations. Canada consistently advocated multilateralism during the Cold War, largely because multilateralism gave it an opportunity to participate in cooperative efforts and institutions, giving Canada a voice in international affairs. Canada also took an independent stand toward Cuba, and established good diplomatic relationships and a positive reputation in much of the developing world. However, successive Canadian governments took care not to alienate the United States; Canadian criticisms of U.S. policy in Central and South America and Vietnam were muted as a result, with one notable exception: Lester Pearson's ill-received speech at Temple University, Philadelphia, in 1965, when he called for a cessation of the American bombing campaign in Vietnam.

SEE R. WHITAKER AND S. HEWITT, *CANADA AND THE COLD WAR* (TORONTO: LORIMER, 2003) AND, FOR AN INTERESTING COLLECTION OF ESSAYS INCLUDING FEMINIST VIEWPOINTS, SEE R. CARELL, ED., *LOVE, HATE AND FEAR IN CANADA'S COLD WAR* (UNIVERSITY OF TORONTO PRESS, 2004).

communist victory in China in 1949, Chinese coercion against Tibet, numerous Taiwan Strait crises, and the Korean War in 1950. The Cold War era was also characterized by mass decolonization as the former European empires finally crumbled, and both superpowers competed for allies among newly independent countries.

Europe, which would be the focal point of the superpower competition for much of the Cold War, was divided. The United States and other Western governments feared that the Soviet Union might gain control of Western Europe, either through direct conquest or by having Communist Parties taking control in the war-devastated region. To prevent this, the United States launched the **Marshall Plan**, a program of U.S. financial assistance to rebuild the economies of Western Europe. The most prominent confrontations of the early Cold War were centred on the status of Berlin. Germany was split into what would become the Federal Republic of Germany (FRG) or West Germany and the German Democratic Republic (GDR) or East Germany. West Berlin, a small enclave of the city controlled by West Germany, was surrounded by East German territory. The Berlin crises of 1948 and 1961, in which the Soviet Union attempted to gain full control of the city, led to armed standoffs, but not to war. Across Germany, a fenced and guarded line—which Winston Churchill called the *iron curtain* in 1946—dramatically symbolized the division of Europe. In 1961, East Germany built the **Berlin Wall**, separating East and West Berlin, and forcibly preventing Berliners from communicating or travelling across this divide.[15]

In 1949, the United States, Canada, and several European allies established NATO, a formal alliance arrangement that solidified the American and Canadian commitment to Western Europe. Throughout the Cold War, half the world's total defence spending would be devoted to the superpower standoff in Europe. It was along the inter-German border that the military forces of NATO (including soldiers from European NATO countries and the United States and Canada) would face the military forces of the Warsaw Pact. In this respect, NATO was a classic alliance, a collective defence arrangement made to counter a common threat. However, NATO also served other functions. First, it guaranteed that U.S. forces would be involved immediately if the Soviet Union attacked Western Europe. NATO thus bound Western Europe and the United States together. Second, NATO also provided for the safe, albeit slow, reintegration of West Germany back into European politics. West Germany would become a member of NATO in 1951. NATO thus served a collective security purpose, providing confidence that Germany did not pose a threat in Europe. And so, in the iconic (and today perhaps ironic) words of NATO's first Secretary-General, Lord Ismay, NATO was established to "keep the Russians out, the Americans in, and the Germans down."

In China, the nationalists under Chiang Kai-shek and the communists under Mao Zedong (or Mao Tse-tung) had battled invading Japanese forces during World War II. However, the evacuation of the forces of the defeated Japanese left the nationalists and the communists to battle over control of China. Despite assistance from the United States, Chiang Kai-shek was defeated by the communists and forced to flee to the island of Formosa, now known as Taiwan. The United States extended political and security guarantees to Taiwan, and to this day U.S. support for Taiwan remains a source of tension between China and the United States. On October 1, 1949, the People's Republic of China (PRC) was proclaimed. To the capitalist West, the "loss" of China to communism was the first of what have been called the *two shocks of 1949* (the second shock was the explosion of the first Soviet atomic bomb). However, ideological differences, distrust, and Chinese resentment of what they perceived as domineering Soviet attitudes led to the Sino–Soviet split of the early 1960s. Thereafter, the Soviet Union and China were geopolitical and ideological competitors. During the rest of the Cold War, the

Attention. You are now leaving West Berlin. The Berlin Wall, seen here from West Berlin looking into East Berlin in the background, was a symbol of the Cold War division of Europe and the East–West confrontation. The Brandenburg Gate, at the centre of the picture, was in the zone dividing Berlin. (AP PHOTO/CP Images)

Soviet Union devoted approximately one-third of its military resources to guarding the Sino–Soviet frontier. The two countries also engaged in rhetorical sparring matches, each claiming to represent the true path to communism. The threat posed by Soviet power even prompted China to establish a rapprochement with the United States, which culminated in a visit by U.S. President Nixon in 1972. Nixon was deftly dealing the Soviets a moral blow with his historic trip. Again, ideological preferences gave way to geopolitical considerations.

In June 1950 the Korean War broke out when communist North Korea attacked South Korea. In response, the United States and 15 allied countries sent military forces to South Korea. This deployment was achieved under the collective security provisions of the United Nations, although in practice the United States dominated both the political and military direction of the war. The U.S.S.R. had walked out of the Security Council over the issue of Chinese representation and so was absent (and could not cast a **veto**) when the decisive vote was taken to give UN authorization to the U.S.–led collective security operation. (The Soviet Union would never walk out of the Security Council again!) As the war progressed, allied forces pushed the North Koreans back toward the Chinese border, with the intent of unifying the country. China then intervened, sending more than 300 000 "volunteers" into North Korea, who pushed allied forces back in retreat. A stalemate followed near the original border along the 38th parallel, and the war ended in a truce in 1953 (see Profile 3.3). The Korean War

PROFILE 3.3 Canada and the Korean War

On June 25, 1950, North Korea invaded South Korea. The next day, under request from the U.S., the UN Security Council passed a **resolution** calling on member states to respond to halt North Korean aggression. The Canadian government agreed in principle with the U.S. position, but was noncommittal about sending troops. Initial Canadian contributions involved naval vessels and transport planes. Not until August 7 did the St. Laurent government, under criticism at home for its inaction, commit ground troops to Korea. Canada was anxious that the operation in Korea be controlled and managed by the UN. It was thought that multilateral management of the conflict would restrain American impulsiveness. However, the Korean War was fought largely by American and South Korean forces, and the political decision making was dominated by Washington. This situation led to some criticism in Canada that the Canadian government was too closely tied to that of the United States, a critical theme that persisted throughout the Cold War. Canadian troops joined the 27th Commonwealth Infantry Brigade in February 1951 and later formed the 25th Canadian Infantry Brigade Group operating as part of a Commonwealth Division. Canadian troops took part in a number of battles, and by the war's end on July 27, 1953, Canadian troops had suffered 312 killed and 1577 wounded in what came to be known as Canada's "forgotten war."

SEE J. MELADY, *KOREA: CANADA'S FORGOTTEN WAR* (TORONTO: MACMILLAN, 1983); AND T. BARRIS, *DEADLOCK IN KOREA: CANADIANS AT WAR, 1950–1953* (TORONTO: MACMILLAN, 1999).

heightened Western fears of communist expansionism and revealed that conventional wars could still occur in an era of nuclear weapons.

After this period of crisis and the death of Stalin in 1953, the Cold War thawed to some extent. Nikita Khrushchev emerged as the new general secretary of the Communist Party of the Soviet Union. The first U.S.–Soviet Summit meeting was held at Geneva in 1955. However, the spirit of Geneva did not last long. In 1956, the Soviet Union crushed a rebellion in Hungary. In the Suez Crisis of the same year, Israel, France, and Great Britain invaded Egypt. The European states were clinging to imperial prestige and resented Egypt's **nationalization** of the Suez Canal. The Soviet Union threatened to intervene on behalf of Egypt, one of its allies in the region. The United States, which opposed the actions of its allies in Egypt, compelled them to accept a proposal forwarded by Canadian Foreign Minister Lester B. Pearson for a ceasefire and a UN interpositionary force in the region. Great Britain and France withdrew, and Israel pulled its forces back. Though peace in the region would be short-lived, the Suez Canal crisis signalled the end of European dominance in world affairs, the beginning of superpower management of crises, and the introduction of modern peacekeeping.

Cold War intrigue also spread to the Caribbean, where the United States attempted to overthrow Fidel Castro's revolution by supporting the **Bay of Pigs** invasion by Cuban exiles. The invasion failed, serving only to drive Castro further into the Soviet camp. In 1960, an American U-2 spy plane was shot down over the Soviet Union. These incidents culminated in the 1962 Cuban Missile Crisis in which the United States and the Soviet Union came closer to all-out nuclear conflict than they would at any time during the Cold War.[16] The crisis was precipitated by the construction of medium-range ballistic missile launch sites on the island of Cuba. These sites, built to offset Cuba's strategic inferiority and to help deter another invasion of the island, were detected by U.S. aerial reconnaissance. Soviet merchant vessels carrying missiles were also detected as they sailed to Cuba. U.S. President John F. Kennedy imposed a naval blockade of Cuba to prevent the landing of the missiles and to force the removal of the bases. Thus the world was dangerously close to nuclear war when the U.S.S.R. agreed not to station missiles in Cuba in return for an American promise not to invade the island. The fear prompted by the Cuban Missile Crisis led both superpowers to establish closer ties, agreeing in 1963 to a Limited Test Ban Treaty that banned atmospheric nuclear tests, as well as to a Moscow–Washington hotline, and a variety of scientific, cultural, and space and aviation agreements.

However, Cold War competition continued around the world (see Profile 3.4). Both the United States and the Soviet Union supported insurgency movements in the allied and client states of the other superpower. The pattern of support did not necessarily reflect ideological positions. In many cases, the United States supported governments and movements that were authoritarian and undemocratic (though not opposed to the investment of American capitalists), while the Soviet Union often supported governments and movements that could scarcely be called communist. Proxy wars continued, the largest of which occurred in Vietnam, where warfare had persisted since World War II during the painful retreat of French colonialism. In the Vietnam War, the United States backed a succession of authoritarian governments in Saigon against an internal insurgency mounted by the Viet Cong and supported by communist North Vietnam (which in turn was supported by the Soviet Union and China). The United States, concerned with expanding communist influence in Asia, committed itself to preventing a communist takeover in Vietnam.

The visual evidence, 1962. The scene in the United Nations Security Council on October 25, 1962, as U.S. Ambassador Adlai Stevenson provides evidence of missile launch sites being built in Cuba. The launch sites were intended for Soviet ballistic missiles aimed at the United States. (AP Photo/CP PHOTO)

PROFILE 3.4 The Domino Theory and Other Zero-Sum Views

During the Cold War, successive American administrations committed the United States to combating the spread of communism whenever and wherever it took place, a perspective that was shared to varying degrees in many other Western capitals. This commitment grew from the fear that if one country in a region fell under communist rule, the other countries in that region would also be at risk. Therefore, communism had to be prevented from taking root in even the smallest and remotest of countries. This concept came to be called the *domino theory*, by analogy with dominos standing up on end close together, tipping over one another until all have fallen: once one country fell, its neighbours would inevitably fall as well. This fear contributed to American efforts to prevent the spread of communism around the world, most prominently in Korea and Vietnam. Another analogy was *salami tactics*, in which the world was represented as a salami. Communism was taking over the world slice by slice, country by country. Yet another instrument was the use of world maps that showed communist countries in red. As more countries fell to communism, more red appeared on the map. This method contributed to the fear that the Soviet Union was "painting the map red." All these conceptualizations were based on a zero-sum view of the Cold War, that a gain for one side was an equivalent loss for the other side, so both superpowers found themselves engaged in struggles for countries whose citizens often knew or cared little about the broader Cold War context.

In the face of continued communist successes in South Vietnam, what was initially a small U.S. involvement (in the form of military advisors) soon escalated to the deployment of more than 540 000 U.S. troops by 1968. However, the U.S. military was designed to fight the Soviet military, not a counterinsurgency campaign against a lightly equipped enemy using the jungle for concealment. In an attempt to use superior firepower to win an insurgency war, the U.S. military conducted a massive saturation bombing campaign against North Vietnam and Cambodia, and made widespread use of chemical defoliants such as Agent Orange and other "rainbow herbicides" to remove the jungle canopy in parts of Vietnam. This was a modern variation of a practice called **ecocide**: the deliberate destruction of the environment for military purposes. The use of chemical defoliants in Vietnam also left a legacy of increased rates of disease, cancer, and birth defects for the U.S. soldiers and Vietnamese civilians exposed to these chemicals. However, despite superior technology and firepower, the United States failed to defeat the insurgency. The Vietnam War divided the American public and compelled the Nixon administration to seek a withdrawal of U.S. forces. The Paris Peace Accords of 1973 led to the withdrawal of all American troops from South Vietnam, which fell to the North in 1975. Approximately 58 000 Americans were killed in Vietnam, and more than one million Vietnamese perished. The Vietnam War had a profound impact on the American psyche, as many questioned the rightness of the war and were hesitant to support the deployment of U.S. forces in the future. This hesitation came to be called the *Vietnam syndrome*, and arguably it was never fully exorcized until the 1990 to 1991 Persian Gulf War.

In 1979 another Cold War crisis erupted when the Soviet Union invaded Afghanistan. U.S. President Jimmy Carter responded by enunciating the Carter Doctrine, which committed the United States to protecting its interests in the Persian Gulf by any means necessary, including military force. He also organized a **boycott** of the 1980 Moscow Olympics, suspended U.S. grain exports to the Soviet Union, and dramatically increased defence spending. The invasion of Afghanistan was to prove as much of a quagmire for the Soviet Union as Vietnam had been for the United States. The Soviet Union was unable to fully suppress Afghan resistance to the invasion, and the Soviet army was to suffer 13 000 dead and 35 000 wounded by the resistance fighters, who were given financial and weapons support from the U.S. through Pakistan. Some of this support would later come back to haunt the United States: among some of the benefactors of U.S. assistance were those who would later rule Afghanistan in the Taliban government. It was this government that provided sanctuary to terrorists, including Osama Bin Laden and Al-Qaeda, the group responsible for the September 11, 2001, terrorist attacks.

If the invasion of Afghanistan soured U.S.–Soviet relations, the election of President Ronald Reagan in 1980 ushered in a period sometimes referred to as Cold War II. President Reagan and his supporters came to power with a very hostile view of the Soviet Union, which was reflected not only in his public speeches and proclamations (most famously, he repeatedly referred to the U.S.S.R. as an *evil empire*) but also in the policies of his administration. The Reagan administration accelerated the military buildup initiated by President Carter, proposed the development of the Strategic Defense Initiative, and enhanced U.S. support to insurgency movements in Soviet client states (particularly in Nicaragua and Angola). Escalating tensions between Washington and Moscow fuelled increasing concerns about the possibility of war and growing opposition to the nuclear arms race in the form of a growing anti-nuclear movement.

THE END OF THE COLD WAR: POWER POLITICS DESCENDANT?

The combination of the superpower confrontation during the Cold War, the regional wars that broke out around the world, and the nuclear arms race all served to provide ample ammunition to realists. The Cold War seemed to confirm much of the premise and dynamics of the power politics approach to IR. However, as we will explore over the next few chapters, some significant new trends began to take shape in the Cold War world, including the development of an increasingly interdependent world economy, the growth of international institutions and organizations, heightened concern over the environment, increased international travel and communication, and the widening gap between the rich and the poor. These trends began to challenge the accuracy of the realist framework.

Nevertheless, it was the end of the Cold War that removed the shadow of the superpower rivalry and brought these trends to the front of the international agenda. Few international events have been as dramatic as the end of the Cold War. The revolutions against communist rule in Eastern Europe, the reunification of Germany, and the collapse of the Soviet Union itself took place within a startlingly short time—from mid-1989 to the end of 1991—and changed the face of global politics. The Cold War ended not with a hegemonic war (as many had feared and anticipated) but with the disintegration of one of the two poles of power. It is crucial to explore the question of why this occurred.

The Soviet Union experienced increased economic stagnation during the rule of Leonid Brezhnev. By the time Mikhail Gorbachev came to power in 1985, the problems facing the Soviet Union were enormous. The economy was performing poorly and in some sectors was actually shrinking. By the 1980s Japan had overtaken the U.S.S.R. as the world's second-largest economy. Soviet central planning had created an economic structure that was inefficient, obsolete, and incapable of meeting the demand for food and even basic consumer items.

The Soviet Union's two vital energy resources, coal and oil, were becoming more difficult to extract. The U.S.S.R. had become the world's largest importer of grain, with a quarter of its own crops rotting in the fields because of a poor distribution system. The military budget was absorbing approximately 20 to 25 percent of the country's Gross National Product (GNP), as well as 33 percent of the country's industrial force, 80 percent of its research and development personnel, and 20 percent of its energy output. In addition, the Soviet Union subsidized its allies, spending more than US$20 billion a year. The workforce suffered from poor morale, with strikes and demonstrations taking place in many cities. Food rationing had to be reintroduced. Life expectancy and infant mortality compared unfavourably with those of the West. The closed nature of the Soviet system, which restricted access to information and controlled television, newspapers, and books, was unable to take advantage of the computer and information revolution.[17]

Gorbachev's solution to these problems was to implement a reform program based on three elements: **glasnost** (openness) to broaden the boundaries of acceptable political discussion; **perestroika** (restructuring) to reorganize the old economic system by introducing limited market incentives; and **democratization** to increase the involvement of the people in the political process. It was Gorbachev's hope that this program would revitalize the Soviet economy while the Communist Party remained in power. Gorbachev never envisioned that his reforms would fundamentally alter the nature of political power in the U.S.S.R.; he was a reformer, not a revolutionary (see Profile 3.5). To embark on this program of domestic reform, Gorbachev required a favourable international environment. He required good relations with the West to obtain Western aid so that resources could be diverted from military spending to the civilian economy. Gorbachev embarked on a foreign policy that saw him reach out to the West with arms control proposals and summits with Western leaders. He also withdrew Soviet forces from Afghanistan. In so doing, Gorbachev changed the tone of the East–West relationship, and even became something of a celebrity in the West. Gorbachev's arrival on the international scene marked the beginning of the end of the Cold War.

However, Gorbachev's domestic program did not yield the desired results. In fact, the opposite occurred, as the standard of living of the average Soviet citizen actually began to fall. By the end of the 1980s, the contradictions in the Gorbachev reform program were evident. In the attempt to reorganize the economy, the old system was dismantled, while no new legal or reformed banking system was put in place to allow market forces to operate. The result was economic decline, unemployment, and a drop in production. Glasnost served to expose the inefficiencies and corruption of the economic system and increasingly of the government and the Communist Party itself. Within the U.S.S.R., some wanted to slow reform and maintain many of the characteristics of the old economic system, while others wanted to accelerate reform and remove the old system entirely. Gorbachev was increasingly isolated politically between these two factions and his credibility and influence began to wane.

By the late 1980s the end was near. The last gasps of the Soviet Union began in 1989. In a series of revolutions in Eastern Europe—some peaceful, others violent—the ruling Communist Parties in those states were swept away with no response from Gorbachev. The Berlin Wall, the symbol of the Cold War division of Germany and the division of Europe, was officially opened up on November 7, 1989, although citizens of both countries had been singing and dancing on the wall and taking picks and hammers to it for days. Germany, divided during the Cold War, was reunified on October 3, 1990. The Warsaw Pact, the Soviet Union's alliance system in Eastern Europe, was dissolved. Although Germany and Eastern European countries would

Mikhail Gorbachev

Hailed in Canada. Former Soviet Union President Mikhail Gorbachev presents the James S. Palmer Lecture at the University of Calgary, October 12, 2000. (CP PHOTO/Adrian Wyld)

The last leader of the Soviet Union (from March 11, 1985 to December 25, 1991), Mikhail Gorbachev was the architect of the reform program that initiated a chain of events that was to culminate in the collapse of the U.S.S.R. After studying law in Moscow (graduating in 1955), Gorbachev worked his way through the ranks of the Communist Party organization, eventually becoming responsible for agriculture. He became a full **Politburo** member in 1980, and after the deaths of Brezhnev's successors (Yuri Andropov and Konstantin Chernenko), Gorbachev became General Secretary of the Central Committee of the Communist Party of the Soviet Union. He embarked on an ambitious program of political and economic reform, what he called *the new political thinking* on domestic and foreign policy issues. This reform was dramatically displayed in Gorbachev's approach to arms control, a cooperative relationship with Europe, and a hands-off approach to the Eastern European countries (even when they were throwing off communist rule).

While Gorbachev's international diplomacy earned him international acclaim and the Nobel Peace Prize in 1990, at home he was increasingly unpopular, and his reform program had unleashed forces that were soon spiralling out of control. Central control over the economy was lost, nationalism spread and intensified, the constituent republics of the U.S.S.R. began to agitate for more autonomy, and the political spectrum in the U.S.S.R. diverged into radical reformers and conservatives. Ultimately, the reform program was rendered obsolete by the political events surrounding the breakup of the Soviet Union.

In retrospect, Gorbachev was one of the great reformers in world history, but his efforts were inadequate in the face of a system that required transformation rather than mere reform. Outside contemporary Russia, Gorbachev is remembered as the Soviet leader who did more than any one individual to make the end of the Cold War peaceful by acquiescing to the freedom of Eastern Europe. However, within Russia, Gorbachev is often vilified as the man who caused the collapse of the Soviet Union and increased the misery of the average citizen. The last leader of the Soviet Union remains far more popular abroad than in his own country.

SEE HIS BOOK *GORBACHEV: ON MY COUNTRY AND THE WORLD*, TRANS. GEORGE SHRIVER (NEW YORK: COLUMBIA UNIVERSITY PRESS, 1999).

now have to struggle with political and economic reform and the legacy of more than 40 years of communist rule, the Europe of the Cold War had vanished.

Within the U.S.S.R., increasing disaffection with the central leadership in Moscow led to demands for an increased devolution of powers to the constituent republics. A new Union

People power defeats the Berlin Wall. Germans from East and West Berlin celebrate the fall of the Berlin Wall, November 10, 1989. The wall was removed and the Brandenburg Gate was restored. (AP Photo/CP Photo)

Treaty was to be signed on August 20, 1991, that would have weakened the power of the centre. However, on August 19, a coup attempt was mounted while Gorbachev was away on (an apparent) vacation, and an eight-person council took power.[18] The coup failed, largely because key elements of the internal security apparatus and the military refused to support it. Instead, many backed Boris Yeltsin, a former Communist Party official who had been elected chairman of the Supreme Soviet of the Russian Republic in May 1990 and president of the Russian Republic (the largest of the 15 republics) in June 1991. Faced with public opposition and without control of the army, the coup plotters caved in, and Gorbachev was brought back to Moscow. However, the central government began to simply wither away as governments in the republics gathered increasing power in their own jurisdictions. Gorbachev was quite literally president of a federal bureaucracy detached from the republics and possessing little real authority. The final blow fell with the Ukrainian vote for independence on December 1, 1991, which effectively scuttled attempts to revive a Union Treaty. Declarations of independence from other republics followed. On December 8 the **Commonwealth of Independent States (CIS)** was formed as a coordinating framework for most of the former republics of the U.S.S.R. (only the Baltic States were non-members). In the last week of December 1991, the Soviet flag was taken down from the Kremlin in Moscow. The Soviet Union had disintegrated, and the Cold War was over.

PONDERING THE END OF THE COLD WAR

For almost half a century, the Cold War defined global politics. Virtually everything deemed internationally newsworthy was directly or indirectly related to the Cold War, whether it was the announcement of new, profligate spending for defence projects, the hopeful negotiation of another arms control agreement, or the outbreak of a distant proxy war. Everyone feared the ever-present threat of nuclear conflict and the unspeakable yet certain devastation such a war would bring. Indeed, it is possible to speak of a Cold War generation for whom nuclear anni- hilation was a constant possibility (it still is, but thankfully the threat is much less intense). The Cold War affected domestic politics as well. In the democratic industrialized world, the fear of communism led to suspicion and often suppression of domestic communist movements. In some countries, witch hunts were conducted to purge government, the arts, and society of communist influences. The most famous of these efforts took place in the United States in 1952 and 1953 under Senator Joseph McCarthy, whose use of accusation and innuendo with no substantial evidence gave rise to the term *McCarthyism*, an extreme example of the general tendency during the Cold War to regard with suspicion those who were sympathetic to or sup- portive of communism, the Soviet Union (or China), or left-wing policies in general. In other countries, anti-communism was used as an excuse to suppress dissident movements, commu- nist or non-communist, often with the larger purpose of maintaining a political and military elite in power. For example, hundreds of thousands of people died in Indonesia as a result of a bloody anti-communist purge by the Suharto government in 1965. In communist countries, political freedoms were almost non-existent, and state-controlled media emphasized the evils of the capitalist West. The brutal repression of dissent in the Soviet Union and China (and many of their client states) was a vivid illustration of the gulf between the theories and dreams of Karl Marx and the reality of life in most so-called communist states.

Intellectually, the Cold War contributed to a sense of predictability and order in world affairs. The most predominant concern was maintaining a stable superpower relationship and keeping the Cold War cold. A consensus (although by no means universal) emerged in most countries with respect to foreign affairs and defence policy. Broadly supported by their publics, governments maintained their alliance commitments and a certain level of defence spending. In scholarly circles, the Cold War seemed to vindicate much of the realist perspective, and academic work concentrated on issues such as strategic stability, deterrence, and arms control. The Cold War fed an interest in the history and politics of the Soviet Union, and Kremlinology became an important area of study. This does not imply that scholarship during the Cold War was stale or uniform. On the contrary, major theoretical debates took place. An increased interest in economic interdependence fostered the rise of liberal perspectives, and a growing academic voice from low-income countries pushed theories about imperialism, decoloniza- tion, and dependency to the fore.

The Cold War was characterized by periods of high tension, crises, proxy wars, and a con- ventional and nuclear arms race between the superpowers and their allies. Why did these dif- ferences and confrontations not lead to an omnicidal war between the United States and the Soviet Union? First among the reasons was the nuclear stalemate between the two countries. The leaders of both countries knew that if a conflict between them developed into a war, there was a very good chance that the war would escalate to the use of nuclear weapons, resulting in a strategic nuclear war that would at the very least devastate both societies. The Cuban Missile Crisis proved to be the catalyst for a growing realization that to avoid a nuclear war, the super- powers would have to manage their relationship more carefully. The superpowers established a hotline between Washington and Moscow to facilitate communication in a crisis. Over time, informal rules were established between the two countries, such as the acknowledgment of spheres of influence in which the other would not overtly interfere, and the employment of consultation and communication during times of war or crises in regions such as the Middle East and Asia. The leaders of both countries met in summits, arrived at cooperative arrangements such as cultural exchanges and **trade** agreements, and signed several arms control treaties. All these efforts served to enhance the communication and cooperation between the United States and the Soviet Union and were a reflection of the awareness of both countries that the Cold War had to be kept cold.

Because the end of the Cold War meant the end of conditions that had been so pervasive and all encompassing, it left a conceptual and intellectual aftershock. Political leaders, scholars, and the public began to ask fundamental questions about the nature of global politics, questions that were seldom asked during the Cold War. Little thought had been devoted to what a post–Cold War world would be like. No plans were made for such an eventuality, and some, like John Mearsheimer, suggested that we would come to miss the Cold War, with its familiarities and certainties.[19] In contrast Francis Fukuyama suggested that the end of the Cold War represented the final triumph of liberal democracy and market economics over **authoritarianism** and central planning. For Fukuyama, this meant the "end of history," the end of the historical ideological struggle over how human society would be organized.[20] However, in the former communist world, the end of the Cold War was much more traumatic. Economic hardship, social decay, and environmental problems afflicted most of the former Soviet Union and Warsaw Pact countries, and these problems have not been resolved in many of these regions even today.

The collapse of the Soviet Union left many people in Russia wondering what had happened. Post-Soviet Russia embarked on a rapid program of economic reform designed to bring capitalism to the country. The reforms, coupled with the resistance of powerful bureaucratic and industrial interests, caused massive disruptions in the economy. While a few new rich prospered, life for most Russians improved only slightly, and for many it became worse. The sense of pride associated with being citizens of one of only two superpowers vanished, replaced by the country's fragmentation and the humiliation of declining standards of living and an erosion of personal safety in the face of growing crime rates. The formerly well-funded sectors of Russian society and industry were also deeply troubled. A poorly led, poorly prepared, and cash-starved military performed badly in the suppression of Chechnya, a small region in the Caucasus that sought independence. Scientists who worked in the huge Soviet military–industrial complex struggled to support their families. Some feared that the state of affairs in Russia was disturbingly similar to 1920s **Weimar Germany**, and those conditions were instrumental in enabling Adolf Hitler to rise to power. Indeed, the government of the former Russian President Vladimir Putin (who came to power in March 2000 and was re-elected under controversial circumstances to another term as president in 2012) has been characterized by an enthusiasm for centralized power, suppression of dissent, control of the media, structural corruption, and disregard for the rule of law. Fear that a new Cold War may be emerging between Russia and the West is discussed in Chapter 13.

WHY DID THE SOVIET UNION COLLAPSE?

Realism and neorealism have been attacked for their failure to predict the end of the Cold War. However, none of the theoretical frameworks employed by IR scholars can claim a better record in this regard. We can isolate several factors that offer possible explanations for the fall of the Soviet Union. In general, these factors point to a superpower that was in increasingly dire straits, a superpower that had become a "Potemkin Village" and was facing an unpromising future (see Profile 3.6).

In retrospect, many observers in the West were well aware of the problems facing the U.S.S.R. However, they underestimated the extent to which these forces were undermining the Communist Party of the Soviet Union, which after all could call on massive military forces, a large internal security apparatus, and state control of political and economic life to maintain its power and keep order in the country. The autopsy following the collapse of the U.S.S.R. has yielded the following perspectives and explanations for this dramatic event:

- *A victory for containment.* One explanation is that the grand strategy of containment by the United States worked. The costs of the nuclear arms race, maintaining a massive military establishment, and supporting allies in Eastern Europe and overseas bankrupted the Soviet Union. Unable to devote resources to the revitalization of its civilian economy and boost sagging consumer and agricultural production, the U.S.S.R. simply spent itself into its grave. Many realists in the West (particularly in the United States) take this position and argue that the policy of firm containment and high defence spending contributed to the end of the Cold War and a Western victory. In contrast, liberals argue that the containment policies of the West may have prolonged the Cold War. Soviet leaders could use the threat posed by the West as a rallying point for political support and as an excuse to maintain high levels of defence spending and centralized control over the economy. Without an external threat to distract attention from domestic hardships, the U.S.S.R. may have embarked on reform (or even collapsed) far earlier. As George Kennan, the original author of the doctrine of containment, argued in 1992, "The general effect of Cold War extremism was to delay rather than hasten the great change that overtook the Soviet Union at the end of the 1980s."[21]

- *Soviet imperial overstretch.* Another explanation can be found in the theories of power transition and imperial decline. Using the theories publicized by Yale historian Paul Kennedy, this explanation suggests that empires tend to expand until they overstretch themselves. The costs of these commitments burden the economy at home, which undercuts the long-term capacity of the economy to sustain itself. By this

PROFILE 3.6　The Potemkin Village Analogy

The Potemkin Village analogy originates with the story of a Russian prince named Grigori Potemkin, a favourite of the famous tsarina of Russia, Catherine the Great. Potemkin had helped organize her imperial tour of the southern provinces of the Russian Empire in 1787, taking great efforts to make the tour as spectacular as possible. This effort included the construction of attractive false fronts, or façades, for many of the buildings and towns along the tsarina's route, to impress Catherine with the prosperity of the empire, a prosperity that was at least in part an illusion manufactured by Potemkin. This story is used as an analogy for the state of the Soviet Union by the 1980s, a superpower that was in truth a superpower in military terms only. This façade of strength, while significant, obscured the fact that the Soviet Union was sliding deeper into economic decline, with most of its citizens cynical about the political and economic system and struggling to maintain their meagre standard of living.

explanation, the U.S.S.R. took on too many commitments in the world, which forced it to devote scarce resources to client states such as Cuba, Syria, and Vietnam. The war in Afghanistan burdened the economy even more in the early 1980s. The costs of these commitments drew already scarce resources out of the country, resources that could have been used to reinvigorate the Soviet economy.

- *The economic and social decline of the U.S.S.R.* The most widely accepted explanation of the collapse of the Soviet Union is that the communist system simply did not work very well. The command economy that had been so successful in guiding the rapid industrialization of the Soviet economy later served to hinder reform and innovation. Consumers suffered from shortages of even basic goods and endured long lineups for food items. Industries in the civilian sector turned out poorly manufactured goods developed and built not for the consumer but to fulfill production quotas set by the state. Agricultural techniques stagnated and led to poor distribution and massive waste. Worker morale declined, as exhibited in the famous Soviet workers' proverb: "They pretend to pay us, and we pretend to work." New technologies and techniques could not be absorbed into the Soviet economic system, which became increasingly entrenched in a heavily bureaucratized political system that favoured the elite few—the *nomenklatura*—but was resistant to change. The collapse of the Soviet Union was therefore the result of a failed economic system, one that could not sustain itself, let alone compete with the West, which was entering the electronic and information age.

- *The failure of Gorbachev's reforms.* Another explanation argues that the reform program of Mikhail Gorbachev was the most important reason behind the collapse of the U.S.S.R. Gorbachev sought a middle way to reform between the command economy and market forces. However, no middle way was to be had, and the poorly conceived reform program was doomed from the beginning. This misdirected reform effort made an already bad situation worse, creating such desperation and discontent that the centre lost its grip on power. A different reform program might have succeeded. The Soviet system was badly rundown, but in trying to fix the system, Gorbachev broke it.

- *The triumph of democracy and the market.* Finally, liberals argue that the collapse of the Soviet Union represented a victory for democracy and the market as systems of governance. The virtues and advantages of an open political system, the efficiencies of a market economy, and the capacity to innovate and adapt to changing conditions and technology served as a standard against which all other systems were measured. Clearly, the communist system did not measure up. The average Soviet citizen was becoming increasingly aware of the living standards enjoyed in the West, and this was a source of increasing concern and embarrassment to the Soviet leadership. This explanation argues that soft power played an important role in the end of the Cold War.

It is tempting to argue that everything changed when the Cold War ended. However, as we saw in the previous chapter, major historical tidal waves leave both changes and continuities in their wake. From a global perspective, the end of the Cold War can be described as the third defining event of the 20th century, following the shocks of World War I and World War II. Just as the interwar period and the Cold War years saw changes and continuities, so have the post–Cold War years. We will turn to the issues of contemporary global politics in Part Two of this book, but turn now to examine one of the most visible intellectual legacies of the Cold War, the development of foreign policy analysis as a subfield of international relations.

THE STUDY OF FOREIGN POLICY DECISION MAKING

During the Cold War, IR scholars began to take an interest in how states (and, to a lesser extent, other actors) made foreign policy decisions. This growing interest created a distinct area of study that continues to fascinate.[22] Scholars have a natural interest in how governments reach decisions that might have devastating consequences, and how miscalculation and error might lead to crises or even wars. They have borrowed ideas and concepts from psychology (with its interest in motives and perception), economics (which examines the decisions of consumers in terms of trade-offs and preferences), and business administration (with its interest in efficiency and organizational culture). The field was originally grounded in rational choice theory, which makes certain controversial assumptions about decision makers, but has since expanded to include a vast array of theories, variables, and actors. The field is notable for its focus on people, politics, and processes within governments. As Mark Shafer and Scott Crichlow note, "The [foreign policy decision making] program takes us inside the state."[23]

In general terms, foreign policy is "the concrete steps that officials of a state take with respect to events and situations abroad … [it is] … what individuals representing the state do or do not do in their interactions involving individuals, groups, or officials elsewhere in the world."[24] Foreign policy can also be described as the public policy of a state implemented in the international environment. However, this definition excludes non-state actors and the influence of domestic politics. We must remember that non-state actors, such as terrorist groups, multinational corporations, and humanitarian relief organizations, also make decisions relevant to events and situations in global politics, and that seemingly "domestic" decisions can have foreign policy consequences. In fact, the boundary between domestic and international issues has been eroding steadily. In short, foreign policy decision making often involves more than just the consideration of the actions of governments.

As defined by James Dougherty and Robert Pfaltzgraff Jr., "decision making is simply the act of choosing among available alternatives about which uncertainty exists."[25] The primary concern of decision-making theory is process, rather than outputs or actual decisions. When actors make decisions, these decisions are made in a larger context, which influences the nature of the decision. This context includes the following:

- *The external environment.* The broader setting in which the decision must be made includes the kind of issue confronting the actor, the position and power of the actor with respect to others, and the influences and pressures the latter exert on the actor.

- *The internal environment.* The domestic setting in which the decision must be made concerns the nature and structure of the political system, the role of key decision makers, the influence of public opinion or interest groups, the influence of domestic political factors (such as elections), and the role of certain bureaucracies in foreign policy decision making.

- *The perceptions of the decision makers.* The perceptual lenses of individual decision makers can have a major influence on decision making. How individuals in the process see the world and the actors in it is a key determinant of actor behaviour.

- *The decision-making process.* The rules governing how decisions are made can be a crucial influence. Is one individual making the decision? Is the decision made by majority vote or the achievement of consensus among a leadership group? Was the decision taken with wide consultation and democratic input?

- *The time constraints.* The temporal setting (the amount of time the decision makers have in which to reach a decision) is crucial. If a decision is required quickly, it will be made in a different way than if the decision involves long-term planning.

In order to analyze foreign policy decisions, students and scholars of global politics must account for this context if they are to have a complete picture of why a decision was made.

An important constraint on students of decision making is access to information. In many cases, vital documents may be held as state secrets, sometimes for decades. Interviews with key decision makers may yield self-serving interpretations of events. Incomplete media reports can lead to erroneous conclusions or the development of conspiracy theories. Propaganda and misinformation may lead analysts astray. As a result, the study of decision making often involves revisions to supposed facts and truths, and reassessments of explanations once thought to be above reproach. Of course, all of this makes it very difficult to engage in analysis of recent decisions. The more recent the decision under analysis, the less information will be available on how the decision was made.

In order to make sense of how decisions are made, a variety of different models have evolved. Two main models of decision making are used, and they offer alternative explanations of how decisions are made by actors in the international system (although they are primarily focused on states). The **rational actor model** argues that decision makers make decisions in a self-optimizing, rational fashion. The **bureaucratic politics model** suggests that decision outputs are the result of competition and bargaining among different organizations within government. While many other models are examined in this textbook, including constructivist frameworks for the development of foreign policy, we expand on these two here, since they are most closely associated with the central debates on foreign policy decision making.

THE RATIONAL ACTOR MODEL

Recall that the realist perspective, which dominated academic discourse on IR during the Cold War, assumes that states are rational, unitary actors. Liberals also make the same basic assumption about individuals. In the rational actor model of decision making (also called the *classical model*), decisions are regarded as the product of a largely unified and purposeful process based on considerations of available alternatives aimed at selecting the best option. In other words, decisions are the result of a rational process of choice designed to maximize outcomes. The rational choice process has four steps:

1. *Recognize and identify the problem.* Recognizing that a decision must be made, and identifying the nature of the problem, is the first step in any rational process of decision making.

2. *Establish objectives and aims.* The next step involves considerations of one's goals with respect to the issue at stake. These goals must be established on the basis of judgments about interests and preferences, in addition to expectations about prospects for success.

3. *Establish options.* Next, possible alternative decisions must be formulated and considered in the context of available resources, capabilities, and potential reactions by other actors.

4. *Select an option.* Finally, the best option available—in terms of satisfying the goals of the actor and having the best chance of success—will be selected.

As a result, this model contends that decisions are—or, certainly, should be—the product of a careful cost–benefit analysis process.

As an example, take the decision of the Canadian government under Brian Mulroney to pursue and then sign the Canada–U.S. Free Trade Agreement, which came into force on January 1, 1989. The rational actor model would explain this decision beginning with the belief of the prime minister and his Cabinet that the country faced a looming crisis: the Canadian economy could not be competitive in the future or sustain a high living standard for Canadians by serving the small Canadian market. In fact, this was the conclusion of the influential Macdonald Royal Commission in 1985. With the problem established, the rational actor model suggests the Canadian government would then have formulated its objectives, which included developing markets for Canadians products abroad (in order to expand the demand for Canadian products). The relevant decision makers would then have examined their options. Canada could have pursued increased trade liberalization through multilateral trade negotiations. However, multilateral negotiations were slow and cumbersome. Canada might have pursued bilateral trade agreements with Europe or Japan. However, the limited demand for Canadian products in Europe or Japan and the constraint of transportation costs reduced the viability of this option. Another option was to seek a free trade agreement with the United States, the largest market in the world and already the destination of the vast majority of Canadian products. A free trade agreement would secure Canada's access to the U.S. economy, and pre-empt economic nationalists in the United States from erecting protectionist trade barriers that would shut Canadian products out of the U.S. market. On the "cost" side, however, there was concern across Canada that signing a free trade agreement would threaten Canadian sovereignty, diminishing its cultural distinctiveness and compromising Canadian policies on health and environmental regulations. The rational actor model suggests that the Canadian government would have weighed the advantages and disadvantages of each option, and then selected the option that it considered best: that option was pursuing a free trade agreement with the United States. The rational actor model thus provides us with one possible explanation of the Canadian government's decision-making process. The next step for the analyst is to test the accuracy of the model, by conducting research to determine whether the Canadian government really did act in this "rational" manner.

However, decision making in the real world can seldom exist in such a pure or comprehensive theoretical form; it is impeded or constrained by a number of factors, a phenomenon known as **bounded rationality**.[26] The ability of individuals to process information and operate effectively under pressure varies. The information decision makers receive may be incomplete or inaccurate. Decisions may also be made based on **satisficing**,[27] which occurs when decision makers examine their available alternatives until they encounter one that meets their minimum standards of acceptability. They then select that alternative without proceeding to examine any further options, even though better ones may be available. Other decision makers may choose to make small, incremental decisions and so avoid having to undertake a fundamental review of an existing policy or make a decisive decision on a current issue. Finally, decision makers will seldom select an option that carries a high level of risk. Instead, they will bypass such options and decide on those that entail fewer prospects for gains but also fewer risks.[28]

Decision makers are generally risk-averse rather than risk-acceptant; even Saddam Hussein's decision to invade Kuwait in 1990 may be explained with reference to the idea that he did not realize he risked an American counteroffensive. Time constraints may also force decision makers to make choices under pressure without the advantages of careful deliberation. Indeed, during crises rational decision-making processes tend to break down.[29] Very little time is available to gather information and assess its accuracy, and communications between individuals and groups may be disrupted. Insufficient time may be available to formulate a comprehensive set of options and to consider their advantages and disadvantages. Decision makers tend to fall back on their own ideological predispositions, prevailing views, or assumptions, and ignore or dismiss contrary opinions or information. Stress and sleep deprivation may also affect their ability to make reasoned choices. Emotions become more intense and are a greater factor in decisions. Mistakes and errors are made with greater frequency, with fewer opportunities to catch and correct them. As a result, at a time when the issues at stake are very important and when the need for an effective decision is most urgent, the decision-making procedures and systems designed to make effective, reasoned outputs might break down. All of these factors suggest that human variables will compromise the extent to which decisions can be made in a perfectly rational manner. However, decision makers may still be acting rationally, in accordance with the four steps outlined above. The idea that rationality may be bounded does not challenge the rational actor model; it simply reminds us that there are limits to what decision makers can know and how perfectly rational they can be.[30] As Mark Shafer and Scott Crichlow observe,

> The decision process within a state is quintessentially a human process, fraught with those things that are human: biases, errors, emotions, interpretations, projections, personalities, and many others. This does not mean that actors within states are irrational. Nor does it mean that actors are not trying to maximize interests. Of course they are. But they are human beings, and they have human limitations.[31]

Furthermore, government officials do not make decisions in a vacuum. In liberal democracies such as Canada, two variables often have immense influence: interest groups and public opinion. Interest groups comprise individuals who share common perspectives and goals on particular issues and seek to influence the decisions made on such issues. For the leaders of states, these societal interests must often be accommodated, although in practice the influence of various groups and the openness of the political system to such groups vary considerably. Interest groups can take a wide variety of shapes and forms, including political parties, professional associations, business coalitions, labour unions, churches, senior citizens, veterans' groups, and activist organizations such as human rights or environmental groups. These groups engage in two levels of activity: lobbying and public awareness campaigns.

Lobbying occurs when representatives of interest groups meet with decision makers in an attempt to change or influence their views on an issue. In some cases rewards might be offered to the decision maker in return for taking a particular stand on an issue. In countries where corruption is a serious problem, rewards might take the form of bribes or favours of various illicit kinds. In other cases, interest groups might take their case directly to the public in an effort to influence public attitudes and wishes about certain issues. In this way, interest groups can achieve their aim by compelling decision makers to respond to larger public pressure. Public awareness campaigns can take the form of written or electronically disseminated material, protest rallies and marches, Web-based awareness campaigns, and community or "town hall" seminars. For example, non-governmental organizations raised international awareness of the global land mines problem by using all these techniques. The profile of this campaign encouraged the governments of states such as Canada to respond to the issue with the creation of a global land mines treaty. In practice, interest groups do not always reflect the views of a majority; in fact, many have goals or views that clash with the beliefs or values of broader society (however those might be defined), and wealthy clients can afford to hire top-rated lobbyists, who are often more effective at playing the lobbying game. To return to our example of Canada and free trade with the United States, during the private and public deliberations leading up to the Canada–U.S. Free Trade Agreement, interest groups lobbied the Canadian government in an effort to influence the outcome of the decision. Most (though not all) corporations, business associations, and provincial governments were prominent supporters of free trade, and lobbied the government to reach an agreement. On the other hand, most labour unions, social activist groups, and environmental NGOs were opposed, or wanted it to address their key concerns (this would occur, to some extent, with NAFTA, signed several years later). And so, one interpretation of the Canadian government's decision to enter a free trade agreement with the United States is the superior lobbying power of Canadian business interests, a power derived from close connections in government and large monetary resources. The influence of such interest groups has often been derided as counterproductive and a threat to representative decision making in a democratic society.

Public opinion is a general reference to the range of attitudes held by the people in society, and is especially important in democratic political systems, although not irrelevant in authoritarian states. To win public support for their foreign policies, governments will launch information or propaganda campaigns. These campaigns can vary considerably, from efforts by governments to explain and justify their actions to blatant distortions and falsifications of evidence. In democracies, public opinion can be gauged through polls, which can influence government action, although such polls can be misleading if they are sloppy or abused. In some cases, autocratic and democratic governments may embark on a foreign policy venture to increase their popularity or to distract the public from domestic problems. This has been called the *diversionary theory of war* or *wagging the dog*, after a popular movie released in the 1990s.[32] An example of this phenomenon is the 1982 Falklands War, in which the military government of Argentina seized Las Malvinas (the Falklands) in an effort to revive its sagging popularity at home. It worked, but only for a short time, as Great Britain retook the islands by force. The Argentine government fell shortly thereafter. The same argument might be applied to the British government of Margaret Thatcher, which was low in the polls before the crisis and may have used the British military response to bolster its domestic popularity.

As any pollster knows, public opinion is rarely monolithic. Frequently, public opinion can be uninformed and tend toward simplistic views and beliefs, which can complicate the efforts of decision makers to explain their policies or the constraints facing the country on a certain issue. As a result, public opinion can send mixed or contradictory signals to government decision makers. Public opinion can also shift dramatically and influence governments to act in haphazard and unpredictable ways. For example, in 1992 media coverage of the civil war and famine in Somalia put public pressure on the U.S. government to lead a multinational force (which included Canada) to support an aggressive relief effort and end the war. Less than a year later, 18 U.S. soldiers were killed in an ambush and one soldier's body was dragged through the streets of Mogadishu. Immediately, U.S. public opinion shifted dramatically against involvement in Somalia, and the U.S. withdrew shortly thereafter. However, it would be a mistake to assume that governments are always at the mercy of swings in domestic public opinion; governments can (and often do) pursue foreign policy actions that either lack a broad base of support or are deeply unpopular.[33] For example, the Spanish and Italian governments both supported the invasion of Iraq in 2003, despite widespread domestic protests. However, the Spanish government was voted out of office in March 2004, as public opposition to its domestic policies grew, especially in the wake of a series of bombings against commuter trains in Madrid, which left 191 people killed and over 1800 injured. The recent financial crisis in Europe is another example of the interaction between public opinion and foreign policy decision making. In 2011 and 2012, a financial crisis in Greece prompted European governments to establish a large bailout loan package for the country in an effort to prevent the collapse of the Greek economy and the possible collapse of the common European currency, the Euro. However, the bailout package was very unpopular, especially in Germany, where there was widespread resentment about the use of German taxpayer's money to support Greece. In Greece, the terms of the bailout package (which included major cuts in government spending and the imposition of fiscal austerity programs) proved very unpopular with the Greek population, and led to the fall of the Greek government and a period of domestic political uncertainty and unrest. Public opinion in many European countries has constrained the freedom of action of state leaders as they seek a solution to the crisis, while many people in Europe call on their leaders to be more responsive to their economic needs at home rather than what they see as the abstractions of the European Union and the Euro.

Historically, public opinion has not exerted the same level of influence on foreign policy as it has on domestic issues. Foreign policy decision makers generally have more autonomy from both public scrutiny and public input, because diplomacy tends to be both less visible and more secretive: international affairs is often regarded as the exclusive reserve of a foreign policy elite, composed of elected and unelected government officials, some business elites, journalists, military leaders and advisors, lobbyists, and experts. Advocates of the rational actor model argue that it remains the best explanation of how decisions get made because distinct decision makers can be identified; others argue the elitist and secretive nature of foreign policy makes the application of the model difficult and highly subjective.

THE BUREAUCRATIC POLITICS MODEL

The bureaucratic politics model makes very different assumptions about the nature of the decision-making process. This model suggests that decision-making outputs do not reflect a process of the rational consideration of alternatives by individuals but rather are the result of the process of competition or bargaining among bureaucratic units with divergent perspectives on the issues.[34] One of the most famous works on decision making was *Essence of Decision: Explaining the Cuban Missile Crisis*, written by Graham Allison in 1971.[35] Allison argued that state decisions would be the result of "pulling and hauling" between competing government agencies. What bureaucratic interests are involved in this process? Governments have become increasingly dependent on foreign policy bureaucracies, which provide a source of expertise on the issues and have the staff and instruments at their disposal to execute the decisions of governments. Many of these bureaucratic units are engaged in the decision-making process. In Canada, for example, the Prime Minister's Office, the Department of Foreign Affairs and International Trade, the Department of National Defence, the Department of Finance, and parliamentary committees have input into foreign policy decision making.

The bureaucratic politics model assumes that those who represent different bureaucratic interests within the decision-making structure will hold different views on the issue confronting the decision makers. This assumption is premised on the idea that where an individual stands on an issue depends on where that individual sits in the process. For example, individuals representing the Department of Foreign Affairs and International Trade may have a very different view of how the Canadian government should act than individuals representing the Department of Finance or those from the Canadian International Development Agency. Also at stake in this bureaucratic process—whether it involves struggling or bargaining—are the prestige, influence, and perhaps the budget, of the bureaucratic agencies themselves. The final decision of the Canadian government will reflect the outcome of a competition and/or bargaining among bureaucratic units, each seeking to convince government decision makers that their preferences are the best possible course of action for the country. The bureaucratic politics model provides us with a method of generating fascinating hypotheses and explanations for state decision making. The decisions of the notoriously opaque North Korean regime with respect to nuclear warhead and missile testing (among other tension-raising foreign policy actions) are often attributed to internal bureaucratic politics within the government. These politics intensified when Kim Jong-un came to power in 2011, and the subsequently erratic decision making of the regime (which oscillates between conciliatory gestures and provocation) may reflect an internal struggle for influence under the new leader.

Another influence that organizations can exert on decision making is through the *organizational process* by which they implement or execute decisions. The organizational process model suggests that decisions are neither the result of a rational process of choice nor the result of competition or bargaining among bureaucracies. Instead, decision-making outcomes are the result of the constraints imposed on decision makers by the bureaucratic organizations that execute the decisions of policymakers. These constraints come in the form of standard practices or routines called *standard operating procedures* (SOPs). Because these SOPs reflect what an organization is prepared or equipped to do, they can limit the range of choices available to the decision maker. In other words, the organization responsible for executing a decision may not be capable of performing the desired tasks. In effect, the capabilities, preparedness, and contingency plans of an organization often determine the range of choice available to decision makers.

Returning to our example of the Canadian government's decision to pursue a free trade agreement with the United States, the bureaucratic politics model would explain the decision-making process very differently than the rational actor model. The decision of the Canadian government would have been the outcome of "pulling and hauling" between organizational units of the Canadian government. The Department of Foreign Affairs and International Trade, the Department of Finance, Industry Canada, Natural Resources Canada, the Prime Minister's Office, and myriad other departments and agencies of the Canadian government would have advanced their own positions on the issue of free trade depending on their bureaucratic interests. At the end of the day, the bureaucratic units in favour of a free trade agreement with the United States prevailed. This perspective thus challenges the notion that foreign policy decisions are the result of a process of rational deliberation. Instead, they are the result of bureaucratic and organizational interests engaged in a process characterized by a lack of unity among the key departments and agencies in state governments.

THE INDIVIDUAL, THE GROUP, AND THE ROLE OF PERCEPTION

Perception plays a crucial role in the decision-making process. Perception can have an impact on decision making on two levels: the level of the individual and the level of the group or organization. At the level of the individual, all decision makers have different and often unique life experiences, preconceptions, personal beliefs, value systems, prejudices, and fears that influence their perspective of the world and how they process information about it. As a result, considerable attention has been devoted to the perceptions of individual decision makers and the link between these perceptions and their decisions.[36] This study can be done through content analysis (the exploration of themes in speeches and writings), examinations of personal histories, or the discovery of operational codes in which routine and method act as an influence on personal beliefs.[37] In addition, leadership style can have an important influence on decisions, especially when a single leader dominates the decision-making process.[38]

In short, we all possess perceptual lenses through which we view the world. Individuals examine and process information through these perceptual lenses, which leads to some of the following tendencies in decision making:

- *Worst-case analysis.* Decision makers tend to regard their own decisions as objective responses, while attributing hostile motives to the decisions of others.

- *Mirror imaging.* Decision makers can form similar images of each other ("we are peaceful, they are warlike," etc.) that reinforce mutual hostility. Decision makers can also make the mistake of believing that other decision makers are mirror images of themselves and that they will act in the same manner.

- *Wishful thinking.* Decision makers may have a personal attachment to a certain outcome, and may overestimate the chances of achieving that outcome.

- *Historical analogy.* Frequently, decision makers will employ history as a guide to policy, a process that can be beneficial or counterproductive, depending on the appropriateness of the analogy and the similarities with the current issue.

- *Affective bias.* All decision makers have learned or intuitive preconceptions of issues or actors. Decision makers tend to be more accepting of information that confirms their predispositions and less accepting of information that challenges those preconceptions.

- *Grooved thinking.* Decision makers may categorize information or events into a few basic types, and in some cases information and events may be unsuitably categorized, which can lead to inappropriate foreign policy responses.

- *Uncommitted thinking.* Decision makers may have no opinions on certain issues and questions and may vacillate or flip-flop among different views of the issue and the different options available to respond to it.

- *Committed thinking.* Alternatively, decision makers may have a strong commitment to certain beliefs and views that remain consistent over time and are difficult to change.

At the group level, the dynamics that take place between individuals within a decision-making body (whether it be the foreign policy team of a state or the decision-making body of a non-state actor) can also influence the decision-making process. In some circumstances, the influence of group dynamics can promote a rigorous and systematic approach to the problem by accounting for a number of individual differences expressed by those in the group. In effect, the group can promote rationality by encouraging deliberation and debate. However, group dynamics may also interfere with the rationality of a decision-making process. Groups can develop shared mindsets or belief systems—in essence, dominant views—that individuals within the group are afraid to challenge. Psychology experiments have shown that when a group of six people are shown two lines on a screen and five of the six people (who are accomplices to the experiment) say that the lines are of equal length when in fact they are not, the sixth individual is likely to agree with the group rather than make the correct assessment. This phenomenon is called **groupthink**.[39] In extreme cases, those who advocate policies at odds with the prevailing view may be ostracized or isolated from the group.

In addition, groups and organizations have their own cultures, perceptual lenses, and value systems, and information and ideas that are in accordance with these belief systems are passed up the organizational ladder, while others are subjected to intense scrutiny or even discarded by junior officials, who may try to anticipate what senior decision makers want to hear or read. This is called **anticipatory compliance**.[40] In the wake of the Iraq War in 2003, there were questions in both the United States and the United Kingdom concerning prewar intelligence reports on Iraqi weapons of mass destruction. Iraq did possess chemical weapons in the 1980s and in fact used them on numerous occasions, especially during the Iran–Iraq War. However, no evidence was ever found to support the claims of U.S. and British intelligence that Iraq had possessed vast stocks of chemical and biological weapons in the 2000s. This intelligence was a crucial component of the case for war presented by former U.S. President George Bush and former British Prime Minister Tony Blair. Some have accused the two leaders of engineering a deliberate deception in order to gain domestic and international support for the war. Others have suggested that political interference from senior government officials distorted the intelligence reports, and this distorted evidence was presented to the political leadership as accurate information. It is also possible that decision makers in both governments experienced groupthink. It is also possible that intelligence officials engaged in anticipatory compliance when passing intelligence information up the ladder to senior government officials. In any case, this example is likely to occupy the attention of many analysts for a long time.

The development of constructivism as a theoretical framework in the study of global politics (see Chapter 1) has increased the attention paid to the role of constructed belief systems in decision making. As David Patrick Houghton points out, "A full appreciation of foreign policy decision making surely requires that we understand both individual construction (cognitive psychological approaches) and collective construction (social construction)."[41] When U.S. President John F. Kennedy and his advisors chose to establish a naval blockade of Cuba during the Cuban Missile Crisis, they did so for a combination of reasons informed by their own individual constructions about what was the best option as well as their wider social constructions about the superpower rivalry and the Soviet threat. When U.S. President George W. Bush and his advisors made the decision to go to war in Iraq, that decision was informed by their individual constructions about Iraq as well as their broader social constructions about the Middle East and America's role in the world. Constructivism thus promises to bring the study of social construction into the wider debate over foreign policy decision making.

The conceptual models of decision making introduced in this chapter can be valuable instruments for students of global politics, useful for deriving alternative explanations of why decisions were made. To use another example, in May 1998, India tested a series of nuclear warheads, tests that established India as a declared nuclear power. Why did India conduct these tests? One explanation is derived from the rational actor model. From this perspective, India tested nuclear warheads because the government felt it was the best option in the face of India's security concerns about Pakistan and China. Furthermore, the tests would bolster India's power and prestige in the world. The tests could also be interpreted as a dramatic signal of India's antipathy toward the Nuclear Non-Proliferation Treaty, which India has long regarded as privileging the Western great powers. Another explanation can be derived from the bureaucratic politics model. From this perspective, the tests were the outcome of competing interests within the Indian state, with the pro-test factions led by the military and nuclear science establishments emerging victorious.

How did this group make decisions? Former U.S. President George W. Bush and his National Security Council meet the day after the September 11, 2001, terrorist attacks on America. From left to right, CIA Director George Tenet, Secretary of Defense Donald Rumsfeld, Secretary of State Colin Powell, President Bush, Vice-President Dick Cheney, Chairman of the Joint Chiefs of Staff General Henry Shelton, and National Security Advisor Condoleezza Rice. Were these individuals rational actors or bureaucratic actors? What were their views of the world and their perceptions of the attacks that had taken place the day before? (AP Photo/Doug Mills/CP Photo)

Alternatively, the tests could have been an effort (and a successful one at that) to appeal to Indian pride and nationalism in order to rally public support behind the new Bharatiya Janata Party government. In other words, the tests might have been driven by domestic political considerations. By using these decision-making models to analyze historical and contemporary events, we can gain a richer understanding of the nature of the decisions made in the arena of global politics.

PLAYING GAMES

Yet another instrument used to study the decisions of policy-makers is **game theory**, which is derived from a rational choice model. Game theory is a branch of mathematics concerned with modelling behaviour and outcomes under certain prescribed conditions. Two or more actors are provided with a set of alternative policy choices, and each is provided with a set of payoffs that are dependent on both their policy choice and the policy choices of others. In other words, the expected utility (the payoff or gain) is influenced by the decisions of others. Therefore, the policy choices of the players are influenced not only by their own preferences but also by their expectations about the preferences of others. Game theory attempts to predict the outcomes of games by anticipating the preferences of the players. The outcomes of games can also be affected by altering the payoffs or gains that the actors receive. Some games are zero-sum games in which a loss by one actor is considered a gain for the other. Other games are non-zero-sum games in which it is possible for both players to gain (or to lose).[42]

Game theory is employed by some scholars of IR to model the behaviour of states under certain conditions. It should not surprise us that realists often employ models that assume rationality and utility maximization. In particular, a game called **Prisoner's Dilemma** is used by realists to demonstrate how the character of an environment can lead actors to make rational, self-interested choices that will actually leave them worse off than if they were to cooperate with one another. The actors in the game do not cooperate because no basis for trust exists among them; this situation is roughly equivalent to the context of anarchy and the security dilemma discussed in the previous chapter.

Prisoner's Dilemma is the most commonly used game theory model. It is based on a story of two prisoners who have jointly committed a crime, such as armed robbery. The two prisoners are placed in their own cells, unable to communicate with each other. The prosecutor knows that they have committed the crime but requires a confession to get a conviction on the charge of armed robbery. Otherwise, the prosecutor has enough evidence only to get a conviction on the lesser charge of possession of a gun. The prosecutor offers the following deal to each prisoner:

> If you confess, and your partner does not, you will go free and your partner will go to jail for armed robbery for 10 years. If your partner confesses, and you do not, your partner will go free and you will go to jail for armed robbery for 10 years. If you both confess, you will split the penalty for armed robbery, and you will each go to jail for 5 years. If you both do not confess, you will both be convicted for gun possession and will serve a penalty of 1 year.

The game assumes there is no possibility for retaliation, that this is an isolated case, and that the prisoners care only about their own individual interests. Given these payoffs, the outcome of the game is clear: both prisoners will confess to the crime of armed robbery. The logic for such a decision is based on the following calculation of individual interest by each prisoner:

> I should confess, because if I confess and my partner does not, I will go free and my partner will go to jail. If I confess and my partner also confesses, I will still go to jail, but for a shorter term than I would if I didn't confess and my partner did. Under no circumstances should I not confess, for I cannot trust my partner to do the same.

Both prisoners will serve fairly long sentences when they could have served a short one by trusting each other to keep quiet. The Prisoner's Dilemma game can be represented by the following chart:

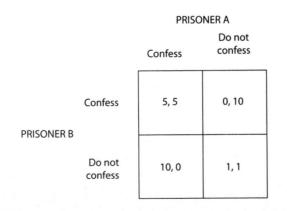

This chart, called a *payoff matrix*, illustrates the choices and payoffs facing each prisoner. As you see, if both prisoners confess, they each get five years in prison. If prisoner B confesses and prisoner A does not, prisoner B goes free while prisoner A receives ten years in prison for armed robbery. If both prisoners do not confess, they receive one year in prison for gun possession charges. In IR theory, this game has been used to illustrate how countries may find themselves in arms races. It is in the interest of both countries not to engage in an arms race, for they will expend vast sums of money and yet end up no more secure than they were before. However, neither country can afford to trust the other by not arming itself, for if one country arms and the other does not, then the unarmed country will be at a disadvantage. So both countries arm, even though both would do better to avoid an arms race altogether.

Another game often employed by IR scholars is called Chicken, drawn from a practice allegedly popular among North American teenagers in the 1950s and immortalized by James Dean in the movie *Rebel Without a Cause*. Two cars are driven toward one another, on a collision course, at high speed on a narrow stretch of road. The first to swerve to avoid the imminent collision is "chicken" and suffers a corresponding drop in prestige. The driver who does not swerve wins an increase in prestige at the cost of the other driver's reputation. If both drivers swerve, they both lose prestige but not as much as they would have if they had swerved alone. If they both do not swerve, they will collide and be killed or seriously injured. As they approach each other, the two drivers may take actions designed to signal their commitment to stay on course, such as accelerating, raising their hands off the steering wheel, or—most dramatically—removing the steering wheel and throwing it out the window (entirely removing the ability to swerve).[43] The following payoff matrix applies:

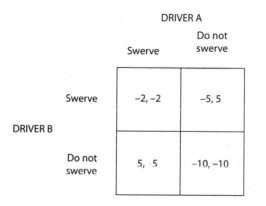

This game is used to model international crises in which countries are on a collision course toward war; the country that blinks or backs down first "loses." If neither country backs down, the outcome may be a costly or devastating war.

As mentioned earlier, the study of decision making grew rapidly in popularity among scholars during the Cold War. This interest grew largely because the decisions made in Washington and Moscow affected everyone: they could have led to conflict or even nuclear war. The study of foreign policy decision making remains of vital importance today, as analysts and students evaluate the circumstances of the Bush administration's decision to go to war in Iraq in 2003, the Canadian decision to send troops into Afghanistan but not into Iraq, the debate over intervention in Syria, or the Canadian decision to withdraw from the Kyoto Accord on climate change. More than ever, we seek to understand the causes and implications of foreign policy decisions in an uncertain world characterized by widespread concern over war, climate change, trade, poverty, human rights, and myriad other issues. Normative perspectives will affect our evaluation of decisions (asking whether a decision was the "right" thing to do, in ethical terms), but we also need a mental map to understand why and how decisions were made.

CONCLUSIONS

This chapter began with an examination of the various themes and dynamics of the Cold War, an omnipresent reality in global politics after World War II, which influenced virtually every aspect of international life. The tense relationship between the superpowers and the nature of the nuclear arms race fuelled the growth of decision-making analysis as a subfield of the study of IR. However, as we will see in later chapters, the international system began to experience some significant changes in the latter half of the Cold War period, changes that served to challenge the accuracy and applicability of the power politics approach. We now turn to an examination of such changes, including the growth of economic interdependence, and increasing inequality, in the global economy.

Endnotes

1. R.S. McNamara, "The Military Role of Nuclear Weapons: Perceptions and Misperceptions," *Foreign Affairs* 62 (1983), 59–80.

2. J. Isaacs and T. Downing, *Cold War: An Illustrated History* (Toronto: Little, Brown, and Company, 1998), 232.

3. The term *Cold War* originates in the 14th century and refers to the long conflict between Muslims and Christians for the control of Spain.

4. See J.L. Gaddis, *The Long Peace* (New York: Oxford University Press, 1987); and J.L. Gaddis, "Great Illusions, the Long Peace, and the Future of the International System," in C.W. Kegley Jr., ed., *The Long Postwar Peace* (New York: Harper Collins, 1991), 25–55.

5. Quoted in C.W. Kegley Jr. and E.R. Wittkopf, *World Politics: Trend and Transformation*, 5th ed. (New York: St. Martin's Press, 1995).

6. R.W. Tucker, "1989 and All That," *Foreign Policy* 69 (Fall 1990), 94.

7. See D. Smith, *Diplomacy of Fear: Canada and the Cold War 1941–1948* (Toronto: University of Toronto Press, 1988).

8. L. Freedman, *The Evolution of Nuclear Strategy* (London: Macmillan Press, 1983).

9. For excellent reading on the nuclear arms race, see R. Rhodes, *Arsenals of Folly: The Making of the Nuclear Arms Race* (New York: Alfred A. Knopf, 2008).

10. R. Reagan, "Speech on Military Spending and a New Defense," in D.P. Lackey, ed., *Ethics and Strategic Defense* (Belmont, CA: Wadsworth, 1989), 36.

11. For a review of some of the contending perspectives on SDI, see C. Snyder, ed., *The Strategic Defense Debate: Can "Star Wars" Make Us Safe?* (Philadelphia: University of Pennsylvania Press, 1986); and H. Binnendijk, ed., *Strategic Defense in the 21st Century* (Washington, DC: Center for the Study of Foreign Affairs, 1986).

12. X [George F. Kennan], "The Sources of Soviet Conduct," *Foreign Affairs* 25 (July 1947), 566–82. For an excellent biography of George Kennan, see J.L. Gaddis, *George F. Kennan: An American Life* (New York: The Penguin Press, 2011).

13. Quoted in J.L. Gaddis, *Strategies of Containment: A Critical Appraisal of Postwar American National Security Policy* (New York: Oxford University Press, 1982), 64–5.

14. Ibid., 40.

15. For a history of the Berlin Wall, See F. Taylor, *The Berlin Wall: A World Divided 1961–1989* (New York: Harper Perennial, 2006).

16. See M. Dobbs, *One Minute to Midnight: Kennedy, Khrushchev, and Castro on the Brink of Nuclear War* (New York: Alfred A. Knopf, 2008), and L.V. Scott, *The Cuban Missile Crisis and the Threat of Nuclear War: Lessons from History* (London and New York: Continuum Publishing, 2007).

17. D. Mackenzie and M.W. Curran, *A History of the Soviet Union*, 2nd ed. (Belmont, CA: Wadsworth, 1991), 474–5.

18. In a rather embarrassing episode, Canadian government officials decided to reach out to the coup leaders, stating they would communicate with them in the near future.

19. J. Mearsheimer, "Why We Will Soon Miss the Cold War," *Atlantic Monthly*, August 1990, 35–50.

20. See F. Fukuyama, *The End of History and the Last Man* (New York: Free Press, 1992).

21. G. Kennan, "The G.O.P. Won the Cold War? Ridiculous," *New York Times*, October 21, 1992, A21.

22. For a discussion of the development of foreign policy analysis, see W. Carlsnaes, "Foreign Policy," in W. Carlsnaes, T. Risse, and B.A. Simmons, eds., *Handbook of International Relations* (London: Sage, 2002), 331–49. See also V.M. Hudson, *Foreign Policy Analysis: Classic and Contemporary Theory* (Lanham, MD: Rowman and Littlefield, 2007).

23. M. Shafer and S. Crichlow, *Groupthink versus High-Quality Decision Making in International Relations* (New York: Columbia University Press, 2010), 8.

24. J.N. Rosenau, "The Study of Foreign Policy," in J.N. Rosenau, K.W. Thompson, and G. Boyd, eds., *World Politics: An Introduction* (New York: Free Press, 1976), 16.

25. J.E. Dougherty and R.L. Pfaltzgraff Jr., *Contending Theories of International Relations: A Comprehensive Survey*, 4th ed. (New York: Longman, 1996), 457.

26. H.A. Simon, *Models of Bounded Rationality* (Cambridge, MA: MIT Press, 1982).

27. See H.A. Simon, *Models of Man* (New York: Wiley, 1957).

28. J.S. Levy, "An Introduction to Prospect Theory," *Political Psychology* 13 (June 1992), 171–86. See also Y. Vertzberger, *Risk Taking and Decision-making: Foreign Military Intervention Decisions* (Stanford: Stanford University Press, 1998).

29. M. Brecher, *Crises in World Politics: Theory and Reality* (New York: Pergamon Press, 1993).

30. For a discussion of the role of individual psychology and judgment in decision making, see S.A. Renshon and D.W. Larson, *Good Judgment in Foreign Policy: Theory and Application* (Lanham, MD: Rowman and Littlefield, 2003).

31. M. Shafer and S. Crichlow, *Groupthink*, 9.

32. See J.S. Levy, "The Diversionary Theory of War: A Critique," in M. I. Midlansky, ed., *Handbook of War Studies* (Boston: Unwin Hyman, 1989), 259–88.

33. For more on public opinion and U.S. foreign policy, see E.R. Wittkopf and J.M. McCormick, eds., *The Domestic Sources of American Foreign Policy* (Lanham, MD: Rowman and Littlefield, 2003).

34. For an overview, see M.H. Halperin, P. Clapp, and A. Kanter, *Bureaucratic Politics and Foreign Policy* (Washington, DC: The Brookings Institution, 2006); and D.A. Welch, "The Organizational Process and Bureaucratic Politics Paradigms: Retrospect and Prospect," *International Security* 17 (1992), 112–46.

35. G.T. Allison, *Essence of Decision: Explaining the Cuban Missile Crisis* (New York: Harper and Row, 1971). See also G.T. Allison and P. Zelikow, *Essence of Decision: Explaining the Cuban Missile Crisis*, 2nd ed. (New York: Longman, 1999); and J. Bendor and T.H. Hammond, "Rethinking Allison's Models," *American Political Science Review* 86 (1992), 301–22.

36. For a discussion of psychological factors in the study of decision making, see J.E.C. Hymans, *The Psychology of Nuclear Proliferation: Identity, Emotions, and Foreign Policy* (New York: Cambridge University Press, 2006), and J.G. Stein, "Psychological Explanations of International Conflict," in W. Carlsnaes, T. Risse, and B.A. Simmons, eds., *Handbook of International Relations* (London: Sage, 2002), 292–308.

37. See R.G.L. Waite, "Leadership Pathologies: The Kaiser and the Fuhrer and the Decisions for War in 1914 and 1939," in B. Glad, ed., *Psychological Dimensions of War* (Newbury Park: Sage, 1990), 143–68; and A. George, "The 'Operational Code': A Neglected Approach to the Study of Political Leaders and Decision-Making," *International Studies Quarterly* 13 (1969), 199–222.

38. See M.G. Hermann, T. Preston, B. Korany, and T.M. Shaw, "Who Leads Matters: The Effects of Powerful Individuals," *International Studies Review, Special Issue* 3 (Summer 2001), 83–131.

39. I.L. Janis, *Victims of Groupthink: A Psychological Study of Foreign-Policy Decisions and Fiascoes* (Boston: Houghton Mifflin, 1972). See also P.A. Kowert, *Groupthink or Deadlock: When Do Leaders Learn from Their Advisors?* (Albany, NY: State University of New York Press, 2002).

40. E.K. Stern and B. Sundelius, "Understanding Small Group Decisions in Foreign Policy: Process, Diagnosis, and Procedure," in P. t'Hart, E.K. Stern, and B. Sundelius, eds., *Beyond Groupthink: Political Dynamics and Foreign Policy Making* (Ann Arbor: University of Michigan Press, 1997), 123–50.

41. D.P. Houghton, "Reinvigorating the Study of Foreign Policy Decision Making: Toward a Constructivist Approach," *Foreign Policy Analysis* 3, no. 1 (January 2007), 42. See also V. Kubalkova, ed., *Foreign Policy in a Constructed World* (Armonk: M.E. Sharpe, 2001).

42. P. Allan and C. Schmidt, *Game Theory and International Relations: Preferences, Information, and Empirical Evidence* (Brookfield, VT: Edward Elgar, 1994).

43. In the movie, James Dean and his opponent race toward a cliff in separate cars; the one who jumps out of the car first loses. In the movie, however, Dean's opponent is killed when his door jams and he goes over the cliff, introducing a further element of tragedy to the scene. This may be a more appropriate analogy in the study of arms races and war.

Political Perspectives on the World Economy

The British taste for tea ... could not have been cultivated in that damp little island had it not been able to export its cheap textiles to Southern Asia, albeit to sell them in captive colonial markets, along with common law, cricket and railways.

—Malcolm Waters

Goodbye to the sovereignty of nation-states. The world dances to the music of money, and the only frontier that matters is the one that separates the gardens of the rich from the deserts of the poor.

—Lewis Lapham

Many people now take an integrated world economy for granted, regard it as the natural state of things, and expect it will last forever. Yet the bases on which global capitalism rests today are not much different from what they were in 1900, and the potential for their disruption is as present today as then. Globalization is still a choice, not a fact.

—Jeffry Frieden[1]

AN INTRODUCTION TO INTERNATIONAL POLITICAL ECONOMY

Historians, economists, and anthropologists alike remind us that long before the advent of the modern state era, the spread of ideas, technology, and culture was facilitated first and foremost by the growth of trade between people in groups ranging in size from small communities to nations and empires. The development of modern capitalism in Europe and its subsequent global expansion established European dominance in the global economy by the 17th century. Following the two world wars and the decline of European imperial power, the United States became the dominant state actor in the world economy, and the leading proponent of liberal economics. Today capitalism remains the primary socioeconomic system in the world, and the principles of liberal economics guide the theory (if not always the practice) behind the economic policies of most states, **international financial institutions (IFIs)** and banks, and corporations. Trade agreements, financial flows, technology, IFIs, and increased communications traffic all suggest the world economy is a place of great convergence, and that increasingly open and competitive global markets are making room for vast improvements in the quality of life on this new "flat earth."[2]

For advocates of liberal economics, the spread of capitalism is seen as a positive phenomenon, bringing greater wealth and quality of life to the world's population and reducing the prospects for war as trade and investment promote international interdependence and cooperation. However, many analysts, students, and activists dispute this view. Critics argue that the world economy is unfair, unstable, and unsustainable. The growth of wealth in some highly protected locales has come at the expense of poverty, dislocation, and violence in other areas, and has uniformly damaged the natural ecosystems on which it is based. The world is increasingly polarized between the rich and poor, and this polarization is at the root of the North–South debate, reflected in different opinions about IFIs, and in diplomatic disputes at international conferences on environmental and development issues. An emergency conference on soaring food prices in June 2008 brought these differences to the fore once again. Many wonder whether there is any long-term hope for those people Paul Collier has labelled the "bottom billion" who live in **absolute poverty**.[3] For neo-Marxists and many other critical theorists, this polarization of wealth is seen as the inevitable outcome of the evolution of global capitalism.

These wildly different visions of the future are at opposite ends of the divide that exists within the field of International Political Economy (IPE). Those who study the vast field of IPE are interested in the relationship between economics and politics at the international level. Robert A. Isaak defines IPE as "the study of the politics behind the economic relations among peoples and nations in order to assess their relative wealth and power."[4] Theodore H. Cohn suggests that IPE is "concerned with the interaction between 'the state' and 'the market.' The state and the market, in turn, are associated with the (political) pursuit of power and the (economic) pursuit of wealth."[5] The famous political economist, Karl Polanyi, once argued that states and markets are analytically inseparable.[6] Thomas Oatley defines IPE as "the study of how economic interests and global processes interact to shape government policies."[7] While many scholars and students of IPE explore the relationship between states and markets, others focus on specific but integral aspects of the world economy, such as the transformational role played by women, the position of trade-dependent states such as Canada, or ecological economics. This chapter will begin with an examination of the ascendance of IPE in the study of global politics, followed by a discussion of both mainstream and alternative theories of IPE. We then present a condensed version of the evolution of the world economy, setting the stage for our examination of contemporary IPE issues and debates in Chapter 8. This chapter thus explores the conceptual and historical foundations of the modern world economy, and thus the origins of globalization and marginalization.

ECONOMIC POLITICS ASCENDANT?

We make no attempt here to educate the reader on pure microeconomics or macroeconomics. A wealth of literature written by economists is readily available.[8] Rather, our focus is on the interaction between political and economic forces, forces that are so interwoven that it is often difficult to discern between the two. In fact, any debate on whether politics drives economics or economics drives politics is at least partially artificial. The realm of politics and the realm of economics almost always overlap.[9] The United Nations, for example, is well known as a political institution. Yet, through the work of its development agencies, the World Bank, and the associated **International Monetary Fund (IMF)**, it is certainly an economic actor as well. When the prime minister of Canada personally promotes increased trade in the Pacific region, he or she is acting in the capacity of a political actor, although an economic agenda is being followed. At the same time, economic matters can transcend political matters and vice versa. A particularly dramatic example of the separation of commerce from politics occurred in the Crimean War of 1854 to 1856. While England was at war with Russia, London banks floated loans for the Russian government! Today, despite ongoing tensions between the governments of Taiwan and China over the vexing issue of Taiwanese independence, high levels of mutual investment and business cooperation continue.

The study of IPE did not always have a high profile among students and scholars of global politics. Realists characterized IPE as a subject of "low politics" rather than "high politics." From a realist perspective, the two world wars illustrated the dominance of military security issues, and the subsequent Cold War was defined by the geopolitical, military, and ideological competition between the superpowers. Nuclear weapons were thought to have transformed IR, and it was believed that both conventional weapons and economic dimensions of power would be less important as a result. For realists, IPE in the postwar period was defined by American economic power, which offered a stable market for world production and provided the foundation for a system of international institutions, regimes, rules, and norms. However, by the early 1970s, the profile of international economic issues began to increase, attracting greater attention from scholars and students. By the 1990s economic issues were arguably the leading priority for most states. The ascendance of IPE in global politics can be attributed to the following factors:

- *Increasing global interdependence.* It became visibly evident by the 1960s that economic activity in the form of merchandise trade, financial flows, and monetary policies, facilitated by advances in communications technology, was linking the economies of states to an unprecedented extent. This interdependence was reflected in the increased importance of the economic institutions, organizations, and agreements designed to promote economic transactions across states. These organizations became just as prominent as international institutions with military security objectives (and in some instances more so).

- *The decline of the U.S. economy.* For much of the early Cold War, the United States was the world's only economic superpower (the closest competitor was the Soviet Union, with an economy half the size of the U.S. economy). However, in the latter half of the Cold War, the U.S. economy entered a period of what some describe as decline, and many observers concluded that the era of U.S. economic dominance was over. The implications of this decline are still hotly debated, even as a general consensus emerged that the United States was no longer in as dominant an economic position as it had been when the postwar international economic system was established. In the 2000s, the American dollar continued its slide against the euro, the yen, and the Canadian dollar, prompted by concerns about America's economic performance and high levels of public debt. The global financial crisis of 2008 to 2009, which was precipitated by highly questionable practices in the U.S. banking sector, raised new doubts about the role of American leadership.

- *The rise of other state economies.* During the Cold War, other states recovered from the devastation of World War II and became increasingly important actors. The economies of Western Europe and Japan emerged as economic centres of power, and several countries in East Asia—led by the Four Tigers of Hong Kong, Taiwan, Singapore, and South Korea—experienced high levels of economic growth. China's emergence as an economic power in the late 1980s led to much speculation that the Chinese economy may one day rival that of the United States, with dramatic implications for global politics. By 2010, China boasted the second largest economy in the world, and Brazil and India were emerging economic powerhouses.

- *The rise of multinational corporations (MNCs).* The emergence of MNCs—corporations with operations in several countries—as global economic actors challenged prevailing views about the dominance of states in IPE. There are over 60 000 MNCs in the world economy, accounting for approximately one-third of world trade. As the size and resources of MNCs grew, so did debates about their impact on global trade and their role in the economic development of poor countries.

- *The oil shock.* In 1960, a group of oil-producing states formed the **Organization of the Petroleum Exporting Countries (OPEC)** to coordinate their oil production. Their objective was to resist pressure from consuming countries for lower prices and to ensure steady oil revenues for producers. In 1973, OPEC had a profound influence on global politics through the imposition of an oil embargo against the U.S. and other countries in retaliation for their support of Israel in the 1973 Arab–Israeli War. The embargo caused economic chaos in the U.S. and other countries, raised the international significance of the oil-producing states, and increased the attention paid to the economic dimension of IR. Oil remains an important subject in global politics today, with any increases in oil prices affecting all aspects of the global economy. Concerns over climate change have raised many further questions about fossil fuel dependence and the politics of oil extraction and transportation.

- *European integration.* In 1951, France, West Germany, Italy, Belgium, the Netherlands, and Luxembourg formed the European Coal and Steel Community (ECSC) to coordinate their production and trade policy in these sectors. Buoyed by their success, and mindful of the ongoing need to reinforce cooperation to prevent Franco–German conflict and to strengthen Western Europe against the Soviet threat, in 1957 these six countries established the European Economic Community (EEC). In 1993, an expanded community of 15 states renamed itself the **European Union (EU)**. On May 1, 2004, ten new states joined the EU, followed by two more in 2007, continuing a process that remains the leading example of economic and political integration in the world.

- *Growing awareness of global disparities.* While poverty and wealth disparity predate the modern world economy, the wave of decolonization in the post–World War II period led to the creation of a large number of newly independent countries that for the most part were ill prepared to meet the economic challenges they faced. Beset by high levels of poverty, poor infrastructure, economies dislocated by colonialism, a lack of modern technology, and political instability, these countries were automatically at a disadvantage in the world economy. The wide disparity between the wealth and power of the rich industrialized countries of "the North" and the great majority of **less-developed countries (LDCs)** in "the South" emerged as one of the most serious challenges in global politics, and remains so today.

- *The collapse of the Soviet Union.* The fall of the Soviet Union dramatically illustrated the importance of economics as a foundation for state power. As discussed in Chapter 3, the

U.S.S.R.'s decline and eventual collapse were due largely to the failure of its economic system. As well, the fall of the U.S.S.R. removed the military and ideological threat to the West, and as a result economic issues became more prominent on the global stage.

Chapters 2 and 3 focused on a historical and political perspective that emphasized the politics of war and peace. IPE scholars tend to see global history differently. They focus on the relationship between economics, politics, society, and power. However, while this focus unites all scholars of IPE, there are vast differences in their theoretical orientations and how they describe and explain events in the global economy. In Chapter 1, we explored the core differences between these theoretical perspectives, and we now turn to an explanation of how they approach the subject of IPE.

REALIST APPROACHES TO IPE: MERCANTILISM AND ECONOMIC NATIONALISM

In Chapter 1, we explored the foundations of realist thought, with its emphasis on the state and the survival and security of the state in an anarchic international environment. Realist approaches to IPE are consistent with this view of global politics. The state is the most important actor in international economic affairs, and states act to secure and advance their economic interests defined in terms of economic power. This is critical because economic power is regarded primarily as a foundation of state power. Realists argue that states are concerned with **relative gains** in economic strength across states. So, if states A and B both experience gains in wealth (that is, they both experience **absolute gains**) but state A experiences a greater gain in wealth than state B, it is this *relative* gain that matters in terms of the power relationship between these two states. Realists thus tend to see the world economy as a **zero-sum** competition: gains experienced by one state are a proportionate loss to another. Relative gains and economic competition are therefore crucial components of the struggle for survival and power among states.[10]

This focus on the state in IPE does not mean realists completely dismiss the relevance of non-state actors such as MNCs or NGOs (non-governmental organizations). However, since these actors must operate in an international system with regulations defined by states, non-state actors do not possess the kind of power or significance that liberals would ascribe to them. Similarly, realists argue that international economic organizations are built and managed by states, especially the most powerful states, and as such are primarily forums for state action and arenas for state competition. Why then do states cooperate on trade and financial matters? For realists, states cooperate because of the need for self-help: when the interests of states converge, cooperation is possible. When the interests of states diverge, cooperation is not possible, and conflict is likely.

The origins of the contemporary realist perspective on IPE can be found in **mercantilism**. *Mercantilism* is a term derived from the writings of Adam Smith, who criticized the economic practices of the mercantile system that prevailed in Europe between 1500 and 1750. Mercantilists argued that the accumulation of gold and silver in a state treasury would provide the foundation for military strength and political influence. In order to accumulate such wealth, states sought not only to acquire more precious metals but also to export more goods than they imported. If they could achieve this, more money would flow into the state compared with that flowing out. Mercantilists were therefore early advocates of **balance of trade** surpluses. The desire to accumulate gold and silver to increase state power was also a primary driver of European colonialism, as trade surpluses with colonial economies and the precious metals of the colonies helped fill the treasuries of the European imperial states. Today, states remain concerned about the status of their trade balance as well as their balance of payments (see Profile 4.1).

In the wake of the Industrial Revolution, when industrialization and the development of manufacturing capabilities were seen as crucial to state power, mercantilist practices evolved into what today are generally referred to as neomercantilist or economic nationalist practices. Neomercantilists and economic nationalists emphasize the building of state power not through the accumulation of precious metals, but almost entirely through economic practices aimed at generating balance of trade surpluses. This is achieved through the stimulation of domestic production and the promotion of exports.[11] However, a balance of trade surplus can come only at the expense of one's trading partners (who must then have a trade **deficit**). As a result, neomercantilism is often referred to as a **beggar-thy-neighbour** economic policy. Richard Rosecrance described the evolution of "trading states," intervening in economic affairs to secure trade surpluses and to ensure that national economic interests are protected and promoted.[12] Neomercantilists and economic nationalists also emphasize the importance of advanced industrial development and technological innovation. Put simply, there is a hierarchy of economic activity in the global economy: high-technology industries are preferable to steel or textile industries, which are in turn preferable to agricultural production and natural resource exports. Those states that position themselves as industrial and technological leaders in the world economy will be best placed to maintain and increase their power in global politics.

PROFILE 4.1 The Balance of Payments

The **balance of payments** is an accounting system for recording a state's financial transactions with the outside world. The balance of payments comprises two accounts: the current account and the capital and financial account. The first includes exports and imports of merchandise (cars, radios, CD-ROM drives), exports and imports of services (management consulting, information), investment income and payments (dividends and interest income earned from foreign investments along with payments to foreigners who have invested in the home country), and foreign aid and other transfers (humanitarian relief, loans and grants, the sale of military weapons). The capital and financial account includes short-term and long-term investment inflows (foreign investment in the home state) and outflows (investment abroad). States with a highly troubled balance of payments may borrow money from the International Monetary Fund or sell bonds to make up the difference. One other account is important: a state's official reserves, which represent the foreign currencies, gold, and other financial assets accumulated by its central bank to pay for imports and meet other financial obligations. In 2011, Canada had a current account balance of payments deficit of $48 394 000 000 (down from a surplus of 12 722 000 000 in 2007) and a capital account balance of payments surplus of 55 843 000 000. The current account deficit reflects the impact of the global economic recession and the high Canadian dollar on Canadian exports, while the capital and financial account surplus reflects the confidence of investors in the strength of the Canadian economy.

See Statistics Canada, "Canada's Balance of International Payments (Current Account)," at http://www.statcan.gc.ca/tables-tableaux/sum-som/l01/cst01/econ01a-eng.htm and "Canada's Balance of International Payments (Capital and Financial Account) at http://www.statcan.gc.ca/tables-tableaux/sum-som/l01/cst01/econ01b-eng.htm.

How do neomercantilists and economic nationalists translate these principles into government practice? In general, states pursuing this approach employ a combination of **protectionism** and export promotion. **Tariffs** are essentially taxes charged to goods as they enter a country, and the cost of the tariff is generally passed on to the consumer, thus making that product more expensive and therefore less desirable compared with a domestically produced alternative. Domestic producers thus benefit, and consumer money stays in the country rather than going to a foreign producer. Today, tariffs are still an instrument of protectionism, but international trade agreements between states have eliminated or lowered tariffs on most products as states try to derive greater economic benefits from trade. This has led to the use of non-tariff barriers to trade, which include safety, health, labelling, or environmental standards that may serve to exclude foreign products and shield domestic firms from foreign competition. Non-tariff barriers to trade have been a major issue in global trade negotiations, with champions of free trade arguing that international rules need to be put in place so government policies cannot be used as barriers to trade. However, critics of free trade have argued that international trade agreements restricting the use of non-tariff barriers place excessive restrictions on government powers and threaten the ability of governments to set appropriate rules for safety, health, and other social standards.

States following neomercantilist practices also employ **subsidies**, government programs that provide direct financing, low-cost loans, or tax exemptions to particular high-value industries in order to encourage their development and their international competitiveness or to protect them from foreign competition. The extensive use of subsidies in the world economy today has led to the use of countervailing duties (taxes imposed on imports from a state accused of using illegal subsidies) and anti-dumping duties (taxes imposed on imports that are allegedly being exported into a foreign market and sold at a price below the cost of production). States can also impose **quotas** on imported products, which serve to limit the number of any given product that is imported into the country. A common practice is for states to negotiate "voluntary" export quotas, in which exporting states essentially agree to voluntarily restrict their exports to a particular country, usually in return for similar concessions from their negotiation partners. Taken together, all of these measures are tools (or weapons) employed by states as they seek economic survival and economic gain in an anarchic world. Of course, states with the greatest economic power will have a structural advantage when wielding these instruments, and will have a greater capacity to influence international organizations and use coercion and reward to further their economic objectives. In reality, most states in the global economy pursue some neomercantilist or economic nationalist policies some of the time. Some, such as Japan, have been considered especially mercantilist, because they strongly protect their domestic markets, allowing limited foreign goods and services, while actively promoting their products abroad. Even less traditionally "mercantile" countries such as Canada have maintained high levels of protectionism on some products while promoting exports abroad.

Despite the limited success of the **General Agreement on Tariffs and Trade (GATT)** negotiations in reducing tariffs in the 1950s and 1960s, the 1970s ushered in a new era of protectionism, which resulted from several events. The boom in oil prices brought on by the OPEC cartel, the shift from fixed to flexible **exchange rates** that occurred as the United States finally gave up its role as the guarantor of international monetary stability, rising competition from export-led industrializing states such as Japan and the newly industrialized countries (NICs), and increased trade subsidies and barriers imposed by the European Economic Community all created a climate of economic uncertainty. A major recession in the early 1980s, brought on partly by another steep rise in the price of oil, further contributed to this uncertainty.

Those threatened by job displacement in the industrialized northern states put considerable pressure on governments to slow the pace of trade liberalization and impose protectionist measures to protect vulnerable sectors of the economy. A notable example was the agricultural sector in Western European states. Economic nationalist practices therefore have a powerful domestic constituency in many countries. In difficult economic times, economic nationalist policies become more popular as groups in society look to governments for protection.

Neomercantilists insist that the state is still the primary actor in the global political economy and that MNCs are largely instruments of the states in which they house their headquarters. They also claim that the opening of the world economy to increased trade has led not to a borderless world, as the proponents of globalization proclaim, but to one in which the state continues to act as a protectionist force. Free trade agreements simply reflect the fact that certain states believe that some free trade will benefit them and increase, rather than decrease, the power they wield in the world. As we shall see in Chapter 8, economic nationalism remains an influential perspective in most states, despite ongoing efforts to expand international trade and deepen regional and global free trade agreements. This was especially true in the wake of the economic recession that began in 2008. Anti–free trade movements have maintained or increased their popularity in most countries, supported by individuals and groups concerned about jobs, social programs, culture, and ecology.

LIBERAL APPROACHES TO IPE: CLASSICAL LIBERALISM, KEYNESIANISM, AND INSTITUTIONALISM

The principles of economic liberalism form the foundation of the contemporary global economy, including the international trade system and its related organizations such as the **World Trade Organization (WTO)**. Liberal economics have also determined the shape of the international monetary system. MNCs, as well as smaller firms, conduct their global economic affairs in accordance with liberal market principles. The predominant development strategy directed at LDCs is based on liberal approaches to the generation of wealth and the promotion of economic growth. It is not an exaggeration to suggest that a liberal orthodoxy has dominated the theoretical and policy discourse on global economic affairs.

The foundation of the liberal approach to IPE rests on the work of Adam Smith (1723 to 1790), most specifically in his classic work *An Inquiry into the Nature and Causes of the Wealth of Nations*. Smith's writings were motivated by his opposition to mercantilism, which he argued was not only poor economics but also a source of "discord and animosity" in international affairs.[13] In contrast, Smith supported the establishment of open markets in which individuals would be free to engage in commerce. The "invisible hand" of unfettered markets could maximize prosperity, and free trade would create "a bond of union and friendship" among nations.[14] From these intellectual beginnings, liberal approaches to IPE emphasize the market and the promotion of individual wealth over protectionism and the accumulation of state power. For liberals, economic actors (whether individuals, firms, or households) will engage in mutually beneficial exchange if given the freedom to do so. While states and their governments will be required to establish laws and enforcement provisions concerning private property and economic transactions, liberals argue that resources are allocated most efficiently through free market activity unburdened by excessive state regulation. Therefore, governments should pursue a hands-off or *laissez-faire* (literally "let do") approach to economic management, permitting individuals, households, and firms the freedom to make their own decisions on economic matters.

The headquarters of the World Trade Organization (WTO) in Geneva, Switzerland. The WTO replaced the General Agreement on Tariffs and Trade (GATT) in 1995, but both were designed to reduce barriers to trade in accordance with liberal economic principles. (AP Photo/Donald Stampfli/CP Archive)

Liberals reject the zero-sum-game characterization of realist approaches to IPE, trusting instead that all states can benefit from trade. However, there are significant differences of opinion within the liberal perspective on IPE.[15] We describe these differences in terms of classical liberalism, Keynesianism, and liberal institutionalism.

Classical liberals, like Adam Smith, emphasize *laissez-faire* economic policies and the efficiency of the market in determining the exchange and allocation of money, goods, and resources. Classical liberals are champions of free trade in global politics. In a market-driven international economy, every state will find an economic niche by specializing in the production of goods it can produce most efficiently and trading for those goods it cannot produce efficiently. This **absolute advantage** would mean that every state would gain from free trade with other states. Why waste resources producing goods inefficiently when you can trade for those goods by selling the goods you do produce efficiently? For example, if Canada can produce wood products more efficiently than India, but India can produce cloth more efficiently than Canada, both countries will benefit from specialization and trade. Each country will no longer waste resources on inefficient production. As more and more states engaged in such trade, the collective use of their resources would become more and more efficient, and they would all accumulate greater wealth as a result.

Another classical liberal, David Ricardo (1771 to 1823) took Smith's logic a step further. Ricardo's work *On the Principles of Political Economy and Taxation* (1817) outlined his theory of **comparative advantage**, which remains the foundation of trade theory to this day.[16] Ricardo's theory of comparative advantage is crucial because it demonstrates why states will and should trade, even if no absolute advantage exists between them. What if state A and state B contemplated a trade relationship, only to find that state A produced *all* goods more efficiently than state B? Would this not mean that neither state would benefit from trade? Ricardo argued that both states could in fact benefit from trade, because state B would still produce some goods comparatively more efficiently than state A. In other words, even though state A produces all goods more efficiently than state B, not all of these goods will be produced with the same margin of efficiency over the goods produced in state B. It is this comparative margin, or difference, that is the basis for a mutually beneficial trade relationship (see Profile 4.2).

Classical liberal economic theory has been challenged in a number of ways. A significant challenge is the unequal distribution of the gains from trade. While liberals typically acknowledge that not all individuals, firms, households, or states will gain equally from free trade, over time these unequal gains can create large asymmetries in wealth and economic development. Another significant challenge to classical liberal economic theory is the widening gap between those who benefit least (the very poor) and those who benefit the most (the very rich). Smith's work was completed before the advent of mobile, transnational capital, which today can usually relocate production processes while seeking the lowest wages, resource prices, and environmental standards. For critics of liberal economic theory, these processes have exacerbated

PROFILE 4.2   Comparative Advantage: An Illustration

To illustrate the theory of comparative advantage, we will use a hypothetical example involving Canada and Mexico. (In his *On the Principles of Political Economy, and Taxation*, Ricardo used the example of England and Portugal.) We will pick two products (wheat and cloth) and one production input (labour). The table below provides the hypothetical amount of labour (hours of work) required to produce one bushel of wheat and one roll of cloth in Canada and Mexico.

	ROLL OF CLOTH	BUSHEL OF WHEAT
Canada	9 hours	7 hours
Mexico	3 hours	6 hours

Mexico therefore has absolute advantage over Canada in the production of both wheat and cloth, because it requires fewer labour hours to produce both products. However, Canada has a comparatively small labour disadvantage in wheat production, and Mexico has a greater comparative advantage in cloth. The two countries can specialize and achieve gains from trade by emphasizing what they produce most efficiently. If Canada were to divert 100 hours of labour from cloth production to wheat production, wheat production would rise by approximately 14 bushels (100 divided by 7), and cloth production would fall by approximately 11 rolls (–100 divided by 9). If Mexico were to divert 50 hours of labour from wheat production to cloth production, cloth production would increase by nearly 17 rolls (50 divided by 3) and wheat production would fall by approximately 8 bushels (–50 divided by 6). So, through greater specialization and trade, Canada and Mexico would together produce 6 more rolls of cloth and 6 more bushels of wheat!

	ROLL OF CLOTH	BUSHEL OF WHEAT
Canada	–11	+14
Mexico	+17	–8
Gain	+6	+6

Of course, this is a simplified example. In the complex world of global economics, states have many trading partners, not just one. There are many goods produced, not just two. And there are more inputs into production costs than labour time expended, including social and environmental costs. Nevertheless, this basic concept of comparative advantage forms the foundation of liberal trade theory: in theory, all states benefit from free trade.

the economic division between the richest and poorest peoples on the planet. Finally, classical liberal economics was never confronted with the large-scale environmental costs associated with free market activity on a global scale. The relationship between environmental degradation and economic growth is now a major point of concern and controversy.

In contrast to classical liberalism, **Keynesian liberalism** is based on the ideas of John Maynard Keynes (1883 to 1946). One of the most influential liberal economists of his time, Keynes was critical of both neomercantilism and classical liberal economics.[17] In his view, the classical liberal argument that the pursuit of mutually beneficial exchange in a largely unregulated market would lead to gains for all and society as a whole was flawed. Keynes drew his argument from the experience of the Great Depression, which he believed demonstrated that unregulated market activity would lead to economic instability (such as the 1929 stock market crash) and perpetuate high levels of unemployment (which persisted well into the 1930s). This unemployment in turn would lead to a downturn in the economy (because people had less to spend) and a consequent fall in production and investment. In his most important book,

The General Theory of Employment, Interest, and Money (1936), he challenged the conventional economics of the time, arguing that governments needed to intervene in economic activity to a much greater extent than classical liberals would ever contemplate. Keynes argued that a *laissez-faire* philosophy was harmful during economic downswings and that the state should intervene in the economy, encourage low interest rates, and adopt a fiscal policy that injects money into the economy through increased public expenditure or lower taxes. Keynes's solution to the Depression was for governments to stimulate demand through large public works projects. While this might require running budget deficits in the short term (in effect, governments would borrow money to spend on public works projects), this would benefit society in the long run by increasing employment, and therefore demand, production, and investment. The increased tax revenue generated by a growing economy could then be used to pay off the deficits incurred by government borrowing. In effect, Keynes argued that government intervention in the economy was required to ensure economic stability and the larger social good, which could not always be guaranteed by classical liberal economic policy.

Keynes extended his idea to include international economic affairs. He was a critic of the harsh economic prescriptions of neomercantilism. In *The Economic Consequences of the Peace* (1919), Keynes questioned the wisdom of the postwar settlement that imposed heavy reparations on Germany. Although he was generally supportive of free trade, he argued that

The more, the better? Trade has increased dramatically over the decades, and ports such as Vancouver and Halifax are busier than ever. However, while some economies have benefited from trade, others have not. Gains from trade are unevenly distributed, and environmentalists question the ecological sustainability of economic growth. (CP Photo/Chuck Stoody)

governments had to be willing to manage such trade, and intervene when necessary to ensure that free trade did not damage domestic employment levels. Keynes thus saw a positive role for restrictions on imports under certain circumstances. International economic activity, he argued, should be managed and planned through multilateral negotiations, in order to ensure international economic stability and the effective coordination of macroeconomic policies. As an economic advisor to the British government, Keynes drafted proposals for the establishment of an International Clearing Union after World War II. In this system, nations with trade deficits would be able to maintain participation in the global economy by drawing on the union, which other states would help fund. The IMF and the **International Bank for Reconstruction and Development (IBRD**; now known as the **World Bank)** perform a function similar to that of Keynes's proposed union. Although the Keynesian outlook fell into serious disrepute among industrial countries when it was discovered that undisciplined deficit spending by governments led to high levels of public debt, the idea that it is the government's responsibility to create jobs to keep an economy healthy survives, advocated by famous economists such as Canadian-educated John Kenneth Galbraith. Keynes thus established the principles for a more interventionist, managed approach to liberal economics. As Theodore H. Cohn has argued,

> Despite his divergence from liberal orthodoxy, Keynes remained firmly within the liberal-economic tradition, believing in the importance of individual initiative and the inherent efficiency of the market. Greater management, in Keynes's view, would facilitate rather than impede the efficient functioning of world market forces. Thus, Keynes favoured intervention by the government, not to replace capitalism but to rescue and revitalize it. Keynes's views, calling for greater government intervention in the economy, gave rise to the interventionist strand of liberalism.[18]

Finally, **liberal institutionalism** emphasizes the importance of international organizations and regimes in the global economy. We discuss international organizations and regimes in greater detail in Chapter 5, so here we will focus only on the significance of liberal institutionalism in IPE. Regimes are "sets of implicit or explicit principles, norms, rules, and decision-making procedures around which actors' expectations converge."[19] In other words, over time sets of principles, norms, and rules can be established that serve to regulate and guide state behaviour in some issue areas, such as transportation and communication.[20] Liberal institutionalists argue that this desire for reliable coordinating instruments is a logical consequence of cooperation. As states experience gains from cooperation, it is to their mutual benefit to develop mechanisms to govern and regulate their relationship. In IPE, liberal institutionalists point to the creation and rapid growth of regimes established since World War II to regulate economic affairs between states. This wide array of rules determines what kinds of economic activities are allowed or disallowed. Of course, it helps to have these principles, norms, and rules written down, and so it should be no surprise that the world economy is also characterized by a wide array of international agreements, treaties, regulatory agencies, and organizations that serve to manage global economic activity. The relationship between regimes and IGOs is symbiotic. For example, today the WTO and regional trade organizations are part of the global trade regime. These organizations also contribute to the deepening and widening of this regime, as organizations establish new rules and invite new states as members.

For liberal institutionalists, these regimes and organizations matter a great deal, because they serve to entrench liberal economic practices. The greater the cooperation between states, and the more states that participate, the stronger—more resilient to changes and shocks—regimes become. States are increasingly bound together in an ever-deepening and ever-widening interdependence, reinforcing the benefits of economic cooperation and the prospects for peace. However, realists and Marxists are less complimentary about the role of regimes. For realists, regimes are merely instruments created and employed by the most powerful states to control international economic activity to their advantage. It is not a coincidence that the United States was the founder and principal maintainer of most of the economic regimes in the world today. On the other hand, Marxists argue that regimes are merely part of the mechanisms of control wielded by economic elites in service of their efforts to exploit others. Like states themselves, regimes and organizations serve the interests of dominant economic classes.

MARXIST APPROACHES TO IPE: DEPENDENCY THEORY AND WORLD SYSTEMS THEORY

In our discussion of Marxism in Chapter 1, we outlined the core elements of the Marxist approach to global politics. As we have seen, Marxism is grounded by a historical materialist view: economic developments have driven political developments in world history. Marxism is an evolutionary perspective based on transitions from one mode of production to another, holding in common the exploitation of a poor, politically subordinate peasant or working class by a rich, politically dominant landowning or factory-owning class.[21] History is the history of class struggle, as the subordinate class struggles to achieve its liberation from oppression and exploitation. In capitalist systems—the dominant mode of production in modern times—the bourgeoisie (the capitalist class) dominates and exploits the proletariat (the workers). The state is merely an instrument of the bourgeoisie: it is used to maintain their power and privilege, and authorities employed by the state are socialized to adopt conducive values.[22] For Marx, this exploitation cannot end until the capitalist system, the economic foundation of the political order, is overthrown in a revolution of the proletariat that will usher in a classless society free from inequality and therefore free of social conflict.

Karl Marx (1818 to 1883) never developed a comprehensive theory of international politics, but many others have developed Marxist theories of IPE. It was left to activists and theoreticians such as Vladimir Lenin (1870 to 1924) and Rosa Luxemburg (1870 to 1919) to build on the work of Marxist and non-Marxist economists (such as John A. Hobson) to develop a theory of imperialism.[23] Marx had predicted that capitalist systems would collapse because of overproduction. As production exceeded demand, employment and wage prospects for the working class would diminish. The proletariat would thus live in growing hardship, and this would eventually spark revolution and the overthrow of the bourgeoisie in the advanced capitalist countries (most notably Germany). However, the revolution did not seem imminent, and Lenin explained this by arguing that the age of European imperialism had delayed the revolution. The colonies of the capitalist states of Europe had brought new sources of cheap labour, raw materials, capital, and new markets to consume products. As a result, the predicted crisis in capitalism had not occurred. However, Lenin argued that the imperial powers' desire for more labour, resources, and markets would drive them into a zero-sum game of competition for imperial possessions, leading to a war that would precipitate the revolution and overthrow capitalism. Although it was not his own idea, Lenin's theory of imperialism was the foundation for subsequent neo-Marxist work on IPE. The ideas that capitalism was extended around the world, and that there was a dominant set of capitalist imperial states that dominated and exploited their colonies, would establish the foundation for dependency theory and world systems theory.

Dependency theory developed in Central and South America in the 1960s, and was almost exclusively concerned with development in relatively impoverished countries (specifically those in Latin America). An important authorial link between Marxism and dependency theory was Paul Baran, who argued that the economic elites in advanced capitalist states used developing states as "source countries" for raw materials and opportunities for corporate profit and investment.[24] Dependency theorists agreed with Baran, pointing to the position of Latin American economies within the economic orbit of the United States, and argued that economic elites in "core" countries such as the United States kept "periphery" countries such as those in Latin America in a subordinate position of "underdevelopment."[25] This dominance was facilitated by cooperation between Latin American landowners, export merchants, and American economic elites. What dependency theorists called a **compradore** class thus controlled Latin American countries. The interests of these *compradores* were not in the economic development of their country but in the maintenance of their own power and privilege, which was directly linked to the subordinate and exploited status of their country.[26] Although some countries might experience more economic growth than others in this environment, poor countries remained poor by virtue of their subordinate roles in an international capitalist system run by economic elites in core countries, in cooperation with *compradores* in the periphery countries.

Dependency theory was powerfully influenced by the economic and political role of the United States in Latin America before and during the Cold War. This role frequently took the form of indirect interference and outright intervention in the affairs of Caribbean and Central and South American countries. For example, the U.S. military occupied the Dominican Republic between 1916 and 1924. Although the occupation came in the wake of successive dictatorships, it also created a political climate favourable to U.S. investment.[27] In another example, the United States engineered the overthrow of the Guatemalan government of Jacobo Arbenz in 1954. Arbenz had been elected in 1950 on a platform of socioeconomic reforms. Fearing (with little justification) that a nationalist, communist regime was taking root, the U.S. Central Intelligence Agency embarked on a campaign of subversion that eventually forced Arbenz to resign and flee the country. The CIA installed Castillo Armas in power, beginning a long period of successive Guatemalan dictators who would be responsible for some of the worst human rights abuses in the Americas. However, the most famous example of U.S. intervention in Latin America involved Chile. In 1970, Salvador Allende Gossens, a self-proclaimed Marxist, was elected president over a candidate favoured by the U.S. government and U.S. businesses in Chile (including Kennecott Copper, Anaconda Copper, International Telephone and Telegraph, and Pepsi-Cola, among others). The Nixon Administration despised the Allende government, both for its rhetoric (which was highly critical of the U.S.) and for its economic policies (which included the nationalization of some

Still influential. Though few states espouse Marxism as an ideology today, its central proponents continue to inspire political activity around the world. Here, members of the Lebanese Communist Party march through Beirut on May Day, 2008. (AP Photo/Hussein Malla/CP Archive)

foreign businesses and factories). With the cooperation of U.S. firms, the United States began a campaign to destabilize the Allende government, by cutting off sources of finance and pressuring other countries not to purchase Chilean products. The Chilean economy weakened, and protests began to grow against the government. Finally, in 1973 Allende was overthrown and killed in a military coup led by Augusto Pinochet. The Pinochet regime (which would receive the support of the U.S.) would go on to become one of the most brutal in South America.[28] Given this record, and the example set by the Cuban revolution, it is not hard to see why dependency theory developed in Latin America, and why it received considerable support in a region that could see for itself what the "core" could do to countries in the "periphery."

World systems theory shares many similarities with dependency theory, but as we indicated in Chapter 1, it is now considered to subsume dependency theory within its wider theoretical scope. The focus of analysis is the world system, a global economy organized largely according to the logic of capitalism. Much of world systems theory is drawn from the work of Immanuel Wallerstein, who argued that "there is one world system. It is a world-economy and it is by definition capitalist in form."[29] Like dependency theorists, world systems theorists argue that the world is divided between a dominant "core" and an exploited "periphery." As Wallerstein went on to argue, "capitalism involves not only appropriation of the surplus value by an owner from a labourer, but an appropriation of surplus of the whole world-economy by core areas."[30] World systems theorists thus argue that the world economy mimics domestic capitalism on a global scale. Economic elites in the rich industrialized world, using the power of states that they control, discipline labour and dominate and exploit the poor of the world. The instruments of control are the institutions and non-state actors of the global economy: international organizations and agencies, multinational corporations, and the network of regimes that perpetuates the hegemony of the core.

World systems theory differs from dependency theory in several respects. First, while dependency theory tends to focus on periphery states, especially those in Latin America, world systems theory examines the entire system, including relations among the core countries. Second, world systems theory allows for some movement by states across the categories of core, periphery, and what world systems theorists call *semi-periphery* countries. These semi-periphery countries are more powerful and economically advanced than periphery countries, and enjoy more autonomy from the core. While semi-periphery countries are still dependent on the core, world systems theorists suggest that countries can on occasion move across these categories, while dependency theorists argued that periphery countries could not escape their subordinate status without revolution. Dependency theory and especially world systems theory continue to be relevant perspectives in the contemporary study of IPE. As we shall see, these perspectives play a powerful role informing the views of those critical of liberal theories of progress in low-income countries. Many of the antiglobalization perspectives we will explore in Chapter 8 are informed by dependency or world systems interpretations of the global economy.

Finally, many neo-Marxist IPE scholars are influenced by the Gramscian perspective discussed in Chapter 1, and emphasize the significance of the spread of liberal economic beliefs and value systems at the global level. The world political order at any given time in history is determined by the social relations of production, which include not only economic relations but also a set of accompanying beliefs and value systems, reinforced and perpetuated by political, cultural, and social institutions, including formal and informal education systems. In our time, the political order is characterized by capitalism and the accompanying dominance of liberal economic ideas. These ideas have constructed an international hegemonic belief system. Although pockets of active resistance to this liberal orthodoxy exist, the inexorable spread of capitalism is aided by the widespread intellectual acceptance of market values, corresponding legal codes, and the doctrines of economic growth and globalization. The word *hegemony* is therefore used in a different context here than when employed by realists or liberals. A leading proponent of this view of IPE is the Canadian scholar Robert Cox.[31]

FEMINIST, ECOPOLITICAL, AND CONSTRUCTIVIST APPROACHES TO IPE

From a feminist perspective, the evolution of the global economy has marginalized women and placed them in a condition of economic and social disadvantage and underrepresentation. Discrimination against women is evident across a broad range of economic and social indicators, from land ownership to share of private wealth to equal pay for equal work. Relatively few women are present at the upper levels of the corporate world or the institutions of global economic governance. In contrast, women are disproportionately represented among poor and exploited populations. Feminists also observe that the mainstream study of IPE is reflective of patriarchy and the dominance of the male experience in economic matters. Liberal economic theory has emphasized individual self-interest and rational choice, and de-emphasized the role of lived experience, differences in power, and other behaviour motivations such as concern for family, community, and social health. These concerns are often more (though not exclusively) the priorities of women and have not been the focus of mainstream economic thought.[32]

Furthermore, economic theory focuses on production and accumulation of money and goods, and the exchange of those goods. Feminists argue that less attention has been paid to reproduction, family, and provisioning, all roles much more commonly associated with women. The result has been the systematic devaluation of domestic work, childbearing and child rearing, and community service, with the consequent devaluation of the status of women in economic and political life. Male and female "jobs" and "work" have thus been viewed differently and rewarded unequally in a male-dominated society. Feminists believe that our notions of what constitutes "production" and the value we associate with "work" have to be changed to achieve gender equality in practice and in economic thought. Feminists also point out that the expansion of global trade has precipitated a deep and often painful social transition in most countries. Issues such as labour rights and labour mobility, the expansion of the financial and services sector, and the social impact of economic crises, including a burgeoning sex trafficking industry, are having a very real impact on women, and an analysis and response to these issues should include gendered perspectives.

Ecopolitical perspectives in the study of IPE first emerged during the 1960s, when the health and ecological impact of pollution from industry and agriculture became increasingly apparent. Rachel Carson's book *Silent Spring*, published in 1962, detailed the impact of pesticides on the environment and is often credited with starting the modern environmental or "green" movement.[33] The ecopolitical perspective in IPE observes that liberal economic theory does not account for the environmental costs of resource extraction, production, trade, and transportation. In effect, economic growth and development has been decoupled from the ecological costs of economic activity: these costs have been externalized and are not factored in the final costs of any product or service. In an effort to maximize economic efficiency, businesses and industries actually have a disincentive to protect the environment, because doing so would create costs (for waste treatment, for example) that could make a business or industry uncompetitive in a fluid international investment context. However, untreated waste can have severe impact on the biosphere, local ecology, and human welfare. As a result, on its own the liberal economic system fails to include the importance of ecological endowments that provide the very basis for human, animal, and plant welfare, as well as the existence value of habitat and biodiversity. Of course, this criticism can also be applied to other economic systems. During the Cold War, the Soviet Union was steeped in polluting industries and environmentally harmful resource extraction and agricultural practices. The imperatives of industrialization and competition with the West coupled with control of the media and suppression of dissent left little room for the expression of environmental concerns.

The ecopolitical perspective on IPE argues that we must include the environment in our economic calculations, in the costs of doing our business, and in decisions related to what we consume and how we travel. Part of the solution is government regulation and enforcement to ensure that pollution is minimized. However, much of the ecopolitics approach calls for a shift to new models of economic thinking, away from big business and big markets and toward an emphasis on localized and community-based economic activity.[34] Local sourcing for resources and food strengthens community bonds, reduces waste, and minimizes transportation costs. This perspective was best articulated in E.F. Schumacher's famous 1973 book *Small Is Beautiful: Economics as If People Mattered*, which called for a new balance between human activity and the environment.[35] The green movement and ecopolitical perspectives on IPE grew in significance with increased awareness that there were—to adopt the title of a popular report published in 1972—"limits to growth."[36] We turn to these issues in Chapter 10, but it is important to note that the global character of environmental issues was beginning to seep into the study of IPE well before climate change emerged as the overarching issue it is today.

Constructivist approaches to IPE focus on the power of concepts and ideas to influence thought and policy. For constructivists, concepts such as the state, the market, and capitalism (among many others) reflect assumptions about a set of patterns and behaviour that are built on contestable foundations. The social process leading to the construction of these assumptions may differ from person to person or across time and place. Someone living in Niger or in Belarus is going to have very different views of what the state, the market, and capitalism mean than most people living in Canada or Japan. How can there be eternal truths to comparative advantage, mutually beneficial exchange, or the "invisible hand" of the market if these concepts lack meaning or mean different things to different people? Constructivists also remind us that liberal economic theory and IPE concepts are interwoven into normative assumptions about how markets and capitalism are "good" things to be encouraged and developed, and how economic growth and development are "inevitable" or how there are no alternatives to "globalization." In other words, value systems are inextricably linked with concepts, practices, and historical developments in the study of IPE. The entire discourse of liberal economic theory privileges certain ideas and perspectives over others, creating a dominant perspective that is difficult to challenge. It is this dominant perspective that guides the decision making of key governments and international institutions, a clear illustration of the power of ideas in policy practice. We next briefly discuss one such dominant idea, that of hegemonic stability.

HEGEMONIC STABILITY THEORY AND IPE: IS THE UNITED STATES IN DECLINE?

In Chapter 2, we introduced the theory of hegemonic stability, which holds that a dominant state can exert a stabilizing influence over international affairs, and lead the management of the world economy, by providing certain public goods for the international community. This theory has been one of the most hotly debated and politically significant concepts in the study of global politics since the end of World War II, largely because it has profound implications for the policies (and the very future) of the United States. Although hegemonic stability theory is grounded in realism, there are liberal scholars who support and criticize the theory; it is something of a special case, having won praise and condemnation across theoretical boundaries.

Hegemonic stability theory is grounded in the realist concept of the distribution of power. When one state is so powerful compared to all the others in the system, that state is described as "hegemonic" or a "hegemon." Robert Gilpin characterizes a hegemonic system as one in which "a single powerful state controls or dominates the lesser states in the system."[37] However, the concept of hegemony has been extended beyond the traditional measures of power employed by realists. Wallerstein describes a hegemonic environment as one in which "one power can largely impose its rules and wishes (at the very least by effective veto power) in the economic, political, military, and diplomatic and even cultural arenas."[38] As discussed in the preceding section, Gramscian and constructivist thought extends the idea of hegemony even further to include the dominance of certain ideas and belief systems (such as capitalism and liberal economic theory). Hegemonic states and hegemonic ideas have a symbiotic relationship, each serving to reinforce the dominance of the other. In this way, the status quo is maintained, both in the realm of state power and in the realm of ideas.

In the conventional use of the term, *hegemonic stability theory* holds that the existence of a dominant state, willing and capable of exerting leadership, is essential for the development and maintenance of a stable international economic order. The hegemon uses its preponderance of power in the system to establish rules, institutions, and regimes, and provides the **public goods** necessary for the maintenance of the system. The implications of hegemonic stability theory are therefore quite stark: when there is no hegemon, or when a hegemon is in decline, the prospects for the creation or maintenance of a stable, open international economic system are poor. As Robert Keohane has argued, "Hegemonic structures of power, dominated by a single country, are most conducive to the development of strong international regimes whose rules are relatively precise and well obeyed … [T]he decline of hegemonic structures of power can be expected to presage a decline in the corresponding international regimes."[39] Some (but not all) liberals regard hegemons as a benevolent presence because the hegemon must be willing to pay a price for its dominant position, and bears a disproportionate share of the burden of its maintainance.[40] In contrast, realists tend to see the hegemon as more coercively inclined, while neo-Marxists tend to see the it as an exploitative actor, and feminists regard the concept of **hegemonic power** as emblematic of the focus on very male-centric interpretations of power.

For liberals, hegemons perform two valuable functions that serve to maintain an open and stable international economic order. First, liberals argue that hegemons will provide public goods in order to maintain an open trading system. Public goods (sometimes referred to as collective goods) are goods that, once created, benefit everyone, including those who do not pay to create or maintain the good; it is difficult or impossible to restrict their use to some while excluding others. Public parks and sidewalks are examples of domestic public goods. For liberals, an open international economy is a public good established and maintained by the current hegemon (the United States) from which all states derive benefit, whether they contribute to its maintenance or not. Second, because public goods can be used by everyone and exclusion is difficult, the natural tendency of all users is to free ride; that is, to continue to use a public good while contributing nothing to maintain it. Of course, if everyone adopted this approach, the public good (whether a public park, a sidewalk, or the international economic system) could decline into disrepair until it was no longer usable. For liberals, the corrosive impact of free riding on public goods is minimized when a hegemon takes it upon itself to maintain the public good. A hegemon can also reduce free riding by encouraging or threatening other states to bear at least some of the burden of maintaining the good. Therefore, hegemons help to reduce the harmful effects of self-interested free riding. If there is no hegemon, or a hegemon disappears, free riding becomes more likely, and the prospects for maintaining public goods become rather poor.

And so, for most liberal economists, the post–World War II United States has carried a disproportionate share of the burden of maintaining the public good of an open, international economic order, from which all other capitalist states benefit. Liberals argue that the U.S. supplies its currency as the central unit of account and reserve in the world economy, and must therefore maintain a money supply that benefits all, not just U.S. interests. The United States must also maintain a relatively open domestic market, even though more cheaply produced goods are free to enter from abroad, thus threatening domestic interests and jobs. In other words, the U.S. must tolerate balance of trade deficits in order to maintain a global free trade regime. The United States has also had to take the lead coordinating the macroeconomic policies of the world's largest economies, and providing credit as a lender of last resort (via the IMF) when states need to finance deficits or when economic shocks threaten to destabilize the world economy. In short, for liberals a hegemon gives as well as receives in its role, and without U.S. hegemony an open international trading system may never have been built or maintained. However, realists and neo-Marxists have less benevolent views of hegemons. For realists, hegemons maintain their dominant position through the power of reward and threat, and derive a highly disproportionate advantage from this status as compared with any burdens they need to bear. For neo-Marxists, the provision of public goods is merely another instrument of hegemonic control over world capitalism. The hegemon establishes and maintains an open trading system because it is the mechanism through which its elites exert their dominance over structurally disadvantaged countries and the working classes, and transnational economic elites in the periphery collude in this system.

Historically, hegemons rise and decline. The period of British hegemony began to decline in the 1870s and disappeared after World War II. The period of U.S. hegemony began during World War II. Today, the question is whether America's hegemonic power has eroded to the point where using the term *hegemon* to describe it is anachronistic. The question is extremely significant, for two reasons. First, debate over U.S. decline obviously strikes a chord in America, as it calls into question the future of American power, American foreign policy, and America's role in the world; it also has direct implications for Canada, which shares a continent and relies heavily on trade with the United States. Second, the debate over U.S. decline calls into question the future of the international economy, for if the hegemon is in decline, would this not mean the future of the global economic system is in question?

Why do hegemons decline? Periods of hegemony are temporary because of slow but steady changes in the economic fortunes of the most powerful states. Changes in the international distribution of economic power arise from technological innovation and changes in economic efficiency, production costs, and economic competitiveness between states. Eventually, the economic position of a hegemon begins to erode relative to new centres of economic growth and dynamism. As Robert Gilpin suggests, "With the inevitable shift in the international distribution of economic and military power from the core to the rising nations ... the capacity of the hegemon to maintain the system decreases."[41] In addition, in their effort to maintain the international order, hegemons suffer from what Paul Kennedy has termed *imperial overstretch*. Hegemons tend to take on a large number of international commitments, especially military commitments. The investment in these military capabilities draws resources away from economic revitalization and domestic economic development, thus contributing to and even accelerating hegemonic decline. Paul Kennedy's 1987 book titled *The Rise and Fall of the Great Powers* began the enduring debate over U.S. hegemonic decline.[42]

The debate was particularly intense in the 1990s, when the U.S. share of global economic output fell to 20 percent from 50 percent in 1947.[43] The United States went from being the leading creditor nation to the leading debtor nation, failed to invest in public infrastructure and education, and overstretched itself with large military budgets and extensive overseas military commitments. However, those who disputed the notion that the United States was in decline criticized the declinist thesis. "Revivalists" or "renewalists" argued that the drop in the U.S. share of global output could be explained by the recovery of the war-devastated economies of Europe and Japan after World War II. The U.S. economy was still more than twice as large as any other in the world. As for high levels of U.S. debt, the U.S. economy remained large and robust enough to sustain such a debt burden. U.S. military spending (historically maintained at approximately 3 percent of GDP) was not an unbearable burden. Furthermore, the United States still led the world in cultural influence, innovation, and ideas, and was therefore the world leader in "soft" power.[44] This declinist–revivalist debate continues in the context of the financial and political costs of the "War on Terror" and the Iraq War (see Chapter 6), and the economic consequences of the U.S. financial crisis and recession (see Chapter 13).

Globalization has brought a new energy to theoretical debates in IPE, and concern over the future of the global economy has never been more widespread. In Chapter 8, we will explore globalization and the theoretical debates that surround it in more detail. But to get there, we need a rough composite of from whence we came. We now turn to a discussion of how the modern world economy developed, and how the principles of liberal economics, in particular, became embedded in the structure and institutions of the contemporary world economy. As we indicated in our overview of civilizations and war and peace in Chapter 2, this is also a necessarily brief discussion and cannot claim to be a complete historical account.

THE EVOLUTION OF THE GLOBAL ECONOMY

Throughout history, groups of people have traded with one another. Trade over wide geographic areas developed around 200 BCE with the rise of the Roman and Han Empires. Trade flourished within these empires, and luxury goods were traded between the empires via the famous Silk Route and by sea routes connecting Indian and Persian ports with those in the Mediterranean. Trade nearly collapsed after the fall of the Roman Empire and the invasion of India and China by "barbarian" peoples. Long-distance trade routes were reopened between 570 and 1000 CE. With increased trade came the rise of merchant cities such as Bruges, Venice, Baghdad, Samarkand, and Hangchow. A variety of products, ranging from Asian spices to Flemish woollens, were in heavy demand, and merchants began travelling to sell them. As economic activity and wealth grew, demand for exotic luxury items increased. By 1100 CE, trading centres had been established all over Europe, from Italy to the Baltic, from England as far east as Bohemia. In 1317 the Venetians produced the Flanders galleys, commercial flotillas that made regular passage between the Adriatic and the North seas. In the 1400s, trade flourished in Europe, and financial empires based on international banking rose in importance (for example, the Fuggers of Augsburg and Medicis of Florence).

Extensive long-distance maritime trade did not begin until about 1500. With the adoption of the mariner's compass and improvements in ship design and building, it became possible to sail the open seas, out of sight of land, and still get—roughly—where one wanted to go. The Portuguese were the first to build a sea-based commercial and political empire, but all the major European nations, including the Spanish, Dutch, and French, would soon follow. As a result, just as the Westphalian state system was extended through the expansion of the European empires (see Chapter 2), the economic system of Europe was extended around the world in a similar fashion. Through the 1500 to 1750 time period, the economic principles of mercantilism prevailed, as states sought balance of trade surpluses and the accumulation of gold and silver. Colonialism and mercantilism were thus closely linked, as some overseas colonies provided markets, cheap labour, and resources, and others (especially in Central and South America) provided gold and silver. The economic and trading systems of non-European empires and civilizations initially survived (and even thrived), but increasingly they were reduced to colonial status by the political and economic dominance of the European empires. In this way, the seeds of the current North–South debate were sown.

Asia had long been a source of many highly valued commodities, such as silk and cotton fabrics, rugs, jewellery, porcelains, sugar, and spices. (The remarkable rise of Asia–Pacific trade today is not so surprising when we take this historical context into consideration.) But the new sea route to the East and the discovery of America in the late 1400s brought a vast increase in trade not only in luxury items but also in bulk commodities such as rice, sugar, and tea. Older commercial activities were transformed by the widening of markets. Trade had become a way of life for many people by the middle of the past millennium.

Arguably, the opening of the Atlantic in the 16th century marked the real beginning of a global economy. In this period, the economic dominance of the Mediterranean and the Middle East receded, as western and northern Europe became the new centres of economic activity with trade links to the Americas, Africa, and Asia. The Portuguese and Spanish were the first to profit, and they retained a near-monopoly through most of the 16th century, but their eventual commercial and military decline made room for the British, French, and Dutch empires. However, this economic activity had a dark side. First, the slave trade was one of the largest activities in the world economy. The arrival of European traders in Africa greatly increased the traditional sub-Saharan and Arab slave trades; between 1500 and 1850, white traders forced almost 10 million Africans to the Americas, most of them to the newly opened plantations of the Caribbean, Brazil, and the United States. Second, the colonial powers were adamant about protecting their trade routes and markets. For example, the famous Opium War (1839 to 1842) was caused primarily by British traders, who insisted on trading opium to addicts of the drug in China despite official Chinese protests. In 1839, opium in British warehouses was destroyed, and in retaliation the British sent warships and troops to attack China's coastal cities (such as Hangchow, Hong Kong, and Canton). Eventually, the victorious British received a $20 million indemnity and temporary colonial possession of Hong Kong, and they opened ports to the opium trade. The Opium War also weakened Imperial China, leaving it vulnerable to demands for treaty ports and trading concessions by Russia, Japan, France, and Germany. Hong Kong was finally returned to Chinese rule at the end of June 1997.

Another great expansion of international trade took place when systems of delivery—ships and trains—acquired new capabilities in the 19th century. As a result of the innovations of the Industrial Revolution, world trade grew threefold between 1870 and 1913, before being curtailed by World War I. Most trade at that time took place between imperial powers and their colonies; the latter would export primary products such as natural resources, and the parent country would export finished products (this pattern of trade persists today in many sectors). Opening up borders to trade was not an easy development, since governments were highly protective of domestic markets and could use the colonies to attain raw materials instead of trade with each other. The defeat of the Corn Laws, which had imposed high tariffs on imports of grain into England, was one of the first major victories for free trade. The Anti–Corn Law League, established in 1838, was composed mostly of industrialists and wage earners, all of whom sought to establish lower corn prices with freer trade. The British landowning aristocracy, however, wanted to protect English agriculture from the onslaught of cheaper, continental products. Pressure from the League and a famine in Ireland ultimately led to the Corn Law's repeal in 1846. Great Britain, by that time an emerging economic state, would become dependent on imports for food and was thus committed to an interdependent (albeit imperial) global economic system of increased free trade.

However, it was not just the movement of goods that was shaping the emerging global economy. Between 1845 and 1914, some 41 million people migrated to the Americas, especially the United States, from Europe. Others went to Australia and South Africa (see Chapter 11). This migration and the stagnation of industrialized European economies led to the export of capital. British, Dutch, French, Belgian, Swiss, and eventually German investors tried to increase their incomes by buying the stocks of foreign business enterprises and the bonds of foreign businesses and governments. They organized companies of their own to operate in foreign states; and banks began granting loans to each other across the Atlantic. As early as the 1840s, half the annual increase of wealth in Great Britain was going into foreign investments. By 1914 the British had US$20 billion in foreign investments, the French about US$8.7 billion, and the Germans about US$6 billion (these were huge sums of money at the time). The sums went into the Americas, the less affluent regions of Europe, and then after 1890 to Asia and Africa. However, in World War I the British lost about a quarter of their foreign investments, the French about a third, and the Germans everything.

Investment, trade, and monetary policy in the 18th, 19th, and 20th centuries were largely influenced by capitalist principles. **Capitalism** involves the ownership of means of production and the employment of labourers to produce goods that are then sold on domestic and international markets. As an economic system, capitalism is prone to cycles of boom and depression, the most notable example of the latter being the long depression that set in about 1873 and lasted to about 1893. The growth of capitalism depended partly on the technological changes that ushered in the Industrial Revolution, but in the strict economic sense it was contingent also on a willingness to grant credit and gamble with it. Sometimes this gamble works, in the sense that profits are realized and loans are paid back; other times it does not, and the willingness to loan and gamble recedes. During times of recession, governments began to take a more active role in the economy. Previously, governments had adopted a hands-off or *laissez-faire* approach to their economies, except in the case of tariffs. Governments began taking measures to combat the essential insecurity of private capitalism, adopting additional protective tariffs and social insurance and welfare legislation, and allowing trade unionism to grow in some areas. After 1880, the old orthodoxy of 19th-century unregulated, *laissez-faire* capitalism diminished in an era of interventionist governments.

Investment and trade were both facilitated by the near-universal adoption of the gold standard. England had adopted the gold standard in 1816, when the pound sterling was legally defined as the equivalent of 113 grains of fine gold. This standard led many investors to keep money in London in the form of sterling on deposit. This money, and the military defeat of Napoleon in 1815, established London's reputation as the centre of the world economy and signalled the beginning of Britain's hegemonic status. Western Europe and the United States (the latter was growing into a major economic power, though the American Civil War would delay its emergence) adopted an exclusively gold standard in the 1830s; a person holding any "civilized" money (defined by the Eurocentric sentiments of the time as pounds, francs, dollars, marks, etc.) could turn it into gold, which could in turn be converted to hard currency (money). Thus citizens from states with different currencies could trade with confidence that their money could change hands in this manner. Until 1914 exchange rates between the currencies remained very stable, though the gold standard was hard on countries with little gold, and it produced a gradual fall in prices, especially between 1870 and 1900, because (until the gold discoveries in South Africa, Australia, and Alaska in the 1890s) the world's production of gold lagged behind the expanding production of industrial and agricultural goods.

In the 15 years before World War I, world trade increased dramatically. German exports grew more rapidly than British exports at this time, and some historians feel this severe economic competition was one of the primary factors leading to the "war to end all wars." The war would help usher in another economic system, put in place by Lenin's Bolsheviks after the Russian Revolution in 1917 (see Chapter 2). This rejection of capitalism by the Soviet Union produced a wave of fear that other states in Europe or North America might experience a similar revolution. The new Soviet state would pronounce itself owner of all the means of production and, after World War II, would participate in an alternative trade system involving itself and other states based on the socialist economic model.

After World War I, production was at an all-time high, due especially to the mass production of the automobile in the United States. However, much of the postwar boom was based on credit and stock market speculation. The Great Depression began as a stock market crisis in New York in October 1929. The crisis was related to speculation: stockbrokers (and many ordinary citizens as well) had purchased large amounts of stock on credit, pushing up stock prices. When prices began to fall, owners of stock had to sell off enough stock to pay back the money they had borrowed, and this snowballed into a huge selloff: between 1929 and 1932, the average value of 50 industrial stocks traded on the New York Stock Exchange dropped from $252 to $61, and 5000 American banks shut down.[45]

As Americans stopped exporting capital and buying foreign goods, world trade decreased. The failure of a leading bank in Vienna in 1931 sent shockwaves throughout Europe. Massive unemployment was experienced across the globe, and states adopted policies designed to protect themselves. The gold reserve in Britain that had supported the pound sterling declined, and investors converted their pounds into other currencies they felt would be safer. By 1931 Britain had devalued the pound and gone off the gold standard, and other countries soon followed suit. Governments manipulated their currencies to keep up exports (that is, they devalued their currencies, making it cheaper to buy their goods). In response to this global economic crisis, states turned away from multilateral free trade to protectionism, in an effort to insulate their hard-hit industries and labour forces from foreign competition. Tariffs were raised, first by the United States in the famous Smoot–Hawley tariff of 1930 (see below) and then by other countries, which had the effect of almost eliminating trade in some commodities (such as agricultural products), while quotas were introduced for others. World trade fell from US$35.6 billion in 1929 to US$11.9 billion in 1932. This decline in trade exacerbated the economic crisis and made economic recovery much more difficult and slower than it could have been. An International Monetary and Economic Conference was convened in London in 1933, but participants were unable to negotiate a reversal of these restrictions on trade as the world sank deeper into the Depression.

In Germany, Adolf Hitler rose to power on a wave of post-Versailles discontent and tremendous inflation rates. The German economy, in shambles after World War I, did begin to recover as a result of the Dawes Plan. In 1924 an American banker, Charles G. Dawes, proposed a plan under which war reparations would be lowered and bank loans would be extended to

Germany to enable it to pay the reduced reparations. Money flowed into Germany from the United States, financing economic recovery and the payment of reparations to Great Britain and France. These reparation payments were in turn used to pay off the debts these countries owed to the United States. The importance of the U.S. economy in this arrangement was highlighted in 1929, when the stock market crash stopped the flow of U.S. dollars to Europe. When the Germans could no longer pay their reparations, the British and French could no longer pay their war debts to the United States. To pay these debts, the British and French governments sought to increase their exports to the United States to obtain the needed currency. However, protectionist sentiment (to protect domestic industry) in the United States was high, and the Smoot–Hawley tariff of 1930 raised tariffs against foreign imports to their highest levels ever. The result was that British and French exports were shut out of the United States. The Smoot–Hawley tariff hampered international trade, blocked collection of war debts, and initiated a chain reaction of protectionism around the world, including the 1932 Ottawa Agreements, which established favourable tariff agreements for the Commonwealth. The Smoot–Hawley tariff also exported the Depression to Europe, which, without U.S. dollars, could not finance its debt burdens. The result was economic disaster; businesses closed and unemployment soared. Just as it did in Germany, economic nationalism contributed to political nationalism and the rise of extremist movements, which capitalized on the frustration and resentment

On to Ottawa! Canada did not escape the hardships of the Depression. Thousands of unemployed "rode the rails" in search of jobs. In 1935, many unemployed did so in protest against the conditions in government work camps. Then, as now, there was a direct relationship between economic hardship and political instability. (CP PHOTO/Toronto Star)

over high unemployment and falling living standards. Democratic governments fell in Japan, Austria, and Eastern Europe (with the exception of Czechoslovakia).

The rise of fascism in Spain, Germany, and Italy, and Japanese expansionism in Asia, would eventually lead to World War II, but many analysts argue that the effect of the Great Depression and the fall of the multilateral trading system as it had evolved to that point were also partly responsible for the war. During World War II, economic production became war oriented. According to Alvin and Heidi Toffler, the United States manufactured nearly six million rifles and machine guns, more than 300 000 planes, 100 000 tanks and armoured vehicles, 71 000 naval vessels, and 41 billion rounds of ammunition.[46] The U.S. had built up considerable gold reserves during the 1930s and benefited further from trade with the allies. As a result, the most powerful military power emerged as the most powerful economic power after the war.

BRETTON WOODS AND THE DEVELOPMENT OF THE WORLD MONETARY SYSTEM

The instability that characterized the interwar period is often attributed to U.S. reluctance to join the League of Nations and assume a leadership role in the world economy. The United States refused to accept the mantle of hegemon and fill the void left by the diminishment of the British Empire, which had previously wielded great power within the world economy through the common use of the pound sterling.[47] After World War II the U.S. emerged as the most powerful economic and military power in the world, especially given the devastation and war-exhaustion of most European and Asian economies. In contrast to the interwar period, the United States was willing to assume the role of a hegemonic power, and to exert leadership in establishing postwar monetary and trade institutions and regimes. In July 1944, even before the end of World War II, representatives of 44 countries met at Bretton Woods, New Hampshire, to construct a stable postwar international economic arrangement. This system came to be called the **Bretton Woods system**, and until 1971 the plans developed at Bretton Woods were to form the foundation of what would be called the **Liberal International Economic Order (LIEO),** the international economic system of the non-communist world.

The first priority of the Bretton Woods conference was to establish an international financial structure based on fixed currency rates. Floating exchange rates were blamed for the instability and ultimate collapse of the international economy in the interwar period. At Bretton Woods, all countries agreed to fix (or peg) their currencies to the U.S. dollar at a specified rate of exchange and to maintain that rate. The U.S. dollar, in turn, was fixed (or pegged) to gold, at an exchange rate of US$35 an ounce. The United States pledged that it would exchange dollars for gold at any time. As a result, all countries knew the value of their currency in U.S. dollars (and ultimately in gold). They knew this value would not fluctuate unpredictably, because states could borrow from the International Monetary Fund (IMF; see below) to prevent a weakening of their currency and because any change in exchange rates required international negotiations. As a result, the international monetary system would be predictable and stable. The U.S. dollar became the central unit of account in the international system, used by states to maintain the value of their currency (by using dollars to sell or buy their own currency internationally), to purchase products needed for postwar reconstruction, and to store financial reserves.

The Bretton Woods negotiations also established two institutions to help manage the system and perform central banking functions. The IMF was created to facilitate trade. The IMF had to approve changes in the fixed exchange rate system and possessed a credit fund of US$8.8 billion to lend to countries that were experiencing downward pressure on the value of their currencies. The IBRD, now known as the World Bank, was created to assist war-torn countries in rebuilding their economies by providing short-term financing (see Profile 4.3). Later, both the IMF and the World Bank became prominent lenders to developing countries, a role they still perform today, although not without criticism. In particular, the decision-making systems of both institutions have been accused of being undemocratic and unrep-resentative. In the IMF and the World Bank, decisions are made by a vote in the Board of Governors or the Executive Board, whose members are nominated (in the former) and elected (in the latter) by member states. The weight of each board member's vote is determined by the contribution that state makes to the financial resources of the institution. As a result, the richer countries (especially the United States, Japan, Germany, France, and Britain) have the greatest influence in the IMF and World Bank and tend to dominate decisions. Together, the IMF and the IBRD are known as the "twin institutions" of the Bretton Woods system. It was clear soon after the war that the Soviet Union, with its commitment to a non-capitalist path, would not participate in the building of the LIEO. It was also clear that all the other states with large economies, most of which required a great deal of reconstruction, were willing to accept American leadership. Resource-rich Canada was also posed to benefit from an American-led global economy.

PROFILE 4.3 The IBRD (the World Bank)

The IBRD (commonly referred to as the World Bank or World Bank Group) was established at the Bretton Woods conference in 1944 and is located in Washington, D.C. After the postwar reconstruction of Europe, the Bank began to focus on development issues. The Bank operates on a weighted voting system, meaning that the more a state contributes, the more say it has in what the Bank does and does not do. Obviously, decisions are dominated by the United States, Japan, Germany, and other wealthy contributing states. In 2011, Canada was among the ten largest shareholders in the Bank, possessing a voting share of 2.51 to 3.38 percent (depending on the specific decision- making forum within the Bank). In 1957 the Bank established the International Finance Corporation (IFC) to assist poorer states in obtaining finance from private lenders, and in 1960 the International Development Association (IDA) was established to loan to poorer states. The Bank also includes the Multilateral Investment Guarantee Agency, and the International Centre for Settlement of Investment Disputes. Collectively, these institu-tions are now called the World Bank Group.

In the 1970s the activities of the Bank acceler-ated under a campaign to eliminate poverty. However, the Bank's aid was linked to economic and social reforms, many of which harmed the most vulnerable members of society. Critics charge that the Bank has contributed to the perpetuation of poverty by favouring large-scale infrastructure projects that benefit the wealthy and cause environmental damage. The Bank has attempted to reform its policies to account for these negative experiences. Nevertheless, it remains a target of critics who argue that its policies remain harmful and counterproductive to development. For example, in 1995 the "Fifty Years Is Enough" campaign demanded the sus-pension of all World Bank activities, while the "Make Poverty History" campaign has called for the restructuring of the Bank to make it more democratic. Today, one of the Bank's core activi-ties is to advance the Millennium Development Goals discussed in Chapter 8.

For more on Canada's official position at the Bank, see Department of Finance Canada, *Canada at the IMF and World Bank Group 2011: Report on Operations under the Bretton Woods and Related Agreements Act*, at http://www.fin.gc.ca/bretwood/pdf/bretwd11-eng.pdf.

Indeed, the United States provided much of the funding for the creation of the United Nations, the IMF, and the IBRD, and came to the aid of the Bretton Woods system when it was threatened in 1947, when an international dollar shortage became a serious problem. As discussed above, dollars were in demand for a number of crucial functions, but if not enough dollars were in circulation, what then? More dollars had to be disbursed into the international system if Bretton Woods was to survive. The answer was a massive program of aid to foreign countries so that they would be able to buy the U.S. goods they required for reconstruction. The most famous of these programs was the Marshall Plan, under which 16 Western European countries received more than US$17 billion between 1948 and 1952. The United States also tolerated trade protectionism in Europe and Japan to revive the European and Japanese economies (and thus create more consumers for U.S. products in the future). As a result of the Marshall Plan and trade protectionism abroad, the United States experienced massive balance of payments deficits; that is, more money was flowing out of the country than was coming in. Although this deficit was not a concern in the late 1940s and early 1950s, by the late 1950s it was becoming a problem, and by 1960 the Bretton Woods system was again in trouble.

GATT AND THE DEVELOPMENT OF THE WORLD TRADING SYSTEM

Negotiations on the principles and structure of the postwar trading system began between the United States and Great Britain as early as 1942, with multilateral discussions beginning in 1945. An open trading system was naturally in U.S. interests because it would allow the United States to export products overseas. An open trading system would also allow European and Asian economies to export products to the United States, thus facilitating postwar economic development. There was also an additional interest. Most governments believed the Depression had been prolonged and deepened by protectionism. An open trading system, established by treaty and maintained by the hegemonic United States, would prevent protectionism from stalling economic recovery after World War II. And so, in 1947 the General Agreement on Tariffs and Trade (GATT) was established. GATT was a treaty binding its members to certain rules concerning international commerce. Only 23 countries attended the first GATT conferences in 1947. Originally, the authors of the Bretton Woods system had intended to establish a powerful International Trade Organization (ITO). However, the U.S. Congress objected to an exception for imperial trading systems, which effectively killed the ITO proposal. The GATT system proceeded without the ITO, focusing on a series of trade negotiations. The aim of GATT was to increase trade liberalization. For its part, Canada was an avid supporter of the GATT regime.[48]

GATT was initially designed to promote trade liberalization in two ways. First, because it was an intergovernmental process, GATT provided an important forum for states to negotiate reductions in barriers to trade. GATT was an ongoing process and provided a steadily expanding body of rules and agreements to build upon as more states joined the GATT process (see Profile 4.4). Second, GATT established (and continually developed) sets of norms and rules governing international trade. For the first 30 years of GATT's existence, these norms and rules focused on the reduction of tariffs. The average tariff on a manufactured good among the governments belonging to GATT after World War II was 40 percent. After successive negotiations in GATT, in the early 1970s the average tariff on manufactured goods had fallen to 9 percent.[49] The result was an increase in trade among GATT countries as falling tariffs led to falling prices for imported manufactured goods, which in turn increased demand for imported and exported products.

PROFILE 4.4   Multilateral Negotiations under GATT and Number of Participants

1. Geneva, 1947: 23 states
2. Annency (France), 1949: 13 states
3. Torquay (Britain), 1950–51: 38 states
4. Geneva, 1955–56: 26 states
5. Dillon Round, 1960–61: 26 states

6. Kennedy Round, 1964–67: 62 states
7. Tokyo Round, 1973–79: 102 states
8. Uruguay Round, 1986–94: 123 states
9. Doha Round (WTO), 2001-?: 155 states

In order to ensure that the GATT system was fair, GATT rules included the principles of **non-discrimination** and **reciprocity**. The principle of non-discrimination specifies that all members of GATT must treat all other members of GATT the same with respect to trade policy. For example, a GATT member could not have a low tariff on a good imported from country A and impose a higher tariff on the same good imported from country B (assuming both country A and country B are members of GATT). The tariff would have to be the same for both countries, and any changes to the tariff would have to be applied equally to all members of GATT who produced that good. In principle, this ensures there is no discrimination in how states treat one another in GATT. This convention is also known as the **Most Favoured Nation (MFN)** principle. The principle of reciprocity specifies that all members of GATT should make approximately the same value of concessions to each other when making trade policy. For example, if Canada were to reduce its tariffs on rice imported from Japan, Japan should reciprocate by reducing its tariffs on a product it imports from Canada, such as wood products. Moreover, this Japanese reciprocity should lead to approximately the same value of increased trade for Canada in wood products as the Canadian tariff reduction did for Japanese rice. These two principles were crucial for GATT, because they entrenched the idea that all members should benefit from trade, and they should all benefit as equally as possible. In this way, it was hoped that neomercantilist temptations would be minimized.

As GATT evolved and expanded, and world economic activity grew in scope and complexity, member states began to negotiate and implement measures on a variety of other issues related to trade liberalization. One of the first issues to be addressed was **dumping**, the practice of exporting goods to a country and selling them at below the cost of production (in order to seize market share by bankrupting competing producers prior to increasing prices). Dumping was made illegal under GATT, although accusations of dumping remain commonplace in the global economy. By the 1980s, **non-tariff barriers** to trade were under discussion. There was growing concern that countries were using health and safety regulations, labelling laws, and government contracting rules as barriers to trade (that is, to exclude foreign products from their market to favour domestic producers). This of course led to debates on whether such regulations were unfair trade practices or justifiable efforts by governments to regulate their economies and societies. Under the Tokyo and Uruguay Rounds of GATT, some progress was made on the issue of non-tariff barriers, but, as we shall see, this debate continues to rage today. The Uruguay Round also began to create rules governing **Intellectual Property Rights (IPR)**. Intellectual property involves creations of the imagination subject to ownership, including artistic works, literature, symbols and logos, among many others. The holder of the patent or copyright for such creations has the exclusive right to profit from a piece of music, computer software, image, or brand name. Since the 1980s, copyright infringement and piracy has emerged as a major issue. Companies in some parts of the world turn out counterfeit, unlicensed versions of these creations at low cost for their own profit, costing the patent holder thousands, millions, or billions of dollars in lost revenue and reducing the incentives to produce creations of imagination in the first place. As we shall see in Chapter 8, the negotiation of **Trade-Related Intellectual Property Rights (TRIPs)**, which require member states to create and enforce copyright rules, has been a controversial issue in IPE. Some critics charge that TRIPs agreements protect the profits of large firms, and high licensing or user fees prevent developing countries from using technology and ideas that might improve their social condition. The advent of the Internet and near-infinite downloading capacity has further complicated the issue.

The Uruguay Round also created a **General Agreement on Trade in Services (GATS)** to govern the growing international trade in the service sector. Services are economic activities such as banking, insurance, tourism, and transportation, to name a few. The expansion of the service sector in the 1980s was addressed in GATT because service sector companies were finding it very difficult to operate in other countries. The GATS agreement began the process of liberalizing trade in services, an effort that continues today, though not without controversy. GATT was also forced to confront a growing problem in the world economy: the divide between rich countries and poor countries. Decolonization brought a large number of new (and generally poor) states into the international system, and large numbers of these states joined GATT. The poor states of the developing world called for greater access to the markets of rich states, through the lowering of tariffs on products exported by developing countries. Greater access to rich world markets would enable lower-income countries to generate increased revenues through increased exports. For the most part, rich states were reluctant to do this because of threats the (generally cheaper) goods of the developing world posed to domestic industries and agriculture. While a **Generalized System of Preferences** was established in GATT in the 1960s (allowing industrialized states to lower tariffs on imports from developing countries to levels below the tariffs imposed on the same goods from developed countries), this system never succeeded in addressing the North–South divide in the global economy. As we shall see in Chapter 8, this issue has only intensified in contemporary debates over globalization.

Agreements in GATT were not reached without considerable debate at the intergovernmental level, and of course most governments faced domestic political opposition to many new measures. GATT agreements reached at the end of each round always reflected what was possible through negotiation. States sought to protect their economic and social interests in the GATT negotiations, and realists would remind us that GATT agreements reflected these interests (while constructivists would suggest the perception of those interests changed as the system evolved). States negotiated exemptions for certain sectors of economic and social activity. For example, many countries (including Western European states, the United States, and Canada) have protected their agricultural sector from high levels of trade liberalization, enabling them to maintain subsidies and high tariffs in this politically sensitive sector. Canada and other countries (especially France) fought to protect their cultural sector against the perceived threat of U.S. cultural influences. Of course, states also found themselves in trade disputes with other GATT members. Trade disputes arise when one or more states feel that other GATT states are engaging in economic or public policy that is against the letter or the spirit of GATT rules. Trade disputes became a central feature of global politics. Major disputes, such as those between the United States and Japan over automobile imports, and the United States and the EEC over agricultural trade, received considerable media and public attention.

Though the successive rounds of GATT succeeded in reducing tariffs and facilitating increased levels of world trade, the 1970s and 1980s saw a rise in protectionism. The final concluded round of GATT negotiations (the eighth) may have been the most difficult. The Uruguay Round began in 1986 and initially involved 107 countries. Only the Soviet Union and China sat out the negotiations. On April 15, 1994, at Marrakesh, Morocco, the final result of these lengthy negotiations (some refer to GATT as the "General Agreement to Talk and Talk") was released to the public. Under this new world trade agreement, 123 countries (the membership of GATT by 1994) agreed on a set of rules that would reduce tariffs by approximately one-third. Since 1994, more states have signed the agreement, and the countries that are party to the Uruguay Round agreement account for 90 percent of world trade. Finally, the agreement also established the World Trade Organization (WTO) to replace the GATT, which now includes China (2001) and Russia (2012). We will explore the WTO further in Chapter 8.

THE DECLINE AND FALL OF THE BRETTON WOODS SYSTEM

By 1960, the problems facing the Bretton Woods system were in many ways different from the ones it faced in 1947. The persistent balance of payments deficits experienced by the United States meant that more and more dollars were in circulation in the international system. The dollar shortage had turned into the dollar glut. In 1960, for the first time, more dollars were in circulation than there was gold in U.S. reserves. This imbalance meant that the United States would not be able to exchange gold for dollars at $35 an ounce. Not surprisingly, many began to question the strength of the U.S. dollar as a reserve currency and feared that it would be devalued. As a result, many holders of U.S. dollars began to convert their dollars into gold, creating the first dollar crisis.

Other developments also threatened the position of the dollar. The economies of Western Europe and Japan had recovered from the war, and the need for U.S. dollars and U.S. products lessened. The IMF was moving away from reliance on the U.S. dollar toward Special Drawing Rights (SDRs), a basket of major currencies that could be drawn on by countries in search of financing. (Because SDRs were a blend of currencies, they were seen as more stable than gold or U.S. dollars.) The expenditures of the Vietnam War and President Lyndon Johnson's War on Poverty had also eroded the competitiveness of the U.S. economy. And finally, in 1971, the United States experienced a balance of trade deficit (with more goods imported into the country than were exported) for the first time. This deficit threatened jobs at home and increased international tensions, as the U.S. government blamed Western Europe and Japan for maintaining undervalued currencies (currency values that did not reflect the true cost of goods and services in those countries). This undervaluing in turn made foreign products more attractive for consumers in the United States, which contributed to the U.S. balance of trade deficit.

On August 15, 1971, the Nixon administration responded to the eroding position of the U.S. economy by announcing that it would no longer exchange dollars for gold. A tariff was placed on goods entering the United States, and the U.S. dollar was devalued to increase exports.[50] For all intents and purposes, the Bretton Woods system had collapsed. This collapse had two general consequences. First, the international monetary system was transformed. With the collapse of the fixed exchange rate system, the value of currencies now floated freely in international financial markets. The value of a currency was now based on perceptions of the strength and health of a state's economy; market forces, rather than government intervention, determined a currency's value. The financial predictability of Bretton Woods vanished, replaced with the volatile financial markets we are familiar with today (see Profile 4.5). Second, it was apparent by 1971 that the United States could no longer unilaterally regulate the global economic system. Economic power had become more dispersed in the international system, and although the United States was still by far the world's largest economy, it was no longer capable of exerting leadership unilaterally, and other countries were no longer willing to unconditionally accept that leadership. The management of the international economy began to shift from a hegemonic management system to an increasingly multilateral management system. Of course, this shift to a new international monetary system had implications for other countries, including Canada (see Profile 4.6).

THE POLITICS OF OIL

The global economy faced another challenge in the wake of the collapse of Bretton Woods: the formation of OPEC in 1960 by four Middle Eastern states and Venezuela. OPEC was established to fight proposed oil price cuts by oil companies and later to pressure transnational oil corporations to give host-country governments a greater share of the immense profits the industry was generating. By the early 1970s OPEC was winning significant concessions and had raised the price of oil. It is important to keep in mind that oil has been the predominant fuel of industrialization since the latter half of the 20th century, especially in the United States, Western Europe, and Japan. The pursuit of oil, its role in the global economy, and the geopolitical and environmental implications of humanity's extraordinary dependence on this substance has inspired a great body of literature.[51] OPEC is a **cartel**, a producer's organization that seeks to raise the price of a good by reducing its supply through controls on production. In 1973, in reaction to U.S. support for Israel in the 1973 Arab–Israeli War, OPEC countries initiated a cutback in oil production and imposed an oil embargo against the United States. World oil prices rose dramatically, from $2.50 a barrel in 1973 to $11.65 in 1974. (A barrel is a standard measure for petroleum, equivalent to 42 U.S. gallons or 159 litres.) The oil shock created havoc in the West and particularly in the United States, the world's leading importer of oil. A global recession followed, as countries had to spend more for energy. Dollars also flowed to OPEC countries in such huge amounts ($70 billion in 1974 alone) that the supply of "petro-dollars" in the international system depressed the value of the dollar still further, and encouraged cash-heavy banks to take large risks loaning money to low-income states.

Some equilibrium was achieved when oil prices began to decline in the late 1970s due to a fall in demand through conservation efforts, reduced consumption, the discovery of new deposits elsewhere, and a shift to alternative sources of energy. However, another oil shock followed after the Iranian revolution in 1979, as world prices of oil shot up to $50 a barrel. Global recession once again followed, although, again, conservation measures and the exploitation of new sources of oil eventually reduced pressure on world oil prices. However, many of the world's leading industrial economies (especially those in Europe and Asia) remain reliant on Middle Eastern oil. In fact, many would argue that the war in the Persian Gulf in 1991 and the Iraq War in 2003 were related directly to the strategic importance of oil. Oil is also a key factor in the politics of export-dependent states such as Nigeria and Venezuela; some analysts refer to states with large oil reserves and military governments as "petro-tyrannies."[52] As we shall see in later sections of this textbook, the shock of high oil prices in 2008, combined with newfound awareness of climate change issues and the environmental impact of exploiting less accessible reserves, may be the beginning of a profound revolution in human affairs as we adjust to a post-oil global economy. However, we are some way off from this achievement and the current importance of this special commodity cannot be overemphasized.

PROFILE 4.5   Money and Floating Exchange Rates

Toronto Stock Exchange. Photo by Gordon Powley taken c. June 17, 1952. (© Toronto Star Syndicate 2003. All rights reserved. CP Photo)

Money performs several different functions in the international economy. Currencies must be accepted and recognized so that actors possessing currency can use it to purchase goods and services from other actors. Money serves as a store of value, and as a standard of deferred payment so that actors will be willing to lend money knowing that the money will still have purchasing power when the loan is repaid. This belief is important because the value of money can erode through inflation. Inflation occurs when the supply of money exceeds the value of goods and services produced in an economy. As a currency becomes inflated, it loses purchasing power and becomes a poor store of value and less acceptable as an exchange for the payment of debts. As a result, governments try to keep inflation as low as possible.

Changes in currency exchange rates occur when international evaluations of a country's economy and its ability to maintain the value of its money change due to political or economic events or trends. If a country has a healthy and growing economy, its currency will rise relative to other currencies (one unit of the currency will buy more of another currency) because it becomes more desirable as a store of value or a medium of exchange. If, however, a country's economy is performing poorly, its currency will fall relative to other currencies (one unit of the currency will buy less of another currency) because it is less desirable as a store of value or a medium of exchange. Of course, since all currencies are floating relative to each other, the exchange rates between them are dependent on the relative performance of their economies. Who makes these international evaluations of the performance of state economies? International organizations, governments, banks and financial institutions (such as investment houses), corporations, and individuals all contribute to the general appraisal of a state's economy (although certain institutions play a greater role than others). Much of the activity in international financial markets is based on **currency speculation**, an effort to make money by buying it and selling it at a profit. In essence, speculators gamble (based on economic and political indicators) that the value of a currency will increase in the future: they will buy the currency, store it, and sell it when the value of the currency is higher (thus making a profit).

As a result, the capacity of a state government to influence the value of its own currency is limited, because the value of the currency is based on what others think of the state's

(continued)

PROFILE 4.5 Money and Floating Exchange Rates (*continued*)

economy. However, governments will try to act in support of their currencies, because the value of a currency (and especially its stability relative to other currencies) is extremely important for exporters and importers of goods and services, since they must purchase or sell their goods and services across state borders in accordance with current exchange rates. Governments will therefore try to follow responsible fiscal policies so as not to damage the value of their currency. Governments intervene by buying or selling their own currency in the international system, thereby increasing or decreasing the value of the currency by affecting the international demand for it. One of the great challenges of the post–Bretton Woods system was adjusting to the fact that the value of currencies could fluctuate quite dramatically and that this fluctuation was due to forces largely out of state control. Today, even small changes in the value of currencies are important knowledge, whether you are planning an international holiday or managing a government's financial reserves.

PROFILE 4.6 Canada and Floating Exchange Rates

The value of the Canadian dollar, like that of most other currencies, is largely determined by financial markets. Currency traders, buyers, speculators, banks, and foreign governments evaluate the attractiveness of the Canadian dollar (popularly known as the Loonie, after the dollar coin introduced in 1987) on the basis of the health of the Canadian economy, the economic policies of Canadian federal and provincial governments, and political developments in Canada. If the Canadian economy shows disappointing trends (such as lower growth), the Canadian dollar is less attractive to foreign-currency holders and the value of the Canadian currency will decline. Similarly, if the Canadian government follows economic policies viewed as fiscally irresponsible (such as increased budget deficits), the value of the Loonie will decline. Political developments may also cause the value of the Canadian dollar to fluctuate. For example, in the 1997 federal elections in Canada, early returns indicated a possible minority government for the Liberal Party. A minority government may have meant instability in Canada's political scene, and the value of the Loonie dropped as speculators, banks, and governments found it less attractive. As the election results showed a slim Liberal majority government, the dollar rebounded somewhat on international markets. Canada, like most countries, is faced with two dilemmas in this market-oriented monetary environment. Canadian governments must make economic policy with an eye on the possible reaction of international financial markets, which constrains the government's ability to make decisions on the basis of domestic needs. The Canadian government must also decide when to intervene to prop up the dollar by buying Canadian dollars on international markets (creating a demand for Canadian dollars, which increases the value of the currency). Doing this, of course, costs money. Because Canada is a major exporter and importer, currency fluctuations are of tremendous importance to the Canadian economy. Between 2003 and 2007, the increasing value of the Canadian dollar relative to the U.S. dollar (the dollar reached parity with the U.S. dollar in 2007) caused consternation among Canadian exporters, as the higher Canadian dollar made Canadian exports more expensive to consumers (especially consumers in the United States). On the other hand, many imported products dropped in price, to the pleasure of many Canadian consumers! By 2012 the Canadian dollar had again settled to a value slightly below that of its American counterpart.

PART ONE: ORIGINS

THE GROUP OF SEVEN (AND THEN THERE WERE EIGHT)

Since 1975, a very exclusive forum has met to discuss and reach agreement on economic issues. The **Group of Seven (G7)** countries are Canada, France, Germany, Great Britain, Italy, Japan, and the United States. Initially known as the Group of Five (G5) before the admission of Canada and Italy in 1976, the G7 is not a formal international organization. Rather, it is a forum for discussion and coordination on a wide range of political and economic issues. In short, the G7 has a deliberative function (members meet to create understanding and awareness), a directive function (summits establish agendas and priorities), and a decisional function (members reach joint agreements on programs, targets, and timetables). Summits of the leaders of the G7 countries are held on a yearly basis. In the early years of the G5/G7, the primary role of the forum was to coordinate the management of exchange rates and domestic interest rates. This role is significant because it signalled the inability of the United States to manage the global economic system on its own, and it committed the largest economies of the free world to cooperation on economic policy to attempt to manage the international economy. In addition, the early meetings marked the return of Japan to global prominence.

The G7 summit in 1994 was held in Naples, where leaders agreed to revitalize international economic institutions and integrate the former communist countries into the global economic system more rapidly. This summit was also notable for the fact that Russian President Boris Yeltsin was invited. Although Russia was not invited to become a full economic member of the forum, it has attended the G7 summits every year since Naples (leading some to refer to the G7 as the G8 or simply the Eight; the president of the EU also participates). In 1995 the G8 summit was held in Halifax, where leaders discussed the collapse of the Mexican peso and the progress achieved in creating new financial institutions. In recent years, G8 summits in St. Petersburg, Russia (2006), Heiligendamm, Germany (2007), Toyako, Japan (2008), La Maddalena, Italy (2009), Muskoka, Canada (2010), Deauville, France (2011), Camp David, U.S.A. (2012), and Fermanagh, Northern Ireland (2013), have addressed a wide range of political issues, including terrorism and security challenges, the environment, food and oil prices, and development. This raises questions about whether the G8 is becoming something akin to an elitist concert of powers (similar questions have been raised about the high-level meetings of economic elites in Davos, Switzerland, each year).

Membership in the G8 has also become an issue. As a forum for the world's largest democratic market economies, the G8 membership is rather anachronistic. If economic size were the sole measure of membership, for example, Canada would no longer be a member of the group; China, India, and Brazil certainly would. Canada's continued membership in the G8 is a reflection of Canada's international diplomatic profile, its tradition of involvement in international economic and political issues, and the unwillingness of other G8 countries to discuss the politically sensitive issue of membership criteria. In part, this led then–Canadian Prime Minister Paul Martin to propose the creation of the Group of Twenty (G20) forum. The G20 first met in 1999 as a forum of finance ministers and central bank governors from the 20 largest economies in the world (including the European Union). The G20 devotes most of its attention to financial and development policy coordination among member states. It met at the Heads of Government level for the first time in November 2008, possibly indicating that its role may be enhanced and become more significant in the future. In another relatively exclusive forum, the **Trilateral Commission**, economic experts from North America, Europe, and Japan meet to discuss future relations. The 29 states in the

Organisation for Economic Co-operation and Development (OECD) carry out research and consultations on promoting free trade and economic efficiency. OECD countries produce two-thirds of the world's goods and services. The organization is often criticized as a rich countries' club, though Mexico and South Korea have both won admission.

As we have seen, the global economy has evolved considerably since the end of World War II, through a combination of long-term trends (such as economic growth, trade, technological innovations, and the decline of U.S. dominance, or hegemony, in the system) and short-term shocks (such as the collapse of Bretton Woods, the oil shocks, and the fall of the Soviet Union). In general, the politics of the global economy have evolved from a largely unilateral or hegemonic management of the system to a multilateral management effort. The global economy we live in today is the product of a conscious effort to create an open trading system at the end of World War II based on liberal economic principles, and of the subsequent political and economic events that shaped the 20th century.

CONCLUSIONS

As the Cold War ended, the global economy was as complex as ever. A clear dividing line remained between rich and poor, largely in North–South terms. However, it was becoming quite apparent that the Soviet Union and the Eastern European states were in economic disarray. They had to be integrated into the world economy somehow, and they embarked on a program of privatization that, initially at least, caused a great deal of hardship. China was charting a new course toward greater privatization and was experiencing rapid economic growth based on cheap labour and increased exports. Other Asian countries were also continuing down the export-led development path with record growth, although the Asian financial crisis of 1997 (see Chapter 8) would slow growth down for a few years. Canada had entered into NAFTA with the U.S. and Mexico, and Europe was forging ahead with its problematic economic and political integration. Many states in Sub-Saharan Africa and Latin America were mired in development dilemmas. The environmental problems that had resulted from years of global industrialization and population growth became topics of great concern as the world prepared for the United Nations Conference on Environment and Development, held in Rio de Janeiro, Brazil, in 1992. MNCs were growing in number and in size, which raised questions about the impact such firms were having on trade and development.

Poverty and wealth, arguably the two central themes of economic history, continue to coexist. So, too, do the central perspectives on IPE we have outlined. In this chapter, we have emphasized several divergent perspectives: neomercantilism, liberalism, neo-Marxism, feminism, global ecopolitics, constructivism, and hegemonic stability theory. We have provided a brief outline of the recent evolution of trade and finance in the international economy and the principles on which this system is based. In Chapter 8, we will look at the modern world economy and discuss some of the prevalent concerns facing those who study IPE today. We turn now to an examination of what many analysts feel are the principal potential facilitators of both peace and economic progress on a global scale: international institutions.

Endnotes

1. M. Waters, *Globalization* (London: Routledge, 1995), 66–7; L. Lapham, "Notebook: Estate Sale," *Harper's Magazine*, May 2008, 9–12, 11; J. Frieden, *Global Capitalism: Its Fall and Rise in the Twentieth Century* (New York: W.W. Norton and Company, 2006), xvi.

2. T. Friedman, *The World Is Flat: A Brief History of the Twenty-First Century* (New York: Farrar, Straus and Giroux, 2005).

3. P. Collier, *The Bottom Billion: Why the Poorest Countries are Failing and What Can Be Done about It* (Oxford: Oxford University Press, 2007).

4. R. Isaak, *Managing World Economic Change: International Political Economy*, 3rd ed. (Upper Saddle River, NJ: Prentice-Hall, 2000), 2.

5. T. Cohn, *Global Political Economy: Theory and Practice*, 2nd ed. (Toronto: Longman, 2003), 6.

6. K. Polanyi, *The Great Transformation: The Political and Economic Origins of Our Time* (New York: Beacon Press, 1944).

7. T. Oatley, *International Political Economy: Interests and Institutions in the Global Economy* (New York: Pearson Education, 2004), 3.

8. See, for example, P. Krugman, and M. Obstfeld, *International Economics: Theory and Policy* (New York: HarperCollins, 1991); and J.D. Richardson, *Understanding International Economics: Theory and Practice* (Boston: Little, Brown and Company, 1980). For a study of the interaction between politics and economics, see J. Grieco and J. Ikenberry, *State Power and World Markets: The International Political Economy* (New York: W.W. Norton, 2003).

9. C.E. Lindblom, *Politics and Markets: The World's Political Economic Systems* (New York: Basic Books, 1977).

10. R. Gilpin, *The Political Economy of International Relations* (Princeton University Press, 1987).

11. See R.S. Walters and R.H. Blake, *The Politics of Global Economic Relations*, 4th ed. (Englewood Cliffs, NJ: Prentice-Hall, 1992).

12. For a classic text, see R. Rosecrance, *The Rise of the Trading State: Commerce and Conquest in the Modern World* (New York: Basic Books, 1986).

13. A. Smith, *An Inquiry into the Nature and Causes of the Wealth of Nations*, vol. 1, bk. 4 (London: Dent and Sons, 1910), 436.

14. Ibid., 436.

15. Cohn suggests there are three variants of liberalism: orthodox, interventionist, and institutional. Cohn, *Global Political Economy*, 93; Michael Doyle writes of liberal institutionalism, commercial pacifism, and liberal internationalism in his *Ways of War and Peace: Realism, Liberalism, and Socialism* (New York: W.W. Norton, 1997).

16. For a discussion of international trade theory and its evolution, see D. Irwin, *Against the Tide: An Intellectual History of Free Trade* (Princeton University Press, 1996).

17. For a discussion of the impact of Keynes's ideas, see P. Hall, ed., *The Political Power of Economic Ideas: Keynesianism across Nations* (Princeton University Press, 1989).

18. Cohn, *Global Political Economy*, 98.

19. S. Krasner, "Structural Causes and Regime Consequences: Regimes as Intervening Variables," in S. Krasner, ed., *International Regimes* (Ithaca, NY: Cornell University Press, 1983), 2. See also M. Zacher, "Toward a Theory of International Regimes," *Journal of International Affairs* 44, no. 1 (1990), 139–58; and O. Young, "The Politics of International Regime Formation: Managing Natural Resources and the Environment," *International Organization* 43, no. 3 (1989), 349–75.

20. See, for example, M. Zacher with B. Sutton, *Governing Global Networks: International Regimes for Transportation and Communication* (Cambridge, UK: Cambridge University Press, 1996); P. Kien-hong Yu, *International Governance, Regimes, and Globalization: An East Asian Perspective* (New York: BrownWalker, 2008).

21. K. Marx and F. Engels, *The Communist Manifesto* (New York: International Publishers, 1948). Much more important, from a theoretical viewpoint, was Marx's landmark study, *Das Capital*, and his earlier, more philosophical work.

22. R. Miliband, *The State in Capitalist Society* (New York: Basic Books, 1969).

23. See V.I. Lenin, *Imperialism: The Highest Stage of Capitalism: A Popular Outline* (New York: International Publishers, 1939); and R. Luxemburg, *The Accumulation of Capital* (London: Routledge, 2003).

24. See P. Baran, *The Political Economy of Growth* (New York: Monthly Review Press, 1962), 12. On the political history of what is often referred to as the *Third World*, see L.S. Stavrianos, *Global Rift: The Third World Comes of Age* (New York: William Morrow, 1981).

25. See, for example, A.G. Frank, *Latin America, Underdevelopment or Revolution: Essays on the Development of Underdevelopment and the Immediate Enemy* (New York: Monthly Review Press, 1970). For an excellent review of dependency theory, see M. Blomstrom and B. Hettne, *Development Theory in Transition, The Dependency Debate and Beyond: Third World Responses* (London: Zed Books, 1984); and P. Evans's classic *Dependent Development: The Alliance of Multinational, State, and Local Capital in Brazil* (Princeton University Press, 1979). For an African perspective, see S. Amin, *Accumulation on a World Scale: A Critique of the Theory of Development*, vols. 1 and 2 (New York: Monthly Review Press, 1974).

26. See F. Cardoso and E. Faletto, *Dependency and Development in Latin America*, trans. M. Urquid (Berkeley: University of California Press, 1979).

27. See P. Gleijeses, *The Dominican Crisis: The 1965 Constitutional Revolt and American Intervention*, trans. L. Lipson (Baltimore, MD: Johns Hopkins University Press, 1978).

28. See R. Sandford, *The Murder of Allende and the End of the Chilean Way to Socialism*, trans. A. Conrad (New York: Harper and Row, 1976). For more on U.S. foreign policy in Latin America, see R. Pastor, *Exiting the Whirlpool: US Foreign Policy toward Latin America and the Caribbean* (Boulder, CO: Westview Press, 2001).

29. I. Wallerstein, "The Rise and Future Demise of the World Capitalist System: Concepts for Comparative Analysis," in I. Wallerstein, ed., *The Capitalist World-Economy* (New York: Cambridge University Press, 1979), 35. See also F. Braudel, *Civilization and Capitalism: 15th–18th Century*, 3 vols. (New York: Harper and Row, 1981, 1982, 1984).

30. Ibid., 18–19.

31. R. Cox, *Production, Power, and World Order: Social Forces in the Making of History* (New York: Columbia University Press, 1987).

32. See G. Waylen, "Gender, Feminism, and Political Economy," *New Political Economy* 2, no. 2 (July 1997), 205–20; and J.A. Nelson, "Feminism and Economics," *The Journal of Economic Perspectives* 9, no. 2 (Spring 1995), 131–48.

33. R. Carson, *Silent Spring* (Boston: Houghton Mifflin, 1962).

34. See E. Helleiner, "International Political Economy and the Greens," *International Political Economy* 1, no. 1 (March 1996), 59–78.

35. E.F. Schumacher, *Small Is Beautiful: Economics As If People Mattered* (New York: Harper Perennial, 1973).

36. This was the famous Report to the "Club of Rome," a group of scientists established in 1968 to evaluate the state of international affairs and the impact of human activity on the earth. The Club of Rome still exists: see their website at http://www.clubofrome.org/?p=326; for the Canadian chapter, see http://www.cacor.ca/.

37. R. Gilpin, *War and Change in World Politics* (Cambridge, UK: Cambridge University Press, 1981), 29.

38. I. Wallerstein, "The Three Instances of Hegemony in the History of the Capitalist World Economy," in I. Wallerstein, ed., *The Politics of the World-Economy: The States, the Movements, and the Civilizations* (Cambridge, UK: Cambridge University Press, 1984), 38.

39. R. Keohane, "The Theory of Hegemonic Stability and Changes in International Economic Regimes, 1967–1977," in O. Holsti, R. Siverson, and A. George, eds., *Change in the International System* (Boulder, CO: Westview Press, 1980), 132.

40. See C. Kindleberger, *The World in Depression, 1929–1939* (Berkeley: University of California Press, 1973).

41. Gilpin, *The Political Economy of International Relations*, 78.

42. P. Kennedy, *The Rise and Fall of the Great Powers* (New York: Random House, 1987).

43. D. White, "Mutable Destiny: The End of the American Century?" *Harvard International Review* 20 (Winter 1998), 42–7.

44. For examples of revivalist writings, see J. Nye Jr., *Bound to Lead: The Changing Nature of American Power* (New York: Basic Books, 1990); and S. Strange, "The Persistent Myth of Lost Hegemony," *International Organization* 41, no. 4 (Autumn 1987), 551–74.

45. On the causes and consequences of Black October 1929, see J.K. Galbraith, *The Great Crash: 1929* (1954; Boston: Houghton Mifflin, 1988).

46. A. Toffler and H. Toffler, *War and Anti-War: Survival at the Dawn of the 21st Century* (Boston: Little, Brown and Company, 1993), 40. See also N. Polmar and T. Allen, *World War II: America at War, 1941–1945* (New York: Random House, 1991).

47. Kindleberger, *World in Depression*.

48. See F. Stone, *Canada, the GATT and the International System* (Montreal: Institute for Research on Public Policy, 1984).

49. Oatley, *International Political Economy*, 20.

50. See F. Block, *The Origins of International Economic Disorder* (Berkeley: University of California Press, 1977). This tariff increase especially angered Ottawa, since Canada and the United States had such a close trading relationship by that time.

51. See, for example, A.A. Kubursi and S. Mansur, "The Political Economy of Middle Eastern Oil," in R. Stubbs and G. Underhill, eds., *Political Economy and the Changing Global Order* (Toronto: McClelland and Stewart, 1994), 313–27, 324. See also D. Yergin, *The Prize: The Epic Quest for Oil, Money and Power* (New York: Simon and Schuster, 1991).

52. See J. Bacher, *Petrotyranny* (New York: Science for Peace, 2000).

International Institutions and Law

We the Peoples of the United Nations, determined to save succeeding generations from the scourge of war ... and to reaffirm faith in fundamental human rights, in the dignity and worth of the human person, in the equal rights of men and women and of nations large and small, and to establish conditions under which justice and respect for the obligations arising from treaties and other sources of international law can be maintained, and to promote social progress and better standards of life in larger freedom ... HAVE RESOLVED TO COMBINE OUR EFFORTS TO ACCOMPLISH THESE AIMS.

—Preamble, The Charter of the United Nations, 1945

The globalization of law is an integral aspect of the globalization of capitalism. The law globalizes rules that facilitate transnational patterns of capital accumulation, attenuating certain regulatory capacities of states, while advancing others.

—A. Claire Cutler[1]

INTRODUCTION

There are many ways of looking at international organizations (IOs) and international law (IL), and there is some truth to all of them. IOs and IL can be seen as the conceptual and regulatory core of the international society of states, as the instrumental arm of what is popularly termed **global governance**. Liberal institutionalists tend to view IOs and international regimes as institutional solutions to anarchy and market failure problems, reducing uncertainty and promoting further cooperation. Realists are rather less enthusiastic about the purpose and prospects of international institutions and law, which they view primarily as vessels or forums for the pursuit of national interests. Realists ascribe little autonomy to IOs, and little causal significance to IL, but certainly recognize the potential of IOs to intervene in conflict situations, and to present both obstacles and opportunities to rational decision makers. Neo-Marxists and Gramscians would argue that important elements of what Marx would call the "superstructure" of the capitalist system—the institutions and ideologies enforcing and justifying the socioeconomic order—can be found at the IO and IL level. Historically, law has protected property, including of course the territorial right to sovereignty held by states (or by those elites who determine the national interest for states). At the same time, however, many constructivists and feminists see the UN (United Nations) and IL as possible conduits for serious reforms toward a more equitable world order, instruments for enhancing the observation of human rights standards, and the global redistribution of wealth. Constructivists argue that by participating in IOs such as the European Union (EU) or African Union (AU), states slowly change their own self-identities, and thus their estimation of self-interest in the process.

Taken together, the study of IOs, IL, and other forms of multilateral cooperation is increasingly referred to as *global governance*. Of course, this term does not refer to an extant, or even the future existence, of a world government, but to efforts to manage global problems with decentralized yet coordinated political authority and regulation. However, the subfield of international organization still revolves largely around what Jack Plano and Roy Olton term a "formal arrangement transcending national boundaries that provides for the establishment of institutional machinery to facilitate cooperation among members in security, economic, social or related fields."[2] Generally, two types of IOs exist: **intergovernmental organizations (IGOs)** and non-governmental organizations (NGOs).

All IGOs share a number of characteristics. First, they are composed of states and only states (although in some cases non-state actors may be represented, or have "observer" status). Second, IGOs are created by treaties between states and, therefore, have legal standing under IL; they have, for example, the right to immunity from jurisdiction of state courts for acts and activities performed by the organization. Third, they hold regular meetings attended by delegates from member states. Those delegates represent the policies and interests of their respective countries. Fourth, IGOs have permanent headquarters and an executive secretariat that runs the day-to-day activities of the organization. Finally, IGOs have permanent administrative employees who work for the organization and do not represent their governments. Although these international bureaucrats do not renounce their citizenships, they serve the organization, not their respective states. Such organizations have proliferated in number, especially in the 20th century. In 1909, there were 37 IGOs; in 1960, there were 154; in 1987, there were 381; and there are currently more than 400. As we will see, these organizations perform a wide variety of functions in the international system, and states have increasingly interacted and cooperated with each other through the mechanisms provided by IGOs. In addition, such institutions are vital to less powerful states, such as Canada, that have many connections to the international diplomatic scene but a limited capacity to influence international events on their own. Many Canadians, such as Lester Pearson, Yves Fortier, Stephen Lewis, Elizabeth Dowdeswell, Douglas Roche,

He really gets around. Secretary-General of the United Nations Ban Ki-Moon speaking while on a visit to the European Council in Brussels. Based in New York, the Secretary-General leads an active diplomatic life, travelling often. (© Peter Cavanagh/Alamy)

Louise Arbour, Maurice Strong, and Louise Fréchette, have played high-profile roles at the United Nations.

It is important to recognize the wide scope of activities in which international organizations engage. The UN, for example, is involved in issue areas as diverse as international and civil war, economic development, technology transfer, gender relations, humanitarian assistance and disaster relief, literacy, pollution abatement, decolonization, human rights and IL, disarmament, important treaties such as the nuclear **Non-Proliferation Treaty,** and significant conferences such as the 2012 London Summit on Family Planning. We have also seen the rise of a particular single actor, the UN **Secretary-General**, from the preconceived role of an international bureaucrat to that of a globetrotting mediator and spokesperson for global issues such as climate change and poverty.

Several types of IGOs exist. The UN is a *multipurpose, universal-membership* organization. It serves many functions and can be joined by all states in the international system, providing the Security Council's permanent members and two-thirds of the General Assembly agree.[3] Importantly, the UN universe includes more than 30 major agencies and programs such as the International Labour Organization (ILO), the **Food and Agriculture Organization (FAO)**, the **UN Educational, Scientific and Cultural Organization (UNESCO)**, the International Maritime Organization (IMO), the **UN Conference on Trade and Development (UNCTAD)**, the **UN Development Programme (UNDP)**, the International Research and Training Institute for the Advancement of Women, the UN Population Fund, the UN Office for the Coordination of Humanitarian Affairs, the International Civil Aviation Organization, the World Intellectual Property Organization, all of the UN-mandated peacekeeping operations in effect around the globe, UNAIDS, and many others.

Multipurpose, universal-membership organizations may be contrasted with *regional* and *functional* organizations, which manage issues at a regional level or are designed for a specific purpose. In fact, most IGOs fall into the latter category. The most famous regional IGO is the European Union, which was known as the European Community (EC) before 1994; indeed, the EU has coordinated policies to such a degree that it is often called a *supranational* institution. Other multipurpose regional organizations include the **Organization of American States (OAS)**, the African Union (AU), the Association of Southeast Asian Nations (ASEAN), and the **Arab League**. Single-purpose, or functional, regional organizations include the **Asian Development Bank**, the North Atlantic Treaty Organization (NATO), the **Northwest Atlantic Fisheries Organization (NAFO)**, and the Organization of the Petroleum Exporting Countries (OPEC).

Lest we think only the UN has potential global membership, we should keep in mind the existence of open-membership organizations that have single functions, such as the various UN agencies[4] mentioned above, the **International Organization for Migration (IOM)**, and the International Whaling Commission (IWC). Not all states have joined these organizations, but they may apply for membership if they desire—and if they are willing to pay membership fees when accepted.

INTERNATIONAL ORGANIZATIONS AND REGIMES IN HISTORY

Anyone who watches the Olympic Games may be surprised to learn that the Games, originally organized to conduct peaceful athletic competition among Greek city-states, were in effect a very early ancestor of the modern IO.[5] But when we speak of modern, formal IOs and related networks, such as the League of Nations (1919 to 1946) and the current UN system (1945 to present), we are discussing relatively recent developments.

Both the League and the UN were established for two primary reasons. The first was sheer practicality. Once the nation-state system was established and contacts between states expanded, it became clear that governments would have to maintain linkages that facilitated communication and coordination. As economic **interdependence** between states grew, it became necessary to establish new lines of communication and to reduce the probability of unexpected events. Trade relations are very dependent on order, the ability to expect payment for goods, fair treatment in foreign markets, freedom from piracy, and other factors. Secondly, IOs can serve a much broader purpose, such as the establishment or maintenance of world order and peace—this is the official mandate of the UN itself, which was established following the most destructive war in global history. However, we should stress how these rationales complement each other. Simply put, most functional organizations are based on some set of guiding principles (or ideals), but their creation is also necessitated by the practical circumstances surrounding them. For example, two early IOs still in operation today are the **International Telecommunication Union (ITU)** (1865) and the **Universal Postal Union (UPU)** (1874), both created for rather specific purposes (telegraphs and postage between nations).[6] Another early IO with a clear functional purpose was the **International Office of Weights and Measures**, established in 1875. Yet behind this functional cooperation was a belief, held by participating government and industry representatives, that telegrams, mail, and common measurement standards were good for business, if not for world peace itself. Liberal values on international political economy, as discussed in the previous chapter, surface again here: increased trade and communication is assumed by many to be the best path toward a peaceful international system, and IOs provide the regulatory standards and predictability that trade and communication systems require.

It is tempting to conclude that IOs provide a wide range of functions similar to those of domestic governments. In many respects this is true, but ultimately IOs operate under the cardinal principles of state sovereignty. The extent to which states are willing to sacrifice some sovereignty in return for the benefits of increased cooperation through institutions is one of the most fascinating debates in global politics and a subject of intense debate in many states. For example, there is considerable concern in many European countries that governments are ceding too much authority to the institutions of the EU, which lack democratic accountability to the people. IL can also be seen as providing a similar range of functions as domestic law. IL, which we examine later in this chapter, evolved alongside international institutions, though it has a much more complex history predating the contemporary era. International treaty law is especially important, since it often establishes the legality of IOs themselves.

THE LEAGUE OF NATIONS

As discussed in Chapter 2, the **League of Nations** was created at the end of World War I, inspired by idealism and the associated hope for a world free from war. Two basic principles underlay the League's system of peace maintenance. First, members agreed to respect and preserve the territorial integrity and political independence of other states. Second, any war or threat of war was considered a matter of concern to the entire League. While the major emphasis of the League's Covenant was on maintaining international peace and stability, some recognition was also given to promoting economic and social cooperation. The Covenant did not provide any special machinery for overseeing these efforts, though a commitment was included for the establishment of one or more organizations to secure "fair and humane conditions of labor for men, women and children" (Article 23), and an autonomous International

Labor Office (ILO) was established as part of the **Treaty of Versailles** (the ILO is still in existence as the International Labour Organization).

League organization centred around three major organs: the Assembly, to which all member-states belonged; the Council, to which a select few belonged; and the Secretariat. The League also established a Permanent Court of International Justice in 1921 to resolve disputes between members of the international community. From the outset the Permanent Court's role was not considered of primary importance, mirroring the present International Court of Justice in the UN system, which retains some symbolic significance but is not a decisive factor in world affairs. The League Assembly and the Council were the two main deliberative organs of the League. In both organs, each member-state possessed one vote. The Assembly was primarily responsible for discussing important issues confronting either individual members of the League or the international community as a whole. The Council was primarily responsible for discussing the maintenance of peace. Originally, the Council was to be composed of five permanent and four elected members. However, despite the fact that U.S. President Woodrow Wilson was the primary champion of the League, the United States never joined the organization (the U.S. Senate did not ratify the Treaty of Versailles, preferring its old isolationist foreign policy). As a result, Great Britain, Italy, Japan, and France were the original permanent members. Germany was given Permanent Council status on its admission to the League in 1926, and the Soviet Union was given the same status in 1934. Germany and Japan would eventually withdraw from the League, and the Soviet Union was expelled in 1939 for its invasion of Finland.

Despite the failure of the League to prevent war, the operations of the Secretariat, which was charged with administrative duties, were widely regarded as a success. As Egon Ranshofen-Wertheimer has observed, "The League has shown that it is possible to establish an integrated body of international officials, loyal to the international agency and ready to discharge faithfully the international obligations incumbent upon them. It was not for lack of executive efficiency that the League system failed."[7] Beyond this administrative precedent, the League of Nations established or incorporated bureaus and committees dealing with disease, communications, traffic in arms, slavery, drugs, labour, women, and children. In 1925, it played an important role in bringing about the peaceful resolution of the Greek–Bulgarian border dispute. By 1921, 48 members had joined the League and by mid-1929, 46 states had ratified the 1928 Kellogg–Briand Pact, in theory committing signatories to the peaceful settlement of disputes. The League considered 66 disputes and conflicts between 1920 and 1939, and in 35 of them, it was able to contribute to a peaceful resolution. The League was linked to several semi-autonomous organizations, such as the Economic and Financial Organization, the Health Organization, the Organizations for Communications and Transit, the High Commissioner for Refugees, and the Intergovernmental Committees on the Drug Traffic, Traffic in Women, the Protection of Children, and Intellectual Co-operation. Nevertheless, despite the Wilsonian idealism that surrounded the formation of the League, its "primary purpose, like that of the Concert of Europe, was to assist in the management of a multipolar balance of power, not to replace it with a universal system."[8]

Unfortunately, the League's ability to alleviate serious disputes was limited. As discussed in Chapter 2, when the Japanese launched a series of attacks against Manchuria in 1931, some Council members, including Great Britain and France, were unwilling to apply economic and military sanctions, which seriously undermined the League's ability and willingness to discourage members of the international community from resorting to arms to achieve their objectives. Another serious blow to the League's credibility came in 1935, when the League was unable to deter Italy's invasion of Ethiopia, although the economic sanctions imposed on Italy were the first on behalf of the international community, setting an important precedent for the use of economic sanctions by the UN.

Several reasons have been advanced for the League's demise. Some attribute it to the absence of the United States and, during shorter periods, to the absence of the Soviet Union and Germany (this lack of leadership helped give rise to theories about hegemonic stability discussed in previous chapters). Its collapse can be linked to the inherent deficiencies of its Covenant, including Article 5, requiring unanimity on all major Assembly and Council decisions. Yet, in the critical tests, such as Japan and Ethiopia, it appeared to be the lack of political will among the members of the League, rather than the available machinery, that was primarily responsible for the League's failings. Finally, the aggressive foreign policies of the Axis powers made a successful League impossible. The League of Nations, reduced to insignificance by the cataclysm of World War II, was officially disbanded in April 1946. Realists often cite the demise of the League as evidence of the inherent limitations of international institutions and international law in an anarchic world.

THE UNITED NATIONS ORGANIZATION

Plans to create the UN began during World War II. The term *United Nations* originated in the Washington Declaration of 1942 in which 26 allied countries pledged to fight Germany, Japan, and Italy; before that, the Declaration of Principles (the **Atlantic Charter**) expressed similar concerns. By October 1943, the governments of the United States, Great Britain, the Soviet Union, and China were prepared to issue a clear statement of their intention to establish a general IO. That year, further steps were taken to create several agencies that would eventually fall under the auspices of the UN or that would come to be closely associated with it. The FAO would be established in 1945, and, as a result of the Bretton Woods conference in 1944, the IMF and the IBRD were created. At the Dumbarton Oaks Conference of August 21, 1944, representatives from the United States, Great Britain, and the U.S.S.R. (China participated in the second phase of negotiations) began to map out a blueprint for a new world body. At the famous **Yalta Conference** of February 1945, progress was made on filling several of the technical gaps that remained open at Dumbarton Oaks. Two more important conferences took place before the organization was officially born. In February and March 1945, representatives from the United States and its Latin American allies met in Mexico City to discuss their plans for a general IO. At the same time, a committee of jurists representing virtually all the states that would attend the San Francisco conference met in Washington to discuss the creation of an International Court of Justice (ICJ), which would replace the Permanent Court of International Justice established under the League of Nations.

Inis Claude argues that it was important to begin discussing plans for the creation of the United Nations before the end of war for two main reasons. First, as former U.S. Secretary of State Cordell Hull pointed out, if negotiations for an IO had been left to the end of the war, it would have been much more difficult to reach a consensus on how to create the organization, since politicians would be too preoccupied with political, economic, and social issues at home. Second, it was extremely important to avoid creating an unnecessarily close relationship between the UN and the peace settlement. In other words, the founders of the UN did not want it to appear as if the rights and obligations contained in the UN Charter were being imposed on states as part of the peace settlement, which appeared to be the case with the League. Rather, the UN was to be created expressly for "all peace loving nations," which

Canadian delegation to the United Nations conference in London, January 1946. Vincent Massey, Canadian High Commissioner to the United Kingdom (left), stands next to Minister of Justice Louis St. Laurent, Secretary of State Paul Martin Sr., and Associate Under-Secretary of State for External Affairs Hume Wrong. (CP PHOTO)

opened up the possibility of accepting bids by postwar Germany and Japan to join in the hope of bringing about lasting peace.[9]

In addition, it is important not to dismiss the psychological and political factors motivating diplomats from countries such as Canada to support the creation of the UN. Canadians, for example, believed that—in contradistinction to the League of Nations experience—the United States had to be engaged in postwar affairs, and saw the UN as a means to ensure this. Yet a close reading of the UN Charter indicates that although this document is approximately four times longer than the League's Covenant, it nonetheless contains many of the same features. Not unlike the Covenant, the Charter refers to the principal organs of the UN and the functions each should perform. Moreover, it clearly sets out the primary purpose of the UN, the maintenance of international peace and security, and how this commitment can be fulfilled. Furthermore, like the Covenant, the Charter emphasizes the inherent responsibility of all member states to deter aggression.

The climactic event in the long and arduous process of building a new IO took place in San Francisco in the spring of 1945. Representatives from 50 nations deliberated for two months before they could agree on the final version of the UN Charter. On June 26, 1945, the Charter was signed, but it was not until January 10, 1946, that the first session of the General Assembly was held in London. Eventually, UN headquarters would be moved to its permanent home in New York City, a building now easily recognized around the world (see Profile 5.1). Although initial hopes for the organization were high (especially in Canada), the superpower confrontation effectively paralyzed the UN's capacity to mount collective security efforts. This incapacity did not mean that the UN was inactive. On the contrary, the UN performed many other crucial functions, most prominently in the process of decolonization, peacekeeping, and aid and development.

The UN has six principal organs (see Figure 5.1). At its heart is the **General Assembly** (GA), a forum in which all states can send representatives to sit in session, present opinions, and vote on resolutions, which need a two-thirds majority to pass (see Profile 5.2). Resolutions passed by the GA are non-binding recommendations and the Assembly cannot force UN members to comply with them; however, since those resolutions are considered by many to carry the weight of world opinion, they remain significant. The GA also makes key decisions regarding who gets to join the organization, what the Economic and Social Council (ECOSOC) does, and the spending powers of the organization. The GA has exclusive authority over the budget of the UN and elections to the Security Council and ECOSOC, but needs a recommendation from the Security Council to take action on the appointment of the Secretary-General, UN membership, and amendments to the Charter. The Assembly and Security Council are jointly responsible for electing the judges of the International Court of Justice (ICJ).

The **Security Council**'s five permanent members are the People's Republic of China, France, the Russian Federation, the United Kingdom, and the United States. Each of these

PROFILE 5.1　Locating the United Nations

What if you had built a world organization on which a new global order was to be based but didn't know where to put it? Locating the UN was, in fact, one of the first problems faced by the organization. This issue was obviously important in 1945 since it was initially believed that a truly global organization should not be located anywhere closely affiliated with a major power, such as in Washington or Moscow, and it would be unsafe to locate it in an unstable state where political authority itself was contested, such as in China or soon-to-be-independent India. In all probability, the idea of locating the UN in a Southern state was never taken seriously; the first southern hemisphere location of a UN agency was in Nairobi, Kenya, and this was the headquarters of the UN Environment Programme established in the early 1970s. Germany, Japan, and Italy were (of course) out of the question as hosts of the new UN, as was any truly neutral place, such as the inaccessible Antarctic. The Swiss, hosts to the League of Nations and the first temporary location of the General Assembly of the UN, were reluctant to assume the responsibility of long-term UN involvement; they refused to host a UN capable of making decisions related to the use of force, which is of course precisely what Chapter 7 of the UN Charter authorizes the Security Council to do. (Switzerland joined the UN in 2002 and hosts many UN agencies.) Europe was in a state of financial chaos and most of its capital cities were literally in physical ruin. The only country in a position of relative economic strength was the United States, and it was the American philanthropist John Davison Rockefeller Jr. who supplied the initial capital for the UN building site in New York City. However, most specialized agencies and Conventions have Secretariats in other world cities, such as Geneva, Vienna, Rome, Paris, Nairobi, and Montreal.

states has a veto over any substantive matter that comes before the Council. There are also ten non-permanent members (originally there were six), elected by the General Assembly in accordance with an agreed-upon geographical formula for two-year terms. A substantive matter (as opposed to a procedural one) requires nine positive votes and the absence of a veto to pass in the Council. The resolutions passed by the Security Council are considered binding on UN members. The Council meets whenever the Secretary-General decides a matter has come up that demands its attention. Simultaneous translation allows it to operate in six official languages: Arabic, Chinese, English, French, Spanish, and Russian. Sydney Bailey and Sam Davis write that one diplomat, Victor Andres Belaunde of Peru, "used to choose a language to suit his mood: French when he wanted to be precise, English when he wanted to understate, Spanish when he wanted to exaggerate."[10] The Security Council is still the primary organ dealing with questions of international peace and security, and in particular collective security, a concept embraced originally by the UN's founders despite its apparent failure during the interwar period (see Profile 5.3 on page 171). Canada has been elected six times to a non-permanent seat on the Security Council: 1948 to 1949, 1958 to 1959, 1967 to 1968, 1977 to 1978, 1989 to 1990, and 1999 to 2000. Canada's bid for election to the Security Council in 2010 failed, sparking a national debate on the direction of Canadian domestic and foreign policy.

The **Economic and Social Council (ECOSOC)** comprises 54 members elected by the General Assembly for a term of three years. ECOSOC has established several regional and functional commissions and other bodies, considers general policy questions regarding economic and social development, and makes recommendations. The **Trusteeship Council** was set up to help

Figure 5.1 The United Nations System

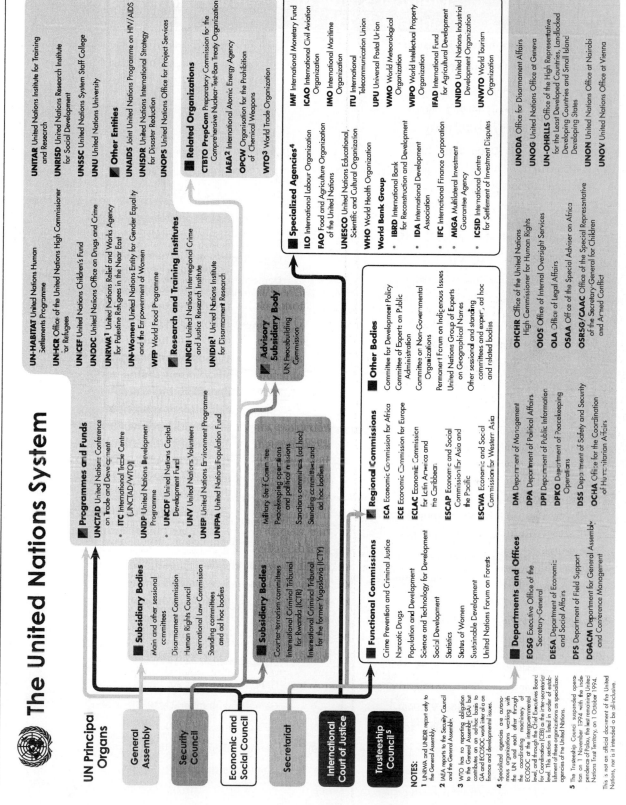

The United Nations System

UN Principal Organs

General Assembly

Security Council

Economic and Social Council

International Court of Justice

Trusteeship Council[5]

NOTES:

[1] UNRWA and UNIDIR report only to the General Assembly.

[2] IAEA reports to the Security Council and the General Assembly.

[3] WTO has no reporting obligation to the General Assembly (GA) but contributes on an ad-hoc basis to GA and ECOSOC work inter alia on finance and developmental issues.

[4] Specialized agencies are autonomous organizations working with the UN and each other through the coordinating machinery of ECOSOC at the intergovernmental level, and through the Chief Executives Board for Coordination (CEB) at the inter-secretariat level. This section is listed in order of establishment of these organizations as specialized agencies of the United Nations.

[5] The Trusteeship Council suspended operation on 1 November 1994 with the independence of Palau, the last remaining United Nations Trust Territory, on 1 October 1994.

This is not an official document of the United Nations, nor is it intended to be all-inclusive.

■ Programmes and Funds

UNCTAD United Nations Conference on Trade and Development
· **ITC** International Trade Centre (UNCTAD/WTO)
UNDP United Nations Development Programme
· **UNCDF** United Nations Capital Development Fund
· **UNV** United Nations Volunteers
UNEP United Nations Environment Programme
UNFPA United Nations Population Fund

■ Subsidiary Bodies

Main and other sessional committees
Disarmament Commission
Human Rights Council
International Law Commission
Standing committees and ad hoc bodies

■ Subsidiary Bodies

Counter-terrorism committees
International Criminal Tribunal for Rwanda (ICTR)
International Criminal Tribunal for the former Yugoslavia (ICTY)
Military Staff Committee
Peacekeeping operations and political missions
Sanctions committees (ad hoc)
Standing committees and ad hoc bodies

■ Advisory Subsidiary Body

UN Peacebuilding Commission

■ Functional Commissions

Crime Prevention and Criminal Justice
Narcotic Drugs
Population and Development
Science and Technology for Development
Social Development
Statistics
Status of Women
Sustainable Development
United Nations Forum on Forests

■ Regional Commissions

ECA Economic Commission for Africa
ECE Economic Commission for Europe
ECLAC Economic Commission for Latin America and the Caribbean
ESCAP Economic and Social Commission for Asia and the Pacific
ESCWA Economic and Social Commission for Western Asia

■ Other Bodies

Committee for Development Policy
Committee of Experts on Public Administration
Committee on Non-Governmental Organizations
Permanent Forum on Indigenous Issues
United Nations Group of Experts on Geographical Names
Other sessional and standing committees and expert, ad hoc and related bodies

■ Departments and Offices

EOSG Executive Office of the Secretary-General
DESA Department of Economic and Social Affairs
DFS Department of Field Support
DGACM Department for General Assembly and Conference Management
DM Department of Management
DPA Department of Political Affairs
DPI Department of Public Information
DPKO Department of Peacekeeping Operations
DSS Department of Safety and Security
OCHA Office for the Coordination of Humanitarian Affairs
OHCHR Office of the United Nations High Commissioner for Human Rights
OIOS Office of Internal Oversight Services
OLA Office of Legal Affairs
OSAA Office of the Special Adviser on Africa
OSRSG/CAAC Office of the Special Representative of the Secretary-General for Children and Armed Conflict
UNODA Office for Disarmament Affairs
UNOG United Nations Office at Geneva
UN-OHRLLS Office of the High Representative for the Least Developed Countries, Landlocked Developing Countries and Small Island Developing States
UNON United Nations Office at Nairobi
UNOV United Nations Office at Vienna

UN-HABITAT United Nations Human Settlements Programme
UNHCR Office of the United Nations High Commissioner for Refugees
UNICEF United Nations Children's Fund
UNODC United Nations Office on Drugs and Crime
UNRWA[1] United Nations Relief and Works Agency for Palestine Refugees in the Near East
UN-Women United Nations Entity for Gender Equality and the Empowerment of Women
WFP World Food Programme

■ Research and Training Institutes

UNICRI United Nations Interregional Crime and Justice Research Institute
UNIDIR[1] United Nations Institute for Disarmament Research
UNITAR United Nations Institute for Training and Research
UNRISD United Nations Research Institute for Social Development
UNSSC United Nations System Staff College
UNU United Nations University

■ Other Entities

UNAIDS Joint United Nations Programme on HIV/AIDS
UNISDR United Nations International Strategy for Disaster Reduction
UNOPS United Nations Office for Project Services

■ Related Organizations

CTBTO PrepCom Preparatory Commission for the Comprehensive Nuclear-Test-Ban Treaty Organization
IAEA[2] International Atomic Energy Agency
OPCW Organisation for the Prohibition of Chemical Weapons
WTO[3] World Trade Organization

■ Specialized Agencies[4]

ILO International Labour Organization
FAO Food and Agriculture Organization of the United Nations
UNESCO United Nations Educational, Scientific and Cultural Organization
WHO World Health Organization
World Bank Group
· **IBRD** International Bank for Reconstruction and Development
· **IDA** International Development Association
· **IFC** International Finance Corporation
· **MIGA** Multilateral Investment Guarantee Agency
· **ICSID** International Centre for Settlement of Investment Disputes
IMF International Monetary Fund
ICAO International Civil Aviation Organization
IMO International Maritime Organization
ITU International Telecommunication Union
UPU Universal Postal Union
WMO World Meteorological Organization
WIPO World Intellectual Property Organization
IFAD International Fund for Agricultural Development
UNIDO United Nations Industrial Development Organization
UNWTO World Tourism Organization

PROFILE 5.2 — Member States of the United Nations as of January 2013

MEMBER (DATE OF ADMISSION)

Afghanistan (November 19, 1946)

Albania (December 14, 1955)

Algeria (October 8, 1962)

Andorra (July 28, 1993)

Angola (December 1, 1976)

Antigua and Barbuda (November 11, 1981)

Argentina (October 24, 1945)

Armenia (March 2, 1992)

Australia (November 1, 1945)

Austria (December 14, 1955)

Azerbaijan (March 9, 1992)

Bahamas (September 18, 1973)

Bahrain (September 21, 1971)

Bangladesh (September 17, 1974)

Barbados (December 9, 1966)

Belarus (October 24, 1945)

Belgium (December 27, 1945)

Belize (September 25, 1981)

Benin (September 20, 1960)

Bhutan (September 21, 1971)

Bolivia (November 14, 1945)

Bosnia and Herzegovina (May 22, 1992)

Botswana (October 17, 1966)

Brazil (October 24, 1945)

Brunei Darussalam (September 21, 1984)

Bulgaria (December 14, 1955)

Burkina Faso (September 20, 1960)

Burundi (September 18, 1962)

Cambodia (December 14, 1955)

Cameroon (September 20, 1960)

Canada (November 9, 1945)

Cape Verde (September 16, 1975)

Central African Republic (September 20, 1960)

Chad (September 20, 1960)

Chile (October 24, 1945)

China (October 24, 1945)

Colombia (November 5, 1945)

Comoros (November 12, 1975)

Congo (September 20, 1960)

Costa Rica (November 2, 1945)

Côte d'Ivoire (September 20, 1960)

Croatia (May 22 1992)

Cuba (October 24, 1945)

Cyprus (September 20, 1960)

Czech Republic (January 19, 1993)

Democratic People's Republic of Korea (September 17, 1991)

Democratic Republic of the Congo (September 20, 1960)

Denmark (October 24, 1945)

Djibouti (September 20, 1977)

Dominica (December 18, 1978)

Dominican Republic (October 24, 1945)

Ecuador (December 21, 1945)

Egypt (October 24, 1945)

El Salvador (October 24, 1945)

Equatorial Guinea (November 12, 1968)

Eritrea (May 28 1993)

Estonia (September 17, 1991)

Ethiopia (November 13, 1945)

Fiji (October 13, 1970)

Finland (December 14, 1955)

Former Yugoslav Republic of Macedonia (April 8, 1993)

France (October 24, 1945)

Gabon (September 20, 1960)

Gambia (September 21, 1965)

Georgia (July 31, 1992)

Germany (September 18, 1973)

Ghana (March 8, 1957)

(continued)

| PROFILE 5.2 | **Member States of the United Nations as of January 2013 (*continued*)** |

Greece (October 25, 1945)

Grenada (September 17, 1974)

Guatemala (November 21, 1945)

Guinea (December 12, 1958)

Guinea-Bissau (September 17, 1974)

Guyana (September 20, 1966)

Haiti (October 24, 1945)

Honduras (December 17, 1945)

Hungary (December 14, 1955)

Iceland (November 19, 1946)

India (October 30, 1945)

Indonesia (September 28, 1950)

Iraq (December 21, 1945)

Ireland (December 14, 1955)

Islamic Republic of Iran (October 24, 1945)

Israel (May 11, 1949)

Italy (December 14, 1955)

Jamaica (September 18, 1962)

Japan (December 18, 1956)

Jordan (December 14, 1955)

Kazakhstan (March 2, 1992)

Kenya (December 16, 1963)

Kiribati (September 14, 1999)

Kuwait (May 14, 1963)

Kyrgyzstan (March 2, 1992)

Lao People's Democratic Republic (December 14, 1955)

Latvia (September 17, 1991)

Lebanon (October 24, 1945)

Lesotho (October 17, 1966)

Liberia (November 2, 1945)

Libyan Arab Jamahiriya (December 14, 1955)

Liechtenstein (September 18, 1990)

Lithuania (September 17, 1991)

Luxembourg (October 24, 1945)

Madagascar (September 20, 1960)

Malawi (December 1, 1964)

Malaysia (September 17, 1957)

Maldives (September 21, 1965)

Mali (September 28, 1960)

Malta (December 1, 1964)

Marshall Islands (September 17, 1991)

Mauritania (October 7, 1961)

Mauritius (April 24, 1968)

Mexico (November 7, 1945)

Micronesia (Federated States of) (September 17, 1991)

Monaco (May 28, 1993)

Mongolia (October 27, 1961)

Montenegro (June 28, 2006)

Morocco (November 12, 1956)

Mozambique (September 16, 1975)

Myanmar (April 19, 1948)

Namibia (April 23, 1990)

Nauru (September 14, 1999)

Nepal (December 14, 1955)

Netherlands (December 10, 1945)

New Zealand (October 24, 1945)

Nicaragua (October 24, 1945)

Niger (September 20, 1960)

Nigeria (October 7, 1960)

Norway (November 27, 1945)

Oman (October 7, 1971)

Pakistan (September 30, 1947)

Palau (December 15, 1994)

Panama (November 13, 1945)

Papua New Guinea (October 10, 1975)

Paraguay (October 24, 1945)

Peru (October 31, 1945)

Philippines (October 24, 1945)

(continued)

PROFILE 5.2 — Member States of the United Nations as of January 2013 (*continued*)

Poland (October 24, 1945)

Portugal (December 14, 1955)

Qatar (September 21, 1971)

Republic of Korea (September 17, 1991)

Republic of Moldova (March 2, 1992)

Romania (December 14, 1955)

Russian Federation (October 24, 1945)

Rwanda (September 18, 1962)

Saint Kitts and Nevis (September 23, 1983)

Saint Lucia (September 18, 1979)

Saint Vincent and the Grenadines (September 16, 1980)

Samoa (December 15, 1976)

San Marino (March 2, 1992)

Sao Tome and Principe (September 16, 1975)

Saudi Arabia (October 24, 1945)

Senegal (September 28, 1960)

Serbia (November 1, 2000)

Seychelles (September 21, 1976)

Sierra Leone (September 27, 1961)

Singapore (September 21, 1965)

Slovakia (January 19, 1993)

Slovenia (May 22, 1992)

Solomon Islands (September 19, 1978)

Somalia (September 20, 1960)

South Africa (November 7, 1945)

South Sudan (July 14, 2011)

Spain (December 14, 1955)

Sri Lanka (December 14, 1955)

Sudan (November 12, 1956)

Suriname (December 4, 1975)

Swaziland (September 24, 1968)

Sweden (November 19, 1946)

Switzerland (September 10, 2002)

Syrian Arab Republic (October 24, 1945)

Tajikistan (March 2, 1992)

Thailand (December 16, 1946)

Timor-Leste (September 27, 2002)

Togo (September 20, 1960)

Tonga (September 14, 1999)

Trinidad and Tobago (September 18, 1962)

Tunisia (November 12, 1956)

Turkey (October 24, 1945)

Turkmenistan (March 2, 1992)

Tuvalu (September 5, 2000)

Uganda (October 25, 1962)

Ukraine (October 24, 1945)

United Arab Emirates (December 9, 1971)

United Kingdom of Great Britain and Northern Ireland (October 24, 1945)

United Republic of Tanzania (December 14, 1961)

United States of America (October 24, 1945)

Uruguay (December 18, 1945)

Uzbekistan (March 2, 1992)

Vanuatu (September 15, 1981)

Venezuela (November 15, 1945)

Viet Nam (September 20, 1977)

Yemen (September 30, 1947)

Zambia (December 1, 1964)

Zimbabwe (August 25, 1980)

manage trust territories after World War II but is no longer an active body. The **Secretariat** is the administrative arm of the organization, comprising the Secretary-General and staff appointed by that person. Staff members are supposed to act as truly international civil servants, discarding any national obligations they may have toward their home state. The Secretariat has been trusted with increasingly important matters since the formation of the UN, and the Secretary-General has participated in, or has had representatives participate in, many diplomatic missions through the "good offices" function. The sixth principal organ of the UN, the **International Court of Justice (ICJ)**, is discussed in our examination of IL later in the chapter.

The demands placed on the UN are quite extraordinary. In addition to its diplomatic and moral role in global politics, the UN and its related program and agencies employ approximately 63 450 people worldwide. The UN deployed over 97 000 uniformed police, military experts, and troops in peacekeeping operations in mid-2012.[11] The Office of the High Commissioner for Human Rights has eleven country offices and seven regional offices. The UN Development Program has a presence in almost 170 countries. Each year, on average, the World Food Program delivers food aid to over 90 million people in 70 countries. However, despite the UN's profile in the world, and despite the wide variety of political, economic, and social functions it performs, the organization operates in a state of permanent financial crisis. The regular budget of the UN for 2012 to 2013 was US$5.15 billion, although adding the separate peacekeeping budget, the expenditures of all funds and programs, and the budgets of the specialized agencies, the entire UN system spends approximately US$15 billion a year (excluding the IMF and the World Bank). Compared to the spending of other institutions the UN budget is remarkably modest. For example, the City of New York planned to spend over US$68 billion in 2012.[12]

The money in the UN regular budget is paid to the UN in the form of dues from member states (peacekeeping costs are assessed separately). The UN is often in financial crisis because many members fail to pay their dues. During the 1990s, the biggest debtor was the United States, although it has paid up much of its debt—after prolonged negotiations. The Americans argued that the mechanism used to determine dues was unfair. Member states are expected to contribute a certain percentage of the UN budget based on the size of their gross national product (GNP). As a result, because the United States had typically generated about a third to

---

PROFILE 5.3 Collective Security and the UN

Collective security is a system of international order in which all states respect recognized territorial boundaries and in which aggression by any state is met by a collective response. In other words, an attack on one will be considered an attack on all and dealt with accordingly. This ideal differs from collective defence systems, which are traditional alliances aimed at potential aggressors outside the membership of the alliance. Though both the League of Nations and the UN are based on formal collective security arrangements, the concept remains an unrealized ideal. The UN rarely exercised its collective security provisions during the Cold War, due to the use (or threatened use) of the veto. It came close to doing so in the Korean War, but the Soviet Union was absent from the Security Council vote on Korea. Some argue that the response to Iraq's invasion of Kuwait in 1990 to 1991 was an instance of collective security in action; others insist it was merely an example of American-orchestrated power. NATO chose to avoid the Security Council altogether when it launched its air war over Serbia in 1999, aware that the Russians and Chinese would most likely veto military action; and the United States did not seek final Security Council authorization before it and the United Kingdom launched the invasion of Iraq in 2003. The Security Council did approve the international intervention in the Libyan Civil War in 2011, although Russia and China would later claim that the NATO–led coalition had overstepped its mandate by actively supporting the overthrow of the Gaddafi government, and would go on to veto strong action on Syria in the summer of 2012.

a quarter of world GNP, it was expected to pay much more than other states. However, with the increased growth in the economies of Europe and Japan over the past two decades, the United States argued that it was paying more than its share, and demanded that its contribution be capped at 22 percent. This was agreed to in 1999, and the U.S. began paying back some (though not all) of its dues. Many other countries are also in arrears to the UN. As of October 2011, the UN was owed US$867 million in unpaid dues to the regular budget and US$4.3 billion in unpaid dues to all budgets (including the regular and peacekeeping budgets).[13] In addition, over the past few decades the United States has on occasion unilaterally withdrawn funding for various agencies, such as the United Nations Population Fund, which promotes family planning and contraception. Given the enormous responsibilities and tasks the UN is assigned by its member states, it is a source of great shame and frustration for UN advocates around the world that inadequate funding continues to plague the organization.

The UN has also been criticized for being unrepresentative, with the composition of the Security Council reflecting the old distribution of power and excluding important countries (especially Japan, Germany, Brazil, and India), and for being overly bureaucratic. In recent decades there has been much discussion of UN reform. Some substantive developments include the creation in 2005 of a Peacebuilding Commission and a Peacebuilding Fund to increase the ability of the UN to engage in post-conflict reconstruction. In 2006, the UN Security Council passed resolution 1674 on the Protection of Civilians in Armed Conflict, for the first time affirming the "Responsibility to Protect" doctrine (see Chapter 7).[14] A Human Rights Council was created in 2006 (replacing the Human Rights Commission) in order to strengthen the UN's role in monitoring and promoting human rights. A Department of Field Support was created in 2007 to enhance the ability of the UN system to provide logistics assistance to peacekeeping and other UN missions. Many other reforms were made to UN structures, procedures, and programs. However, the solution to the major issue of reforming the UN Security Council has proven elusive.

Ultimately, the UN can be only as effective as its members want it to be. National interests, concerns over protecting sovereignty, and economic and political disputes between states continue to plague the United Nations. Indeed, many political leaders (often from lower-income states) want to avoid a stronger UN; they are concerned that the UN might become an instrument used by rich states to dominate or intimidate others. A vocal domestic anti–UN political current has also marked the American approach to the UN, and this was especially evident during the George W. Bush administration. However, contrary to the conspiratorial allegations of some individuals and groups, the UN is nowhere close to becoming a world government with any substantive supranational authority, though myths of "UN hegemony" (and even a UN army) persist.

For the most part, smaller states such as Canada tend to be supportive of the UN, showing generally consistent dedication to paying their dues and contributing to peacekeeping missions.[15] Many countries view the UN as the cornerstone of an international legal system, and Security Council authorization is often seen as the most important form of legitimation for collective security–related military operations. However, a large rift has grown between theory and practice, since neither NATO's attack on Serbia in 1999 nor the "coalition" invasion of Iraq in 2003 were given explicit Security Council approval. Nonetheless, the UN and its agencies perform so many valuable functions the organization can make an excellent case for its relevance and value.[16] In the end the UN does what its members allow it to do, and the political will and resource capacity of its members establishes its limitations.

NON–UN IGOS

The UN, of course, is not the only IGO in the international system. Arguably, the most advanced supranational institution is the European Union: it can be seen as an ongoing experiment in political integration, challenging many aspects of the sovereign statehood that have long characterized the European system. The EU is a much more demanding institution than the UN, since it has more regulatory and legal powers within member states. But there are other IGOs of great significance as well. While space does not permit an exhaustive survey, here is an overview of some other prominent IGOs.

- *The North Atlantic Treaty Organization.* NATO (also informally called the *Atlantic Alliance*) was established in 1949 to deter a Soviet invasion of Western Europe and to solidify American leadership (Canada was a founding member.) After the Cold War, NATO adopted a New Strategic Concept, which reduced its standing military forces and created a force structure oriented toward crisis response. NATO has established close relationships with other European institutions and was actively involved in peace-keeping operations in the former Yugoslavia in the 1990s. In a controversial action, NATO embarked on a bombing campaign against Serbia in 1999 in response to human rights abuses in the Serbian province of Kosovo. In 2003, NATO took over responsibility for the International Security Assistance Force (ISAF) in Afghanistan, a mission that has caused controversy among and within member states. In 2011, NATO assumed operational control of the intervention in the Libyan Civil War. NATO has grown since the end of the Cold War: Poland, Hungary, and the Czech Republic joined in 1999 and seven more countries—Bulgaria, Estonia, Latvia, Lithuania, Romania, Slovakia, and Slovenia—joined in 2004. In 2009, Albania and Croatia joined the Alliance, bringing NATO membership to 28 states. NATO's headquarters are in Brussels, Belgium.

- *The Commonwealth.* The origins of the Commonwealth lie in the British Empire. World War I, the adoption of the famous Balfour Declaration at the 1926 Imperial Conference, and the institution's formal creation in 1931 under the Statute of Westminster were the defining events in the formation of the Commonwealth and the independence of its early members (which included Canada and Newfoundland). The Commonwealth expanded during the decolonization era, though South Africa was expelled, and in 1965 a Secretariat was established. A major issue facing the Commonwealth during the Cold War was the apartheid regime in South Africa; its eventual collapse led to the readmission of South Africa in 1994. Today, human rights, democracy, and good governance are the major concerns of the Commonwealth (see Profile 5.4), which now has a membership of 54 states. The organization has suspended several members in the recent past, usually for a failure to meet standards of democratic rule; Zimbabwe withdrew in late 2003, and Fiji was suspended in 2009. Another important cultural and diplomatic organization, with ties to Canada's French colonial past, is La Francophonie.

- *The Organization of American States.* According to its own literature, the OAS is the oldest regional intergovernmental organization in the world, with its origins in the 1826 Congress of Panama. The Charter of the present OAS was signed in 1948 and entered into force in 1951. The OAS has a troubled history, both because of the political instability of Central and South America and because of the disturbing tendency of the United States to engage in unilateral action (including invasions and interventions)

PROFILE 5.4 Membership in the Commonwealth

The 54 Commonwealth states have an estimated 1.7 billion citizens. Members are listed below:

Antigua & Barbuda	Kiribati	Singapore
Australia	Lesotho	Solomon Islands
Bangladesh	Malawi	South Africa
Barbados	Malaysia	Sri Lanka
Belize	Maldives	St Kitts & Nevis
Botswana	Malta	St Lucia
Brunei Darussalam	Mauritius	St Vincent & the Grenadines
Cameroon	Mozambique	Swaziland
Canada	Namibia	Tanzania (United Republic of)
Cyprus	Nauru	The Bahamas
Dominica	New Zealand	The Gambia
Fiji Islands (suspended)	Nigeria	Tonga
Ghana	Pakistan	Trinidad & Tobago
Grenada	Papua New Guinea	Tuvalu
Guyana	Rwanda	Uganda
India	Samoa	United Kingdom
Jamaica	Seychelles	Vanuatu
Kenya	Sierra Leone	Zambia

in the region. As a result, the OAS has been frequently maligned as ineffective and dominated by Washington. Today, the principal activities of the OAS are focused on democratic values, trade, and economic development. The OAS has also played a minor role in political oversight and mediation, frequently deploying election observers and negotiating teams. The OAS had 35 members in 2012 (Canada joined in 1990) and is headquartered in Washington, D.C.

- *The African Union.* In 2002, the 54-member AU was established from the foundations of the Organization of African Unity (OAU), which had failed to respond to the crises in Rwanda, the Congo, and Somalia. The AU vision is to strengthen cooperation on African security affairs, trade, development, and corruption. Notably, it explicitly recognizes the right to humanitarian intervention. The AU deployed peacekeeping missions in Burundi and Darfur in 2003 (the latter in cooperation with the UN), in Somalia in 2007, and in Mail in 2013. An AU force restored stability to the Comoros in 2008. The AU oversees the New Partnership for Africa's Development (NEPAD), which establishes partnerships with industrialized countries to increase the economic development of Africa. However, the AU is beset with problems familiar to many international organizations. It relies on consensus of its members in order to act, and this has weakened the organization's ability to respond to human rights problems in Africa, such as the governance of Zimbabwe and continued violence in the Sudanese region.

The finances of the AU are beset by problems of unpaid dues and heavy dependence on funding from non-African (mainly Western) states.

NON-GOVERNMENTAL ORGANIZATIONS

In Chapter 4, we mentioned the growing importance of non-state actors in world affairs. An important distinction must be made between multinational corporations (MNCs) and international Non-governmental Organizations (NGOs), which are sometimes referred to as "INGOs." MNCs are profit-generating businesses with operations in more than one country. NGOs are not-for-profit organizations of individuals dedicated to a particular cause and/or representing particular social movements. In this chapter we focus on NGOs, but private-sector actors are obviously heavily involved in global politics and global governance efforts. Indeed, James Rosenau has written of the "bifurcation of global structures into the old state-centric world and the relatively ascendant multicentric world, composed of sovereignty-free actors including MNCs, ethnic minorities, subnational governments and bureaucracies, professional societies, and transnational organizations."[17] While we should not forget the significance of MNCs and related organizations such as business and trade associations, the rising influence of NGOs such as Amnesty International, CARE, Friends of the Earth, Médecins sans Frontières, OXFAM, International Rescue Committee, 350.org, and the International Committee of the Red Cross/Red Crescent is viewed as a significant development by liberals and critical theorists alike. Labour unions are increasingly internationalized as well, and are major voices in global activism on working conditions and the rights of labourers, among many other issues. While NGOs may not have the military power or diplomatic resources of states, they do possess an inherent ability to react swiftly, adapt to changing conditions, and use their resources efficiently, all valuable assets in humanitarian and environmental work. NGOs frequently coordinate their efforts with each other and with governments, forming networks for activism and information sharing. The IOs that form the core of state-centric diplomacy, in particular the UN system, often act as channels or conduits between states and the NGO community.

While NGOs may not have access to the same resources as states, they are increasingly important and visible actors in the global system. Most are private organizations, founded by individuals or groups and funded from donations, grants, IGO budgets, or governments. These individuals or groups do not formally represent their states or governments, although they continue to be citizens of states, and many do collaborate extensively with governments. It is impossible to list the wide variety of NGO activities here, but a partial list would include the following:

- *Humanitarian NGOs.* These NGOs undertake aid efforts to assist in the alleviation of human suffering. The **International Committee of the Red Cross (ICRC**, or "Red Crescent" in Muslim societies) provides medical assistance to victims of war and armed conflict. CARE International provides developmental and emergency care to poor peoples and victims of natural disasters and conflicts. Save the Children focuses on alleviating child poverty.

- *Human rights NGOs.* Human rights NGOs monitor and investigate human rights abuses worldwide and put pressure on governments to improve their human rights records or take action against other governments with poor human rights records. The most prominent example is Amnesty International.

- *Corporate lobby groups.* Corporations typically pool their money and expertise to create lobby groups with international reach. Examples include the Trilateral Commission, the European Roundtable of Industrialists, the Canadian Business Council on National Issues, the Davos World Economic Forum, and the International Chamber of Commerce.

- *Scientific and technical organizations.* Scientific and technical NGOs work to increase scientific cooperation, achieve standardization, and promote research and development. Examples include the Council of Scientific Unions, the International Peace Research Institute, and the European Space Agency.

- *Sports bodies.* Sporting organizations manage international sporting events and frequently find themselves involved in global politics, as sport is often employed for political purposes (such as the former ban on South African athletes, or boycotts and protests related to the Olympic Games). The International Olympic Committee (IOC) is the most prominent sports-related NGO.

- *Professional associations.* These exist to promote the interests of their members and interaction among them. Examples include the International Federation of Airline Pilots, the Canadian Aquatic Invasive Species Network, and the International Studies Association (a favourite of many IR scholars!).

- *Environmental groups.* Environmental NGOs promote awareness on environmental issues and often mount protests and publicity campaigns to this end. Well-known environmental NGOs include Greenpeace, 350.org, the International Fund for Animal Welfare, and Friends of the Earth.

- *Women's issues NGOs.* These NGOs exist to promote the political and economic advancement of women. Examples include the parallel Women's Forum of the ECOSOC Commission on the Status of Women, and the Associated Country Women of the World, MADRE, and the Global Fund for Women.

- *Philanthropic organizations.* A large number of trusts and foundations provide grants and sponsor projects on a variety of international issues. Although not strictly international NGOs because they are chartered under the domestic law of one state, organizations such as the Ford Foundation, Rockefeller Foundation, Bill and Melinda Gates Foundation, and the Clinton Global Initiative have supported the NGO community and many global causes.

- *Religious organizations.* A large number of religious NGOs exist, including the Roman Catholic Church and the World Jewish Congress. Multifaith NGOs include the International Association for Religious Freedom and the World Congress of Faiths. They promote religious activities and are often directly involved in transnational political campaigns related to lifestyle and other moral choices.

NGOs perform many functions in global politics: they facilitate communication between interested individuals; act as pressure groups to change government policies; offer information-gathering resources, often when no other reliable source exists; distribute humanitarian aid, services, and knowledge; and play an important role in the formulation of state or IGO policy in cooperation with governments. Indeed, there is a growing tendency toward institutionalized interaction between official multilateral organizations and NGOs with more specific agendas. Such hybrids include the Arctic Council, which is composed of eight Arctic states—Canada, Denmark (for Greenland), Finland, Iceland, Norway, the Russian Federation, Sweden, and the United States—as well as six initial permanent participant groups—the Inuit Circumpolar Conference, the Saami Council, the Russian Association of Indigenous Peoples of the North, the Aleut International Association, the Arctic Athabascan Council, and the Gwich'in Council International. It is not insignificant that these groups have been guaranteed a permanent status on the Council, even if they will have less influence than the formal governments involved. The Council is supposed to be a "high-level permanent intergovernmental forum to provide for co-operation, co-ordination and interaction among the Arctic states, the Arctic indigenous communities and other Arctic inhabitants on common Arctic issues [including] economic and social development, improved health conditions and cultural well-being."[18] In another, somewhat ironic example, even legislators have an NGO, called *Parliamentarians for Global Action.* Here we see the ultimate meshing of the public sector and the nonprofit NGO.

At the UN, NGOs have consultative status in many agencies. As A. LeRoy Bennett writes,

> The most sought-after consultative status is granted by the Economic and Social Council. The breadth of ECOSOC's mandate explains the large number of NGOs that have been granted consultative status, including more than 800 organizations divided into three categories according to the extent of their involvement in ECOSOC's program. … The relationships between United Nations agencies and hundreds of NGOs demonstrate the impossibility of effectively separating public from private organizations.[19]

Bailey and Daws argue that NGOs play an important role within ECOSOC, "so long as they do not try to usurp the functions of governments."[20] Meanwhile, David Keen, who is concerned with refugees' rights, argues that while NGOs can contribute immensely to such UN–related activities as humanitarian relief,

> this trend nevertheless carries risks. It represents a shift in welfare responsibilities away from government-funded bodies in the UN towards organizations largely funded from private contributions. … Linking the welfare of millions with private charity—which is unpredictable and makes planning difficult— seems a poor alternative to establishing an international system in which refugees' rights to welfare are guaranteed by regularized public contributions and clear legal obligations.[21]

Some analysts even suggest that transnational environmental activist groups, such as the World Wildlife Fund, Friends of the Earth, Greenpeace, Conservation International, and Earth Island Institute are formative agents in the development of a new **global civil society,** both as part of and in opposition to the evolution of global governance.[22] A wide variety of NGOs cluster around certain issue areas and coordinate their activities. For example, the annual meeting of the International Whaling Commission habitually attracts representatives from more than 90 NGOs. Similarly, in the political arena, groups such as Amnesty International and Human Rights Watch play a key role in monitoring and exposing violations of human

Marching for fish. Greenpeace members at the 2012 Earth Day celebration in San Diego express their concern for marine conservation. (© ZUMA Press, Inc./Alamy)

rights by governments. A number of NGOs dedicated to human rights issues cooperate under a loose framework known as the social justice movement. Others, such as CARE International, play a constructive role in both long-term and emergency development and relief efforts. And NGOs, domestic and international, have always been the active force behind what has been broadly labelled the **peace movement** in both international and domestic contexts.[23] However, the tendency to equate NGO activity with the broader political concept of global civil society may be criticized as an oversimplification. Some active organizations (such as the U.S.–based National Rifle Association) would not identify themselves as part of this conception of global society, while others (such as racist and hate groups) would reject the very principles upon which the idea of civil society is built.

Throughout the remainder of this text we will refer often to various NGOs that have been involved in global politics. Whether we are on the verge of a new global civil society is highly debatable, but we are undeniably living in an era in which non-state actors have increased their ability to influence the work of governments and IOs alike. According to English school realists, all of these organizations operate in an *anarchical society*, a complicated environment dominated by sovereign states that are loosely bound together with institutions, non-state actors, and a growing set of norms and rules that constitute a social system. We turn next to those formal rules that form the basis of international law.

INTERNATIONAL LAW

Many would argue that IL has its origins in the Roman Empire, when Roman judges settled disputes between persons of different regions with conflicting local customs. Roman law held that no custom was necessarily right—that a higher universal law existed that was inherently fair and would apply to all. This **natural law**, or law of nature, would arise from human reason and nature itself, and it would derive its force from being enacted by a proper authority. This authority, attributed (not surprisingly) to the emperor, was called *majestas,* or sovereign power. Thus the central question of IL remains the achievement of global standards that can be applied within the context of respect for the individualism of different localities and geographic areas of the world (see Profile 5.5). In addition, the international legal system, like the Westphalian state system and the international economic system, resulted from the expansion of the European empires. As a result, Western values and legal concepts dominate IL and are often the source of considerable friction between Western countries and the Islamic and Asian world.

IL is often dismissed as a weak force in world politics because it is based on voluntarism, or states' willingness to commit themselves to its realization, rather than on any physical body capable of enforcing it. Though no legal authority exists that can enforce IL in the same way domestic courts can enforce national laws, as A. LeRoy Bennett writes, an assessment "of the deficiencies of IL may lead erroneously to the conclusion that no legal principles operate across national boundaries, but an inadequate system does not signify the absence of any system."[24] Most scholars of IL accept its inherent weakness (as the price of protecting state sovereignty), but do not dismiss its potential as a unifying and even pacifying force.

PROFILE 5.5 Hugo Grotius (1583–1645)

Grotius was a Dutch jurist and diplomat (in Swedish service). His most famous work, *De jure belli ac pacis (On the Law of War and Peace)*, is regarded as one of the intellectual foundations of IL. Grotian thought offers an alternative perspective on international relations from that of Machiavelli or his English contemporary, Thomas Hobbes. This perspective, referred to as the *Grotian tradition*, seeks to establish order and escape anarchy in the international system through the creation of IL. For Grotius, the origins of IL rested in natural law principles and in treaties and covenants established between states. In addition, Grotian thought recognizes the existence of values and norms that influence the behaviour of states and help to maintain order among them. Grotius believed that IL should be binding on states even in the absence of a central authority to enforce them. In this sense, Grotius was advocating the building of a world as it ought to be, rather than describing the world as it existed.

Four key Grotian ideas have had an enduring legacy in international relations:

1. States should refrain from interference in the internal affairs of others, by not seeking to impose their ideologies (in Grotius's time, Catholicism and Protestantism) on others.

2. A law of nature exists that is higher than human affairs but can be known through reason.

3. Acceptance of the principles of this natural law is the only escape from anarchy.

4. An assembly of nations ought to be created to enforce such laws.

Grotius is recognized as one of the key founders of the constitutive concepts behind IL and IOs. In international relations theory, the Grotian perspective is similar to that of the English School/liberal realists discussed in Chapter 1.

SOURCE: L. VAN SOMEREN, *UMPIRE TO THE NATIONS: HUGO GROTIUS* (LONDON: DENNIS DOBSON, 1965); S. TARZI, "THE ROLE OF NORMS AND REGIMES IN WORLD AFFAIRS: A GROTIAN PERSPECTIVE," *INTERNATIONAL RELATIONS*, VOL. 14, NO. 3 (1998), PG. 71–84.

Formal public international law encompasses the affairs of states, while private international law largely concerns the transactions of companies doing business in the international arena. The latter is the more lucrative for aspiring lawyers, while the former, arguably, has more important implications for global politics. We should further distinguish between the progressive development of IL and the codification of IL. The first aims at developing new law (*lex ferenda*), while codification aims essentially at clarifying existing law (*lex lata*). In practice, a bit of both occurs. Finally, many analysts distinguish between hard law, codified by treaties and enforced by some sort of punishment mechanism, and soft law, which consists mainly of declaratory statements emerging from the GA and elsewhere.

IL is derived from many sources, including treaties, customs, and legal scholarship. Of these, treaties are the most demanding, since they are largely seen to bind states to agreements. Tens of thousands of bilateral and multilateral agreements exist today, a sign of the spread of diplomatic activity as well as faith in IL. Treaties are assumed to be binding on successor governments, no matter how those governments come into power. Many treaties, however, have escape clauses that permit states to withdraw their obligations without penalty, and other clauses that allow disputants to use the International Court of Justice (often referred to as the World Court) to settle arguments over their interpretation.

Arguably, the most important treaty is the Charter of the United Nations, which not only outlines the formal structure of the UN but also enshrines the primacy of the principle of state sovereignty while asserting the need for collective responses to international issues. For example, although states that sign the UN Charter do commit themselves to collective security and in theory surrender some of their sovereign authority to make foreign policy decisions to the greater body called the United Nations, it is the Security Council, consisting of a mere 15 members (five of which, we will recall, have disproportionate power as permanent members with a veto), that ultimately decides when collective security has been breached and when the UN can take action. In addition, in practice many states have not contributed to collective security or peacekeeping efforts by the UN. Participation is largely voluntary, and no system exists to force or compel states to contribute to UN operations. Another example of the protection of sovereignty in the Charter is the contrast between supranational jurisdiction and two conflicting perspectives on the legitimate prosecution of crimes. The territorial principle suggests that courts in the country where the crime is committed should have first crack at prosecution. The nationality principle implies that states can assert their jurisdiction over the conduct of nationals anywhere, including outside their home state.

IL is also derived from **customary law**, which stresses the validity of repeated modes of interaction over time. In what is known as the positivist view, customs that occur over time can be said to constitute some form of law, while natural law or divine law (said to have come from the heavens) is rejected. Customary law has an important psychological element in the sense that it requires "a conviction felt by states that a certain form of conduct is permitted by international law."[25] For example, in the so-called Fisheries Case in the International Court of Justice (*United Kingdom vs. Norway, 1949–51*), the United Kingdom complained that Norway had reserved an exclusive fishing zone for its nationals within a four-mile zone (about 6.5 kilometres) that had been drawn according to several fixed points along the coastline instead of using the configuration of the actual coastline itself. The Court found that Norway had been using this method for decades without any objections by other states and that, therefore, it was permissible under customary IL. The ICJ can also refer to legal scholarship, the judgments of international arbitrational bodies such as itself, as well as the writings of highly respected experts in the field, when arriving at decisions.

If no global police force exists to enforce IL, are there mechanisms at least to encourage compliance? The short answer is yes. States that reject or deliberately disobey IL can be subject to **reprisals**, whereby actions that would have been illegal under IL may be legal if taken in response to the illegal actions of another state. The most extreme example of this action is the outright declaration of war on a state, as was seen when Iraq violated the sovereignty of Kuwait, and the Security Council voted in November 1990 to authorize the use of force against Iraq. (Cuba and Yemen voted against the relevant resolution, and China abstained.) Bilateral or multilateral sanctions can also be applied.[26] In the bilateral case a state will suspend or reduce its customary diplomatic and/or trade relationship with another state, and in the multilateral case a number of states will join to impose sanctions on a target state. As we will see in Chapter 7, the efficacy of sanctions is a hot topic of policy debate. For example, some say sanctions helped change apartheid South Africa, while others (such as former British Prime Minister Margaret Thatcher) argue that South Africa changed despite them. On the other hand, multilateral sanctions will usually have a greater impact on the offending state than will bilateral sanctions. A sanctioned state can, over time, assume the status of a pariah in the world community. Nigeria, Burma, Iraq, Iran, Serbia, Sudan, Zimbabwe, and Libya are examples of states that at one time or another have achieved this dubious distinction. (Libya temporarily rehabilitated itself by renouncing weapons of mass destruction in 2004.) However, the world community does much less when more powerful states violate IL. Russia's activities in Chechnya, China's actions in Tibet, and the American/British invasion of Iraq are all, arguably, violent examples of breaches of global norms without direct legal consequences.

Certain conventions related to international diplomacy also have international legal status. Embassies in foreign states are considered part of the embassy state's territory. As a result, the laws of the embassy state apply there, not the local laws of the land. When Iranian students seized and occupied the American embassy in Iran in 1979 following the Islamic revolution there, it was widely considered a breach of IL. Since host governments are expected to use force to protect the sanctity of embassies, the Iranian government was condemned as an accomplice. Another important convention is the extension of diplomatic immunity to foreign diplomatic staff (though there are some constraints on their right to travel). Because this means the law of the local state does not apply to foreign diplomats, the worst a state can do to a diplomat suspected of engaging in criminal acts is expel that person from the country. This treatment opens up room for espionage activities and can elicit a rather indignant response among the local population.

There are other bodies of IL as well. International criminal law has been defined as a "complex set of norms and conflict-resolving mechanisms adhered to by sovereigns within a particular jurisdictional unit, through agreement or the use of sanctions."[27] As such, it encompasses slavery, terrorism, hijacking, drug trafficking, genocide, piracy, acts against the peace, acts of aggression, and war crimes. International humanitarian law, on the other hand, refers to laws designed specifically to limit the harm to non-combatants during wartime. A great deal of jurisdictional overlap exists between this body of IL and domestic law in most states. This jurisdictional overlap sometimes creates tensions between those advocating prosecution under domestic law and those advocating prosecution under IL. A major development in the realm of international criminal and humanitarian law occurred in 1997 when the Treaty of Rome established the **International Criminal Court (ICC)**. The ICC has the unique ability to prosecute individuals charged with crimes against humanity, and began hearing cases in 2008 (we examine the ICC in more detail in Chapter 9).

Another distinction should be made between international public law (which we have discussed so far) and international private law, which refers to legal contracts between individuals and, more often, firms engaged in trade and investment. The vast majority of international lawyers are in fact employed by MNCs, though they must understand international public law in order to represent their clients. Sometimes, the concerns of private and public IL converge in a single case. For several years, three judges from the United States, three from Iran, and three from other countries met to negotiate the issue of financial compensation following the Iranian revolution in 1979. The Iran–United States Claims Tribunal convened in an unmarked building on the outskirts of The Hague, Netherlands. As Abner Katzman writes, "Despite the backdrop of political bitterness, the daily hearings in the marble and wood-paneled chambers have resolved almost 4000 cases arising from expropriations, the freezing of assets, and broken contracts. That has meant about $2.1 billion (U.S.) for American claimants and about $9 billion to Iranians, with a billion more in interest." The tribunal also facilitated the settlement of a $61.8 million payment the Americans made to Iran after the cruiser USS *Vincennes* shot down an Iran Air A-300 Airbus over the Persian Gulf on July 3, 1988. The Airbus case had been before the ICJ for years before both sides agreed that it would be easier to deal with through the tribunal.[28]

However, this case is by no means typical, since political divisions will often undermine attempts to achieve consensus and healthy compliance levels with IL. The prevalent cynicism about the efficacy of IL is understandable. However, that a body of legal thought and historic precedents pertaining to international relations exists at all is impressive. In a speech to the General Assembly of the UN in New York, the former president of the ICJ, Judge Nagendra Singh, argues we should not be

> mesmerized by the simplistic notion of politics and law as antipoles. On the contrary, the law made by treaties is a law made by political decisions; the law codified in conventions is a law confirming the *opinio juris* of political entities; while the law of custom registers the regularity of State conduct. But in all three the keynotes are balance and reconciliation, tolerance and mutual regard: in a nutshell, the evidence that politics can, and must, transcend the partisan, the provisional, and the parochial.[29]

Others, such as Theodore Couloumbis and James Wolfe, are less sanguine:

> Without worldwide consensus on vital international issues, without central global authorities, without a legislature, without effective courts, given the existence of large autonomous subjects with powerful military establishments, given further the permanent companion of human history called war ... in these circumstances, all that international law can hope to accomplish is to limit violence [and] to substitute for it at times.[30]

The UN has developed a complex network of international legal specialists and governmental representation over the years. Two important bodies are the International Law

Commission, which is an independent body of 34 legal experts who meet once a year in Geneva to work on the codification of existing laws (often taking the advice of the expert NGO International Law Association), and the Sixth Committee of the General Assembly, the Legal Committee. The Legal Committee is filled with governmental representatives who report to the GA on current developments in IL and also draft conventions. Although many other parts to the giant puzzle of contemporary IL exist, the most prominent institution is the International Court of Justice, also known as the World Court.

THE INTERNATIONAL COURT OF JUSTICE

Established in 1946, the ICJ is the principal judicial organ of the UN and meets at the Peace Palace in The Hague, Netherlands. Its 15 judges are elected by separate votes (simple majorities required) in the Security Council and the General Assembly, and they are intended to reflect the world's leading civilizations and judicial systems. The judges serve nine-year terms. Decisions are taken in private by a majority vote, the quorum being nine. Cases are brought before the ICJ voluntarily when both states seek a ruling, but the Court also provides **advisory opinions** at the request of the General Assembly, individual states, or any of the specialized agencies. All members of the UN belong to the Court, although many have opted out of accepting its compulsory jurisdiction (the ability to call states before it at will and enforce decisions). Article 36 of the ICJ Statute says that states may agree in advance to adhere to compulsory jurisdiction. In 1946 the United States made a reservation (known as the Connally Amendment) that asserts the right to exclude disputes believed to fall under domestic jurisdiction, and most states have adopted similar reservations. Thus the ICJ is nothing like a domestic court of law.

Most states have signed the treaty establishing the Court, but only about one-third have signed the Optional Clause, which would give the Court unconditional jurisdiction in certain cases.[31] The United States withdrew from the Optional Clause when it refused to allow the Court's 1986 decision regarding the mining of Nicaraguan harbours to affect its foreign policy. Israel has withdrawn its acceptance of the Optional Clause as well. Canada put forth a reservation over the issue of extending Canadian sovereign jurisdiction in Arctic waters in the early 1970s.[32] However, literally hundreds of bilateral and multilateral treaties contain clauses agreeing that the parties will submit any disputes over terms of the treaty to the ICJ. And the Court has jurisdiction over a number of specialized human rights conventions, including the Convention on Genocide, the Supplementary Convention on the Abolition of Slavery, the Slave Trade and Institutions and Practices Similar to Slavery, the Convention on the Political Rights of Women, the Convention Relating to the Status of Refugees, and the Convention on the Reduction of Statelessness. The ICJ also works in conjunction with other legal bodies. For example, the European Convention for the Protection of Human Rights and Freedoms (1950) allows individuals to petition the European Commission on Human Rights, which may ask the European Court of Human Rights to enforce the relevant UN convention.

In some cases, states employ the ICJ as a mediator. For example, in 1992, El Salvador and Honduras used the Court to settle territorial disputes along six stretches of border, three islands, and territorial waters. The disputes had been one of the causes of a war in 1969. The commonly accepted five-judge panel was headed by a Brazilian, and included judges from El Salvador, Honduras, Britain, and Japan. The Court drew borders in the ruling that gave about two-thirds of the total land to Honduras and split the territorial waters among both countries and Nicaragua, and all the relevant governments pledged to abide by the decision.

The World Court at work. The ICJ convenes on September 8, 2008, to hear charges of harassment and persecution brought by the government of Georgia against the government of Russia. The charges opened up a legal front in the armed conflict between Georgia and Russia over the territories of South Ossetia and Abkhazia in 2008. (AP Photo/Evert-Jan Daniels/ CP Images)

Thus, a potentially violent conflict was avoided by the use of the ICJ. Canada and the United States have similarly used the Court to determine fishing rights off the East Coast.

The Court has also gone beyond its role as mediator and passed commentary. In 1996 it found that the use or threat to use nuclear weapons, which by definition implies mass murder or genocide, is "generally illegal under international law." The Court added that it was impossible to say whether the weapons would be illegal to use in self-defence, however. This hardly challenges the theory of deterrence, which, as we saw in Chapter 3, is based on the idea that nuclear weapons would be used only in self-defence anyway. This opinion was also a non-binding one sought by the General Assembly, and the presiding judge, Mohammed Bedjaoui of Algeria, had to break a 7–7 tie on crucial paragraphs of the ruling. Yet, despite all this ambiguity, many have interpreted the Court's ruling as a strong push toward the negotiation of a Comprehensive Test Ban Treaty, which was signed in 1996. Canada's former disarmament ambassador, Douglas Roche, believes the Court was telling the nuclear five "to get on with it."[33] However, it is rather contestable whether an ICJ ruling on such a matter will have any significant influence when it comes to a topic state leaders tend to hold so dear to national security. For example, the 2004 ruling condemning the construction of a "security fence" by Israel in the Occupied Territories has been ignored. Canada abstained from the GA vote calling for the trial, claiming it was asking the Court to render a political, and not a legal, decision. However, the distinction between these two modes of decision remains unclear.

THEORY AND INTERNATIONAL ORGANIZATIONS

Three interpretations of the role and influence of IOs stand out in the literature. The central question pursued here is how much influence and autonomy IOs have in global politics. We have seen already that both IGOs and NGOs have increased in size and scope. But has this change resulted in a commensurate increase in their abilities to affect human or state behaviour? Are IGOs actually capable of making independent decisions, free from the constraints of members' objections, or do they merely, and ephemerally, reflect cases where the interests and expectations of various actors converge? Likewise, do NGOs influence global politics in decisive ways, constituting the emergence of a global civil society that transcends the state, or are they primarily reflective of existing patterns of power and privilege in the world?

First, MNCs and NGOs have some automatic freedom from governments since they are not official representatives of states and exist to pursue their own objective, be it profit, charity, or value promotion. However, powerful though they may be, they are still subject to the national laws that exist where they operate, as well as the constraints imposed by the international system. But what about intergovernmental organizations themselves? The three main perspectives regarding the role of IGOs are simplified immediately below. Keep in mind that one can view the question of the effect of IL in much the same manner.

- IGOs are seen as mere instruments of foreign policy: they are little more than political arenas in which members (states) pursue their self-interest.
- IGOs are seen as "intervening variables"; that is, IGOs and international regimes intervene between causes and outcomes in world politics. As a result, they have some limited influence in global politics.
- IGOs can be seen as autonomous and influential actors, able to command their own resources and significantly alter the international system.[34]

As mentioned in the introduction to this chapter, both realists and Marxists tend to reject the notion of IO autonomy. For realists, IGOs merely reflect the character of power politics and the dynamics of cooperation as a form of self-help in an anarchic world. Like alliances, IGOs will form or dissolve when states decide to create them or eliminate them. When IGOs act in global politics, these actions reflect the extent to which states are willing to cooperate. Realists argue that this is why IGOs frequently fail to act in response to global events or only act in limited ways. No international institution can act without the agreement of its member states, and most decisions are the result of consensus or the lowest common denominator among the membership (see the discussion of decision making in Chapter 3). For realists, NGOs lack true power and rely on lobbying state publics and governments to obtain their goals. Ultimately, NGOs rely heavily on states to adopt their beliefs, implement their policy prescriptions, and fund their programs in order to make change in global politics. For neo-Marxists, IGOs and some NGOs merely reflect the character of global capitalism and the interests of the rich elites and the rich states. Both are part of the global power structure characterized by dominance and exploitation. Gramscian approaches argue that NGOs and IGOs also act as conduits for the dissemination of liberal value systems that are part of the power structure of global capitalism. Some NGOs, however, have fairly clear counter-hegemonic agendas.

In contrast, liberals tend to see the most potential for IOs, so much so that the literature refers to liberal institutionalism as a genuine perspective (see Chapter 1). The core belief held by liberal institutionalists is that international regimes and institutions can facilitate agreements among states. IOs operate as modifiers of state behaviour or, as Stephen Krasner and others put it, as "intervening variables." Although diplomacy is still the prerogative of states, the IOs to which they belong (and, in the broader sense, the regimes) at least partially shape their behaviour. Some would suggest that IOs are perhaps even supplanting the state in importance as global governance progresses. In other words, IOs are gaining autonomy from the governments that send representatives to them and have an independent voice in world affairs. Within the liberal perspective we may identify at least two historically prevalent strains of theory: **functionalism** and **regime theory.**

FUNCTIONALISM

Integration theorists have written of the gradual establishment of supranational governments, be they along federal or confederal lines. Functionalism, with roots in the writings of David Mitrany, emerged as a branch of such thinking following World War II.[35] Functionalists envisioned global political integration as a process arising out of technical cooperation among nation-states. Meanwhile, neo-functionalists stressed the role of mutual self-interest in the construction of regional institutions whose success would "spill over into other areas of inter-action."[36] Functionalists believed that positive experiences with cooperation between peoples and governments would encourage further cooperation and increased institutional and pol-itical integration; in this sense they were to some extent constructivist in orientation. In the development of larger political communities, form should follow function. IOs should be con-structed according to the specific needs they can satisfy for the citizens of states, and eventually those citizens will come to realize that their loyalty to the nation-state is itself misplaced. The European Union has been the traditional source of empirical inspiration for functionalism and neo-functionalism (see Profile 5.6). Regional economic arrangements are heralded as embryonic political communities, since a "regional market's institutional machinery, its har-monization of economic policies, and the spillover effect of its successes may help create an awareness within the region of the advantages of the integrative process."[37]

For functionalism to make sense, it has to be manifested at the institution-building level: the granting of authority to supranational entities in which a scientific or technocratic con-sensus determines policy. Although examples of this authority occur in limited areas, it is impossible to talk seriously of apolitical international relations. First, policies will reflect the operative ideologies of the decision makers, regardless of how objective their research and sug-gestions might be. Second, the sacrifice of state sovereignty such institutions demand can be viewed as a short-term commitment, rather than the kind of permanent obligation required to transform global politics. Third, aware of the possibility that political interests will usu-ally interfere with scientific or technocratic calculations, political scientists have been rather skeptical about the idea of functionalist bodies capable of freeing themselves from the political demands of individual members. Neo-functionalists argue that, in some cases, self-interest will be best pursued by such cooperation, which will then spill over into other areas. However, the evidence in terms of a neo-functionalist trend in the continuing evolution of the European Union (often considered the most fertile proving ground for neo-functionalism) seems rather bleak.[38]

One observation that flows from the functionalist literature has a special resonance for global politics today: the notion that the modern state is poorly equipped to deal with the daily needs of contemporary citizens. In a certain sense, little doubt exists that a growing number of states, due to ecological and other problems, are incapable of effective governance. Lynton Caldwell writes of the potential spread of what he terms *socioecological insolvency*, wherein "a state has exhausted its material means of self-support and no longer provides to its people the elementary services of government."[39] Furthermore, functionalism stresses the possible emergence of some form of global technocratic social democracy and predicts the formation of groups of international scientists acting in concert to influence policy. These groups are commonly referred to as "epistemic communities."[40] However, none of these developments necessarily means the end of the sovereign state system or the end to conflicts between states.

REGIME THEORY

It is more common today for students of IOs to discuss institutionalism rather than integration, accepting the inconvenient fact that the nation-state just will not go away. Oran Young's dif-ferentiation between institutions ("social practices consisting of easily recognised roles coupled with clusters of rules or conventions governing relations among the occupants of those roles") and organizations ("material, extant entities that possess legal sovereignty and physical artifacts, such as office buildings") is helpful.[41] The first category is currently manifested in academic

PROFILE 5.6 The European Union

The EU is widely regarded as the most advanced case of contemporary political integration among states. It began with three largely functional "communities" established by post–World War II Western European states: the European Coal and Steel Community (1952), the European Economic Community (1957), and the European Atomic Agency (EURATOM) (1957). In 1967 these three institutions merged and became the European Community. Increased integration at the economic and political level prompted the establishment of the European Union in 1993. The original membership included France, Germany, Italy, Belgium, the Netherlands, and Luxembourg. The United Kingdom, Denmark, and Eire (Ireland) joined in 1973; Greece in 1981; Spain and Portugal in 1986; Austria, Finland, and Sweden in 1995. In May 2004, a group of 10 states joined the EU: Estonia, Latvia, Lithuania, Poland, the Czech Republic, Hungary, Slovakia, Slovenia, Malta, and Cyprus. In 2007, Bulgaria and Romania joined, as did Croatia in July 2013. Even Turkey might join in the future, although consideration of Turkey raises interesting questions about what exactly it means to be "European." Collectively, the 28 countries of the EU have over 500 million citizens and account for almost a third of world economic output. The EU has developed many common policies. It is a single market, providing for the free movement of people, goods, and finance within its borders. It maintains common trade, agricultural, and fisheries policies. And it maintains a regional development policy to assist economically weaker areas in the Union. The EU is the most highly institutionalized international organization in the world: the European Commission is composed of member states and is the executive branch of the EU; the Council of the EU and a European Parliament compose the legislative branch; the European Court of Justice manages legal affairs; and the European Central Bank manages monetary policy. The EU is increasingly an actor on the world stage. Member states will often forge common positions on issues, and then represent themselves as a single, united block in international negotiations. For example, the EU has forged common positions on climate change, global trade rules, and genetically modified organisms.

The EU can be seen as a bold experiment in political integration, involving the forging of a new identity that supersedes the identities of its collective units. However, the EU has always encountered resistance to its integration plans. Governments have often proved reluctant to agree to certain proposals or policies, attempting to block them outright or refusing to adopt them. And many people in Europe are skeptical of too much economic integration and are even more skeptical of too much political integration. This has resulted in widespread suspicion and even hostility to the EU, often expressed by nationalist elements, who feel that Brussels has acquired too much influence over sovereign state affairs. Indeed, EU regulations cover everything from recycled beer cans to the enforcement of the European Convention on Human Rights. Although the EU principle of *subsidiarity* suggests that the European Council should intervene only when lower jurisdictions cannot deal adequately with issues, this has not been sufficient to satisfy anti-EU sentiments. The adoption of the "Euro" as a single currency by many EU states was controversial and continues to be so in light of the financial crisis engulfing the EU in 2012 (see Chapter 8). The enlargement of the EU has also been controversial; many have argued that the entry of Eastern European states has harmed the EU's economy, as millions of labourers flood westward looking for work. As a result, deepening and strengthening European integration has proved to be a difficult task in recent years. In 2005, French and Dutch voters rejected a new EU constitution that would have strengthened EU institutions and foreign policy machinery. The Libson Treaty of 2009 (which introduced many reforms, including the establishment of the European External Action Service) was initially rejected by Irish voters in a referendum. Concerns about sovereignty and democratic accountability, along with the deepening of the European financial crisis in 2012, has plunged the future of European integration into uncertainty.

For more on the EU, see the *Journal of European Integration*, an academic journal dedicated to the study of European cooperation and institution building.

inquiry by what has been popularly labelled *regime theory*, stemming from the liberal preoccupation with the concept of interdependence in world politics. To cope with this interdependence, states form regimes, defined succinctly by Stephen Krasner as sets of norms, principles, rules, and decision-making procedures around which actors' expectations converge. Regimes do not change the fundamental structures of political power, but they may influence the ultimate outcome of behaviour emanating from the international system.[42] Of course, one may be more or less enthusiastic about just how "intervening" these variables are. This intervention does not always seem to matter in its current usage; the term *regime* has acquired fantastic flexibility. A loose definition of what exactly constitutes a regime or institution—a tight definition would be unnecessarily constraining—leads to the conclusion that most areas of international collaboration are regimes whether or not some hegemonic leader provides the "public good" of leadership. What were once functionalist projects, for example, have become regimes.[43]

Regime analysis may seem a shallow, even cosmetic, perspective by those obsessed with grand theories that attempt to explain everything. Others argue that any study of regimes must reflect the social constructions or normative contexts that influence these interactive activities. The identification of the latter can be only an imprecise enterprise, perhaps largely determined by the intellectual perspective of the observer. This contribution belongs to the constructivists mentioned in Chapter 1, who suggest that agents and structures co-evolve as participants acquire intersubjective understandings of each other and themselves. Prolonged exposure to certain institutions will affect the perceptions of policymakers and thus their policies, for better or for worse. Feminists also tend to be supportive of regime building, which can promote greater awareness and understanding of gender issues in global politics, as well as establishing international laws and norms to address the political and economic marginalization of women and issues ranging from international humanitarian law to the sex trade.

International institutions do help us define acceptable behaviour, though this is not an inherently progressive function. This process of definition may involve delegitimation: redefining certain types of behaviour as illegitimate and attempting to proscribe them. In these cases we see the development of **global prohibition regimes**: they are guided by norms that "strictly circumscribe the conditions under which states can participate in and authorize these activities and proscribe all involvement by nonstate actors."[44] Slavery is often used as an example of an international activity that came to be viewed as inhumane by key actors in the global system, which led to a global prohibition regime outlawing the world slave trade (although that trade persists in many forms today). At the same time, regulatory regimes have a corresponding positive function: to legitimize behaviour that is taking place. This legitimization could include, for example, behaviour that is arguably hazardous to environmental health, such as the spread of nuclear power, which is one of the stated goals of the **International Atomic Energy Agency (IAEA)**. The tendency to equate regime formation with a progressive evolution in world affairs overlooks the dual nature of institutions and organizations that have both promotional and regulatory roles. Finally, mainstream regime theory is often criticized for overlooking the contemporary role of non-governmental actors, despite the fact that the rise of such actors helped promote thinking about interdependence.

CONCLUSIONS

This chapter has argued that IOs are highly relevant in global politics. We offered a brief historical look at international institutions in history, including the development of the League of Nations and the United Nations. Next, we discussed international law and some of its key terminology before turning to the International Court of Justice. Though IL has limited direct utility and relies on consent rather than any strong coercive powers, it contributes to the popularization of important issues, such as the validity of nuclear weapons, and can promote human rights and compliance with regime agreements designed to preserve the environment. However, certain government leaders will consider themselves above the law, and this belief leads to a crisis of legitimacy for institutions such as the ICJ. As the noted scholar Martin Wight once commented, IL has a tendency to "crawl in the mud of legal positivism."[45] Yet IL remains a core component of efforts to build a more tightly knit global society—for better or for worse.

We finished the chapter by discussing theoretical perspectives pertaining to the role of IOs and IL. Realists and neo-Marxist theorists feel that IOs and IL serve the interests of the more powerful states or classes. Liberal institutionalists, constructivists, and feminists hold a more positive view of institutions and organizations, regarding them as important actors that can be used to lower levels of conflict and promote greater understanding and well-being. Students might reflect on the question of the influence and autonomy of IOs when reading the remainder of this book, since IOs (and IL) factor into all of the issue areas we examine. One of the more fundamental questions concerns whether we can speak appreciably about a new era of global governance today, or whether unilateralism in foreign policy, ongoing points of divergence among rich and poor states, the privatization of security forces, and other factors make the very notion of global governance problematic, at least at this time. This question is a dominant one for experts examining contemporary global politics, and we turn to these issues in the next section of this book.

Endnotes

1. A.C. Cutler, "Historical Materialism, Globalization, and Law," in M. Rupert and H. Smith, eds., *Historical Materialism and Globalization* (London: Routledge, 2002), 230–56, 231.

2. J. Plano and R. Olton, *The International Relations Dictionary*, 4th ed. (Santa Barbara: ABC-CLIO, 1988), 416. For more resources see the journal *International Organisation* and (for a constructivist take) M. Barnett and M. Finnemore, *Rules for the World: International Organizations in Global Politics* (Ithaca: Cornell University Press, 2004). On global governance see J. Rosenau and E. O. Czempiel, eds., *Governance without Government: Order and Change in World Politics* (Cambridge: Cambridge University Press, 1992); the flagship journal of the Academic Union for the Study of the UN System, *Global Governance: A Review of Mulitlateralism*; J. Muldoon, *The Architecture of Global Governance: An Introduction to the Study of International Organizations* (Cambridge, MA: Westview, 2004); and P. Diehl and B. Frederking, eds., *The Politics of Global Governance: International Organizations in an Interdependent World*, 4th ed. (Boulder: Lynne Reinner, 2010). The standard realist response has become J. Grieco, "Anarchy and the Limits of Cooperation: A Realist Critique of the Newest Liberal Institutionalism," *International Organization* 42 (Summer 1988), 485–507.

3. States can also be expelled, though this is rare. It is still a matter of some contention regarding which states belong to the UN, since China has resolutely disallowed the Republic of Taiwan from joining, claiming it is still part of mainland China. Despite hosting many of its key institutions, Switzerland refused to join the UN for many years, protecting its policy of neutrality (since collective security would commit it to taking sides in a UN–approved war). However, after a national referendum on the subject, Switzerland finally officially joined in 2002. Yet another controversy is related to the unilateral declaration of independence by Kosovo, which now seeks its own seat in the General Assembly; the International Court of Justice delivered an advisory opinion in July 2010 that Kosovo's earlier Declaration of Independence from Serbia was not in violation of international law, but with Russia's veto at the Security Council it is unlikely that Kosovo will attain a GA seat soon.

4. This difference may lead to understandable confusion for the non-specialist. The agencies of the UN (WHO, UNESCO, etc.) are in and of themselves IOs, with working constitutions and general and

executive assemblies. However, they are generally considered part of a larger organizational entity, the UN Organization. On the UN system see P. Baehr and L. Gordenker, *The United Nations: Reality and Ideal*, 4th ed. (New York: Palgrave Macmillan, 2006).

5. The games were held from 776 BCE to 393 CE, every four years at Olympia, in honour of Zeus; they resumed in their present format in 1896. At present, the International Olympic Committee is a universal-membership, single-purpose IO, with headquarters in Lausanne, France. Recent corruption scandals have plagued the IOC.

6. The ITU was originally created as the International Telegraph Union; the title was changed in 1934. The ITU became a UN specialized agency in 1947. Headquarters are in Geneva. See G. Codding and A. Rutkowski, *The International Telecommunication Union in a Changing World* (Dedham, MA: Artech House, 1982). The UPU was established when the first International Postal Convention was signed, creating the General Union of Posts; its name was changed to the UPU four years later. Stamp collectors will recognize the importance of the Convention, which gave every member-state full use of postal services throughout the world. Headquarters are in Bern, Switzerland, where the International Copyright Union is also stationed. See G. Codding, *The Universal Postal Union* (New York University Press, 1964).

7. *The International Secretariat* (Washington, DC: Carnegie Endowment for International Peace, 1945), 428. For a first-hand account of the role of secretariats, see J. Mathiason, *Invisible Governance: International Secretariats in Global Politics* (New York: Kumarian, 2007). Another excellent text, focused on environmental issues and the complex role of secretariats, is F. Biermann and B. Siebenhuner, eds., *Managers of Global Change: The Influence of International Environmental Bureaucracies* (Cambridge MA: MIT Press, 2009).

8. B. Hughes, *Continuity and Change in World Politics: The Clash of Perspectives*, 2nd ed. (Englewood Cliffs, NJ: Prentice-Hall, 1994), 73.

9. Claude's classic text is *Swords into Ploughshares*, 4th ed. (New York: Random House, 1971). See also L. Goodrich, "From League of Nations to United Nations," *International Organization*, February 1947, 3–21; and for a recent account, P. Kennedy, *The Parliament of Man: The Past, Present and Future of the United Nations* (New York: Random House, 2006).

10. *The United Nations: A Concise Political Guide*, 3rd ed. (London: Macmillan, 1995).

11. Office of Management and Budget, *The City of New York Budget Summary: Fiscal Years 2010–2014* (May 6, 2010). http://www.nyc.gov/html/omb/downloads/pdf/sum5_10.pdf (accessed July 19, 2012).

12. Data from "Contributions to United Nations Peacekeeping Operations," June 30, 2012. http://www.un.org/en/peacekeeping/contributors/2012/june12_1.pdf (accessed July 19, 2012).

13. United Nations Security Council Resolution 1674, S/RES/1674 (April 28, 2006).

14. Data from United Nations Department of Management, Program Planning, Budget and Accounts Fact Sheets, available at http://www.un.org/en/hq/dm/budget_factsheets.shtml (accessed July 20, 2012).

15. See F.H. Suward and E. McInnis, "Forming the UN, 1945," in D. Munton and J. Kirton, eds., *Canadian Foreign Policy: Selected Cases* (Scarborough, ON: Prentice-Hall, 1992), 4–18, for more on the initial Canadian position.

16. For a concise summary, see J. Rosenau's article "Normative Challenges in a Turbulent World," *Ethics and International Affairs* 6 (1992), 1–20. A (much) lengthier exposition is found in his *Turbulence in World Politics: A Theory of Change and Continuity* (Princeton University Press, 1990). On the private sector, see D. Fuchs, *Business Power in Global Governance* (Boulder, CO: Lynne Rienner, 2007); on the role of various actors in modern conflict zones, see M. Duffield, *Global Governance and the New Wars: The Merging of Development and Security* (London: Zed, 2001).

17. See "Frequently Asked Questions" on the UN website: http://www.un.org/en/faq/index.shtml.

18. Canada, Department of Foreign Affairs and International Trade, press release, September 19, 1996.

19. A. LeRoy Bennett, *International Organizations: Principles and Issues*, 6th ed. (Englewood Cliffs, NJ: Prentice Hall, 1995), 272.

20. S. Bailey and S. Daws, *The United Nations: A Concise Political Guide*, 3rd ed. (Lanham, MD: Barnes and Noble, 1995).

21. D. Keen, *Refugees: Rationing the Right to Life* (London: Zed, 1992), 40.

22. P. Wapner, "Politics beyond the State: Environmental Activism and World Civic Politics," *World Politics* 47 (1995), 311–40; J. Fisher, *The Road from Rio: Sustainable Development and the Nongovernmental Movement in the Third World* (Westport, CT: Praeger, 1993); J. McCormick, *Reclaiming Paradise:*

The Global Environmental Movement (Bloomington: Indiana University Press, 1989); and P. Willetts, ed., *"The Conscience of the World": The Influence of Non-Governmental Organizations in the UN System* (Washington, DC: Brookings, 1996); on the role of IL, see R. Falk, *Law in a Merging Global Village: A Post-Westphalian Perspective* (Ardsley, NY: Transnational Publishers, 1998). See also the review essay by R. Reitan, "A Global Civil Society in a World Polity, or Angels and Nomads Against Empire?" *Global Governance* 13 (2007), 445–60.

23. R. Angell, *Peace on the March: Transnational Participation* (New York: Van Nostrand Reinhold, 1969); for a Canadian history, see T. Socknat, *Witness against War: Pacifism in Canada 1900–1945* (Toronto: University of Toronto Press, 1987).

24. A. LeRoy Bennett, *International Organizations*, 180.

25. M. Akehurst, *A Modern Introduction to International Law*, 3rd ed. (London: George Allen and Unwin, 1977), 35. See also A. Cassese, *International Law* (Oxford: Oxford University Press, 2001); G. von Glahn, *Law Among Nations: An Introduction to Public International Law* (New York: Macmillan, 1965); and M. Byers, ed., *The Role of Law in International Politics: Essays in International Relations and International Law* (Oxford: Oxford University Press, 2000).

26. On sanctions, see especially M. Doxey, *Economic Sanctions and International Enforcement*, 2nd ed. (New York: Oxford University Press, 1980); and D. Drezner, *The Sanctions Paradox: Economic Statecraft and International Relations* (Cambridge: Cambridge University Press, 1999).

27. C. Bassiouni and V.P. Nanda, eds., *A Treatise on International Criminal Law: Crime and Punishment.* vol. 1 (Springfield, IL: Charles Thomas, 1973), 5.

28. A. Katzman, "U.S., Iran Claims Settled Quietly," *The Globe and Mail*, March 20, 1996.

29. Reprinted in *The International Court of Justice*, 3rd ed. (The Hague: ICJ, 1986), 144.

30. T. Couloumbis and J. Wolfe, *Power and Justice: Introduction to International Relations*, 3rd ed. (Englewood Cliffs, NJ: Prentice-Hall, 1986), 259.

31. This is Article 36 of the Statute of the ICJ, which provides in Section 2 that any party can recognize as compulsory the jurisdiction of the Court in legal disputes concerning the interpretation of a treaty; any question of international law; the existence of any fact that, if established, would constitute a breach of an international obligation; and the nature or extent of the reparation to be made for the breach of an international obligation. By July 1993, only 56 states had filed declarations of acceptance of the Optional Clause.

32. See K. Kirton and D. Munton, "Protecting the Canadian Arctic: The Manhattan Voyages, 1969–1970," in K. Kirton and D. Munton, eds., *Canadian Foreign Policy: Selected Cases* (Scarborough, ON: Prentice-Hall, 1992), 205–26, 220.

33. *The Globe and Mail*, July 9, 1996, A8. For a broad discussion of this important theme, see N. Singh and E. McWhinney, *Nuclear Weapons and Contemporary International Law*, 2nd ed. (Dordrecht, Netherlands: Martinus Nijhoff, 1989).

34. For another summary, see C. Pentland, "International Organizations," in J. Rosenau, K.W. Thompson, and G. Boyd, eds., *World Politics* (New York: The Free Press, 1976), 624–39.

35. Mitrany's classic text is *A Working Peace System: An Argument for the Functional Development of International Organisation* (London: RIIA, 1943).

36. Most famously, see E. Haas, *Beyond the Nation-State* (Stanford: Stanford University Press, 1964); and A. Groom and P. Taylor, eds., *Functionalism: Theory and Practice in International Relations* (London: University of London, 1975).

37. R. Riggs and J. Plano, *The United Nations: International Organizations and World Politics* (Chicago: Dorsey, 1988), 290.

38. See, in particular, M. Huelshoff and T. Pfeiffer, "Environmental Policy in the EC: Neo-Functionalist Sovereignty Transfer or Neo-Realist Gate-Keeping?" *International Journal* 47, no. 1 (1992), 136–58. See also B. Rosamond, *Theories of European Integration* (New York: St. Martin's Press, 2000).

39. L. Caldwell, *International Environmental Policy: Emergence and Dimensions*, 2nd ed. (Durham: Duke University Press, 1990), 328. We expand on this theme in Chapter 11.

40. See P. Haas, "Introduction: Epistemic Communities and International Policy Coordination," *International Organization* 46, no. 1 (1992), 1–35; and on the role of epistemic communities in policy convergence see D. Drezner, "Globalization and Policy Convergence," *International Studies Review* 3 (2001), 53–78; and for an interesting take on a "counter-epistemic community" see J. Youde, "The Development of a

Counter-Epistemic Community: AIDS, South Africa, and International Regimes," *International Relations* 19 (2005), 421–39.

41. O. Young, *International Cooperation: Building Regimes for Natural Resources and the Environment* (Ithaca, NY: Cornell University Press, 1989), 32. For example, the University of British Columbia is an organization, and the Canadian postsecondary school system is an institution; the International Atomic Energy Agency is an organization, and the non-proliferation regime is an institution; the Las Vegas Wedding Chapel is an organization, and marriage is an institution. However, analysts often refer to UN agencies and other international organizations as institutions as well, as the term *liberal institutionalism* suggests.

42. For standard texts, see S. Krasner, "Structural Causes and Regime Consequences: Regimes as Intervening Variables," in S. Krasner, ed., *International Regimes* (Ithaca, NY: Cornell University Press, 1983), 1–22; R. Keohane, *After Hegemony: Cooperation and Discord in the World Political Economy* (Princeton University Press, 1984); M. Zacher, "Toward a Theory of International Regimes," *Journal of International Affairs* 44, no. 1 (1990), 139–58; and O. Young, "The Politics of International Regime Formation: Managing Natural Resources and the Environment," *International Organization* 43, no. 3 (1989), 349–75.

43. For example, see P. Sands, "EC Environmental Law: The Evolution of a Regional Regime of International Environmental Protection," *Yale Law Journal* 100, no. 8 (1991), 2511–23.

44. E. Nadelmann, "Global Prohibition Regimes: The Evolution of Norms in International Society," *International Organization* 44, 4 (1990), 481–526.

45. M. Wight, "Why Is There No International Theory?" in H. Butterfield and M. Wight, eds., *Diplomatic Investigations* (Cambridge, MA: Harvard University Press, 1968), 29.

PART TWO

CURRENTS

This section explores the central issues and ongoing debates that characterize contemporary global politics. In the preceding section we presented an overview of the historical and intellectual roots that have contributed to the evolution of the international system and our understanding of it. We now turn to an examination of current international security issues, contemporary conflict management efforts, the globalization of the world economy, the problem of inequality, and human rights. As we will see, the dual process of convergence/divergence continues to define the political landscape and challenge our ability to make safe assumptions about the future, and all of the theoretical perspectives we introduced in Chapter 1 retain their relevance.

International Security After the Cold War

The supreme importance of the military instrument lies in the fact that the ultimate ratio of power in international relations is war.

—*Edward Hallett Carr (1942)*[1]

War [has] penetrated the years with its rhythms, opening and closing the gates of time. Even when fighting was over, it asserted a hidden pressure, surviving underground.

—*Fernand Braudel (1996)*[2]

INTRODUCTION: THE CHANGING NATURE OF INTERNATIONAL SECURITY

What is *security*? What does it mean to be *secure*, and whose security matters? Put another way, what are the threats to security that we need to address in order to pursue it? Traditionally, *international security* has focused on the security of states, and *national security* is most frequently conceptualized as the protection of a state from external threats to its territorial integrity and political independence. For realists, the most important challenge has been the military threat posed by other states, although revolutionary movements, secessionist movements, and terrorist groups have also been long regarded as threats to national security. However, this rather restrictive view has been challenged in recent decades, both by theoretical schools that do not accept a state-centric interpretation of global politics, and by changes in the structure of the international system itself.[3]

As a result, the subject matter of security studies now includes a range of threats that are not state-centric or military in nature. For example, environmental degradation, food security, foreign cultural influences, economic modernization, energy security, organized crime, and the migration of peoples may be interpreted as threats to the well-being or even the survival of societies. Furthermore, the study of security is increasingly focused on actors and forces other than the state: ideologies, individuals, groups, or even socio-economic conditions existing within or across state boundaries may represent a threat to human communities. Of course, states are still highly relevant actors: as Peter Andreas argues, "clandestine transnational actors" are shifting conceptions of borders and security away from military defence and toward policing, and therefore "territoriality is persisting—but with a shift in emphasis."[4] Furthermore, states still go to war, and threaten the security of individuals or groups through a variety of repressive measures including the use of force and discriminatory political and economic policies. Nevertheless, in moving the reference point of security away from a focus purely on the state and military power, liberal, neo-Marxist, and feminist scholars have all contributed to an expansion of the concept of security. Constructivists have also made a significant contribution to security studies in the form of securitization theory, emphasizing that security is not an objective term but is constructed through social processes. Certain issues are "securitized" through speech, the media, and other forms of social dialogue, becoming security issues because they are represented as such in a society, thus influencing how people subsequently approach them.[5]

The end of the Cold War had a profound effect on the study of international security. The focus on the superpower rivalry vanished, and a wide range of other security concerns moved to centre stage. Many of these concerns were not new, but the end of the Cold War served to bring them to the forefront. Profile 6.1 illustrates this shift. Today, several issues occupy the attention of most international security scholars and analysts:

- *The origins and causes of conflict in the international system.* This work now includes a growing literature on the origins of civil wars and ethnic conflicts, as well as research into the link between poverty and war, environmental degradation and war, and economic incentives for war.

- *National security.* Interstate security concerns have not vanished, and state governments continue to grapple with a broad range of security threats to their territorial integrity, the independence of their political institutions, and their way of life. Other interests may include defending strategic territory and allies, combating international criminal organizations, and securing access to vital resources such as oil or natural gas (often referred to as "energy security").

- *Group security.* The focus of this growing area of study is ethnic, religious, clan, or factional groups and issues such as minority rights, economic and political grievances, **self-determination**, and in some cases separatism.

- *Nuclear weapons safety and nuclear weapons proliferation.* While the safety and security of existing nuclear arsenals continue to receive attention, so do the possibility of a nuclear war between India and Pakistan, the development of nuclear weapons technology in so-called rogue states such as North Korea and Iran, and the remote though much-feared prospect of a terrorist attack using nuclear weapons.

- *Chemical and biological weapons proliferation.* The spread of chemical and biological weapons and their possible use by states and/or terrorist groups is now a prominent security concern in global politics, demonstrated by the significance of accusations that the Syrian government used chemical weapons against rebel forces in 2012 and 2013.

- *The spread of conventional weapons.* While a great deal of attention is placed on nuclear, chemical, and biological weapons (sometimes collectively referred to as **weapons of mass destruction** or **WMD**), conventional arms buildups are a major concern in many regions. Most organized political violence is conducted with so-called conventional weapons, mostly small arms and light weapons such as assault rifles or rocket-propelled grenades.

PROFILE 6.1	**The International Security Agenda: Cold War and Contemporary**			
COLD WAR		**CONTEMPORARY**		
East–West	Preoccupation with super-power confrontation as the source of the next world war	North–South	Growing awareness of global disparities and poverty as a source of conflict	
Interstate	Study of wars between states	Intrastate	Study of wars within states: ethnic, religious, and factional conflicts between substate actors	
Nuclear strategy	Focus on deterrence and nuclear weapons programs	Nuclear, biological, and chemical weapons proliferation	Concern with the spread of nuclear weapons to states and substate groups	
Alliances	Study of alliance formation, East and West blocs	Zones of peace and instability	Study of actors and structures (especially institutions) in peaceful regions as compared with warring regions	
Military	Focus on military security and military as foreign policy instrument	Economic, social, and environmental	Examination of security implications of economic conflict, resource scarcity, environmental degradation, and organized crime	
High-intensity conflict (HIC)	Focus on large-scale wars between powerful states and development of sophisticated weapons	Low-intensity conflict (LIC) and counterterrorism	Focus on insurgency wars, peace support and stability operations, and combating terrorist groups	
War in Europe	Concern with NATO/Warsaw Pact HIC in Europe	Regional conflicts	Concern with outbreak and spread of war and instability in the world's regions	
Superpower arms control	Effort to control super-power arms race especially with agreements on nuclear weapons	Global arms control	Effort to control spread of weapons around the world	

- *Terrorism.* While terrorism has been an international security issue for decades, since the September 11, 2001, attacks on the United States, it has become the highest security priority of the U.S. and Canadian and many other governments.

- *Global criminal activity.* International organized crime, especially in the form of piracy and human- and drug-trafficking syndicates, threatens the legitimacy of states and the well-being of human communities.

- *Human security.* The focus is on the individual as the object of security. The objective is the freedom of individuals from violent or non-violent threats to their rights, safety, and lives. The human security agenda includes efforts such as the Ottawa Treaty to ban land mines, the work of the International Criminal Court, and international agreements on war-affected children.

- *Environmental security.* The focus is on the impact of ecological degradation on individuals and human communities, acts of ecocide, and the links between resource scarcity and armed conflict (see also Chapter 10).

- *Food security.* Billions of people lack stable access to sufficient levels of safe, nutritious food. This has been blamed on war, chronic poverty, economic recession, currency fluctuations, biofuel production, and high energy costs.

This chapter first explores the more traditional problems of interstate and intrastate war. We will then address some of the newer security challenges outlined above: the proliferation of weapons, terrorism, and the growth of international organized crime.

WAR IN CONTEMPORARY GLOBAL POLITICS

War or armed conflict is a period of armed hostilities within or between states or other collectives (such as ethnic groups or political factions). The historian John Keegan has devised what may be the most concise definition of war: collective killing for a collective purpose.[6] In his famous work *On War*, Karl von Clausewitz characterizes war as a "continuation of politics by other means" and therefore focuses on armed conflict as a political act. However, a debate rages over the relative importance of politics, economics, history, and culture in the origin and fighting of wars.[7] Armed conflict has caused immeasurable suffering and destruction in human history: one estimate suggests that between 1816 and 2007 there were approximately 655 wars in the international system.[8]

Between 1946 and 2011, there were 248 armed conflicts in the world.[9] During this period there were no wars between great powers, although they were certainly involved in wars (such as Korea, Vietnam, the Falklands, and the Gulf War). Instead, most wars have taken place between or within smaller countries in the Middle East, Africa, and Asia. Another trend is the increased frequency of wars within states, known as *intrastate conflicts* (see Figure 6.1). Overall, the frequency of armed conflict is in decline: in 2011, there were 37 armed conflicts in the world.[10] Although this was an increase from the 31 reported armed conflicts in 2010, this is a decline from the post–Cold War peak of 52 in 1991 to 1992.[11] Finally, though war-related casualties are also on the decline, civilians are more likely to be its victims: in World War I, 15 percent of the fatalities were civilians, and in World II, this percentage rose to 65 (including Holocaust victims). In wars since 1945, however, more than 90 percent of casualties have been civilians.[12]

Governments continue to spend enormous sums of money on their armed forces. In the years immediately following the end of the Cold War, there was an encouraging decline in global military spending. Most of this decline came from the dramatic fall in military expenditures in Eastern Europe and the former Soviet Union.[13] However, since 1998 world military spending has steadily increased. In 2010, world military expenditures totalled over US$16 trillion, amounting to 2.6 percent of world gross domestic product (GDP) and representing US$236 per person on the planet. Most of the increase in world military spending is due to the surge in U.S. expenditures following the September 11, 2001, attacks and the wars in Afghanistan and Iraq. Between 2001 and 2010 U.S. military spending increased by 81 percent, compared to 31 percent in the rest of the world. Indeed, the United States accounted for 43 percent of world military expenditures in 2010. The top five countries (the U.S., China, the United Kingdom, France, and Russia) account for approximately 61 percent of global military spending.[14]

Figure 6.1 Number of Armed Conflicts by Type, 1946–2011

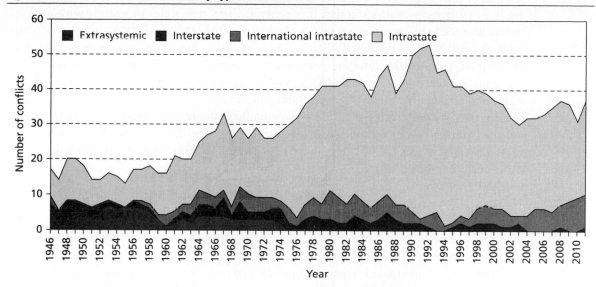

SOURCE: LOTTA THEMNÉR & PETER WALLENSTEEN, "ARMED CONFLICT, 1946–2011," *JOURNAL OF PEACE RESEARCH*, VOL. 49, NO. 4, 2012.

THEORIZING ABOUT THE ORIGINS OF WAR

Not surprisingly, many efforts have been made to understand the phenomenon of war and explain its causes. The difficulty with this enterprise is our inability to confidently generalize from one war to the next, since every war has unique and multifaceted causes. As Quincy Wright has observed, "A war, in reality, results from a total situation involving ultimately almost everything that has happened to the human race up to the time the war begins."[15] We can, however, build narrower categories of possible explanations by exploring the three levels of analysis introduced in Chapter 1: causes of war at the individual level, the state or group level, and the systemic level.

Using the individual level of analysis, we would find the cause of war in ourselves, in our nature as a species. But where does this nature come from? Early psychologists suggested that humans are inherently aggressive and war is therefore inevitable. In a letter to Albert Einstein, Sigmund Freud suggested that humans possess a death instinct, a desire to destroy and kill.[16] Konrad Lorenz, an anthropologist, referred to humans as killer apes, one of very few species that kills its own kind.[17] On the other hand, behavioural sociologists suggest that aggressive and violent behaviour is not innate but learned. Human society developed in such a way as to reward aggressive individuals and social organizations, and these traits were in turn passed on to future generations. Some feminists have argued that aggression is related to gender, with most males being more aggressive than females (whether through biology or social conditioning). Still other theories suggest that the origins of war lie in confrontational individual personalities or in the misperceptions of decision makers.[18]

The state or group level of analysis suggests that the cause of war is to be found in social and political characteristics; put simply, some states or groups are more prone to war than others. Cultural determinists such as anthropologist Margaret Mead argue that war is an invention and that some cultures never experienced war, such as some of the indigenous peoples of the South Pacific.[19] An enduring debate exists over what kinds of states or groups are inherently more warlike. Today, it is generally held that states or groups with authoritarian internal structures are more warlike because the leaders of such states are isolated from the will of their peoples and lack any checks or controls on their exercise of power. In contrast, democratic states are regarded as inherently peaceful, an assumption we will examine further in the next chapter. However, in the past monarchies were regarded as stable and responsible forms of government while republics were seen as impetuous, aggressive, and dangerous. During the Cold War, capitalist states regarded themselves as inherently peaceful and so-called communist states as inherently aggressive, while the latter regarded capitalist states as warlike, seeking markets abroad through imperialism. In other words, the conception of what is a war-prone state or group has changed over time and according to political or ideological perspectives.

Finally, the system level of analysis finds the origins of war in the nature of international politics itself. As discussed in Chapter 1, this view is widely held by structural realists. The principal source of war is anarchy and the distribution of power. Wars arise not necessarily from belligerence, but because, as Kenneth Waltz argues, "There is nothing to prevent them."[20] The insecurity of an anarchic environment will lead to the security dilemma, arms races, and competing alliances (see Chapter 2). One of the more popular systemic-level explanations is the concept of hegemonic war. Some realist scholars have suggested that history oscillates between **long cycles** of war and peace between great powers, with a general war breaking out approximately every 100 years.[21]

Long-cycle theory is based on the rise and decline of hegemonic powers. As hegemonic powers decline due to overextension, costs of empire, and the rise of challengers to their position, the pre-eminence of the hegemon is delegitimized, and war breaks out between the declining hegemon and its challengers. At the conclusion of the war, a new hegemon emerges (or the old one survives) and the cycle begins anew. Smaller wars, such as the Vietnam conflict in the 1960s and 1970s, are seen as proxy wars among competing hegemons.

War has been a central subject of debate between the principal theoretical frameworks employed in the study of global politics. While realists argue that war is inevitable due to the lack of trust and the primacy of self-interest in an anarchic international system, liberals see war as a reflection of weak global governance mechanisms and the existence of authoritarian governments. For liberals, war is not inevitable: it can be prevented through the development of effective international institutions and law, and the spread of economic interdependence and democracy. In contrast, neo-Marxists regard war as an extension of the interests of rich elites, who use the power of the states they control (including military power) to protect and promote their own interests. War is therefore an extension of imperialism. Constructivists assert that wars are caused by socially constructed belief systems such as historical grievances, political or religious ideologies, nationalism, and racism. Wars can be avoided by challenging and exposing these constructions through education and improved understanding of the "other" in order to undermine the stereotypes born of ignorance and prejudiced social discourse. Feminists point out that war is a product of male perspectives on power and security, perspectives that are further illustrated by the long history of violence against women in wartime. The answer to war is to challenge male approaches to power by emphasizing the importance of cooperation and the security of individuals and communities. Arguments based on these perspectives are in evidence whenever war is publicly discussed, illustrating the ongoing relevance and importance of theoretical debates in global politics.

INTERSTATE WARFARE: THE 2003 IRAQ WAR

The 2003 Iraq War demonstrated the ongoing significance of interstate war in global politics. After the terrorist attacks of September 11, 2001, terrorism became the primary security threat to the United States. Terrorism, and the states that supported it, became the focus of a "war on terror" launched by the new administration of George W. Bush. Initially supported by widespread public and government opinion, and backed by UN Security Council resolutions, the U.S. identified al-Qaeda and its leader, Osama Bin Laden, as the group responsible for the attacks. A U.S.–led coalition, which included Canada, launched a war to overthrow the Taliban government in Afghanistan. (We examine terrorism and September 11 later in this chapter.) However, the war on terror would not stop in Afghanistan. On January 29, 2002, in his State of the Union address, President Bush referred to North Korea, Iran, and Iraq as an "axis of evil" that threatened the United States and world peace. For many senior officials in the new Bush administration, Iraq—and specifically its leader Saddam Hussein—was the most important security threat facing the United States.[22] Despite the lack of evidence suggesting a substantive link between al-Qaeda and Saddam Hussein, the Iraq agenda and the war on terror began to converge in Washington. The Bush administration began an effort to build international support against Iraq, based on two allegations: the link between the Iraqi government and al-Qaeda, and Iraq's efforts to develop WMDs. The U.S. received considerable diplomatic support from the U.K., and British Prime Minister Tony Blair would be a forceful spokesperson for the case against Iraq and the decision to go to war.

Making the case against war. A peace march moves through London's Piccadilly toward Hyde Park on February 15, 2003, as part of the global "Day of Action" in protest against the eventual invasion of Iraq. (AP Photo/Kirsty Wigglesworth/CP Archive)

However, there was considerable opposition to U.S. efforts. Many governments simply did not agree that Iraq was an immediate threat to American or world security, did not believe that Iraq was close to acquiring WMDs, and did not see any connection between the September 11 attacks and Saddam Hussein. There was widespread suspicion of American motives, particularly in the Middle East, where American policy was seen as an expression of a U.S. desire to remove Saddam Hussein and control Iraqi oil. Moreover, the prospect of American-led military action against Iraq was deeply unpopular in almost all countries. As the threat of war grew so did anti-war protests, which culminated in a global "Day of Action" on February 15, 2003, a worldwide protest of millions of people coordinated over the Internet. There was also a growing concern over the policies of the Bush administration and the direction the war on terror was taking. At a speech at West Point Military Academy in June 2002, President Bush stated that U.S. security would require Americans "to be ready for preemptive action when necessary."[23] A new national security strategy document released in September 2002 stated that "while the United States will constantly strive to enlist the support of the international community, we will not hesitate to act alone, if necessary, to exercise our right of self-defense by acting preemptively against such terrorists, to prevent them from doing harm against our people and our country."[24] These proclamations increased suspicion that the U.S. was moving toward a unilateral, pre-emptive approach to its security priorities in general and Iraq in particular.

Prior to the outbreak of war, there was a period of frantic and often acrimonious diplomacy. The Bush administration sought to obtain a UN Security Council resolution authorizing force against Iraq to increase the legitimacy of military action and bolster domestic and international support for war. It proposed a draft resolution with a strict deadline and an authorization to use force if Iraq did not comply fully with its UN weapons inspection obligations. France was opposed to such a resolution, and instead proposed a call for the return of UN inspectors to Iraq, but with no firm deadline and no commitment to use force. The UN Security Council passed Resolution 1441, an awkward compromise between the French and U.S. positions, and weapons inspectors did return to Iraq in November. However, by January 2003 the head of the UN inspection commission, Hans Blix, estimated that their work would take another year to complete.[25] Seeking to speed up the process and obtain UN authorization to use force, in February the United States, Spain, and the United Kingdom drafted a resolution explicitly authorizing force against Iraq. The U.S. Secretary of State Colin Powell made a lengthy presentation to the Security Council on February 5, 2003, in which he outlined the suspected Iraqi WMD programs, Iraq's circumventions of UN sanctions, connections to al-Qaeda, and human rights violations by the Iraqi government.[26] France, Russia, and China were opposed to the draft resolution, believing that Iraq should be given more time to comply with UN resolutions. France even threatened to use its veto to stop any resolution authorizing force against Iraq. When it became clear that the Security Council would not pass a resolution authorizing force against Iraq, the diplomatic effort at the UN was over. On March 17, 2003, U.S. President George Bush gave Saddam Hussein 48 hours to leave Iraq.

The military campaign against Iraq began on March 19, 2003. Of the 30 countries that openly supported the effort diplomatically, only the United States, Britain, and Australia contributed military forces, while some countries in the Gulf allowed their airspace or territory to be used by coalition forces. Turkey, a traditional ally of the United States, refused to permit coalition forces to use Turkish land bases for the attacks on Iraq. Canada, another traditional ally of the United States, also refused to directly participate in the war in the absence of a UN Security Council resolution. No Middle Eastern or Muslim countries contributed military forces. Nevertheless, the military campaign was swift and successful. With air supremacy gained almost immediately, U.S. and British forces moved into Iraq from Kuwait on March 20. In the north, U.S. Special Forces, airborne troops, and Kurdish fighters advanced on regime strongholds north of Baghdad. U.S. forces advancing from the south reached Baghdad by April 3. By April 9, the regime in Baghdad had ceased to function, Saddam Hussein had fled, and U.S. troops controlled the city. On May 1, beneath an enormous banner reading "Mission Accomplished" hanging from the control tower of the U.S. aircraft carrier *Abraham Lincoln*, President Bush declared that major combat operations were over. Saddam Hussein was captured in a small, underground hideaway on December 13, and executed in 2006.

Despite President Bush's optimistic declaration, the Iraq war did not come to an end in May 2003. The institutions and capacities of the Iraqi state essentially collapsed after the invasion, leaving a governance and security vacuum. The situation was exacerbated by poor preparation and decision making by the Bush administration and U.S. civilian and military leaders responsible for governing Iraq.[27] Violence initially took the form of crime and looting, but

Making the case for war. The scene in the United Nations Security Council on February 5, 2003, as U.S. Secretary of State Colin Powell (seated at round table, first from left) presents evidence of Iraq's weapons of mass destruction program. He would later regret this moment. (© Action Press gmbh & co kg [2002] All rights reserved.)

soon an al-Qaeda–led and al-Qaeda–inspired insurgency emerged, followed by sectarian violence between Iraq's main religious communal groups, the Kurds, Shias, and Sunnis. To make matters worse, tribal factions also fought each other, resulting in a complex pattern of violence that included criminality, kidnappings, assassinations, attacks on United States and coalition forces, sectarian terrorism, and political feuds. From 2005 through 2009, U.S. and coalition forces in Iraq (complemented by a slowly reconstituted Iraqi military) struggled to maintain order and security. All-out civil war was a distinct possibility, as violence increased and the Iraqi government was deeply divided along sectarian lines and proved largely incapable of governing. Some observers suggested that the formation of a successful national unity government was impossible.[28] The U.S. government's own 2007 National Intelligence Estimate for Iraq warned that a significant deterioration in the security situation might lead to state collapse with three possible outcomes: partition into Kurdish, Shia, and Sunni territories; the emergence of a Shia "strongman"; or the anarchic fragmentation of Iraqi society.[29]

The Iraq War has left students and analysts of global politics with many enduring questions. First, what were the human and monetary costs of the war? At its peak, the U.S. led coalition deployed over 500 000 personnel, over 90 percent of these being American. When President Bush declared the war over on May 1, 2003, the coalition had suffered 172 fatalities. However, by June 2009 over 4200 U.S. military personnel had been killed in Iraq, and over 30 000 wounded. (The United Kingdom had suffered 174 deaths, and other coalition countries a total of 133.)[30] Estimates of Iraqi military and civilian casualties vary: one conservative estimate based on confirmed press reports of civilian deaths provides a range of between 108 593 and 118 669 Iraqi civilian deaths from violence between 2003 and August 2012.[31] However, another report based on household surveys estimated that approximately 1 033 000

Iraqi civilians were killed between 2003 and August 2007.[32] Meanwhile, the monetary costs of the Iraq war to the U.S. treasury are staggering. The U.S. Congressional Budget Office released a report in October 2007 estimating that the Department of Defense had spent US$413 billion in Iraq between 2003 and 2007.[33] A study by Linda Bilmes and Nobel Prize winner Joseph Stiglitz estimated that the Iraq War would cost America US$3 trillion.[34] It is worth remembering that cost estimates issued by the Bush administration prior to the war ranged between US$50 billion to US$200 billion.

Second, what was the Bush administration's motive for going to war? It seems likely there were a number of factors. The perceived threat of weapons of mass destruction unified the administration, even if this perception was based on the flimsiest of evidence. Certainly, Iraq was already on the agenda of a number of leading figures in the administration. In fact, some critics have charged that the administration was so focused on Iraq that it ignored the threat posed by al-Qaeda prior to September 11.[35] Still others saw a war as an opportunity to reorder the Middle East, by affecting regime change in Baghdad and installing a "democracy" in the region.[36] Much was made of the U.S. desire to control Iraqi oil (the "No War for Oil" slogan was a popular feature of the anti-war protests) and of the Bush administration's connections with the oil industry.[37] Certainly, controlling Iraq would make the politics of the international oil market much more favourable to the United States. However, although oil was a motive, it was likely not the only one: if it had been, America might have reasonably decided to cut a deal with Saddam Hussein. Earlier U.S. governments had done so, and had made similar arrangements with other authoritarian regimes. All these motives seem to have combined to take Bush and his senior advisors toward war.[38]

Third, was the Iraq War a "war of necessity"? In making the case for war, the Bush administration maintained that the war was necessary. However, as more information came to light this became an increasingly improbable argument. The evident enthusiasm for the military option within the administration rode roughshod over any alternatives, and belies the notion that war was undertaken as a last resort. Alternatively, a policy of "vigilant containment" may have been more appropriate.[39] Above all else, Saddam Hussein was interested in maintaining his own power, and therefore it was unlikely he would support or initiate an attack against the United States with weapons of mass destruction that would invite his own destruction in return. The Iraq War also diverted enormous resources and extensive diplomatic energy away from more immediate terrorist threats and the ongoing effort to rebuild Afghanistan. Certainly, the failure to obtain UN Security Council authorization was a major blow to the legitimacy of the war. For all of these reasons, the Iraq War may have been, as one of its critics suggested, "the wrong war, in the wrong place, at the wrong time, against the wrong enemy."[40]

Fourth, what happened to the weapons of mass destruction? Bush administration officials had repeatedly claimed there was "no doubt" that Iraq possessed chemical weapons, and was close to acquiring biological and nuclear weapons. Therefore, Iraq was an "immediate threat" to United States and global security. And yet, after the war was over, inspectors found no evidence that Iraq possessed weapons of mass destruction. This has led to charges that President George Bush and Prime Minister Tony Blair had engaged in a deliberate deception. Attention has also been focused on the U.S. National Intelligence Estimate on Iraq that proved to be systematically inaccurate for a number of reasons. The starting assumption was that Iraq would never give up its weapons of mass destruction. However, by the mid-1990s it appears that Saddam Hussein had decided to scale down his WMD program to avoid detection. This change in policy was apparently missed by intelligence agencies. Furthermore, when UN inspectors left Iraq in 1998, the primary source of intelligence gathering and verification dried up, leaving intelligence officials relying on suspect information that could not be independently confirmed. Lacking good data, they began to rely on their assumptions concerning Iraqi intentions. In an exhibition of "groupthink" behaviour, the Bush administration was clearly receptive to information that confirmed its beliefs about Saddam Hussein, and doubted or rejected contrary intelligence information. Efforts appear to have been made to manipulate intelligence by selecting certain pieces of information for reports to senior officials while excluding others. Finally, the Bush administration has been accused of distorting intelligence reports to enhance the public case for war. Administration officials would cite "worst-case" estimates from intelligence reports, but not the estimates considered most likely by the intelligence community. This is an especially damaging accusation for, if true, it represents a deliberate effort to mislead not only the American public but also world governments and world opinion.[41]

Fifth, why was the United States so poorly prepared to stabilize and rebuild postwar Iraq? The U.S. and its coalition partners encountered enormous problems dealing with stability in postwar Iraq. There was no clear transition government ready to put in place, there were an insufficient number of troops available to maintain order and prevent theft and looting, and there were insufficient resources available to repair infrastructure and rebuild institutions and government agencies. Critics charged that the Bush administration was unprepared for the challenges of governance in postwar Iraq. In fact, a great deal of planning for rebuilding Iraq had been done in the U.S. government. As early as late 2001, what would become the Future of Iraq Project was already under way in the State Department, preparing for a possible postwar Iraq scenario. In the year prior to the war, experts inside and outside government had warned Congressional committees that the challenges of postwar Iraq would be greater than the challenges of defeating the Saddam Hussein regime. The United States Agency for International Development formed an Iraq Working Group that accumulated the experience of U.S. non-governmental organizations in postwar environments. The U.S. Army conducted studies on the numbers of soldiers necessary to invade Iraq and maintain order afterward. The problem was not that these studies had never been carried out, or that the studies had failed to anticipate the postwar challenges correctly. The problem was that senior officials in the Bush administration ignored or dismissed these studies and reports, and chose to treat warnings about the challenges of postwar Iraq as anti-war sentiment.[42] Subsequently, the U.S. lost immeasurable credibility both inside and outside Iraq, and the Iraqi people endured a great deal of unnecessary suffering.[43]

Can the image of the United States recover? Perhaps the greatest criticism that can be brought to bear on the decision to launch the Iraq War is the damage it has done to the legitimacy, prestige, and image of the United States. In the wake of September 11, the U.S. received the sympathy and support of most governments and most peoples around the world. Unprecedented advances in cooperation on counterterrorism and intelligence gathering followed. The vast majority of the world's governments supported the war in Afghanistan. And yet, in less than two years, the United States had effectively squandered that sympathy and political support.[44] The credibility of the U.S. has been further damaged worldwide by revelations of the torture of Iraqi prisoners held by U.S. forces in prisons such as Abu Ghraib, civilian casualties, and the careless use of deadly force by some private security contractors operating in Iraq. The war has had a very negative impact on popular opinion of the United States in most countries, especially in the Middle East.[45] According to the U.S. government's own 2006 National Intelligence Estimate, the Iraq War has exacerbated anti–U.S. sentiment in the Islamic world, increased sympathies with extremist movements, and facilitated terrorist recruitment.[46] The Iraq war was also increasingly unpopular in the United States; in a poll conducted in November of 2007, 62 percent of Americans believed the Iraq War was a mistake.[47]

Loss of credibility. U.S. President George W. Bush is depicted with a Pinocchio nose on a float in the annual carnival parade in Düsseldorf, Germany, in February 2004. The writing on the nose reads, "Iraq possesses weapons of mass destruction." (CP Photo/Frank Augstein/CP Images)

The future of Iraq remains uncertain. While the end of the Saddam Hussein regime should not be lamented, the future of Iraq may be characterized by ongoing violence and social upheaval, the division of the country into Kurdish, Shiite, and Sunni blocs, or the emergence of another authoritarian ruler. Of course, one must dare to hope that the future of Iraq will be a better one, where a democratic system and economic development can offer a better choice than extremism and violence. The challenges are formidable, and depend on the willingness of Iraq's political leadership to overcome their differences and the willingness of countries (especially the United States) to commit the resources necessary for the length of time necessary to consolidate peace and stability.[48] In February 2009 U.S. President Obama announced that the U.S. combat mission in Iraq would end in August 2010, and in December 2011 the U.S. completed its formal troop withdrawal from Iraq.

The Iraq War of 2003 reminds us that interstate wars may still occur in an era of intrastate conflict and transnational security concerns. In 2011, there was one interstate conflict in the world, a border dispute between Cambodia and Thailand. However, examples abound of high levels of tension and rivalry between states in the contemporary international system that could lead to future wars:

- Greece and Turkey both claim control over islands in the Aegean Sea and have clashed over the control of Cyprus, an island divided between Greek Cypriots and Turkish Cypriots.

- India and Pakistan have fought three wars since the end of World War II and continue to clash over territorial and religious issues. In 1998, both countries tested nuclear weapons, raising the prospect of a nuclear war in South Asia.

- China, Vietnam, Malaysia, Brunei, and the Philippines are the principals in a dispute over the Spratly Islands, a chain of small volcanic outcroppings in the South China Sea. Small violent clashes have occurred over the possession of these islands and the right to exploit fishing and mineral resources and conduct oil exploration in the territorial limit around them.

- China and Taiwan have an unresolved conflict over the status of Taiwan, with Taiwan unilaterally claiming (though not declaring) independence.

- Israel and Syria have fought each other in the Arab–Israeli wars, and continue to dispute possession of the **Golan Heights**. Their interests and allies also clash in Lebanon, and the intense conflict in Syria could easily spill over.

- North Korea and South Korea have not fought each other since 1953, but a very high level of tension remains on the Korean peninsula, especially after two North Korean nuclear tests in 2006 and 2009.

- Peru and Ecuador have clashed over their disputed border since their last major war in 1941. The latest border skirmishes took place in 1995.

- Ethiopia and Eritrea fought a war over territory and economic issues between 1998 and 2000. The war ended in December 2000, and a UN peacekeeping force was deployed to the border between the two states. However, the underlying territorial and economic issues remain unresolved.

- Venezuela, Ecuador, and Colombia became embroiled in a crisis in 2008 when Colombian troops crossed the border into Ecuador to combat insurgents. All three countries sent military forces to their borders and the crisis was only defused through diplomatic efforts at the Organization of American States.

- Russia and Georgia fought a war in August 2008 over two separatist regions of Georgia, Abkhazia and South Ossetia. The status of these territories, which Georgia claims as part of its sovereign territory and Russia recognizes as independent states, continues to be a source of tension between the two governments.

- Sudan and South Sudan fought border skirmishes and nearly went to war in 2012 over the issues of borders and oil revenues. The Republic of South Sudan became an independent state in July 2011 after a long civil war, but the same issues that fuelled the civil war are now fuelling conflict between the two states.

Realists remind us that warfare between these states remains a very real possibility, and of course other interstate wars could break out almost anywhere with little warning.

INTRASTATE CONFLICT

As indicated earlier in this chapter, one of the most noticeable trends in international security is the extent to which traditional conflicts between states—interstate conflicts—have been less frequent, while conflicts within states—intrastate conflicts, often referred to as civil wars—have increased in frequency. These conflicts are often generically referred to as **ethnic conflicts**, but not all intrastate conflicts reflect ethnic strife. In many cases, they may be conflicts between religious communities, clans, or political factions. We use the term **communal conflicts** to describe wars that take place between communal groups, or between communal groups and governments, at the substate level.[49]

Communal groups come in many forms, but they all share one important quality: a sense of common identity. Ted Robert Gurr calls this shared sense of identity a "psychological community" that is enduring and differentiates the group from others.[50] This sense of identity gives the group internal solidarity and the capacity for collective action. Without this quality (if group identification is weak) there is seldom the potential for organized collective action by the group. Communal identities can be based on one or more of the following characteristics: ethnicity, historical experience or myth, religious beliefs, region of residence, or familial ties (clan systems).

Communal groups are fluid entities, and their self-identities may vary over time. Some may be assimilated into larger ones; and the unity of some groups may be influenced by their position within a larger society. If a group comes under external pressure (by, for example, a threat to its religious beliefs or social customs), its sense of identity and capacity for communal action may increase; if the group has its basic desires accommodated within a larger social structure, the identity and capacity for action may decline. Communal identity can also be affected over time by other social constructions. Myth and legend, passed down from generation to generation, can keep beliefs, values, and shared history alive, and reinforced through schooling and social life. Nation-states often aspire to a high level of communal identity and popular loyalty to state nationalism: many modern states spend time and money on fostering solidarity at the national level. Often, as in the former Yugoslavia or the former Czechoslovakia, the effort fails completely as substate communal loyalties persevere and triumph over state nationalism.

EXPLAINING COMMUNAL CONFLICT

Why do communal conflicts erupt? It is tempting to point to a particular causal factor and declare that it is the sole cause. In some cases, this declaration may be accurate. But in most cases, while some may be more readily apparent than others, multiple causal factors exist. Communal conflicts may originate in one or more of the following situations:

1. *Grievances.* One communal group within a society may have a grievance against other groups or against the state itself. These grievances may take several forms, including the following:

    *   *Economic grievances*, including conflicts over entitlements, resources, and the right or power to control them. Communal conflicts are often struggles against entrenched economic discrimination; one group may control these resources and the means of distributing them, leading to conflict between the advantaged and the disadvantaged groups.

    *   *Political grievances*, mainly conflicts over political rights and freedoms. In this sense, these conflicts are struggles against political discrimination, which may take the form of efforts to gain the right to vote, practise a religion, travel, organize, or secure protection from human rights abuses. In addition, the conflict may be a struggle for representation in the institutions of the state, government, the army, the police, or the bureaucracy.

2. *Autonomy and independence.* Conflict may develop out of the desire of a communal group for greater political and cultural autonomy or independence and statehood. Most communal groups regard a certain defined territory (which they may or may not

occupy) as part of their ethnic endowment or as their natural homeland. Conflict may develop between rival communal groups or communal groups and governments that claim the same stretches of territory.

3. *Social change.* Conflict may erupt when a communal group feels threatened by change, such as modernization. This change may take the form of the threat posed by industrialization or commercialization or by government policies that threaten their political, economic, territorial, or cultural position in society. In such cases, communal groups will mobilize in defence of their way of life.

4. *Primordialism.* Communal conflicts may reflect deeply entrenched historical animosity. Long memories of past injustices perpetrated generations ago perpetuate cycles of violence. This explanation suggests that communal conflicts start at the grassroots level between peoples.

5. *Incitement by leaders.* Alternatively, conflicts may originate with self-aggrandizing leaders who mobilize public support for their goals of territorial expansion or ethnic purification by vilifying other communal groups, creating scapegoats for economic and social hardships, or inciting conflict between groups to justify oppressive state control. This "instrumental" explanation suggests that communal conflicts begin at the *elite* level, not at the grassroots level.

6. *State nationalism versus ethnonationalism.* The nation-state is built on an internal tension between sovereignty based on territorial demarcation and the imposition of this sovereignty on the ethnic, cultural, and religious divisions of the world. In an effort to achieve domestic social unity, political leaders may seek to emphasize a sense of common identity based on loyalty to the state. However, this effort may threaten communal group identity and loyalty, sparking conflict.

7. *Power vacuums.* A structural explanation suggests that when central governments collapse or fail, communal groups become enclaves plunged into a condition of anarchy. A **security dilemma** can develop as groups perceive external threats, and attempts to protect group security become interpreted as hostile acts by neighbours, starting (or renewing) a cycle of mistrust or hostility.

8. *Symbolic politics.* Symbolic politics is "any sort of political activity focused on arousing emotions rather than addressing interests."[51] Ethnic conflicts begin when symbolic politics involving hostile myths and ethnic fears are mobilized in the absence of a political centre willing and capable of stopping this mobilization. When this happens, people make decisions increasingly on the basis of emotional attachments to ideas and values, preconceptions of enemies and heroes, and interpretations of right and wrong. This can lead toward confrontation and war.

THE NATURE OF COMMUNAL WAR

Intrastate wars have a very different profile than the wars of the past. As Kalevi Holsti has observed,

> There are no declarations of war, there are no seasons for campaigning, and few end with peace treaties. Decisive battles are few. Attrition, terror, psychology, and actions against

civilians highlight "combat." Rather than highly organized armed forces based on a strict command hierarchy, wars are fought by loosely knit groups of regulars, irregulars, cells, and not infrequently by locally based warlords under little or no central authority.[52]

The violence and brutality of contemporary communal conflicts has shocked and appalled most observers, and this sentiment is in no small part responsible for the many international efforts to terminate or manage these conflicts. However, wars have always been brutal, even so-called good or just wars. In World War II, for example, entire cities were laid waste in an effort to destroy manufacturing facilities and to weaken the morale of the civilian population. Massacres and rapes were not uncommon. What is it about communal conflicts that strike such a chord of repulsion? Is it the way these wars have been presented to viewers on television or the Internet? Is it because the relatively small number of casualties involved enables us to sympathize with the victims on an individual level in a way that we cannot with the abstraction of high casualties? Or is there a qualitative difference between these wars and interstate conflicts?

One significant difference may be the extent to which civilians are intentional targets in communal conflicts. Civilians are the centre of group power, the source of soldiers, food, and support, and so they are attacked to weaken the military potential of communal groups. Furthermore, in communal conflicts territory is considered conquered only when all or most members of the other ethnic group have been removed and people of the victor's ethnic group have been brought in to replace them; forcing populations to leave is a cornerstone of military campaigns in communal conflicts. The term **ethnic cleansing** has been coined to refer to this practice (see Chapter 9). The instruments of ethnic cleansing include forced deportation, mass murder, the destruction of homes and property, and the spread of fear and terror. Sexual violence has also been used as a weapon in such conflicts, most notably in the former Yugoslavia, Rwanda, Sudan, the Congo, and Syria. Beyond the obvious pain and trauma to individuals, rape spreads fear among the female population, compelling women to flee. In recognition of the significance of rape in armed conflict, in June 2008 the UN Security Council classified rape as a tactic of war and a threat to international security. The International Criminal Court's 1998 Rome Statute recognizes rape as a potential war crime. For all these reasons, the violence of communal conflicts is regarded as especially brutal, even by the standards of behaviour found in the history of warfare.

Finally, ethnic conflicts often have a powerful economic component that is sometimes overlooked. While the tendency of the observer is to focus on political, territorial, and religious aspects of the conflict, these may in fact be secondary to the economic gains the continuation of a war can bring to certain groups or individuals. Mats Berdal and David M. Malone suggest that civil wars of all kinds, including ethnic wars, have been "driven not by a Clausewitzian logic of forwarding a set of political aims, but rather by powerful economic motives and agendas."[53] For example, a rebel leader in Liberia was estimated to have made more than US$400 million a year from the war between 1992 and 1996. In Angola, the rebel group controlled 70 percent of the country's diamond production, creating an international reaction against "conflict diamonds" that were financing an ongoing war. In Cambodia, senior commanders in the rebel groups and the government's army alike were often more interested in reaping the profits of illegal logging and trading in gems than in the politics of the war.[54] As David Keen has suggested,

Conflict can create war economies, often in the regions controlled by rebels or warlords and linked to international trading networks; members of armed gangs can benefit from looting; and regimes can use violence to deflect opposition, reward supporters or maintain their access to resources. Under these circumstances, ending civil wars becomes difficult. Winning may not be desirable: the point of war may be precisely the legitimacy which it confers on actions that in peacetime would be punishable as crimes.[55]

This connection between ethnic conflict, civil wars, and economic gain must of course be addressed in any conflict management efforts designed to end such wars.

The case studies below provide some illustrations of the dynamics of specific communal conflicts. While many similarities exist across all intrastate conflicts, understanding the origins and dynamics of each conflict requires careful consideration of the circumstances unique to each war.

- *The collapse of Yugoslavia.* Yugoslavia was a federal state composed of eight republics and provinces, presided over by the dictator Josef Tito. It was a multiethnic state, composed of Serbians, Croatians, Muslims (Bosniacs), Slovenians, Albanians, and a variety of other communal groups. When Tito died in 1980, the federal structure and the federal army became increasingly dominated by Serbia, alienating the republics of Slovenia and Croatia, which sought to leave the federation and declare independence. Violence broke out in 1990 and Slovenia and Croatia declared independence in June 1991. The Serbian-dominated federal army was instructed by Serbian President Slobodan Milošević to use force to keep Slovenia and Croatia in the federation, but this effort failed. In April 1992, war spread to Bosnia, where the Bosnian Muslim government, having declared independence, wanted to preserve a multiethnic state. However, nationalist movements in the Serbian and Croatian regions of Bosnia sought independence and eventual amalgamation with Serbia and Croatia respectively. Months of heavy fighting followed, characterized by ethnic cleansing, artillery bombardment of cities, and battles for control of ethnic enclaves. The initial success of the Bosnian Serbs, supported by the Milošević government in Serbia, was reversed by a combination of a Muslim–Croat alliance, the withdrawal of support from Serbia (the result of UN sanctions), and the intervention of NATO in support of the UN. At the end of 1995, after more than three years of war, a peace was brokered for Bosnia, leading to the Dayton Agreement and the deployment of 60 000 heavily armed NATO troops authorized to use force to maintain the peace. While communal tensions remain high in Kosovo (see Chapter 7), an uneasy peace now exists in what is essentially an ethnically divided Bosnia. Slovenia and an ethically cleansed Croatia are now member states of NATO.

- *Somalia.* Somalia emerged from colonialism as an independent state in July 1960. However, it was deeply divided along clan lines. In 1969, Major-General Mohammed Siad Barre seized power and attempted to establish a socialist state. Barre was ousted in 1991 by a coalition of opposition clans. This coalition soon collapsed and months of war followed, destroying what was left of the infrastructure of Somalia. A humanitarian disaster of enormous proportions gained the attention of the UN and the international community, which responded in an effort to bring humanitarian relief and peace to Somalia. Yet while the humanitarian relief effort was largely successful, the peace efforts were not, and UN peacekeepers and American-led coalition forces engaged in armed clashes with local clan militias. The international presence was withdrawn in March 1995, and the country remains deeply divided between rival political movements based on clan divisions; it is often described as a "failed state" with no effective central government and poor prospects for long-term peace and development. Somalia is a continuing source of regional instability: the outbreak of armed conflict in 2006 between an alliance of warlords and Islamic militias led to Ethiopian intervention in the war. The chaotic environment in Somalia has also made the country a haven for drug and arms trafficking, terrorists, and pirates who seize merchant ships and their crews off the coast of Somalia for their cargoes and for ransom.

• *Israel and the Palestinian people.* This decades-old conflict has defied repeated efforts to build a permanent peace. In September 1993, a peace process culminated in the signing of an agreement between Israel and the Palestine Liberation Organization (PLO). However, the peace process began to unravel after the assassination of Israeli Prime Minister Yitzhak Rabin in November 1995. Another attempt to forge peace under the "Road Map" plan devised by the Bush administration in 2002 also failed (see Chapter 7). Little progress has been made on outstanding issues such as the future of Jerusalem, the return of refugees, Israeli settlements, and division of territory and land. A number of Palestinian terrorist groups have employed suicide bombers and rockets against civilian and military targets in Israel. The Israeli government has responded with a hard-line policy of doubtful legality including air strikes, military incursions into Palestinian self-rule areas, economic coercion, and restrictions on Palestinian freedom of movement. These policies have in turn inflamed Palestinian sentiment toward Israel. In 2002, Israel began construction of a "security fence," which became another source of tension between Israel and Palestinians. Unilateral Israeli withdrawal from the Gaza Strip in 2005 and the subsequent seizure of the territory by the Islamist movement Hamas in 2007 led to further armed conflict, including rocket fire by Hamas militias in Gaza against Israeli towns and Israeli attacks against Hamas targets, punctuated by armed incursions into Gaza by the Israeli Army. Violent conflict erupted again in 2012.

• *The Sudan.* The intrastate war in Sudan has waged since 1956, apart from a nine-year break in the 1970s. The war has pitted an Arab Muslim government in the north against African Christian and animist militias in the south and west. The conflict has been waged over territory, religious practices, separatist claims, and oil. In 2002, peace talks began between the government and rebel groups, and significant progress was made by 2003 when the two sides had agreed on regional autonomy for the south, the sharing of oil revenues, and religious practices. A peace agreement was finally signed on May 26, 2004. As noted above, South Sudan gained independence from Sudan in July 2011, and many of the issues that drove the intrastate war are now creating conflict between the two states. Another communal conflict and humanitarian disaster emerged in the Darfur region of western Sudan in 2003. Two political movements composed of local African communal groups rebelled against the government. In an effort to defeat the rebellion, the Sudanese government armed and supported an Arab "Janjaweed" militia, which conducted an ethnic cleansing campaign against the African population of Darfur. The violence began to diminish in 2009 and talks between the government and rebel groups led to the signing of the Darfur Peace Agreement in July 2011, but violence had intensified again by the summer of 2013. Estimates of the death toll vary widely, largely on the basis of whether deaths from disease and malnutrition are included with war deaths. According to one respected estimate, between 178 258 and 461 520 people in Darfur died, and over two million were displaced.[56]

- *Syria.* The civil war in Syria has its origins in the broader wave of revolutions and uprisings (commonly referred to as the **Arab Spring**) that swept across the Middle East beginning in December 2010. Governments in Tunisia, Egypt, and Yemen were overthrown by popular revolts, while the government of Libya was overthrown by an armed revolution with the assistance of a foreign military intervention (see Chapter 7). Several other governments across the Middle East experienced major protests that were suppressed with a combination of military and police repression and political concessions. In Syria, the civil war began in March 2011, with mass demonstrations calling for the end of the five decades of one-party rule and the resignation of President Bashar al-Assad. The Syrian military was deployed to quell the demonstrations, and in the face of increasing levels of violence against protestors, the demonstrations developed into an armed rebellion, pitting supporters of President al-Assad (largely members of the Alawite minority that controlled the ruling party) against a fragmented opposition composed of Syrian opposition politicians, defectors from the al-Assad regime, former Syrian army soldiers, and increasing numbers of foreign fighters. As violence escalated into a civil war in 2011, multiple efforts by the Arab League and the United Nations to broker a ceasefire or a political settlement failed. Repeated efforts to secure

A partial victory. Rebel fighters take control of Raqqa, Syria, in March of 2013. Despite a bloody civil war, the international community has been able to muster a coordinated response, and rebel groups are themselves often in conflict over how to govern cities they have conquered. Human rights abuses and war crimes have been reported on both sides of the conflict. The international community has NOT been able to muster a coordinated response. (Unimediaimages Inc - ADC / Rex Features)

international support for some form of intervention in the Syrian Civil War also failed, largely due to the reluctance of most governments to intervene and the active opposition of Russia and China to any UN Security Council Resolution authorizing intervention. In December 2012 reports began to emerge that chemical weapons had been used in the conflict, and in June 2013 the United States, France, and Great Britain accused the Assad regime of using chemical weapons against rebel forces. However, these accusations remained unconfirmed as this edition was going to press. Hundreds of thousands of refugees have fled Syria to neighbouring countries, and widespread human rights abuses have been reported across the country. Whatever the outcome of the civil war, the future of Syria will be at the very centre of efforts to establish stability in the Middle East.[57]

The cases we have examined here represent only a small percentage of the number of ongoing intrastate, communal conflicts. Every year, new conflicts emerge and many descend into violence. As a result, one of the core questions facing international conflict management is how such conflicts can be avoided and stopped. We will explore this question in Chapter 7. Of course, even a casual observer of the world's interstate and intrastate conflicts cannot help but notice the availability of weapons. We turn now to a discussion of the weapons proliferation problem in global politics.

THE PROLIFERATION OF WEAPONS

The proliferation, or spread, of weapons is a major international security issue. While most attention is directed toward weapons of mass destruction (nuclear, biological, and chemical), the spread of conventional weapons is also a matter of grave concern. Conventional weapons include a wide variety of weapons systems such as aircraft, naval vessels, missiles, and armoured vehicles, as well as individual small arms and light weapons such as assault rifles, rocket-propelled grenades, and land mines. The proliferation of weapons is regarded with anxiety because regional arms races can exacerbate existing tensions or raise levels of distrust and hostility, and should war break out the combatants will be equipped with more destructive weaponry. Furthermore, the possibility that substate groups such as terrorist organizations might acquire increasingly sophisticated weapons, including chemical and biological weapons, is a major international security concern. As a result, the control of the spread of weapons systems and weapons technology is regarded as an important contribution to both preventing war and reducing the level of violence in the international system.

THE PROLIFERATION OF NUCLEAR WEAPONS

Today, nine countries possess nuclear weapons, with one of them an undeclared nuclear power. (Israel has never formally acknowledged the possession of nuclear weapons.) Four other countries had acquired nuclear weapons but subsequently relinquished them (see Profile 6.2). Many other countries had active nuclear weapons programs at one time. Today, the two most prominent proliferation concerns are North Korea and Iran. Some scholars—in particular, some structural realists—have argued that nuclear weapons can have a steadying effect on regional stability.[58] As Kenneth Waltz argues, "The presence of nuclear weapons makes states exceedingly cautious. Why fight if you can't win much and might lose everything?"[59] However, the prevailing view is that the spread of nuclear weapons is inherently dangerous.[60] Beyond the temptation afforded by their availability as military options, the prospects for accidental or

PROFILE 6.2	**Nuclear-Weapons States: Past, Present, and Future**		
NUCLEAR-WEAPONS STATES	**FORMER NUCLEAR-WEAPONS STATES**	**STATES WITH PAST NUCLEAR-WEAPONS PROGRAMS**	**FUTURE NUCLEAR-WEAPONS STATES?**
United States (1945)	South Africa[c]	Iraq[e]	Iran
Russia (1949)	Ukraine[d]	Libya[f]	
United Kingdom (1952)	Belarus[d]	Argentina	
France (1960)	Kazakhstan[d]	Brazil	
China (1964)		South Korea	
Israel (1969)[a]		Taiwan	
India (1974)			
Pakistan (1998)			
North Korea (2006)[b]			

[a] Undeclared nuclear weapons state. The precise year of acquisition is unknown, and it is not known if Israel has conducted a test.
[b] In April 2003, North Korea informed U.S. officials it possessed a nuclear bomb. North Korea conducted one nuclear test in 2006 and another in 2009.
[c] South Africa developed nuclear weapons in the 1970s but unilaterally dismantled the weapons and the program in 1991.
[d] Ukraine, Belarus, and Kazakhstan all inherited the nuclear weapons on their soil after the collapse of the Soviet Union, but all three relinquished possession of those weapons.
[e] A significant nuclear weapons program was disrupted by the 1990 to 1991 Gulf War. Ceasefire terms required Iraq to eliminate all nuclear-related facilities and materials. No nuclear weapons were found at the conclusion of the 2003 Iraq War.
[f] Renounced its secret nuclear weapons program in 2003.

unauthorized nuclear weapon release will increase, especially as many new nuclear weapons states may not invest the same effort or resources into effective command and control systems. In addition, small nuclear arsenals may be more vulnerable to pre-emptive strikes, thus increasing the incentives to use nuclear weapons first in crisis or war. Finally, the monetary and environmental costs of nuclear arms races are tremendous, as the Russians and Americans are well aware.

Several rationales may motivate state leaders to develop a nuclear weapons capability. First, they may want to acquire nuclear weapons for security reasons, perceiving a threat from another country and seeking the bomb to act as a deterrent or as a weapon of last resort. Certainly, these were important considerations in the respective decisions by the Soviet Union and by Pakistan to develop a nuclear capability. Second, state leaders may seek the prestige such a capability lends: nuclear weapons are equated with power, modernization, and development. This was a factor in the Chinese and Indian nuclear weapons programs. Others might be seeking security, autonomy, and independence—the ability to be militarily self-reliant. This was important in the motivation behind the development of France's *Force de Frappe*. Alternatively, some countries might develop (or attempt to develop) nuclear weapons because of isolation (South Africa) or ambition (Iraq). As we saw in Chapter 3, another possible explanation is the influence of domestic politics: nuclear weapons may be acquired to advance the interests of domestic groups, industries, and bureaucracies.[61]

For any country seeking to develop nuclear weapons, several steps must be taken. First, the political will to develop the weapons must exist. Canada, for example, could build nuclear weapons quite quickly, but successive Canadian governments have decided not to do so.

Second, governments must acquire the knowledge base required, either by developing their own nuclear scientists and technicians or purchasing the services of foreigners. Third, the nuclear, industrial, and manufacturing infrastructure required to build a bomb, including the construction of a nuclear reactor, uranium enrichment facilities, and laboratories and manufacturing plants, must be developed. All this infrastructure takes time to build, is costly, and may be detected if the program is a clandestine one. Fourth, the necessary fissile material—highly enriched uranium or plutonium—is needed; a difficult acquisition for would-be nuclear states, since this rare material must be purchased from abroad or mined and enriched at home. Finally, a bomb design must be adopted and a decision made to assemble and deploy the weapons. A test may be necessary, although computer models have improved to the point where a country can have a high expectation that its bomb will work even if it is not tested. We will explore international efforts to prevent the proliferation of nuclear weapons in the next chapter, but the greatest obstacles to the spread of nuclear weapons remain the technical difficulty, costs, and lengthy time frame associated with a nuclear weapons program.

A small number of states have recently attempted to secretly develop nuclear weapons, and have resorted to building clandestine nuclear facilities with the help of international smuggling networks. Dr. Abdul Khan, the chief of Pakistan's nuclear weapons programs since the 1970s, headed the most famous of these networks. The "Khan network" operated out of Pakistan, using companies in Japan, Germany, Turkey, South Africa, Dubai, Switzerland, South Korea, Thailand, China, and the Netherlands as intermediaries. The Khan network provided assistance to Iran, Libya, and North Korea in the form of uranium separation and enrichment equipment components. The network was exposed in 2004, but Dr. Khan, a national hero in Pakistan for his role in developing Pakistan's nuclear arsenal, was pardoned. More recently, two of the countries assisted by Khan's network—North Korea and Iran—have been the focus of proliferation fears.

North Korea began its nuclear weapons program in 1964. Under increasing international suspicion, North Korea was accused of having produced plutonium for a nuclear bomb in the early 1990s. The international response was to call for inspections of nuclear facilities, which North Korea refused to permit. In 1994 negotiations between the United States and North Korea led to a Framework Agreement in which the North Korean government agreed to stop its nuclear weapons program and accept international inspectors in return for assistance in building replacement reactors for civilian use and regular supplies of fuel oil. In October 2002 North Korean officials admitted to having a program to enrich uranium, a violation of the 1994 agreement. In April 2003, a North Korean official informed U.S. representatives that North Korea had at least one nuclear weapon.[62] The already tense situation became a crisis when North Korea conducted a nuclear test on October 9, 2006. The precise motive behind the test remains unclear: perhaps the Kim Jong-Il government felt a test would allow the impoverished and isolated North Korea to negotiate from a position of strength; perhaps the test was a domestic political statement reinforcing Kim Jong-Il's power; or perhaps North Korea's government feared a pre-emptive attack on their nuclear facilities. Whatever the motive, the test certainly gained the world's attention and resulted in international condemnation (even from China, North Korea's only ally) and the imposition of additional sanctions.

The U.S. government had traditionally taken a hard line on North Korean nuclear proliferation, but in the wake of the North Korean test it changed course and began direct negotiations with the Kim Jong-Il government. This shift in policy led to the resumption of the so-called Six Party Talks (China, North Korea, South Korea, Japan, Russia, and the U.S.), a mechanism used to negotiate with North Korea since 2003. On February 13, 2007, an agreement on a

Denuclearization Action Plan was reached in which North Korea agreed to shut down its nuclear weapons facilities and accept International Atomic Energy Agency (IAEA) inspectors. In return, the Six Party Talks members agreed to provide economic, energy, and humanitarian assistance to North Korea, and Japan and the U.S. agreed to move toward the normalization of political relations with the Kim Jong-Il government. However, in May 2009 North Korea conducted another nuclear test, which raised tensions and threw the future of the Denuclearization Action Plan into doubt. The death of Kim Jong-Il in 2011 and the transition to power of his son, Kim Jong-un, has raised yet more concerns about the future of North Korea's nuclear weapons program. On December 12, 2012, North Korea successfully launched a long-range missile that delivered a payload into orbit, an act that was universally condemned and raised fears that North Korea was close to developing a missile that could deliver a nuclear warhead as far as the west coast of North America.

Similarly, tensions over Iran's nuclear program have risen dramatically over the past few years. Unlike North Korea, Iran has neither declared nuclear status nor carried out a test. Iran is considered a proliferation concern because it possesses a nuclear energy program, refuses to stop uranium enrichment, and refuses to allow unrestricted inspection of its facilities. The U.S., Israel, and many other countries fear that Iran's nuclear energy program is being used to develop a bomb. The UN Security Council has repeatedly called on Iran to suspend its enrichment activities and cooperate fully with the IAEA. The president of Iran at the time, Mahmoud Ahmadinejad, rejected these resolutions, arguing that Iran's enrichment program was entirely peaceful. However, the Iranian government has been less than cooperative on the issue. In 2003 Iran had signed an Additional Protocol arrangement with the IAEA, resulting in some of its equipment being sealed in special storage sites under IAEA supervision. Iran also agreed to additional regular IAEA inspections of its nuclear facilities to verify their strictly civilian use. In 2006 Iran withdrew from this agreement, broke the seal on the storage sites, and resumed enrichment activity. In December 2006 the UN imposed sanctions on Iran.

Divisions between the United States, Israel, Europe, China, and Russia on how to deal with the Iranian nuclear crisis have complicated international diplomacy toward Iran. Israel and the U.S. have been the most insistent on diplomatic pressure and sanctions. European governments have emphasized dialogue and negotiation, while Russia and China have been more reluctant to exert pressure on Iran. The Obama administration sought to deepen international sanctions against Iran, and additional sanctions were imposed in 2012, this time on Iranian oil exports. At the same time, the Obama administration conducted a clandestine cyber-attack campaign using software viruses to cripple Iranian nuclear facilities. However, neither of these efforts has led to the cessation of uranium enrichment in Iran or a change in Iran's negotiating position. As the crisis has intensified, there has been growing concern that Israel or the United States might carry out a pre-emptive military strike on Iranian nuclear facilities despite serious practical challenges and political risks.[63] However, any military strike against Iranian nuclear facilities would risk wider repercussions in a volatile region already beset with the aftermath of the Arab Spring uprisings and the civil war in Syria. In Iran, President Ahmadinejad used the nuclear issue as a means of rallying domestic support and positioning himself as a defender of Iranian national pride and technological prowess.[64] As a result, an uneasy stalemate developed, with the international community divided on how to proceed and Iran "playing it by ear."[65] The election of President Hassan Rouhani in June 2013 raised hopes for progress on negotiations with Iran, while some cautioned that the country's nuclear program has deep support within the ruling elite and no significant changes in Iranian policy could be expected.

Of course, states are not the only actors that may be interested in acquiring nuclear weapons. Concern is increasing that nuclear weapons may proliferate to substate groups, especially terrorist organizations. This fear has been magnified by concern over the security of weapons grade materials, technology, and warheads from the former Soviet Union and Russia.[66] Yet the likelihood of a terrorist organization acquiring a nuclear device or the capability to produce one is often overstated.[67] Terrorist organizations may not be able to achieve their goals with a weapon so destructive, and its use (or the threat of its use) might be counterproductive. Developing nuclear weapons is costly and, as noted above, requires a large physical infrastructure. Stealing a weapon is also a difficult proposition, but even if a warhead could be obtained, the terrorists would still have to find someone with the knowledge to detonate the bomb, which is a rare talent. Nevertheless, the threat of nuclear terrorism cannot be ignored, because the use of even trace amounts of plutonium or other highly radioactive substances in a "radiological" or "dirty" bomb would have enormous implications.

A NUCLEAR SOUTH ASIA

One of the most significant developments in nuclear weapons proliferation occurred in May 1998. From May 11 to 13, India conducted five nuclear tests, and Pakistan followed suit with six tests between May 28 and 30. While India had tested a nuclear device in 1974 and Pakistan was thought to have nuclear weapons by 1992, these tests heightened tensions in South Asia and increased awareness of the dangers of nuclear proliferation. International condemnation was swift, as countries such as the United States, Japan, Australia, and Canada imposed sanctions on India and Pakistan. The sanctions hurt both economies (especially Pakistan's), but neither country showed any indication of renouncing its nuclear weapons program. Although both countries were accused of violating international norms on nuclear testing and damaging the non-proliferation regime, Indian and Pakistani officials argued that such accusations were hypocritical. After all, they argued, most of their accusers possessed nuclear weapons or benefited from the security provided by them. Did not India and Pakistan have the same right as sovereign states to respond to their own security requirements?

As we indicated in Chapter 3, the relevance of nuclear deterrence did not end with the Cold War. Nuclear deterrence is alive and well in South Asia, raising fears that two countries that have fought three wars might fight a fourth war with nuclear weapons. These concerns were exacerbated by the development of ballistic missiles by both countries. However, the nuclear tests have imposed the same threat of mutual annihilation on India and Pakistan that existed between the superpowers during the Cold War. Indeed, on February 20, 2000, the leaders of India and Pakistan inaugurated the first bus service between the two countries in 50 years, using the occasion to reinforce their desire for peace and to avoid a nuclear war. Could nuclear weapons compel the two states toward a closer political relationship, much in the same way the United States and the U.S.S.R. established a closer (though still antagonistic) relationship? In the summer of 2000, a border skirmish in Kashmir between Pakistani-backed separatists and the Indian military increased tensions between the two countries. In late November 2008, terrorist attacks in Mumbai, India, were linked to Pakistan. These incidents illustrate that the possession of nuclear weapons will not necessarily prevent conflict between India and Pakistan.

In Chapter 3 we discussed varying explanations for why India and Pakistan tested nuclear weapons in 1998. Several factors played a role in India, including the enthusiasm of nuclear scientists, the Indian government's desire to increase domestic support, the threat from Pakistan and China, and the desire to be seen as a great power. Pakistan's government was under enormous pressure to respond to the Indian tests and not appear weak. Growing conventional military inferiority meant nuclear weapons promised security from India. And the Pakistani military, a strong force in Pakistani politics, was largely in favour of the tests, as was public opinion, with large crowds celebrating in an atmosphere of national fervour. Yet there were dissenters: in 1998, thousands of protestors marched in India and Pakistan. It is possible that these groups will be the beginning of growing regional antinuclear movements similar to those that existed in the West during the Cold War. As one Indian commentator lamented, "A country that has nearly half its population living in absolute poverty, that has an illiterate population more than 2.5 times that of sub-Saharan Africa, that has more than half its children over the age of four living in malnourishment can never be a superpower."[68] Furthermore, increased violence and instability in Pakistan have raised concerns about the safety and security of the country's nuclear weapons. If Pakistan were to become a failed state, what would happen to its nuclear arsenal?

THE PROLIFERATION OF CHEMICAL AND BIOLOGICAL WEAPONS

Although the proliferation of nuclear weapons has attracted the attention of scholars, government officials, and the public, the proliferation of chemical and biological weapons may be a more urgent concern. Chemical and biological warfare involves the dissemination of chemicals or living organisms over military or civilian targets. The primary vector—that is, the medium through which the chemical or biological warfare agent reaches a human being—is the atmosphere, although these agents can be transmitted to humans through water and skin contact as well. Chemical agents include mustard gas, phosgene, cyanide, and the nerve agents sarin, soman, and tabun, among many others. Biological weapons are living organisms that multiply within the host, eventually killing it, including plague, dysentery, typhus, anthrax, smallpox, yellow fever, and botulism. Research and development have produced newer and deadlier chemicals, and innovations in microbiology and genetics have led to the development of various engineered bacteria and viruses.

Chemical weapons were used extensively in World War I. The Imperial Japanese Army used chemical and biological weapons in China during World War II. Chemical weapons were used by the United States in Vietnam, in the form of napalm, defoliants, and tear gas. There were persistent allegations of chemical weapons use by the Soviet Union in Afghanistan. During the Iran–Iraq War (1980 to 1988), Iraq used chemical weapons at the front against Iranian troops and also used chemical weapons against a Kurdish rebellion in northern Iraq. In 1995, nerve gas was used in a terrorist attack in the Tokyo subway system. Chemical weapons have limited utility against well-trained and well-equipped military personnel. Against such forces, they are largely of nuisance value, forcing soldiers to wear hot, cumbersome, and restrictive protective clothing. Biological weapons have a limited battlefield utility, as they take time to incapacitate or kill and are hard to confine to a specific target area. However, both chemical and biological weapons can be devastating against unprotected military personnel or civilians, which is why they are classified as weapons of mass destruction.

Some countries may acquire such weapons for use on the battlefield, particularly if their prospective opponent is not well equipped with protective clothing. The use of gas by Iraq during the Iran–Iraq War demonstrated the utility and effectiveness of such weapons against unprepared opponents. Other countries may acquire these weapons for deterrent purposes. Compared to nuclear weapons, chemical and biological weapons are relatively inexpensive to develop and produce. (As a result, they are often considered the poor state's nuclear weapon.)

Furthermore, the technology is readily available because it is very similar to that used in the fertilizer or chemical industry, and the precursors, or component chemicals, are common industrial compounds that can be purchased openly on the international market. Research facilities need not be large or expensive: one U.S. study managed to build a small biological weapons facility for US$1.6 million.[69] Unfortunately, deadly chemical or biological WMDs may be seen as effective and economical alternatives to nuclear weapons (see Profile 6.3).

THE PROLIFERATION OF CONVENTIONAL WEAPONS

Although WMDs get more publicity, small arms and light weapons, such as military rifles, grenades, rocket launchers, and land mines, have been responsible for the overwhelming majority of war-related deaths and casualties since 1945. Conventional weapons proliferation has two dimensions: the legal international arms trade and the covert or illicit arms trade. Many of the conventional weapons that change hands do so through the perfectly legal international arms trade, either between governments or directly between corporate manufacturers and governments. The international arms trade continues to grow: the volume of all international arms transfers in the five-year period between 2006 and 2010 was 24 percent higher than the volume of all arms transfers in the previous five-year period between 2001 and 2005.[70] Five countries—the United States, Russia, Germany, France, and the United Kingdom—accounted for 75 percent of the supply of arms between 2006 and 2010.[71] The U.S. was the world's largest arms exporter in this period, accounting for approximately 30 percent of the international trade in major conventional weapons. Russia followed with 23 percent, Germany at 11 percent, France at 7 percent, and the United Kingdom at 4 percent. Between 2006 and 2010, Asia imported 43 percent of all arms transfers, while Europe accounted for 21 percent and the Middle East 17 percent. The value of international arms transfers is extremely difficult to estimate, due to different accounting practices and the recent decision by the United Kingdom and Israel (two major arms suppliers) to cease publishing data on the value of their arms exports.

Another point of concern is the quality of many weapons now being purchased. Particular concern exists over the spread of ballistic missile capabilities, which could be used to deliver

PROFILE 6.3	**States with Chemical and Biological Weapons**	
	CHEMICAL WEAPONS	**BIOLOGICAL WEAPONS**
KNOWN	Iran, North Korea, Syria	
PROBABLE	China, Egypt, Ethiopia, Israel, Myanmar, Pakistan, Russia, Taiwan	China, Cuba, Egypt, Iran, North Korea, Russia, Syria
POSSIBLE	Algeria, Cuba, Sudan, Taiwan, Vietnam	Algeria, India, Israel, Pakistan, Sudan, Taiwan
FORMER	Canada, France, Germany, India, Iraq, Italy, Japan, Libya, South Africa, South Korea, United Kingdom, United States, Yugoslavia (Federal Republic of)	France, Germany, Iraq, Japan, South Africa, United Kingdom, United States

SOURCE: CHEMICAL AND BIOLOGICAL WEAPONS: POSSESSION AND PROGRAMS PAST AND PRESENT, JAMES MARTIN CENTER FOR NONPROLIFERATION STUDIES, MONTEREY INSTITUTE FOR INTERNATIONAL STUDIES. FOUND AT: HTTP://CNS.MIIS.EDU/CBW/POSSESS.HTM (ACCESSED 28 JUNE 2004).

conventional, nuclear, chemical, or biological weapons in various regional settings. Many countries are acquiring sea-skimming anti-ship missiles, modern tanks, new fighter aircraft, submarines, and precision-guided munitions, and the spread of lethal drone technology cannot be far behind. Competition has led arms companies to offer generous offset packages to prospective buyers, which take a variety of forms. The importing country might be permitted to manufacture certain components of the weapon domestically under licence (and perhaps in time the entire weapon). Some offset packages permit the permanent transfer of technology to the recipient country. Governments may assist their own arms industries by lifting export restrictions on certain armaments. In other cases, governments may offer financing or credit to prospective buyers to secure the contract for their own arms industry.

The arms industry itself is also in the process of transformation. Just as global economic interdependence has facilitated the internationalization of civilian business, finance, and manufacturing, it has also facilitated the internationalization of the arms industry. Weapons systems consist of components and technology from a variety of countries and corporations; transfers of weapons technology between corporate subsidiaries are increasingly common.[72] Why do governments help domestic weapons manufacturers sell their product abroad? In some cases, hard currency is the main motivation, especially if that country is in dire need of cash. For some countries (such as Russia), military hardware is a significant export and hard-currency earner in the country's economy. Jobs are another incentive: governments will encourage arms exports to maintain production and commensurate employment. As long as the production line is busy, the skilled workforce, design teams, and manufacturing facilities (the **Defence Industrial Base**) will remain intact. If the production line has to close down, these assets may be lost. Finally, producers may want to encourage sales abroad to lower the unit cost of the weapon, which is reduced with mass production, making the weapons system more affordable, both for foreign buyers and for domestic purchasers. In early April 2013, the UN General Assembly voted to adopt a new Global Arms Trade Treaty (it will come into force after 50 states ratify it). It places a series of demands on governments to play a more active role in regulating the arms trade, ensuring that arms exports are not ending up in war zones and that arms brokers are subjected to greater scrutiny. Though the Treaty creates a new Secretariat to which states will have to report their exports of everything from battle tanks to pistols, most observers are skeptical that it will really reduce the global trade in weapons.

One reason for this skepticism is that, in comparison to the legal arms trade, the covert arms trade is harder to track. The value of the covert trade in armaments (or **gunrunning**, as it is sometimes called) is estimated at between US$2 billion and US$10 billion per year.[73] International arms dealers (often referred to as *brokers*) purchase and stockpile weapons for sale on the black market, or broker sales between sellers and buyers. The weapons may have been purchased legitimately, sold illegally, stolen from military stocks, diverted from their original destinations, or purchased in war-torn regions from individuals or groups that have a large surplus of weapons available for sale to any bidder. The weapons are then transported through transshipment points to their buyers.

The challenge of responding to the illegal trade in weapons is illustrated by the case of Victor Bout, the notorious "Merchant of Death." For two decades, Bout supplied weapons to many of the world's conflicts, often in violation of UN arms embargoes. Bout also supplied weapons to dictators and terrorist groups. Wanted since 2002, Bout evaded capture for years by exploiting the gaps between national and international laws and weak enforcement capacities. In March 2008 authorities in Thailand arrested Bout, but inevitably others will rise to take his place.[74]

INTERNATIONAL TERRORISM

Terrorism: few words generate such an emotional impact today. The surprise that attends most acts of terrorism is key; without warning, a plane is hijacked, a bomb explodes, or individuals are kidnapped or taken hostage. And yet, many more cases go unnoticed or unreported. Terrorism directly or indirectly affects the policies of all actors in global politics, and terrorist activity often stretches across borders and regions. In this sense, it is a transnational security concern. Huge sums are spent every year on counterterrorism and security measures at airports, government buildings, business facilities, and public places. The terrorist attacks committed against the United States on September 11, 2001, brought all of the debates about terrorism and counterterrorism into sharp relief and raised the profile of international terrorism to an unprecedented level. The United States and many other countries now regard international terrorism as the most important security threat they face. Canada has been relatively unscathed by terrorist attacks: although 25 Canadians died in the September 11 attacks, and there can be no doubt that international terrorists use Canada as a travel conduit, a location for fundraising, and a place where a small minority of sympathetic individuals might be found, incidents of international terrorism in Canada have been rare.

Terrorist incidents, or the causes that motivate them, often have deep historical roots. Traditionally, non-state terrorism has been the weapon of the weak, employed as a political instrument by individuals or groups seeking to reject authority, generate social change, promote revolution, or spread fear. Historical examples of the use of terrorism include the Zealots, a Jewish sect that appeared in BCE 6 and used assassinations in an effort to force the Roman Empire out of Palestine. In the Middle East between 1090 and 1275 CE, Muslims known as *hashashin* (from which the word *assassin* originates) carried out many political and religious killings on behalf of their political and spiritual leaders. In 1605, a group of English Catholics conspired to blow up James I of England, in the failed "gunpowder plot." At the end of the 19th century, political assassinations by anarchists claimed U.S. President William McKinley, French President Sadi Carnot, the Empress Elizabeth of Austria, and Spanish Prime Minister Antonio Canovas. World War I began with an act of terrorism—the assassination of Austrian Archduke Franz Ferdinand—by a Serbian terrorist organization called the Black Hand. In an eerie precursor to contemporary car bombings, in 1920 a horse-drawn cart exploded on Wall Street in New York City, killing 40 and injuring 300 in an attack that remains unsolved. In 1946, the Jewish Irgun Tsvai-Leumi bombed the King David Hotel, the headquarters of the British Secretariat in Palestine, killing 91 people. At the 1972 Olympics in Munich, the Palestinian group Black September killed 11 Israeli athletes. Also in 1972, "Bloody Friday" claimed 9 lives and injured 130 as 22 bombs planted by the Irish Republican Army exploded in and around Belfast. In 1980, government-backed death squads in El Salvador killed a Catholic priest and four U.S. nuns. In a rare Canadian example, in 1985 a bomb placed on board Air India Flight 182 by Sikh extremists at Vancouver International Airport killed 329 people, most of them Canadians of Indian descent. North Korean agents planted a bomb on Korean Airlines Flight 858 in 1987, killing all 115 on board. In 1993, a car bomb exploded in the underground parking lot of the World Trade Center Towers in New York, killing six. In 1995, a Japanese cult named Aum Shinrikyo released sarin nerve gas in the Tokyo subway system, killing 12 and injuring 5000. In the same year, 168 people were killed when Timothy McVeigh and his associates detonated a truck bomb outside a federal building in Oklahoma City. In 1999, Ahmed Rassam, an Algerian national, was arrested crossing the Canada–United States border with explosive materials for a bomb intended to attack Los Angeles International Airport. These incidents are a small fraction of the terrorist acts perpetrated over the years, but illustrate how terrorism as a historical phenomenon cuts across countries, regions, and cultures.

There is no universally accepted definition of terrorism in international law. Definitions of terrorism are notoriously difficult to construct, in part because *terrorism* is a politically charged word, and is often used inappropriately for political purposes. The familiar adage, "one person's terrorist is another's freedom fighter," illustrates the relative nature of the term. Many different types of terrorism occur, and it is difficult to establish a single definition that accounts for all of them. Walter Laqueur defines terrorism as "the substate application of violence or threatened violence intended to sow panic in a society, to weaken or even overthrow the incumbents, and to bring about political change."[75] Cindy Combs defines terrorism as "a synthesis of war and theatre, a dramatization of the most proscribed kind of violence—that which is perpetrated on innocent victims—played before an audience in the hope of creating a mood of fear, for political purposes."[76] Paul Wilkinson's definition is more comprehensive:

> Terrorism is the systematic use of coercive intimidation, usually to serve political ends. It is used to create and exploit a climate of fear among a wider target group than the immediate victims of the violence, often to publicize a cause, as well as to coerce a target into acceding to terrorist aims. Terrorism may be used on its own or as part of a wider conventional war. It can be employed by desperate and weak minorities, by states as a tool of domestic and foreign policy, or by belligerents as an accompaniment or additional weapon in all types and stages of warfare. A common feature is that innocent civilians, sometimes foreigners who know nothing of the terrorist's political quarrel, are killed or injured.[77]

Many definitions of contemporary terrorism also reflect the "stateless" quality of some terrorist acts. As Suman Gupta argues, for many terrorist acts "the motives and/or agencies and/or effects cross the boundaries of nation-states, and are not necessarily conducted (certainly seldom directly) at the behest of any nation-state."[78]

Paul Wilkinson's definition reminds us that individuals and groups are not the only perpetrators of terrorism. Although the image of the small terrorist cell operating in a clandestine fashion in the city or countryside is the most popular conception of terrorism, much of the terrorism in the world is planned and executed by states against their own citizens. **State terrorism** is employed by states within their own borders to suppress dissent and silence opposition. Such campaigns frequently involve massive human rights violations, an issue we shall return to in later chapters. State terrorism also has deep historical roots. The Roman emperor Nero killed large numbers of suspected political opponents, including members of his own family. In the French Revolution, state terrorism was employed as a tool of the French Republic to get rid of its enemies. During the years of racial segregation, or apartheid, in South Africa, government hit squads killed political opponents of the regime to spread fear and to intimidate others. In the late 1970s, the Khmer Rouge in Cambodia systematically murdered approximately 1.5 to 2 million people in an effort to fulfill a bizarre ideological purification of the country. The military government of Argentina was responsible for the deaths of almost 10 000 people in 1976 and 1977 alone. In the 1980s, the government of Guatemala used death squads to conduct assassinations and kidnappings of political opponents. Accusations of state terrorism have been directed against Israel for its actions against Palestinians. Such state terrorism differs from **state-sponsored terrorism**, which is the support of international terrorist individuals or groups by a government. Libya once provided sanctuary and assistance to the Abu Nidal Organization, and Iran has supported the operations of Hamas and Hezbollah, among others. Many accusations of state-sponsored terrorism have been directed against the United States: the arming and training of the Contras in Nicaragua in their effort to overthrow the Sandinista government is but one example.

THE ORIGINS AND CAUSES OF TERRORISM

State terrorism is designed to eliminate political opposition, and the killers and torturers who engage in it are paid for their work, which can even become routine for them. But what causes the non-state terrorist to commit acts of violence against innocent people? If appropriate and effective counterterrorist strategies are to be developed, an understanding of these motives is essential. Studies of terrorism and terrorists suggest that terrorism can be explained by the following factors:

Individual and Group Psychology

Some researchers suggest that the root cause of terrorism is the psychological makeup of the individuals who participate in terrorist activities. In particular, personal motivations such as the desire for glory, romantic visions of sacrifice and struggle for a cause, feelings of obligation or duty to family or community, the sense of identity and community found in terrorist cells, or a desire for revenge are powerful explanations for terrorist actions. Some psychologists and psychiatrists suggest that personality disorders or even mental illness may explain terrorist activity.

Ideological Fanaticism

Terrorism can originate from the commitment of individuals and groups to a particular political idea and their efforts to promote social change through violence. Ideologies such as Marxism–Leninism, fascism, and extreme racism offer a framework for interpreting social injustice and inequality and identifying those responsible, and provide a program of action to build a better society.

Religious Fanaticism

Terrorist acts may originate in religious extremism, drawn from literal interpretations of religious beliefs. Often, religious fanaticism employs a belief system that is in fact a perversion of the principles of that religion. Terrorist acts are carried out by individuals or groups seeking to advance their religious views, secure religious rights or freedoms, or wage a holy war against their religious enemies.

Grievance and Cycles of Violence

Terrorist acts may originate with the grievances of a particular group. This group may be the target of discrimination and repression, which may include economic, political, or religious persecution. In some instances, this persecution may be violent. Although the relationship between poverty and terrorism is uncertain, the combination of economic and political grievances can create angry and resentful individuals, who can then be recruited and indoctrinated to carry out acts of violence against the perceived enemy.

Nationalism and Separatism

Terrorism may also originate from the desire of individuals within a larger community for greater political autonomy or even full independence. While this desire often originates with a history of grievances, the specific aim of the terrorist activity is to advance the political independence of a group. The FLQ (Front de libération du Québec) was a classic Canadian example.

Activist Fanaticism

Terrorist activity may also originate from a very specific issue or controversy that provokes certain individuals or groups to violence. The aim of such violence is to prevent certain political or social activity or to force their belief systems on others. Such issues include abortion, animal rights, racial superiority, and environmental protection.

Despite the shock and horror terrorism evokes, it is seldom successful in achieving its stated objectives. While terrorist activity is designed to promote a cause, it can often have the opposite effect, alienating other supporters of the cause and discrediting moderates. While a harsh backlash against terrorists by a central authority can drive more people to the terrorists' cause, these measures can also lead to persecution and repression of the people or group the terrorist organization is supposedly fighting for.

9:03 a.m., September 11, 2001. United Airlines Flight 175 strikes the south tower of the World Trade Center in New York, just 18 minutes after American Airlines Flight 11 hit the north tower. Both towers subsequently collapsed. (AP Photo/Moshe Bursuker/CP Images)

SEPTEMBER 11, 2001

On the morning of September 11, 2001, nineteen terrorists used box cutters and verbal threats to hijack four civilian airliners in the United States. Two of the aircraft were deliberately crashed into the twin towers of the World Trade Center in New York, which subsequently collapsed on live global television. The third hijacked plane was crashed into the Pentagon, the headquarters of the U.S. Department of Defense. The fourth plane, whose target was believed to have been either the Capitol Building or the White House, crashed into a field in Pennsylvania, apparently when the passengers tried to overpower the hijackers. Over 3000 people were killed that morning. For most, it was a day of profound shock and dismay, as well as fear and uncertainty of what might happen next. All civilian airline traffic in the United States was grounded, and most flights inbound from other parts of the world were diverted to Canada. The Canada–United States border was closed, bringing cross-border travel and commerce to a halt. In the following days, as transportation systems in North America resumed operation and cleanup efforts started to remove rubble and human remains, expressions of sympathy and support were extended to the United States from around the world.

Though many reasonable questions remain about the origin and execution of the September 11 attacks, they are generally assumed to be the result of years of planning and preparation by al-Qaeda, a terrorist group led by Osama Bin Laden. As early as two days after the attacks, official suspicion fell on al-Qaeda, as the organization had been responsible for the bombing of the World Trade Center in 1993, the bombings of U.S. embassies in Africa in 1998, and an attack on a U.S. warship in 2000. With operations and terrorist cells in over 50 countries, al-Qaeda engaged in the planning and execution of attacks, fundraising efforts, and training thousands of terrorist fighters (primarily in bases in Afghanistan). Days later, Osama Bin Laden was formally accused as the perpetrator of the attacks. On September 20, President George W. Bush declared, "Our war on terror begins with al-Qaeda, but it does not end there. It will not end until every terrorist group of global reach has been found … and defeated."[79]

The motive for the September 11 attacks has been the subject of considerable debate and controversy. The increasing resentment directed against the United States in large parts of the world in general and the Islamic world in particular was well understood by observers of global politics (though not the American population at large). Anti-American sentiment was built on a wide array of grievances that include U.S. support for Israel (and therefore complicity in the repression of the Palestinian people), U.S. assistance to repressive regimes in the Islamic world, the growing cultural influences of the United States, and a reaction against Western modernization and globalization, which is led in large part by Washington. The world perspective of Osama Bin Laden and the al-Qaeda ideology used an extreme interpretation of these grievances, and combined them with a particular brand of Islamic fundamentalism, to recruit and train young volunteers for a perverse form of *jihad* or holy war against America and the West. However, there may also have been a broader political purpose behind the attacks. Al-Qaeda had long regarded most Middle Eastern governments as enemies of Islam. The September 11 attacks may have been intended to precipitate an American reaction that would lead to a general uprising and revolution across the Arab world. Critics of U.S. foreign policy also pointed out that Bin Laden (virtually unknown at this time) and other extremists had received U.S. assistance during the Cold War in their fight against the Soviet occupation of Afghanistan.[80]

Of course, any suggestion that American foreign policy may have been even partially responsible for the September 11 attacks was rejected by Washington, which quickly cast the attacks as an act of unjustified aggression by extremists. In one sense, this sentiment is understandable, as none of the 3000 people who were killed in the attacks had any hand in the real or imagined grievances of the attackers. It is also hard to imagine any political leader acknowledging that a terrorist attack might have been understandable. Moreover, one cannot blame U.S. foreign policy in isolation from other factors, including the hate- and ambition-inspired motives of terrorist leaders and the propaganda and invective they employ to guide others to kill in the name of faith or politics. It is difficult to imagine any political initiatives that could satisfy al-Qaeda, whose spokesman, Suleiman Abu Ghaith, stated that there could be no truce until four million Americans had been killed.[81] However, in another sense this rejection of responsibility by the American government is a counterproductive sentiment, for it absolves the United States of any critical reflection on its role in the world. The U.S. cannot detach itself or its policy decisions from the political and economic grievances that even now are being used to preach hatred and violence against it, and to recruit future generations of poor, desperate, ignorant, angry, and easily misled youth to be the next generation of terrorists.

THE WAR IN AFGHANISTAN

Once al-Qaeda was identified as the perpetrator, the United States began to move against the group's primary base of operations in Afghanistan, which was then ruled by the Taliban, a predominantly Pashtun group that had seized power over much of the country in 1997 (with the exception of anti-Taliban regions in the north). Composed largely of students of religious schools preaching an extremist form of Islam, the Taliban government was already isolated from the international community for its harsh imposition of Islamic law and its treatment of women. The U.S. accused the Taliban government of harbouring al-Qaeda terrorists and Osama Bin Laden and demanded they be handed over to American authorities. The Taliban government refused, and the diplomatic efforts of Pakistan and Saudi Arabia to change the Taliban government's position were unsuccessful. The Bush administration began a war against Afghanistan on October 7, 2001, with the stated objectives of destroying al-Qaeda, capturing Osama Bin Laden, and overthrowing the Taliban government.

The war in Afghanistan received considerable international support. Thirty-three countries offered military forces, and many others offered political support. (For an explanation of Canada's role in Afghanistan, see Profile 6.4.) There was, however, controversy over the legalities of military action against Afghanistan. Critics charged that the operation did not have the explicit authorization of the UN Security Council and was therefore illegal. Others argued that because the United States was responding to the September 11 attacks, military action against Afghanistan was legal under the right of self-defence. While legal experts deliberated, the military campaign moved swiftly. Through a combination of Special Forces personnel on the ground cooperating with anti-Taliban forces in the north, and the extensive use of airpower, the U.S.–led coalition successfully overthrew the Taliban government in November. Many senior Taliban and al-Qaeda figures were captured or killed, but Osama Bin Laden himself eluded capture until he was killed in a raid by U.S. special operations soldiers at his hiding place in Abbottabad, Pakistan, on May 2, 2011.

Political events also moved swiftly. Under the Bonn Agreement of December 2001, an Afghan Interim Authority was established, beginning a process designed to establish a new government in Afghanistan. In January 2002 a UN International Security and Assistance Force (ISAF) deployed to Kabul to assist in providing security in the area around the capital, while U.S.–led coalition forces under Operation Enduring Freedom fought surviving Taliban and al-Qaeda forces in the west and south of Afghanistan. In 2003 the North Atlantic Treaty Organization (NATO) assumed control over ISAF (a transition authorized by the UN Security Council). Although Taliban and al-Qaeda resistance continued, the Bonn process led to the adoption of a new constitution and the election of Hamid Karzai as president in 2004. NATO expanded ISAF operations across the country between 2003 and 2006, establishing Provincial Reconstruction Teams (PRTs) under the control of NATO member states in most Afghan provinces. The PRTs were designed to provide security assets and development resources that together would defeat the Taliban insurgency. However, in recent years the efforts of NATO, international aid organizations, and the Afghan government have encountered many obstacles and challenges. NATO–led combat forces (with the exception of training experts and special forces personnel) are due to leave Afghanistan by the end of 2014, and there are serious doubts about the long-term prospects for peace and stability in the country after the withdrawal.

Overall, the security situation in Afghanistan has deteriorated steadily since 2001.[82] The number of violent incidents and civilian deaths in the country continues to increase, with 2010 the worst year for civilian deaths since the conflict began. A resilient insurgency has shifted tactics from larger-scale operations to suicide bombings, the use of improvised explosive devices

PROFILE 6.4   Canada in Afghanistan

In the wake of the September 11, 2001, attacks, Canada added its voice to the international condemnation of Afghanistan, and supported U.S. diplomatic efforts to pressure the Taliban government into surrendering Bin Laden and the al-Qaeda leadership. When the U.S.–led military campaign began in October 2001, Canada deployed a naval task force to the Persian Gulf in support of coalition operations in the region. In February 2002 a battle group of 800 personnel were deployed to Kandahar Province in Afghanistan to assist U.S. and coalition forces in the U.S.–led Operation Enduring Freedom against the Taliban and al-Qaeda fighters. There was some opposition to Canada's participation in the war in Afghanistan: some felt Canada was abandoning its peacekeeping tradition and following Washington too closely. However, for the most part there was widespread support for Canada's contribution as a justifiable response to terrorism and an expression of Canada's commitment to the United States. The Canadian battle group was withdrawn from Afghanistan in July 2002. In February 2003 the Canadian government announced it would send Canadian troops back to Afghanistan. The decision was widely viewed as a tactic to avoid the deployment of Canadian ground forces in the Iraq War. From August 2003 to December 2005, Canada's military commitment was based in Kabul, as part of the NATO–led, UN–mandated International Security Assistance Force (ISAF), which was to provide the security required for the rebuilding of Afghanistan (Canada would

command ISAF for much of 2004). In August 2005, Canada assumed responsibility for the Kandahar Provincial Reconstruction Team (PRT), and Canadian forces were redeployed from Kabul to the volatile southern province. The Canadian effort in Kandahar was multidimensional: in addition to providing security, the PRT was responsible for assisting Afghan reconstruction and development. The Canadian government formally ended Canada's combat military mission in Afghanistan at the end of 2011, pledging to contribute personnel to the NATO effort to train the Afghan National Army and police until 2014.

The mission in Afghanistan was a high-profile component of Canadian foreign policy: it was the longest overseas deployment of Canadian troops since the Cold War, and from 2005 Afghanistan was the largest recipient of Canadian development assistance funding. Afghanistan became a major political issue in Canada. Supporters of the mission argued that Canada had an interest in the stability of the country and should honour its commitments to its NATO allies. Critics argued the conflict was too closely connected to the U.S. "war on terror," and was beset with poor planning, inadequate resources, and insufficient efforts to rebuild the country. The cost has been high: between 2002 and 2010, 158 Canadian soldiers were killed in Afghanistan.

FOR AN ACCOUNT OF THE POLITICS OF CANADA'S ENGAGEMENT IN AFGHANISTAN, SEE J. G. STEIN AND E. LANG, *THE UNEXPECTED WAR: CANADA IN KANDAHAR* (TORONTO: VIKING CANADA, 2007).

(IEDs), and smaller-scale "hit and run" attacks. While these tactics are incapable of holding territory against NATO forces, they are difficult to counter and have increased the sense of insecurity in the country, especially in the southern and eastern provinces. The conflict in Afghanistan is best described as an **insurgency** war, with ISAF troops and Afghan government forces trying to defeat a resurgent Taliban and maintain or establish a safe and secure environment for reconstruction and development efforts, efforts regarded as essential to gaining victory over the insurgency by winning the "hearts and minds" of the Afghan people.

However, attempts to improve the security situation have met with a number of challenges. The mountainous terrain of Afghanistan is ideal for insurgency warfare. The complex social structures of the country rooted in ethno-linguistic and tribal relations have complicated political reconciliation and federal and provincial governance. The historical antipathy of the Afghan people to foreign involvement in their country (drawn from experiences with the British Empire and the Soviet Union) has been an obstacle to trust and cooperation between ISAF and the Afghan government and people.[83] Civilian casualties caused by NATO air strikes have provoked much additional resentment. Despite having as many as 132 000 troops in the country at the end of 2010, ISAF has lacked sufficient resources to effectively control the countryside. Some NATO governments have been reluctant to commit their militaries to the more dangerous, combat-intensive mission in the southern part of the country, leading to tension within the alliance. Finally, the Taliban have relatively safe sanctuary in western areas of neighbouring Pakistan, which they have used as a base of operations and a recruitment ground for new fighters. In response, U.S. air and drone strikes and Pakistan military campaigns against the Taliban in western Pakistan accelerated between 2008 and 2013. However, these efforts have not proven decisive in the ongoing fight against the Taliban insurgency, and U.S. drone strikes have been deeply unpopular in Pakistan.

One of the most serious challenges facing Afghanistan and the international effort in that country is the narcotics trade. Poppy growth and cultivation has increased steadily since 2001. Afghanistan is responsible for over 90 percent of the world's production of opium, with the annual crop accounting for about one-third of the country's gross domestic product (GDP) in 2007.[84] Afghanistan has become a "narco-mafia state," with the economy of some areas dominated by poppy cultivation and drug-related corruption reaching the highest levels of government.[85] Proposed responses have ranged from eradication (which risks alienating local populations, harming local ecology, and plunging farmers into poverty) to legal purchase of opium for codeine and morphine (which would not yield the same return as opium for the drug trade). And reducing demand in the primary market for Afghanistan's opium—Europe—would also help.

The prospects for stability and economic development in Afghanistan ultimately depend on effective governance. Initial optimism for the Karzai government has changed to skepticism, largely due to the lack of capacity of the government, its poor or even nonexistent control over large parts of the country, and persistent problems with corruption. Positive developments are in evidence: GDP grew by 8 percent in 2006, enrolment in school increased dramatically between 2001 and 2008, and cultural life (virtually nonexistent under the Taliban) experienced a renewal.[86] There is widespread agreement that strengthening the institutions of the Afghan government, as well as the Afghan National Army and the Afghan National Police, are essential if ISAF is to be able to withdraw from a country that is relatively stable and secure. To feminists, however, women and girls' rights remain a serious issue, to which we will return in Chapter 9.

A Canadian soldier on patrol in Arghandab, Kandahar Province. In 2008, there were approximately 2500 Canadian soldiers serving in the International Security Assistance Force (ISAF) in Afghanistan. Canada's combat military mission in Afghanistan ended in 2011. (AP Photo/Alluaddin Khan/CP Images)

INTERNATIONAL TERRORISM AFTER SEPTEMBER 11

Terrorism continues to be a major focus in the security strategy of many states and a domestic concern for governments worldwide. Recent discourse in most industrialized countries has focused on what has been called *Islamist terrorism*, a reference to terrorist groups and acts inspired by extremist or fundamentalist interpretations of Islam. In particular, attention has focused on al-Qaeda, the organization held responsible for the attacks on September 11, 2001. On the one hand, this emphasis on Islamist terrorism and al-Qaeda is understandable, given the focus on Iraq, Afghanistan, Pakistan, and other Islamic countries in the U.S. war on terror. Numerous terrorist groups are guided by extremist Islamic ideology and operate in countries from Mali to Indonesia. Furthermore, al-Qaeda has proved to be a resilient and dangerous entity, inspiring and conducting acts of violence in many parts of the world. On the other hand, the emphasis on Islamic-inspired terrorism has led to an unfortunate and inaccurate association of Islam with terrorism, a dangerous assumption that the "clash of civilizations" thesis (see Chapter 13) is now a reality, and a relative neglect of other forms of terrorism (especially state and state-sponsored). Critics of the war on terror and other national counterterrorism campaigns have argued that the focus on "Islamic terrorism" has led to prejudice and racial profiling against Muslims and people of Arab descent, and counterterrorism tactics are threatening the civil liberties essential to a free and democratic society.

In the past few years, al-Qaeda has continued to be the primary focus of global counter-terrorism efforts, largely because these efforts are led (or greatly influenced) by American policy. It is sobering to consider that after years of effort to eradicate al-Qaeda, it has survived, largely due to its evolution from a relatively coherent and structured organization based in Afghanistan to a decentralized network. Terrorist attacks attributed to al-Qaeda are rarely planned or executed by a central leadership, but instead are carried out by local or "home-grown" individuals or "franchise" groups sympathetic to al-Qaeda's visions and goals.[87] Using the Internet, al-Qaeda has remade itself into a global conduit for two basic messages: a simple narrative of Muslim oppression at the hands of unbelievers, and a call for violent "resistance" through jihad. The narrative of the oppression of Muslims is characterized by references to Western occupation of Muslim lands (particularly Iraq and Afghanistan), anti-Israeli and anti-Jewish sentiments, a deep hatred of America, and calls for the overthrow of existing secular governments in the Islamic world such as Saudi Arabia, Egypt, and Pakistan. While most Islamic scholars and imams generally understand *jihad* as a personal struggle for spiritual purity, jihad in the al-Qaeda formulation is literally a call to violent action to overthrow the oppressors of the Islamic world. This potent combination of a narrative of grievance and a call to violence by an evasive Web-based ideology with little or no centralized command or leadership has proven a difficult challenge for governments throughout the world.[88] As Audrey Kurth Cronin argues,

> Al-Qaeda's most potent sources of strength are its powerful image and carefully crafted narrative, assets constructed through … a sophisticated effort to build popular support for the cause. … Al-Qaeda is at heart a brilliant propaganda and image machine whose primary purpose has been to convince Muslims that they can defeat the West and in this way solve their problems.[89]

Around the world, there is growing concern that al-Qaeda's message is finding a sympathetic audience among some alienated and disaffected Muslim youth, sparking national debates on the assimilation and integration of Muslims into society and the role of racism and religious bigotry in social attitudes toward Muslim immigrant communities. The Boston Marathon bombing was a vivid illustration of these themes. On April 15, 2003, two pressure cooker bombs exploded on the route of the Boston Marathon, killing three and injuring 264. The bombers were motivated by a combination of radical Islamist beliefs, opposition to the wars in Iraq, Afghanistan, and their homeland of Chechnya, and alienation from mainstream American life. The bombers learned to build the bombs from an online magazine published by an al-Qaeda affiliate.

U.S. counterterrorism strategy has emphasized the use of military power projection and the physical security of American territory. While some successes have been achieved, such as the killing or capture of many senior al-Qaeda leaders, the U.S. war on terror has been heavily criticized. It has been widely interpreted in the Muslim world as a Western "crusade" against Islam, provoking increased anti–U.S. and anti-Western sentiment. The emphasis on military power in U.S. counterterrorism policy has been criticized as misplaced and counterproductive, marginalizing the importance of intelligence, policing, and political and social policy as responses to terrorism. The war on terror has sparked global protest over U.S. violations of human rights and international law. Examples include the maintenance of a detention centre at the U.S. military base in **Guantanamo Bay** where detained terrorist suspects were held without protection under the Geneva Conventions or U.S. domestic law, the practice of **"extraordinary rendition"** (the transport of terrorist suspects to third countries for interrogation and torture) by the Central Intelligence Agency outside of legal procedures, and the use of **"enhanced interrogation"** techniques that include sleep deprivation and "waterboarding" (a torture technique that simulates drowning). Finally, U.S. counterterrorism policy has raised serious civil liberties concerns, particularly with respect to the Patriot Act of 2001, which increased the powers of intelligence and law enforcement agencies. Significantly, establishing a timetable for closing Guantanamo Bay and banning waterboarding were among the first acts of the Obama administration, which also discontinued the use of the term *war on terror* and replaced it with *Overseas Contingency Operation*. The Obama administration has continued to follow a strong counterterrorism strategy, especially through the use of controversial drone strikes against al-Qaeda leaders, particularly in western Pakistan and Yemen, and the use of large-scale electronic surveillance, including the National Security Agency's controversial "PRISM" program, which mines data from Internet traffic and large service providers such as Google and Facebook. The existence of PRISM was revealed in 2013 when a former employee leaked documents about the covert agency's operations to the press.

As noted earlier, the attention placed on al-Qaeda and on "Islamic-inspired" terrorism has obscured the fact that terrorism is a much wider phenomenon. For example, in recent years terrorist attacks have been carried out by Tamil Tiger separatists in Sri Lanka, *Fuerzas Armadas Revolucionarias de Colombia* (FARC) rebels in Colombia, the *Ejercito Popular Revolucionario* (EPR) in Mexico, and Basque *Euskadi Ta Askatasuna* (ETA) separatists in Spain. (In October 2011, ETA announced it was abandoning its armed struggle for a Basque homeland.) Furthermore, governments have carried out acts that can be described as state terrorism, such as the policies of the Sudanese government in Darfur or the attempts by many countries in the Middle East to suppress the Arab Spring uprisings. Terrorism is likely to remain a feature of global politics in the future, enhanced by the use of Internet communication and Web-based information dissemination.[90] Concerns remain that terrorists might acquire and use chemical and biological weapons (see Profile 6.5) or perhaps even radiological and nuclear weapons.[91] However, it is more likely that the current trend toward globally inspired but locally derived terrorist activity using bombs and suicide bombers will continue to be the dominant form of terrorism in the future. Some analysts have argued that globalization is enhancing the terrorist threat: Audrey Kurth Cronin contends that "the current wave of international terrorism, characterized by unpredictable and unprecedented threats from nonstate actors, not only is a reaction to globalization but is facilitated by it."[92] However, others claim that globalization also provides opportunities to combat terrorism. As Kendall Hoyt and Stephen G. Brooks argue, "Many of the most effective tools for dealing with the terrorist threat are themselves partly the product of globalization."[93]

Another trend is the emergence of many terrorist groups that have somewhat different motivations than traditional terrorist groups. Most terrorism is motivated by a set of goals that can be quantified in terms of land, political power, or independence. However, the objectives of what Walter Laqueur has called *postmodern terrorism* are inspired by religious or cult beliefs or by racial hatred. These motives are not so amenable to conflict management efforts or negotiated settlements, and so there is considerable concern that such groups cannot be addressed by responding to root causes or by offering concessions. Perhaps most disturbing of all is the fact that these groups seem to have turned away from hijackings and the targeting of specific individuals and toward more indiscriminate killing.[94]

September 11 has led counterterrorism experts into a dangerous game of speculation as to what types of attacks terrorist groups may undertake in the future. Since September 11, terrorists have attacked nightclubs and street markets, civilian aircraft, embassy buildings, and train stations, to name a few. They might attack nuclear power plants or chemical industries with potentially devastating effects. Port facilities might be attacked using bombs planted on commercial ships or small civilian craft. National transportation infrastructure such as bridges, pipelines, power cables, dams, subways, and railways are all considered vulnerable. Portable

---

PROFILE 6.5 The Tokyo Subway Attack

In March 1995, 12 people were killed and more than 5000 injured by a sarin nerve gas attack on several Tokyo subway lines. The attack was carried out by members of a religious cult known as *Aum Shinrikyo* (Supreme Truth), a well-financed organization with more than 10 000 members in Japan and some 100 000 abroad. Asahara Shoko founded the cult in 1994, and his teachings spoke of an imminent Armageddon for modern society, which he believed was corrupt. Although many more casualties have been caused by terrorist bombings and shootings around the world, the *Aum Shinrikyo* acts are especially disturbing. For the first time, chemical weapons have been used on a large scale in an urban terrorist act. The cult maintained front companies and laboratories that employed highly skilled technicians and graduate microbiologists to develop and produce the gas used in the subway attack. In addition, the cult was a religious organization, not a political one, and was interested in promoting a theological outcome, not one designed to advance a political agenda or extract concessions from the Japanese government. As such, its actions cannot be responsive to political change designed to eliminate the root causes of terrorism. Asahara Shoko was found guilty of murder in 2004 and was sentenced to death. His appeal was denied in 2006, but in 2012 his execution was postponed.

Terrorism in Libya. A burnt car outside the U.S. consulate in Benghazi, Libya. On September 11, 2012, U.S. Ambassador Christopher Stevens and three embassy staff were killed as they rushed away from the consulate building, stormed by al-Qaeda–linked gunmen. In the remaining days of the 2012 presidential election, the incident was played out by Republicans as evidence that the Democrats were weak on security. (REUTERS/Esam Al-Fetori)

surface-to-air missiles might be used against civilian airliners. More ominously, terrorists with chemical or biological weapons might attack water supplies, public places, or urban areas using "crop duster" aircraft intended to spray agricultural pesticides. The anthrax attacks in the United States after September 11 used the postal service to deliver anthrax spores to a range of individuals in letter-sized envelopes. It is also possible that terrorists will turn to weapons of mass disruption in the future, choosing to attack computer and telecommunications networks in what are sometimes called *cyber attacks.*[95] The mere threat that a bomb exists or an attack is imminent can cause mass fear and disruption of transportation systems. In other words, wherever we look we are likely to see opportunities for terrorists. While such an exercise can be prudent if it leads to sound security improvements, it can also lead to an exaggerated sense of vulnerability and fear, suspicion and prejudice, and the expenditure of large amounts of resources to defend against an attack that may never come.

COMBATING TERRORISM: APPROACHES AND METHODS

Can international terrorism be stopped? Can a war on terrorism be won? Asking this question demands some humility, for terrorism has been an enduring feature of the history of human violence. However, terrorist groups can be defeated with a combination of sound policies. To the extent that terrorism is rooted in grievances, injustices, and a desire for autonomy or independence, efforts to address such grievances or desires might reduce or eliminate terrorist activity. Of course, particularly radical or extremist individuals or groups might not be satisfied with any level of accommodation short of their objectives; these individuals and groups would be increasingly isolated from their broader community, and easier to combat with law enforcement efforts. Of course, in many cases, governments and publics are committed to preserving the status quo, and are highly resistant to making economic, political, or social changes. Furthermore, in many regions of the world, poverty, despair, hatred, and other social ills are so pervasive that eliminating related terrorism would require revolutionary changes beyond the resources as well as the political will of governments. The motives of terrorists must also be understood if responses are to be effective: if terrorists are motivated by political aims, certain responses may be effective, but if terrorists are motivated by affective or emotional ties to each other and the group, different responses may be in order.[96]

Second, governments can employ military or police forces, or both, against terrorist organizations or the states that sponsor their activities. Such counterterrorist operations might include the use of highly trained teams of police or military personnel in large-scale search operations or the bombing of terrorist training grounds and facilities from the air. However, the usefulness of the military against terrorist organizations is limited. Terrorist organizations are hard to track and target because they are often small, and compartmentalized into highly secretive cells. Military operations against terrorists also face tactical and political obstacles. Terrorist facilities are often located in sponsoring states, and any attack against them would have to take into account the military capability of the host state as well as the political repercussions of attacking its territory. Often, military force is a very blunt instrument, and attacking terrorists or their facilities can lead to the deaths of innocent individuals; the use of military force can create new grievances and new martyrs for the terrorist cause. Furthermore, constructivists remind us that using the language of war influences our thinking about counterterrorism: by declaring a war on terror, the Bush administration captured a mood of sadness and anger that prevailed in the United States immediately after September 11, but also (intentionally or unintentionally) militarized the campaign against terrorism. The language of war focused discussion on military responses, while reducing the importance of non-military responses, international law, and the need to address the root causes of terrorism.

Third, efforts can be made to reduce vulnerability to terrorist attacks. Security can be increased at prominent government buildings and transportation infrastructure such as airports, and public places and events; computer networks can be protected; and surveillance of public places can be effective, if intrusive. Immigration and refugee applicants can be screened more thoroughly, and visitors to a country can be subjected to a higher level of search and investigation. However, these measures all carry the risk of infringing on people's rights, the selective application of security measures to certain minority groups, and the creation of obstacles to the free movement of goods and services. There is also a practical limitation on efforts to increase the physical security of a society: the scale of cross-border traffic and trade is simply immense, and security measures are at odds with the economic advantages of the free flow of people, goods, and services.

Fourth, governments can seek to strengthen international cooperation on counterterrorism. In order to meet the threat posed by international terrorist networks, states must design comprehensive and integrated strategy incorporating economic, political, legal, diplomatic, cultural, and military responses. Intelligence agencies must share information and coordinate law enforcement efforts and work with financial institutions to combat terrorist financing. States can establish bilateral agreements on **extradition** of terrorists for trial. For example, the political offence exception rule in extradition law allows defendants accused of terrorist acts to claim that they were engaged in political acts of conscience so that they are not subject to extradition. Bilateral agreements, such as the United States–United Kingdom extradition treaty, can remove this exception from certain acts of terrorism, such as skyjacking. A number of international multilateral treaties on terrorism also exist, though many states have yet to sign them (see Profile 6.6). However, in democratic societies, strengthening domestic law to combat terrorism is a serious matter, raising the danger of excessive restriction of freedoms and a slide into authoritarianism in the name of combating subversion.

Finally, publicity is a major objective behind terrorist activities, which brings attention not only to the attack itself but also to the individuals and groups who carried out the act, the cause or aim they purport to achieve, and the grievances or injustices they are struggling against. Terrorism attracts the attention of the media, the public, and government officials and elected leaders. The role of the media in covering terrorist incidents is controversial. Some argue that media coverage of terrorist incidents encourages terrorism (by providing terrorists with the publicity they seek) and that such coverage lacks sophistication and a high level of informed comment. Others argue that a free media is an essential component of a free society and that media reporting on terrorism, as long as it remains within appropriate ethical and legal boundaries, should not be constrained. Few would advocate complete media censorship today.

PROFILE 6.6 International Agreements on Terrorism

There are 14 major multilateral conventions on terrorism. In addition, there are many other instruments, treaties, and agreements between states on counterterrorism.

1963	Convention on Offences and Certain Other Acts Committed on Board Aircraft (Tokyo Convention)
1970	The Hague Convention for the Suppression of Unlawful Seizure of Aircraft (Hague Convention)
1971	Convention for the Suppression of Unlawful Acts against the Safety of Civil Aviation (Montreal Convention)
1973	Convention on the Prevention and Punishment of Crimes against Internationally Protected Persons, Including Diplomatic Agents
1979	International Convention on the Taking of Hostages (Hostages Convention)
1980	Convention on the Physical Protection of Nuclear Material (Nuclear Materials Convention)
1988	Convention for the Suppression of Unlawful Acts against the Safety of Maritime Navigation
1988	Convention for the Suppression of Unlawful Acts of Violence at Airports Serving International Civil Aviation
1988	Protocol for the Suppression of Unlawful Acts against the Safety of Fixed Platforms Located on the Continental Shelf
1991	Convention on the Marking of Plastic Explosives for the Purpose of Detection
1997	International Convention on the Suppression of Terrorist Bombings
1999	International Convention for the Suppression of the Financing of Terrorism
2005	International Convention for the Suppression of Acts of Nuclear Terrorism (Nuclear Terrorism Convention)
2010	Convention on the Suppression of Unlawful Acts Relating to International Civil Aviation

INTERNATIONAL ORGANIZED CRIME

Traditionally, organized crime has been regarded as a domestic political problem. Yet criminal activity has become increasingly internationalized, and organized crime is now considered a serious global security issue and a threat to the social, economic, and political stability of societies worldwide. International organized crime manifests itself in many forms, including trafficking in human beings, drugs, endangered species, toxic waste, and weapons, as well as money laundering, prostitution, kidnapping for ransom, and piracy. The increased attention placed on transnational organized crime is reflected in international agreements. At the 1995 G7 summit in Halifax, the participating states declared that organized crime represented a growing threat to the security of the G7 countries.[97] In December 2000, the United Nations Convention against Transnational Organized Crime was established, obligating member states to cooperate on extradition, mutual legal assistance, and joint investigations. Member states are also obligated to establish domestic laws against participation in international criminal groups, money-laundering activities, corruption, and obstruction of justice. Two optional protocols to the convention cover trafficking in humans and the exploitation of women and children for sexual activities or sweatshop labour. In October 2003, the United Nations Convention against Corruption was established, aimed at eliminating the growing threat presented by criminal activity to election and political party financing, judicial neutrality, and fair government contracting. Transnational crime has been identified as an international security issue for the following reasons:

- International criminal activity accounts for huge illegal profits worldwide. For example, an often-cited UN report estimated the value of the global drug trade at US$320 billion in 2005, while the value of world trade in opiates and cocaine alone was estimated at US$68 billion and US$85 billion respectively in 2009.[98]

- Organized crime has expanded into international banking, investment, finance, and business activity. **Money laundering** (the conversion of illicitly gained property or money into legal property and currency) is a major international enterprise, estimated at 2 to 5 percent of the global economy.[99] The volume of money involved has compromised some banking institutions. For example, before it was exposed the infamous Bank of Credit and Commerce International (BCCI) served as a money-laundering and criminal finance system for organized crime, although for most of its 1.4 million depositors, the BCCI was a bank like any other. (Notably, international criminal organizations are not the only actors that conduct illegal financial activities. Bank and government officials often commit fraud and conduct illegal transactions.)[100]

- Criminal organizations threaten governments. The Italian Mafia has used violence to intimidate the Italian government and law enforcement authorities; Colombian drug cartels have killed judges and politicians. In Mexico, tens of thousands of people have been killed in drug-trafficking-related violence since 2006, and threats and attacks against government officials have become commonplace.

- Criminal organizations can erode the social fabric of a country, undermining political authority and corrupting the economic and political leadership. In some cases, however, this is because criminal organizations actually improve the standard of living of rural workers or inner-city youths, whereas governments neglect them.

- In some countries, organized crime represents a threat to the conventional economy and the ability of the government to manage it. In Russia, organized crime accounts for a major portion of economic activity that is beyond government regulation and taxation. For example, organized crime figures are believed to exert a considerable influence over the energy sector in Russia.

- Worrisome indications exist that organized crime may be involved in the sale of materials required for the production of weapons of mass destruction, in particular nuclear materials, which have appeared in small quantities for sale in Europe.

- The distinction between organized crime and terrorist and revolutionary movements is blurring as terrorist and revolutionary organizations obtain funding from the sale of drugs and as governments funnel money from illegal arms sales to revolutionary militias. International criminal organizations are allegedly facilitating illicit transfers of weapons and financing to terrorist and insurgency groups.[101]

Organized crime exists in virtually all societies in all regions of the world, but the United States, Canada, Mexico, Colombia, Italy, Russia, China, and Japan harbour particularly powerful criminal organizations. Many of these organizations have been increasing their cooperation with one another across state and regional boundaries. In North America and Italy, the Mafia, or Cosa Nostra—with operations in 40 other countries—dominates organized crime. Its activities include drug trafficking, union control and corruption, loan sharking, illegal gambling, prostitution, and financial fraud. Mexican crime organizations smuggle drugs on behalf of the South American drug cartels and smuggle illegal immigrants (with the assistance of the Chinese Triads) into the United States. In Russia, the Russian *mafiya* has expanded rapidly, making inroads into North America and Europe. Its activities include slavery, theft, extortion, murder, money laundering, and poppy production (for the world heroin market). In Asia, the Six Great Triads (based largely in Hong Kong and Taiwan) form the largest and perhaps oldest criminal network in the world. They are involved in drug trafficking, arms trafficking, illegal immigration, gambling, prostitution, fraud, and product piracy. The Japanese *boryokudan*, or *yakuza* (the name used in the West for Japanese organized crime syndicates), also operate throughout Asia.

The expansion of, and growing communication and uneasy cooperation among, organized crime syndicates has been facilitated by the growth of global interdependence. Other contributing factors include the collapse of communism in the Soviet Union and the growth of capitalism in China, which have removed social barriers to criminal activity in those countries. The establishment of free trade areas and customs unions (especially in North America and Europe) has facilitated the flow of criminal goods and services across borders. The weakening of state authority in many countries has eroded the capacity of police and judicial systems to combat organized crime, though some governments have a long history of close ties with criminal elements.

As the operations of criminal organizations have become increasingly international, the effort to combat them has involved greater cooperation and coordination of effort between countries. The United States, for example, has developed a very high level of cooperation with many South American countries to assist in the effort against the drug cartels, including agreements on punishments and extradition, law enforcement coordination, intelligence sharing, and—most controversially—military cooperation. As international crime is likely only to increase, measures such as these may become increasingly common as governments seek to join forces to combat criminal organizations that possess resources greater than those of many states. Meanwhile, unless the demand for drugs in the United States is reduced, there is little hope that the drug trade can be defeated, even as the U.S. continues to wage a largely futile "war on drugs" in the Caribbean and South America. In 2000, the United States committed US$1.3 billion to "Plan Colombia," an effort to eradicate that country's coca production. This plan was expanded under the Bush administration in 2001 and again in 2004, to include a controversial increase in military aid, larger numbers of U.S. military advisors and private security contractors, and aerial fumigation of crops. Critics charge that this military aid is undermining Colombian democracy, ignoring the social plight of Colombia's poor, promoting ecocide, and supporting paramilitary groups that have been accused of human rights violations. Mexico has also been embroiled in a drug war since 2006, but despite high levels of cooperation between the United States, Canada, and Mexico and the deployment of tens of thousands of Mexican army troops, drug trafficking and its attendant violence show no signs of abating.

CONCLUSIONS

In this chapter, we have explored some of the major issues facing international security in contemporary global politics. One positive is that the likelihood of a great-power war remains low. However, in much of the rest of the world, there has been no respite from regional wars or the threat of their outbreak. Indeed, it is possible to speak in terms of zones of peace and zones of instability. Zones of peace, such as North America and Western Europe, enjoy relative freedom from the threat of war, a high level of prosperity, and high levels of economic and political cooperation. Within zones of instability, wars and revolutions and other forms of political violence threaten individual and social well-being. Will more regions become increasingly stable and free of conflict, or will instability and violence spread? We have also looked at weapons proliferation, intrastate conflict, international terrorism, and transnational organized crime. These are just some of the issues that are currently shaping the international security field, and we will encounter others in subsequent chapters. We now turn our attention to the efforts made to prevent, control, or manage warfare and international security challenges, efforts collectively known as *conflict management.*

Endnotes

1. E.H. Carr, *The Twenty Years' Crisis 1919–1939: An Introduction to the Study of International Relations* (London: Macmillan, 1942), 139.

2. F. Braudel, *The Mediterranean: And the Mediterranean World in the Age of Philip II, Volume II* (Berkeley: University of California Press, 1996), 836.

3. See, for example, K. Krause and M.C. Williams, "Broadening the Agenda of Security Studies? Politics and Methods," *Mershon International Studies Review* 40 (1996), 229–54; S. Smith, "The Increasing Insecurity of Security Studies," *Contemporary Security Policy* 20 (1999), 72–101; P. Stoett, *Human and Global Security: An Exploration of Terms* (Toronto: University of Toronto Press, 2000); and C. Bildt, "Address to the IISS 50th Anniversary Dinner," in *Perspectives on International Security.* Adelphi Paper 48, nos. 400–401 (New York: Routledge, October 2008), 29–34.

4. P. Andreas, "Redrawing the Line: Borders and Security in the 21st Century," *International Security* 28 (Fall 2003), 78. See also C. Coker, *Globalisation and Insecurity in the Twenty-First Century: NATO and the Management of Risk,* Adelphi Paper 345 (Oxford: Oxford University Press, 2002); and B. Buzan, O. Waever, and J. de Wilde, *Security: A New Framework for Analysis* (Boulder, CO: Lynne Rienner, 1998).

5. See M.C. Williams, "Words, Images, Enemies: Securitization and International Politics," *International Studies Quarterly* 47 (December 2003), 511–31; T. Farrell, "Constructivist Security Studies: Portrait of a Research

Program," *International Studies Review* 4 (Spring 2002), 49–72; and the groundbreaking book by D. Campbell, *Writing Security: United States Foreign Policy and the Politics of Identity* (Minneapolis: University of Minneapolis Press, 1992).

6. J. Keegan, *A History of Warfare* (New York: Alfred A. Knopf, 1993).

7. See, for example, Keegan op. cit.; *A History of Warfare* (New York: Alfred A. Knopf, 1993); and J.A. Lynn, *Battle: A History of Combat and Culture* (Boulder, CO: Westview Press, 2003).

8. See M.R. Sarkees and F.W. Wayman, *Resort to War: A Data Guide to Inter-state, Extra-state, Intra-state and Non-state Wars, 1816–2007* (Washington: CQ Press, 2010), 562. See also M.R. Sarkees and F.W. Wayman, "Inter-state, Intra-state, and Extra-state Wars: A Comprehensive Look at Their Distribution over Time, 1816–1997," *International Studies Quarterly*, 47 (March 2003), 60, 65.

9. L. Themnér and P. Wallensteen, "Armed Conflicts, 1946–2011," *Journal of Peace Research* 49 (July 2012), 565.

10. The most typical threshold for identifying an armed conflict is 25 battle-related deaths per year. Major armed conflicts are typically identified using the threshold of 1000 battle-related deaths per year. For more information, see the Uppsala Conflict Data Program at http://www.pcr.uu.se/research/ucdp/program_overview/.

11. See L. Themnér and P. Wallensteen, "Armed Conflicts, 1946–2011," 565; and L. Harbon and P. Wallensteen, "Armed Conflict, 1989–2006," *Journal of Peace Research* 44 (September 2007), 623.

12. See G. Strada, "The Horror of Landmines," *Scientific American*, May 1996, 40.

13. Stockholm International Peace Research Institute, *SIPRI Yearbook, 2003* (Oxford: Oxford University Press, 2003), 109.

14. Stockholm International Peace Research Institute, *SIPRI Yearbook, 2011* (Oxford: Oxford University Press, 2011), 158, 181–3.

15. Q. Wright, *A Study of War*, vol. 1 (Chicago: University of Chicago Press, 1942), 17.

16. S. Freud, *Civilization, Society, and Religion*, ed. A. Dickson, trans. J. Strachey (New York: Penguin Books, 1985), 357.

17. K. Lorenz, *On Aggression* (New York: Harcourt Brace, 1966). See also P. Shaw and Y. Wong, "Ethnic Mobilization and the Seeds of Warfare: An Evolutionary Perspective," *International Studies Quarterly* 31, no. 1 (1987), 5–32.

18. See J.G. Stoessinger, *Why Nations Go to War*, 10th ed. (Belmont, CA: Wadsworth Publishing, 2007); R. Jervis, *Perception and Misperception in International Politics* (Princeton University Press, 1976), 154; and M.G. Hermann, "Explaining Foreign Policy Behaviour Using the Personal Characteristics of Political Leaders," *International Studies Quarterly* 24 (March 1980), 8.

19. See the discussion in J. Keegan, *A History of Warfare*, 86–9.

20. K. Waltz, *Man, the State, and War* (New York: Columbia University Press, 1959), 232.

21. See G. Modelski, *Exploring Long Cycles* (Boulder, CO: Lynne Rienner, 1987); and W. Thompson, *On Global War: Historical–Structural Approaches to World Politics* (Columbia, SC: University of South Carolina Press, 1988).

22. For an interesting prewar assessment of U.S. interests and objectives, see P.H. Gordon, M. Indyk, and M.E. O'Hanlon, "Getting Serious about Iraq," *Survival* 44 (Autumn 2002), 9–22. For another prewar assessment, see C. Kaysen et al., *War with Iraq: Costs, Consequences, and Alternatives* (Cambridge, MA: American Academy of Arts and Sciences, 2002). For further background material on the Iraq war, see M.L. Sifry and C. Cerf, eds., *The Iraq War Reader: History, Documents, Opinions* (New York, Touchstone Books, 2003); and A.H. Cordesman, *The Iraq War* (Westport: Praeger, 2003).

23. Remarks by the president at 2002 Graduation Exercise of the United States Military Academy, West Point, New York, June 1, 2002.

24. "The National Security Strategy of the United States of America," September 2002, 6, 14, http://www.informationclearinghouse.info/article2320.htm (accessed June 18, 2013).

25. See G. Forden, "Intention to Deceive: Iraqi Misdirection of UN Inspectors," *Jane's Intelligence Review* 16 (March 2004), 30–9.

26. Remarks to the United Nations Security Council by Secretary of State Colin L. Powell, New York City, February 5, 2003.

27. For an excellent overview see T.E. Ricks, *Fiasco: The American Military Adventure in Iraq* (New York: Penguin Books, 2007).

28. For example, see P.W. Galbraith, "After Iraq: Picking up the Pieces," *Current History* 106, no. 705 (December 2007), 403–08.

29. "Unclassified Key Judgments of the National Intelligence Estimate," *Prospects for Iraq's Stability: A Challenging Road Ahead* (Washington, DC: Office of the Director of National Intelligence, 2007), 8–9.

30. Data from "Iraq Figures since 2003," *The Associated Press*, February 4, 2008, and www.globalsecurity.org/military/ops/iraq_casualties.htm.

31. "Iraq Body Count," http://www.iraqbodycount.org (accessed September 8, 2012).

32. See "Opinion Research Business Survey of Iraq War Casualties," http://en.wikipedia.org/wiki/ORB_survey_of_Iraq_War_casualties (accessed June 25, 2013).

33. See "Estimated Costs of U.S. Operations in Iraq and Afghanistan and of Other Activities Related to the War on Terrorism," CBO testimony before the Committee on the Budget, U.S. House of Representatives, http://www.cbo.gov/publication/19202 (accessed June 25, 2013).

34. L. Bilmes and J.E. Stiglitz, *The Economic Costs of the Iraq War: An Appraisal Three Years after the Beginning of the Conflict*, Working Paper no. 12054 (Cambridge, MA: National Bureau of Economic Research, February 2006); and J. E. Stiglitz and L. J. Bilmes, *The Three Trillion Dollar War: The True Cost of the Iraq Conflict* (New York: W.W. Norton, 2008).

35. See R.A. Clarke, *Against All Enemies: Inside America's War on Terror—What Really Happened* (New York: The Free Press, 2004).

36. A.R. Norton, "Making War, Making Peace: The Middle East Entangles America," *Current History* 103 (January 2004), 3–7.

37. See L. McQuaig, *It's the Crude, Dude: War, Big Oil, and the Fight for the Planet* (Toronto: Doubleday, 2004).

38. For different accounts of the decision making within the Bush administration, see D.J. Feith, *War and Decision: Inside the Pentagon at the Dawn of the War on Terrorism* (New York: Harper Collins, 2008); and M. Isikoff and D. Corn, *Hubris: The Inside Story of Spin, Scandal, and the Selling of the Iraq War* (New York: Random House, 2006).

39. On the case for vigilant containment, see J.J. Mearsheimer and S.M. Walt, "An Unnecessary War," *Foreign Policy* 134 (January/February 2003), 50–59.

40. Former U.K. Defence Minister Peter Kilfoyle, quoted in N. Watt and M. White, "Wrong War, Wrong Time, Wrong Enemy, Warns Labour Rebel," *The Guardian*, March 19, 2003.

41. Kenneth M. Pollack, "Spies, Lies, and Weapons: What Went Wrong," *The Atlantic Monthly*, January/February 2004, 78–92.

42. James Fallows, "Blind into Baghdad," *The Atlantic Monthly*, January/February 2004, 52–74.

43. Norton, "Making War, Making Peace," 4.

44. For a collection of observations, see "A Special Survey: U.S. Foreign Policy, Seen from the Other Side," *Bulletin of the Atomic Scientists* 60 (March/April 2004), 18–34.

45. See, for example, *A Year after Iraq War: Mistrust of America in Europe Ever Higher, Muslim Anger Persists* (Washington, DC: The Pew Research Center for the People and the Press, 2004), and PEW Global Attitudes Project, "Conflicting Views in a Divided World 2006" (Washington, DC: The Pew Research Center, 2006).

46. "Declassified Key Judgments of the National Intelligence Estimate," *Trends in Global Terrorism: Implications for the United States* (Washington, DC: Office of the Director of National Intelligence, 2006), 2.

47. "American Majority Sees Iraq War as a Mistake," *Angus Reid Global Monitor: Polls and Research*, http://www.angus-reid.com/polls/view/american_majority_sees_iraq_war_as_a_mistake (accessed June 18, 2013).

48. See J.S. Yaphe, "Iraq: Are We There Yet?" *Current History* 107 (December 2008), 403–9; D. Byman, "Constructing a Democratic Iraq: Challenges and Opportunities," *International Security* 28 (Summer 2003), 47–78; and A. Sorensen, "Iraq's Reluctant Nation Builders," *Current History* 102 (December 2003), 407–10. For a broad discussion of postwar issues, see "From Victory to Success: Afterwar Policy in Iraq," *Foreign Policy* 137 (July/August 2003), 50–72.

49. This term is employed by T.R. Gurr, *Minorities at Risk: A Global View of Ethnopolitical Conflicts* (Washington, DC: United States Institute of Peace, 1993).

50. Gurr, Minorities at Risk, 3.

51. See S.J. Kaufman, *Modern Hatreds: The Symbolic Politics of Ethnic War* (Ithaca, NY: Cornell University Press, 2001).

52. See K.J. Holsti, *The State, War, and the State of War* (Cambridge, UK: Cambridge University Press, 1996), 20.

53. M. Berdal and D.M. Malone, "Introduction," in M. Berdal and D.M. Malone, eds., *Greed and Grievance: Economic Agendas in Civil Wars* (Boulder, CO: Lynne Rienner, 2001), 4.

54. Ibid., 5.

55. D. Keen, *The Economic Functions of Violence in Civil Wars*, Adelphi Paper 320 (Oxford: Oxford University Press, 1998), 11–12.

56. See O. Degomme and D. Guha-Sapir, "Patterns of Mortality Rates in Darfur Conflict," *The Lancet* 375 (January 2010), 294–300. See also International Institute for Strategic Studies, *Strategic Survey 2008* (New York: Routledge, 2008), 250.

57. See Emile Hokayem, "Syria and its Neighbours," *Survival*, vol. 54 (April–May 2012), 7–14.

58. See B. Bueno de Mesquita and W.H. Riker, "An Assessment of the Merits of Selective Proliferation," *Journal of Conflict Resolution* 26 (June 1982), 283–306; J. Mearsheimer, "The Case for a Ukrainian Nuclear Deterrent," *Foreign Affairs* 72 (Summer 1993), 50–66; and K. Waltz, "Nuclear Myths and Political Realities," *American Political Science Review* 84 (September 1990), 731–45.

59. K. Waltz, *The Spread of Nuclear Weapons: More May Be Better*, Adelphi Paper 171 (London: International Institute for Strategic Studies, Autumn 1981), 5.

60. See L. Dunn, *Containing Nuclear Proliferation*, Adelphi Paper 263 (London: Oxford University Press, 1991); K. Kaiser, "Non-Proliferation and Nuclear Deterrence," *Survival* 31 (March/April 1989), 123–36; and S. Miller, "The Case Against a Ukrainian Nuclear Deterrent," *Foreign Affairs* 72 (Summer 1993), 67–80. See also N. Tannenwald, *The Nuclear Taboo: The United States and the Non-Use of Nuclear Weapons since 1945* (Cambridge: Cambridge University Press, 2008).

61. For three models of weapons proliferation incentives, see S. Sagan, "Why Do States Build Nuclear Weapons? Three Models in Search of a Bomb," *International Security* 21 (Winter 1996/97), 54–86. See also E. Solingen, *Nuclear Logics: Contrasting Paths in East Asia and the Middle East* (Princeton University Press, 2007).

62. See P. Kerr, "North Korea Crisis Chronology," *Arms Control Today* 33 (June 2003).

63. T. Ripley, "Mission Improbable: Could Israel Attack Iran?" *Jane's Intelligence Review* 19, no. 11 (November 2007), 26–31.

64. See A.M. Ansari, *Iran Under Ahmadinejad: The Politics of Confrontation*, Adelphi Paper 393 (London: Routledge and the International Institute for Strategic Studies, 2007), 50.

65. S. Chubin, *Iran's Nuclear Ambitions* (Washington, DC: Carnegie Endowment for International Peace, 2006), 13.

66. See R. Molander and P. Wilson, "On Dealing with the Prospect of Nuclear Chaos," *The Washington Quarterly* 17 (1994), 32; and J.B. Wolfstahl and T.Z. Collina, "Nuclear Terrorism and Warhead Control in Russia," *Survival* 44 (Summer 2002), 71–84.

67. R.M. Frost, *Nuclear Terrorism After 9/11*, Adelphi Paper 378 (London: Routledge and the International Institute for Strategic Studies, 2005).

68. T. Singh, "Get Back to Basics," *India Today*, June 8, 1998.

69. See J. Miller, S. Engleberg, and W. Broad, *Germs: Biological Weapons and America's Secret War* (New York: Simon and Schuster, 2001), 297–8.

70. Stockholm International Peace Research Institute, *SIPRI Yearbook, 2008* (Oxford: Oxford University Press, 2008), 295.

71. Stockholm International Peace Research Institute, *SIPRI Yearbook, 2011* (Oxford: Oxford University Press, 2011), 271.

72. N. Cooper, "What's the Point of Arms Transfer Controls?" *Contemporary Security Policy* 27, no. 1 (2006), 123.

73. "The Covert Arms Trade," *The Economist*, February 12, 1994, 21. For more information on small arms and light weapons see *Small Arms Survey 2008: Risk and Resilience* (Cambridge: Cambridge University Press, 2008).

74. See "Merchant of Death Arrested in Thailand," http://www.globalwitness.org/library/ %E2%80%9Cmerchant- death%E2%80%9D-arrested-thailand (accessed June 20, 2013).

75. W. Laqueur, "Postmodern Terrorism," *Foreign Affairs* 75 (September/October 1996), 24–36.

76. C. Combs, *Terrorism in the Twenty-First Century* (Upper Saddle River, NJ: Prentice Hall, 1997), 8.

77. P. Wilkinson, "A European Viewpoint on Terrorism," in J.S. Nye Jr., Y. Satoh, and P. Wilkinson, *Addressing the New International Terrorism: Prevention, Intervention, and Multilateral Cooperation*, Report to the Trilateral Commission (Washington, DC: Trilateral Commission, 2003), 21.

78. S. Gupta, *The Replication of Violence: Thoughts on International Terrorism after September 11th 2001* (London: Pluto Press, 2002), 1.

79. U.S. President G.W. Bush, "Address to a Joint Session of Congress and the American People" (Washington, DC: Office of the Press Secretary, September 20, 2001).

80. See S. Coll, *Ghost Wars: The Secret History of the CIA, Afghanistan, and Bin Laden: From the Soviet Invasion to September 10, 2001* (New York: Penguin Books, 2005). See also R. Gutman, *How We Missed the Story: Osama Bin Laden, the Taliban, and the Hijacking of Afghanistan* (Washington, DC: United States Institute of Peace Press, 2008).

81. Quoted in International Institute for Strategic Studies, *The Military Balance, 2003–2004* (London: Oxford University Press, 2003), 356, and Graham Allison, *Nuclear Terrorism: The Ultimate Preventable Catastrophe* (Cambridge: Times Books, 2004), 12.

82. For a review of the security challenges facing Afghanistan, see C. Hodes and M. Sedra, *The Search for Security in Post-Taliban Afghanistan*, Adelphi Paper 391 (London: Routledge and the International Institute for Strategic Studies, 2007), and Adam Roberts, "Doctrine and Reality in Afghanistan," *Survival* 51, no. 1 (February/March 2009), 29–60.

83. For a historical account of Afghanistan's struggles with governance and foreign occupation, see M. Ewans, *Afghanistan: A Short History of Its People and Politics* (Hew York: Harper Collins, 2002).

84. See "Policing a Whirlwind," *The Economist* 385, December 2007, 33.

85. See C. Hodes and M. Sedra, *Search for Security*, 8; and J. Wright, "Blood Flowers: Afghanistan's Opium Industry Remains Robust," *Jane's Intelligence Review* 21, no. 1 (January 2009), 38–43.

86. The International Institute for Strategic Studies, "Afghanistan: Spreading Insurgency," *Strategic Survey 2007* (New York: Routledge, 2007), 370.

87. B. Riedel, "The Return of the Knights: Al-Qaeda and the Fruits of Middle East Disorder," *Survival* 49, no. 3 (Autumn 2007), 107–20.

88. N. Labi, "Jihad 2.0," *The Atlantic Monthly* 297, no. 6 (July/August 2006), 102–8. See also M. Sageman, *Leaderless Jihad: Terror Networks in the Twenty-First Century* (Philadelphia: University of Pennsylvania Press, 2008).

89. A.K. Cronin, *Ending Terrorism: Lessons for Defeating al-Qaeda*, Adelphi Paper 394 (London: Routledge and the International Institute for Strategic Studies, 2008), 53. See also B. Singh, *The Talibanization of Southeast Asia: Losing the War on Terror to Islamist Extremists* (Westport, CT: Praeger Security International, 2007).

90. See G. Weimann, *Terror on the Internet: The New Arena, The New Challenges* (Washington, DC: The United States Institute of Peace Press, 2006).

91. On chemical and biological weapons terrorism, see A. Stenersen, "Chem-Bio Cyber Class: Assessing Jihadist Chemical and Biological Manuals," *Jane's Intelligence Review* 19, no. 9 (September 2007), 8–13. On nuclear terrorism, see R.M. Frost, *Nuclear Terrorism after 9/11*, Adelphi Paper 378 (London: Routledge and the International Institute for Strategic Studies, 2005); and J.M. Acton et al., "Beyond the Dirty Bomb: Re-thinking Radiological Terror," *Survival* 49, no. 3 (Autumn 2007), 151–68.

92. A.K. Cronin, "Behind the Curve: Globalization and International Terrorism," *International Security* 27 (Winter 2002/2003), 30.

93. K. Hoyt and S.G. Brooks, "A Double-Edged Word: Globalization and Biosecurity," *International Security* 28 (Winter 2003/2004), 124.

94. Laqueur, "Postmodern Terrorism," 25.

95. S.J. Lukasik, S.E. Goodman, and D.W. Longhurst, *Protecting Critical Infrastructures against Cyber-Attack*, Adelphi Paper 359 (Oxford: Oxford University Press, 2003).

96. M. Abrahms, "What Terrorists Really Want: Terrorist Motives and Counterterrorism Strategy," *International Security* 32, no. 4 (Spring 2008), 78–105. See also B.L. Nacos, *Terrorism and Counterterrorism: Understanding Threats and Responses in the Post–9/11 World* (New York: Penguin, 2006).

97. Robert Chote and Peter Norman, "Leaders Zero In on Crime and Nuclear Safety," *Financial Times*, June 19, 1995, 5.

98. See *World Drug Report 2005* (New York: United Nations Office on Drugs and Crime, 2005); and *World Drug Report 2011* (New York: United Nations Office on Drugs and Crime, 2011), 16, 17.

99. See P.A. Schott, *Reference Guide to Anti-Money Laundering and Combating the Financing of Terrorism*, 2nd ed. (Washington, DC: The International Bank for Reconstruction and Development and the International Monetary Fund, 2006), I-6.

100. See A.A. Block and C.A. Weaver, *All Is Clouded by Desire: Global Banking, Money Laundering, and International Organized Crime* (Westport, CT: Greenwood Publishing, 2004).

101. See *Overview of the Law Enforcement Strategy Used to Combat International Organized Crime* (Washington, DC: U.S. Department of Justice, April 2008), 3.

Conflict Management in Global Politics

Since the end of the Cold War the UN has led an upsurge of international activism that has played a critical role in reducing the number of violent conflicts.

—*Human Security Report*[1]

For most of history, war has been a more or less functional institution, providing benefits for those societies that were good at it, although the cost in money, in lives, and in suffering was always significant. Only in the past century have large numbers of people begun to question the basic assumption of civilized societies that war is inevitable and often useful.

—*Gwynne Dyer*[2]

RESPONDING TO THE INTERNATIONAL SECURITY AGENDA

In Chapter 6, we examined some of the key security issues and challenges facing the contemporary international system. In this chapter we discuss the range of instruments available to prevent, manage, and resolve conflict in global politics, which include diplomacy, arms control and disarmament, the concept of human security, international organizations (IOs) and law, peacekeeping operations, humanitarian intervention, sanctions, and democratization. Our aim in this chapter is to evaluate what might be called the *international conflict management tool kit*. To what extent have these instruments been useful or found wanting? While international news coverage is dominated by warfare, terrorism, and crisis, this can blind us to the reality that most conflict in global politics is managed or even resolved without resorting to violence.

The theoretical frameworks discussed in Chapter 1 provide many insights into the nature of conflict management in global politics. Realism is not overly optimistic about the prospects for managing or reducing conflict: states will establish alliances and treaties, international institutions, and laws in an attempt to avoid conflict, but this cooperation is merely a form of self-interest and will not endure if states feel it is no longer in their best interests. For realists, war can be deterred through military power (at least for a period of time), but in general conflict management efforts are prone to failures due to the distrust and hostility endemic in an anarchic international system. Liberals are much more optimistic about the prospects for successful conflict management, convinced it is possible to make progress toward a more peaceful and stable world by addressing the root causes of war and other security challenges: distrust, insecurity, and authoritarian governments. Liberals generally believe that economic interdependence, international institutions, law, and the spread of democracy will promote peace and security.

Critical theorists take a different approach to conflict management. Neo-Marxists argue that most conflict management efforts fail to address deep economic and political inequities; war and other security challenges will never be resolved until the stark inequities of the capitalist system are addressed. Constructivists seek to understand the deeply embedded value systems that cause insecurity and conflict, and emphasize the transformative potential of education, dialogue, and the promotion of norms less rooted in prejudice, intolerance, fear, and other social constructions that contribute to insecurity and conflict. Feminists see most conflict management approaches as a reflection of masculine conceptions of conflict and military security that de-emphasize or devalue the importance of women, community, and social health: more women should become engaged in conflict management at all levels, and emphasis should be placed on human security and more community-oriented paths to peace. The ecopolitical viewpoint suggests that our treatment of local ecosystems, natural resources, and the global environment must change if social and political harmony are to be achieved.

All these perspectives shed light on our conflict management tool kit, and you should bear them in mind as you read this chapter. We begin our examination of conflict management instruments with the nature and practice of diplomacy.

THE NATURE OF DIPLOMACY

Diplomacy has survived many changes in international relations from the ancient world to today.[3] The study of diplomacy has traditionally been confined to statecraft and the activities of professional diplomats, and defined simply as *purposeful communication between states*. However, the definition is widening to include diplomatic activities conducted by non-state actors, as well as individuals who may not be in formal positions of political power. In more traditional approaches, the concepts of representation and communication are fundamental components of diplomatic activity. Representatives of states are acting on behalf of the government of that state, and are almost always acting under the instructions of their government; one study has even suggested that diplomats adopt the identity of their state as part of their own personal identities.[4]

Public and private diplomatic affairs are highly formalized events, characterized by painstaking attention to protocol. This allows states to interact with one another using established and mutually acceptable procedures. For example, when a **head of state** makes a formal visit to a foreign country, an elaborate reception protocol demands a formal reception at the airport, a red carpet, a greeting line of dignitaries, an honour guard (dutifully inspected), a band (playing the national anthem of the visitor's country), an escorted motorcade to a hotel or the seat of government, and usually one formal state dinner. While the receptions for visitors or diplomats of lesser rank are not as elaborate, they are no less established as conventions. Though many of the trappings of past diplomatic practice have been discarded, most of the key traditions, such as diplomatic immunity, endure. As we discussed in Chapter 5, states that have embassies in foreign countries can legitimately lay claim to that space as part of their own territory. This principle of **extraterritoriality** is a cornerstone of diplomatic tradition. According to Garret Mattingly, it evolved in the early days of the Westphalian state system, when states "found they could only communicate with one another by tolerating within themselves little islands of alien sovereignty."[5] Diplomatic protocols help avoid individuals, groups, and states from clashing on issues of symbolism and prestige and maintain the image that diplomats, officials, and leaders of equivalent rank are treated as equals. Formality and protocol also reduce the chance that personality conflicts might interfere with communication between governments. Nevertheless, personalities are often a crucial influence on affairs of state. Canadians, for example, have an interest in the personal relationship between their prime minister and the president of the United States, with some expressing anxiety when the two leaders do not get along, and others upset when they seem to get along too well.

Despite its adherence to tradition, diplomacy has undergone some significant changes, particularly in the latter half of the 20th century. Decolonization and increased global interdependence have forced diplomatic services to adjust to larger numbers of states and a much wider variety of language and cultures. The increasing number of states buttresses the relevance of multilateral and conference diplomacy: the process of diplomatic exchange simply becomes more efficient if all of the states involved are represented around a single table (although this does not mean the chances of an agreement are any greater). Furthermore, the growing complexity of the diplomatic agenda requires very specific technical knowledge on matters as varied as satellites to coral reef management. As a result, communication and dialogue between government agencies other than foreign ministries (sometimes called *paradiplomacy*) has become ever more common.[6]

Indeed, the essential character of diplomatic life has changed as modern communications technology has made contact between governments and their representatives abroad virtually instantaneous. Long gone are the days when mailed diplomatic pouches would outline broad policy and give a diplomat considerable leeway to make decisions; texts, email, and cellphones (often subject to interception) are today's norm. Another change is the expanding, unprecedented contact and involvement with non-state actors such as humanitarian and aid organizations, multinational corporations, private military companies, and communal groups. Frequently, diplomatic activity today is conducted through informal social contacts between individuals and groups in two or more countries. This is sometimes called *track-two diplomacy*, which has proven its value as a means of communication between governments that do not have formal diplomatic ties or have a very poor political relationship.

As indicated in Chapter 3, foreign policy remains a relatively closed area of government activity. Nevertheless, increased access to information has made diplomacy a much more public affair. Public opinion may compel leaders to act in ways that are contrary to the advice of the diplomatic service, tempting politicians with rash or dangerous diplomacy designed primarily to capture public loyalty or votes. Finally, another change in diplomacy is the increasing importance attached to **summit diplomacy**, the formal meeting of heads of state and government. This can enable leaders to establish a personal rapport and remove the frustrating constraints of the slow and bureaucratic diplomatic process. The **Camp David** accords, the product of a summit between Egyptian President Anwar el-Sadat and Israeli Prime Minister Menachem Begin at U.S. President Jimmy Carter's official Maryland retreat in 1978, were a success because of the face-to-face meetings between the two leaders. However, summitry can lead to ill-advised decisions made by leaders without adequate consultation with experts or time for reflection. At the Yalta Conference in 1945 (discussed in Chapter 2) between Winston Churchill, Franklin Roosevelt, and Josef Stalin, Roosevelt acquiesced to an agreement that would divide Europe into spheres of influence and pave the way for Soviet domination of Eastern Europe (although there is debate about how much of a choice Roosevelt had). Summits have also been criticized as being little more than photo opportunities and high-security cocktail parties celebrating the signing of agreements worked out in advance by diplomats. Summits can also attract large protest gatherings, as demonstrated during the annual G8 Summits, which are invariably accompanied by large demonstrations. These protests against the pace of globalization, the lack of development aid, and the failure to address human rights concerns are indicative of the gap between formal state-level diplomacy and the wishes, priorities, and policy prescriptions of a growing international civil society movement of activists and NGOs.

DIPLOMATIC TECHNIQUES AND CONFLICT MANAGEMENT

While diplomacy is an everyday feature of global politics, it is also the foundation of efforts to prevent, contain, and manage international conflict. Of course, diplomacy may also be quite bellicose and militaristic, and even diplomatic efforts intended to avoid war can use threats and intimidation to achieve state objectives.[7] The effectiveness of diplomatic techniques as conflict management instruments depends heavily on whether a set of proposals is preferred over the consequences of reaching no agreement at all or resorting to violence. At its complex heart, conflict management diplomacy is about facilitating and encouraging the development of negotiated agreements, using the techniques of signalling, bargaining, and third party mediation.[8]

SIGNALLING

States and groups use signals to communicate intent, commitment, and displeasure. Signals may take the form of speeches or written statements by political leaders or foreign ministries, or direct diplomatic contact with individual representatives of other states or groups. Official statements expressing the Canadian government's concern about human rights in China or its wishes for a transition to a democratic Syria are examples of direct government-to-government signalling. At other times, signals may be less overt, and may come in the form of deliberate symbolic actions such as unofficial visits, the recall of ambassadors, or displays of military power. The problem with all signals is that they can be misunderstood or misinterpreted and sometimes missed altogether. Some signals can be very circumspect; in a particularly famous example, in 1971 the Chinese government invited the U.S. table tennis team to visit China. After some deliberation, the U.S. government decided (correctly) that this was an overture by the Chinese leadership to improve relations between China and the United States. Thus, the term *Ping-Pong diplomacy* was coined.

BARGAINING AND NEGOTIATION

Another technique is the use of bargaining, an attempt to reach an agreement on how symbolic and substantive desires and aims will be exchanged and divided among the parties to a dispute: negotiations are in essence acts of formal bargaining. Not all agreements will be equally beneficial to all sides; parties to a dispute bring different forms of leverage to the bargaining process. As realists would quickly remind us, leverage originates mainly with power capabilities, and can allow stronger parties to offer rewards, issue threats, or appeal to sentiments of friendship, allegiance, or shared ideology or religion; unequal arrangements are frequently (though not always) the result.[9] Over time, several tactics for successful negotiation have emerged:

- Discourage zero-sum (win–lose) views of the issues.
- Establish a fair compromise to ensure a lasting settlement.
- Avoid ultimatums and posturing; encourage dialogue and debate.
- Avoid humiliating one's opponents.
- Blend rewards and threats.
- Avoid personal *ad hominem* attacks on the other party.
- Look for bridges: solutions acceptable to both sides but different from the positions taken at the beginning of negotiations.
- Look for **nonspecific compensation**, in which one side gets what it wants but gives up something that was not part of the original dispute or discussion.
- Divide the issue into separate and more manageable subjects for agreement.

THIRD-PARTY MEDIATION

Third parties, whether individuals, groups, organizations, or states, can be invited by the parties to assist the process of reaching a settlement. Mediation is a more common form of diplomatic conflict management than bilateral negotiations between parties.[10] Third parties can offer a number of services, which include

- providing **good offices** (acting as a conduit for communication), a role often performed by the UN Secretary-General;
- providing a neutral site for negotiations (a role often performed by Switzerland, and specifically the city of Geneva);
- clarifying facts and evidence (which may involve providing figures or conducting fact-finding missions);
- acting as a mediator by becoming active in negotiations, making suggestions that might be agreeable to all sides, and breaking deadlocks when they occur;
- acting as an arbitrator (making a judgment on the dispute and establishing a fair settlement) with the consent of the parties; and
- acting as an adjudicator (making a judgment with reference to international law).

Naturally, any actor entrusted with such roles must be acceptable to all sides, be perceived as neutral with little or no agenda, and be capable of performing such tasks. In the end, the parties to the conflict retain the power to decide on outcomes: despite the best efforts of a mediator, the parties to a conflict may choose to abandon mediated talks or to reject some or all of the terms of any agreement. This is also true of international law in general, as discussed in Chapter 5, though states can submit to the arbitration of the ICJ (International Court of Justice) or other bodies, including the Permanent Court of Arbitration, also located at The Hague in the Netherlands.

DIPLOMACY AND CONFLICT MANAGEMENT IN GLOBAL POLITICS

The record of diplomatic efforts to prevent, control, or manage conflicts is mixed. Certainly there have been spectacular failures, such as in the weeks before the outbreak of World War I. (When wars commence, any diplomatic efforts to prevent them have by definition failed.)

However, there have been successful cases of diplomatic conflict management. For example, in 1987, Costa Rican President Oscar Arias designed a peace accord for Central America involving Costa Rica, El Salvador, Nicaragua, Honduras, and Guatemala. All parties agreed to eliminate restrictions on dissent, offer political amnesty to rebel movements, hold national elections, negotiate ceasefires between governments and rebel groups, deny the use of their territory to rebel groups from other countries, and cut off superpower aid to rebel groups. It was a remarkable achievement, and although never fully implemented, the Arias Plan won Oscar Arias the 1987 Nobel Peace Prize. In another example, India and Pakistan were poised on the brink of war in 2002, with the threat of nuclear hostilities hovering. However, diplomatic interventions from abroad and exchanges between the two countries defused the crisis, though the underlying issues remain unresolved. Two of the most high-profile diplomatic conflict management efforts in recent years have been the Middle East peace process and the Northern Ireland peace process. Thus far, these two efforts have yielded different outcomes, illustrating both the limits and possibilities of diplomacy as a conflict management instrument.

DIPLOMACY AND CONFLICT MANAGEMENT IN THE MIDDLE EAST

Since the late 1940s, the key obstacle to peace and stability in the Middle East has been the Israeli–Palestinian conflict. Other actors such as Iran, Iraq, Syria, and Egypt, as well as armed groups in Lebanon and the Syrian Civil War, are also part of the conflict management equation, but a lasting peace remains heavily dependent on an Israeli–Palestinian accommodation. Both Israelis and Palestinians claim the same territory, and conflict management efforts have concentrated on issues such as control of land, Palestinian independence and statehood, control of Jerusalem (which both sides regard as their indivisible capital as well as a holy centre), the return of Palestinian refugees to their homes in Israel, Israeli settlements on the West Bank, freedom of movement for Palestinians, and access to water resources. For decades, this conflict resisted all international efforts to achieve a diplomatic resolution between the Palestine Liberation Organization (PLO) and the government of Israel. The conflict has been characterized by acts of terrorism, assassinations, military action, civil disturbances (such as the Palestinian youth uprising, or **Intifada**), and economic coercion.

A diplomatic breakthrough occurred in September 1993. Israeli and PLO officials had been meeting in secret in Oslo, Norway. With the third-party mediation of the Norwegian government, negotiators reached agreement on a Declaration of Principles signed in Washington by Israeli Prime Minister Yitzak Rabin (who was assassinated in 1995) and PLO Chairman Yasser Arafat on September 13, 1993. In this declaration, Israel recognized the PLO as the legitimate representative of the Palestinian people, and the PLO recognized Israel's right to exist and renounced terrorism. The declaration also included the goals of future negotiations, the most important of which was Israeli withdrawal from the Gaza Strip and the West Bank, and self-rule for Palestinians in those territories under a new Palestinian Authority. However, the hope that the Oslo Accords might pave the way to peace was soon dashed. While some parts of the agreement were partially implemented, disputes over outstanding issues such as sovereignty over Jerusalem and the border between Israel and a future Palestinian state began to erode support for the agreement on both sides. The continued construction of Israeli settlements in the West Bank caused consternation among Palestinians, and renewed terrorist attacks by Palestinian groups caused outrage in Israel. Israel criticized the Palestinian Authority for not doing enough to stop the attacks and suspended implementation of the agreement. The best chance to save the Oslo Accords occurred in July 2000, when Israeli Prime Minister Ehud Barak and Yasser Arafat held a summit mediated by U.S. President Bill Clinton, but this meeting failed to resolve the key issues.[11]

As frustration with the peace process grew, the economic hardships facing Palestinians were mounting, Israeli settlements were still being built, and terrorist attacks continued. Some Palestinian leaders began to call for an uprising to compel Israel to agree to a separate Palestinian state, while the Israel Defense Forces (IDF) prepared to crush any Palestinian uprising. All that was needed was a spark, and that spark came when the Likud party leader Ariel Sharon (an accused war criminal) visited the Temple Mount/Haram al-Sharif, a site considered holy to both Muslims and Jews, in the fall of 2000. Palestinians were outraged that Sharon would visit a site considered holy to Muslims, while many conservative Israelis were outraged at the idea that Sharon should not be able to visit a site holy to Jews. In the wake of the visit, neither side showed any restraint: the El-Aqsa Intifada was launched in September 2000, and the IDF responded with a massive campaign to suppress it.[12] Suicide bombings by Palestinian militant groups increased, while the Israeli army conducted frequent raids into Palestinian areas, killing terrorist suspects and civilians, destroying buildings and homes, and arresting suspected militants.

The ongoing violence renewed international efforts to find a resolution to the conflict. The new U.S. president, George W. Bush, called for an end to the construction of Israeli settlements in the West Bank, a cessation of Palestinian attacks, and the creation of a Palestinian state. However, active U.S. economic and military support for Israel, efforts to undercut the leadership of Yasser Arafat, and muted criticisms of Israeli military action against Palestinians

A moment of hope. The signing of the 1993 peace accords by Israeli Prime Minister Yitzhak Rabin and PLO Chairman Yasser Arafat with U.S. President Bill Clinton in the background. This agreement was achieved with the mediation assistance of Norway and the United States. (AP Photo/Ron Edmonds/CP Images)

continued to frustrate the Palestinian leadership and most of the Arab world, and undermined the ability of the United States to break the negotiation deadlock.[13] In February 2002 Saudi Arabia proposed a "grand bargain" that called for Israeli withdrawal to pre-1967 boundaries in exchange for full normalization of relations with all Arab states. The U.S. signalled its support for the proposal, but Israel was less enthusiastic as the proposal called for a Palestinian capital in East Jerusalem and openly supported the El-Aqsa Intifada. Any momentum the Saudi Arabian proposal may have had died away in a renewal of suicide bombings and Israeli reprisals.[14]

In early 2002, Israel began construction of a "security fence" designed to close off the border between Israel and the West Bank, with five crossing points for Palestinian workers and tourists. The wall, which the Israeli government maintains is a necessary barrier to prevent the movement of terrorists into Israel, not only cuts through communities and separates many Palestinians from their work in Israel, but also cuts into the West Bank and therefore is seen by Palestinians as an effort by Israel to annex land.[15] The deterioration of the situation prompted another round of international efforts to achieve a settlement. In April 2003, yet another peace plan was unveiled. Known as the "Road Map," this plan was designed and endorsed by the United States, Russia, the EU, and the UN. It called for a comprehensive settlement of the Israeli–Palestinian dispute by 2005. In the agreement, a ceasefire would be established; the Palestinian Authority would carry out reforms; Israel would dismantle illegal settlements set up since 2001; a Palestinian state would be created; and negotiations would be conducted on final borders, the status of Jerusalem, and the right of return for Palestinian refugees. However, the "road map to nowhere" achieved little.[16] Dozens of terrorist attacks had to be thwarted during the supposed ceasefire, and Israel dismantled only a few of the illegal settlements and continued building the "security fence."

Since 2004, dramatic developments in Palestinian politics have altered the conflict management environment. In November 2004, Yasser Arafat, the leader of the Palestinian Authority and for decades the most visible international symbol of the Palestinian cause, died. This set the stage for a power struggle within Palestinian politics, between the "Fatah" movement once led by Arafat and the rival Islamic-based "Hamas" movement. Presidential elections in 2005 brought Mahmoud Abbas to the Palestinian Authority presidency. Abbas (also called Abu Mazen) was considered a moderate Fatah leader and his election created hope for progress in peace talks. However, in parliamentary elections held in January 2006 it was Hamas, not Fatah, that gained a majority in the Palestinian parliament and Hamas' Ismail Haniya became prime minister. The election of the militant and openly anti-Israeli Hamas (the movement refuses to accept Israel's right to exist) stunned many international observers, but in retrospect the results were a reflection of Hamas' efforts to build goodwill in the Palestinian population, widespread frustration with the corruption of Fatah, and divisions within the Fatah movement that divided their voters between too many candidates.[17] The international reaction to the election of Hamas was swift: the United States rejected the election results and halted most of its aid to the Palestinians, Israel cut ties to the Palestinian Authority, and Europe (traditionally more supportive of the Palestinian cause) withdrew much of its support as well.

The election of Hamas also created conflict among the Palestinian people. The Palestinian Authority was now deadlocked between a Fatah president (Abbas) and a Hamas prime minister (Haniya) who disagreed fundamentally on a wide range of issues. Tensions between Fatah and Hamas grew and violence between their respective supporters broke out in 2006, escalating to include daily assassinations and gun battles by the end of the year. Bolstered by U.S. and Israeli support, President Abbas began a buildup of Fatah's security forces to

Map 7.1 Israel with the West Bank, Gaza Strip, and Golan Heights

Infrastructure of conflict. A view of part of Israel's controversial "separation barrier" in the West Bank town of Abu Dis. Israel says the projected 723 kilometres (454 miles) of steel and concrete walls, fences, and barbed wire are needed for security. Palestinians view it as a land grab that undermines their promised state. (© ZUMA Press, Inc./Alamy)

wrestle control of the Palestinian Authority from Hamas. However, in June 2007 Hamas militias struck first, overwhelming Fatah supporters in the Gaza Strip, which since an Israeli withdrawal in August 2005 had been controlled by the Palestinian Authority. In response, President Abbas dissolved the unity government, rounded up Hamas supporters, and appointed an emergency cabinet controlled by Fatah with no Hamas representation. As a result, the Palestinian government and people were now clearly divided between the Fatah-controlled West Bank and the Hamas-controlled Gaza Strip.

The Hamas coup in Gaza took international observers and governments by surprise and has seriously complicated conflict management efforts in the region. The governments of the United States, Europe, and Israel are pursuing a "West Bank first" strategy of supporting Fatah, but this seems to be more of a reactive policy rather than a coherent approach to the conflict.[18] This strategy has resulted in diplomatic support for President Abbas. In contrast, the Hamas-controlled Gaza Strip has been isolated politically and economically and is surrounded by fences and barriers and virtually cut off from the world by an Israeli land, air, and sea blockade. A cycle of violence has developed between Hamas and the Israeli government, characterized by periods of rocket fire from Gaza into Israel, and Israeli air strikes and military incursions into Gaza. In December 2008 and January 2009, a period of violence called the Gaza War resulted in over a thousand civilian casualties in Gaza and some 13 Israeli deaths. Despite a ceasefire and negotiations facilitated by Egypt, the underlying conflict remained unresolved. In November of 2012, an eight-day war of airstrikes and rocket fire resulted in the deaths of over 150 Palestinians and 6 Israelis. Both of these violent outbreaks left much of Gaza in physical ruins, and served to exacerbate an ongoing humanitarian crisis reflecting Gaza's isolated position. Unemployment is high, and a large proportion of Gazan households live in extreme poverty. Due to the ongoing Israeli blockade of Gaza, essential goods are often in short supply, and electricity and water services are often interrupted. Basic health services are difficult to provide, and hospitals are short of medicines and diagnostic and surgical resources.[19] The humanitarian situation in Gaza has brought international condemnation against Israel, but the Israeli government continues to attempt to isolate Hamas, citing the ongoing threat of rocket attacks and the refusal of Hamas to make political concessions, most fundamentally on the issue of Israel's right to exist.

In the meantime, the considerable international support that has been extended to Fatah in the West Bank has not yielded any progress on an Israeli–Palestinian peace. The fundamental issues continue to plague efforts at establishing a formula for a lasting settlement. Despite a growing awareness in the U.S. government that the Israeli–Palestinian conflict both is central to Middle East peace and continues to fuel Islamic extremism and anti-Americanism in the region, efforts by the United States to broker even an interim agreement between the Palestinian Authority and the government of Israel have failed. Saudi and Egyptian efforts have met with a similar lack of success. At times, the magnitude and scope of the dispute seems overwhelming. Land, borders, Israeli settlements, religion, violence, the security fence (often referred to as the *apartheid wall*), the status of Jerusalem, Palestinian refugees, and now a divided Palestinian leadership are all obstacles in the path of conflict management efforts. The vote of the UN General Assembly in November 2012 to recognize Palestine as a non-member observer state was a significant symbolic measure, but is unlikely to encourage diplomatic movement on the fundamental issues that divide Palestinians and Israelis. To complicate matters further, the overthrow of several Middle Eastern governments in the Arab Spring, most notably in Egypt, may have a long-term effect on conflict management diplomacy. The future will bring new challenges but also new opportunities, and we must dare to hope that an agreement and ultimately a resolution can be found. This may require a committed international political intervention, especially by the U.S. government. This, at least, is one thing on which most Israelis and Palestinians can agree.

DIPLOMACY AND CONFLICT MANAGEMENT IN NORTHERN IRELAND

The conflict in Northern Ireland has its origins in the Protestant English conquest of Catholic Ireland in the early 17th century. Although English control over Ireland was consolidated by the victory of William of Orange at the Battle of the Boyne in 1690, Catholic resistance and revolt continued through to the early 20th century. After the famous Easter Rising in 1916, sentiment in England for Home Rule in Ireland increased. Irish Protestants opposed this idea as a recipe for absorption into the Catholic majority. After the Irish Civil War (1919 to 1921) between the British and the Irish Republican Army (IRA) ended in a truce and the independence of Southern Ireland in 1922, sectarian violence in the North continued between Catholic Nationalists or Republicans, who wanted the six counties of Northern Ireland united with the South, and Protestant Loyalists or Unionists, who wanted Northern Ireland to remain under British rule.

The period between 1922 and 1969 was relatively calm, but sectarian violence returned in what has been called the modern "time of troubles" in which more than 3200 people were killed. The revived IRA began a campaign of violence against Protestants, and the British Army returned to Northern Ireland to restore stability. However, most Catholics regarded the British Army as an occupying force, especially after the shooting of unarmed protestors in Londonderry in 1972 (known as *Bloody Sunday*). Bombings and shootings by the IRA and extremist Protestant organizations continued through to the early 1990s. As with so many conflicts, most people and parties in Northern Ireland wanted a peaceful settlement, but extremist violence polarized the two sides and made compromise and reconciliation difficult. Many diplomatic efforts were made to resolve the conflict, but they foundered because one or more of the parties refused to negotiate or because acts of violence derailed peace initiatives.

A new round of peace talks began in 1996, under the mediation of U.S. Senator George Mitchell; the IRA announced a ceasefire and joined the Irish and British governments at the table in 1997. Working under a deadline imposed by Mitchell, a diplomatic breakthrough occurred on April 10, 1998. The settlement was called the Belfast Agreement, but it is commonly called the Good Friday Agreement, and came into force on December 2, 1999. Northern Ireland would remain a part of Great Britain as long as a majority of people wanted it; an assembly would be established in Northern Ireland for self-governance, institutions would be established to develop more cooperation between Northern Ireland and the Republic of Ireland, and the civil rights of Catholics would be established and protected. The agreement went to a referendum and passed by a large majority. Elections were held for the new assembly in June. However, bombings, assassinations, and attacks on property continued. Tensions rose during the infamous annual "Orange Marches," which commemorate the Battle of the Boyne. In late 1999, the implementation of the Good Friday Agreement stalled, and the British government suspended the new assembly when the IRA refused to disarm.

Attempts to revitalize the Good Friday Agreement in 2000 and 2001 were not very successful. Each side accused the other of non-compliance with the Agreement, and it seemed as if the process had failed.[20] However, in the wake of the September 11 attacks in the U.S., the IRA was under increased pressure to meet its commitments to decommission its weapons and disarm.[21] In an effort to save the peace process, the British and Irish governments issued joint declarations in October 2003, calling on all sides to disarm, halt violence, and establish a power-sharing arrangement between Republicans and Unionists. The IRA became increasingly isolated as its refusal to disarm and continued acts of violence committed by its members alienated the Irish public, including most Catholics. In July 2005 the IRA announced it was forsaking violence. Although staunch unionists remained skeptical of IRA assurances, elections for the Northern Ireland Assembly took place in March 2007. In May, the leaders of the rival factions reached a historic power-sharing agreement and local government finally came to Northern Ireland. In 2008, the ten-year anniversary of the Good Friday Agreement, Northern Ireland was at peace and reconciliation efforts were under way to try to slowly heal the wounds of decades of sectarian violence. However, in January 2009 a proposed plan to compensate the families of those killed in the "troubles" encountered stiff resistance, because many families believed it unjustly extended the same compensation to the families of dead "terrorists" as it did to the families of the "victims." In March 2009 gunmen killed two soldiers and wounded several civilians in an attack on a military base. In January 2012, riots broke out in Belfast over a decision by the City Council to cease flying the British Flag on City Hall, except for special occasions. This angered the Protestant community, which regarded the measure as an effort by Catholics to attack Loyalist symbols. The riots were also a reflection of economic hardship and high unemployment, which have created a new generation of angry and disaffected youth. These events are an illustration of the fragility of the peace and the ongoing enmity and hostility that endures in Northern Ireland, and the need for vigilance.

DISARMAMENT AND ARMS CONTROL

The main assumption behind disarmament and arms control efforts is that weapons contribute to the likelihood of armed conflict, a position juxtaposed with the realist view that peace and stability can be attained only through balances of power and preparation for war.[22] Advocates argue that the frequency of war can be reduced by eliminating threatening or destabilizing weapons, preventing arms races that increase tensions and hostility and absorb financial resources, promoting mutual trust and confidence, and limiting the destructiveness of war if it does occur. An important distinction must be made: disarmament efforts seek to drastically reduce or eliminate weapons as an important step toward the elimination of war itself, while arms control efforts seek to reduce stockpiles of existing weapons or prevent their use to reduce the risk of war through stabilizing the status quo, building confidence between states and groups, encouraging the peaceful dispute resolution, and discouraging the use of force. As one analyst observes, "Arms control is fundamentally a conservative enterprise. Disarmament seeks to overturn the status quo; arms control works to perpetuate it."[23]

Not surprisingly, only a few historical examples of disarmament efforts exist. In 6th-century BCE China, several states formed a disarmament league that contributed to a century of peace. In 1817, Great Britain and the United States signed the Rush–Bagot Treaty which demilitarized the Canada–U.S. border. At the end of World War I, U.S. President Woodrow Wilson called for national disarmament to the lowest point consistent with domestic safety (a provision later watered down to disarmament to the lowest level consistent with national safety, which could mean almost anything). The League of Nations sponsored a World Disarmament Conference in 1932, which attempted to ban offensive weapons, but foundered on the definition of which weapons were defensive and which were offensive. Finally, the UN has sponsored a number of special sessions on disarmament since its inception in 1945, although with limited results.

In contrast, the historical record of arms control agreements is vast and varied. In almost all cases, arms control efforts have attempted to ban the production or deployment of a specific weapon (or a variant of a weapon) or to restrict the number of weapons a signatory is allowed to possess. For example, in the 11th century an effort was made by the Second Lateran Council to ban crossbows, and in 1868 the St. Petersburg Declaration banned explosive bullets. The 1899 and 1907 International Peace Conventions at The Hague banned a number of weapons (including poisonous gas). At the Washington Naval Conferences (1921 to 1922), the United States, Great Britain, Japan, France, and Italy agreed to fixed ratios for the number of capital ships in their battle fleets, a production moratorium on new ones, and the scrapping of a significant number. During the Cold War, two broad types of arms control agreements existed. The most prominent of these were the bilateral agreements established by the two superpowers. In addition, several multilateral arms control agreements involving other countries were established. Some of these multilateral arrangements were directly related to the Cold War, while others were intended to have a wider, universal effect. Many of these agreements survive to this day and form the foundation of contemporary efforts to address contemporary security issues.

ARMS CONTROL IN GLOBAL POLITICS

Contemporary arms control efforts are focused largely on preventing the proliferation of weapons (see Chapter 6) and banning the use, production, or stockpiling of specific weapons systems. Some new agreements have been established to meet new concerns, but for the most part older Cold War agreements have been revisited in an effort to adapt them to new international conditions (see Profile 7.1). The immediate priority was nuclear arms reductions and securing the nuclear arsenal of the former Soviet Union. After the collapse of the U.S.S.R., the Russian government either did not, or simply could not, account for all of the nuclear weapons on Russian territory, and it certainly could not negotiate on behalf of the former republics of Ukraine, Belarus, and Kazakhstan, which suddenly possessed weapons on their own territories. After a period of intense negotiation (in particular with Ukraine, which had a powerful domestic constituency favouring the retention of nuclear weapons), all three countries agreed to eliminate all nuclear weapons on their territories and sign the Non-Proliferation Treaty (NPT). They have now joined South Africa as the only states to dispossess themselves of nuclear weapons. In June 1992, at a summit in Washington, President Bush and President

PROFILE 7.1	**Major Multilateral Arms Control Treaties and Agreements**

DATE	AGREEMENT	PRINCIPAL AIMS
1959	Antarctic Treaty	Prohibits military use of the Antarctic, including nuclear weapons testing
1963	Limited/Partial Test Ban Treaty	Prohibits testing nuclear weapons in the atmosphere, underwater, and in outer space
1967	Outer Space Treaty	Prohibits testing or stationing any weapons in space, and bans military manoeuvres in space
1967	Treaty of Tlatelolco	Creates Latin American nuclear weapons–free zone
1968	Nuclear Non-Proliferation Treaty	Prohibits transfer of nuclear weapons and technology to (Revised in 19 non-nuclear states)
1971	Seabed Treaty	Prohibits deployment of weapons of mass destruction (including nuclear weapons) beyond a 12-mile (20-kilometre) coastal limit
1972	Biological Weapons Convention	Prohibits production and stockpiling of biological weapons
1977	Environmental Modifications	Bans use of technologies that can alter weather patterns or ecology
1981	Inhumane Weapons Convention	Prohibits or restricts certain fragmentation weapons, incendiary weapons, and treacherous weapons
1985	South Pacific Nuclear Free Zone	Prohibits testing, acquisition, or deployment of nuclear weapons in the South Pacific
1986	Confidence Building and Security	Requires prior notification and onsite inspection of military exercises in Europe (CDE) Agreement
1987	Missile Technology Control	Restricts export of ballistic missiles and technology
1990	Conventional Forces in Europe	Limits numbers of five categories of weapons in Europe (extended to former Soviet Union states in 1992)
1992	Open Skies Treaty	Permits surveillance and verification flights over signatory countries
1993	Chemical Weapons Convention	Requires all stockpiles and production facilities to be destroyed within 10 years
1993	UN Register of Conventional Arms	Calls on states to submit sale and receipt information on seven categories of conventional arms to a central registry
1996	Comprehensive Test Ban Treaty	Requires all signatories not to test nuclear weapons
1997	Global Land Mines Treaty	Requires all signatories to destroy stocks of land mines and not produce or export them
2008	Cluster Munitions Convention	Requires all signatories to eliminate the use, production, stockpiling, and transfer of all existing and future cluster bombs
2013	Global Arms Trade Treaty	Requires all signatories to closely monitor arms exports and transactions, creates a secretariat to collect reports

Yeltsin surprised the world by agreeing to a Joint Understanding under the START agreement that would reduce the nuclear arsenals of the superpowers by 60 percent—to 3000 warheads for Russia and 3500 warheads for the United States—by the year 2003 (later 2007). This understanding was formalized as a treaty in the START II Agreement in January 1993. On May 24, 2002, U.S. President George W. Bush and Russian President Vladimir Putin signed the Strategic Offensive Reductions Treaty (SORT). The treaty restricted each country to possessing no more than 1700 to 2200 strategic warheads by December 31, 2012. While significant, the treaty did not address warhead destruction or reductions in non-strategic (sometimes called *tactical*) nuclear warheads. Nevertheless, SORT resulted in further cuts to the nuclear arsenals of the United States and Russia, which expires in 2021, also tightens verification measures.

Another immediate concern after the Cold War was securing Russia's nuclear warheads, fissile material, and nuclear weapons infrastructure. The collapse of the Soviet Union left the security and safety of vast numbers of nuclear warheads in doubt. Many Soviet nuclear scientists and weapons technicians were suddenly unemployed, raising fears that they would accept jobs developing nuclear weapons in other countries. In 1991, the United States passed the Nunn–Lugar Act, otherwise known as the Cooperative Threat Reduction Program. This program, initiated with the cooperation of the Russian government, provides U.S. financial assistance to Russia for the identification, securing, and destruction of Russian nuclear (and chemical) weapons, as well as assisting Russian nuclear scientists to find work in peaceful industries. Among other accomplishments, in the first 10 years of the program, 6212 warheads were removed from their missiles and many were dismantled and the fissile material secured.[24] Concern over worsening relations between Russia and the West have renewed calls for more aggressive nuclear arms control efforts, including nuclear disarmament. In 2007 several former high-ranking U.S. officials called for a world free of nuclear weapons.[25] In April 2009 U.S. President Barack Obama delivered a speech in Prague committing the United States to pursue nuclear disarmament. While the lofty expectations of that speech have yet to be realized, in 2010 the United States and Russia negotiated the New START agreement, which came into force in 2011 and commits both countries to reduce their strategic nuclear warhead numbers to 1550 and their respective ballistic missile and heavy bomber arsenals to a total of 700 for each country, by the year 2018.

While stockpile reductions remain an important objective, today the focus of nuclear arms control is on proliferation. Two agreements figure prominently in the global effort to control the spread of nuclear weapons: the Non-Proliferation Treaty (NPT) and the Comprehensive Test Ban Treaty (CTBT). Under the NPT, signed in July 1968, nuclear weapons states are obligated not to transfer nuclear weapons or related technology to non–nuclear weapons states. In turn, non–nuclear weapons states are obligated not to try to acquire nuclear weapons or related technology. Materials related to nuclear energy are exempt from these provisions, because the NPT was originally designed to facilitate the spread of peaceful nuclear technology. For the same reasons, "peaceful" nuclear explosions are permitted. All signatories to the NPT pledge to work toward universal nuclear disarmament. The International Atomic Energy Agency (IAEA) is charged with verifying compliance with the NPT through constant monitoring of nuclear facilities in signatory countries and the use of onsite inspections.

The NPT has been the subject of considerable criticism. First, as an international treaty it binds only its members, and not all nuclear weapons states are signatories (Israel, Pakistan, and India are not members of the NPT, and North Korea withdrew in 2003). Despite the efforts of the IAEA, some non-nuclear weapons states have managed to build significant nuclear weapons development programs. For example, Iraq possessed a sophisticated program during the 1980s, which was exposed after the end of the 1990 to 1991 Gulf War. North Korea managed to develop a nuclear bomb while a member of the NPT. Iran has conducted a number of clandestine nuclear activities that violate the terms of its agreement with the IAEA. These examples fuel accusations that the IAEA is ineffective as a **verification** and compliance mechanism because it lacks (among other things) sufficient resources and an enforcement capacity. Furthermore, the NPT and the IAEA are criticized for their role in encouraging the spread of nuclear energy. This role has raised environmental concerns, and civilian reactor programs can be the first step in acquiring a bomb. Finally, countries such as India have argued that since the NPT also obligates nuclear states to work for disarmament, it is hypocritical of nuclear weapons states to criticize countries such as India for developing nuclear weapons. However, these criticisms should not obscure the fact that the NPT does maintain the norm that the spread of nuclear weapons is inherently dangerous. This norm is nearly universal: as of 2012, 189 countries were signatories to the NPT (Taiwan has also signed on, though it is not formally recognized as a state). Along with a network of agreements among suppliers of nuclear technology, the NPT does add another obstacle to nuclear ambitions.[26]

The CTBT also has a long history. Since the late 1950s, periodic efforts have been made to ban all nuclear tests. A Partial Test Ban Treaty signed in 1963 by the United States, Britain, and the U.S.S.R. (and joined by France in 1974 and China in 1980) did not include underground tests, a step that would constrain the development of new types of nuclear weapons. In the 1990s, several countries (including the United States) followed unilateral moratoriums on testing. With the signing of the CTBT on September 24, 1996, more than 90 countries committed themselves not to test nuclear weapons.[27] The CTBT had 183 signatories in 2012 with 157 countries having ratified the treaty. It also prohibits peaceful explosions, closing an important loophole in the NPT. However, India and Pakistan have refused to sign the CTBT. India has argued that the treaty provisions violate its sovereignty, and Pakistan will not sign until India does as well.

Chemical and biological weapons proliferation is another focus of contemporary arms control efforts. The two most important mechanisms designed to address these problems are the Chemical Weapons Convention (CWC) and the Biological Weapons Convention (BWC). The CWC, signed in January 1993 and in force by April 1997, is an ambitious and forward-looking treaty, aimed at disarmament rather than arms control. Bargaining was especially complicated, since many chemicals used in weapons are "**dual use**" chemicals also used in industry and agriculture. The signatories to the CWC were obligated to declare and complete the destruction of all of their chemical weapons and production facilities within 10 years of the treaty coming into force. Signatories are also obligated to declare whether they have received chemical weapons from another country or whether they have transferred them to another country. The CWC also has a complex verification system in which countries may mount challenge inspections in other countries to verify compliance. As of 2012, 188 countries had signed the CWC (186 had ratified the treaty). Of course, the CWC binds only its signatories, and the ease with which chemical weapons can be manufactured has led to suspicion that clandestine chemical weapons facilities might evade the attention of the world community.

The BWC was signed in 1972 and came into force in 1975. It prohibits the development, production, and stockpiling of biological weapons, although it does not explicitly ban their use since the 1925 Geneva Protocol for the Prohibition of the Use in War of Asphyxiating, Poisonous, or Other Gases and of Bacteriological Weapons of Warfare had already done so. However, the BWC has been heavily criticized for lacking a verification system and allowing signatories to continue research on biological weapons and protective measures for defensive purposes. In recognition of the limitations of the BWC and the increasing threat posed by biological weapons, in 1995 an Ad Hoc Working Group of governments began discussions to strengthen the BWC. Over six years later, the working group drafted a proposed protocol to the BWC that would require signatories to declare the existence and location of treaty-relevant facilities, and put in place a system of verification inspections. However, in 2001 the United States rejected the draft protocol, arguing that it did not cover enough relevant facilities, would be applied mostly to Western states and not those states most suspected of developing biological weapons, and might be used as an instrument of industrial espionage against U.S. biotech companies. The U.S. rejection of the proposed protocol met with a great deal of condemnation; supporters of the treaty dismissed the concerns of the U.S. government as unwarranted and even inaccurate. However, the U.S. rejection of the protocol effectively erased any hopes for strengthening the BWC. As of 2012, 165 states had signed the BWC, with 153 **ratifications**.

As concern over the spread of conventional weapons has increased, greater attention has been placed on establishing controls over such weapons. Some prominent examples are the Conventional Forces in Europe (CFE) Treaty, the Missile Technology Control Regime (MTCR), and the UN Register of Conventional Arms. The CFE Treaty was signed by 23 European states in November 1990. The treaty entered into force in 1991 and was extended to include the newly independent states of the former Soviet Union in 1992. The treaty classifies weapons into five broad categories of Treaty Limited Equipment (TLE) in a geographic area from the Atlantic Ocean to the Ural Mountains in Russia (the so-called Atlantic to the Urals, or ATTU, zone). All countries have allowable limits in TLE, which they cannot exceed, although in practice most countries maintain arsenals lower than they are permitted under the CFE. The CFE treaty has recently become a victim of the deteriorating relationship between Russia and NATO. In July 2007, Russia suspended its observance of the treaty, upset with a variety of issues including NATO enlargement, plans for the deployment of a U.S. missile defence system in Eastern Europe, and the refusal of NATO to make changes to the treaty to allow Russia more flexibility in deploying military forces in the ATTU zone.

The MTCR is an informal, voluntary arrangement designed to control the spread of **ballistic missile** technology. As such, it is not a treaty, nor is it legally binding on its membership. Formed in 1987 by seven producers of ballistic missile technology, the MTCR initially covered nuclear-capable missiles and was expanded in 1993 to include chemical-capable and biological-capable missiles as well. The MTCR now consists of 34 states. In 1993, China (which had pledged to abide by the provisions of the MTCR) was found to have transferred ballistic missile components to Pakistan. India, Pakistan, Iran, and North Korea continue to develop their ballistic missile programs, and all have received at least some international assistance in doing so. On the other hand, the MTCR has contributed to the cancellation of some ballistic missile development programs, by making it difficult to acquire certain technologies or creating a political environment that condemns such efforts. Brazil, South Korea, Taiwan, Argentina, Egypt, and South Africa have all stopped or suspended ballistic missile development efforts. In 2002, the International Code of Conduct against Ballistic Missile Proliferation was established. This agreement is non-binding, and calls for restraint in the production, testing, and export of ballistic missiles. With 134 signatories in 2012, the Code of Conduct has a wider number of signatories but weaker provisions than the MTCR, which remains an export control group of producing countries.

The UN arms register was created in 1991 by a UN General Assembly resolution. The register is an attempt to establish an information service to track arms shipments around the world in seven categories of weapons: tanks, armoured combat vehicles, heavy artillery, combat aircraft, attack helicopters, warships, and missiles and missile systems. Ideally, states submit transparent information on all exports and imports of weapons, and this reduces the secretive nature of arms transfers and the tensions and suspicions this secrecy can create. Critics of the registry argue that it places no limits on the transfer of weapons and is entirely dependent on the willingness of states to provide information about their arms sales and purchases. In addition, it can compile information only on the open arms trade and has no capacity to address the covert arms trade. A Global Arms Trade Treaty was reached at the UN in early April of 2013, but it too contains many loopholes and will not go into force until it is ratified by 50 signatories.

In addition to these mechanisms, other arms control instruments do exist, but they are unilateral, or measures agreed to by relatively small groups of states, lacking the near-universal quality of global arms control treaties. In the Western Hemisphere, 20 countries have signed the Inter-American Convention on Transparency in Conventional Weapons Acquisitions, which requires signatories to report their regional weapons sales and purchases. States can impose arms embargoes against other states, and impose arms sales codes of conduct on their domestic producers. Groups of states can agree not to transfer certain technologies to other states: for example, the 40 countries of the Wassenaar Arrangement on Export Controls for Conventional Arms and Dual-Use Goods and Technologies have agreed to exchange information on certain weapons transfers to encourage the responsible transfer of weapons and related technologies. In an effort to manage the flow of weapons in Central Africa, the Central African Convention for the Control of Small Arms and Light Weapons was signed in April of 2010. All of these mechanisms have their limitations, and the challenges facing arms control agreements in general have raised questions about the effectiveness of arms control efforts.

CRITICS OF ARMS CONTROL

Both disarmament and arms control efforts have been subjected to several critical themes:

- Arms control is risky and even dangerous because success depends on trusting one's opponents not to cheat.
- Compliance has to be verified, a complicated and difficult task.
- Arms control agreements will be violated in times of crisis or war.
- Weapons cannot be effectively banned, because the knowledge to manufacture them exists.
- Some restricted weapons may have minimal military utility.
- Arms control agreements channel production into weapons-system types that are not banned or restricted, further legitimizing the highly lucrative arms trade.
- Technological developments can render agreements obsolete or ineffective.
- Making agreements with authoritarian governments is ill advised, because they are more apt to cheat and more able to conceal this cheating.
- Arms control agreements bind only signatories, not non-signatories, who may proceed with arms buildups or the manufacture of certain banned weapons.

In response, advocates of disarmament and arms control maintain that states and groups have entered into arms control negotiations with deceitful purposes, seeking to consolidate an advantage in the possession of certain weapons. Advocates also point out that states enter arms control arrangements as public relations exercises. Until governments around the world are committed to the idea of disarmament and arms control for the mutual long-term benefit of all, the impact of disarmament and arms control measures will be limited.

There is not much optimism that arms control efforts will lead to a fundamentally more peaceful world in the future, for several reasons. First, governments continue to direct more resources toward researching and developing new weapons. Second, military and political leaders remain wary of disarmament and arms control as a means of strengthening their security. As a result, military preparedness remains a primary instrument of state security. Third, leaders are reluctant to engage in arms control either because they want to attain a certain military capability (whether nuclear weapons or ballistic missiles) and are unwilling to commit themselves to an agreement not to acquire it, or because they possess a superiority in a certain military capability and see no reason why they should accept constraints on it. Fourth, many developing states view the effort to prevent the spread of certain weapons as discriminatory acts by the rich nations anxious to perpetuate their military superiority. Fifth, a growing number of states are becoming capable of developing and manufacturing sophisticated weapons systems, making the process of reaching an arms control agreement among a larger and larger number of states an increasingly difficult proposition. Sixth, the 2003 war in Iraq (fought largely on false allegations of Iraqi weapons of mass destruction) has complicated global diplomacy on arms control by undermining the credibility of subsequent allegations against suspected treaty violators.[28] Finally, arms control cannot be regarded as a panacea, for true international security "depends not as much on arms or arms control as on reducing as much as possible the sources of conflict in international situations and on finding effective non-violent means of resolving the conflicts that remain."[29]

HUMAN SECURITY AND ARMS CONTROL

We introduced the concept of *human security* in Chapter 6, but expand on it here because much of the human security agenda is in fact a conflict management agenda. Human security is an idea that calls for a shift in thinking from the level of the state to the level of the human individual. In essence, it proposes a new global hierarchy of security priorities, placing the security of individuals above state sovereignty and territorial integrity, particularly if a state proves unwilling or unable to provide for the human security of its population. The first formal appearance of human security was in the UN Human Development Report in 1994: "Human security can be said to have two main aspects. It means, first, safety from chronic threats such as hunger, disease and repression. And second, it means protection from sudden and hurtful disruptions of daily life—whether in homes, in jobs, or in communities."[30] Former Canadian Foreign Affairs Minister Lloyd Axworthy was one of the leading advocates of the human security approach. Axworthy defined human security as "security against economic deprivation, an acceptable quality of life, and a guarantee of fundamental rights ... [this] requires that basic needs are met, but it also acknowledges that sustained economic development, human rights and fundamental freedoms, the rule of law, good governance, sustainable development, and social equity are as important as arms control and disarmament."[31] The human security concept did attract some governments, such as Canada and Norway, who made it a prominent component of their foreign policies. A Human Security Network was established in 1998, which currently consists of 13 states, and many NGOs in the arms control, humanitarian, and aid communities have adopted the term.

The concept has been criticized, most notably for a lack of precision. *Human security* is by nature a very vague term that covers a wide range of issues and topics. While this makes it politically useful, it also makes it a poor guide for establishing priorities. As Roland Paris argues, "Human security is like 'sustainable development'—everyone is for it, but few people have a clear sense of what it means."[32] In Canada, the human security concept was accused of promoting "pinchpenny diplomacy" (diplomacy on the cheap) and "pulpit diplomacy" (preaching morality while alienating allies).[33] Nevertheless, human security did establish a role and a voice for Canada before it was largely abandoned.[34] Human security was also a driving intellectual force behind a number of concrete initiatives that culminated in international treaties or agreements, most notably the Ottawa Treaty (see Profile 7.2) and the **"Responsibility to Protect"** doctrine.

In a significant development for human security and arms control advocates, on May 28, 2008, an agreement was reached to ban cluster bombs, a weapon that disperses small "bomblets" over a wide area. Arms control advocates had been calling for a ban for years, arguing that many of these bomblets fail to explode immediately and become a hazard to civilians days, weeks, and months later. The Cluster Munitions Convention was signed by 111 states. The U.S., China, Russia, Israel, India, and Pakistan (all major producers of the weapons) refused to attend the treaty conference or sign the agreement, arguing that the weapons were needed for military operations. Nevertheless, advocates of the ban were pleased with the result, and hoped it would have a similar effect as the 1997 Ottawa Treaty, which reduced land mine use even by countries that had not signed it. Human security and arms control advocates also hope to develop arms control agreements on the proliferation of small arms and light weapons. Human security will continue to have a place in the policy initiatives of some states and NGOs. The lasting significance of human security may well be the entrenchment of the idea that security cannot, and should not, always be defined in state-centric terms.

INTERNATIONAL LAW AND CONTROLS ON WAR

Efforts to prevent or control war through international law have pursued two strategies: the prohibition of war as an instrument of policy, and the imposition of rules and regulations to establish lawful conduct in war. Many qualified efforts have been made to prohibit war. The Hague Conventions of 1899 and 1907, for example, bound signatories to seek a peaceful resolution to their disputes before resorting to force. Presumably, if no peaceful resolution could be found, war was permissible. The Bryan Treaties of 1913 to 1914 banned declarations of war by one state against another before an arbitration committee had met to consider the circumstances of the conflict. The Covenant of the League of Nations bound League members to renounce aggression, and the signatories to the 1928 Kellogg–Briand Pact forfeited the right to go to war (see Profile 7.3). The Charter of the UN (Article 2/4) prohibits the use or threat of force in the international system, and a 1974 General Assembly resolution banned aggression. However, none of these efforts has succeeded in achieving the real goal of eliminating war.

Partly because of the historical record of attempts to prohibit war, much of the body of international law on war concerns its conduct. As early as 1400 BCE, agreements had been established concerning the treatment of prisoners, and poisoned weapons were outlawed in what is now known as India in 500 BCE. Modern legal efforts to control war are founded on the Geneva Conventions of 1948, and the additional Protocols of 1977. This body of law, sometimes referred to as the laws of war or International Humanitarian Law (IHL), has focused on establishing rules of conduct that include distinguishing between combatants and non-combatants

PROFILE 7.2

Weapons Proliferation and Human Security: The Global Land Mines Problem

The Ottawa Treaty. The signing of the Convention on the Prohibition of the Use, Stockpiling, Production and Transfer of Anti-personnel Mines and on Their Destruction, December 3, 1997. From left are International Campaign to Ban Landmines representative Jody Williams, President of the International Committee of the Red Cross Cornelio Sommaruga, UN Secretary-General Kofi Annan, Foreign Affairs Minister Lloyd Axworthy, and Prime Minister Jean Chrétien. (CP PHOTO-Tom Hanson/CP Images)

Anti-personnel land mines (APLs) are designed to explode automatically in response to pressure or tripwires. Because they are easy to make and deploy, and are cheap (as little as $3 to $15 for simpler mines), they have become very common in intrastate wars. In the mid-1990s, an estimated 60 million to 110 million land mines were buried in 64 countries. More mines were laid every year, while extraction rates were low: every year UN or private deminers took out just 10 000 mines. The human costs of land mines were horrific: indiscriminate land mines killed or wounded an estimated 26 000 people a year through the late 1980s to the mid-1990s. Mine injuries are painful and crippling, involving costly treatment and lengthy rehabilitation. They are also an obstacle to post-conflict recovery and development, rendering land unusable for crops or grazing and preventing safe travel, and represent a serious threat to human security in countries such as Cambodia, Angola, Bosnia-Herzegovina, Mozambique, and Afghanistan.

Efforts to ban the stockpiling, production, and export of land mines grew in the 1990s.

A UN resolution called for a moratorium on land mine exports (with then Secretary-General Boutros Boutros-Ghali giving the matter his personal attention), and NGOs such as the International Committee of the Red Cross and the International Campaign to Ban Landmines increased their pressure on governments. By 1996 Canada had begun to exert international leadership on this issue, imposing a unilateral moratorium on the production, export, and operational use of anti-personnel land mines. In 1997 Canada led a successful campaign to conclude a global anti-personnel land mine treaty, which was signed in Ottawa on December 2, 1997. The treaty bans the use, production, transfer, and stockpiling of anti-personnel mines and obligates signatories to destroy their stockpiles. States contribute funds for mine clearance, medical treatment, rehabilitation, and artificial limbs. However, key countries have not signed the treaty, including the United States, Russia, China, India, Pakistan, Israel, and Iran. New wars have seen increased mine use and casualties in countries such as Libya, Pakistan, Sudan, South Sudan, and Syria. Nevertheless, the treaty has proved to be a major diplomatic and arms control success and a significant breakthrough for the human security concept. By 2013, 161 countries had acceded to the treaty. Land mine use has declined, production of land mines has fallen, the global trade in land mines has virtually ceased, demining efforts continue (with 1700 square kilometres of land and 3.1 million mines removed between 2001 and 2011), and, while the number of victims per year is still appalling (4286 in 2011), casualties have decreased by one-third between 2001 and 2011.

SOURCE: "THE UNITED NATIONS AND MINE CLEARANCE," OVERVIEW - JUNE 1995, UNITED NATIONS DEPARTMENT OF HUMANITARIAN AFFAIRS, INTERNATIONAL MEETING ON MINE CLEARANCE, GENEVA, 5-7 JUNE 1995; ARMS CONTROL ASSOCIATION FACT SHEET: THE OTTAWA CONVENTION: SIGNATORIES AND STATE PARTIES. WASHINGTON D.C.: THE ARMS CONTROL ASSOCIATION, 2004; LANDMINE MONITOR REPORT 2003: TOWARD A MINE FREE WORLD. INTERNATIONAL CAMPAIGN TO BAN LANDMINES (NEW YORK: HUMAN RIGHTS WATCH, 2003).

PROFILE 7.3 **The Kellogg–Briand Pact**

The Kellogg–Briand Pact, formally known as the Treaty Providing for the Renunciation of War as an Instrument of State Policy, was originally agreed to by the governments of the United States and France in 1927. U.S. Secretary of State Frank B. Kellogg and French Foreign Minister Aristide Briand agreed to outlaw war between their two states. The enthusiasm of the U.S. government led to an open offer to other governments to sign the treaty; by 1934, 64 states (most of the states in the world at that time) were signatories. However, the hopes of the treaty were never realized. Most signatories placed caveats on their commitment to the renunciation of war; Japan, for example, insisted on the right to wage war in self-defence, while Great Britain insisted on its right to intervene militarily in areas of the world of interest to it (namely, its colonies). The treaty contained no enforcement mechanism and was unable to respond to acts of aggression. The treaty was also signed by states that had clear expansionist or revisionist ambitions. As a result, it has been derided as an example of the emptiness and futility of efforts to outlaw war.

SOURCE: R. FERRELL, *PEACE IN THEIR TIME: THE ORIGIN OF THE KELLOGG-BRIAND PACT* (NEW HAVEN: YALE UNIVERSITY PRESS, 1952).

(civilians), the treatment of prisoners of war, defining an indiscriminate attack, restrictions on carpet bombing, extra judicial executions, and the establishment of war zones. International law has also focused on defining war crimes such as genocide (see Chapter 9), and on the prohibition or restriction of specific types of weapons.[35] Modern efforts at the latter are largely derived from two special UN conferences on conventional weapons held at Lucerne in 1974 and Lugano in 1976. These conferences laid the foundation for the three protocols of the 1981 Inhumane Weapons Convention, which banned different types of weapons systems. Protocol I covers fragmentation weapons, banning the use of toxic fragments and fragments that are undetectable by X-ray. Protocol II covers treacherous weapons, prohibiting booby traps, the use of mines against civilians, the placement of mines, and requiring recorded maps of minefields. Protocol III covers **incendiary weapons**, prohibiting attacks on the natural elements (unless they are used as cover for military movements) and the use of incendiary weapons against civilians.

Despite the letter of international law, these provisions are frequently violated. Many states and substate groups violate IHL out of ignorance, or choose to violate it knowing the chances of enforcement are slim. Few robust enforcement mechanisms exist to support the observation of international law in war. Non-state actors such as the International Committee of the Red Cross and Red Crescent Societies have filled this gap, but can only call attention to violations of IHL and lack the formal or practical capacity to enforce it. The efforts to build and apply war law—the Nuremberg and Tokyo war crimes trials and the international tribunals on atrocities committed in the former Yugoslavia and Rwanda—have been criticized as victors' justice, imposed on the losers of a conflict by the winners (see Chapter 9). The International Criminal Court (ICC) was a notable development but it too has serious limitations. International law also has difficulty keeping up with technological developments, and many new weapons systems and their deployment are not explicitly covered by international law. For example, the use of missile-firing drones by the United States against terrorist targets in other countries has sparked an intense debate on the legality of such attacks. Nevertheless, international law on war establishes norms of conduct and seeks to ban certain weapon systems that are especially inhumane; to violate these norms is to invite international condemnation.

INTERNATIONAL ORGANIZATIONS AND CONFLICT MANAGEMENT

As liberal institutionalists remind us, IOs perform several tasks and roles that are both directly and indirectly related to conflict management. IOs can act as a forum for debate and discussion, reducing the chances of misunderstanding or misinterpretation. IOs can also act as a steam valve, permitting political leaders to accuse and condemn their opponents without resorting to violence. This ability can be particularly useful when public opinion back home demands some form of response, especially in cases in which doing nothing best serves the interests of peace. Of course, governments can be accused of avoiding substantive action on an issue by raising it in an international forum but doing little else. IOs can also provide third-party **mediation** services in times of crisis or war. Because they are established actors with a permanent location and membership, they can provide physical facilities, staff, and diplomatic support for negotiations. Other members of an IO can also encourage the parties to a dispute to come to a settlement and offer rewards and threats to that end. IOs can establish fact-finding and information missions designed to obtain more objective sources of evidence and information. In other cases, the staff or leadership of the organization itself (such as the UN Secretary-General) may become involved in facilitating an agreement. Finally, with the agreement of the parties to a dispute, IOs may act as arbitrators.

IOs can also provide legitimacy to the policies of a state or a group of states, and can serve to constrain unilateralism. To act as a collective, IOs require the consensus of their membership (depending on the voting procedure of the organization). If states or groups want to act as a collective, with the advantages of added legitimacy that joint action provides, then some states or groups will have to compromise or alter their positions so that a common stance can be reached. Therefore, organizations can help alter outcomes in such a way as to enhance peace by inhibiting or restraining certain members from aggressive actions. The Iraq War proved that in some cases states will act without the legitimacy provided by an IO (in this case, the UN). However, the relatively low level of international support for the United States-led war was in part attributable to the lack of a UN Security Council resolution authorizing the invasion.

IOs can promote peace and stability by establishing norms and principles of conduct and governance among their members. Members must often commit to the rejection of aggression and military force as means of resolving disputes. Over time, this norm of non-violence may become so pervasive that governments and substate groups will no longer regard military force as an option in the conduct of their affairs with each other. Karl Deutsch referred to such groups of countries as "security communities," which share common values, predictability of behaviour, and mutual responsiveness (the capability and willingness to respond quickly to one another).[36] The European Union (EU) is an example of an IO that can be described as a security community. In addition, IOs often seek to promote domestic values and systems of governance that are regarded as stabilizing and nonaggressive. Examples include the **Organization for Security and Co-operation in Europe (OSCE)**, which is built on the promotion of the principles of democracy and the protection of human rights, and the Organization of American States (OAS), which maintains a unit for the promotion of democracy. Of course, realists remind us that these organizations are nothing more than the creations of states and will act only when states agree to act. In contrast, neo-Marxists reject security communities and democracy promotion as strategies of Western imperialism.

In recent years, emphasis has shifted toward regional organizations as conflict management instruments. The hope is that they may contribute to regional peace and security by encouraging and facilitating cooperation among their members, establishing norms for the peaceful resolution of disputes, and acting as conduits for regional efforts to manage conflict. Examples include the following:

- *The North Atlantic Treaty Organization (NATO).* Founded in 1949 to defend Western Europe against a Soviet attack, NATO has altered its political purpose to the maintenance of stability and has changed its military structure to respond to crises. The alliance now has 28 members, and has created a number of consultative instruments to strengthen cooperation between its members and neighbouring states. NATO enforced the peace in Bosnia between 1995 and 2004, and launched an air war against Serbia in 1999 over the issue of human rights violations in Kosovo. In August 2003, NATO assumed command of the International Security Assistance Force (ISAF) in Afghanistan. In March 2011, NATO assumed control over the international intervention in the Libyan Civil War that ultimately led to the overthrow of the Gaddafi government. Although political tensions and disagreements are common in the alliance, it remains the most powerful military organization in the world.

- *The Organization of American States (OAS).* Founded in 1948, the OAS was preoccupied with the issue of the spread of communism to Latin America during the Cold War. Post-Cold War, the central tasks of the OAS have been the promotion of mutual security, regional economic and social development, non-intervention and sovereign equality, the peaceful settlement of disputes, and democracy and human rights. In 1994, the OAS initiated the Summit of the Americas process, designed to bring the 34 member states together to solve regional issues. The OAS was involved in the termination of several insurgency conflicts in Central America in the 1990s. In 2001, it adopted the Inter-American Democratic Charter, aimed at promoting regional democracy. Subsequent Summits have focused on economic development and good governance.

- *The African Union (AU).* The **African Union** is built on a previous organization called the Organization of African Unity (OAU). Established in 1963, the OAU reflected the concept of Pan-Africanism and efforts to encourage decolonization and economic development. The OAU had some success in mediating conflicts. However, it has failed to address more complex interstate and intrastate disputes such as the Nigerian Civil War, the Ethiopia–Somalia War, and the civil wars in Angola and Mozambique. In 2002, the OAU was replaced by the AU, which has deployed peacekeeping missions in Burundi, Darfur, Somalia, and Mali. An AU force restored stability to the Comoros in 2008. However, the peacekeeping efforts in Somalia, Darfur, and Mali have been characterized by inadequate troop contributions and a lack of equipment and financial resources. Another African regional organization, the **Economic Community of West African States (ECOWAS)**, dominated by Nigeria, has had mixed results in its efforts to manage the conflicts of West Africa and needed assistance from France and the AU in Mali.

- *The Arab League.* Formed in 1945 and now consisting of 22 states, the Arab League was designed to promote cooperation between Arab countries on economic and social affairs, communications, culture, and health. Egypt was expelled for making peace with Israel in 1979 but was readmitted in 1987. As a mechanism for conflict management, the Arab League has not been very successful; most of its proclamations and plans have gone unheeded. It was unable to broker a resolution in the events leading up to Iraq's invasion of Kuwait and authorized its member states to cooperate with the United States-led coalition against Iraq in 1990 to 1991. Subsequent disagreement over the maintenance of sanctions against Iraq kept the League divided. The League has been criticized for its failure to respond effectively to the Iraq War and the Syrian Civil War.

• *The Association of Southeast Asian Nations (ASEAN).* ASEAN was formed in 1967 and now consists of 10 member states. Formally a mechanism for regional cooperation, ASEAN has addressed a widening range of issues from trade liberalization to refugees to the drug trade. ASEAN has moved slowly into the realm of security issues. It played a significant role in ending the Vietnamese occupation of Cambodia. Today, ASEAN is the basis for regional political and security arrangements, including joint military exercises. ASEAN members are involved (often as a collective) in larger Pacific-wide cooperation initiatives, such as the Asia-Pacific Economic Cooperation (APEC) arrangement. In 1993, ASEAN expanded its security role with the creation of the ASEAN Regional Forum (ARF). However, there has been little progress on deepening security cooperation in this forum, and the embryonic Trans-Pacific Partnership appears ready to eclipse ASEAN as a trade arrangement.

In part, this trend toward regionalism in conflict management is due to the perennial challenges facing the UN (see Chapter 5). Short of money and resources, the UN has found it increasingly difficult to maintain its current obligations and programs and even harder to undertake new operations and tasks. However, the turn to regional organizations is also a function of the belief that they are more effective as conflict management instruments within their respective regions than universal organizations such as the UN.

Regional organizations do have advantages when addressing local crises. Their members will be more familiar with local disputes than diplomats in the distant hallways of UN headquarters, and they may not be constrained by wider disagreements among UN members, especially if regional consensus exists on an appropriate response to a crisis. Regional organizations, by virtue of their geographic proximity, can respond faster than UN peacekeeping or intervention forces. In some cases, regional organizations may have better capabilities than the UN and a more streamlined political and military decision-making structure (this is certainly the case with NATO). However, local actors may pursue their own interests in the crisis; parties to a dispute may feel that local actors and regional organizations lack the requisite neutrality and impartiality to act as mediators or facilitators. Regional organizations are often incapable of offering sufficient rewards (such as economic aid) or acting on threatened punishments (such as economic sanctions). Most lack the economic resources and military capabilities to undertake significant action. In many cases they are unable under their respective charters to undertake such actions, or to enforce their will on states by any means other than moral appeal. The members of such organizations are often deeply divided, and a meaningful consensus is often very difficult to achieve. Nonetheless, the potential certainly exists for regional organizations to play an increased role in conflict management, especially in cooperation with other organizations, as explicitly envisioned in the UN Charter.

FROM UNITED NATIONS PEACEKEEPING TO HUMANITARIAN INTERVENTION

From its inception, the UN was first and foremost a security institution, designed to establish peace in the post–World War II world. As stated in the first sentence of the Preamble to the Charter, the UN was intended to "save succeeding generations from the scourge of war."[37] The UN was designed as a collective security system, and the UN Charter committed member states to resolve their differences peacefully and refrain from the use of force.[38] However, it also recognized the limitations of collective security as experienced by the League of Nations. Under Article 51 of the UN Charter, member states retain the right of self-defence, and under Article 52, they retain the right to engage in regional arrangements (such as alliances) to protect their security.

The conflict management provisions of the UN are found in Chapters 6 and 7 of the UN Charter. Chapter 6, entitled "Pacific Settlement of Disputes," calls on member states to resolve their disputes through "negotiation, enquiry, mediation, conciliation, arbitration, judicial settlement, resort to regional agencies or arrangements, or other peaceful means of their own choice." Chapter 7, entitled "Action with Respect to Threats to the Peace, Breaches of the Peace, and Acts of Aggression," is the heart of the collective security function of the UN. Article 40 empowers the Security Council to call on the parties to a dispute to abide by related resolutions; Article 41 empowers it to call on member states to observe measures directed at the parties to a dispute that do not involve the use of force (most commonly, some form of sanctions). Finally, if these measures prove inadequate, the Security Council can invoke Article 42, which reads:

> Should the Security Council consider that measures provided for in Article 41 would be inadequate, it may take such action by air, sea, or land forces as may be necessary to maintain or restore international peace and security. Such actions may include demonstrations, blockade, and other operations by air, sea, or land forces of Members of the United Nations.

Chapter 7 also specifies the obligation of member states to provide forces, facilities, and transit rights for such operations.

During the Cold War the UN was unable to perform its collective security function because of disagreements between the United States and the Soviet Union in the Security Council. Only the Korean anomaly (see Chapter 3) stands as an example of UN collective security in action during the Cold War. The 1990 to 1991 Persian Gulf War is the only clear post–Cold War example, although (as with the Korean case) there is considerable debate over whether it can rightfully be called a *collective security action*. Rather, the most visible and significant conflict management role performed by the UN since its creation has been peacekeeping. Between 1948 and 2012, the UN created 67 peacekeeping operations, a remarkable achievement considering that peacekeeping was an improvisation and is not even mentioned in the UN Charter. The origin of UN peacekeeping lies in the use of observer and truce supervision missions, a tradition drawn from the experience of the League of Nations.[39] The UN established observer missions in 1947 during the Greek Civil War, in 1948 after the Arab–Israeli War, and in 1949 after a war between India and Pakistan. However, the term *peacekeeping* was not coined until 1956, when Canadian Secretary of State for External Affairs Lester B. Pearson suggested a UN Emergency Force be established to manage the Suez Crisis (see Profile 7.4).

These early experiences laid the foundation for UN peacekeeping. Over time, a set of conventions about the composition, aims, and tasks of peacekeeping operations emerged, which were for the most part followed. These conventions came to be called *traditional* peacekeeping:

- *Impartiality.* No side should be favoured by UN peacekeepers. Unlike Chapter 7 collective security operations, UN peacekeeping did not identify an aggressor.

PROFILE 7.4 The United Nations Emergency Force

The Suez Crisis was precipitated by the nationalization of the Suez Canal by Egypt on July 26, 1956. Three months later, Israel, France, and Great Britain invaded Egypt. Israel sought to damage the Egyptian military in a pre-emptive war, while France and Great Britain were attempting to seize the canal. The invasion was widely condemned by the international community, including the U.S. Under pressure from domestic opposition and from Washington, the warring parties agreed to a ceasefire on November 6 to 7. In previous weeks, Canada had proposed the creation of a UN force and had supplied a draft resolution and presented it to the General Assembly for approval. The creation of the United Nations Emergency Force (UNEF) satisfied many interests. France and Great Britain were spared some of the embarrassment of being forced to obey the United States; the United States achieved an end to the war without direct intervention. Canada prevented a serious rift between the United States and Great Britain, Egypt secured the canal, and Israel obtained a ceasefire after damaging the Egyptian armed forces. Launched on November 4, 1956, under a UN General Assembly resolution, the mission was mandated to secure and supervise the cessation of hostilities and facilitate the withdrawal of France, Great Britain, and Israel from Egyptian territory, and to serve as a buffer between Egyptian and Israeli forces. UNEF began to deploy after the ceasefire was in place. It reached a strength of 6000 personnel, from Brazil, Canada, Colombia, Denmark, Finland, India, Indonesia, Norway, Sweden, and Yugoslavia. UNEF I was the beginning of the prominent role Canada would play in UN peacekeeping missions throughout the Cold War. However, UNEF I was expelled from Egypt in 1967, and another Arab–Israeli war soon followed.

- *Non-hostile and lightly armed personnel.* As UN peacekeepers were not present to engage in offensive military operations and could not appear to be a coercive presence, UN peacekeepers were unarmed or lightly armed (generally with service rifles and side arms) for self-defence only.

- *Consent.* Respect for state sovereignty required the UN to obtain the consent of the parties to a dispute before a UN force could be dispatched, deployed, and maintained.[40]

- *A peace to keep.* UN peacekeepers could not forcefully create peace: it had to be in place before the peacekeeping operation was deployed.

- *Military personnel.* UN operations were carried out primarily by soldiers.

- *Proper authorization.* UN peacekeepers had to be dispatched under UN authorization (or by organizations authorized to do so by the UN). In practice, this has generally meant the Security Council, which also established the mandate (the legal and operational boundaries of the mission) and the rules of engagement (the legal and operational boundaries of the personnel).

- *Reliance on member states.* As the UN had no army, UN peacekeeping operations were entirely dependent on contributions of money, personnel, and equipment from member states. Suggestions that the UN should possess its own army have always been rejected because governments fear the creation of a military instrument under UN control and the great expense involved in creating it.

- *Non-territoriality.* Peacekeeping personnel patrolled a zone or line that had been negotiated by the parties to a dispute. They had no legal claim to that territory, nor did they exercise sovereignty over it.

Confusion in Cyprus. United Nations soldiers patrol the UN "Buffer Zone" in Nicosia, which splits Cyprus, July 2, 2010. Suspected Russian agent Christopher Robert Metsos skipped bail on the Mediterranean island, and fears have been expressed that he may have escaped via northern Cyprus, a breakaway state recognized only by Ankara. The area does not have extradition treaties with other countries. (Katia Christodoulou/EPA/Newscom)

The tasks of traditional UN peacekeepers included positioning themselves between belligerents, gathering information and facts, observing ceasefire lines and reporting violations, supervising the withdrawal of belligerent forces, defusing tensions, preventing or controlling the outbreak of violence, assisting in the maintenance of order, acting as mediators, and engaging in humanitarian tasks. UN peacekeeping operations occupied a middle ground between Chapter 6 and Chapter 7 of the UN Charter, described by former UN Secretary-General Dag Hammarskjöld as "Chapter Six-and-a-half" operations. Peacekeeping was one of the most visible and respected of UN functions, and UN peacekeepers were collectively awarded the Nobel Peace Prize in 1988.

However, the character and qualities of peacekeeping operations began to change by 1990 to 1991 for several reasons. First, intrastate conflicts began to dominate the international security agenda, and the UN became engaged to an unprecedented degree in civil wars and so-called failed states in many parts of the world. Second, the Security Council, freed from the constraints of the Cold War, was more capable of reaching agreements on the creation of peacekeeping forces; with the end of the Cold War there was much optimism that the UN would finally be able to perform as the instrument of international peace and security that the drafters of the UN Charter had intended. This optimism was reflected in *An Agenda for Peace*, a document prepared in 1992 by Secretary-General Boutros Boutros-Ghali, in which he proposed to enhance the role of the UN in international peace and security:

> In these past months a conviction has grown, among nations
> large and small, that an opportunity has been regained to

achieve the great objectives of the Charter—a United Nations capable of maintaining international peace and security, of securing justice and human rights and of promoting, in the words of the Charter, "social progress and better standards of life in larger freedom." This opportunity must not be squandered. The Organization must never again be crippled as it was in the era that has now passed.[41]

As a result, the number of peacekeeping operations mounted by the UN surged. In 1988, the UN was operating five missions, consisting of a total of 13 000 personnel, at a cost of US$266 million; by 1994 there were 17 missions, 76 500 personnel, and a cost of over US$3.3 billion.[42] Peacekeeping had become the preferred method of responding to the many intrastate conflicts that confronted UN member states in the early to mid-1990s. Not only did UN missions experience a surge in frequency but also the missions themselves experienced a number of qualitative changes.[43] These changes included the following:

- *Increased size.* The size of many UN operations increased dramatically, as they were deployed over larger areas, and occasionally across entire countries. The big three UN operations of the post–Cold War period—the UN Transitional Authority in Cambodia (UNTAC), the UN Protection Force in the Former Yugoslavia (UNPROFOR), and the second UN Operation in Somalia (UNOSOM II)—all deployed more than 20 000 personnel at their peak. During the Cold War, only the UN Operation in the Congo (ONUC) approached this size.

- *Lack of consent.* Many UN peacekeeping operations were now taking place in states experiencing intrastate war, or in failed states with little or no central government, where humanitarian crises were underway or imminent (see Chapter 6). In these cases, consent was difficult to obtain because governments were either nonexistent or opposed to UN action. Often the UN sought consent from the next-highest level of authority: the warring communal groups themselves. However, this was difficult to achieve, and the UN faced a stark choice: deploy a mission without consent or fail to respond to humanitarian crises. In reality, missions were often deployed without the consent of one or more of the warring factions.

- *Operations in hostile environments.* Many UN peacekeeping missions were now deployed to countries or areas where there was no peace to keep. Negotiated arrangements among the warring factions were either nonexistent or fragile. As a result, UN contingents attempting to facilitate the delivery of humanitarian relief or to establish safe areas for refugees have encountered obstruction and threats, and have come under armed attack both from organized groups and from lawless bands of armed individuals not under firm political control.

- *Increased use of force.* The UN has also demonstrated a greater willingness to employ force and the threat of force during peacekeeping missions, in part because of the erosion of the principle of consent. The UN was widely criticized (particularly in UNPROFOR and UNOSOM II) for standing by while humanitarian relief supplies were blocked, human rights abuses were perpetrated, and UN personnel were obstructed and abused. In response, the UN employed a greater level of force against warring parties, and UN contingents became more heavily armed. However, this placed UN peacekeepers at risk of retaliatory attacks and undermined the impartiality of the UN force.

- *Proliferation of mission tasks.* UN missions began to perform a much wider range of tasks: electoral support or management, judiciary and policy reform, refugee resettlement, aiding the delivery of humanitarian relief supplies, disarmament of warring factions and weapons cantonment, mine clearing and education, and protection of safe areas. UN operations now involve close cooperation with a wide variety of capacity building and humanitarian aid agencies.

- *Peacebuilding and national reconstruction.* Many UN missions have been assigned a wide variety of tasks designed to facilitate post-conflict recovery and development. As Boutros-Ghali put it, "UN operations now may involve nothing less than the reconstruction of an entire society and state. This requires a comprehensive approach, over an extended period. Security is increasingly understood to involve social, economic, environmental, and cultural aspects far beyond its traditional military dimension."[44] This objective has transformed UN peacekeeping operations from almost exclusively military operations to missions coordinating a vast aid and development effort.[45]

As a consequence of the changing nature of peacekeeping operations and the different environments in which they were operating, UN peacekeeping experienced what can only be described as a time of troubles in this period. Highly publicized UN failures in the former Yugoslavia, Somalia, and Rwanda revealed the mismatch between traditional peacekeeping and the intrastate communal conflicts of the post–Cold War world.

Yugoslavia. The UN experience in Yugoslavia was, at best, mixed. Although the UN Protection Force (UNPROFOR) succeeded in facilitating the delivery of humanitarian relief to the civilian population, the UN failed to end hostilities in Bosnia-Herzegovina. UN personnel were the targets of intimidation and harassment, were fired upon, and were taken hostage. All sides routinely defied the UN. In one incident that has become a symbol of UN futility in Bosnia, Dutch peacekeepers protecting a UN safe area near Srebrenica found themselves outgunned by Bosnian Serb militia and withdrew, and an estimated 7000 Muslim men were subsequently massacred. It was the shifting nature of the military balance on the ground, the intervention of NATO, and the use of air strikes that prompted the signing of the Dayton Agreement in 1995. The implementation of the settlement was facilitated by the deployment of 60 000 NATO troops.

A sad return. Roméo Dallaire, right, returns to Kigali, Rwanda, on April 5, 2004, the 10th anniversary of the beginning of the Rwandan genocide. Dallaire is the retired Canadian general whose UN peacekeepers had to stand by helplessly as the slaughter unfolded. Now a Senator in the Canadian parliament, he has emerged as one of the leading public proponents of humanitarian intervention in Sudan and elsewhere. (AP Photo/Sayyid Azim//CP Images)

Somalia. The UN experience in Somalia was almost a complete failure. UNOSOM I was initially deployed to facilitate the delivery of humanitarian relief supplies. The obstruction of UN and aid agency efforts and the continued fighting in Somalia prompted the creation of the United States-led Unified Task Force (UNITAF), authorized under Chapter 7 of the UN Charter. While UNITAF was initially successful in achieving order, it became embroiled in a shooting war against one of Somalia's factions. Because of casualties to U.S. forces, UNITAF was deactivated and replaced by UNOSOM II. However, the failure to establish a peace settlement and the continued fighting in Somalia led to the withdrawal of UNOSOM II in March 1995. Although many lives were saved, Somalia is no closer to political stability today than it was before UN intervention.

Rwanda. The call for the creation of a UN force for Rwanda came on the heels of the Somalia imbroglio. A conflict between the Hutu government and the Tutsi-led Rwandan Patriotic Front (RPF) had been raging for decades. A peace settlement (the Arusha Accords) was signed in August 1993, and the UN Assistance Mission for Rwanda (UNAMIR) began deploying later that year. However, in 1994 an orchestrated genocide began in Rwanda. The UN force commander, Canadian General (and now senator) Roméo Dallaire, has often argued that if he had been given more troops and an appropriate mandate, he could have prevented the worst of the genocide. In fact, neither was forthcoming, several Belgian peacekeepers were slaughtered, and UN member states—remembering the Somalia experience and refusing to acknowledge that genocide was under way—actually reduced the size of UNAMIR. By then, at least 500 000 people had died, and many more would die as the world watched and did nothing.[46]

The UN reinforced peace in Cambodia (UNTAC), Angola (UNAVEM), and Mozambique (UNOMOZ), and made some progress in restructuring the police and the judiciary in El Salvador (ONUSAL). However, the high-profile failures in Yugoslavia, Somalia, and Rwanda—and, later, the DRC (Democratic Republic of Congo)—received most of the attention, and undermined the credibility of the UN as an effective conflict management instrument. Former UN Assistant Secretary-General for Political Affairs Giandomenico Picco argued, "Neither the post–Cold War climate nor civil wars can rightfully be blamed for the failures that have beset the United Nations since 1991. One must look to the workings of the United Nations itself."[47] Saadia Touval was more specific:

> It is increasingly apparent that the United Nations possesses inherent characteristics that make it incapable of effectively mediating complex international disputes. It does not serve well as an authoritative channel of communication. It has little real political leverage. Its promises and threats lack credibility. And it is incapable of pursuing coherent, flexible, and dynamic negotiations guided by an effective strategy.[48]

The UN has also been criticized for its inability to manage the peacekeeping operations it has mounted. UN peacekeeping missions have been plagued by a variety of operational problems, including a shortage of long-range transportation and tactical airlift; the uneven quality of troop contributions and incompatibility of equipment; little or no capacity to gather information or intelligence; and slow reaction times, with as much as six months passing before a UN operation is ready to be deployed.

While much of this criticism is justified, blaming the UN is somewhat misleading. Certainly, the organization struggled to manage the increase in peacekeeping operations, and there are bureaucratic and structural shortcomings within the UN system. However, it is member states that authorize peacekeeping missions (or refuse to do so), provide the mandates, resources, troops, and diplomatic support, and decide whether those missions are to be renewed or increased or decreased. Often, blaming the UN is a tactic states use to evade responsibility for their actions or inactions. The capacities of the UN are largely dependent on the commitment of member states, and so the UN can hardly be held solely accountable for failures in peacekeeping. As early as 1993, Boutros-Ghali warned, "Our renaissance remains in question; demands made upon the United Nations are not being matched by the resources to do the job."[49]

In the face of such problems, some attempts have been made to improve the capacity of the UN to create and deploy peacekeeping missions. The Department of Peacekeeping Operations (DPKO) has created a 24-hour situation centre that provides UN headquarters with command, control, and communications capabilities. In 1992, a Humanitarian Early Warning System was created. In 1993 a UN Standby Arrangements system established a list of forces member states were willing to contribute to UN operations. A logistics base stockpile was established at Brindisi, Italy. Prompted by a Canadian study conducted after the failure in Rwanda, in 1995 the UN established a rapidly deployable peacekeeping headquarters designed to react swiftly in times of need. In August 2000, the UN released the *Report of the Panel on UN Peacekeeping Operations*, otherwise known as the Brahimi Report. As a result, DPKO was restructured and in June 2007 a new Department of Field Support was established to strengthen the logistics support available to UN field missions. The UN introduced a new operational guidance document in 2008 to establish formal norms and rules governing peacekeeping.[50] These reform efforts have all had some positive impact, but due to monetary shortages and political opposition they must be described as relatively modest developments.

With the UN increasingly regarded as unsuited to the challenges of major regional conflicts and gross violations of human rights, states have turned to regional organizations or "coalitions of the willing" that are unburdened by the constraints of the UN system. In such cases, the UN no longer exerts direct control over the military mission or the political process, and in effect becomes a legitimating device for the coalitions or regional organizations that are conducting the operation through their own means and according to their own counsel. Nevertheless, UN peacekeeping continues to make a valuable contribution to conflict management efforts worldwide. The past few years have seen an increase in the number of missions and the number of deployed peacekeepers. In October 2012, the UN deployed 15 peacekeeping missions with some 115 374 personnel (95 223 of them military), the largest number of deployed personnel in the history of peacekeeping. In the 2012 to 2013 UN fiscal year, the peacekeeping budget was approximately US$7.23 billion, a trifle compared to virtually any measure of world military spending but nevertheless the largest annual budget allocation for peacekeeping in history. As of January 2013, the largest UN peacekeeping missions (each deploying over 7000 military, police, and civilian personnel) were in Liberia, the DRC, Lebanon, Côte D'Ivoire, Haiti, South Sudan, and Darfur.[51]

However, peacekeeping continues to face daunting challenges. Operating 15 simultaneous missions has placed a heavy burden on administrative capacity. The UN continues to rely on member states for troops, equipment, and adequate funding, and these are not always forthcoming. Peacekeeping personnel deployed into unstable areas such as Darfur, the DRC, and Lebanon have been threatened and attacked. Contributions of troops from rich, industrialized countries have declined: in December 2012 the leading troop contributors were Pakistan, Bangladesh, and India, while no industrialized countries were in the top ten. Canada, despite a long tradition of participation in UN missions, ranked 55th. In some missions, sexual misconduct and corruption has damaged the UN's reputation. In others, such as Sudan and Lebanon, missions have been accused of political bias. In addition, high-profile counterinsurgency operations in Iraq and Afghanistan, as well as the use of terminology such as *stability operations* and *peace support operations* has led to confusion over the distinction between **counterinsurgency** and peacekeeping. The effectiveness of peacekeeping in the future will be determined by at least three factors: (1) the careful consideration of the demands of a proposed mission and the mandates and capabilities required to carry it out; (2) the willingness of contributing states to offer money and resources, including troops; and (3) the willingness of the parties to a dispute to stop fighting and begin the process of building a peace.

The UN has become increasingly active in peacebuilding, which "is aimed at preventing the outbreak, the recurrence, or continuation of armed conflict and therefore encompasses a wide range of political, developmental, humanitarian, and human rights programmes and mechanisms."[52] The emergence of peacebuilding coincided with the need to develop the means to consolidate the gains of peace settlements. Why deploy costly, risky UN peacekeeping missions if the underlying causes of conflict were not resolved, and there was no basis for a lasting, self-sustaining peace? By the mid-1990s, the UN peacekeeping missions were engaging in demobilization, disarmament, and the reintegration of militias; refugee return; democratization; restoration or introduction of market activity; institution building; promoting dialogue and reconciliation; police and judicial reform; trauma recovery; and development assistance. Peacebuilding is largely based on the promotion of liberal values in societies torn by war or deep social conflict, and the assumption that a lasting peace can be achieved through the instruments of the liberal peace formula. In 2005, the UN established a Peacebuilding Commission and a Peacebuilding Fund to help manage and coordinate post-conflict reconstruction.

However, peacebuilding has also been criticized. The premise that political and economic liberalization will lead to peace has been challenged as an attempt at "social engineering" that might in fact lead to more conflict in a society as "both democracy and capitalism encourage conflict and competition—indeed, they thrive on it."[53] Many countries in the developing world are suspicious of peacebuilding, worried that it could lead to intervention in the domestic affairs of a society. Peacebuilding, like peacekeeping, relies on the contributions of states: if governments do not support peacebuilding efforts with diplomatic backing, funding, and adequate resources, then UN efforts to build sustainable peace in war-torn societies will be unsuccessful.[54] The sheer magnitude of the task is also significant, demanding nothing less than rebuilding a viable and sustainable country out of the ashes of war and the trauma of violence. Peacebuilding efforts must promote economic and social development, good governance and institutional reform, and social reconciliation and justice, while at the same time dealing with "spoilers" who might wish to derail the peace efforts for their own gain.[55] Perhaps this is why early assessments of peacebuilding success are not encouraging.[56] Nevertheless, peacebuilding remains critically important: without it, international military forces will have to remain in war-torn countries indefinitely (as has been the case in Cyprus), and the possibility of a return to violence will threaten long-term development efforts.

THE WAR IN LEBANON AND THE UTILITY OF PEACEKEEPING

The conflict in Lebanon is one of the many tragedies of Middle East politics. Since achieving independence at the end of World War II, the country experienced long periods of peace and prosperity, developing a reputation as a centre of banking and tourism. However, Lebanon's turbulent and often violent history includes conflict between the religious factions (Shia, Sunni, and Druze Muslims, and Christians) that inhabit the country. In particular, the Lebanese Civil

War (1975 to1990) devastated the economy and worsened sectarian and political divisions in the country. To make matters worse, Lebanon has also served as a battleground for competing regional interests between the United States, Israel, Syria, and Iran, which have supported Lebanese factions to achieve their own objectives. Finally, the PLO used Lebanon as a base of operations for attacks against Israel during the Lebanese Civil War, and Israel invaded and occupied Lebanese territory in 1978 and again in 1982. An uneasy stability returned to Lebanon after 1990, and economic development and national reconstruction saw the return of financial activity and a revival of the tourist trade.

Lebanon's tragedy continued in July 2006 when Hezbullah fighters attacked an Israeli military patrol, killing three soldiers and taking two others hostage. Hezbullah is a Shia Muslim organization (supported by Iran): a political party with representation in the Lebanese parliament, and a military organization dedicated to advancing Shia interests in Lebanese politics and the destruction of Israel. Many Western countries, including the United States and Canada, consider Hezbullah a terrorist organization. In response to the attack and kidnappings, Israel launched a military campaign in Lebanon, consisting of extensive air strikes and a naval bombardment of Lebanese infrastructure and Hezbullah installations in the south of the country. Hezbullah responded by firing over one hundred missiles per day into Israel (forcing the evacuation of 300 000 to 500 000 people in northern Israel). Hoping to achieve a decisive victory against Hezbullah, Israel launched a ground offensive into southern Lebanon. The Israeli army encountered stiff resistance from well-prepared and heavily armed Hezbullah fighters. In the meantime, the damage done to southern Lebanon by Israeli air strikes, increasing civilian casualties, and the possible collapse of the Lebanese government in the face of the Israeli invasion brought more energy to international conflict management efforts.

When the war broke out there was considerable condemnation of Hezbullah within Lebanon and in Europe and the Middle East; the kidnapping of the Israeli soldiers was seen as a foolish provocation. This condemnation created an opportunity for Israel (with the support of the U.S.) to continue the military effort to destroy Hezbullah. However, as civilian casualties and media images of human suffering and destroyed buildings and infrastructure in Lebanon increased, opinion turned against Israel and the United States. As hopes for a military victory faded, Israel and the U.S. became more interested in international conflict management efforts. Hezbullah, weakened by the fighting and losing political support in Lebanon, was also willing to consider a ceasefire. Negotiations resulted in a UN Security Council Resolution of August 11, 2006, calling for the withdrawal of Hezbullah and Israeli forces from southern Lebanon and the deployment of a new UN peacekeeping force. A truce between Hezbullah and Israel came into force on August 14. The 33-day war caused considerable human casualties and infrastructure damage. Approximately 1140 Lebanese civilians (a third of them children) and 43 Israeli civilians were killed.[57] Heavy damage was inflicted on Lebanese infrastructure by the Israeli bombing campaign: thousands of homes and apartments were destroyed along with dozens of bridges, roads, and power facilities. Unexploded munitions and cluster bomblets posed a danger to hundreds of thousands of civilians returning to their homes.[58]

The UN Interim Force in Lebanon (UNIFIL) is a prime example of both the limitations and continued relevance of peacekeeping in global politics. The original UNIFIL mission had been deployed along the Lebanese–Israeli border since 1978, but was powerless (in both the legal and the military sense) to prevent the Israeli invasion of Lebanon in 1982. Similarly, when the July War broke out, UNIFIL was powerless to stop it, and five peacekeepers were killed observing the conflict and providing humanitarian assistance. However, when interest in a ceasefire grew, all parties recognized the need for an impartial peacekeeping mission to facilitate and support the provisions of the truce agreement. As a result, when an agreement was approved, the UN Security Council authorized the deployment of a larger UNIFIL to southern Lebanon. The new UNIFIL began deployment in mid-September, with French, Italian, and Spanish troops joining the contingents from Ghana and India already in place. As of November 2012, UNIFIL had 12 250 military, police, and civilian personnel deployed in southern Lebanon. Despite criticism from both Israel and Hezbullah that UNIFIL operations have been biased in favour of one side or the other, the mission has played an important conflict management role in the region, although it is incapable of resolving the underlying causes of the conflict along the Israeli–Lebanese border.

THE RESPONSIBILITY TO PROTECT

The concept of human security has a complex and controversial relationship with the concept of humanitarian intervention. The genocide in Rwanda was a benchmark in the development of human security because of the recognition that at least 500 000 people were slaughtered while the international community stood by and did nothing. The lesson of Rwanda was that a relatively small military force could have conducted a humanitarian intervention that would have saved many of the lives that were lost. (Of course, this would have meant intervening in the internal affairs of Rwanda.) The genocide prompted efforts to grapple with the question of when violations of state sovereignty and armed interventions against states would be permissible in the cause of protecting people threatened by gross violations of human rights. However, there was limited enthusiasm for this venture in the UN, where the vast majority of states (especially those in the developing world) stood firm on the principle of sovereignty, arguing it was one of their few protections against interference from powerful states. This prompted an effort to develop a dialogue outside the UN system, which led to the **International Commission on Intervention and State Sovereignty (ICISS)**. This commission consisted of leading experts and practitioners, and, with the support of several governments, including Canada, the commission published its final report in December 2001. The final report, titled *The Responsibility to Protect*, argued that

a. state sovereignty implies responsibility, and the primary responsibility for the protection of its people lies with the state itself;

b. where a population is suffering serious harm, as a result of internal war, insurgency, repression or state failure, and the state in question is unwilling or unable to halt or avert it, the principle of nonintervention yields to the international responsibility to protect.[59]

In 2006, the UN Security Council passed Resolution 1674 on the Protection of Civilians in Armed Conflict, for the first time affirming the "responsibility to protect" doctrine.[60] However, this has not resulted in a reliable, universal norm: humanitarian intervention remains very contentious, both in concept and in practice. Can intervention ever be solely humanitarian? Is it appropriate to use military force in which non-combatants will be killed, even if the aim is to restore peace? Is it right to intervene in some cases, but not in others? Who decides when an intervention is humanitarian (or not)? Is humanitarian intervention simply a political tool used to justify interventions by rich and powerful countries into poor, weak countries? The following examples of humanitarian intervention illustrate the limitations, controversies, and moral dilemmas associated with the implementation of this concept.

NATO AND HUMANITARIAN INTERVENTION AGAINST SERBIA

Since the creation of Yugoslavia, Kosovo had been a predominantly ethnic Albanian province of Serbia. Tensions grew between the Albanian majority, which called for greater autonomy or outright independence, and the Milošević government in Belgrade. Violence broke out between Albanian separatists (later called the Kosovo Liberation Army, or KLA) and the Serbian police in the early 1990s. The violence intensified in 1998 and 1999 as an increasingly indiscriminate government campaign aimed at suppressing the KLA escalated into ethnic cleansing disturbingly similar to the kind witnessed in the Bosnian War just a few years earlier. Incidents of mass murder became ever more frequent, and a serious refugee crisis developed inside and outside Kosovo. NATO threatened Serbia with air strikes unless the campaign against ethnic Albanians stopped. The Serbian government agreed to attend talks at Rambouillet, France, but refused to sign a peace agreement that would have given Kosovo considerable autonomy and provided for a future referendum on independence. On March 24, 1999, NATO began a bombing campaign against Serbia that would last 78 days until, on June 10, the Milošević government accepted NATO demands to withdraw its security forces from Kosovo. On June 12, NATO began deployment of Kosovo-force (K-FOR) to restore law and order, demilitarize the KLA, and assist with the restoration of civilian authority.

NATO's campaign against Serbia remains a vivid illustration of the dilemmas associated with humanitarian intervention, the right of self-determination, statehood, and international law. Critics charge that NATO acted illegally, as no UN resolution was ever passed authorizing the air campaign (K-FOR did have UN approval). Critics also argued that not enough time or effort was given to diplomacy. The bombing campaign itself was criticized as excessive and more damaging to civilian targets than to the Serbian military. NATO had violated the rights of a sovereign state and had in effect severed Kosovo from Serbia by force. Supporters of the NATO campaign argued that Serbia had violated international law, rejected diplomatic overtures, and had engaged in ethnic cleansing, which demanded a swift reaction before more Albanians died and the region became destabilized. To do nothing, supporters argued, would allow ethnic cleansing to continue and risk human rights violations on the scale of those in Bosnia. The air campaign was conducted to avoid civilian casualties as much as possible, and in any case Milošević could have stopped the bombing by agreeing to terms far earlier. Serbia may have been a sovereign state, but by committing violations of human rights, it had given NATO countries little choice and every right to intervene. The government of Canada was confronted with the decision of whether to contribute to the war, and Foreign Affairs Minister Lloyd Axworthy, who was a champion of human security, grappled with the conflicting morals of intervening and killing Serbian civilians, or not intervening and allowing ethnic cleansing to continue. In the end, Canada participated in the war.

The final status of Kosovo has been uncertain since the intervention, which left the province of Serbia a de facto protectorate of NATO. Since 1999 Kosovo has been governed though a UN administration in cooperation with elected Kosovar Albanian representatives. Efforts to resolve the final status of Kosovo stumbled on a key point: the government of Serbia maintained that Kosovo was part of Serbia while Kosovar Albanians wanted independence and statehood for Kosovo. Complicating the dispute was the existence of a Serbian minority in Kosovo (approximately 10 percent of the population), which largely refused to accept independence, and the periodic violence between Albanians and Serbians in Kosovo that inflamed tensions between the two groups. The refusal of either party to compromise led to years of diplomatic stalemate. In 2006 a UN Special Envoy (former Finnish President Martti Ahtissari) acted as a third-party mediator to facilitate a diplomatic settlement. Ahtissari's efforts failed and in the end he submitted a plan to the UN Security Council in March 2007 that called for the independence of Kosovo.

The government of Serbia opposed the Ahtissari plan because Kosovo was legally a province of Serbia and any forced independence of the province would violate Serbian sovereignty and constitute a breach of international law. On the other hand, the Ahtissari plan was welcomed by the Kosovo Albanian leadership, which argued that Kosovo Albanians clearly wanted self-determination and could not be expected to live in Serbia after the atrocities of 1999. UN Security Council Resolution 1244 (which ended NATO's military campaign against Serbia in 1999) complicated matters, for it recognized the sovereignty of Serbia but also called for a final settlement based on the will of the people! This classic demonstration of the inherent tension between the rights of sovereignty and the rights of self-determination sparked a conflict between Russia (which supported its traditional ally, Serbia) and most Western democracies, which supported Kosovo's independence. Russia used its Security Council position to block proposed resolutions on Kosovo's independence. In the absence of an agreed-upon international framework, Kosovar Albanians took matters into their own hands and declared independence on February 17, 2008. By 2013 one hundred countries (including Canada) had diplomatically recognized Kosovo, but its long-term stability is very uncertain.[61]

AUSTRALIA AND HUMANITARIAN INTERVENTION IN EAST TIMOR

East Timor was a Portuguese colony for almost 500 years. In 1975, it was invaded by Indonesia and subjected to a brutal occupation that saw at least 200 000 deaths between 1975 and 1980 alone from executions, starvation, and military operations. East Timor became a symbol of the world's failure to respond to human rights disasters. In 1998, a leadership change in Indonesia opened the way for a UN-supervised referendum on independence. However, violence perpetrated by pro-Indonesian militias supported by the Indonesian Army required the postponement of the referendum. Finally, on August 30, 1999, an extraordinary 98 percent of registered voters went to the polls despite threats of physical violence. Almost 80 percent voted against remaining tied to Indonesia. The pro-Indonesian militias reacted with a campaign of violence and intimidation, which rapidly escalated into the pillaging of East Timor. Faced with a humanitarian crisis, an Australian-led coalition developed plans for an intervention force to restore order and protect the East Timorese people. The proposed force received UN Security Council authorization on September 15, and on September 20, an Australian-led force of 8000 personnel began arriving in East Timor with the grudging consent of the Indonesian government. Troops moved quickly to establish order and forced the militias out of East Timor. In February 2000 the Australian-led force withdrew, replaced by a UN peacekeeping force. On May 20, 2002, East Timor became fully independent and changed its name to Timor-Leste, and joined the UN as the 191st member state.

It is difficult to find a critic of the Australian-led humanitarian intervention in East Timor because of the circumstances of the intervention, which included a clear moral purpose, UN authorization, and the consent of the Indonesian government. In this case, the circumstances were quite different from those confronted by NATO in Kosovo. However, some critics wonder why it took so long for the international community to respond to Indonesia's brutality in East Timor (which had lasted for almost 25 years). For most of that time, governments traded with Indonesia, participated in IOs with Indonesia, and held summits with Indonesian leaders. It took a change in East Asia's security environment (a consequence of the end of the Cold War), a change in the Indonesian government, the collapse of the Indonesian economy in the Asian financial crisis, and another humanitarian crisis to create the conditions for the international community to respond to one of the longest-lasting human rights outrages in the world.[62]

HUMANITARIAN INTERVENTION IN DARFUR

Sudan has experienced numerous civil wars rooted in regional inequality, grievances over access to land and resources, culture and religion, and population movement and climate change. The war in the North, West, and South Darfur provinces (collectively referred to simply as *Darfur*) received considerable international attention, a reflection of the scale of human suffering, the spread of the conflict to neighbouring Chad and the Central African Republic, and the spotlight the Beijing Olympics cast on China's support for the Sudanese government. The conflict in Darfur broke out in 2003, when two political movements composed of local African tribal groups rebelled against the government. In an effort to defeat the rebellion, the Sudanese government armed and supported an Arab "Janjaweed" militia that conducted an ethnic cleansing campaign against the African population of Darfur. Approximately 300 000 people in Darfur were killed, and over two million displaced.[63] Villages throughout the region were destroyed, and massacres and rape were commonplace.[64] Many humanitarian organizations referred to the conflict as a *genocide,* a description echoed by U.S. President George Bush in June 2005.[65] The situation was complicated by the evolution of the conflict, as noted by the International Crisis Group: "The Darfur conflict … evolved from a rebellion with relatively defined political aims to a conflict increasingly overshadowed by shifting alliances, defections, regional and international meddling and a growing, complex tribal dimension."[66]

Efforts to stop the conflict in Darfur met with limited success largely due to the inability of the Sudanese government and rebel groups to reach a negotiated settlement, and the reluctance of the Sudanese government to accept international involvement without significant constraints. UN sanctions imposed on the country in 2004 and 2005 failed to stop or reduce the level of violence. In 2004, negotiations between the Sudanese government and the AU resulted in the deployment of a 7000-strong African Union Mission in Sudan (AMIS). However, AMIS was unable to quell the violence due to a lack of military capacity (especially transport) and the reluctance of the government and the rebels to stop fighting. As the conflict began to spread to neighbouring countries (most notably Chad) and rebel factions began to fight among themselves, international efforts to mediate an end to the war increased. After seven unsuccessful attempts at negotiation since 2003, a peace agreement was signed between the government and one of the main rebel factions in May 2006. However, the settlement quickly broke down and violence resumed across Darfur, with frequent attacks on civilians, aid workers, and AMIS personnel. As a result, the Sudanese government came under intense international pressure to agree to the deployment of a UN peacekeeping force in Darfur to support AMIS. The government finally agreed to accept such a force in June 2007, and a UN Security Council Resolution on July 31 established the United Nations/African Union Mission in Darfur (UNAMID), a hybrid mission jointly operated by the two organizations. In 2012, UNAMID deployed over 25 000 troops, military observers, and police (mostly from African counties) and a large civilian peacebuilding component, making it one of the largest peace-keeping missions ever mounted. However, the Sudanese government has been largely unco-operative with UNAMID and continues to receive diplomatic support from China, Russia, and some Arab states. The ICC formally charged the president of Sudan, Omar al-Bashir, with genocide in July 2010. However, Bashir remained president as of July 2013 and has openly visited other African countries, challenging the ICC's fragile legitimacy.

No one said peacekeeping would be easy. In April of 2010, UNAMID peacekeepers patrol the area surrounding a polling station at Abou Shouk refugee camp, on the outskirts of the north Darfur capital of el Fasher, Sudan. (AP Photo/Nasser Nasser)

HUMANITARIAN INTERVENTION IN LIBYA

The origins of the Libyan Civil War lie in the frustration and resentment that had built up within Libyan society over the 41 years of dictatorial rule by Colonel Muammar Gaddafi. The spark for the uprisings that eventually overthrew Gaddafi was the arrest of a human rights activist on February 15, 2011. Mass protests broke out in many parts of the country, and the Libyan security apparatus responded by firing into crowds of protestors. As the protests grew, in some parts of the country Libyan government forces were overwhelmed and lost control of key cities, including Libya's second-largest city, Benghazi. Governments around the world began to take notice, and U.S. Secretary of State Hillary Clinton stated, "The world is watching the situation in Libya with alarm. We join the international community in strongly condemning the violence in Libya."[67] On February 26, the UN Security Council passed Resolution 1970, which imposed an arms embargo against Libya and referred the situation to the ICC. These measures failed to encourage the Gaddafi government to desist its military campaign against the protestors or open negotiations with the newly formed Libyan National Council, which united the anti-Gaddafi protest movements in Libya under one political organization. As violence escalated between the Libyan security forces loyal to Gaddafi and the poorly equipped and disorganized militia of the Libyan National Council, a diplomatic dialogue began on the possibility of a military intervention in Libya to protect civilians, support the Libyan National Council, and overthrow Gaddafi.

On March 17, the UN Security Council passed Resolution 1973, calling on member states to enforce a no fly zone and "take all necessary measures … to protect civilians and civilian populated areas … while excluding a foreign occupation force of any form on any part of Libyan territory."[68] The wording of Resolution 1973 has become the subject of considerable

Map 7.2 Sudan, South Sudan, and the Darfur Region

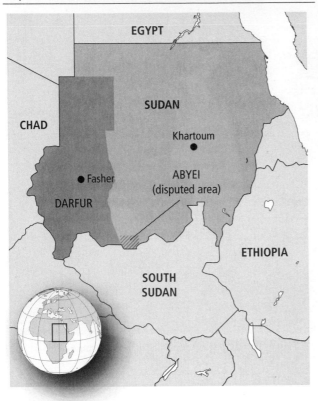

controversy. Russia and China maintain that the resolution was only intended to protect civilians and civilian areas from attack by Libyan forces: it was not an authorization to attack military targets across the country or a mandate to overthrow Gaddafi. Other governments, such as France, U.K., and the U.S., maintained that the resolution empowered the intervention to do much more than simply defend civilian areas. Decisively, it was these governments that determined the course of military strategy under Resolution 1973. Air strikes against Libyan forces loyal to Gaddafi began shortly after the resolution was passed, conducted mostly by aircraft from a coalition of France, the U.K., and the U.S. Through March 24 to 27, NATO assumed control over the intervention, and a Canadian General, Lt. General Charles Bouchard, served as operational commander. With the assistance of NATO airstrikes, Libyan opposition militias slowly made progress against Gaddafi's forces, and ultimately seized the capital, Tripoli, on August 23; Gaddafi himself fled into hiding but was discovered on October 20 and beaten and shot by his captors. While few mourned the passing of Gaddafi, the political future of Libya is far from certain. The intervention created a political rift between NATO and Russia and China, making both countries reluctant to support intervention options in the subsequent Syrian Civil War.[69] As this edition went to print, this diplomatic rift, as well as the broader legal, moral, and political implications of the Responsibility to Protect doctrine, were an important part of the debate over humanitarian intervention in Syria.

SANCTIONS AND CONFLICT MANAGEMENT

Economic sanctions are "deliberate government actions to inflict economic deprivation on a target state or society, through the limitation or cessation of customary economic relations."[70] Economic sanctions, therefore, are coercive instruments. Nevertheless, they have been employed as instruments of conflict management in the international system. Economic sanctions may include trade boycotts, embargoes, or restrictions on financial interactions (such as blocking access to overseas assets or international financial institutions). Sanctions may be imposed unilaterally by one state, or multilaterally, by a group of states (or by the membership of an IO). When sanctions are imposed, the sending or initiating countries might have a number of possible goals or aims:

- *Compliance:* "to force the target to alter its behaviour to conform with the initiator's preferences"
- *Subversion:* "to remove the target's leaders or overthrow the regime"

- *Deterrence:* "to dissuade the target from repeating the disputed action in the future"
- *International symbolism:* "to send messages to other members of the world community"
- *Domestic symbolism:* "to increase its domestic support or thwart international criticism of its foreign policies by acting decisively"[71]

The use of sanctions has deep historical roots. In his history of the Peloponnesian War, Thucydides describes a trade embargo put in place by Athens against Megara, a Spartan ally. Under Napoleonic domination, most of continental Europe limited grain sales to Great Britain. However, the use of sanctions increased dramatically in the 20th century. One study found that between World War I and 1990, economic sanctions were used 120 times, with 104 occurring since World War II.[72] The increased use of economic sanctions as an instrument of policy can be explained by their attractiveness as a policy choice. Diplomatic measures, although they may carry the weight of the displeasure of one country against another or the force of global or world opinion, tend not to have the same strength as other instruments for two reasons: (1) the leverage one can exert against a target state is limited; and (2) the sending or initiating countries incur few costs, so diplomatic measures are less credible as expressions of will or commitment. On the other hand, military measures are both costly and risky. Therefore, sanctions are often an attractive option because although costs are involved (the severing of some or all economic ties with the target state), they do not carry the burdens of military action and have more credibility than mere diplomatic measures.

Despite the frequency of their use, the effectiveness of economic sanctions in achieving their goals has been limited at best. The consensus is that when results are measured against goals and objectives, economic sanctions usually fail and often harm the most vulnerable people in target states. One study found that between 1914 and 1989, "although sanctions were successful in 34 percent of 115 cases … success has become increasingly elusive in recent years. … The success rate among [the 46] cases begun after 1973 was a little less than 26 percent."[73] Several possible explanations exist as to why the success rate of economic sanctions is so low:

- The target state is usually able to find alternative sources of supply or markets for its exports. (For this reason, unilateral sanctions are frequently ineffective, and most sanction efforts are multilateral in nature.)

- In target states, sanctions may provoke nationalist sentiments and a willingness to sacrifice in the name of resistance against outside interference.

- Sanctions may harm the very people they are supposed to benefit; rulers who care little for the hardships of their people will not be swayed by sanctions. Jim Hoagland has observed: "The logic of the policy seems to be to make unarmed citizens desperate enough to rise up and throw off the brutal regimes that other powers are not willing to use the world's best armies to topple."[74]

- Sanctions are often undercut by the actions of domestic companies and foreign corporations, or by foreign governments. The longer sanctions last, the greater the likelihood that they will erode and collapse or be undermined.[75]

- The imposition of sanctions can actually increase the power of undesirable political elites in the target state, as the sanctions can be used to justify increased control, or create a lucrative environment for informal markets. Sanctions can also create a "rally around the flag" effect that can boost their popularity.

- The public can have inflated expectations about the utility of sanctions. Economic deprivation has never been a reliable means of forcing change; the political context is usually a more important factor in the political outcome.[76]

The success of sanctions appears to depend on several variables. The relationship between the state (or states) sending the sanctions and the target is very important. If the target state is less economically powerful, or is a close trading partner, economic sanctions tend to have a greater effect. When countries impose sanctions quickly and decisively, and do not involve significant economic hardships for sending countries, they will have greater credibility because they will be sustainable over time. Clear communications are vital: target state leaders must understand why the sanctions were imposed and what actions they must undertake to have them lifted. Furthermore, if objectives are broad and general, sanctions will not have the same chance of success as if the objectives are specific and clearly defined. Sanctions should, therefore, be imposed to give the target country an incentive to change certain specific policies rather than as a general punishment for a broad range of actions. Finally, sanctions will be

---

PROFILE 7.5 Sanctions

QUALIFIED SUCCESS AND THE CASE OF SOUTH AFRICA

The South African apartheid regime was a prominent human rights issue during the Cold War. Apartheid institutionalized racial separation and discrimination against the black majority, and to end this system sanctions were imposed on South Africa from a variety of sources. The UN imposed a voluntary arms embargo against South Africa in 1963, and this was made mandatory in 1977. Many other countries, including Canada, began to impose stronger unilateral sanctions against South Africa as well. In addition, campaigns in many countries led many corporations and social institutions (such as universities) to divest themselves of their interests and operations in South Africa. However, stiffer multilateral sanctions could not be imposed because of the opposition of Great Britain and the United States. Both countries argued that sanctions would hurt only the black majority. Critics charged that the U.S. was being soft on South Africa because of its importance as a source of raw minerals and its opposition to communism in Africa. However, in 1985 Congress overrode a presidential veto and imposed harsh economic sanctions. In 1989, F.W. de Klerk came to power in South Africa, intent on reform.

He released the long-time jailed leader of the **African National Congress (ANC)**, Nelson Mandela. In 1993, apartheid was dismantled, and sanctions subsequently lifted.

Did sanctions succeed in this case? The consensus is that they played a role. The South African economy was certainly damaged by sanctions, as trade fell, debt rose, loans were not renewed, and foreign investment and growth rates declined. Two questions remain: How much of this economic damage was due to sanctions, and how much was due to falling world prices for gold (a key South African foreign-exchange earner)? What would have happened had a hardline South African leader determined to resist sanctions come to power, instead of the reform-minded de Klerk? In any event, the South African example stands as a success story for sanctions.

QUALIFIED FAILURE AND THE CASE OF IRAQ

When Iraq invaded Kuwait in 1990, the international community responded with diplomatic expressions of opposition and economic sanctions organized through the UN, including a total ban on imports and exports to and from Iraq, with the exception of humanitarian imports such as medicine and some foodstuffs. Iraq was a

(continued)

PROFILE 7.5 Sanctions (*continued*)

vulnerable target, as its main export was oil, and it was heavily dependent on food imports. The stated goal of sanctions was to compel Saddam Hussein's government to withdraw from Kuwait. However, military force was eventually used to eject Iraqi forces from Kuwait.

After the end of the Gulf War, sanctions remained in place against Iraq. The goal of the sanctions was to compel Saddam Hussein to cooperate with UN Special Commission (UNSCOM) weapons inspectors seeking to destroy Iraq's weapons of mass destruction program. Between 1991 and 1998, UN inspectors continued their work of compiling information on Iraq's programs and destroying discovered weapons and weapons-related infrastructure, all in the face of Iraqi efforts to hide evidence and obstruct the inspectors' work. However, the sanctions became increasingly controversial. Critics charged that the sanctions were causing extensive human suffering inside Iraq due to shortages of medicine, food, and basic industrial needs. On the other hand, supporters argued that sanctions remained the only lever available (other than the use of force) to pressure Iraq to give up its WMD and to prevent

more aggressive behaviour by the Iraqi regime. International support for the sanctions began to waver, and public protests against sanctions grew in many countries. In an effort to reduce the human impact of sanctions, the UN authorized the delivery of humanitarian supplies (including food) to be paid for by authorized sales of Iraqi oil (which was otherwise under embargo by the sanctions). By August 1998, Iraq announced that it would no longer cooperate with the inspector teams, which were withdrawn in November. American and British air strikes followed, and a renewed weapons inspections program was mounted by the creation of the United Nations Monitoring, Verification, and Inspection Commission (UNMOVIC) in 2001. Meanwhile, the "food for oil" program was never successful in striking a balance between sanctions and human suffering in Iraq, and it was abandoned in 2001. By then, several countries were openly calling for an end to sanctions. It is unlikely that sanctions would have worked in the case of Iraq, but ultimately we can never be sure, as the 2003 Iraq War and the overthrow of the Baathist regime ended the sanctions debate.

more effective if an internal faction exists within the target state that supports their imposition and can thereby exert extra domestic pressure against the government; this was an instrumental factor in the case of apartheid South Africa (see Profile 7.5).

Overall, sanctions will likely continue to be frequently used instruments in conflict management, valuable tools to signal disapproval and important alternatives to the use of military force. However, the controversy and harm associated with their use is leading to an evolution of sanctions policy toward targeting political and economic elites rather than entire societies. Whether such "smart sanctions" will be successful is uncertain.[77]

A DEMOCRATIC PATH TO PEACE?

The idea that democracies are inherently peaceful forms of government is not unique to the post–Cold War era. Immanuel Kant suggested that constitutional governments and their respect for international law would be a constraint on war; we explore this line of thought in greater length in the section on liberalism in Chapter 1. However, the idea of a "democratic peace" took on a new significance after the Cold War. A belief prevails in most Western countries that democracies rarely, if ever, fight one another (although they do fight non-democratic states). It follows that if the number of democracies increases, so will the prevalence and likelihood of peace. This was one of the pillars of U.S. foreign policy during the Clinton administration, which promoted the concept of "enlargement of the world's community of market democracies" as a replacement for the Cold War strategy of containment.[78] According to former President Clinton, "enlargement" is in the interests of the United States because "democracies rarely wage war on one another."[79]

The argument is based on two assumptions. First, the domestic institutional structures of democratic states act as a constraint on war. Ideally, democratic governments answer to their citizens, and the financial and human costs of war might result in a government losing the next election. In addition, there are constraints on leaders in democracies. The checks and balances that exist in parliamentary and republican systems will help prevent warlike or renegade leaders from coming to power. Authoritarian governments, in contrast, have fewer constraints, and are thus more likely to engage in aggressive or warlike behaviour. Second, the norms of democratic governance promote the peaceful resolution of disputes. Democracies are governed by the rule of law and principles that seek to establish a balance between the rights of the individual and the common good. As a result, they are more likely to use **adjudication** and bargaining to avoid violent conflict. As Bruce Russett suggests, "The culture, perceptions, and practices that permit compromise and the peaceful resolution of conflicts without the threat of violence within countries come to apply across national boundaries toward other democratic countries."[80] Michael Doyle agrees, suggesting that democracies "presume foreign republics to be also consensual, just and therefore deserving of accommodation."[81]

However, democratic peace theory has been challenged. First, critics argue that institutional constraints will not necessarily prevent wars between democracies. If they did, they would prevent democracies from going to war against any kind of opponent. The fact that democracies have often gone to war (although not necessarily with other democracies) raises doubts about the salience of democratic constraints on war. Public opinion has, in fact, often favoured war: American public opinion favoured war with Spain in 1898, and, according to popular historical accounts, the publics of Europe enthusiastically welcomed war in 1914. Second, democracies have nearly gone to war with each other on numerous occasions. In one study, Christopher Layne argues that in four cases of near-war between democracies (the U.S. and Great Britain in the Trent Affair of 1861, the U.S. and Great Britain in the Venezuela Crisis of 1895–96, France and Great Britain in the Fashoda Crisis of 1898, and France and Germany in the Ruhr in 1923), war was avoided only because one side backed down due to fears that a war would end in defeat or quagmire.[82] Third, there have been very few democracies in history, and as a result there have been fewer opportunities for conflict and warfare between them (and, since most states are rarely at war, it should be no surprise that democracies are generally not either).[83] Fourth, democracies have actually fought one another. Or have they? Here the problem is the definition of democracy. World War I saw democratic states fight one another. However, some debate exists as to whether Germany was a democracy and how democratic any of the combatants were in the realm of foreign policy decision making.[84] In another ambiguous case, the U.S. Civil War occurred *within* a democracy, and assumed the character of an interstate conflict. Why did the democratic institutions of the United States not save the country from civil war?

The debate over the idea of a democratic peace has profound policy implications. For example, should Canada support the spread of formal democracy in the hope that it will lead to a more peaceful world? Is it not possible that the effort to encourage or promote democracy will drag Canada (or other countries) into interventions and even wars, thus increasing global insecurity? After all, one of the stated objectives of the U.S.-led Iraq War was to democratize the country, and similar language is used to justify continued intervention in Afghanistan.

CONCLUSIONS

This chapter has explored some of the conflict management instruments available to actors in global politics; they remain plagued by several obstacles, most notably the interrelated problems of compliance, trust, and self-interest. Many actors sign international agreements or take on obligations but do not abide by them. Others refuse to engage in bilateral or multilateral conflict management because they do not trust other countries to live up to their obligations, or simply do not believe it is in their best interests to pursue such a course. Conflict management is by its very nature a cooperative enterprise, and, as we have seen, cooperation in a world that is at least in part anarchic is problematic. Yet, despite the less-than-illustrious history of conflict management, some cause for optimism remains. Emerging transnational security issues may compel international actors—especially states—to increase their efforts to establish more rigorous and effective conflict management mechanisms in the future.

Endnotes

1. *Human Security Report 2005* (Oxford: Oxford University Press, 2005), 146.
2. G. Dyer, *War: The New Edition* (Toronto: Vintage Canada, 2004), 2.
3. C. Jönsson, "Diplomacy, Bargaining, and Negotiation," in W. Carlsnaes, T. Risse, and B.A. Simmons, eds., *Handbook of International Relations* (London: Sage, 2002), 121.
4. See A. Faizullaev, "Diplomacy and Self," *Diplomacy and Statecraft* 17, no. 3 (September 2006), 517.
5. G. Mattingly, *Renaissance Diplomacy* (Baltimore, MD: Penguin, 1964), 244.
6. See J. Melissen, "Introduction," in J. Melissen, ed., *Innovation in Diplomatic Practice* (London: Macmillan; New York: St. Martin's Press, 1999).
7. A.L. George, *Forceful Persuasion: Coercive Diplomacy as an Alternative to War* (Washington, DC: United States Institute of Peace Press, 1991).
8. For a highly readable and general text on negotiation, see R. Fisher and W. Ury, *Getting to Yes: Negotiating Agreement without Giving In* (Boston: Houghton Mifflin, 1981). For studies of diplomacy and conflict management see B.G. Ramcharan, *Preventive Diplomacy at the United Nations* (Bloomington, IN: Indiana University Press, 2008); and S. Hideo, *Containing Conflict: Cases in Preventive Diplomacy* (Tokyo and New York: Japan Center for International Exchange, 2003).
9. See K. Boulding, *The Three Faces of Power* (Newbury Park, CA: Sage, 1990); and W. Habeeb, *Power and Tactics in International Negotiation: How Weak Nations Bargain with Strong Nations* (Baltimore: Johns Hopkins University Press, 1988).
10. See J. Berkovitch, ed., *Resolving International Conflicts: The Theory and Practice of Mediation* (Boulder, CO: Lynne Rienner, 1996).
11. J. Pressman, "Visions in Collision: What Happened at Camp David and Taba?" *International Security* 28 (Fall 2003), 44–77.
12. For a study on the El-Aqsa Intifada, see H. Gordon, R. Gordon, and S. Taher, *Beyond Intifada: Narratives of Freedom Fighters in the Gaza Strip* (Westport, CT: Praeger, 2003).
13. For a discussion of the U.S. role in the Middle East, see S. Telhami, *The Stakes: America and the Middle East* (Boulder, CO: Westview Press, 2002).
14. For a discussion of the unravelling of the peace process, see N. Kozodoy, ed., *The Mideast Peace Process: An Autopsy* (San Francisco: Encounter Books, 2003). See also B. Wasserstein, *Israel and Palestine: Why They Fight and Can They Stop?* (London: Profile Books, 2003).
15. For a discussion of the issues surrounding the security fence, see J. Rynold, "Israel's Fence: Can Separation Make Better Neighbors?" *Survival* 46 (Spring 2004), 55–76.
16. Ibid., 56.
17. G.E. Robinson, "The Fragmentation of Palestine," *Current History* 106, no. 704 (December 2007), 421–2.
18. See International Institute for Strategic Studies, *Strategic Survey 2007* (New York: Routledge, 2007), 238.
19. From United Nations Office for the Coordination of Humanitarian Affairs (OCHA), *Gaza Humanitarian Situation Reports*, January–March 2008, http://www.ochaopt.org/?module=displaysection&section _id–11&format=html (accessed April 18, 2008); and Robinson, "Fragmentation of Palestine," 423.

20. For an overview, see S. Wolff, "The Peace Process since 1998," in J. Neuheiser and S. Wolff, eds., *Peace at Last? The Impact of the Good Friday Agreement on Northern Ireland* (New York: Beghahn Books, 2002).

21. M. Fitzduff, *Beyond Violence: Conflict Resolution Process in Northern Ireland* (Tokyo: United Nations University Press, 2002).

22. See R. Johansen, "Swords into Plowshares: Can Fewer Arms Yield More Security?" in C. Kegley Jr., ed., *Controversies in International Relations Theory: Realism and the Neoliberal Challenge* (New York: St. Martin's Press, 1995), 224–44.

23. J. Kruzel, "Arms Control, Disarmament, and the Stability of the Postwar Era," in C. Kegley Jr., ed., *The Long Postwar Peace* (New York: HarperCollins, 1991), 249.

24. Remarks by Senator Richard G. Lugar, Chairman, Committee on Foreign Relations, at the Chemical and Biological Arms Control Institute Tenth Anniversary Symposium, November 19, 2003. (Washington, DC: Bureau of International Information Programs, U.S. Department of State, 2003).

25. See G.P. Schultz, W.J. Perry, H.A. Kissinger, and S. Nunn, "A World Free of Nuclear Weapons," *The Wall Street Journal*, January 8, 2007.

26. For a discussion of the issues facing the NPT, see J. Dhanapala, *Multilateral Diplomacy and the NPT: An Insider's Account* (Geneva: United Nations Institute for Disarmament Research, 2005). See also *Arms Control Today: Atoms for Peace Anniversary Issue* 33 (December 2003).

27. See R. Johnson, "The In-comprehensive Test Ban," *Bulletin of Atomic Scientists* 52 (November/December 1996), 30–35.

28. See W. Sidhu and R. Thakur, eds., *Arms Control after Iraq: Normative and Operational Challenges* (Tokyo: United Nations University, 2006).

29. Kruzel, "Arms Control," 268.

30. United Nations Development Programme, *Human Development Report, 1994* (New York: Oxford University Press, 1994), 22.

31. L. Axworthy, "Canada and Human Security: The Need for Leadership," *International Journal* 52 (Spring 1997), 184.

32. R. Paris, "Human Security: Paradigm Shift or Hot Air?" *International Security* 26 (Fall 2001), 88.

33. See R.K. Nossal, "Pinchpenny Diplomacy: The Decline of 'Good International Citizenship' in Canadian Foreign Policy," *International Journal* 54 (Winter 1998–99), 88–105; and F.O. Hampson and D. Oliver, "Pulpit Diplomacy: A Critical Assessment of the Axworthy Doctrine," *International Journal* 53 (Summer 1998), 379–407.

34. F.O. Hampson, N. Hillmer, and M.A. Molot, eds., *The Axworthy Legacy: Canada Among Nations 2001* (Oxford: Oxford University Press, 2001).

35. For examinations of war law, see R. Gutman et al., eds., *Crimes of War 2.0: What the Public Should Know*, rev. upd. ed. (New York: W.W. Norton, 2007); and R. B. Byers, *War Law: Understanding International Law and Armed Conflict* (Vancouver: Douglas and McIntyre, 2005).

36. See K. Deutsch, *Political Community and the North Atlantic Area* (Princeton University Press, 1957).

37. See *Charter of the United Nations and Statute of the International Court of Justice* (New York: United Nations), 1.

38. See Article 2/4, *Charter of the United Nations and Statute of the International Court of Justice*, 4.

39. For case studies of peacekeeping before the creation of the UN, see A. James, *Peacekeeping in International Politics* (New York: St. Martin's Press, 1990).

40. For more discussion of these principles and their interrelated nature, see F.T. Liu, *United Nations Peacekeeping and the Non-Use of Force*, International Peace Academy Occasional Paper Series (Boulder, CO: Lynne Rienner, 1992).

41. *An Agenda for Peace: Preventive Diplomacy, Peacemaking, and Peacekeeping* (New York: United Nations, 1992), 1–2.

42. Data from UN Department of Public Information and Global Policy Forum, http://www.globalpolicy.org/security/peacekpg/index.htm (accessed June 18, 2013).

43. For discussions of the changing nature of peacekeeping, see I. Rikhye, *The Politics and Practice of United Nations Peacekeeping: Past, Present, and Future* (Toronto: Brown Book Company, 2000); and O.P. Richmond, *Maintaining Order, Making Peace* (New York: Palgrave, 2002).

44. B. Boutros-Ghali, "Beyond Peacekeeping," *New York University Journal of International Law and Politics* 25 (Fall 1992), 115. See also M. O'Hanlon and P.W. Singer, "The Humanitarian Transformation: Expanding Global Intervention Capacity," *Survival* 46 (Spring 2004), 77–100.

45. See E. Newman and O.P. Richmond, eds., *The United Nations and Human Security* (New York: Palgrave, 2001).

46. See R. Dallaire, *Shake Hands with the Devil: The Failure of Humanity in Rwanda* (Toronto: Vintage Canada, 2003). Most estimates put the number of deaths at 800 000.

47. G. Picco, "The UN and the Use of Force: Leave the Secretary-General Out of It," *Foreign Affairs* 73 (September/October 1994), 14.

48. S. Touval, "Why the UN Fails," *Foreign Affairs* 73 (September/October 1994), 45.

49. Quoted in P. Lewis, "United Nations Is Finding Its Plate Increasingly Full but Its Cupboard Is Bare," *The New York Times*, September 27, 1993, A8.

50. See *United Nations Peacekeeping Operations: Principles and Guidelines* (New York: United Nations, 2008).

51. Peacekeeping data from the United Nations Department of Peacekeeping Operations, http://www.un.org/en/peacekeeping/resources/statistics/factsheet.shtml (accessed January 16, 2013).

52. See United Nations Security Council, S/PRST/2001/5, February 20, 2001.

53. R. Paris, "Peacebuilding and the Limits of Liberal Internationalism," *International Security* 22 (Fall 1997), 56.

54. See E.M. Cousens, C. Kumar, and K. Wermester, *Peacebuilding as Politics: Cultivating Peace in Fragile Societies* (Boulder, CO: Lynne Rienner, 2001).

55. See S.J. Steadman, "Spoiler Problems in Peace Processes," *International Security* 22 (Fall 1997), 5–53.

56. A.G. Sens, "From Peacekeeping to Peacebuilding: The United Nations and the Challenge of Intrastate War," in M.W. Zacher and R.M. Price, eds., *The United Nations and Global Security* (New York: Palgrave Macmillan, 2004), 141–60.

57. "Timeline of the July War 2006," *The Daily Star Lebanon*, February 21, 2008.

58. For a compilation of facts and figures from various sources from the July War, see "Middle East Crisis: Facts and Figures," *BBC News*, http://news.bbc.co.uk/2/hi/middle east/5257128.stm (accessed May 6, 2008).

59. *The Responsibility to Protect: Report of the International Commission on Intervention and State Sovereignty* (Ottawa: International Development Research Centre, 2001), xi.

60. United Nations Security Council Resolution 1674, S/RES/1674, April 28, 2006. See C. Badescu, *Humanitarian Intervention and R2P: Security and Human Rights* (London: Routledge, 2011); and A. Bellamy, *Responsibility to Protect: The Global Effort to End Mass Atrocities* (New York: Polity, 2009).

61. See "Kosovo's First Month," *International Crisis Group Europe Briefing No. 47*, March 18, 2008. See also B. Posen, "The War for Kosovo: Serbia's Political-Military Strategy," *International Security* 24 (Spring 2000), 3–50; W. Arkin, "Smart Bombs, Dumb Targeting?" *Bulletin of the Atomic Scientists* 56 (May/June 2000), 46–54; and A. Roberts, "NATO's Humanitarian War over Kosovo," *Survival* 4 (Autumn 1999), 102–23.

62. See J. Cotton, "The Emergence of an Independent East Timor: National and Regional Challenges," *Contemporary Southeast Asia* 22 (April 2000); and James Traub, "Inventing East Timor," *Foreign Affairs* 79 (July/August 2000), 74–89.

63. For a short description of war crimes in Sudan and their link to the ICC see P. Stoett, "Justice, Peace, and Windmills: An Analysis of Live Indictments by the International Criminal Court," in H. Carey and S. Mitchell, eds., *Trials and Tribulations of International Prosecution* (Lanham, MD: Lexington Books, 2012), 117–31.

64. See International Institute for Strategic Studies, *Strategic Survey 2007* (New York: Routledge, 2007), 263.

65. J. VandeHei, "In Break with UN, Bush Calls Sudan Killings Genocide," *The Washington Post*, June 2, 2005.

66. "Darfur's New Security Reality," *International Crisis Group Africa Report No. 134* (November 26, 2007), 27.

67. Secretary of State Hilary Clinton, "Libya Has a Responsibility to Respect the Universal Rights of the People," *DipNote, US Department of State Official Blog*, February 21, 2011, http://blogs.state.gov/index.php/site/entry/clinton_libya_statement (accessed May 26, 2011).

68. See United Nations Security Council Resolution 1973, March 17, 2011, 3, http://www.un.org/ga/search/view_doc.asp?symbol=S/RES/1973(2011) (accessed January 19, 2013).

69. For an overview of the intervention and an assessment, see D. Barrie, "Libya's Lessons: The Air Campaign," *Survival*, vol. 54 (December 2012–January 2013), 57–65.

70. D. Leyton-Brown, "Introduction," in D. Leyton-Brown, ed., *The Utility of International Economic Sanctions* (New York: St. Martin's Press, 1987), 1–4.

71. J. Lindsay, "Trade Sanctions as Policy Instruments: A Re-examination," *International Studies Quarterly* 30 (June 1996), 153–73.

72. See G. Hufbauer, J. Schott, and K. Elliott, *Economic Sanctions Reconsidered: History and Current Policy*, 2nd ed. (Washington, DC: Institute for International Economics, 1990).

73. K. Elliot, "Sanctions: A Look at the Record," *Bulletin of the Atomic Scientists* 49 (November 19), 32–5.

74. See J. Hoagland, "Economic Sanctions Sometimes Do More Harm Than Good," *The State* 11 (November 1993), A12.

75. See Hufbauer et al., *Economic Sanctions Reconsidered*, 100–101.

76. Ibid., 94.

77. See J.M. Farrall, *United Nations Sanctions and the Rule of Law* (Cambridge: Cambridge University Press, 2007); and R. Eyler, *Economic Sanctions: International Policy and Political Economy at Work* (New York: Palgrave Macmillan, 2007).

78. Anthony Lake (former U.S. National Security Advisor), "From Containment to Enlargement," *Dispatch* 4, no. 39 (Washington, DC: United States Department of State, Bureau of Public Affairs, September 1993), 3.

79. W. Clinton, "Confronting the Challenges of a Broader World," *Dispatch* 4, no. 39 (Washington, DC: United States Department of State, Bureau of Public Affairs, September 1993), 3.

80. B. Russett, *Grasping the Democratic Peace: Principles for a Post–Cold War World* (Princeton University Press, 1993), 31.

81. M. Doyle, "Kant, Liberal Legacies and Foreign Affairs: Part One," *Philosophy and Public Affairs* 12 (Summer 1983), 205–35, 230.

82. C. Layne, "Kant or Can't: The Myth of a Democratic Peace," *International Security* 19 (Fall 1994), 5–49. See also A. Geis, L. Brock, and H. Müller, eds., *Democratic Wars: Looking at the Dark Side of Democratic Peace* (Basingstoke and New York: Palgrave Macmillan, 2006).

83. D. Shapiro, "The Insignificance of the Liberal Peace," *International Security* 19 (Fall 1994), 50–86.

84. Layne, "Kant or Can't," 40–44.

The Global Economy: Growth, Prosperity, Crisis, and Inequity

If present trends continue, economic disparities between industrial and developing nations will move from inequitable to inhuman.

—James Gustave Speth, UN Development Programme Administrator, 1996[1]

INTRODUCTION: THE GLOBAL ECONOMY TODAY

Our convergence/divergence theme is vividly illustrated by an examination of the state of the global economy today. While more people enjoy a higher standard of living than at any time in human history, there has been a discernibly widening gap between rich and poor states, and wealthy and impoverished people, since 1945. While the global economy can be viewed from a distance as a growing phenomenon related to globalization, up close it often looks more like a series of worldwide or regional crises, more on the verge of collapse than universal prosperity. Convergence seems rampant: increased world trade and financial flows, regional economic integration (especially in Europe and North America) and free trade agreements between states, and the World Trade Organization (WTO), which by 2012 boasted 157 members. Yet divergence persists, sustained by monetary crises, endless trade disputes, the potential rise of exclusionary trade blocs, imbalanced investment flows, and the vast difference in life experiences of low-income people from those of economic elites. All of these long-term developments and trends took place within the context of a global **recession** that began in earnest in 2008 and lingered well into the 2010s, punctuated with an economic meltdown in the European Union, especially in several states (Greece, Spain, Italy, Ireland, Portugal) with severe balance of payments, unemployment, and deficit problems.

The enormous gap in the quality of life, health, education, and general welfare remains a prominent reality in global politics, and indications are that while overall our aggregate wealth continues to increase, economic disparities remain as wide as ever. The majority of the wealth is controlled by the so-called developed world; these countries accounted for 64 percent of world GDP (Gross Domestic Product) in 2010, down from almost 70 percent in 1980. Average

GDP **per capita** income in developed countries was 11 times higher than average GDP per capita income in low-income countries in 2010.[2] If we were to divide global income in 2012 in half, the richest 8 percent of the world's population would take one-half, while the other 92 percent would take the other half. If we were to divide it into fifths, the richest 1.7 percent of the world population would take one-fifth, while the poorest 75 percent would take one-fifth.[3]

Perhaps the gap between rich and poor countries can be best illustrated using the Human Development Index (HDI) employed by the UN. In 2011, Canada (a "high human development" country) ranked sixth in the world on the HDI with a "score" of 0.908. This high ranking (recall there are over 190 countries today; ranking sixth is not a bad score!) reflected Canada's high life expectancy of 81 years, a literacy rate of over 99 percent, a 93.4 percent primary and secondary school enrolment rate, and a GDP per capita of US$34,567. In contrast, Niger ranked 186th on the HDI list, with a "score" of 0.295, with life expectancy at 54.7 years, a low literacy rate, primary and secondary school enrolment of 31.3 percent, and a GDP per capita of only US$626.[4]

Such blatant inequality fuels the ongoing debate about the human impact of globalization, a term we attempt to define later in this chapter. Some economists argue that globalization and liberal development strategies are having, or will soon have, a widespread positive impact on the standard of living in typically impoverished states. For example, in his book *The World Is Flat: A Brief History of the 21st Century*, Thomas Friedman takes a rather rosy view of globalization, suggesting that the removal of barriers to competition are the key to further economic and thus human development.[5] In one sense this is undeniable: more people around the world have higher incomes and a better quality of life than ever before. However, a large number of states and people are being left behind, unable to take advantage of the bounty others enjoy. In *The Bottom Billion: Why the Poorest Countries Are Failing and What Can Be Done About It*, Paul Collier (winner of the prestigious 2008 Lionel Gelber Prize) argues that the status and future of the 50-odd "failed states" at the bottom of the economic tree are the main issues facing contemporary global politics. For Collier, the world needs a new, concerted approach to poverty, and globalization is actually making the situation in these countries worse. Suggested remedies include preferential trade policies and the elimination of corruption (by international intervention if necessary).[6]

Many other voices are considerably less sanguine than Friedman, or even Collier.[7] Despite the expanded economies of the so-called BRIC states (Brazil, Russia, India, China), the international system has simply not been responsive to the issue of chronic disparities in wealth and well-being, and the global recession of the late 2000s only exacerbated this disparity, as the poorest countries suffered the worst drops in economic growth and living standards. We are certainly not on track toward achieving all of the Millennium Summit Goals (discussed later in this chapter), although significant progress has been made on some of the targets according to the UN's *Millennium Development Goals Report of 2012*. While the total number of people affected by chronic hunger has risen to approximately one billion, there are pockets of actual improvement in some of the traditionally worst-hit areas in sub-Saharan Africa and South Asia. School enrolments have increased, though a gender gap persists in many regions. HIV/AIDS prevention efforts are proving effective in some areas, but in others infection rates and related deaths are still on the increase, and tuberculosis rates have risen dramatically.[8]

There is also widespread concern about economic stability. Financial crises have become commonplace: Mexico, Argentina, India, and Russia all experienced crises in the 1990s; the 1997 to 1998 Asian financial crisis had a ripple effect throughout the world economy; in 2008 and 2009 the world was again in the grip of recession, caused by a serious credit crisis in the U.S. that quickly spread around the globe. All of these crises revealed how banks, foreign investors, and currency speculators play a decisive role in national economies, and when they move their money amid concern over its safety, and when governments use public funds to bail out banks and other major industries, thus incurring large amounts of debt, the chaos can be both immediate and long-lasting. Furthermore, fluctuations in the price of oil caused by increased demand and stock speculation, coupled with prolonged droughts in several major agricultural centres, can contribute to commodity and food price increases that threaten the well-being of millions of people. These crises remind us that the global economy is far from shock-proof despite the existence of institutions designed to prevent such crises.

A number of global economic issues are likely to be important subjects of ongoing discussion and debate. One persistent issue is the debt crisis. Some states have managed to reduce their debt burdens. Canada, for example, managed balanced budgets between 1997 and 2007, although it has run budget deficits from 2008 to 2012 in an effort to counter the recession. However, public or sovereign debt has soared in other countries. In the U.S., the costs of long wars in Iraq and Afghanistan, and the trillion-dollar stimulus packages implemented by the G.W. Bush and Obama administrations in response to the global recession resulted in historic levels of national debt, much of it owed to China. We discuss the sovereign debt crisis in Europe later in this chapter, but suffice it to say that the crisis began in 2009 in Greece but spread rapidly and by 2012, threatened the very existence of one of the world's premier currencies, the euro. However, developing countries have faced overwhelming debt for many decades, and have suffered the financial and social consequences of high interest payments and debt-restructuring policies.

Other developments have reshaped the global economy as well. Women of all ages have become more integrated with the modern production process than ever before, but this is often occurring under exploitative conditions, most notably in the infamous "sweatshops" in many developing countries that produce goods for export. Another issue is the increasing demand for energy, especially fossil fuels, with the rise of the Chinese, Indian, Brazilian, and other newly industrialized economies. Meanwhile, attempts to manage the global economy, from the shelved **Multilateral Agreement on Investment (MAI)** to the meetings of the WTO (including the failed Doha Round), have met with increasing opposition from protest groups and governments concerned with the impact of globalization on societies, cultures, the workplace, employment, and the environment. Finally, innovations such as the Internet, **genetically modified organisms (GMOs)**, and **nanotechnology** have further complicated trade negotiations, international laws on intellectual property rights, and the agenda of protest groups and bioethicists.

This chapter begins with a re-examination of the central perspectives of international political economy introduced in Chapters 1 and 4, placing greater emphasis on more contemporary global economic issues as well as concerns over the role of women in the global economy and environmental problems. We discuss the conceptual and policy challenges posed by globalization. The relationship between globalization, economic activity, and politics is illustrated through an examination of the role of multinational corporations (MNCs) in the world economy. Next, we discuss what various critics argue is the main problem with globalization: marginalization and the perpetuation of extreme poverty. The chapter then examines what some critics consider the main counterpoint to globalization: regionalization. Is the world economy globalizing or regionalizing? Finally, we reflect on the role of energy politics in IPE (international political economy), particularly the politics of oil, which will continue to have a dramatic impact on the global economy.

FROM THEORY TO PRACTICE IN THE CONTEMPORARY GLOBAL ECONOMY

In IPE, realists argue governments are primarily concerned with the health and security of the nation-state itself, and the economy is largely a means to maintain or increase that power: the global economy is part of a broader competitive arena in which states pursue their interests. Thus we can expect only limited progress from world and regional trade talks (the "Doha Round" of the WTO may have proved this point), or from financial institutions and trade organizations that are controlled by self-serving states. Robert Isaac argues that, "although the Cold War has ended, the primacy of insecurity—of the infinite striving for security—has not. Where military security prevails, such as in most of the industrialized democracies, there has merely been a shift in the form of insecurity to the economic or psychological realms, as nations seek to increase economic competitiveness and to reduce unemployment."[9] The spoils of victory will include industrial supremacy, technology and information leadership, and the economic capacity to sustain a modern military. The "losing" states will face the problems created by reduced fiscal resources: unreliable economic growth and a smaller economic pie; permanent relegation to the ranks of the resource extraction, branch plant, or cash-crop economies; second-rate technology and information systems; and a lack of the economic means to escape a cycle of poverty. The economic war between states is, therefore, cast in zero-sum terms; that is, gains for one side are seen as a loss for the other (see Profile 8.1).

Where the economic nationalist sees states struggling to survive or prosper in the world economy, liberals see individuals, households, and firms maximizing their opportunity to pursue mutually beneficial exchanges in the global marketplace. Through comparative advantage,

---

PROFILE 8.1 Survival of the Smartest: Geoeconomic Warfare

Many realists have predicted an increase in economic nationalism in the global economy. In particular, in 1993 Edward Luttwak suggested that "geoeconomics" would come to dominate international economic relations and trigger a "global war for economic power." Luttwak was writing long before the onset of the global recession in 2008 to 2009, but his predictions may have greater significance now than they did in 1993. Luttwak made the following arguments to support his case:

- Geoeconomics is spreading and becoming the dominant phenomenon in the central arena of world affairs, but not all states are equally inclined or equally capable of participating in the new struggle.

- Small but well-educated countries can be much more successful in geoeconomics than they could ever be in global politics, where size always counts and may alone be decisive.

- Reflecting the arguments of structural realists, Luttwak suggests that states will tend to act geoeconomically simply because of what they are: territorially defined entities designed precisely to outdo each other on the world scene.

- When there is no strategic confrontation at the centre of world affairs that can absorb the adversarial orientation of states, those ill feelings may be diverted into the nation's economic relations.

- The emerging geoeconomic struggle for high-technology industrial supremacy among Americans, Europeans, and Asians is eroding their old alliance solidarity. Increased geoeconomic activity will characterize their economic relationship, as opposed to free trade economics.

SOURCE: EDWARD LUTTWAK, "THE COMING GLOBAL WAR OF ECONOMIC POWER," *THE INTERNATIONAL ECONOMY*, VOL. 7 (SEPTEMBER/OCTOBER 1993), PG. 20. REPRINTED WITH PERMISSION.

a world adhering to the principles of free trade will reap the benefits of the efficient use of capital and resources. The institutions of the world economy were built by states in accordance with these liberal economic principles, and through tariff reduction, non-discrimination, national treatment, and the harmonization of regulations, a rules-based trade and financial system has emerged. Some liberals, adhering to **classical liberal** approaches but often referred to today as "neoliberals," argue that state intervention only creates more obstacles to market activity. Liberal institutionalists believe rational actors will converge in common institutions and regimes. This is the heart of the liberal "global governance" approach: a postnationalist international society can emerge with deliberate cooperation and institution building, but the global marketplace should not be subject to extraordinary controls or be responsible for the redistribution of wealth.

In contrast, Keynesian liberal criticism of neoliberal economic philosophy has been especially strong in the wake of the U.S. financial crises that precipitated the global economic recession of 2008. In particular, Keynesian liberals argue that the recession was due at least in part to weak government regulation and oversight of large banks and other financial institutions on Wall Street, and that government deficit-based spending during a financial crisis is the only path to recovery. The stimulus packages pursued by most governments between 2008 and 2012 suggest that, despite rhetoric about fiscal conservatism, many governments agree with these premises. Similarly, relying on harsh austerity measures that severely limit government spending is seen as a colossal error even as Germany inflicts such a policy on the highly indebted EU states. This intra-liberal debate between neoliberals and Keynesians is one of the key features of the dialogue on globalization, with authors such as Joseph Stiglitz and George Soros stimulating dialogue on how the principles of liberal economics should be put into practice.

Meanwhile, neo-Marxists reject both mercantilist and liberal diagnostics and prescriptions: the global economy is characterized by the spread of world capitalism, which is defined by a system that protects wealth and capital while disciplining labour in globally organized modes of production, all to serve a transnational economic elite. The social impact of globalized mass production, cash-crop agriculture, and exploitation of cheap labour has led to increased calls for alternative economic approaches at both the global and local levels. The **neo-Gramscian** perspective, introduced in Chapter 1 and developed by scholars such as Robert Cox and Stephen Gill, retains its allure for graduate students and academics interested in understanding the intersections between empire, intellectual hegemony, and industrial (and post-industrial) production. Some of this work overlaps with postmodern and constructivist calls for a re-examination of economic theory, the principles on which it is based, and the assumptions that make these principles seem legitimate for some but illegitimate for many others.

Feminist and "gendered perspectives" have focused on the role of women in the world economy and what this means for global economic management and the social impact of globalization. More women are participating in the formal workforce than ever. Between 1997 and 2007, 200 million women joined the global labour force (an increase of over 18 percent), and in 2007 there were 1.2 billion women in paid work (in contrast to 1.8 billion men). However, women are more concentrated in informal, subsistence, and vulnerable employment than men, and on average earn 17 percent less than men globally. The global labour force is increasingly feminized, with approximately 60 to 90 percent of the labour-intensive component of the production of fresh produce and clothing in the developing world performed by women.[10] More women are now employed in the service sector worldwide than in agriculture, and they are the main labourers for outsourced corporate services such as call centres.

Women are considered desirable workers in such industries because they can often be extended fewer benefits and paid lower wages, are considered less likely to form unions, and cannot find better work due to discrimination.

Women in the global economy face many other challenges. The increasing trend toward the outsourcing or subcontracting of work to home labourers (referred to as "informal" work) leaves women highly vulnerable to poverty and abusive working conditions. Another challenge comes in the form of the proliferation of **export processing zones (EPZs)**, special territorial enclaves created by governments for industrial and trade activity by domestic and international corporations exempt from national labour and environmental laws. Millions of women work in over 3000 EPZs in over 120 countries worldwide, and therefore fall outside the jurisdiction of whatever minimal labour rights for women might exist in the host country.[11] None of this means the work many women do in the global economy is unimportant. Women grow much of the food consumed locally in most societies and care for the children and elderly in addition to paid work. However, feminists argue that the work many women do has been systematically undervalued in society and by governments and employers, and much of it violates domestic and/or international labour and human rights law. Finally, global trafficking in women (especially for the large international sex trade) is a fixture of the contemporary global economy, and is characterized by kidnapping, deception, and brutal coercion. While gathering data on the number of women affected by international trafficking is extremely difficult, the European Union has suggested that as many as 700 000 women and children are moved across international borders by trafficking rings every year, clearly one the greatest human rights issues of our time.[12]

Meanwhile, the labour force in industrialized states has undergone significant demographic change since women began working in factories during the world wars. Many economies have shifted to a service and information orientation (see Chapter 12), putting more women in positions of decision-making power. Governments have often supported or encouraged this transition with employment equity programs. From a liberal feminist perspective, then, progress has been made—though just how much progress is still a matter of considerable debate. Among academics and politicians alike, much more attention has been paid in recent times to the role of women in development. Countries such as Canada have made women central players in their development assistance programs, though with mixed results. This is part of a more general, and welcome, move away from large infrastructure projects designed to bring Western-style growth to impoverished areas and toward focusing instead on smaller-scale development that involves local communities. International agencies, such as **UNICEF (United Nations Children's Fund)**, have been involved with acquiring bank loans for women in small-business sectors in countries such as Egypt and Pakistan. In many southern states, women have organized cooperatives, income-producing businesses that range from garment production to food processing; the International Labour Organization (ILO) and many regional banks have promoted what is referred to as *women's entrepreneurship development*; and many successful micro-financing (small-loan) programs, such as the Grameen Bank founded in Bangladesh by 2006 Nobel Peace Prize winner Mohammed Yunus, have lifted tens of thousands of women out of absolute poverty.[13] Still, the majority of the malnourished and undereducated children in the world are female, and resistance to the education of girls can take extreme forms: girls seeking educational opportunities have been the targets of homicidal violence in Afghanistan and elsewhere.

Ecofeminists, meanwhile, argue that despite all the media attention paid to the environment, industrialized Western society still does not understand the link between violence against women and environmental exploitation. The world economy remains heavily dependent on the extraction of large amounts of resources, for both fuel and products, while violence against women remains a widespread phenomenon, especially in times of war, as witnessed in the former Yugoslavia in the early 1990s, the DRC (Democratic Republic of Congo) and Sudan in the mid- to late 2000s, and Syria in 2012 and 2013. Ecofeminists argue we need to stop both types of violence together and rethink our approaches to gender and ecology, our tendency to answer complex problems with technical solutions, our efforts at domination instead of collaboration (a heritage of the liberal utilitarian perspective that sees nature as something to be conquered, tamed, and exploited), and our tendency toward monoculture in terms of both agricultural production and intellectual diversity.[14]

While the type of deep change ecofeminists call for is a long way off, economists are recognizing the importance of the environment as both a causal variable and an ongoing concern in their work. The most widely publicized endorsement of the importance of the environment was the 1987 report of the Bruntland Commission, titled our *Our Common Future*.[15] This was followed by the environmental focus of the UN Conference on Environment and Development in Rio de Janeiro in 1992 (see Chapter 10) and subsequent meetings in Johannesburg and Copenhagen, and "Rio+20" in 2012. There is no doubt that the environment is now accepted as a crucial component of the study of the global economy and IPE.[16] Indeed, concerns over the gender dynamic in the international workforce, and the environmental problems resulting from large-scale industrialization and agriculture, are now well reflected in contemporary debates on the meaning, implications, and sustainability of globalization. We turn now to a brief discussion of this widely used but little understood term.

Women have made great strides in terms of economic equality, but feminists argue that many problems remain. For example, large-scale production in a globalized economy often exploits women and children. The match factories of Tamil Nadu, India, rely almost exclusively on female labour working 12-hour days for 15 rupees (less than 30 cents) per day. (AP Photo/Cindy Andrew/CP Images)

WHAT IS GLOBALIZATION?

Globalization is often accepted, without much examination, as an inevitable evolutionary feature of the world economy. But when did we begin thinking about a borderless world in which transnational forces, spurred on by technological developments (especially in the field of communications), are shrinking the globe? One might argue this has been a long-term project that commenced when humans first began communicating; some feel it will end only with the global domination of liberal democracy and capitalism, or a truly global marketplace. Indeed, the state-run economies that formed the "Second World" during the Cold War have largely collapsed. Although some states, such as China and Cuba, retain the rhetorical vestiges of socialism, they too have turned to what we might loosely label **marketization** (characterized ideally by the introduction of private property, free competition between firms, and the acceptance of foreign investment). Seen this way, globalization may be the logical end of history: other stages (the city-state system, feudal Europe, the nation-state system) of human social development have merely been the means to this end. Others, however, reject such a teleological approach, or see the current era as the beginning of a new history, marked by the spread of Western culture, resistance to it, and continued disparities in wealth and opportunity.[17] Some even suggest that global capitalism, driven by its own "manic logic," is creating an inhumane world based on internationalized predatory capitalism.[18]

Perhaps the most succinct definition of globalization is offered by Malcolm Waters in his short but fascinating book on the topic. He defines *globalization* as a "social process in which the constraints of geography on social and cultural arrangements recede and in which people become increasingly aware that they are receding."[19] Waters believes globalization has always been taking place, proceeding through the "fits and starts of various ancient imperial expansions, pillaging and trading oceanic explorations, and the spread of religious ideas." This path was interrupted by the European Middle Ages, a period of "inward-looking territorialism" but then picked up again in the 15th and 16th centuries, when the Copernican revolution convinced humanity that it occupied a globe (instead of a flat, endless plain) and when European expansion took the ideas that today still shape the global economy—market-based trade, for example—to distant lands where people had previously lived in "virtually complete ignorance of each other's existence."[20]

Others, such as renowned Canadian international political economist Robert Cox, argue that the analysis of what he terms the "globalization thrust" must ultimately begin with an understanding of the internationalization of production:

> The internationalizing process results when capital considers the productive resources of the world as a whole and locates elements of complex globalized production systems at points of greatest cost advantage. The critical factor is information on how most profitably to combine components in that production process.... Producing units take advantage of abundant, cheap, and malleable labour where it is to be found, and of robotization where it is not.[21]

While Waters's explanation rests more on the spread of ideas, Cox relies more on a materialist explanation (stressing the political implications of economic forces). Cox also takes a Gramscian approach, suggesting the hegemonic nature of globalization's ideology reflects the preferences of the structurally advantaged.

Globalization is most often associated with a borderless world, a world in which the conventions and norms of the Westphalian system of states are increasingly irrelevant and anachronistic. Globalization is often regarded as beyond the immediate control of state actors, or as an external force to which actors in the international system must respond. This view suggests that we must, perhaps grudgingly, accept the fact that many people will be harmed by globalization even as others gain. After all, this has been a consistent theme in the evolution of economic systems: change tends to harm one part of a society even though society as a whole might benefit. However, another view argues that globalization is hardly an inevitable, impersonal force, but was created and driven forward by the policies of governments, in turn encouraged by financial actors. According to Jeffry A. Frieden,

> [Globalization] is a choice made by governments that consciously decide to reduce barriers to trade and investment, adopt new policies toward international money and finance, and chart fresh economic courses. Decisions made by each government are interconnected; international finance, international trade, and international monetary relations depend on the joint actions of national governments around the world.[22]

The Canadian government, for example, has been very proactive in seeking increased trade opportunities abroad, though its reaction to foreign investment in Canada has differed over time.

In general, IR theorists have very mixed reactions to the assertion that we are in a new stage of world history. Realists point to the stubbornness of the institution of state sovereignty. Anyone travelling across a border and dealing with the officials stationed there to protect it realizes very quickly that borders still exist, and if anything border controls have become tighter after September 11, 2001. Although the functionalist school (see Chapter 5) believed international institutions would eventually supplant the state, they did not have the multinational corporation (MNC) in mind. For their part, Marxists would interpret globalization as the continuation of older forms of **imperialism**. In fact, they would be apt to wonder what all the fuss is about, since this process has been a constant feature of economic and political life since the beginning of the expansion of the ruling elite in ancient societies. The fallen socialist bloc did not stop imperialism, but merely and temporarily stalled its spread. The periphery of the world system continues to be a location for disciplined production and the exploitation of human labour, integrated by core financial institutions and marketplaces, feeding the voracious appetite of global capitalism. For Marxists, global recessions are empirical evidence of the fragility of the world economy and its predatory and merciless character.

Beyond these debates are questions about the important cultural implications of increased trade, investment flows, and telecommunications capacity, a theme to which we return in Chapter 12. In terms of globalization's cultural impact, some would no doubt argue that globalization is the modern equivalent of what development theorists earlier referred to as **modernization**. The latter term was harshly criticized because it implied that only Western states were "modern" and that those developing states that had failed to reach the point of mass consumption societies were "unmodern," perhaps because of geographic, cultural, or even personality traits prevalent in their societies. Thus, one might argue that the pressure to globalize, to become even further involved with the world economy and its regimes, is a destructive one that implies that non-Western societies have no choice, if they want to experience economic growth and development, other than to adopt the conventional attributes of the West: capitalism, commercial culture, secular governance, and an emphasis on the present. Opposition to this cultural set of values is of course common in many regions, and even Western states are concerned about the intrusion of external cultural influences. Canada and France frequently seek to protect culture in world trade talks, for example. For indigenous peoples around the world, the stakes are high: the intrusion of external cultural influences may threaten their very existence. The cultural destruction of indigenous persons (which we discuss as a human rights issue in the next chapter) was an earlier variant of the wide-scale Westernization we see taking place today. And many religious leaders in the Middle East and elsewhere have sought to curb Western influences through an assertion of theocratic power.

Some would insist that the very concept of globalization, and its continual promotion by the corporate elite, belittles the strong cultural differences that exist today. One author argues that the world is still fundamentally divided into at least eight civilization groupings, the Chinese (Confucian–Taoist–Buddhist), Hindu, Islamic, Japanese (Shinton–Buddhist–Confucian), Latin American syncretist, Islamic, non-Islamic African, and Christian.[23] Does a secular vision of globalization, based on markets and investment and common values, do justice to the inherent diversity of humanity? What about the major split, axiomatic to some analysts, between the Eastern and Western, or Islamic and Christian, communities? What about the differences within every nation-state, between rich and poor, between ethnic groups, between male and female? In short, can the forces of globalization overcome the realities of human diversity and environmental diversity? Perhaps **homogenization** is further off than a simplified vision of proliferate Western products and advertisements would have us believe.

Yet the belief in the magic of the marketplace to create wealth still reigns in influential circles. John Williamson coined the term **Washington Consensus** in 1990 to describe a set of policies designed by **international financial institutions** (**IFIs**) based in Washington to stimulate economic growth and development in Latin America.[24] The phrase is now generally used (or, as Williamson himself has argued, misused) to describe the so-called neoliberal approach to economic development, stressing the need for governments to pursue fiscal discipline, cutbacks to non-productive sectors, lower taxes, and the relaxation of controls over interest rates. They should also allow their currencies to float on international financial markets, lower tariffs and encourage trade as well as foreign investment, privatize state-owned industries, deregulate industry and agriculture, and protect the private ownership of property. This agenda, which has been harshly criticized by social activists and others as placing far too much faith in the marketplace, has guided development assistance policies and the terms of the "**structural adjustment**" loans offered by the World Bank and the IMF. Many liberals see this "**conditionality**" as the necessary counterpart to loan guarantees to developing countries: it makes little sense to lend money to countries that are not following sound fiscal and economic policies. However, critics argue that this forces governments to adopt a set of fiscal and economic policies that may be harmful to the most vulnerable sectors of their society, and results in lower government spending on education, health care, environmental protection, and general welfare. A further criticism is that none of the advanced capitalist states have followed the rules themselves: they run deficits, protect their markets, and have their own, often systemic, corruption problems.

The rise of **currency** and **commodity speculation** adds more fuel to antiglobalization viewpoints. Various currencies have experienced great instability, and commodity prices are often artificially inflated, due to speculative investment, which is arguably an inherent element of what Susan Strange termed the *casino capitalism* of the West.[25] This has led to calls for measures to moderate these activities and generate revenue from them for international charitable projects. In fact, the economist James Tobin once suggested that a tax be levied on international currency exchanges.[26] A "Tobin tax," it is often argued, would not only raise hundreds of billions of dollars which could be used for international humanitarian purposes, such as paying for peacekeeping operations or AIDS relief or climate change adaptation, but would also discourage speculation itself. However, it would be difficult to convince market-oriented governments that this type of intervention is justified, and, as an article in *The Economist* points out, unless every state participated, "trading would simply shift to tax-free havens. Also, financial wizards would quickly devise tax dodges: rather than trade yen for dollars, say, they might agree to swap Japanese government bonds for American Treasuries."[27] Finally, the widespread use of the **Internet** for commercial transactions would make such a taxation scheme even more difficult to implement.

One thing remains fairly clear: if the market has won over the hearts and minds of a transnational economic elite, it may not have done so among the millions of people who continue to forge their own path of development somewhere else. It would be a gross overgeneralization to argue that all that is left on the economic menu is global capitalism with minimal state interference. From the quiet fields of agrarian communities to the streets of bustling megacities, people are engaged in forming their own substate arrangements and interpersonal relationships. For example, female workers formed many cooperative ventures to produce textiles in Guatemala; women in Kenya founded the Green Belt movement, planting millions of trees to stop **desertification**; artistic communities in many northern states have formed mutually supportive networks; people rose in widespread protests to halt the privatization of water provision in South and North America and Africa; hundreds of thousands participated in the widespread "Occupy Wall Street" movement in 2011; and unique informal resource-sharing regimes in environmental management are being forged as we grapple with problems of the commons. There is much more to the global political economy than the amorphous entity we refer to as the market, and though the conventional path of authoritarian state socialism may

We are the 99 percent. The Occupy movement began with the Occupy Wall Street protests in 2011, and has since spread into a global movement highlighting social and economic inequality. (Andrew Kelly/Reuters)

well be dead, with its stench of economic failure and political repression, a new, community-centred one may be emerging, built on the survival strategies implemented by people in both hemispheres.[28] However, there is little doubt that the marketplace, as defined by neoliberal ideology, retains a special place in the world view of those who benefit most greatly from globalization. This is best demonstrated with reference to a peculiarly 20th-century innovation with deep consequences, the multinational corporation.

THE CONTROVERSIAL ROLE OF MULTINATIONAL CORPORATIONS

Perhaps one of the most remarkable characteristics of the contemporary global economy is the expansive rise of the MNC. MNCs (also sometimes referred to as *transnational corporations*, or *TNCs*) are businesses with extensive investments or operations in more than one country. Typically, MNCs are headquartered in a home country, and own and operate affiliate businesses in other countries around the world. Larger MNCs may control large product lines and brand names, acquired through strategic corporate alliances, mergers, purchases of other companies, or hostile takeovers. Largely through the operations of MNCs, world production has become increasingly globalized, as production facilities have been constructed and/or relocated overseas and product components are assembled in a wide variety of countries. While some companies are major competitors, MNCs also cooperate extensively, often sharing production facilities and forming partnerships with local firms. American, European, and Asian MNCs are generally the largest and most powerful; today, China operates a constellation of state-owned MNCs that invest trillions of dollars abroad in pursuit of profit.

As early as the 1960s, the power of MNCs led to questions about the primacy of the nation-state.[29] In particular, the dominance of American multinationals has caused Canadians, Europeans, and South Americans to worry about the influence of American corporate commercialism on their cultures. (In the Canadian case, a short-lived spate of Canadian nationalism arose out of these concerns, and apprehensions over foreign investment resurfaced in late 2012 when the Harper Government approved the purchase of major energy companies by state-controlled corporations from China and Malaysia.)[30] MNCs are regarded either as necessary suppliers of investment and technical knowledge or as predatory entities that perpetuate the underdevelopment of poor countries. In either conception, their influence is substantial (see Profile 8.2).

The sheer size of modern MNCs is intimidating. The Toyota Motor Corporation, for example, has manufacturing facilities in 27 countries and employs approximately 326 000 people worldwide. Some MNCs have a large number of subsidiary corporations. For example, Yum! Brands Inc. owns A&W, Pizza Hut, Taco Bell, Long John Silver's, Wingstreet, and Kentucky Fried Chicken, and operates 37 000 restaurants in 117 countries and territories, generating over US$12 billion in revenues in 2011 (see their website at http://www.yum.com/company/). Yum! Brands Inc. was formerly Tricon Global Restaurants, itself a spinoff from PepsiCo in 1997. Corporate mergers and acquisitions have accelerated the growth of many MNCs: in 2000, the French car manufacturer Renault took over Nissan; in the pharmaceutical sector Glaxco Wellcome merged with SmithKline Beecham in an effort to capitalize on the drug potential of the human genome project; and America Online merged with Time Warner, creating a company with a market value of US$340 billion (although the drop in tech stocks in the latter half of 2000 reduced this figure by $140 billion). In 2004, Royal Dutch Petroleum Co. merged with Shell Transport and Trading Company, and in 2006 AT&T Inc. merged with BellSouth Corporation. Each of these corporate mergers and acquisitions had transaction values of over US$70 billion.

PROFILE 8.2 — The Debate over MNCs: Do They Exploit Low-Income Countries?

YES

1. MNCs decapitalize less-developed countries (LDCs). MNCs take more money in profit out of LDCs than they invest.

2. MNCs are obstacles to social progress. The profit motive makes MNCs unresponsive or opposed to progressive political change.

3. MNCs contribute to inequality. MNCs create an elite socio-economic class in LDCs, isolated from the poor majority.

4. MNCs discourage indigenous development. They oppose efforts by LDCs to industrialize, as this would create domestic competition.

5. MNCs create dependence. LDC economies come to depend on MNCs for investment, technology, and markets.

6. MNCs use LDCs as sources of raw materials. MNCs extract raw materials for a low price and manufacture products abroad, forcing LDCs to purchase expensive finished products.

NO

1. MNCs provide investment. MNCs invest a lot of their own money and also attract foreign investors.

2. MNCs support peaceful domestic environments. MNCs require peace to operate effectively, and therefore have an interest in long-term stability.

3. MNCs create jobs. They have an interest in a capable workforce and provide training and education.

4. MNCs promote development. MNCs help create modern infrastructure and share technology and technique, therefore creating conditions conducive to domestic growth.

5. MNCs increase fiscal resources of LDCs. MNCs pay royalties and tax revenues to LDC governments.

6. MNCs give LDCs access to world markets. They provide a channel to markets for products as well as markets for purchase, enabling LDCs to access the global marketplace.

MNCs are extremely powerful economic entities, and their significance in the global economy has grown as world trade has expanded. According to the UNCTAD (UN Conference on Trade and Development) World Investment Report, in 2009, there were over 82 000 MNCs worldwide, with over 807 000 affiliates (often called *subsidiaries*). These MNCs accounted for over a tenth of world GDP and one-third of world exports.[31] It is striking that when the annual revenues of the largest MNCs in the world are compared with the annual GNP (gross national product) of states, more than one-third of the world's largest economic units are MNCs. Even more stark is the fact that while the UN regular budget is approximately US$1.9 billion, over 45 of the largest MNCs have annual revenues over US$100 billion. MNCs are also significant because of their numbers: few countries in the world do not host an MNC or a subsidiary within their territorial boundaries. Furthermore, MNCs have a great deal of control over the global capacity to manufacture products, sell services, and provide finance, and they are leading developers of technology and services. Most of the largest MNCs are in the manufacturing sector (Mitsubishi, Toyota), oil (Exxon, Royal Dutch/Shell Group), and electronics (IBM, AT&T). In other sectors, financial corporations such as the Industrial and Commercial Bank of China (ICBC), Bank of America, Citigroup Inc., and J.P. Morgan Chase are among the world's largest MNCs. The service sector also has many large MNCs, including McDonald's, Giant Tiger, and Walmart, that can change the entire commercial and aesthetic landscape in the towns where they locate, often forcing small businesses into bankruptcy.

MNCs' influence can be measured by the familiarity with which we recognize the household names IBM, Apple, Hitachi, Microsoft, General Electric, Du Pont, PepsiCo, Eastman Kodak,

Toyota, Mitsui, Volkswagen, Bayer, Renault, Michelin, Ciba-Geigy, Seagram, Thomson, Fiat, Philips, Unilever, and others. Billions of dollars are spent on advertising in home and foreign markets so that the products, logos, and advertising campaign themes of these corporations have become part of popular culture in Western states. As these products are marketed around the world, they become visible reflections of Western presence, or what critics would term instruments of **cultural imperialism**.

Obviously, the role played by MNCs in the global economy is a controversial one. Some see MNCs as agents of their home states, used to further their own economic and even political interests. Indeed, some MNCs have become deeply involved in the politics of host countries, even to the point of engineering the overthrow of governments. A famous example of this is the involvement of the U.S. firm International Telephone and Telegraph (ITT) in the events that led to the overthrow of the Allende government in Chile in 1973. Others see MNCs as essentially benign actors, acting in the interests of their shareholders and motivated by profit, and essential to the efficient development, production, and distribution of goods and services in the global economy. Still others see MNCs as exploitative actors, preying on cheap labour markets and raw materials, and selling the resulting products at huge profit margins. For example, in the early 1990s, many Nike shoes were manufactured in Indonesia, where the typical worker was paid $1 a day in 1991 (minimum-wage legislation and labour rights are seldom enforced in Indonesia). In 2008 some 20 000 Vietnamese Nike workers went on strike to protest their $59 per month wages. Meanwhile, one pair of Nike shoes can easily cost $150 in Canada.

This has led to an effort to develop strategies for promoting **corporate social responsibility**, encouraging MNCs to adopt voluntary codes of conduct with respect to working conditions, environmentally sustainable practices, and a variety of other concerns. In 1999, UN Secretary-General Kofi Annan called for the creation of a Global Compact to bring companies together with UN agencies and NGOs to encourage linkage between economic activity and human rights and environmental principles. For example, the International Council on Mining and Metals joins industry and NGOs to promote discussion of sustainable mining practices. Many corporations also cooperate with NGOs to certify their products as "fair trade" or environmentally sustainable. While some activists are hopeful that such programs can make a real difference, others are concerned that the corporate bottom line is based solely on profit maximization and voluntary codes of conduct are no substitute for laws and strict enforcement; rather than collaboration, NGO involvement is seen as co-option.

Certainly, MNCs are major players in many people's lives today, in both the North and the South. But the causes and extent of poverty are much more complex than the dynamics of MNC activity, as our next section will demonstrate.

THE GREAT DIVIDE: THE POLITICAL ECONOMY OF THE RICH AND THE POOR

The gap between the rich and the poor peoples of the world is enormous, whether measured in terms of economic statistics or quality of life. This gap is often described in terms of a generally rich northern hemisphere and a generally poor southern hemisphere. In practice, however, there are significant exceptions to this generalization. For example, North Korea is relatively poor, while Australia is relatively rich. Nevertheless, issues surrounding poverty and development are often cast in terms of a north–south debate. Countries are also classified along "rich" and "poor" lines, with the countries of the developed world having attained a high level of wealth through industrialization and technological development, relatively equitable levels of income distribution, and high standards of living in stable, civil societies. In contrast, countries of the "developing world" have lower levels of wealth, agricultural or subsistence economics, and inequitable income distribution in societies dominated by small elites. From this distinction has grown the term **less-developed country (LDC)**. These supposedly polar opposites—rich and poor, north and south, modern and traditional—are, by and large, misleading caricatures. Indeed, poverty is a serious problem in all of the world's leading industrialized economies, and an extravagantly wealthy upper class is often visible in most lower-income countries. Furthermore, some groups—especially minority groups and working-class women—tend to be more marginalized than others from the benefits of the economy (see Profile 8.3).

If we define the South as including the majority of lower-income states, we find the northern hemisphere contains one-quarter of the world's people but consumes three-quarters of its goods and services, while the southern hemisphere contains three-quarters of the world's people but consumes only one-quarter of its goods and services. The division in global wealth distribution can also be measured by the divergence between "high-income" and "low-income" economies. Of the US$23 trillion world GDP in 1993, US$18 trillion (or over 78 percent) was in the "high-income" economies. By 2002, world GDP had climbed to well over US$32 trillion, with US$26 trillion of this total in the high-income states (or over 81 percent). In 2010, world GDP was estimated at US$63 trillion, with high-income

PROFILE 8.3 The "Third World" and Acute Multidimensional Poverty

Throughout this text, we have generally avoided using the term *Third World* where it is usually employed. Although obvious ethnocentricity has been involved in labelling the developed capitalist states the *First World*, the term *Third World* was first used to indicate a non-American, non-Soviet path of political and economic alignment. Over time, however, it slipped into general usage as representing the southern states with low GNPs, and here it quickly began to make less sense, not only because there are large discrepancies in GNP (and GDP per capita) figures across these states, but also because, with the end of the Cold War, there is no longer a distinct Second World of communist states. Alternative phrases have proliferated over the years, such as *developing states, less-developed states, underdeveloped states*, the *periphery*, the *South*, the *global South*, and the *Majority World*. The broader question is not really which is appropriate, since they all derive from political perspectives, but whether any sort of label is appropriate,

given the diversity of states and peoples in the "developing" world. Enormous differences exist between states in wealth, income distribution, political systems, social structure, and economic organization. In the past, some scholars have suggested differentiating states in the developing world by creating additional categories, such as the **Fourth World**, the *Fifth World*, or the *least developed of the less-developed countries (LLDCs)*. The latest effort to describe the collective poverty of low-income states to receive some acceptance is the "acute multidimensional poverty index," which "captures a set of direct deprivations that batter a person at the same time." This index allows researchers, using indicators derived largely from the MDGs, to aggregate data based on household-level deprivations in education, health, and standard of living.

SOURCE: S. ALKIRE & M. SANTOS, "ACUTE MULTIDIMENSIONAL POVERTY: A NEW INDEX FOR DEVELOPING COUNTRIES," *OXFORD POVERTY AND HUMAN DEVELOPMENT INITIATIVE WORKING PAPER NO. 38*, JULY, 2010. FOUND AT: HTTP://WWW.OPHI.ORG.UK/WP-CONTENT/UPLOADS/OPHI-WP38.PDF.

countries accounting for approximately US$43 billion (or 68 percent).[32] The wealth distribution divide can also be measured in terms of population. In 2008, another UN study revealed that the richest 1 percent of adults owned 40 percent of the world's wealth, while the poorest half of the world's adult population owned just 1 percent of global wealth.[33] The study estimated that a person in the top 1 percent of the world's population was 2000 times richer than a person in the bottom half of the world's population. In 2008, the World Bank estimated that the richest 10 percent of the world's population was responsible for almost 60 percent of world consumption, while the poorest 10 percent was responsible for less than 1 percent.[34]

The relationship between these grim economic figures and quality of life is direct and real. While measures based on monetary shares cannot tell the whole story (some societies with very low per capita GNP rates nevertheless are successful in providing for **basic human needs**), the human dimension of these economic statistics is appalling. At the aggregate level, and at the individual level, global inequality has taken a devastating toll on the human condition in much of the world. Despite recent improvements in global well-being, approximately 1.4 billion people live in abject poverty on an income of less than US$1.25 per day, without access to basic nutritional requirements, health care, waste disposal, or adequate housing. Over a quarter of children in the developing world are suffering from malnutrition. Every year approximately 10 million children die before the age of five, one child every three seconds, mostly from poverty and malnutrition. Infectious diseases claim millions of lives each year, with one million fatalities alone due to malaria. Over 40 million people worldwide are infected with HIV/AIDS and 3 million die each year from this disease.[35] Meanwhile the majority of the people living in abject poverty are women, and 99 percent of maternal deaths occur in low-income countries.[36] The UN has developed a program of action, known as the Millennium Development Goals (MDGs), aimed at reducing these and other shortfalls in human well-being by 2015 (see Profile 8.4), and while progress on some targets has been positive, others will not be met.

In light of these statistics, it might be useful to reflect on how Canada compares to the rest of the world. The UN employs a measure called the Human Development Index, which is based on achievements in basic human capabilities across states. The HDI is measured by life expectancy, educational attainment, and income (GNP per capita). As mentioned in the introduction to this chapter, Canada ranked sixth in 2011 (it had occupied the top spot from 1992 to 1999). These high rankings do not mean that Canada does not face problems associated with poverty, homelessness, or the economic and political marginalization of certain groups in society. Nevertheless, it should give Canadians pause to consider what ethical obligations they might have to work to alleviate global inequalities.

INTERNATIONAL RESPONSES TO GLOBAL INEQUITY AND POVERTY: TOO LITTLE, TOO LATE?

Before discussing contemporary multilateral efforts to ease the plight of the poor, some background is in order. In Chapter 2 we examined how the European empires expanded around the world and how non-European empires also expanded and conquered territories abroad, imposing alien systems of economic and political organization. Many of the problems that beset the southern states have their origins in the nature of this colonial rule. As we have seen, these empires began to collapse after World War II, and many states gained their political independence. However, the end of colonial rule left most of these former colonies woefully

PROFILE 8.4 The Millennium Summit Goals

In 2000, Secretary-General Kofi Annan hosted the Millennium Summit in New York, attended by most heads of state and other officials. He set out a series of challenges, which received a warm welcome and expressions of support from the gathered politicians. However, despite the earnest desire to curb the ill effects of poverty, it would be foolish to suggest we are anywhere near the accomplishment of these goals; the *UN Millennium Development Goals Report of 2011* states that some 837 million people are affected by chronic hunger and undernourishment. Can the global economy possibly achieve these goals without significant or perhaps radical change?

FREEDOM FROM WANT: THE MILLENNIUM DEVELOPMENT GOALS

- *Eradicate extreme hunger and poverty.* Target for 2015: Halve the proportion of the world's people (currently 22 percent) whose income is less than one dollar a day and those who suffer from hunger.

- *Achieve universal primary education.* Target for 2015: Ensure that all boys and girls complete primary school.

- *Promote gender equality and empower women.* Target for 2015: Eliminate gender disparities in primary and secondary education.

- *Reduce child mortality.* Target for 2015: Reduce by two-thirds the mortality rate of children under the age of five.

- *Improve maternal health.* Target for 2015: Reduce by three-quarters the number of women dying in childbirth.

- *Combat HIV/AIDS, malaria, and other diseases.* Target for 2015: Halt, and begin to reverse, the spread of HIV/AIDS, malaria, and other diseases, providing at least 95 percent of young people with access to HIV-prevention services.

- *Ensure environmental sustainability.* Target for 2015: Integrate principles of sustainable development, improve drinking water, improve conditions of slum dwellers.

- *Develop a global partnership for development.* This would involve governments, IOs, civil society, and the private sector.

Urban ecology. Population density is high and living is hard in this *favela* in the Amazon city of Manaus, Brazil. (© Edward Parker/Alamy)

unprepared to govern their political, economic, or social affairs. Although some colonies were better prepared for independence than others, in general they lacked training for the administration of independent government. Furthermore, the arbitrary nature of colonial borders left many newly independent states with complex mixtures of ethnicities, languages, religions, and clans, many of which had historical animosities. The effort to build nationalism around loyalty to the state, as opposed to loyalty to ethnicity or clan, was never very successful, as we saw in our discussion of ethnic conflict in Chapter 6. Finally, a postcolonial dependence lingered: newly independent states needed capital from industrialized states, while industrialized states continued to exploit the natural resources and labour in postcolonial countries. The legacy of imperialism had left the former colonies with the illusion of political freedom but the reality of economic subjugation, which in turn left them vulnerable to political interference and domination. Concern over the north–south divide increased during the 1960s and 1970s, and became a major issue at the UN. Postcolonial states had become stuck in a cycle of underdevelopment, which they felt was perpetuated by the investment activities of large corporations, the accumulation of external debt to rich countries, and the unequal trading arrangement of the world economy. Liberal economists and developed states countered that many postcolonial states followed poor economic practices, spent too much money on their militaries, and suffered from corrupt leadership by economic elites more interested in personal enrichment than the welfare of their people; under such circumstances, states could not be expected to develop.

Efforts to address global poverty began at the Bandung Conference in 1955, a meeting of 25 Asian and African states that condemned colonialism. In 1964 a group of developing states in the UN formed the **Group of 77 (G77)**, which called for the development of favourable terms of trade for developing countries in GATT. The G77 did succeed in creating the pressure behind a **Generalized System of Preferences (GSP)**, an arrangement whereby rich states would permit certain products from the developing world to enter their economies on favourable terms (that is, lower tariff barriers). But this concession was not the decisive or major step the developing world sought. In 1974, the G77 called for the establishment of a **New International Economic Order (NIEO)** that would give low-income states a better position in the world trading system. Many post-colonial states had evolved into what economists have referred to as "one-commodity countries." Some examples included Bolivia (natural gas), Colombia (coffee), Venezuela (petroleum), Botswana (diamonds), Niger (uranium), Zaire (copper), and Fiji (sugar). The price of such items is susceptible to sudden and dramatic shifts in demand, and if the price drops, the country suffers. The NIEO called for commodity agreements that would free states highly dependent on a few products from suffering the effects of wild price fluctuations. It also called for an increase in economic aid from industrialized states; debt relief by forgiving or postponing repayment; the provision of preferential treatment for exports from low-income countries; transfers of appropriate technology; and greater representation for low income countries on the boards of the main financial institutions, such as the IMF and World Bank Group. These demands, and others associated with the NIEO movement, called for heavy state intervention in the global economy, thus contradicting the principles of free trade on which the GATT trade system was slowly evolving. Despite a modest effort to bolster trade opportunities for low-income countries through the European Economic Community in 1975 in the **Lomé Convention** (which currently covers trade with over 70 **African, Caribbean, and Pacific [ACP] States**), the overall thrust of the NIEO plan was so anti-market and demanding from the industrialized world's perspective that it never had a serious chance of being implemented. Today, the G77 countries (which now number more than 120) continue to press for changes to the international trading system, but their profile is no longer what it once was.

As efforts to decisively change the global trading system foundered and **foreign direct investment** proved insufficient, low-income countries increasingly relied on financial aid for development. This aid came from three primary sources: loans from the World Bank Group and the IMF, private capital markets, and Official Development Assistance. Today, the World Bank Group includes the International Bank for Reconstruction and Development (IBRD), the **International Development Association (IDA)**, the **International Finance Corporation (IFC)**, the Multilateral Investment Guarantee Agency (MIGA), and the International Centre for Settlement of Investment Disputes. Together, the Group extended US$46.9 billion in financial assistance commitments in 2011.[37] The money in the bank comes from governments (which pay according to a **quota**) and from borrowing on private financial markets. Loans are extended by a vote, with countries that contribute most to the funds of the Group having increased voting weight. As a result, the United States has disproportionate influence, and the rich countries dominate the voting. The IBRD approves only hard loans, that is, loans that have a good prospect for obtaining returns (repayment with interest). The IFC acts as a bridge between the developing world and private investors and financial institutions, while the IDA assists the world's poorest countries in obtaining soft loans, with easier terms of repayment and lower rates of interest. The IMF has become a crisis lender to governments in immediate need of funds to balance their payments or compensate for a drop in commodity prices, and it has recently convened the Multilateral Consultation on Global Imbalances.

The institutions of the World Bank Group and the IMF have received considerable criticism. Critics charge that the world's richest countries control these institutions (through **weighted voting**), and as a result the institutions lend based not on the need of the developing world but in the interests of capital lenders. The terms of the loans of the World Bank are little better than those from private institutions, and the amount of money dispensed by the Group has never been sufficient to make a decisive difference in low-income countries. Finally, the World Bank Group and especially the IMF are criticized for imposing extensive and often harsh conditions for loans, conditions that critics argue are based on the flawed formula of the Washington Consensus (discussed earlier in this chapter). The **structural adjustment programs (SAPs)** recommended by the IMF and World Bank demand reductions in public spending (which hurt the poor the most) and a focus on trade liberalization and the exportation of natural resources, which harm the environment and curtail more diverse economic development. These measures can increase hardship in low-income states and often create political instability.[38] Liberals argue that conditionality on Bank or IMF loans is put in place to ensure that the money is used properly and in accordance with sound economic practices. Otherwise, the money would be wasted on inefficient government-run industries, or—due to systemic corruption—would not reach the people who need it most.

Through the IFC or private negotiations, governments in the developing world also obtain finance from private lending institutions, primarily the major international banks. In the late 1960s and through the 1970s, private banks extended massive loans to low-income countries. They were more than willing to offload heavy investments from the oil-exporting Arab states, but in the process flooded developing states with short-term infusions of often mismanaged cash. Many of the projects built with these loans failed to yield the expected economic returns, and by the late 1970s and early 1980s, many low-income countries were facing massive debt crises. Defaults on interest charges began to occur, and many loans were extended or simply written off. As a result, today private lending institutions are very careful about lending money, exacerbating capital shortages in poor countries, and prioritizing debt repayment prospects when making loan decisions. Indeed, many poverty activists have long argued that debt relief is a vital first step to help poor states escape the vicious cycle of repayment. Some progress has been made, but in 2006, the total external debt of developing countries was still over 2.1 trillion dollars; and by 2010, reflecting the global recession, it had risen to an astounding 4 trillion.[39]

The third primary source of finance is Official Development Assistance (ODA), which consists of government grants or loans specifically intended for economic development, often used (as during the Cold War) for outright geopolitical purposes. ODA is extended on a bilateral basis or a multilateral basis (through an international organization), and much of it is in fact "**tied aid**," requiring the funds to be spent on products from the contributing country. Although the countries of the North agreed in 1970 (and again in 1992) to maintain ODA targets of 0.7 percent of GNP, they have fallen far short of that goal. Beyond the ethics of tied aid and the dilemmas inherent in fostering further dependence, ODA can also reinforce the power of undesirable regimes. It is hard to find a more glaring example of this than Sudan (whose president has been indicted for crimes against humanity by the International Criminal Court). The Sudanese government routinely calls for and receives international food aid (despite being a leading African exporter of several crops) while people starve in the conflict-ridden Darfur.[40] Other questions are raised about the long-term applicability of aid, suggesting the North is as addicted to it as the South. For example, China and India remain prodigious recipients of aid. While poverty is a serious problem in these two countries, China has sent a man into space and is buying large chunks of business and real estate abroad, while India is often cited as the world's fastest growing high-tech economy and has developed a large nuclear weapons program. Are these countries in need of aid, or is the market for aid-related goods a force of its own?

Further, leaders from developing countries complain of the reverse transfer of technology, or "brain drain," that has often occurred. Developed countries and MNCs have been reluctant to establish research and development and other facilities that employ and train local skilled labour, but have facilitated the emigration of the brightest and most skilled individuals. One study suggested that, between 1960 and 1976, more than 300 000 people migrated from developing countries to work as engineers, scientists, physicians, surgeons, and other technical workers in the United States, Canada, and the United Kingdom alone (see Chapter 11).[41] The loss of these highly skilled workers makes it even more difficult to develop national capacities in these sectors in low-income countries. This perpetuates historical dependencies, and there is no indication that the trend is reversing, as many industrialized countries (including Canada) continue to alter immigration policies to favour persons with certain skills or assets.

Alternatives do exist to the formal economies largely controlled or regulated by states. Indeed, the real growth area in many parts of the world is in the informal sector, characterized by low-paying jobs that offer no form of formal social protection but are often supported by networks of family and friends. The informal sector includes a wide array of economic activity such as street vendors, rickshaw drivers, roadside barbers, garbage collectors, sweatshop workers, and unregistered businesses that are outside the realm of full-time, stable, regulated, and protected work. In the developing world, as much as one-half to three-quarters of all non-agricultural employment is in the informal sector, including 51 percent in Latin America, 65 percent in Asia, and 72 percent in sub-Saharan Africa.[42] In times of economic hardship the informal sector tends to expand, so we can expect the global recession of the late 2000s, and the euro crisis, will only accelerate this trend as the ranks of the unemployed grow across the globe. We have already mentioned the tremendous amount of domestic work, usually performed by women, that offers little monetary compensation but can provide for family needs through local agriculture or barter. Similarly, small communities work to support each other without the help of formal state and international institutions, and the development of microcredit or microfinance lending has enabled millions of poor women to access modest amounts of capital for small business projects. In particular, the Grameen Bank in Bangladesh has had extraordinary success, and is now a model employed worldwide. We must also recognize the fact that transnational organized criminal activity will generate employment as well (see Chapter 6), ranging from illicit drug production to human trafficking to weapons smuggling. Although industrialized states want to deal with these human security issues, which often threaten their own countries, there is reluctance to engage in the kind of sweeping economic reform and development programs that would encourage people to seek livelihood in the formal, rather than informal or so-called black market, economy. For example, in Afghanistan, it is far more lucrative for farmers to grow poppies for drug production than to grow legitimate food crops, and many farmers have their lives and the lives of their families threatened if they do not grow poppies. In a similar situation, what choice would you make? To change this situation will require a combination of economic development, access to markets for legitimate products, security for people against threats, and a significant drop in demand for goods such as drugs and services such as prostitution. Small initiatives will make a difference for some people in the poor parts of the world, but not for all.

Some have suggested that major reforms in international trade rules could offer long-term solutions for the cycles of economic poverty described above, while others contend that more trade liberalization is a possible panacea. Whether or not one accepts the reformist position or the neoliberal premise, recent developments in world trade negotiations are not encouraging. As we saw in Chapter 4, the push toward freer trade continued through the successive negotiation rounds of the General Agreement on Tariffs and Trade (GATT), culminating with the conclusion of the Uruguay Round in 1994. The Uruguay Round agreed to establish a new international organization to manage world trade, and in 1995 the World Trade Organization (WTO) was created. The WTO is an international organization headquartered in Geneva, staffed by a modest secretariat of 640 people; it inherits all of the results of the GATT negotiation rounds. In effect, the WTO replaces GATT, and therefore the organization is built on the principles of liberal trade theory: comparative advantage, tariff reduction, non-discrimination, national treatment, and regulatory harmonization. The WTO is the central forum for world trade negotiations, and WTO agreements reflect the ability of the 155 member states to reach agreement on trade liberalization. Biannual ministerial meetings are supposed to dictate WTO direction, and this ministerial

The Nobel Peace Prize for the Grameen Bank of Bangladesh, 2006. Accepting for the bank is Ms. Mosammat Taslima Begum and the bank's founder, Muhammad Yunus. The bank lends to over 7.5 million people in Bangladesh, 97 percent of them women. Loan recovery rates are 98 percent. The bank's model is now increasingly employed worldwide to provide credit and capital to poor populations, especially in rural areas. However, Yunus faces increasing political hostility in Bangladesh as he campaigns against corruption there, and some critics charge that the Bank ultimately supports a neoliberal agenda, further weakening the role of the state in development. (Kurt Peredersen/Stella Pictures/ABACAPRESS.COM)

council has subsidiary working bodies to administer WTO agreements in specialized areas of trade such as goods, services, the environment, and intellectual property. Countries accused of unfair trading practices must answer to the council, and other states are legally permitted to impose countervailing sanctions and to receive whatever compensation the WTO panel judges deem appropriate (see Profile 8.5). This dispute management system is a significant development, since GATT outcomes were often ignored. However, this process does give rise

---

PROFILE 8.5 **The WTO and Canada: Good News, Bad News**

Decisions made by the WTO will help some governments achieve their goals while hampering others. It will become increasingly difficult to promote free trade in some products and yet remain protectionist with others. Compare the two accounts below for an idea of how the WTO will sometimes give but sometimes take away.

CANADA AND THE JAPAN LIQUOR TAX CASE

In October 1996, the WTO Appellate Body requested that Japan change its liquor tax regime to remove barriers to imports of a wide variety of distilled liquor products (ranging from whiskey to gin). In Japan, imported distilled liquor is taxed at significantly higher rates than competing Japanese distilled spirits such as *shochu*. Canadian, European, and American distillers want to sell their products in Japan at what they consider fair prices. This was the first Appellate Body ruling involving Canada and was the second complaint involving Japanese barriers to imported liquor. (In 1987 a panel under GATT upheld a complaint by the European Commission that Japan's liquor tax law gave a competitive advantage to Japanese distilled liquor. Although Japan changed its law, *shochu* continued to receive preferential tax rates.) Under WTO rules, the Appellate Body report must be adopted within 30 days of being circulated to WTO members. Japan would then have 30 days to notify the WTO Dispute Settlement Body of its plans for implementing the report's recommendation. "I am very pleased with this ruling, a first for Canada," said Art Eggleton, Canada's international trade minister at the time. "It will end a long-standing dispute, and we expect that it will lead to higher Canadian exports to the Japanese distilled liquor market. I urge Japan to carry out the ruling quickly." Japan did not carry out the

ruling quickly, but began lowering taxes and tariffs on imported liquor in 1998.

SOURCE: DEPARTMENT OF FOREIGN AFFAIRS AND INTERNATIONAL TRADE, NEWS RELEASE, OCT. 4, 1996.

CANADA AND THE MAGAZINE CASE

In January 1997, a WTO panel ruled that the Canadian government's efforts to support the Canadian magazine industry violated world trade rules, finding that Ottawa was at fault for preventing the sale of magazines containing mostly U.S. editorial content. The case was filed by the Office of the U.S. Trade Representative at the Geneva-based WTO and followed a prolonged effort by Time Warner Inc. to establish an edition of *Sports Illustrated* magazine in Canada. The decision was regarded as a serious blow to Canadian government efforts to protect the cultural sector from Americanization. The decision by a WTO panel rejected Ottawa's attempts to prevent *Sports Illustrated* from publishing a Canadian edition with mostly U.S. editorial content. However, this was only part of the ruling, since the three-member panel also struck down key policies that supported the entire Canadian magazine industry and protected it from all-out competition, including preferential postal rates, a tariff restriction, and an up to 80 percent tax on split-run magazines. "We lost," said a Canadian governmental official. Canada now faced a choice of either implementing the WTO ruling or allowing Washington to establish trade barriers against Canadian products equivalent to protectionist measures directed against U.S. magazines. Although the Canadian government vowed to fight the ruling, in 1999 the two governments announced an agreement improving the access of U.S. publications to the Canadian market.

SOURCE: D. FAGAN AND L. EGGERTSON, "CANADA LOSES MAGAZINE CASE," *THE GLOBE AND MAIL*, JAN. 17, 1997, PG. A1.

to complaints (by both economic nationalists and antiglobalization activists) that the WTO represents the subordination of national sovereignty to an international organization without accountability to the citizens of individual states.

The WTO is entering a crucial phase in its short history. The current round of trade negotiations launched in November 2001, known as the Doha Round, have proven acrimonious and divisive. In August 2008 the Geneva meetings of the WTO collapsed without an agreement on relaxing trade barriers and lowering agricultural subsidies in wealthy states in order to better assist southern states to engage in world commodity exchanges. This is no small matter: government subsidies given to farmers in the OECD countries have averaged over US$300 billion per year in recent decades, undercutting foreign producers who cannot hope to compete against such massive support. The reduction of tariffs on farm goods would allow developing states' agricultural products to enter the rich countries' markets at a lower price to the consumer, the elimination of agricultural export subsidies by rich states would make developing states' products more competitive, and the reduction in industrial tariffs on certain products (especially textiles) would stimulate industrialization and economic growth in poor countries as their products could get better access to rich markets. The Doha agenda also promised liberalization in the trade of services, and would have established new global rules on the four "Singapore Issues" raised at an earlier WTO meeting: competition, investment, government procurement, and trade facilitation.

What went wrong? Put simply, in round after round of negotiations, countries were unwilling to make the concessions and politically difficult sacrifices necessary to reach agreements. The EU has refused to eliminate export subsidies, and the United States has offered unacceptably low reductions in its own subsidy programs. India argued that it had not agreed to discuss new rules on the Singapore Issues. Japan has refused to contemplate reductions in its tariffs on rice. A group of states led by China, Brazil, and India has insisted on unrealistically deep cuts to agricultural subsidies and liberalization of farm trade by rich countries. Other countries, especially in Africa, are less enthusiastic about liberalizing farm trade, as they believed this would threaten the preferential access they already enjoyed with Europe. Other African countries wanted to see the U.S. eliminate its cotton subsidies (it is the world's biggest exporter of cotton and the source of low world prices for that commodity). The prominence of the "most-favoured-nation status" principle means that a WTO state has to trade with other members as they would with their most favoured partners, and this is especially difficult for many states, such as China, to swallow, who have dubious records related to intellectual property and other contentious issues.

Trying to save the Doha Round. Pascal Lamy, the director-general of the World Trade Organization, has the difficult task of finding common ground among states in order to successfully conclude the negotiations of the Doha Round of trade talks. (© epa european pressphoto agency b.v./Alamy)

Many people—from environmentalists to trade unionists—resent the idea that global trade negotiations and a disconnected body in Geneva can make decisions that have such a large impact on national development issues (see Profile 8.6). Similar opposition, spread through the Internet, was discernible during the failed OECD negotiations for the establishment of the Multilateral Agreement on Investment (MAI), which would have taken the basic principles of trade agreements such as NAFTA and internationalized them, protecting international investors from government interference.[43] At any rate, it is clear that poverty will not

PROFILE 8.6 The Battle in Seattle

A group of Seattle police officers stand in a cloud of smoke near WTO protestors in downtown Seattle, November 30, 1999. Demonstrators temporarily succeeded in delaying the opening session of the WTO. This scene resembles a war zone, or police state, more than a liberal democracy. Is the conflict over trade liberalization leading to further divides in domestic as well as international social structures? (AP Photo/Beth A. Keiser/CP Images)

Civil disobedience is a time-honoured method of expressing one's opposition to government policies. An estimated 40 000 people took to the streets in Seattle in 1999 to register their opposition to the WTO as a regulatory body. Their main concern, although they had an impressive variety of concerns overall, was that the WTO was being granted too much power—the ability to make key decisions affecting people's health, environment, employment, and other issues. For many, the WTO represented the dark side of globalization. The sheer number of protestors surprised local authorities, and when a small minority became violent, the police responded with arrests and tear gas. Inside the WTO meetings, the ministers of member states were unable to reach a consensus on the issues that divided them. The meeting broke up with little in the way of substantive agreements.

The protestors had made their point, and the governments of the world could not make the WTO meetings a success, possibly because of the increased public awareness brought about by the debate over globalization. Similar, though less violent, protests were mounted during the IMF annual meeting in Washington in April 2000 and the Summit of the Americas in Quebec City in April 2001. Seattle, Washington, and Quebec City were just the beginning of a global campaign of protest against the institutions promoting globalization, and major summits and meetings of these institutions now regularly attract large protests and "alternate summits." The "Occupy Wall Street" protest of 2011 was an even broader social phenomenon, attracting hundreds of thousands across the industrialized world disgruntled by the contemporary global economy and income inequality.

be eradicated through trade liberalization alone; even the most successful trading states have great poverty in their midst. Much remains to be done, at all levels, to fight the scourges associated with impoverishment.

REGIONALIZATION IN THE WORLD ECONOMY

Partly as a result of the slow process characteristic of global trade negotiations, states have created a number of regional trade agreements with terms of trade that are preferential to those found in the WTO. That is, the member states of regional trade agreements have negotiated lower tariffs and more liberalized non-discrimination and national treatment regulations than those that exist at the world (WTO) level. This has raised the possibility that the future of trade liberalization rests not in the global arena through the WTO, but in various regions through regional trade agreements.

Much of the free trade debate is, in fact, oriented toward the relative merits of regional trade agreements. These agreements are sometimes called *preferential trade agreements*, because they represent regions, or zones, of preferred terms of trade among participating countries. In Europe, a process of economic integration has been under way since the 1950s. In 1957, the European Economic Community (EEC) created a **customs union** covering all products among its members. In 1967, The EC marked the successful elimination of most of the remaining impediments to the free flow of goods, labour, and capital across the borders of member states. In 1993, the EC became the European Union (EU) after the **Maastricht Treaty** was ratified. The EU has enlarged to a total of 27 member states as of 2012. Under the terms of the Maastricht Treaty, member states developed a monetary union that resulted in the establishment, and partial implementation, of a common currency, the **euro**.

Predictably, the process of integration in Europe has provoked protest over the loss of state control over national economies, social institutions, and culture. These concerns continue to plague the operation of the EU and the ability of governments to reach common policies on controversial issues. In particular, efforts to coordinate political and military policy through the EU have not been particularly successful. In 2005, a new constitution treaty for the EU that envisioned much deeper political and economic cooperation among member states was rejected in referendum votes in France and the Netherlands. This was considered a blow to further integration in Europe, and a statement by European voters that political and economic integration was proceeding too quickly and without due regard for national sovereignty on a host of economic, cultural, and political issues. In 2007, member states signed the Lisbon Treaty, designed to streamline economic and political decision making in the EU. In August 2008 Irish voters rejected the treaty in a referendum vote, but then accepted it in a subsequent referendum, and it came into force in 2009. Despite serious economic turmoil today, the EU remains the most highly integrated and institutionally developed of the world's trading areas, leading some to argue that the EU might one day become a truly supranational organization, perhaps even a "United States of Europe." In reality, the EU is far from this since member countries remain politically sovereign, although they have agreed to share decision-making responsibility and place some authority in the hands of the EU. This strategy is sometimes called **pooled sovereignty**.

The present EU, however, has moved beyond efforts at economic integration and toward monetary union as well, and this has proven to be a major issue with the advent of severe economic downturn and debt crises in several key eurozone states. Monetary union may have seemed a natural step forward, and many EU members had become tired of relying principally on the German economy and its central bank, the Bundesbank, which tends to raise interest rates quickly whenever inflation becomes a possibility.[44] By 2013, the euro was the official currency of 17 out of 27 EU member countries: Austria, Belgium, Cyprus, Estonia, Finland, France, Germany, Greece, Ireland, Italy, Luxembourg, Malta, the Netherlands, Portugal, Slovakia, Slovenia, and Spain. In other words, the euro is the currency in all EU states except the United Kingdom, Denmark, Sweden, and some of the new member states that joined on May 1, 2004, including the Czech Republic, Latvia, Lithuania, Hungary, Poland and Croatia. And yet Europe faces a serious economic crisis and the very future of the euro is at stake.

We have discussed the impact of sovereign debt elsewhere, but in few cases has it been demonstrated with such drama as the eurozone. In December 2008, in response to the global financial crisis of that year (see Chapter 4), the EU authorized a massive economic stimulation plan (200 billion euros). However, this was not sufficient to turn around the hard-hit economies of Spain, Ireland, Italy, and Greece, where government funding was easily outpacing revenue. The Germans had insisted that EU members maintain a certain debt-level ratio before joining the euro, but this had long been surpassed. (In the Greek case, an amazing debt ratio of almost 14 percent of GDP was eventually reported—not by Greece, but by the EU itself—while the requirement for entry into the eurozone had been set at 3 percent; in 2009, Greece admitted to over 300 billion euros in sovereign debt.) Investors were quickly losing faith in the euro, forcing governments to offer extraordinarily high interest rates as they tried to sell bonds. Severe austerity measures were introduced in several eurozone states, but this resulted in increased political instability and changes in government. Concerns rose about the future of all the most heavily indebted euro states, including Greece, Spain, Portugal, and Ireland.

February 7, 2012, austerity protest. Protesters clash with riot police at a rally in Athens, Greece, while trying to enter the Parliament during a 24-hour general strike. Widespread concerns with austerity measures amid high unemployment threw several EU countries into political turmoil. (© Greek photonews/Alamy)

In May of 2010, a 110 billion euro bailout plan for Greece was announced, followed by an 85 billion euro bailout for Ireland. In 2011, EU Ministers established a permanent European Stability Mechanism, renamed the European Financial Stability Facility, a 500 billion euro pool of emergency funding not entirely dissimilar to the IMF. A 78 billion euro bailout for Portugal soon followed, followed by a second, 109 billion euro, bailout for Greece. Austerity measures, including limits on entitlement spending, have been implemented in many of these states, but the crisis continues to unfold despite leaders' promises that the euro will not be permitted to fold and that countries such as Greece will be able to maintain their membership.

Critics argue that austerity is not the answer: government revenue must be provided through tax collection, anti-corruption measures, and increased taxation of the wealthy members of society, but there is no need to severely reduce hard-won entitlements or slash much-needed stimulus spending. Others suggest the euro crisis has served to reveal stark contrasts in national character, financial responsibility, and political stability, and that the implementation of the euro was a premature step in the first place. One thing is certain: especially after this experience, the EU's hazardous movement toward monetary union is unlikely to be repeated elsewhere. For example, it would be difficult to imagine the Federal Reserve of the United States and the Bank of Canada allowing some other agency to determine monetary policy for both states, though it is obvious that American monetary policy has a tremendous impact on the Canadian economy.

At the same time, we can argue that there is a noticeable trend toward regional integration in trade and investment and the creation of political mechanisms to facilitate this in other parts of the world as well. Examples include the **North American Free Trade Agreement (NAFTA)** and the **Association of Southeast Asian Nations (ASEAN)** Free Trade Area. These efforts present a potential tri-regional model of the future world economy centred on the Americas, Europe, and Asia, though we will see later that this makes less sense today than it appeared several decades ago.

Other regional trade arrangements also exist, including the Common Market of Eastern and Southern Africa and the Southern Common Market (also known as **Mercosur**). However, there has also been resistance to these regional trade agreements in member states. A plan to create a Free Trade Area of the Americas (FTAA) floundered amid domestic opposition to such an agreement in many countries and the opposition of several governments.

A regionalized model of trade may have different consequences than the more global approach encouraged by the WTO. Those liberals who argue that peace follows commerce might be concerned that dividing the world into three large trade zones will encourage a tri-polar mentality that might even lead to military conflict as the interests of the three areas begin to be incompatible. Liberals would also point out that a world largely managed by three regional blocs would in effect exclude most poor countries, though the composition of the **Trans Pacific Partnership (TPP)** challenges this assumption. The success of the WTO is therefore regarded as crucial, for the alternative is the greater isolation of lower-income from higher-income states. Others, especially those from the Marxist tradition, contend that each area will be a political empire of the dominant power and its capitalist classes. Thus, imperialism continues in a highly integrated fashion, and imperial powers will inevitably come into conflict as resources grow scarce and expansionism becomes the driving norm (this was, partially, Lenin's explanation of World War I).

Some of globalization's proponents might argue that regional integration is just a step along the road to a harmonized global economy. It occurs simultaneously as the world economy develops as well; the two processes reinforce rather than challenge each other. And, as regional organizations form, the political machinery of multilateralism is created. Though it has become almost habitual among students of international political economy to refer to the EU as the primary example of regional neofunctionalism, other situations exist in which states are engaging. A famous example, of course, is NAFTA, which includes Canada, the United States, and Mexico, and may soon include several Latin American countries as well. The Canada–U.S. Free Trade Agreement was signed in January 1989 between the two countries that exchange more goods and services than any other two in the world. This bilateral arrangement was expanded in 1992 with the addition of Mexico. NAFTA provides for the increased flow of goods and services across the borders of these states, especially in agriculture, automobile products, and clothing and textiles. The agreement was not without considerable controversy, as some Canadians felt that NAFTA posed a threat to Canadian sovereignty and culture and that NAFTA might threaten safety regulations and environmental protection in Canada, as well as social programs such as health care (such concerns continue today). Others were concerned that jobs would leave Canada and the United States and head to Mexico, where salaries are lower. Advocates of NAFTA responded that Canadian sovereignty, social programs, and standards were protected under NAFTA. (And these advocates point out today that there is little or no evidence to suggest that NAFTA has led to job losses in Canada.) Similar concerns about jobs were voiced in the United States, while in Mexico some expressed fears about becoming an economic colony of the United States.

Two side agreements accompanied NAFTA, one on labour and one on the environment. These were made largely to counter opposition on the grounds that NAFTA would promote the degradation of labour standards, wages, and the environment. The environmental agreement created the Commission for Environmental Cooperation (or CEC, headquartered in Montreal), and it has filtered funding to many NGOs that have developed projects related to sustainable development. Examples include a project by the Air and Waste Management Association (Ottawa) to advance air quality in Hamilton, Ontario, and Monterrey, Mexico; the development of non-wood forest products in Oaxaca, Mexico; and a water quality-monitoring project for Colonia residents in El Paso County/Valle de Juarez. However, critics charge that NAFTA, by encouraging investment along the U.S.–Mexican border, is designed primarily to keep Mexicans there (and not migrating northward) and will inevitably result in a lessening of environmental protection in the already heavily polluted maquiladora region.[45] The CEC has been criticized as an ineffective watchdog, having no real power to force any of the states to improve environmental standards.

In Asia, Japan is the regional leader, although the rise of China as the dominant economic power poses an obvious threat to that distinction. In Asia, however, regionalism is far less defined and far less institutionalized. In part, this difference is due to the tradition of bilateral economic diplomacy in Asia, as well as fear of Japanese and/or Chinese political hegemony (with the memory of World War II still fresh in people's memories). Nevertheless, some regional arrangements have taken shape, most notably ASEAN, established in 1967 to promote economic, political, and social cooperation among its members. ASEAN now comprises 10 countries. The Asian financial crisis of 1997, in which many of the large economies in the region suffered meltdowns (huge withdrawals of foreign investment and the crash of currencies, which began in Thailand and spread throughout the region), slowed Asian growth somewhat, but overall this area (and especially "socialist" China) retains the image of a capitalist boom.

More broadly, perhaps the most visible development in the world economy in the past few decades has been the emergence of the Pacific Rim as a major trading area. The Asia-Pacific

Economic Cooperation forum (APEC) was founded in 1989 and currently involves 21 countries that touch the Pacific Rim, states as diverse as Australia, Brunei, Canada, Indonesia, South Korea, Japan, Malaysia, China, Thailand, New Zealand, the Philippines, Singapore, Mexico, Hong Kong, Taiwan, Chile, the United States, and Papua New Guinea. In 1993, at Bill Clinton's suggestion, the conference met with official heads of state in attendance. This brought the leaders of China, Taiwan, and Hong Kong together for the first time (although this did not change the PRC/Taiwan/Hong Kong relationship: Taiwan continues to be denied state status by the Chinese, and Hong Kong became Chinese territory in 1997). However APEC is being transformed—indeed, superseded—with ongoing negotiations, recently joined by Canada (initially left out of the club, much to Ottawa's chagrin) for the establishment of the Trans Pacific Partnership. Other states involved in TPP negotiations include Australia, Brunei, Chile, Malaysia, Mexico, New Zealand, Peru, Singapore, the United States, and Vietnam, though it is expected that Japan and perhaps even China will join at a later date. This agreement zone would surpass NAFTA and the EU in terms of its market size and population. Negotiations so far have been highly secretive and it is difficult to speculate as to what, exactly, will be in the final agreement should one be reached. Meanwhile, Canada has signed a flurry of bilateral free trade deals in recent years (with Colombia, Honduras, Jordan, Panama, and Peru), and is pursuing talks with India, Japan, and other states. This suggests that there is no simple trifecta of regional trade agreements, but select opportunities that have been pursued by governments exhibiting a strong ideological commitment to free trade.

Will these economic regions coalesce into antagonistic trade blocs? Many fear that political and economic friction between countries, as well as pressure from disaffected publics, will promote protectionism and provoke trade wars between regions. Economic regionalism will turn into political regionalism, and the world will become balkanized and divided in a scenario not dissimilar to the interwar experience. Others are more optimistic, arguing that economic regions are beginning to overlap in their membership and that virtually all countries have a stake in the continued health of the global economy.

Barring a major military confrontation, which is always a possibility, trade among nations will probably increase as economic growth continues, which will please most liberals, some economic nationalists, few environmentalists, and even fewer neo-Marxists. Ironically, one of the more widely hailed benefits of international commerce—the idea that with increased trade comes increased mutual vulnerability and understanding, and thus the reduced likelihood of warfare—is often challenged by those who argue globalization is simply redirecting conflicts between states into the realm of economics. Regardless of the architecture of the world economy, however, there are several factors that will inevitably have a tremendous impact on its evolution. We explore many of them in subsequent chapters, but one is so fundamental we elect to introduce it here: the price of energy.

THE POLITICAL ECONOMY OF ENERGY PRODUCTION AND CONSUMPTION

The world economy is powered by a vast infrastructure of energy production, distribution, and consumption; without it, the wheels of the global economy would grind to a halt. The primary sources of energy today remain oil (approximately 33 percent of global energy supply), coal (approximately 27 percent), and natural gas (approximately 21 percent). It is clear that fossil fuels are by far the largest energy sources at present: combustible renewables (biofuels) and waste (10 percent), nuclear power (6 percent), and hydroelectricity (2 percent) make up relatively small shares of world supply, solar and wind power even less.[46] This reliance on fossil fuels continues to have a major impact on global politics in the form of conflicts over oil, disparities in energy access and consumption, and growing concern over the environmental damage caused by large-scale energy production and consumption. While fossil fuels are most often associated with environmental effects (especially with respect to climate change), hydro-electric dams are notorious for creating environmental damage, and nuclear power has proven expensive and produces highly radioactive waste. Global energy consumption patterns are characterized by high levels of disparity. The rich industrialized countries account for almost 50 percent of consumption. Citizens in North America consume far more energy resources per capita than all but a very few countries in the world.[47] Consumption is also very high per capita in Western Europe, Japan, and Australia. By comparison, citizens in South Asia and Africa consume very little energy on an individual basis, but China's unparalleled increase in demand has had a major impact on both oil prices and projections of climate change.

Oil remains synonymous with power and wealth. It is relatively cheap (if environmentally dangerous) to transport; it provides exporters, including Russia, Mexico, Venezuela, Canada and Nigeria, but especially the Persian Gulf states (Kuwait, Saudi Arabia, Iran, the United Arab Emirates, Qatar, Bahrain, Oman, and Iraq), with hard currency. To ensure a steady supply of oil from the Middle East, the area was colonized by the Europeans early in the 1900s and inundated with American MNCs after that. As we saw in Chapter 4, OPEC's oil price increases brought on worldwide confusion and **recession** in the early 1970s and 1980s. Though the George H.W. Bush administration in the United States and the UN Security Council emphasized the importance of protecting Kuwait's sovereignty, it is quite clear that dependence on Middle Eastern oil was an important contributory factor in causing the West to go to war against Iraq in 1991, and oil access was also a factor (though not the only factor) in the decision to invade Iraq in 2003.

As Hanns Maull writes, the two chief concerns regarding the control of oil are price stability and access:

> Price stability does not necessarily mean stable prices; it implies only that prices move smoothly, without drastic jumps, roughly in line with world inflation and towards the cost of alternative sources of energy. Access is defined as the availability of supplies in sufficient quantities over time without major disturbances.[48]

The chairman of Exxon, one of the world's largest oil multinationals, once complained that predicting oil prices was much like "trying to paint the wings of an airplane in flight."[49] When OPEC was founded in 1960, the price of oil was determined by that of Saudi Arabian light, a medium-density oil used as a standard for crude-oil prices until 1980. The price then was about US$2 per barrel. An Arab oil embargo after the Middle East war of 1973 caused widespread panic buying, and OPEC was able to raise the price of crude to US$11.50 a barrel by 1974. By January 1980, after the Iranian revolution induced further panic buying, Saudi Arabian light was selling for as much as US$36 a barrel. These prices not only contributed greatly to the recession of that time but also forced Western states to focus on alternative sources (such as North Sea oil) and conservation. World crude oil demand rose in the 1990s by nearly 12 percent, driving world prices for crude oil to nearly $40 a barrel in late 2000, a price that resurfaced in mid-2004. In the summer of 2008, oil soared to nearly $150 a barrel. For Canadians, this meant paying near $1.50 for a litre of gas (over $4 a gallon for Americans). The price rose due to a number of factors, including political instability in the Middle East, Nigeria, and Venezuela; an enormous boom in oil speculation in world markets; concerns over global warming; and the simple fact that it is becoming more and more difficult to profitably extract oil from the ground. Indeed, Canada is now the largest exporter of oil to the United States, not through conventional drilling techniques, but because of the huge tar sands projects displacing large swaths of the boreal forest in Alberta. The Harper government in Ottawa has referred to Canada as an "energy superpower," but the environmentally costly tar sands remain a contentious topic in both Canada and the U.S. As of 2013 the U.S. State Department had yet to make a final decision about the controversial "Keystone Pipeline" project that would pump Albertan crude south. Meanwhile, controversy about the development of the tar sands accelerated in 2012, due to strong opposition to the Enbridge Northern Gateway Pipelines project. The project proposes to build a twinned pipeline from Bruderheim, Alberta, to Kitimat, British Columbia. At Kitimat, the oil would be transferred to oil tankers bound for Asian markets. The Canadian government has maintained the pipeline is in Canada's economic interests, at it will create jobs and open the markets of Asia for Canadian tar sands oil. However, critics of the project argue that the economic benefits will not be widely spread, various First Nations do not support a pipeline running through their traditional and/or legal territories, and the environmental and economic impacts of a pipeline or tanker spill are simply too great for the project to proceed. Similar controversy has greeted plans to refashion or construct pipelines from west to east.

Over a barrel. Iraq's oil minister and OPEC president Abdul Kareem Luaibi, left, and OPEC Secretary-General Abdallah al-Badri arrive for a news conference after a meeting of OPEC oil ministers at their headquarters in Vienna on June 14, 2012. OPEC kept oil output limits at 30 million barrels a day, powerless to do anything other than hope top producer Saudi Arabia will scale back supplies unilaterally soon to stem a US$30 per barrel slide in prices. (Heinz-Peter Bader/Reuters)

It is difficult to overestimate the significance of a future severe spike in the price of oil, since the global economy is so reliant upon it. While upheaval in rich countries will probably remain confined to protests (such as the protests over fuel prices across Europe in May and July 2008) and the disruption of some industrial production, in many countries violence is possible as high oil prices undermine fragile economies and family incomes and help put food prices out of reach. Others suggest that the record profits recorded by big oil companies are reflective of the predatory capitalism that characterizes the global economy, permitting widely differentiated levels of capital accumulation and human suffering. There is also a demonstrable link between human rights violations and oil, a link reinforced in recent years by China's relationship with Sudan and the activities of Shell Oil in Nigeria.

Looking to the future, the World Energy Council suggests that by 2020, more than 90 million barrels of oil will be consumed daily and that coal output will almost double to seven billion tonnes. So, too, will natural gas demand double, reaching four trillion cubic metres. This huge increase in energy demand will result from the increasing industrialization of the Latin American and, especially, Asian regions.[50] China, the world's sixth-biggest oil producer (ahead of Venezuela), became a net oil importer at the end of 1993. It will have to rely heavily on the Middle East and Africa for its supply, further complicating regional geopolitics in places such as Sudan, and on the prospect of oil deposits in the heavily contested South China Sea. Furthermore, China's energy future is crucial to efforts to control global warming (see Chapter 10). Several factors have emerged, however, since the latest World Energy Council forecast, including the inconclusive continuation of climate change negotiations in Copenhagen and elsewhere; the global recession of 2008 and the euro crisis, which lowered energy demands from various industries; the rise of unconventional gas sources (shale, tight sands, and coalbed methane), not just in North America but in China, Australia, and parts of Europe, along with controversies over hydraulic fracking technology; and two environmental catastrophes: the disastrous BP Gulf of Mexico oil spill in the spring of 2010, and the leak of radioactive material from the Fukushima Daiichi nuclear power facility following the March 2011 Tsunami in Japan. All of these events demonstrate the inherent volatility of energy markets and dangers of energy production.

Ultimately, many analysts believe that a global conversion toward alternative fuel sources must take place, and in particular to the renewable resources such as wind, geothermal, wave, and solar power that many environmentalists have advocated for decades. This conversion is especially important for developing countries: in India, for example, two million small power plants are turning cow dung into electric power and cooking fuel.[51] Efforts to switch to "biofuels," however, have fuelled more debate than cars. Although such programs have been successful in some countries (such as Brazil's sugar cane-to-fuel system) it is phantasmal to think the millions of cars in North America will run on corn any time soon. Moreover, the rush toward biofuel production helps drive food prices upward and raises serious questions about the ethics of producing food for fuel in a world where billions are malnourished. This conundrum hit home in the United States, committed to directing 40 percent of corn production toward biofuels, when a severe drought stumped the harvest in the summer and fall of 2012, driving up food prices.

Optimistically, the push for increased efficiency by environmentalists and managerial elites alike will force states such as China and the United States to mitigate the potential excesses of development and further explore renewable energy sources. Technological improvements and even lifestyle changes in the West have, in some cases, reduced energy consumption, though overall it continues to rise. Most states have an avenue toward energy self-sufficiency; Canada has huge oil and natural gas reserves (including the unexplored reserves under melting

Arctic ice), for example, though its heavy reliance on tar sands oil production is based largely on revenue related to American consumption. The basic fact, despite the proclamations of both presidential candidates in the United States in 2012, is that true energy security is elusive and cannot be confined to a national economy. And yet we have no global mechanisms for energy governance: the International Energy Agency, the G8, the International Partnership for Energy Efficiency Cooperation, the OECD, the IAEA, and other arrangements are basically uncoordinated efforts. As realists would suggest, energy is tied so tightly to national security that it is unlikely a global energy strategy will be formulated any time soon. Yet it is increasingly recognized as a global problem.

Finally, fuel for human movement—the food that sustains and powers us as living organisms—is also rising in price at an alarming rate. There are many reasons for the increase in food prices, including increased demand for meat in the rapidly expanding economies in Asia, increases in oil prices which drive production and transportation costs upward, speculative bidding on food futures markets, prolonged droughts which some scientists attribute to climate change, and the displacement of food crops for the production of biofuels. Rising food prices harm the poor, increase political instability, and force governments and people alike into further debt. The concern with reaching peak oil—a condition whereby extracting oil will simply become too expensive to fuel all the things we now take for granted, from transportation to agricultural production—has given rise to a new literature on coping with a post-oil future, with some authors even suggesting peak oil will lead to the end of globalization.[52] Yet few politicians are willing to publicly discuss this eventuality, and the newfound deposits of shale gas and plans to drill in the Arctic are obscuring this broader discussion. Oil is used to make our clothes, roads, bread, appliances, plastics, and meat, and provide household heating and other daily needs. If we were to find ourselves in a situation where oil was simply not available, through some combination of military conflict, price raises, climate change legislation, and other factors, how would we manage to maintain political stability? How would we adjust? Clearly, we need to get thinking about this!

CONCLUSIONS

This chapter has reinforced the central paradox of global politics. While the global economy displays a trend toward *convergence* in the form of increased trade between countries and peoples, increased levels of global and regional economic cooperation and management, and growing financial interdependence and levels of transactions across state borders, one can also identify trends of *divergence*, in the form of the regionalization of the global economy, the persistence of economic nationalism, serious challenges to the ideals of the EU, and the widening gap between the rich and poor peoples of the world.

All the key variables discussed above, as well as many others, will continue to affect the development of the world economy. We should also keep in mind that other topics discussed in this text, such as resource scarcity, overpopulation, and military spending, will further affect economic outcomes. Indeed, from the vantage point of 2013, it appears that we can expect much more turmoil and hardship in the global economy of the near future. It is unlikely that the promise of liberal economics and short-term Keynesian spending can possibly overcome these challenges, leaving us with the question of how the global economy can be reformed or transformed to enhance social stability and improve the human condition while respecting environmental limits. Ultimately, this is a question pertaining to the quality of human life and dignity, a topic to which we turn in our next chapter.

Endnotes

1. Quoted in *The Globe and Mail*, July 17, 1996, A10.

2. See *Development and Globalization: Facts and Figures 2012* (New York and Geneva: United Nations Conference on Trade and Development, 2012), http://dgff.unctad.org/chapter2/2.1.html (accessed January 21, 2012).

3. Branco Milanovic, "Global Income Inequality by the Numbers: In History and Now, An Overview." *Policy Research Working Paper 6259* (Washington, DC: The World Bank Development Research Group, Poverty and Inequality Division, 2012), 8–9.

4. *Human Development Report, 2011/2012* (New York: United Nations Development Program, 2012), http://hdrstats.undp.org/en/countries/profiles/CAN.html; http://hdrstats.undp.org/en/countries/profiles/NER.html. The 2013 report puts Canada at 11th; Niger remains in last place, at 186th. *Human Development Report 2013: The Rise of the South* (New York: UNDP, 2013).

5. T. Friedman, *The World Is Flat: A Brief History of the 21st Century* (New York: Farrar Straus and Giroux, 2006). See also J. Bhagwati, *In Defense of Globalization* (New York: Oxford University Press, 2004); and M. Wolf, *Why Globalization Works* (New Haven: Yale University Press, 2004).

6. P. Collier, *The Bottom Billion: Why the Poorest Countries Are Failing and What Can Be Done about It* (Oxford: Oxford University Press, 2007).

7. For example, see A. McGrew and N. Poku, eds., *Globalization, Development and Human Security* (Cambridge: Polity, 2007); and B. Milanovic, *Worlds Apart: Measuring International and Global Inequality* (Princeton: Princeton University Press, 2005).

8. See *The Millennium Development Goals Report 2012* (New York: United Nations, 2012).

9. R. Isaac, *Managing World Economic Change: International Political Economy*, 2nd ed. (Englewood Cliffs, NJ: Prentice Hall, 1995), 30. As Michael Mastanduno argues, "Even if nation-states do not fear for their physical survival, they worry that a decrease in their power capabilities relative to those in other nation-states will compromise their political autonomy, expose them to the influence attempts of others, or lessen their ability to prevail in political disputes with allies and adversaries." See M. Mastanduno, "Do Relative Gains Matter? America's Response to Japanese Industrial Policy," *International Security* 16 (Summer 1991), 78.

10. *Who Answers to Women? Gender and Accountability. Progress of the World's Women, 2008/2009* (New York: United Nations Development Fund for Women, 2008), 53–8. See also International Labour Organization, *Global Employment Trends for Women* (Geneva: International Labour Office, 2008), 2, http://www.ilo.org/global/about-the-ilo/newsroom/news/WCMS_195445/lang--en/index.htm (accessed June 30, 2013).

11. *Who Answers to Women? Gender and Accountability*, 61.

12. United Nations Office on Drugs and Crime, *Global Report on Trafficking in Humans* (February 2009), 10; and European Commission, Department of Justice and Home Affairs, *Trafficking in Women: The Misery behind the Fantasy: From Poverty to Sex Slavery: A Comprehensive European Strategy*, http://www.refworld.org/pdfid/4693aa7f2.pdf (accessed June 20, 2013). See also K. Kempadoo, *Global Sex Workers: Rights, Resistance and Redefinition* (London: Routledge, 1998).

13. See J. Bystydzienski, ed., *Women Transforming Politics: Worldwide Strategies for Empowerment* (Bloomington: Indiana University Press, 1992); on microfinance, see http://www.microfinancegateway.org; see also M. Yunus, *Banker to the Poor: Micro-Lending and the Battle against World Poverty* (New York: Perseus, 2007). For a review of feminism and globalization see M.E. Hawkesworth, *Globalization and Feminist Activism* (Lanham, MD: Rowman and Littlefield, 2006).

14. See V. Shiva, *Staying Alive: Women, Ecology, and Development* (London: Zed, 1998); B. Cook, *Women Writing Nature: A Feminist View* (Lanham: Lexington Books, 2007); and R. Ruether, *Integrating Ecofeminism, Globalization, and World Religions* (Lanham: Rowman and Littlefield, 2005); and for a critical analysis, see J. Biehl, *Finding Our Way: Rethinking Ecofeminist Politics* (Montreal: Black Rose Books, 1991).

15. The World Commission on Environment and Development, *Our Common Future* (Oxford: Oxford University Press, 1987). In fact, an entire subfield, referred to as *ecological economics*, has emerged in recent decades. See also R. Paehlke, *Democracy's Dilemma: Environment, Social Equity, and the Global Economy* (Cambridge, MA: MIT Press, 2003).

16. An important work in this direction was J. MacNeil, P. Winsemius, and Taizo Yakushiji, *Beyond Interdependence: The Meshing of the World's Economy and the Earth's Ecology* (Oxford: Oxford University Press, 1992), 32.

17. For an expanded treatment of this section, see P. Stoett, *Human and Global Security: An Exploration of Terms* (Toronto: University of Toronto Press, 2000), 97–118.

18. See W. Greider, *One World, Ready or Not: The Manic Logic of Global Capitalism* (New York: Simon and Schuster, 1997); J. Gélinas, *Juggernaut Politics: Understanding Predatory Globalization* (London: Zed Books, 2003); J. Petras and H. Veltmeyer, *System in Crisis: The Dynamics of Free Market Capitalism* (London: Zed Books, 2003); and T. Smith, *Globalisation: A Systematic Marxian Account* (Boston: Brill, 2006). For discussions of the relationship between globalization and social change see B. Barber, "Jihad vs. McWorld," *Atlantic*, March 1992, 53–63; R. White, *Global Spin: Probing the Civilization Debate* (Toronto: Dundurn, 1995), 127. See also A. Linklater, "Globalization and the Transformation of Political Community," in J. Baylis and S. Smith, eds., *The Globalization of World Politics: An Introduction to International Relations*, 2nd ed. (Oxford: Oxford University Press, 2001), 617–34; and U. Schuerkens, ed., *Globalization and Transformations of Local Socioeconomic Practices* (New York: Routledge, 2008).

19. M. Waters, *Globalization* (London: Routledge, 1995), 3.

20. Ibid., 4.

21. R. Cox, "The Global Political Economy and Social Choice," in D. Drache and M. Gertler, eds., *The New Era of Global Competition: State Policy and Market Power* (Montreal/Kingston: McGill-Queen's University Press, 1991), 335–49, 336.

22. J. Frieden, *Global Capitalism: Its Fall and Rise in the Twentieth Century* (New York: W.W. Norton and Company, 2006), xvi–xvii. For explorations of globalization, see A. MacGillivray, *A Brief History of Globalization: The Untold Story of Our Incredibly Shrinking Planet* (London: Robinson, 2006); S. Dasgupta and R. Kiely, eds., *Globalization and After* (Thousand Oaks, CA: Sage Publications, 2007); L.W. Pauly and W.D. Coleman, eds., *Global Ordering: Institutions and Autonomy in a Changing World* (Vancouver: UBC Press, 2008); and R. Munck, *Globalization and Contestation: The New Great Counter-Movement* (New York: Routledge, 2007).

23. V. Kavolis, "Contemporary Moral Cultures and 'the Return of the Sacred,'" *Sociological Analysis* 49, no. 3 (1988), 203–16.

24. J. Williamson, "What Should the World Bank Think about the Washington Consensus?" (Washington DC: Institute for International Economics, July 1999).

25. S. Strange, *Casino Capitalism* (NY: Blackwell, 1986). On today's currency trade, see A. Balakrishnan, "Daily Currency Trade Equal to Germany's Annual Output," *The Guardian*, September 26, 2007.

26. See M. ul Haq, I. Kaul, and I. Grunberg, eds., *The Tobin Tax: Coping with Financial Volatility* (Oxford: Oxford University Press, 1996).

27. "Floating the Tobin Tax," *The Economist*, July 13, 1996, 84.

28. See, for example, J. Goodman, *Protest and Globalisation: Prospects for Transnational Solidarity* (Annandale: Pluto Press, 2002). On the Occupy movement, see S. van Gelder, ed., *This Changes Everything: Occupy Wall Street and the 99% Movement* (San Francisco: Barrett-Koehler, 2011).

29. R. Vernon, *Sovereignty at Bay: The Multinational Spread of U.S. Enterprises* (New York: Basic, 1971); R. Barnet and R. Muller, *Global Reach: The Power of Multinational Corporations* (New York: Simon and Schuster, 1974). For studies on the role of multinational corporations in world affairs, see S.D. Cohen, *Multinational Corporations and Foreign Direct Investment: Avoiding Simplicity, Embracing Complexity* (New York: Oxford University Press, 2007); L. Cuyvers and F. De Beule, eds., *Transnational Corporations and Economic Development: From Internationalization to Globalization* (New York: Palgrave, 2005); and O. de Schutter, ed., *Transnational Corporations and Human Rights* (Oxford: Hart, 2006).

30. See, for example, K. Levitt, *Silent Surrender: The Multinational Corporation in Canada* (Toronto: Macmillan, 1970). On the controversial Nexen deal, see the CBC report at http://www.cbc.ca/news/politics/story/2012/08/30/pol-weston-cnooc-nexen-oil-china-canada-takeovers.html. Many speculate that China's main interest is not in obtaining access to tar sands oil, but in acquiring the technology needed to develop their own oil sands industry. Though the Canadian government turned down an earlier effort by an Australian firm to buy Potash Corp. of Saskatchewan Inc., the Chinese and Malaysian deals proved harder to reject.

31. *World Investment Report 2010: Transnational Corporations and the Infrastructure Challenge* (New York and Geneva: UNCTD, 2010), http://unctad.org/en/docs/wir2009_en.pdf. See also *World Investment Report 2007: Transnational Corporations, Extractive Industries, and Development* (New York and Geneva: UNCTD, 2007), xvi.

32. See UNDP, *Human Development Report, 1996* (New York: Oxford University Press, 1996), 2; World Bank Indicators Database, see http://www.worldbank.org/topic (accessed June 21, 2013); and *World Development Indicators 2012* (The World Bank, 2012), 209. For explorations of international development issues, see T. Addison, T. Shorrocks, and A. Swallow, eds., *Development Agendas and Insights: 20 Years UN-WIDER Research* (Helsinki: United Nations University, 2005); and J. S. Saul, *Development after Globalization: Theory and Practice for an Embattled South in a New Imperial Age* (Blackpoint, NS: Fernwood Publishers, 2006).

33. J.B. Davies, S. Sandström, A. Sharrocks, and E.N. Wolff, *The World Distribution of Household Wealth*, United Nations University—World Institute for Development Economics Research Discussion Paper no. 2008/03 (February 2008), 7.

34. *2008 World Development Indicators* (Washington, DC: The World Bank, 2008), 4.

35. See The World Bank: Projects and Operations, http://web.worldbank.org/WBSITE/EXTERNAL/EXTABOU TUS/0,,contentMDK:20103853~menuPK:8336850~pagePK:51123644~piPK:329829~theSitePK:29708,00 .html (accessed January 24, 2013).

36. See *The Millennium Development Goals Report 2012* (New York: United Nations, 2012), 4; and *Human Development Report, 2007/2008* (New York: United Nations Development Programme, 2007), 25.

37. *Maternal Mortality in 2005: Estimates Developed by WHO, UNICEF, UNFPA, and the World Bank* (Geneva: World Health Organization, 2005), 1.

38. See T. Lairson and D. Skidmore, *International Political Economy* (Fort Worth, TX: Harcourt Brace, 1993), 65–6; S. George, *The Debt Boomerang* (Boulder, CO: Westview Press, 1992); and S. George, *A Fate Worse Than Debt* (Harmondsworth: Penguin, 1988).

39. See World Resources Institute, *Earthtrends*, http://www.wri.org/project/earthtrends/ (accessed June 30, 2013); and http://data.worldbank.org/sites/default/files/gdf_2012.pdf (accessed May 5, 2012). For an impressive compilation of data on so-called Third World Debt, including the fact that southern states have in effect paid 7.5 Marshall Plans back to northern states in debt financing since 1945, see the website of the Committee for the Abolition of Third World Debt, at http://cadtm.org/IMG/pdf/DEF_Figures_relating_to _the_Debt_Vademecum_2009_FEB_2009.pdf.

40. See J. Gettleman, "Darfur Withers as Sudan Sells a Food Bonanza," *International Herald Tribune*, August 10, 2008.

41. UNCTAD Secretariat, *Technology: Development Aspects of the Reverse Transfer of Technology*, Report of the Secretariat (New York: United Nations, 1979), para. 6.

42. See *Women and Men in the Informal Economy: A Statistical Picture* (Geneva: International Labour Office, 2002), 10.

43. There is a Canadian connection here, since the Council of Canadians, often described as an antiglobalization coalition, was the organization that initially circulated a copy of the proposed MAI over the Internet in April 1997. See T. Clark and M. Barlow, *MAI: The Multilateral Agreement on Investment and the Threat to Canadian Sovereignty* (Toronto: Stoddart, 1997), 21–2.

44. One of the reasons some EU members were fond of the more flexible euro concept is that the Bundesbank has had such a strong anti-inflationary agenda that it has resulted in a "single-minded fixation on price stability [that] has left Europe facing a long-term crisis of joblessness." J. Laxer, "Germans Are Creating a Monetary Quagmire," *Toronto Star*, July 21, 1996, F3. More generally on regionalization, see A. Hülsemeyer, *Globalization in the Twenty-First Century: Convergence or Divergence?* (New York: Palgrave Macmillan, 2003).

45. For a balanced analysis see S. Mumme, "NAFTA and Environment," *Foreign Policy in Focus*, http://www.fpif .org/reports/nafta_and_environment; and K. Gallagher, *Free Trade and the Environment: Mexico, NAFTA, and Beyond* (Stanford University Press, 2004).

46. All data from 2006, in International Energy Agency, *Key World Energy Statistics 2008* (2008), 6, http://www .iea.org (accessed June 18, 2013).

47. See "Energy Consumption: Consumption per Capita," Energy and Resources database, World Resources Institute, http://earthtrends.wri.org (accessed June 20, 2013); and recent Human Development Index Reports.

48. H. Maull, "The Control of Oil," *International Journal* 36, no. 2 (1981), 273–93. For a review of the politics of oil, see F.R. Parra, *Oil Politics: A Modern History of Petroleum* (New York: I.B. Tauris, 2004); and T. Shelley, *Oil: Politics, Poverty and the Planet* (New York: Zed Books, 2005).

49. Quoted in *The Globe and Mail*, March 15, 1994.

50. "Survey," *The Economist*, June 18, 1994, 1–6.

51. P. Sampat, *World Watch*, November/December 1995, 21–3.

52. J. Rubin, *Why Your World is About to Get a Whole Lot Smaller: Oil and the End of Globalization* (New York: Random House, 2009); see also J. Leggett, *The Empty Tank: Oil, Gas, Hot Air, and the Coming Global Financial Catastrophe* (New York: Random House, 2005); more broadly, see D. Lesage, T. van de Graaf, and K. Westphal, *Global Energy Governance in a Multipolar World* (London: Ashgate, 2010); and P. Stoett, *Global Ecopolitics: Crisis, Governance, and Justice* (University of Toronto Press, 2012), 187–9.

Human Rights and Human Security

CHAPTER 9

No one shall be subjected to torture or to cruel, inhuman or degrading treatment or punishment.

—*Universal Declaration of Human Rights, 1948, Article 5*

There is little evidence to suggest that mankind has advanced much beyond [the] level of jungle morality.

—*Robert Gilpin[1]*

INTRODUCTION: CAN WE INSTITUTIONALIZE ETHICS ON A WORLD SCALE?

Few would argue that sovereign governments do not have a "responsibility to protect" their own citizens from the most egregious of crimes. But does the international community have a corresponding responsibility to physically intervene in countries where governments are committing grave violations of human rights (such as genocide, forced migration, or ethnic cleansing)? This high-profile, age-old question has dominated much of the recent discussion on Libya, Syria, Rwanda, and other cases, as well as the broader normative debate on the "responsibility to protect" doctrine, to which we will soon return. But it is important to note also that most human rights violations pass unnoticed or largely ignored, hidden by perpetrators, lost behind more publicized events, or subordinated to more urgent political priorities or national interests. Humanitarian and human rights law (introduced in Chapter 5) is more developed than ever, but as a mechanism to prevent and respond to human rights violations and humanitarian crises it still faces serious challenges: the privileged position of states over individuals, the continued resort to force by both state and non-state actors, the impact of globalization on economic and social rights, and the erosion of civil liberties by counterterrorism policies.

Human rights issues continue to exert influence on the security, economic, and sustainable development agendas, and reflect our twin themes of convergence and divergence in global politics. Although we have discussed **human security** in many other chapters, we will also give it explicit attention here, since the promotion and protection of human rights is a fundamental aspect of its provision, and humanitarian intervention remains one of the most daunting issues on this agenda.

In March of 1995, Canadians mourned the death of Professor John Peter Humphrey, the founder and first director of the United Nations Human Rights Division, a post he held for 20 years. He also founded the Canadian Human Rights Foundation and the Canadian branch of Amnesty International, a non-governmental organization dedicated to protecting citizens from state human rights abuses. However, Professor Humphrey will be most widely remembered for his contributions to the writing of the Universal Declaration of Human Rights.[2] Most observers consider it a largely symbolic work, albeit one of great significance; as a declaration, it does not carry the status of international law attributed to a convention or treaty. This is but one example of the general frustration with international law encountered by those who would aspire to produce a more standardized global human rights regime. As discussed in Chapter 5, some wonder whether law can even be said to exist if there is no formal, coercive mechanism to enforce it. Though states will often engage in punitive measures to attempt to enforce trade agreements, or to punish gross violations of human rights such as the institutionalization of apartheid by the former South African government, it is another thing entirely to speak of a systematic law applied consistently across the globe.

However, the absence of an enforcer does not imply that international law, in a less strict sense, does not exist. One might argue that outside the confines of a domestic legal system, a law that relies on force alone for its legitimacy is essentially tyrannical and bound to be short-lived. International law is a system in which consent-granting state leaders choose to participate not because they have to—though some pressure does exist—but because they believe that it will ultimately benefit them. For realists, this is the essential explanation for the existence of international law: it is an example of self-interested cooperation in an anarchic international system, tied to the emergence of the modern nation state. The Roman and British empires spread law throughout many lands, but it was the law of a coercive empire, not of consensual states. When Hugo Grotius published his *De jure belli ac pacis* (*On the Law of War and Peace*) in 1625, he was writing in an age when the dominant European colonial powers were defining international law and imposing it on the rest of the world (see Chapter 5). The periods of decolonization that followed, especially after World War II, have at least in part changed this perception.

Formal state sovereignty, and its protection in documents such as the UN Charter, ensures that international law is not imposed by Romans or Europeans but has gained the acceptance of self-determining members of the international community. It might be argued that the participation of states in international legal arrangements reflects an even stronger incentive to comply than if that system of law were coercive or imposed. However, one of the problems with this perspective is that in many areas of international law, including questions about human rights, the people most threatened by abuses are the citizens of states, and not those who control the government in power. The principle of territorial sovereignty does not distinguish between democratically elected leaders and tyrants, and many citizens are victims of human rights abuses by authoritarian governments who refuse to respect international human rights law, and then reject international pressure to change their behaviour as interference in their domestic affairs. Another problem is that conceptions of human rights vary, on both philosophical and political grounds. This variation raises the tricky question of whether the international community has an obligation, or for that matter the authority, to institutionalize some universal conceptions of justice, law, and human rights on an international level. However, recent movements toward individual accountability under international law, such as the development of the International Criminal Court (ICC), suggest we may be moving toward a system characterized by both state voluntarism and a potentially viable, if highly controversial, effort to hold state leaders responsible for the more egregious crimes against humanity. We expand on these questions below when we discuss human rights law more specifically. For now we will examine the essential divisions of opinion on human rights. (See Profile 9.1 for recognition of human rights issues throughout the year declared by the United Nations.)

As we noted above, serious philosophical differences of opinion exist regarding human rights. The first debate concerns the subject matter and its definition: do we focus on the political rights of the individual or the socio-economic rights of the collective? The tension between the two has been the source of considerable political controversy in global politics and a mainstay of heated debate. A second debate revolves around the question of whether human rights is a relative or a universal concept. Some charge that the prevalent approach to human rights is an imposed Western idea, and that civilizations, societies, peoples, and groups have different conceptions of the term. Others argue that basic human rights are universal for all peoples. A third debate concerns the usefulness and effectiveness of international laws to protect and promote human rights and human security. As you might anticipate, each theoretical perspective on global politics that we have introduced in this book regards human rights issues from a different vantage point.

INDIVIDUAL VERSUS COLLECTIVE CONCEPTIONS OF HUMAN RIGHTS

During the Cold War (see Chapter 3) it became standard for the two opposing camps to each present their vision of human rights as morally superior. The West insisted that the individual is the most important component of any political system, and that an individual's rights must be protected from encroachment by the state. The Soviet Union naturally rejected this definition of human rights, arguing that collective rights, or those of entire populations, had to come first. The communist parties of the East rejected the right to private property, long taken as a fundamental right in the West. They also rejected the right to practise religion freely, which remains a highly contested right in some societies today where a single religion is instituted as that of the nation-state, such as in Iran. Even in Western states, repetitious references to God and country by political leaders raise concerns about protecting religious diversity and tolerance.

We are engaging in what some might consider excessive dichotomization here. Every society needs some sort of balance between the individual and collective conceptions of rights, such as the right to individual liberties and the right to be free from life-threatening poverty. Individual rights can be superseded in the most liberal states by the need to protect collective rights; for example, in many parts of the United States, a self-declared bastion of civil liberty, state governments can still kill people who are found guilty of certain crimes. Sometimes, the logic of group rights can lead to divisive debate. For example, the Universal Declaration states that "the family is the natural and fundamental group unit of society and is entitled to protection by society and the State" (Article 16/3). This statement remains open to interpretation and can be used to challenge (or support) the legitimacy of same-sex marriage. In Canada, there are competing conceptions of which should take precedence, the individual or groups such as francophones in Quebec or First Nations peoples. States such as Malaysia have argued that Western notions of individual liberty are fine, but they should not be imposed on non-Western states that emphasize collective rights. Human rights groups such as Amnesty International argue

International Days and Weeks Declared by the United Nations Related to Human Rights

Note that most of the days and weeks declared by the UN celebrate some sort of human-rights-related issue. But does all this celebration really advance these causes?

January 27	International Day of Commemoration in Memory of Victims of the Holocaust	Third Tuesday of September	International Day of Peace
February 21	International Mother Language Day	October 1	International Day of Older Persons
March 8	International Women's Day	First Monday of October	World Habitat Day
March 21	International Day for the Elimination of Racial Discrimination	October 10	World Mental Health Day
March 21–28	Week of Solidarity with the Peoples Struggling against Racism and Racial Discrimination	October 16	World Food Day
March 22	World Water Day	October 17	International Day for the Eradication of Poverty
March 23	World Meteorological Day	October 24	United Nations Day
April 7	World Health Day	October 24–30	Disarmament Week
May 3	World Press Freedom Day	November 6	Day for Preventing the Exploitation of the Environment in War and Armed Conflict
May 15	International Day of Families	Week of November 11	International Week of Science and Peace
May 17	World Telecommunications Day/World Information Society Day	November 20	Universal Children's Day
May 31	World No-Tobacco Day	November 20	Africa Industrialization Day
June 4	International Day of Innocent Children Victims of Aggression	November 29	International Day of Solidarity with the Palestinian People
June 5	World Environment Day	December 1	World AIDS Day
June 12	World Day against Child Labour	December 3	International Day of Disabled Persons
June 20	World Refugee Day	December 5	International Volunteer Day for Economic and Social Development
June 26	International Day against Drug Abuse and Illicit Trafficking	December 10	Human Rights Day
July 11	World Population Day	December 18	International Migrants Day
August 9	World's Indigenous People Day	December 20	International Human Solidarity Day
September 8	International Literacy Day		

that there are some things all individuals should be protected from, including repression and **torture** at the hands of the state. This helps form the basic argument that in international law, *jus cogens* (preemptory norms that override all treaties or agreements), universally agreed standards, and protections from the more extreme violations of human rights, do in fact exist. But, beyond the right to life itself (and even this is highly controversial in the abortion debate), which norms or belief systems should receive universal protection?

RELATIVISM VERSUS UNIVERSALISM IN HUMAN RIGHTS

In the African country of Ghana, a few isolated communities still practise an ancient Ewe custom, shared by other communities in Togo, Benin, and southwest Nigeria. The custom holds that for serious crimes against the community such as murder, rape, or theft, "the spirits can be appeased only by the enslavement of young [female] virgins from the offender's family in the shrines of traditional priests." This enslavement of girls as young as 12 includes the expectation that the girls will participate in sexual acts with the priests. Many Ghanaians are campaigning against the practice, which is said to have enslaved "as many as 10,000 girls." But in the Ghanaian coastal village of Tefle, many of the village men insist they have the right to practise what they consider to be a vital custom.[3] This is an extreme case; others, such as child labour, invoke similar feelings of horror among Westerners accustomed to a different set of principles. However, many Africans and South Americans consider the Western tradition of putting older citizens into retirement facilities instead of keeping them at home with extended families to be equally barbaric, and the lack of care for the homeless in major urban centres is viewed with similar disdain. So we realize that there are cultural differences between different societies, as there have always been. The question is whether some practices, often claimed as integral to those cultures, should be universally condemned.

As suggested above, we have to ask also whether it is even appropriate to condemn some states for human rights violations: what gives anyone, or another state, the right to make such pronouncements? Some postmodern theorists reject the premise of a universal moral order, arguing that norms and principles are subject to a specific time and place. In other words, what is morally acceptable today may not be tomorrow; this is certainly the case with some widespread institutions, such as that of slavery in the Americas. It has been suggested that as we progress toward a more civilized world order, we are redefining certain types of behaviour as illegitimate. As described in Chapter 5, the institutionalization of this process of redefinition has been specifically referred to as the social construction of **global prohibition regimes**: they are guided by norms that "strictly circumscribe the conditions under which states can participate in and authorize these activities and proscribe all involvement by nonstate actors."[4] Once we have made some sort of collective decision regarding the immorality of an act or even a sociopolitical system, such as the former apartheid in South Africa, or state repression in Burma, then we should make an attempt to universalize this decision and spread it around the world, through education or outright coercion.

To many, this sounds rather confusing, for while global prohibition regimes may have the most progressive of foundations (such as outlawing slavery, for example), they also imply that the majority (or perhaps merely the strong) has the moral right (or even duty) to impose its will on others. Is this much different from what the imperial powers did during the dark years of colonial administration? Does this simply replace the old political and economic dominance of the West with a new form of **cultural imperialism**?[5] The latter term usually refers to the imposition of one society's values on another, through either the force of law (as in direct colonialism) or the less overt manipulation of minds through the media (television, radio, newspapers, or even the Internet). However, when it comes to standards of international law and human rights in particular, the promotion of Western values with aid policies designed to award liberal democratization are equally suspect, as are rhetoric-laden UN resolutions, which can be seen as the soft law of cultural imperialism.

The idea behind cultural relativism is that ethical values (ostensibly the root cause of governments' human rights policies) vary from place to place and over time. As R.J. Vincent writes, this means "that moral claims derive from, and are enmeshed in, a cultural context which is itself the source of their validity."[6] In other words, beyond condemning the most brutal of practices such as slavery and torture (and even these are subject to relativist definitions), it is intrinsically unfair to criticize the ethical positions of others, since they arise out of the specific conditions faced by them at the time. Japan has always had a strong dependency on seafood, for example; perhaps we should not be surprised or outraged that some Japanese still sell whale meat in restaurants in Tokyo and elsewhere. Amsterdam's "red light" district, where prostitution is on open and legal display, would appear distinctly unethical in many other areas of the world. While the United States often condemns states for engaging in repressive policies, many point to the increasing use of the death penalty and the disproportionately high incarceration of minorities in that country as an indication of regressive public ethics. The role of women has changed rapidly in Western societies, but does this imply that all states should adopt similar legal provisions for women's rights? Since no states are without human rights problems and controversies, it may not be just cultural imperialism to force one's own values onto the international stage; it may be nakedly hypocritical as well.

Even the more obvious cases can become complicated with a close look. For example, the right to food is often used as an example of a universal human right.[7] However, we must ask whether people have a simple right to adequate amounts of food, or to equitable amounts of food within their own societies (few, if any, states would pass that test). We might argue that the right to environmental security should be universally applicable, and that all people should be able to live in a local environment free from profound ecological threats. However, any attempt to ensure this right would not only challenge sovereignty as an institution but also in many cases require the redistribution of resources within societies. At the same time, cultural relativism can become a cloak behind which abusers of basic rights can hide, and we should not let it stop us from analyzing controversial issues. Or, in the words of the distinguished scholar Fred Halliday,

> While an awareness of relativity and difference is essential to an explanation of how and why systems of domination originate and are maintained, such a recognition need not necessarily lead, out of a misplaced anthropological generosity, to denying that forms of oppression do exist and recur in a wide range of societies and historical contexts.[8]

A yet broader issue concerns whether questions of ethics and morality should even be part of the study of international relations.[9] If state sovereignty is sacrosanct, states really have no right to comment on what goes on in other states in the first place. If this were the case, the ethical responsibilities of government leaders would not extend beyond the borders of their own countries.[10] Since the most fundamental principle of international law is state sovereignty, international law reinforces, rather than challenges, this perspective. However, leaving questions of permanence aside, states are almost invariably involved in each other's domestic economies; they often share transnational cultural understandings; and much migration has occurred in the past two centuries. All of this leads us to suggest that, whether they like it or not, government leaders do bear some measure of ethical responsibility for what occurs outside their borders and for what their citizens do outside them as well. While this responsibility has always pertained to the actions of soldiers, it includes the actions of civilians. For example, the Canadian government has joined several other states to make it possible to prosecute Canadians who purchase sex with children when abroad. Similarly, activists have campaigned for MNCs (multinational corporations) to adopt ethical guidelines, or codes of conduct, when operating in low-income regions (see Chapter 8). When a government provides low-cost insurance for firms investing in conflict zones, it is making an ethical decision on the implications of investing there. In fact, most questions related to foreign policy, as well as our own individual interactions with the world, involve the realization and implementation of ethical standards, even if we don't habitually agonize over our choices.

As Sidney Bailey and Sam Daws write, "From a moral point of view, human rights are about the behaviour of individuals. From a legal point of view, human rights are about the responsibilities of governments."[11] Until roughly the mid- to late 19th century, human rights concerns were regarded as within the domestic jurisdiction of rulers. Campaigns to abolish the slave trade and to provide humanitarian care for wounded soldiers helped break this confinement, although the principle of non-intervention maintains its prominent place in the UN Charter today. The human rights field has expanded considerably in scope since the end of World War II, the cataclysmic event that so horrified the world that the international community began to gradually accept the notion that international law might play a role in avoiding future mass atrocities. Where the human rights issue area departs most noticeably from conventional international legal matters, however, is that it forces us to look beyond the usual tradition that defines international law as law for, and by, states. Even in the World Court (formally referred to as the International Court of Justice, or ICJ), states are still recognized as the sole actors in international law. This distinction becomes more difficult to maintain as global human rights movements, conventions and agreements, and the ICC continue to evolve. Increasingly, governments are regarded as having responsibilities beyond their borders. As Kenneth Roth argued in his introduction to the 2009 *Human Rights Watch World Report*, "A government's respect for human rights must be measured not only by how it treats its own people but also how it protects rights in its relations with other countries."[12] Human rights and human security are ultimately about protecting people, not the relatively abstract conceptions we call states.

In recent decades, human rights issues have become increasingly prominent concerns for governments, international organizations, and publics. Why has this happened? In the first place, awareness has increased. Global communications, travel, and print and television media have made us more aware of what goes on in other countries (see Chapter 12). States are no longer as capable of controlling information flows across their borders as they once were, though Marxists argue that media sources are still controlled by elites. Economic interdependence and global communications have provided governments, groups, and individuals with the means to act to promote human rights, through mechanisms such as trade restrictions, boycotts, and public information campaigns and protests. For example, consumer boycotts of MNCs have had some success, as many consumers resist buying products produced by victims of repression. Consumer awareness campaigns directed at Heineken, Carlsberg, British Home Stores, and Liz Claiborne compelled those MNCs to leave Burma. Campaigns have also been mounted against Royal Dutch/Shell for its operations in Nigeria, Total and Unocal in Burma, Nike in Indonesia and Vietnam, Disney in Haiti, and Zenith and General Motors for gender discrimination in Mexico.[13] A long record of human rights abuses directly and indirectly related to economic activity continues to drive calls for more robust corporate social responsibility provisions and "global intergovernmental standards" on business activity and human rights.[14]

The growth of human rights groups has also given interested individuals the opportunity to devote more time and effort to the cause of human rights. Such non-governmental organizations (NGOs) include Amnesty International, Human Rights Watch, the International League for Human Rights, and the International Commission of Jurists. As we discussed in Chapter 5, these NGOs work to create awareness and persuade governments to act on human rights issues. As a result, governments are no longer regarded as the primary means of advancing human rights. In fact, governments are increasingly regarded as serious obstacles to progress. Nevertheless, they remain an essential piece of the effort to develop more effective legal instruments and responses to human rights issues, and as a result human rights groups attempt to raise public awareness to apply pressure on governments for change. (See Profile 9.2 regarding two winners of the Nobel Peace Prize for their contributions to human rights.)

PROFILE 9.2 Human Rights and Nobel Peace Prize Winners

Shirin Ebadi, winner of the Nobel Peace Prize, right, holds up the hand of Narges Mohammadi, wife of Taqi Rahmani, a prominent jailed political activist, during a gathering at the Amir Kabir University in Tehran, Iran, October 29, 2003. In her most biting criticism of the ruling hardline Islamic establishment yet, Ebadi said she owes the award to Cyrus the Great, king of ancient Persia, and those Iranian writers and intellectuals who have been jailed for political reasons. (AP Photo/Vahid Salemi)

Former U.S. President Jimmy Carter right, waves alongside Cuban President Fidel Castro at the airport in Havana, Cuba, May 17, 2002. Carter wrapped up a historic visit after seeking to bring Cuba and the United States closer by challenging both countries to change after more than four decades of enmity. (AP Photo/Gregory Bull)

The Nobel Peace Prize has often been awarded to outstanding members of the human rights community; the assumption is that true peace is impossible without freedom and dignity for all. In 2003, Shirin Ebadi of Iran won the esteemed prize for her work on women's rights and democracy in Iran. She was born in Tehran in 1947, and served as the president of the city court of Tehran, as one of the first female judges in Iran, in the 1970s. After the 1979 revolution, she was forced to resign. She now works as a lawyer and teaches at the University of Tehran; as an activist and researcher she has lobbied for increased rights for refugees, women, and children.

(continued)

PROFILE 9.2   Human Rights and Nobel Peace Prize Winners (*continued*)

She represents a movement called Reformed Islam, and argues for a new interpretation of Islamic law that is in harmony with vital human rights such as democracy, equality before the law, religious freedom, and freedom of speech. She uses Islam as her starting point to promote peaceful solutions, and promotes new thinking on Islamic terms. She has displayed great personal courage as a lawyer defending individuals and groups who have fallen victim to a powerful political and legal system that is legitimized through what many consider an inhumane interpretation of Islam. Ebadi has shown her willingness and ability to cooperate with representatives of secular as well as religious views. Critics charge that she received the prize precisely because her views are in line with Western critiques of Iranian theocracy, but this overlooks her commitment to Islam and her many personal achievements. In 2008 Ebadi argued that the human rights situation in Iran was regressing. She continues to receive death threats against herself and her family.

In contrast, the Nobel Peace Prize winner of 2002 was well known around the world: former U.S. President (1976 to 1980) Jimmy Carter. Carter has long been active, since his defeat by Ronald Reagan, in undertaking various peace diplomacy missions, with mixed results. IIn 2004 he was involved in efforts to calm the Haitian crisis. However, one could as plausibly argue that his Peace Prize reflected the international communities' respect for his work in the human rights field. Founded in 1981, the Carter Center is an Atlanta-based organization devoted to global peace and social justice. Carter has travelled around the globe monitoring elections, promoting human rights, and providing health care and food to the world's poor; the Carter Center is also involved in providing low-cost housing to the poor in the United States. There is always some controversy about the Nobel Peace Prize; some critics felt that a former U.S. president was not a sound choice, given that state's mixed record on promoting human rights abroad. Most, however, felt the Norwegian Nobel Committee got it right this time, rewarding a stalwart defender of rights for the poor and a reliable voice for calm, even if the publication of his 2006 book, *Palestine: Peace Not Apartheid* (New York: Simon and Schuster, 2006), caused many to criticize his views on the Middle East peace process.

See also the website for The Carter Center at http://www.cartercenter.org.

HUMAN RIGHTS AND GOVERNMENTS

The stark reality: many governments continue to perpetuate or tolerate human rights abuses at home and abroad. According to Freedom House, by 2011, 59 countries or territories were described as "Not Free and whose citizens endure systematic and pervasive human rights violations." The very worst violators were identified as Belarus, Cuba, Equatorial Guinea, Eritrea, Iran, North Korea, Turkmenistan, and Uzbekistan.[15] Living conditions in the West Bank and the Gaza Strip have provoked international condemnation against Israel. China has been accused of widespread human rights violations in Tibet. Canada has been condemned for its treatment of indigenous (First Nations) peoples. Amnesty International catalogues a wide range of human rights violations based on the rights enshrined in the Universal Declaration. For example, cases of torture and cruel or inhumane punishment were documented in 101 countries in 2011, and at least 91 countries restricted the freedom of expression in that year.[16]

Governments were slow to react to the human rights abuses in the former Yugoslavia and to the genocide in Rwanda. Governments in Angola and Cambodia have extended amnesty to human rights abusers. The Japanese government remains unwilling to formally compensate for the treatment of approximately 200 000 "comfort women" used as sex slaves for the Japanese military in World War II. Many other countries are struggling with political opposition to the investigation of human rights abuses, and some governments attempt to intimidate human rights advocates, harassing many, imprisoning some, and killing others.[17] The record of governments in human rights issues is, therefore, rather poor; although governments can be important agents of progress, all too often they are obstacles, or the very source of the problem. This fact complicates related diplomatic initiatives. For example, at least two highly murderous regimes have had non-permanent seats on the Security Council (Cambodia, then called Kampuchea, in the mid-1970s, and Rwanda in 1994) even while massive campaigns of genocide were carried out back home. And we should stress the relationship between political power, military control, and human rights abuses: the brutality displayed by the military government led by Robert Mugabe during elections in Zimbabwe in the summer of 2008, the repression following the controversial election in Iran in June of 2009, and abuses committed by Malian government forces in the Civil War in 2012 and 2013, are highly visible examples. This depressing overview illustrates the scale and scope of the human rights situation in the world and the outrages to human dignity that are committed by states on a daily basis.

Human rights are an always controversial factor in foreign policy decision making. Many governments have participated in efforts to build international law and international regimes to promote them, and they have responded to human rights abuses with diplomatic protests and (often limited) economic sanctions (such as those directed against **apartheid** South Africa and against China after the June 1989 Tiananmen Square massacre in which the Chinese military crushed a pro-democracy protest). Other governments have also taken steps to improve human rights in their own societies by prosecuting abusive officials and exposing the stark legacies of their past. For example, the Truth and Reconciliation Commission in South Africa undertook an investigation that implicated top-level officials in the former South African government in the apartheid-era state violence. The Guatemalan government acknowledged past abuses and purged the military and the police of the worst human rights offenders. The government of South Korea has convicted two former presidents for their role in a 1980 massacre of civilians by the South Korean military. The newly formed government of Iraq hanged former leader Saddam Hussein on December 30, 2006, after charging him and his surviving leadership with crimes against the Iraqi people.

Standing up for liberty. In this now-famous photograph, an anti-government protestor stands in front of advancing tanks in Beijing's Tiananmen Square on June 5, 1989, at the height of the pro-democracy protests. Deng Xiaoping is believed to have given the final orders for the military suppression of the 1989 Tiananmen Square pro-democracy protests, which claimed hundreds, perhaps thousands, of lives. Though China has partially liberalized its economy, the Communist Party continues to hold an iron grip on political representation, has actively repressed spiritual groups such as the Falun Gong, and continues its tyranny over Tibet. The 20th anniversary of Tiananmen was celebrated with stony official silence and denial in June of 2009. (AP Photo/Jeff Widener/CP Images)

Governments have often displayed inconsistency and a lack of commitment on human rights issues. In particular, governments around the world (including the government of Canada; see Profile 9.3) appear consistently willing to subordinate human rights concerns to their desire for trade and investment opportunities. Governments have defended this approach by arguing that trade, investment, and interdependence will generate social change

PROFILE 9.3 Talisman and Sudan

The concept of human security was put to an interesting test in a dispute over a Canadian oil firm's investment and operations in the North African state of Sudan. Civil war has raged in that country for over 50 years, and reports of mass displacement and charges of state genocide have been frequent. The northern Arab-dominated National Islamic Front government has been fighting the Christian and animist southern region in a brutal confrontation that has killed some 1.5 million southerners and has seen the use of food as a weapon, concentration camps, and reports of southern villagers being taken into slavery by northern militias. (Western Christian groups have engaged in so-called redemption programs, literally buying back slaves from their oppressors, but this has been criticized as well, since it drives up the price of slaves.) South Sudan achieved political independence in 2011, but violence continues.

In October 1998 Talisman Energy acquired Arakis Energy for C$200 million. This gave Talisman a 25 percent share in the Greater Nile Oil Project, a consortium with China and Malaysia. In southern Sudan, huge oil fields are being drilled and a major pipeline to Port Sudan is planned. The project employs 2000 Sudanese, and more than 100 Canadians have helped train them. However, the southern rebels, in particular the Sudan People's Liberation Army, considered this collaboration with the northern government an affront to their territorial sovereignty and declared such installations legitimate military targets. As a result the Sudanese government, which takes a share of the revenue generated by the oil extraction, employed military

forces to protect the Canadian workers and installations.

Critics charged that a Canadian firm was helping to fund a genocidal war. In response, the Canadian government sent African expert John Harker to investigate the situation, and his report was largely condemnatory. In early 2000 the Canadian government decided that no sanctions would be imposed against Talisman but that the company should be encouraged to carefully monitor the situation and perhaps create a trust fund to help southerners after the conflict is over. Human rights activists, who argued that the conflict would not end as long as the Sudanese government was funded by oil revenues, expressed dismay at this decision. The decision also angered the United States, which has imposed tough sanctions (with some notable exceptions) on Sudan because of suspected terrorist connections. Should the Canadian government have taken steps to force Talisman out of Sudan, or is business just business? Finally, in response to shareholder concerns over human rights abuses, and an American threat to delist the company from the New York Stock Exchange, Talisman agreed in March 2003 to sell its 25 percent stake in Sudan's Greater Nile Oil Project to an Indian state-owned oil company called ONGC Videsh. Indeed, Talisman profited from the sale! The episode heightened awareness of the potential impact of foreign investment, and raised questions about the human costs of promoting "business as usual."

SOURCE: A. NIKIFORUK, "OIL PATCH PARIAH," *CANADIAN BUSINESS*, DEC. 10, 2000, PG. 69; JOHN HARKER, HUMAN SECURITY IN SUDAN: REPORT OF CANADIAN ASSESSMENT MISSION, DEPT. OF FOREIGN AFFAIRS AND INTERNATIONAL TRADE, OTTAWA, JANUARY 2000; S. THORNE, "CANADA CONSIDERS MORE MEASURES TO ENCOURAGE PEACE IN SUDAN," *CANADIAN PRESS*, FEB. 15, 2000.

in countries with human rights problems and that interdependence will create leverage that can later be used to promote human rights. This "**constructive engagement**" strategy has angered critics, who charge that it amounts to a façade of a human rights policy rather than any genuine commitment.[18] Governments also tend to exert human rights pressure on poor states while not doing the same with economically attractive states, and great powers have often continued to provide Official Development Assistance (ODA) and even military aid to some abusive regimes. Governments have also obstructed efforts to reveal the involvement of their own officials in human rights abuses. The U.S. government, for example, has been reluctant to release documents related to the activities of the Central Intelligence Agency (CIA) in Haiti, Honduras, and Guatemala, obstructing the human rights investigations in progress in those countries.

HUMAN RIGHTS AND THE UN SYSTEM

In June 1993, the UN-sponsored World Conference on Human Rights in Vienna declared that "the promotion and protection of all human rights is a legitimate concern of the international community."[19] Similar sentiments had been expressed at previous UN conferences and forums. Yet such declarations conflict with the principle of sovereignty enshrined in the UN Charter. As Stephen Marks has observed, "Human rights in the United Nations has been, to a large extent, the story of tension between the principle that the United Nations cannot intervene in the domestic affairs of states and the principle that states must act with the United Nations to realize fully all rights."[20]

While the UN Charter does call explicitly for international cooperation on economic, social, cultural, and humanitarian matters, and the promotion of human rights and fundamental freedoms (Articles 4 and 55, respectively), it is the Universal Declaration of Human Rights, adopted by the General Assembly in 1948, that has the most impact on legal thinking regarding the obligations of states toward their citizens. More than 60 other human rights instruments have been adopted by the General Assembly since 1948, including the International Covenant on Civil and Political Rights and the International Covenant on Economic, Social and Cultural Rights. These two international covenants and the Universal Declaration of Human Rights are collectively known as the International Bill of Rights. (See Profile 9.4 for a list of UN human rights conventions and protocols.) Despite considerable dissension, the UN-sponsored World Conference on Human Rights in Vienna (the first in a quarter-century) concluded with a commitment to the idea of universal human rights, and established the post of a UN High Commissioner for Human Rights. The Commissioner helped to coordinate the work of the 53-member Commission on Human Rights (a subsidiary body of ECOSOC), and in 2004 a well-respected Canadian jurist, Louise Arbour, was appointed to this demanding post, which she held until the summer of 2008. In 2006, the much-criticized Commission was replaced by the 47-member UN Human Rights Council, which (working closely with the Commissioner) conducts special "periodic reviews" of the human rights records of all UN member states.

In addition, many other bodies in the UN address human rights issues. These include the Committee on the Elimination of Racial Discrimination, the Commission on the Status of Women and the Committee on the Elimination of Discrimination against Women, the High Commissioner for Refugees, the High Commissioner for National Minorities, the International Labour Organization, and the Crime Prevention and Criminal Justice Division in Vienna.

PROFILE 9.4 Selected UN Human Rights Instruments

Note: After each convention appears the year it was opened for signature and the year it came into force. Note that many of these conventions have yet to come into force.

GENERAL HUMAN RIGHTS

International Covenant on Civil and Political Rights, 1966, 1976

Optional Protocol to the International Covenant on Civil and Political Rights, 1966, 1976

International Covenant on Economic, Social and Cultural Rights, 1966, 1976

UN World Conference on Human Rights: Vienna Declaration, 1993

RACIAL DISCRIMINATION

International Convention on the Elimination of All Forms of Racial Discrimination, 1965, 1969

International Convention on the Suppression and Punishment of the Crime of Apartheid, 1973, 1976

International Convention against Apartheid in Sports, 1985

RIGHTS OF WOMEN

Convention on the Political Rights of Women, 1952, 1954

Convention on the Nationality of Married Women, 1957, 1958

Convention on Consent to Marriage, Minimum Age for Marriage and Registration of Marriages, 1962, 1964

Convention on the Elimination of All Forms of Discrimination against Women, 1979, 1981

SLAVERY AND RELATED MATTERS

Convention for the Suppression of the Traffic in Persons and of the Exploitation of the Prostitution of Others, 1949, 1951

Slavery Convention of 1926, as amended in 1953, 1953, 1955

Protocol Amending the 1926 Slavery Convention, 1953, 1955

Supplementary Convention on the Abolition of Slavery, the Slave Trade, and Institutions and Practices Similar to Slavery, 1956, 1957

REFUGEES AND STATELESS PERSONS

Convention on the Reduction of Statelessness, 1949, 1951

Convention Relating to the Status of Refugees, 1951, 1954

Convention Relating to the Status of Stateless Persons, 1954, 1960

Protocol Relating to the Status of Refugees, 1966, 1967

OTHER

Convention on the Prevention and Punishment of the Crime of Genocide, 1948, 1951

Convention on the International Right of Correction, 1952, 1962

Convention on the Non-applicability of Statutory Limitations to War Crimes and Crimes against Humanity, 1968, 1970

Convention against Torture and Other Cruel, Inhuman or Degrading Treatment or Punishment, 1984, 1987

Convention on the Rights of the Child, 1989, 1990

International Convention on the Protection of the Rights of All Migrant Workers and Members of Their Families, 1990, 2003

International Labour Organization Convention on the Worst Forms of Child Labour, 2000, 2000

Convention on the Rights of Persons with Disabilities, 2006, 2008

Declaration on the Rights of Indigenous Peoples, 2007

HUMAN RIGHTS AND REGIONAL ORGANIZATIONS

In addition to efforts to promote human rights through the UN, regional IGOs (intergovernmental organizations) have also made similar efforts, though with varying degrees of commitment and concrete results. In Europe, the foundation for the large body of human rights legislation and institutions is the 1953 European Convention for the Protection of Human

Rights and Fundamental Freedoms, drafted to prevent a recurrence of the Nazi crimes against humanity. Two institutions in Europe have built on the principles of the European Convention. The **Council of Europe** maintains the European Court, which, among other cases, has heard charges against the British government alleging that the laws enacted to suppress the Irish Republican Army (IRA) violated the human rights provisions of the European Convention. The Organization for Security and Co-operation in Europe (OSCE), established in 1994 as a replacement for the Conference on Security and Cooperation in Europe (CSCE), was built on the principles of the Helsinki Final Act of 1975, which provided for the protection of human rights by all signatory governments across Europe (including the U.S.S.R.) and North America. In 1990, the Charter of Paris committed members to observe the human rights provisions of the CSCE Final Act (and any subsequent amendment) and proclaimed human rights as a "legitimate concern" of all signatory governments. The OSCE mounts periodic fact-finding missions to investigate human rights concerns. In addition, much of the European Convention on Human Rights is reflected in the local laws of several EU member states, the most recent being that of Britain.

The Organization of American States (OAS) Charter of 1948 has a Declaration of the Rights and Duties of Man, and in 1978 the American Convention on Human Rights (with an Inter-American Court of Human Rights) came into force. In Africa, the 1981 African Charter on Human and Peoples' Rights (the Banjul Charter) was adopted by the OAU (Organisation of African Unity). In Asia, the Association of Southeast Asian Nations (ASEAN) possesses a human rights commission, and the Asia-Pacific Economic Cooperation (APEC) forum possesses a Human Resources Development Working Group. However, while most of these regional human rights efforts are staffed by dedicated and hard-working personnel, and while many of them perform important roles and tasks on a variety of human rights issues, all of them suffer from the problems of limited financial and human resources and the intransigence (and sometimes the resistance) of member governments.

CONTEMPORARY HUMAN RIGHTS ISSUES

Before looking at specific examples of human rights issues, we should mention the difficulty involved in choosing them. As space constrains us from embarking on anything approaching a comprehensive survey, we have chosen several issues that have had a high public profile in the press in recent years. Although this selection is of course arbitrary, we hope we have covered issues of concern to most contemporary students and encourage you to look elsewhere for information on other pertinent topics, such as freedom of speech, the right to food and education, and gay and lesbian rights. In addition, we have not included a discussion of the refugee crisis (one of the most pressing and challenging human rights issues of our time) in this chapter because we deal with it at length in Chapter 11. We deal with reproductive rights in that chapter as well.

ETHICS AND CONSTRAINTS ON WAR

We include a discussion of the ethical reasoning behind war efforts because war is, at heart, a human rights issue. If war is justified, then killing individual human beings to win one may be justified, and this justification is subject to all the dilemmas inherent in the universal/particular split mentioned above. The relationship between war and ethics has been a complex one.[21] Most of the world's ethical systems (heavily influenced by religion) deplore the act of killing as a general principle. And yet virtually all ethical systems establish sets of conditions under which such killing is justified or permissible. Ethicists, theologians, and philosophers have established the foundations for the ethical rejection of international violence and war, while at the same time their arguments have been used to support or justify international violence and wars; for example, in the name of national liberation or humanitarian intervention.

There is also the sentiment that war is a distinct human activity in which ethics have no place. *Inter arma silent leges*: "In times of war the law is silent." Despite this ethical debate, moral condemnation of the ethics of war tends to be *utilitarian* in nature; that is, the benefits and costs of any act must be judged in moral and ethical terms. As a result, war can be justified in certain cases, such as resisting and punishing aggression, although such wars must still be fought in accordance with certain ethical principles. The problem with utilitarian approaches is that states and groups will manipulate ethical principles to sanction the use of violence, at which point utilitarian ethics may erode into apologies or justifications for the very worst acts of war. *Absolutist* ethics, however, maintain that nothing can justify a certain act, which forms the foundation of the beliefs of pacifists, who maintain that international violence and war are never justified, no matter what the circumstances. The problem with absolutist ethics is that a refusal to use violence or go to war may permit the most horrible acts to take place; inaction itself can be morally bankrupt.

Those who advocate a "just war" doctrine attempt to constrain warfare by establishing the conditions under which it is just to enter into a war and by establishing what level of violence is considered acceptable in the prosecution of that war. This hinges on the distinction between **jus ad bellum** (the justice of a war) and **jus in bello** (the justness of the manner in which a war is fought). In his writing on *jus ad bellum*, Michael Walzer argues that only aggression can justify war, and that wars fought in self-defence are just.[22] The aggressor, once defeated, is to be punished, for punishment will deter future aggression. In society, we punish criminals to deter criminal violence; internationally, aggression is punished to prevent future aggression. From this basic principle are drawn the criteria by which just wars are measured:

- A just war is a war of last resort; all other means of resolution must be explored.

- A just war must be authorized by a legitimate authority, either the state or an international organization.

- A just war must be waged for a just cause, not for aggression or a desire for vengeance.

- A just war must have a good chance of successfully achieving a desirable outcome, and wars fought for good causes that are ultimately hopeless are not justifiable.

- A just war must end in a peace that is preferable to the situation before the outbreak of war.

Jus in bello maintains that a war may also be just or unjust in the manner in which it is fought. A war may have just origins, but it cannot be fought unjustly. Two measures determine the just conduct of a war:

1. A just war must be fought in ways consistent with the principle of proportionality. The potential positives deriving from military activity (such as a bombing campaign) must outweigh the negatives of destruction and death. Military methods must also be limited to the level of violence required to achieve the mission at hand, and any risk to civilians must be proportionate to the military value of the target.

2. A just war must discriminate—combatants and non-combatants must be treated differently. Civilians cannot be the intentional targets of military operations, and civilian casualties must be minimized when this is possible.

Just war doctrine thus argues that wars should be limited and that the conduct of war is (and should be) governed by rules of behaviour and conduct. It is important to remember that in practice few wars meet all of these criteria, and so debates about the justness of a war generally revolve around examples of when certain principles might have been violated or argue to what extent a war can be considered just.

Nuclear weapons, and in particular nuclear deterrence, pose a challenge to ethical constraints on war. During the Cold War, most secular and religious ethicists agreed that nuclear weapons are by their very nature indiscriminate and disproportionate, and so nuclear war was generally regarded as inherently unjust. However, nuclear deterrence, the deployment of nuclear weapons in an effort to deter their use, was more controversial. Is it legitimate or just to threaten an action that would be immoral or unjust if it were carried out? The legitimacy of nuclear deterrence was justified on the grounds that it is necessary to avoid a greater evil (aggression by an enemy or subjugation of the free world at the hands of totalitarianism). However, many argued that the arms race invalidated the moral basis of deterrence as a temporary measure; nuclear deterrence was endangering peace, not contributing to it. So, for example, the United Methodist Council of Bishops argued that "the moral case for nuclear deterrence, even as an interim ethic, has been undermined by unrelenting arms escalation. Deterrence no longer serves, if it ever did, as a strategy that facilitates disarmament. Deterrence must no longer receive the churches' blessing."[23] Although the prominence of this issue has receded somewhat, the ethical status of nuclear weapons remains a subject of intense debate, particularly in the context of proliferation and post-Cold War efforts to ban nuclear weapons.

Critics of just war doctrine charge that since the judges of whether a war is just tend to be the very states, governments, or peoples engaged in the violence, a natural tendency exists to frame whatever one side does in good or just terms and to frame everything the opposition does in bad or unjust terms. Nevertheless, to reject just war doctrine outright would be to invite the separation of morality and war. Furthermore, opposition to war is generally founded on judgments of what is considered just. Opposition to the Vietnam War in the United States was largely built on the view of many that the war was unjust, both in terms of its conduct and its origins. Before the Gulf War of 1990, extensive efforts were made by governments to convince public opinion that the cause was just; this has proven rather more difficult during and after the U.S.–coalition invasion of Iraq in 2003. While many people were willing to accept the war in Afghanistan as a just response to the terror attacks of September 11, the proffered causes for the Iraqi operation—that Saddam Hussein was a viable threat to Western states, capable of developing and using weapons of mass destruction in the near future—were rejected by many as either the consequence of a trigger-happy Bush administration or disinformation. However, to the extent that support for a war is a function of the extent to which it is just, the criteria of just war doctrine would seem to have some value. Furthermore, just war doctrine is a significant part of the debate over humanitarian intervention, which we turn to later in this chapter.

GENOCIDE AND WAR CRIMES

Few words are as connotative as *genocide*. Article II of the Convention on the Prevention and Punishment of the Crime of Genocide, adopted by the UN General Assembly on December 9, 1948, defines genocide as

> any of the following acts committed with intent to destroy,
> in whole or in part, a national, ethnical, racial, or religious

group, such as (a) killing members of the group; (b) causing serious bodily or mental harm to members of the group; (c) deliberately inflicting on the group conditions of life calculated to bring about its physical destruction in whole or in part; (d) imposing measures intended to prevent births within the group; (e) forcibly transferring children of the group to another group.

Article IV goes on to state that persons committing genocide shall be punished whether they are constitutionally responsible rulers, public officials, or private individuals.[24] This definition is important not only because it recognizes a form of collective rights (freedom from discriminatory murder) but also because it implies that the state—traditionally the guarantor of citizens' rights—can at times become the worst enemy of the people. The Convention grew out of the recognition of three types of crimes during warfare: crimes against humanity, crimes against peace, and war crimes.

After World War II, trials were held in which the losers—Germany and Japan—were judged by the victors. At the most famous of these trials, the **war crimes trials** in Nuremberg held from 1945 to 1949 (the Tokyo war crimes trials are less well known), **crimes against humanity** were considered to be murder, extermination, enslavement, deportation, imprisonment, torture, rape, or persecutions on political, racial, or religious grounds committed against any civilian population (including one's own). The term was first introduced in the London Agreement of August 8, 1945 (issued by the United States, the U.S.S.R., Great Britain, and France). **Crimes against peace** included planning, preparing, initiating, or waging a war of aggression and participating in a common plan or conspiracy for the accomplishment of war crimes. Nazi aggression was considered a crime against peace, though its chief architect, Adolf Hitler, had killed himself before the bitter end of the struggle in Berlin, thus escaping trial. **War crimes** were considered murder, ill treatment or deportation to slave labour, killing of hostages, and plunder and wanton destruction with no military necessity.

Obviously some measure of overlap exists in these crimes, but they are considered important legal precedents. Polish jurist Raphael Lemkin coined the word *genocide* during the implementation of Hitler's "final solution." Lemkin had a wide awareness of the atrocities being waged across Europe largely on racial grounds and affecting one ethnic group in particular, the European Jewish community. Thus, he introduced a new term to denote an old practice in its modern development, derived from the Greek word for race or people, *genos*, and the Latin *caedere* (-cide), which means to kill.[25] The Holocaust is still widely considered the ultimate example of genocide. Estimates vary, but at least six million Jews—and many others, including Gypsies, prisoners of war, and German "undesirables," such as people with disabilities and homosexuals—were killed.[26] Due to the massive numbers involved, and the administrative efficiency of such systematic murder, the Holocaust remains a singular event in history, but many examples of genocide exist, such as the murder of millions of Armenians by the Ottoman Turks during World War I.

Two events in the 1990s brought the term *genocide* and the mechanism of the war crimes trial back into public view. The first was the outbreak of war in the former Yugoslavia (see discussion in Chapter 6) and the "ethnic cleansing" (the forced expulsion of particular ethnic groups), concentration camps, mass murders, and rape that characterized the conflict. The second was the outbreak of the carnage in Rwanda in the spring and summer of 1994. This orchestrated campaign of genocide shocked the Western world with images of dismemberment, displacement, starvation, and bloated corpses floating down the Kagera River entering Uganda and Lake Victoria. As a result of just two months of intense violence, UN officials estimated the death toll of unarmed civilians in Rwanda at approximately 800 000.[27] State-employed Hutu militia men are thought responsible for much of the killing, which began after Hutu President Juvenal Habyarimana was killed in a rocket attack on his plane. Rwanda has been plagued with violence, before and after its achievement of independence from Belgian rule in 1962; indeed, it was a massacre of Tutsis in 1959 that originally created an exiled Tutsi community in Uganda, remnants of which returned to Rwanda in an unsuccessful invasion in 1990 and again in 1994 with the currently governing Rwanda Patriotic Front. But nothing in known African history has equalled the recent bloodbath in terms of its scope and, as chilling, the speed with which events took shape.[28] The repercussions of these events spread through the African Great Lakes region in 1996 and 1997, in the form of massive refugee flows and the fall of the long-time president of Zaire, Mobutu Sese Seko, and an escalation in the subsequently established Democratic Republic of the Congo, where millions have died as a result of civil war and related displacement as well.

In 1993, the UN Security Council created the International Tribunal for the Prosecution of Persons Responsible for Serious Violations of International Humanitarian Law in the Territory of the Former Yugoslavia since 1991 (known as the ICTY, or International Criminal Tribunal for the former Yugoslavia), located at The Hague in the Netherlands. In 1995 the Dayton Agreement that ended the war called for the parties to the conflict to cooperate with the tribunal (this has been less than forthcoming, however). After the fall of Slobodan Milošević's regime in 2000, he was put on trial at The Hague, where he erratically defended himself until his death in March of 2006. In July 2008, former Bosnian Serb leader Radovan Karadzic (who, along with General Ratko Mladić, himself arrested in May 2011, is held responsible for the massacre of some 8000 men in the small Bosnian town of Srebrenica) was captured after 12 years of hiding in Belgrade posing as an alternative medicine practitioner. Karadzic was extradited to the Netherlands to face the ICTY on charges of genocide, war crimes, and crimes against humanity, his trial began in 2011, Mladić's in 2012.

In 1994, the Security Council created the International Criminal Tribunal for Rwanda (ICTR). This tribunal operates in Arusha, Tanzania, though it has tried only a tiny fraction of those responsible for the genocide: the governmental elite. The others captured by the Rwandan Patriotic Front in 1994 have certainly suffered a worse fate, as some 80 000 were crammed into a prison system built for 13 000. Many of them were children at the time and are now fully grown men and still imprisoned awaiting trial in 2013 (though efforts to utilize a village justice system in its place, wherein prisoners can return home if their home communities elect to forgive them, show some progress at this stage). The objective of both of these tribunals is to bring the perpetrators of war crimes, crimes against humanity, and genocide to justice, but their progress has been slowed by financial problems, the active opposition of those who fear exposure and retribution, and an inability to physically apprehend many of those charged. Nevertheless, the tribunals have secured convictions. The international community, especially the United States, saw both tribunals as an effort to compensate for the relatively lacklustre response to the carnage that occurred in the Balkans and Rwanda. See Profile 9.5 regarding Canadian Louise Arbour, former UN Human Rights Commissioner, and her involvement in these tribunals. The establishment of a permanent International Criminal Court (discussed later in this chapter) was a response to the crimes committed in the former Yugoslavia and Rwanda and an effort to respond to the weaknesses of the ICTY and ICTR.

On a broader scale, one might argue that the term *genocide* can be used to describe the manifestations of structural violence as well.[29] This is a controversial topic; while we would all agree that the deliberate starvation of entire communities is a war crime or even genocidal, the lack of clean water supplies in the slums of major cities might result in equal misery but few would refer to this as genocidal. Many cases involve mass death inflicted with obvious intent: the destruction of East Timor by the Indonesian military, or of Tibet by the Chinese, or of parts of Indochina by the Americans, or of political opponents of various Soviet regimes, or the drainage of marshes in southern Iraq. By such an expanded definition, war itself could be seen as an inherently genocidal project. Cultural destruction is often referred to as cultural genocide or *ethnocide*, a prime example being the cultural destruction inflicted on the indigenous peoples of the Americas. Similarly, the construction of large-scale dams that displace millions of people, the Himalayan deforestation that has caused floods, and other forms of *ecocide* (see Chapter 10) might be called genocidal when death results. Scholarly and legal debate continues to rage around these expanded definitions of genocide, but we should not ignore the large-scale death and destruction that results from conflict and political actions that are not strictly acts of genocide according to the 1948 Convention.

The advent of the nuclear age takes us further toward an alternative and expanded perspective on genocide. It can be argued that nuclear deterrence, based on the threat of mass annihilation, was based on the threat of implementing the ultimate genocidal policy. Of course, one might argue that the threat of nuclear war introduced a new concept to the lexicon, that of *omnicide*. However, since nuclear strategy was predicated on the destruction of a specific

Where the unthinkable happened. A Christian figure stands between human skulls, August 2003 at the Ntarama church in Nyamata (south of Kigali) where up to 5000 people were killed during the 1994 Rwanda genocide, which claimed the lives of approximately 800 000 Tutsis and moderate Hutus. (AP Photo/Karel Prinsloo/CP Images)

PROFILE 9.5 The Canadian Global Human Rights Commissioner

In 1992 the Security Council of the UN created a Commission of Experts to investigate and report on "the evidence of grave breaches of the Geneva Conventions and other violations of humanitarian law in the territory of the former Yugoslavia" (Res. 780, 1992). After the tabling of an interim report, which clearly indicated that mass murder had taken place, the Security Council established an international tribunal for the prosecution of individuals responsible (UN Doc. S/Res/808, 1993). In March 1996 Canadian Justice Louise Arbour was appointed chief prosecutor for the International Criminal Tribunals for the former Yugoslavia and Rwanda. She had previously been a member of the Court of Appeals for Ontario. The term of chief prosecutor runs four years and is renewable after that; Arbour left for the Supreme Court of Canada in September 1999 and was replaced by Carla Del Ponte of Switzerland. In early 2004, Arbour was appointed UN High Commissioner for Human Rights, a position she held amid great controversy for her stands on many issues, including her condemnation of Israel and relative silence on Russia and China. She retired as high commissioner in July 2008, and was awarded the Order of Canada. In July 2009, Arbour became president and CEO of International Crisis Group, an important NGO working on conflict analysis, prevention, and resolution.

Still speaking out. Louise Arbour speaking in her capacity as president of the International Crisis Group. (AP Photo/Virginia Mayo)

---

enemy, omnicide was not contemplated (though it could well be the end result!). It is this element of intention, or even incitement, that can lead to the labelling of the nuclear arms race as genocidal. If, as UN officials have insisted, we can consider the Rwandan slaughter an instance of genocide because, for example, a Hutu official had given a speech in 1992 in which he "explicitly called on Hutus to kill Tutsis and dump their bodies in the rivers,"[30] then what are we to make of a system of national defence that called on thousands of soldiers to take part, if necessary, in the complete annihilation of hundreds of millions of civilians? Or does international, as opposed to civil, war justify such technique? While The Hague Convention[31] merely states that the "right of belligerents to adopt means of injuring the enemy is not unlimited," it is certainly difficult to argue that the use of hydrogen bombs would be limited in any real manner.[32]

FEMALE GENITAL MUTILATION

One of the more complex human rights issues involves the practice commonly called *female genital mutilation*, also often called *female castration, circumcision,* or *genital cutting*. It refers to the practice in many countries of removing or altering parts of the female genitalia at a certain age as a rite of passage. As you can tell, even the question of which name we assign to this practice is highly controversial, for each carries a strong connotation regarding the legitimacy of the act. Two forms of genital mutilation remain prevalent among certain segments of African women: infibulation, the severing of the clitoris and labia while the two sides of the vulva are sutured (tied together); and clitoridectomy, the partial or complete removal of the clitoris or the removal of both the clitoris and the labia minora. Either procedure comes under severe criticism from many quarters, while it is defended as a cultural priority in others. Several Western states, such as Canada and the United States, have made it illegal for doctors to perform the procedure. This law is not insignificant, since large numbers of recently arrived African women live in both states. No strong opposition to the practice exists at the international level, though UN agencies such as the World Health Organization generally oppose it. According to the United Nations Children's Fund (UNICEF), approximately 70 million girls or women aged 15 to 49 in 29 countries in Africa and the Middle East have undergone this practice.[33]

The medical case against female genital mutilation is a very strong one: it can result in excessive bleeding, infection, and even death when improperly performed; and the after-effects include the risk of childbirth complications and of developing obstetric fistulae—holes between the vagina and the bladder, the rectum, or both. Beyond this, however, it represents to many women an act of oppression because it involves removing part of the clitoris or the entire clitoris and thus denies women a basic form of sexual pleasure.[34] Thus, the issue has become a rallying cry for the feminist movement in general. Some Islamic customs, such as *purdah* (the segregation of the sexes and the covering of the female body) have come under intense criticism by Western feminists, but genital mutilation remains the most widely condemned. The international implications of this condemnation can be seen in Canadian refugee policy, which has periodically adopted the inclusion of women fleeing persecution based on discrimination against their sex as a valid reason to seek asylum. However, most women who undergo the procedure are quite young and are unable to leave their native countries on their own.

Howard French, in an article written for *The New York Times* that explores the issue within the context of the question of cultural relativity, writes about a small group of women in Sierra Leone who are working to ban the practice. One of the group's leaders argues that stopping the practice must be done in as culturally sensitive a manner as possible. For example, genital cutting was traditionally the culmination of a months-long retreat, known as *Bondo*, to mark the passage into womanhood, when older women would share their wisdom with the young. As the years passed, the retreat withered into an increasingly shorter ceremony and was finally represented almost solely by the cutting. Trying to restore the full value of *Bondo* might lead to a greater acceptance of the idea that the circumcision is part of a larger process and may eventually be discarded for hygienic reasons. For many, of course, this approach is far too timid. However, stronger appeals can lead to almost immediate condemnation by religious groups; for example, when a Freetown newspaper published a series of articles critical of the custom, "it became the target of a hostile protest movement by a group of women sworn to defend the rite."[35]

As an issue that forces us to examine the universal/relativist, as well as the gender-related discussions above, female genital mutilation, circumcision, or genital cutting will continue to outrage many communities. However, those who are campaigning to stop it are in a difficult bind: the harder they work, especially when they manage to publicly question or challenge the legitimacy of the practice, the more the pro-traditional forces will be inspired to resist change. Governments will have to seriously consider this matter when directing development assistance toward health programs abroad, and when determining their own operational definition of refugee status.

HEALTH AS A HUMAN RIGHT: HIV/AIDS

It is often argued that one of the most fundamental human rights is access to decent health care. This issue forces the divide between those willing to accept the need for societies to redistribute resources and those who reject this need. In the case of HIV/AIDS (see Chapter 11), questions of equal access to health care have come to represent severe human rights questions because many of the antiretroviral drugs that can mitigate the effects of the disease are still not widely available, especially in sub-Saharan Africa where millions suffer and hundreds die every day from AIDS, despite the relatively low death rates in the West, where such drugs are widely obtainable. Efforts to force pharmaceutical companies to dispense the drugs at cheaper cost met with resistance, but declarations by states such as Brazil and South Africa that they would proceed, despite international patent laws, with their own generic versions of the drugs, have gradually shifted Western perceptions on the matter. The humanitarian NGO Medécins sans Frontiers (Doctors without Borders, or MSF) has been very active on these issues, running an "Access to Essential Medicines" Campaign since 1999.[36]

There are other human rights issues associated with the spread of deadly disease. AIDS victims, in particular, are often subject to ostracism (this is doubly tragic for women who have acquired HIV/AIDS after being raped, which is not uncommon in Rwanda and elsewhere). Many of the fundamental human rights of people living with HIV/AIDS—such as the right to non-discrimination, equal protection and equality before the law, privacy, liberty of movement, work, and equal access to education, housing, health care, social security, assistance, and welfare—are often violated on the basis of their known or presumed HIV/AIDS status. It can also be argued that people living without access to decent health care and related education are more susceptible to acquire the disease in the first place; this would include those caught in the global sex industry, where worker protection is all too often the last of concerns. Other serious health concerns, such as malaria, malnutrition, amputation (common in areas such as Angola and Cambodia where land mines were used extensively during conflicts), and psychological problems, severely hamper the human development of millions, even billions, of people today. (The efforts of former UN special envoy for HIV/AIDS Stephen Lewis to help Africans with AIDS are described in Profile 9.6.) Is the achievement of freedom from these problems to be seen as an essential human right, or a privilege obtainable by only a few? We return to this issue in Chapter 11, where we discuss global public health.

TORTURE

The word *torture* is derived from the Latin word *torquere*, which means "to twist." As a means to ensure the compliance of the people to a ruler's wishes, torture is as old as governance itself. When we mention torture, we are referring essentially to acts committed by governments, though it is clear that non-governmental forces in wars and even terrorist and resistance groups resort to it as well. Torture is an old and tested technique that can be employed to get people to confess to just about anything, whether or not they have committed the act in question. Historians write of the unspeakable brutality inflicted by Ivan the Terrible and the Spanish Inquisition burnings, both during the 1500s. Torture was an accepted form of public punishment during the early development of the European penal systems, and it was employed as a device to facilitate slavery and colonialism.

The 1789 French Declaration of the Rights of Man forbade torture "forever" and the U.S. Bill of Rights forbade "cruel and unusual punishment." As incarceration in prisons began

PROFILE 9.6 **Stephen Lewis, Tireless and Eloquent**

Fighting for medicine. Juno Award–winning artist and humanitarian activist K'naan (left) and Dr. James Orbinski (right), Chair in Global Health, listen to former UN Special Envoy for HIV/AIDS in Africa Stephen Lewis highlight what is at stake in the fight for Bill C-393 on Parliament Hill in Ottawa, Wednesday, March 9, 2011. The bill would have helped provide cheap generic drugs for HIV/AIDS patients abroad. (The Canadian Press/ Adrian Wyld)

Canadian Stephen Lewis is the former UN Secretary-General's Special Envoy for HIV/AIDS in Africa. Lewis previously served as deputy executive director of the United Nations Children's Fund (UNICEF) from 1995 to 1999, former Canadian ambassador to the United Nations, and leader of the New Democratic Party of Ontario. Five key objectives for the global anti–AIDS campaign include preventing the epidemic's further spread, reducing mother-to-child HIV transmission, providing care and treatment to all, delivering scientific breakthroughs, and protecting the vulnerable, especially orphans. Lewis has been a tireless campaigner, employing his well-known eloquence, and celebrities such as Oprah Winfrey and U2's Bono, to chide the northern states to do more for Africa's 11 to 14 million AIDS orphans, and to provide affordable, lifesaving drugs to the poor. *Maclean's* chose him as Canadian of the Year in 2003:

> At the beginning of 2003, frustrated and disheartened by Western nations' willingness to ignore the crisis and commit "mass murder by complacency" while they devoted billions to ousting Saddam Hussein, Lewis agonized over whether he could continue. But he decided to turn his despair and anger to advantage, and push all the harder. "I'm still at the end of my rope because I find myself not handling things well when I travel. I get too distraught, too quickly," says Lewis. "But what is my emotional disarray compared to the hell that is happening? I'm in a great rage now, as I understand how many lives we have lost. But I don't want to leave until I see the breakthrough."

At home, he started the Stephen Lewis Foundation (www.stephenlewisfoundation.org), devoted to providing small-scale funding to communities dealing with the ravages of AIDS. Between 2003 and 2011, the Foundation has distributed over $54 million to 700 initiatives, partnering with over 300 community-based organizations in 15 African countries. Lewis says he has been humbled and revitalized by the outpouring of support. "If our governments were one-tenth as generous as average Canadians, the problem would be solved," he says. "Truthfully, when I see what we can accomplish with money on the ground, it's the only time in my life I have wished I was Bill Gates."

SOURCE: JONATHON GATEHOUSE, "CRUSADE FOR LIFE," *MACLEAN'S*, VOL. 116, ISSUE 52, PG. 20–21, DEC. 29, 2003.

to replace torture as the chief means of punishing criminals (though many would equate imprisonment with torture as well), torture became a less acceptable means of enforcing law and order or extracting confessions. However, it was still widely practised throughout the world, and during World War II was employed by the Nazi Gestapo and the Japanese military (among other organizations). The Soviet state under Stalin was renowned for its willingness to punish dissidents with psychological torture. In fact, it would be difficult, if not impossible, to find a society where some form of state-sanctioned torture has not occurred at some time.

Torture continues to be employed as a means of extracting knowledge from political participants, and is often administered by people who have been specially trained as torturers; the act takes place as a means to something else, be it the suppression of popular dissent or the acquisition of information deemed important by government bureaucrats. Though some individuals involved in its application are no doubt sadistic themselves, they are merely employees in a larger project. This definition helps us distinguish torture in the political sense from that in the criminal sense. Obviously, however, the very definition of torture leaves a great deal open to interpretation. Though the international community has signed many agreements[37] that make the use of torture by governments against the convention of international law, the principle of non-intervention requires that states avoid interfering in the domestic affairs of other states.[38] During the Cold War, many dictatorial or military regimes practised torture, and this was largely ignored for the sake of maintaining alliances (both Western and Eastern). Several Latin American regimes, most notably that of Augusto Pinochet in Chile in the 1970s, were infamous for their human rights abuses and torture techniques, and we should note the complicity of the superpowers themselves in many of these cases. In the post-Cold War era, when the old bloc system can no longer be used to justify the toleration of such excesses, some Western governments are moving toward making the receipt of donor assistance contingent on the pursuit of democratic institutions, which would (one might hope) by definition preclude torture. However, critics have pointed out that the Bush administration's "war on terror" employed torture in various forms, including the incarceration of so-called unlawful combatants at Guantanamo Bay prison, a U.S. naval base on Cuba that remained under American control after the Cuban Revolution in 1959 (still open in 2013, despite promises to shut it down); the use of "waterboarding" (which simulates drowning); and the well-publicized and photographed mistreatment of some prisoners of war in Iraq by U.S. soldiers.

INTERNATIONAL LAW AND THE GLOBAL "WAR ON TERROR"

The post-September 11 years have been trying times for international law. In particular, the U.S. global "war on terror" has called the integrity of international war law and international humanitarian law into question. Of course, war law and humanitarian law have been violated in the past by many states. However, U.S. violations have caused special concern because they have had a global impact and because America's support for international law is seen as vitally important. In the wake of the September 11, 2001, attacks on the United States, the Bush administration made a number of decisions that have had far-reaching impact not only on international law but also on the legitimacy of American counterterrorism efforts. As Roy Gutman, David Rieff, and Anthony Dworkin argue, "In a very short time, the United States went from being the guarantor of the regime of humanitarian law to becoming a major violator of it."[39]

The Bush administration's repeated sidestepping of Supreme Court rulings on the validity of torture and the legitimacy of the Guantanamo Bay prison for "enemy combatants" captured in Afghanistan (including a recently repatriated Canadian, Omar Khadr, who was a child soldier at the time of his apprehension) has also caused concern about the eroding observance of U.S. domestic law. In particular, the CIA has come under criticism for continuing interrogation and detainment practices found to be unacceptable by U.S. courts.[40] The administration argued that captured terrorists (broadly defined) were "unlawful combatants" and were therefore not protected under the provisions of the 1949 Geneva Conventions on the Laws of War. This unilateral "reinterpretation" of the Geneva Conventions set the stage for systematic abuses, including secret detentions and long-term imprisonment without trial in facilities such as Guantanamo Bay. U.S. interrogators have used torture (including waterboarding) to extract information. In a procedure called *extraordinary rendition*, the CIA used secret flights to transfer detainees to other countries for interrogation under torture. Several European countries have been accused of permitting these flights to transit through their airspace or territory. As the 2008 *Annual Report* of Amnesty International noted, "With breathtaking legal obfuscation, the U.S. administration has continued its efforts to weaken the absolute prohibition against torture and other ill-treatment."[41]

Indeed, a central theme in the human rights debates of the past few years has been the relationship between civil liberties and the U.S. global war on terror. The violent and disturbing images from the Abu Ghraib prison, which depicted the torture and sexual humiliation of Iraqi prisoners by American military guards, shocked many, but for many more (especially in the Middle East) simply confirmed the belief that the American military enterprise in Iraq was anything but benevolent in intent. The subsequent military tribunals convened to investigate and prosecute these crimes were limited to low-ranking soldiers only, and ignored the wider political and senior military leadership's role in fostering a culture of indifference and contempt toward human rights and international law.[42] According to Amnesty International, in 2007 the U.S. had detained 600 persons without charge, trial, or judicial review in Afghanistan, and as many as 25 000 in Iraq.[43] Meanwhile, questions have also been raised about the global war on terror and its impact on civil liberties in the U.S. and other liberal democracies. The U.S. Patriot Act of 2001 has raised many concerns about the increased powers of law enforcement and intelligence agencies to conduct surveillance, searches, and detainment of citizens and foreign nationals living in America.

Does the record of the past few years mean that international war law and international humanitarian law have suffered permanent damage? There are encouraging signs despite the seriousness of recent violations. International law has been held as the standard of acceptable behaviour, and by violating those standards the U.S. government has paid a political price. Belatedly, the U.S. government began to recognize the cost of these policies to its legitimacy and how they have served to undermine counterterrorism efforts. The Bush administration came under increasing pressure to close Guantanamo and reassert its commitment to the Geneva Conventions. In his first 100 days, President Obama pledged to close Guantanamo Bay and banned the practice of waterboarding (although rendition was still permissible under certain circumstances); the latter was achieved but the former was not. The Guantanamo Bay controversy also involved Canada, as the last citizen of a Western country (and the youngest) to be held at the facility was a Canadian, Omar Khadr. He had been captured at the age of 15 by U.S. military forces in Afghanistan and was subsequently detained at Guantanamo Bay. His trial, plea agreement, and subsequent repatriation to Canada have been subjects of intense debate and criticism from international agencies, human rights organizations, and the Canadian

PROFILE 9.7   Canada, Human Rights, and Detainee Transfer in Afghanistan

In November 2007, an Amnesty International report accused Canada of complicity in torture. Canadian soldiers fighting in Afghanistan had transferred captured Taliban combatants to Afghan government facilities, where they were subsequently tortured by Afghan military and intelligence personnel (there appear to have been approximately 30 cases involved). Critics in Canada charged that this violated international law, as the Geneva Conventions forbid the transfer of prisoners of war to parties known to use torture. Critics also charged that the Canadian government agreed to a detainee transfer agreement with the government of Afghanistan in 2005 that had very weak visitation or oversight measures (unlike similar British or Dutch agreements), and therefore Canadian officials had few avenues to observe the treatment of transferred detainees. Why were Taliban detainees transferred to Afghan authorities under these circumstances? Did senior Canadian officials and military officers neglect the detainee transfer issue because it was considered a low-priority concern? Did Canadian officials lack sympathy for captured Taliban fighters and turn their backs on how they might be treated? Or did Canadian officials sympathize with U.S. legal interpretations of the rights of detainees and were consequently unconcerned with the Geneva Conventions? There are no clear answers to these questions, but the episode caused controversy in Canada and reminded Canadians of our own obligations under international law. In April 2007, the Canadian government signed a new detainee transfer agreement with Afghanistan that many considered a model agreement; one wonders why such an agreement was not signed in the first place.

Bar Association. Canada has also been criticized for violating the Geneva Conventions in Afghanistan (see Profile 9.7).

HUMAN SECURITY AND HUMANITARIAN INTERVENTION

As we have seen in this text, most of the violent conflicts in the world since World War II have been intrastate wars, and much of the human suffering over the same period has been perpetrated by the governments of states. Many instances of mass killing have been cases of "death by government."[44] In other cases, rebel groups have committed mass murder and other gross violations of human rights against innocent civilians. Either way, the question that often faces the international community is whether, and when, and how to intervene in such cases. The 2001 *Report of the International Commission on Intervention and State Sovereignty*, which has heavy Canadian influence, claimed that the international community has the "responsibility to protect" citizens in complex humanitarian emergencies.[45] How do we draw the line between intervention for the sake of protecting human rights, and intervention that is a thinly veiled effort to assert state interests, such as geopolitical dominance in a certain region? How do we ensure that the impact of intervention does not create a worse situation for those we are attempting to aid? We discussed this topic at length in Chapter 7, but revisit it here because it is central to the challenge of protecting human rights and human security.

One need not be a hard-core realist to accept the proposition that state policies will, by and large, reflect the self-perceived national interests of those who make key foreign policy decisions. Though this may change with time, interests are a vital component of international commitments, and we would be wrong to assert that we can expect states to contribute valuable resources and, more importantly, potential lives, to humanitarian missions if there was nothing at stake. This is why the problem of "selective intervention" will always be with us. Humanitarian interventions will tend to be mounted in contingencies where both interests and values are engaged. Interventions will be less likely to occur when interests are not engaged to the same extent. This explains why NATO intervened in Bosnia and Kosovo, but did not in Albania and Algeria. Some have suggested that this is why the UN needs its own army, an independent military force that could be called into action at the UN's request. Of course, even if such a UN army existed (and it is highly unlikely that it will in the near future), it would be called into action only under Chapter 7 of the UN Charter—in other words, when all of the permanent five members of the Security Council agreed it was either necessary or did not challenge their interests. Even in cases when humanitarian motives were a significant factor in a decision to use military force—such as the NATO air war against Serbia in 1999—interests were engaged, in particular the desire to prevent the conflict from reigniting a wider war and a consensus that Slobodan Milošević had to be removed from power. However, not everyone was convinced of the sincerity of the humanitarian motive: critics saw it as yet another expression of NATO power, and another effort to generate increased military spending in the United States and elsewhere.[46] In other cases, humanitarian rationales can be virtually absent: justifying the wars in Afghanistan and Iraq as humanitarian interventions requires a great stretch of the imagination. These wars were motivated by interests, and while humanitarian rationales may have been a small part of the motivation, or were used to obtain political support, it is highly unlikely either of these wars would have been mounted on humanitarian grounds alone. Even the Russians claimed they were acting on humanitarian grounds when they bombed parts of Georgia in 2008. The NATO mission in Libya in 2011, on the other hand, was widely portrayed as a deliberate effort to aid rebel groups in their fight against the Gaddafi regime, leading others to ask why this effort was not repeated early in the subsequent civil war in Syria. French intervention in Mali in 2013, in contrast, defended the ruling government against advancing Islamist rebel groups.

And yet, there are cases in which the humanitarian argument is certainly a strong one. In Somalia in 1992, a drought and a murderous war between clan factions precipitated starvation and human suffering on a large scale. As we saw in Chapter 7, states responded with a troubled and ultimately unsuccessful intervention that was primarily based on humanitarian impulses. However, in Rwanda, where chaos and genocidal violence created a bloody inferno, an intervention would certainly have been warranted. A similar argument might be made for intervention in the Darfur region of Sudan. It would also have been warranted as a response to violence in the DRC (Democratic Republic of the Congo). And yet, only UN peacekeeping operations with limited resources and mandates were mounted in these cases.

Much intervention is thinly veiled self-interest, such as the United States in Colombia, or Russia in Georgia. The UN is often called upon to clean up the mess or to take over when the dirty work of military action is over. Alternatively, post-conflict security might be provided by private security companies, which are increasingly prominent actors in global politics (see Profile 9.8). There are, of course, notable exceptions to this, as our discussion of the liberation of East Timor indicated. More frequently, however, intervention reflects state leaders' perceptions of opportunity or opportunity costs. India's interventions in West Pakistan (now Bangladesh) and Sri Lanka, Tanzania's invasion of Uganda (overthrowing the notorious Idi Amin), the Vietnamese invasion of Cambodia (stopping the murderous Khmer Rouge regime), and Nigeria's engagement in West Africa are all examples of interventions in which local powers perceived interests as well as opportunities. Although it might be argued that all these actions (most of which occurred outside the parameters of UN diplomacy) had positive

PROFILE 9.8 The Return of the Mercenary?

Observers have noticed a trend in many recent military operations: the employment of private military companies (PMCs). The *mercenary* (a soldier who fights for pay and profit) is an age-old fixture in global politics. Mercenaries have been used by rulers, states, and armed groups to supplement their own military capability. Today, private companies specializing in various aspects of military and police operations are increasingly important actors in armed conflicts and peace and stability missions. Private security contracting is big business in world affairs, with major firms from the United Kingdom, United States, South Africa, and elsewhere engaged in hundreds of operations worldwide. There are over 200 PMCs in the world, providing services that include provision of food and maintenance of equipment, translation and interrogation, land mine clearance and education, personal security, military and police training, guarding installations, and supporting military operations. In the past, companies such as Executive Outcomes and Sandline provided combat capacities (both companies no longer exist). Today, no PMC openly offers combat services, although the U.S.–based company Blackwater once indicated it could provide a battalion of peacekeepers if authorized by the UN. Frequently, these companies are hired by governments and armed forces, but corporations and NGOs also hire PMCs to protect assets and individuals. Although PMCs are active across the world, they were heavily employed in Iraq, where companies such as Blackwater (since renamed Academi), DynCorp, Erinys, Global Risk Strategies, and many others employed over 20 000 personnel in 2006 (the second-largest contingent after the U.S. military).

Unsurprisingly, the employment of PMCs has been very controversial. Many consider such companies little more than mercenary organizations, and the accountability of PMC employees has also been called into question. The laws of war generally cover regular military personnel, and there have been numerous cases of PMC employees committing crimes and escaping punishment because no legal mechanisms exist to prosecute them. In Iraq and Afghanistan, security company personnel were immunized against local prosecution, which has made it difficult, if not impossible, to ensure employees are held accountable for their actions. The use of such personnel has also generated a political debate. PMCs may be effective contributors of personnel and capacity in situations where governments and international organizations are unwilling to contribute adequate resources to peacekeeping and stability missions. On the other hand, they are less subject to control and oversight, making them potential liabilities. For example, in Iraq the careless or blatantly illegal actions of some PMC employees have alienated locals and damaged already-strained efforts of military officials to gain public support.

Perhaps the growth of PMCs should not surprise us, as there has been a shift toward privatized security within many states for several decades: there are more private armed security guards in the United States or Africa than there are police and, even more controversially, many prisons are run as for-profit enterprises.

SOURCE: S. PERCY, *REGULATING THE PRIVATE SECURITY INDUSTRY* (OXFORD: ROUTLEDGE, 2006); M. BARSTOW, "SECURITY COMPANIES: SHADOW SOLDIERS IN IRAQ," *THE NEW YORK TIMES*, APRIL 19, 2004, PG. A1; P. SINGER, *CORPORATE WARRIORS: THE RISE OF THE PRIVATIZED MILITARY INDUSTRY* (ITHICA, NY: CORNELL UNIVERSITY PRESS, 2003).

effects, we cannot expect interests to be separated from the humanitarian intervention equation; they will remain an important part of any decision whether to intervene in humanitarian crises. Further, the immensely complex and expensive process of nation building in post-conflict contexts remains at best an experimental process that can be seen as a cross between humanitarian assistance and cultural imposition; it can be no substitute for local institution building and recovery.

Therefore, the need for conflict prevention through the pursuit of human rights—including minority rights and sustainable development—is paramount in the quest for a more humanitarian world. In other words, the best way to avoid the need for humanitarian intervention, and the debates that surround it, is to avoid the need to intervene in the first place. This is yet another "easier said than done" prospect, but one worth pursuing for the sake of those who have perished and those who might perish in future conflicts.

CHILD LABOUR

As mentioned earlier in this chapter, the international community has condemned slavery for some time, beginning with the major European powers at the Congress of Vienna in 1815. By 1880 more than 50 bilateral treaties on the subject had been concluded. At the Brussels Conference in 1890, an anti-slavery act was signed and later ratified by 18 states. This act instituted a number of mutually-agreed-upon measures to suppress the slave trade both in Africa and on the high seas, including the right of high-seas visits and searches, the confiscation of ships engaged in the trade, and the punishment of their masters and crew. Though slavery is still reported in some parts of the world, such as in the Sudan, it is generally considered a criminal activity, as is the employment of child soldiers by groups such as the notorious Lord's Resistance Army of northern Uganda.

However, some would argue that the international community has done much less, and should do much more, to suppress another form of economic activity that many feel is the modern-day equivalent to slavery: the exploitation of child labour. It is impossible to provide accurate estimates of the number of children working in the world because of disputes over what constitutes exploitative labour and because many countries refuse to participate in surveys. In 2010, the International Labour Organization (ILO) estimated that approximately 215 million children were caught in child labour.[47]

In itself, child labour is nothing new; one might argue that it is only Western notions of adolescence that make the phenomenon recognizable. In other words, before we had anything resembling high school, teenagers simply worked in the fields and factories. It is, therefore, a Western notion of industrial progress that helps us see child labour as abhorrent. However, in some cases we might argue further that there is an unusual level of exploitation involved, since children as young as six are toiling away at repetitive and physically demanding jobs in Africa, Asia, and South America. In Malaysia, some children work up to 17-hour days on rubber plantations enduring insect and snake bites. In Tanzania and Kenya, they pick coffee, inhaling pesticides. In Cote d'Ivoire, young boys (many from neighbouring Mali) have been brutally exploited in the cocoa trade, enduring slave-like conditions to ensure chocolate production.[48] In Portugal, children as young as 12 work on construction sites. In Morocco,

A day in a difficult life. Sex workers dress in their work clothes and put on makeup in the late afternoon before heading out to different parts of the city to attract clients in Bangladesh. (© Alan Rolf/Alamy)

they sew carpets for export. In the United States, children are exploited in sweatshops. Many children end up working to pay off their parents' debts, and their opportunities for education and an escape from the cycle of poverty are virtually nonexistent. Many young female workers (and some young male workers as well) often have to endure the additional burden of sexual abuse, including the sexually transmitted diseases associated with prostitution.

The products of child labour, many of which are in the textile industry and include clothing and rugs, often end up for sale in North America and Europe. In Bangladesh, textile and clothing exports to the United States have doubled since 1990. As a result of American pressure, some 30 000 children were removed from the country's textile industry between 1993 and 1995. However, one problem that Western governments will have an even harder time addressing is that many of these children do not end up in school (indeed, many of them are from regions where school is a luxury for the privileged few) but end up on the street, engaging in begging and prostitution to make a living. As an *Economist* editorial suggested, corporate codes of conduct regarding child labour may not end it at all, but "merely shift it to shadier areas of the economy that are far harder to police."[49] Foreign investors are often criticized for exploiting local labour, which usually includes child labour. In response, Levi Strauss provides schooling for child workers in its suppliers' plants in Bangladesh. This raises yet another ethical dilemma, since one can argue the company is merely reinforcing dependence on it and reaping profits in the process. However, without this schooling, what type of future would the children have?

The question of child labour poses one of the harshest challenges to the concept of universal human rights and human security. Although it may be possible for people in the West to look on child labour as an awful thing, and it is condemned by the ILO and the widely signed UN Convention on the Rights of the Child, people in impoverished regions do not force children to work because they derive pleasure from it (sadly, there are exceptions to this, in both the North and the South); rather, they do so because they have to ensure the survival of a family. The economic conditions of the underprivileged seem to be worsening, not improving, as global economic crises take their toll. It is difficult to conceive of an end to child labour in light of this fact. Consider the remarks of a mother (a sweeper and latrine cleaner) from India:

> Nearly all our girls work as sweepers. Why should I waste my time and money on sending my daughter to school where she will learn nothing of use? ... why not put my girl to work so that she will learn something about our profession? My elder girl who is fifteen years old will be married soon. Her mother-in-law will put her to cleaning latrines somewhere. Too much schooling will only give girls big ideas, and then they will be beaten up by their husbands or abused by their in-laws.[50]

The split is pronounced between the North and South on the general issue of labour standards. The United States and some other Western countries have expressed a desire to use the WTO to fight child labour, unfair (i.e., too low) wages, "union-busting," and other practices that they argue may give other countries an unfair advantage in a world moving toward free trade. Southern politicians and economic representatives argue that this effort is really just old protectionism in new clothing. The ILO has tried to implement a universal code of conduct regarding conditions of employment, but it is up against opposition in the South and North. (See Profile 9.9 regarding Canada's contribution to the ILO to eradicate child labour.) Consumers everywhere can investigate the origin of their products and refuse to purchase those made with child labour, but without simultaneous advances in poverty eradication it is of limited use.

SELF-DETERMINATION

To give a more rounded assessment of the concept of collective rights, we turn now to a discussion of the principle of **self-determination**, defined as either the right of all peoples to choose their own government or the right of all peoples to independence and sovereign statehood. As we will see, this issue area presents all sorts of headaches for national leaders, and cuts to the root of the problems inherent in maintaining a status quo international system while attempting to institutionalize ethics on a global scale.

In 1996, the Nobel Peace Prize was awarded to Bishop Carlos Belo and Jose Ramos Horta of East Timor. They had both worked to restore the right of self-determination to the people of East Timor, which has been occupied by Indonesia for more than two decades. This dedication shows how strong the ethic of self-determination remains today, even if it is still unrecognized in many parts of the world. Woodrow Wilson emphasized the right to self-determination in his famous "Fourteen Points" speech following World War I. It was, and still is in many parts of the world, seen as the principle that would guide the way out of colonial domination. States such as the United States were born of revolution and war; states such as Canada found their way gradually, eventually achieving the self-determination necessary to become recognized (in the Canadian case, in the League of Nations) as a sovereign state. More recently, the dissolution of the Soviet empire can be seen also as the achievement of self-determination by the peoples of the former U.S.S.R. and the former Warsaw Pact countries. Some of them, like the Czechs and Slovaks, decided to split even further. Others, such as the Chechens, have become military targets of Moscow instead. Recently, the East Timorese elected to establish full independence, finally ending years of brutal rule by Indonesia; after protracted and intense conflict, a UN-sponsored Australian peacekeeping force entered the country to try to maintain order despite the opposition of some elements of the Indonesian military (see Chapter 7), and the Timorese have finally obtained independence.

PROFILE 9.9 **Canada and Child Labour**

Prompted by child rights activists, Western governments have spoken loudly about the continued problem of child labour. In 1996, the Canadian government made a contribution of $700 000 to the ILO's International Program for the Elimination of Child Labour (IPECL). In August 1996 in Stockholm, then–Minister of Foreign Affairs Lloyd Axworthy, Senator Landon Pearson, and the Honourable Hedy Fry attended the World Congress against the Commercial Sexual Exploitation of Children, along with 700 representatives from 119 countries, more than 100 participants from other international organizations, 500 NGOs and youth delegates, and 500 media representatives. On April 18, 1996, Bill C-27 was tabled, proposing amendments to the Criminal Code to allow for the prosecution of Canadian citizens and permanent residents who engage in commercial sexual activities with minors while abroad—a practice commonly known as "sex tourism." Canada also ratified ILO Convention 183 on the Worst Forms of Child Labour in 2000. Its projected donation for the IPECL for 2011 was US$1 021 311.

SOURCE: LLOYD AXWORTHY, CANADIAN MINISTER OF FOREIGN AFFAIRS, ADDRESS BEFORE THE PARLIAMENTARY SUB-COMMITTEE ON SUSTAINABLE HUMAN DEVELOPMENT OF THE STANDING COMMITTEE ON FOREIGN AFFAIRS AND INTERNATIONAL TRADE, OTTAWA, OCT. 2, 1996.

PROFILE 9.10 Hawaiian Sovereignty?

We usually think of Hawaii as a popular, if expensive, sunny tropical tourist destination, and as having little in common with often-frigid Quebec. However, an independence movement in Hawaii has gained strength over the years. Dozens of pro-sovereignty organizations have appeared, and in 1993 the state legislature passed several laws and resolutions acknowledging sovereignty as a long-term goal. This has long roots: the islands were annexed as an American territory in 1900, and became an American state in 1959. In 1920, Congress adopted legislation that left the native Hawaiians with a small portion of island territory, most of it on the least desirable stretches of land. The rest went to state control, military control, and private ownership. This has resulted in considerable dissatisfaction, and land ownership remains a pivotal issue in Hawaii today. Native Hawaiians continue to experience many of the problems we find in indigenous communities in the rest of North America, including poverty, widespread substance abuse, and cultural frustration. Their fight for independence continues in 2013, including campaigns by the Hawaii nation to educate American tourists, who are often blissfully ignorant of the fact that Hawaii is in effect an occupied territory.

For more information, see http://www.hawaii-nation.org.

The concept of self-determination remains so thorny, however, because of the collective nature of the right. It raises the further question of just who has the right to self-determination. In the Canadian case, two groups, First Nations peoples and Quebec separatists, argue that they should have the right to self-determination; some of them demand a sovereign state of their own. Even the seemingly monolithic United States has separatist movements in idyllic Hawaii (see Profile 9.10), Puerto Rico, and Texas. The problem is much more acute in areas such as the former Yugoslavia, where pronouncements of sovereignty (and their recognition by the international community) have given rise to ethnic conflict and cleansing. Observers remain concerned that the unilateral declaration of independence from Serbia by Kosovo in late winter of 2008, recognized with approval by many Western governments such as the United States and (belatedly) Canada, but firmly rejected by Russia and China, could spark renewed ethnic violence in the region. Russia's military intervention or invasion of Georgia in August of 2008 (condemned by Western governments) was linked to Russian support for secessionist movements in South Ossetia and Abhkazia, two regions of Georgia seeking independence. South Sudan achieved independence in 2011 but has been targeted by Sudanese military attacks. One can argue that the collective right to self-determination, while acting as a vehicle toward freedom for colonized peoples in the past, invariably creates conflict within, and (just as importantly) among, states.

HUMAN RIGHTS AND THE SPECIAL ROLE OF NGOS

By now you are no doubt aware that one of the trickiest aspects of human rights work is that the perpetrators of crimes are so often the same people or institutions that are supposed to uphold and enforce them—in other words, the state itself. For this reason, many people argue that it is short-sighted to trust governments, and that non-governmental organizations without formal ties to governments can do a better job of providing information about and evidence of human rights violations. For example, many NGOs have participated in the work of the War Crimes Commission of Experts in the former Yugoslavia, including Amnesty

International, the International Committee of the Red Cross, Physicians for Human Rights, Médecins sans Frontières, Helsinki Watch, the International League of Human Rights, the Union for Peace and Humanitarian Aid to Bosnia and Herzegovina, the International Criminal Police Association, the National Alliance of Women's Organizations, and the International Centre for Criminal Law Reform.[51]

Arguably, the most prominent NGO involved in the human rights issue area is Amnesty International, which was started in London in 1961 as a campaign by several lawyers and writers. Peter Berenson drew attention to the campaign with an article in London's *Observer Weekend Review*, in which he suggested that the revulsion we often feel regarding human rights violations could be put to good use: "If these feelings of disgust all over the world could be united into common action, something effective could be done."[52] Amnesty now has more than one million members, subscribers, and donors in more than 150 countries, and it seeks to publicize the plight of people who are held as political prisoners around the world. Other groups, such as Americas Watch, Asia Watch, and Africa Watch, monitor human rights adherence by governments, including their foreign policy activities. Church groups are often involved as well, especially in Latin America. The International Committee of the Red Cross is also a prominent player in the human rights issue area.

NGOs use a wide variety of strategies to call attention to their efforts.[53] They campaign in local settings, exhort members to participate in letter-writing campaigns to pressure public officials to reverse certain decisions, and occasionally participate in protests that result in media coverage as well. Information technology, discussed at greater length in Chapter 12, offers newfound opportunities also. In Thailand, people have referred to the "cellular phone revolution" in which students protesting against the government were joined by relatively affluent Thais with modern phones and fax machines. Protestors used mobile phones to keep in touch after an army crackdown in 1992.[54] During and after the infamous Tiananmen Square massacre of 1989, the Chinese government made a concerted effort to control the flow of information in and out of China. Police monitored incoming faxes, but students were able to use electronic mail on the Internet for some time before authorities detected this and began shutting down computers as well. Indeed, a quick Internet search under the phrase *human rights* will produce a bewildering variety of NGO-sponsored websites and media reports. (See Profile 9.11 concerning Aung San Suu Kyi's efforts for human rights in Myanmar.)

The increased participation of women in international affairs is obvious, especially if one looks at the proliferation of women's groups active in the transnational context.[55] Though many feminists argue that women have yet to influence the real citadels of power in a meaningful way, women's groups have successfully brought women's rights issues onto the agenda of international institutions and have played a role in the creation of many international legal instruments designed to protect women's rights. In particular, women's groups have often pursued their goals through UN mechanisms. In 1946, the 45-member Commission on the Status of Women was established to collect data on women's rights and make recommendations. It had an immediate impact as the Declaration of Human Rights was being drafted; the original text, borrowing ideas from the American Declaration of Independence, had begun, "All men are brothers"; the Commission on the Status of Women objected to this sexist language and the draft was amended to read, "All human beings are created free and equal in dignity and rights."[56] Eleanor Roosevelt, the widow of American President Franklin Roosevelt, played a key role in the writing and passing of the Declaration itself.

In the 1970s, ECOSOC (the UN's Economic and Social Council) created the International Research and Training Institute for the Advancement of Women (INSTRAW). As well, the

PROFILE 9.11 A Human Rights Advocate: Aung San Suu Kyi

Recognition, at last. Myanmar opposition leader Aung San Suu Kyi poses for a photo after being presented the Gwangju Prize for Human Rights at the Kim Dae-jung Convention Center in the southwestern city of Gwangju, South Korea, January 31, 2013. She was named the 2004 winner of the prize but could not receive it because she was under house arrest. (© epa european pressphoto agency b.v./Alamy)

Myanmar is a small Southeast Asian state, known as Burma before a military coup in 1988. Its military dictatorship, self-labelled as the State Peace and Development Council, is known as one of the most oppressive governments on earth, severely curtailing freedom of expression and movement and accused of using the forced labour of its citizens. It has actively suppressed opposition with military means, including the beating and imprisonment of protesting monks, whose colourful robes gave rise to the name "Saffron Revolution" in 2007. Most infamously the government denied any substantial emergency aid to victims of the Cyclone Nigris in the

Irrawaddy Delta in the spring of 2008. In this context, Aung San Suu Kyi, daughter of Aung San, the founder of the Anti-Fascist People's Freedom League, has arisen as the key representative of a democratic voice. She has also been consigned to house arrest and had her movements curtailed. However, she was the winner of the Nobel Peace Prize in 1991, and her status as an international figure has restrained the government from more violent methods of limiting her influence. Aung San Suu Kyi's father was killed in 1947, after leading the struggle for Burmese independence, and she lived in India with her mother and attended Oxford University in England in the late 1960s and 1970s before returning to Burma for the last open multi-party elections there in 1990. Her party won the elections but the government refused to recognize the results. She has never left Burma since and refuses to cease her condemnation of the regime. Sadly, her husband, Michael Aris, died of prostate cancer in London in March 1999, and she was unable to see him. He was denied entry to Burma, and she feared that if she were to go to him, she would not be allowed back in the country to resume her struggle. Thus are the hardships those committed to such demanding causes must endure. On-and-off "house arrests" have become routine events for this activist. However, she survived the cyclone of 2008 and the subsequent political unrest in the country, and in April 2012 she won a seat in the national parliament; later that spring she was granted a passport and allowed to travel for the first time in decades. Whether this reflects a genuine shift in Burmese politics or is a clever ploy to deceive the world, it remains a remarkable individual story of a true hero for democracy.

SOURCE: AUNG SAN SUU KYI, *FREEDOM FROM FEAR AND OTHER WRITINGS*, 2ND ED., ED. M. ARSIS, (NEW YORK: PENGUIN, 1995).

UN Development Fund for Women (UNIFEM), part of the UN Development Programme, was established in 1976 to provide direct support to women's projects. In 1979 the General Assembly passed the Convention on the Elimination of All Forms of Discrimination against Women (CEDAW), and 23 experts were appointed to oversee that convention's implementation. In 1985, the UN Division for the Advancement of Women was set up following the important outcome of a conference in Nairobi, Kenya, a document called *The Forward Looking Strategies for the Advancement of Women to the Year 2000.* The UN has an active Commission on the Status of Women, a 45-member intergovernmental body that meets annually in New York and prepares reports for ECOSOC. On March 8, 1993, International Women's Day, the Commission on Human Rights adopted by consensus a resolution aimed at integrating the rights of women into UN human rights mechanisms; in December of that year, the UN adopted a Declaration on the Elimination of Violence against Women. In September 1995, the UN Fourth World Conference on Women was held in Beijing, and drafted a Platform for Action for women's empowerment. The "Beijing Platform" is aimed at removing obstacles to women's participation in all aspects of public and private life, through a full and equal share in economic, social, cultural, and political decision making.[57] The Beijing Platform has been reviewed and expanded in two subsequent conferences held in 2000 and 2005. All of these initiatives were characterized by the active engagement of human rights and women's NGOs.

It is obvious that NGOs, including women's groups, will continue to develop their role in the human rights issue area. They form part of an expanding and increasingly influential network. However, it is unrealistic to assume that such organizations can battle the very real power of states that continue to grossly violate their citizens' rights; that takes concerted international efforts as well as change from within. The fall of apartheid in South Africa is a brilliant example of how that combination can succeed, but the continuation of poverty and violence there is indicative of the long road ahead.

THE QUESTION OF JUSTICE

Many of the issue areas discussed above lend themselves to a discussion of preventive measures. Although it may be impossible to avoid child labour without eradicating poverty or to stop genital female mutilation without a radical change in cultural perspective, it can be argued that crimes against humanity, such as genocide and torture, can be avoided by pursuing what domestic legal experts and judges call the *power of deterrence.* In other words, if state and military leaders have reason to fear retribution, be it through domestic or international means, they may refrain from excessive atrocities. This was the initial idea behind the Nuremberg war crimes trials, discussed above, and it is one of the main justifications for the two international criminal courts described above, as well as the new International Criminal Court.

Both of the extant courts have received mixed reviews. The International Criminal Tribunal for the Former Yugoslavia (ICTY) has more than 1000 staff members from more than 75 countries, and an annual budget of more than US$90 million. As of April 2012, it had indicted 161 accused and had 35 ongoing trials for various war crimes, including grave breaches of the 1949 Geneva Conventions, violations of the laws or customs of war, genocide, crimes against humanity, and sexual offences. Several individuals have been found guilty, but of course they have the right to appeal and have done so. Slobodan Milošević died while on trial, raising concerns about the pace of the court's proceedings. However, the ongoing relevance of the court was illustrated by the summer 2008 capture and extradition of the former president of the Bosnian Serb Republic, Radovan Karadžić, and the subsequent capture of his chief general, Ratko Mladić, in 2011.

Similarly, the International Criminal Tribunal for Rwanda (ICTR) has become a fairly major operation, with 50 trials completed, including the former prime minister of Rwanda, as well as all senior military leaders and high-ranking government officials, several of whom have been convicted for genocide and crimes against humanity, and many more awaiting trial. While fairly widespread support for both courts exists, they face many problems regarding acquisition of both the indicted and evidence; they are often viewed as partial courts, in which guilty verdicts are inevitable (and thus they are equated with Nuremberg, largely viewed as a "victor's court"). Maintaining adequate funding is an ongoing concern as well; these tribunals were intended as temporary institutions, yet their work is far from complete more than a decade after they were established.[58]

The need for a more permanent tribunal was central to many NGO and state demands in the mid-1990s. States and NGOs met in Rome in 1998 to hammer out a treaty to establish an International Criminal Court, based partly on the ICTY and ICTR experience but also as an effort to deter future acts of state genocide and torture. The resulting Rome Statute was ratified on July 1, 2002, when the required 60 **ratifications** were obtained. Canada ratified the Rome Statute in July 2000, but several key states, including Russia and China, refused to sign. The United States initially refused to sign, did so in December 2000, and rescinded its participation on May 6, 2003. The ICC focuses only on the most egregious crimes, such as genocide, crimes against humanity, war crimes, and aggression (when an agreeable definition of the term is found). Many disputes influenced the adoption of the statute: the permanent members of the Security Council insisted that the Council had ultimate control over the Court, while others wanted a strongly independent chief prosecutor's office. During negotiations, the Americans expressed three main reservations, which determined their decision not to ratify. They felt the ICC would be an untamed animal, with unchecked prosecutorial power, despite the statute's built-in principle of complementarity (ensuring that the ICC is the court of last resort); they believed that the ICC's pledge to be apolitical would undermine the influence and integrity of the Security Council; and they claimed that the ICC threatens American sovereignty. Thus, the United States succeeded in persuading several states to enter impunity agreements that would prevent U.S. nationals accused of genocide, crimes against humanity, or war crimes from being surrendered to the ICC.

Nonetheless, the ICC was established on July 1, 2002, when the Rome Statute came into force. Under the leadership of its then-president, Canadian Philippe Kirsch, and an aggressive prosecutor, Argentine Luis Moreno-Ocampo, it began the trials of several individuals apprehended from Africa and made highly controversial indictments of others. On March 14, 2012, the Court convicted Thomas Lubango Dyilo of war crimes committed while he was the leader of the Union of Congolese Patriots during the conflict in the Ituri province of the Democratic Republic of the Congo from 1999 to 2007. This was the first conviction handed down by the ICC. More convictions are expected; in 2013 the Court was investigating 18 cases. The current president of the ICC is Judge Sang-Hyun Song, and Gambia's Fatou Bensouda was sworn in as the second chief prosecutor in the spring of 2012.[59]

For "security reasons," the UN-backed tribunal on war crimes in Sierra Leone tried former Liberian leader Charles Taylor at The Hague instead of in Africa. The ICC has also indicted the leader of the Lord's Resistance Army in Uganda, Joseph Kony. While this might be seen as a progressive step for international criminal law, the ICC indictment is controversial, because Kony refuses to further negotiate a peace settlement with the Ugandan government while the indictment stands. In July 2008 the prosecutor of the ICC accused Sudanese President Omar al-Bashir of genocide, war crimes, and crimes against humanity. The ICC prosecutor went further in March 2009, when the ICC issued an arrest warrant for President Bashir for war crimes and crimes against humanity, marking the first time a sitting head of state has been indicted by the ICC. However, the decision has revealed the limitations of international law in general and the ICC in particular. The ICC has no means of enforcing its indictment or physically arresting President Bashir in Sudan itself. Many African and Arab governments have called on

The chief prosecutor on the ground. International Criminal Court chief prosecutor Fatou Bensouda speaks to internally displaced persons northwest of Nairobi, Kenya, in October 2012. The Court was investigating the violence that rocked the country following the disputed December 27, 2007, presidential election. (AFP/Getty Images)

the ICC to suspend the indictment for a year, arguing that the ICC decision endangers peace talks between the Sudanese government and resistance movements in Darfur. Human rights advocates argue that many African and Arab governments are wary of the indictment, because they are fearful of being indicted for their own human rights violations. In many countries (especially Sudan), the ICC decision has been framed as an example of Western imperialism and interference in the domestic affairs of a country. The immediate Sudanese government reaction was to expel UN and humanitarian aid NGOs from Sudan, with potentially catastrophic consequences for over one million war-affected people in Darfur who are dependent on international agencies for water, food, and health care. As a result, the ICC indictment has caused great controversy and raised questions about whether it was helpful or harmful.[60] These cases are vivid reminders of the tension that can exist between the need to cooperate with leaders of groups or states to establish peace and deliver humanitarian aid and the need to achieve justice for grave violations of human rights.

Another means to achieve justice is unilateral action, and the case of General Augusto Pinochet of Chile provides a promising, but cautionary, tale. Pinochet assumed control of Chile in a brutal coup in 1973 (the former leader, socialist Salvador Allende, was killed; thousands of opponents were jailed and tortured, many of them disappearing altogether during Pinochet's lengthy rule). Chileans rejected his bid to be installed as president-for-life in 1988, but for the plebiscite on this to take place, an agreement was reached that he would be retained as head of the army and that criminal charges would not be laid against members of his regime. While in London for back surgery in October 1998, he was arrested by British authorities, who planned to extradite him to Spain. The Spanish wanted to charge him with various crimes (in the end these were reduced to the charge of torture) against Spanish nationals during his reign.

The international community was quite divided over this issue, since it is highly irregular to detain a former head of state who can claim diplomatic immunity. Eventually, British authorities (the Home Secretary), concerned with Pinochet's failing health, decided he had the right to return to Chile, where he could have faced charges brought on by his own country. However, his health seemed to fail whenever such a prospect loomed, and he died in December 2006.

At any rate, this was an interesting development, because it involved a former head of state. Other developments (and especially the Sudan case described above) suggest such people will not be immune from prosecution in the future. A judicial investigation has been initiated in Senegal, at the request of a coalition of human rights groups, against the former president of Chad, Hissein Habré, for alleged crimes under international law, including torture, committed during his 1982 to 1990 rule. After initial efforts by the European Union to extradite Habré to Belgium for trial were rejected, Senegal took steps to amend its constitution and legal system to put Habré on trial. As of 2008, evidence was still being gathered by Senegalese authorities. Of course, it could be a chaotic situation if every head of state is brought to justice for crimes committed during his or her rule; few would be exempt, depending on one's definition of crimes. The difficult task of moving on—in Chile's case, difficult indeed, as thousands of relatives and friends of present-day Chileans suffered under Pinochet's iron-fisted rule, and in the case of Cambodia, where over a million citizens were murdered by the infamous **Khmer Rouge** in the late 1970s—remains a challenge for victims and their families.

Another path suggests that South Africa's Truth and Reconciliation Commission (TRC) is a superior way to mend the pain of the past while bringing the negative into the open.[61] However, the effectiveness of the truth-and-reconciliation-commission model is dependent on political conditions and the willingness of both past oppressors and victims (who may prefer to try to forget and move on) to expose themselves to the community at large. Furthermore, many commissions are mandated to extend amnesty to those who participate, which is often opposed by victims and their families. In South Africa, the Commission included three committees. The Human Rights Violations Committee investigated human rights abuses that took place between 1960 and 1994, established the identity of and located the victims, and referred them to the Reparation and Rehabilitation Committee. A President's Fund, funded by parliament and private contributions, was established to pay urgent interim reparation to victims in terms of the regulations prescribed by former president Nelson Mandela. Finally, and most controversially, the Amnesty Committee considered applications for amnesty from those accused of human rights violations. Applicants could apply for amnesty for any act, omission, or offence associated with a political objective committed between March 1, 1960, and December 6, 1993 (the cut-off date was later extended to May 11, 1994). Archbishop Desmond Tutu chaired the Commission, lending his considerable moral weight to the proceedings. Between early 1996 and mid-1998, the commission heard more

Seeking truth and opening wounds. Of the truth and reconciliation process, Chair of the TRC Anglican Archbishop Desmond Tutu wrote in the final report that people "risked opening wounds that were perhaps in the process of healing." (AP Photo/Sasa Kralj)

than 20 000 people give evidence, including members of the ruling ANC party who had resorted to violence during the struggle against apartheid.

This process was, no doubt, constructive for many. Although one might have a hard time equating appeals for amnesty with repentance, and most of the major administrators of apartheid never appeared before the commission (perhaps convinced of their own innocence), it was a progressive step to air old animosities and, importantly, cases in which black South Africans had engaged in abuse were given equal footing. Even Mandela's own party, the ANC (African National Congress), tried to block the final Report's publication in 1998, concerned about allegations of ANC atrocities committed outside South Africa. At the same time, such a public step could unleash a swell of demands for compensation the state cannot possibly provide, and it might inflame an already volatile country. It was certainly a risk, though in South Africa's case it appears to have been worth it. Whether this could be a means used elsewhere, however, is uncertain. For example, it will be difficult for Indonesia to come to terms with the legacy of the Suharto dictatorship, even if his family is forced to pay back some of the hundreds of millions of dollars he effectively stole from the country, since the old political machinery is still largely in place in Indonesia. Cambodia's promise to hold a similar truth committee has been criticized as too little, too late by many; and the trial of Saddam Hussein in Iraq was rejected as "victor's justice" by many in the Arab world—as Milošević's unfinished trial at The Hague was seen by many Serbians.

The call for justice and reconciliation will continue to ring out as long as gross human rights violations take place. Students of international relations will remain interested in how the international system responds to human rights violations, and how, in turn, these responses will shape the ability of international organizations and foreign policies to pursue the objectives of human security.

CONCLUSIONS

Although the split between two competing conceptions of human rights (those that protect the individual and those that seek to protect the collective) remains a strong one, governments no longer have the Cold War to blame for ignoring gross human rights violations. One might argue that the current debate centres on the legitimacy of a universal approach that seeks common ethical themes we can apply across the globe against a relativist conception of rights that argues each state has its own right to make its own domestic laws and apply them as each deems necessary. As we have seen, human rights as an issue area covers a diverse range of topics, but they all point up the difficulty of applying any sort of universal barometer of human well-being at the global level, and the difficulties of ensuring human security in a world largely securitized by the state.

We also examined the important role played by NGOs and women in the evolution of an international human rights regime. While NGOs are still relatively powerless compared with the states they seek to monitor, they can publicize cases that may otherwise remain hidden from the international community. Likewise, while the feminist movement has not altered the fundamental discrepancy in power between men and women, women have made considerable progress in popularizing their causes in international forums such as the UN. What remains to be seen, however, is whether this progress can be sustained as the economic forces of globalization take precedence in government thinking. We looked also at various efforts to affect post-atrocity justice, including international criminal tribunals and courts, unilateral prosecution, and truth and reconciliation commissions. We should note also, however, that many analysts and activists argue that real justice must involve economic factors as well—that the world is still divided between the very affluent, the middle class, and the very poor, and that the international system encourages rather than presents an obstacle to this trend. Further, human rights are of little benefit without a survivable environment in which to enjoy them. We turn to the theme of environmental security in global politics in the next chapter.

Endnotes

1. *War and Change in World Politics* (Cambridge, UK: Cambridge University Press, 1981), 224.
2. For J.P. Humphrey's obituary, see *The Globe and Mail*, March 16, 1995, A20. Interestingly, Humphrey was not originally credited with writing the Declaration: "French human-rights activist Rene Cassin, who claimed authorship of the declaration, was honoured with a Nobel Peace Prize in 1968. Yet when researchers pored over Prof. Humphrey's papers at the McGill library [in Montreal], they discovered the original copy in his handwriting."
3. H. French, "Africa's Culture War: Old Customs, New Values," *The New York Times*, February 2, 1997, E1.
4. E. Nadelmann, "Global Prohibition Regimes: The Evolution of Norms in International Society," *International Organization* 44, no. 4 (1990), 481–526.
5. Note, however, that it can be argued that racist conceptions of universal morality delayed the spread of a universalized conception of human rights. Asbjorn Eide reminds us that "there was a long debate in Spanish theological and philosophical discourse on whether the Indians had a soul. This was also the period in which the theories of racism were gaining ground in Europe. From the simplest efforts at classification of human groups by Kant, Linneaus, and Buffon, to full-fledged racist ideologies like that of Gobineau (mid-1850s), these were obstacles to the evolution of universal human rights, as distinct from the Western 'natural rights' which for a long time was limited to the male Caucasian." See "Linking Human Rights and Development: Aspects of the Norwegian Debate," in I. Brecher, ed., *Human Rights, Development and Foreign Policy: Canadian Perspectives* (Halifax: Institute for Research on Public Policy, 1988), 5–30, 27n6.
6. R.J. Vincent, *Human Rights and International Relations* (Cambridge, UK: Cambridge University Press, 1986).
7. See K. Tomasevski, ed., *The Right to Food: Guide through Applicable International Law* (Dordrecht, Netherlands: Martinus Nijhoff, 1987). See also T. Evans, *Human Rights in the Global Political Economy: Critical Processes* (Boulder, Colorado: Lynne Rienner, 2012).
8. F. Halliday, *Rethinking International Relations* (Vancouver: UBC Press, 1994), 167.
9. See R. Niebuhr, *Moral Man and Immoral Society* (New York: Scribner's, 1947); and T. Nardin, *Law, Morality, and the Relations of States* (Princeton University Press, 1983).
10. Hence the title of Stanley Hoffmann's important book, *Duties beyond Borders* (Syracuse, NY: Syracuse University Press, 1981).
11. S. Bailey and S. Daws, *The United Nations: A Concise Political Guide*, 3rd ed. (London: Macmillan, 1995), 87.
12. *Human Rights Watch World Report 2009* (New York, Human Rights Watch, 2008), 1.
13. *Human Rights Watch World Report 1997* (New York: Human Rights Watch, 1996), xxi.
14. *On the Margins of Profit: Rights at Risk in the Global Economy* (New York: Human Rights Watch and the Center for Human Rights and Global Justice, 2008), 3.
15. See *The Worst of the Worst: The World's Most Repressive Societies, 2011* (New York: Freedom House, 2011), http://www.freedomhouse.org/sites/default/files/Booklet%20for%20Website.pdf (accessed June 2011).
16. Figures from Amnesty International Facts and Figures 2012, http://files.amnesty.org/air12/fnf_air_2012 _en.pdf (accessed January 26, 2013). See also Amnesty International, *Amnesty International Report 2012: The State of the World's Human Rights* (London: Amnesty International, 2012).
17. *Human Rights Watch World Report 1997*, xxvi.
18. *Human Rights Watch World Report 1997*, xiii.
19. World Conference on Human Rights, *Vienna Declaration and Programme of Action*, part I, para. 4.
20. Stephen P. Marks, "Social and Humanitarian Issues," in *A Global Agenda: Issues before the 51st General Assembly of the United Nations* (Lanham, MD: Rowman and Littlefield, 1996), 173. See also J. Mertus, *The United Nations and Human Rights* (London: Routledge, 2005).
21. For an important early treatment of this subject, see Q. Wright, "The Outlawry of War and the Law of War," *American Journal of International Law* 47 (1953), 365–76.

22. Michael Walzer, *Just and Unjust Wars*, 2nd ed. (New York: Basic Books, 1992).

23. See United Methodist Council of Bishops, *In Defense of Creation: The Nuclear Crisis and a Just Peace* (Nashville, TN: Graded Press, 1986).

24. Adoption of the Convention of the Prevention and Punishment of the Crime of Genocide and text of the Convention. General Assembly Resolution 260 (III), A/res/260(III), December 9, 1948, http://untreaty .un.org/cod/avl/ha/cppcg/cppcg.html (accessed June 2013). The last two provisions are related to the policies employed by the Nazi regime regarding forced sterilization and a program to transfer Aryan-looking children into Aryan families.

25. See his landmark *Axis Rule in Occupied Europe* (Washington, DC: Carnegie Endowment, 1944), 79.

26. R. Hilberg, *The Destruction of the European Jews* (New York: Holmes and Meier, 1983); see also H. Fein, *Accounting for Genocide: National Response and Jewish Victimization during the Holocaust* (New York: Free Press, 1979).

27. A United Nations report by three African jurists concluded that the killings were part of a larger plan aimed at exterminating the Tutsis; they also noted that "some reliable estimates put the number of victims at close to one million, but the world is unlikely ever to know the exact figure." *The Globe and Mail*, December 3, 1994, A13. Most experts accept 800 000 as the most likely figure now.

28. See, for example, A. Destexhe, "The Third Genocide," *Foreign Policy* 97 (Winter, 1994–95), 3–17; and A. Des Forges, *Leave None to Tell the Story: Genocide in Rwanda* (New York: Human Rights Watch, 1999). The entire Congo region (formerly known as Zaire) has erupted into violent conflict in the years following the 1994 genocide, and the neighbouring state of Burundi has an equally distressing political past and may be on the verge of similar chaos.

29. See P.J. Stoett, "This Age of Genocide: Conceptual and Institutional Implications," *International Journal* 50, no. 3 (1995), 594–618.

30. *The Globe and Mail*, December 3, 1994, A13.

31. Article 22 of the regulations annexed to The Hague Convention of 1907.

32. To quote two international legal experts: "In light of the multifarious effects of hydrogen-bombs, and particularly the area of devastation from 'fall-out' with its unpredictable genetic effects, it could not be said that a belligerent in resorting to thermo-nuclear weapons was adopting a means of injuring the enemy which was 'limited' in any sense of the word." N. Singh and E. McWhinney, *Nuclear Weapons and Contemporary International Law*, 2nd ed. (Dordrecht, Netherlands: Martinus Nijhoff, 1989), 115–16.

33. *The State of the World's Children, 2011: Adolescence, an Age of Opportunity* (New York: United Nations Children's Fund, 2011), 33.

34. See A. Walker and P. Parmar, *Warrior Marks: Female Genital Mutilation and the Sexual Blinding of Women* (New York: Harcourt Brace, 1993).

35. H. French, "Africa's Culture War: Old Customs, New Values," *The New York Times*, February 2, 1997.

36. For more on MSF, which won the Noble Peace Prize in 1999 and operates with an international budget near $1 billion, see K. Phelan, "From Idea to Action: The Evolution of Médicins sans Frontières," in C. Stout, ed., *The New Humanitarians: Inspiration, Innovations, and Blueprints for Visionaries* (Westport, CT: Praeger, 2008), 1–29; and http://www.msfaccess.org/.

37. The most important of which are the Universal Declaration of Human Rights and the Convention against Torture and Other Cruel, Inhuman or Degrading Treatment or Punishment.

38. Note also that if torture takes place during war, it is considered a crime against humanity.

39. R. Gutman, D. Rieff, and A. Dworkin, eds., *Crimes of War: What the Public Should Know*, rev. and upd. ed. (New York: W.W. Norton and Company, 2007), 10.

40. See *Human Rights Watch World Report 2008* (New York: Human Rights Watch, 2008), 540–4.

41. "Foreword," *Amnesty International Report 2008* (London: Amnesty International, 2008), 5.

42. For a harrowing account of the experience of serving at Abu Ghraib, see P. Gourevitch and E. Morris, "Exposure: The Woman Behind the Camera at Abu Ghraib," *The New Yorker*, March 24, 2008, 44–57.

43. Figures from *Amnesty International Report 2008*.

44. R. Rummel, *Death by Government* (New Brunswick, NJ: Transaction Books, 1994). See also I. Horowitz, *Genocide: State Power and Mass Murder* (New Brunswick, NJ: Transaction Books, 1976); T. Weiss, *Humanitarian Intervention: Ideas in Action* (Cambridge: Polity Press, 2007); M. Finnemore, *The Purpose of Intervention: Changing Beliefs about the Use of Force* (Ithaca: Cornell University Press, 2003); and A. Bellamy,

"Humanitarian Responsibilities and Interventionist Claims in International Society," *Review of International Studies* 29, no. 3 (2003), 321–40.

45. For a positive assessment of the development of "R2P" as a new norm in IR by one of its main proponents, see A. Bellamy, *Responsibility to Protect: The Global Effort to End Mass Atrocities* (Cambridge, UK: Polity, 2009).

46. For a controversial treatment, see Diana Johnstone, *Fool's Crusade: Yugoslavia, NATO and Western Delusions* (New York: Monthly Review Press, 2002). More broadly, see N. Wheeler, *Saving Strangers: Humanitarian Intervention in International Society* (Oxford: Oxford University Press, 2000); E. Newman, "Humanitarian Intervention: Legality and Legitimacy," *The International Journal of Human Rights* 6, no. 4 (2002), 108–30; C. Lu, *Just and Unjust Interventions in World Politics: Public and Private* (New York: Palgrave Macmillan, 2006); and S. Hoffman, *The Ethics and Politics of Humanitarian Intervention* (Notre Dame, IN: University Press, 1996).

47. See International Labour Organization, *Accelerating Action against Child Labour* (Geneva: International Labour Office, 2010), 5. See also United Nations Children's Fund, *Child Protection Fact Sheet: Child Labour* (May 2006); and United Nations Children's Fund, *The State of the World's Children 1997* (Oxford: Oxford University Press, 1997), 26.

48. For a detailed account, see C. Off, *Bitter Chocolate: Investigating the Dark Side of the World's Most Seductive Sweet* (Toronto: Random House, 2006). The chocolate industry, much like the diamond industry, has promised to try to eliminate child labour, but the problem persists.

49. "Child Labour: Consciences and Consequences," reprinted in *The Globe and Mail*, June 5, 1995, A17.

50. N. Burra, *Born to Work: Child Labour in India* (New Delhi: Oxford University Press, 1995), 211.

51. As well, four Canadians participated in a team of 11 women lawyers, sponsored by the Dutch government, who went to the former Yugoslavia to interview victims of sexual assault and collect evidence for the related military tribunals. See also B. Allen, *Rape Warfare: The Hidden Genocide in Bosnia-Herzegovina and Croatia* (Minneapolis: University of Minnesota Press, 1996).

52. P. Berenson, "The Forgotten Prisoners," *Observer Weekend Review*, May 28, 1961, 21.

53. See, for example, V.P. Nanda, J. Scarritt, and G. Shepherd, eds., *Global Human Rights: Public Policies, Comparative Measures, and NGO Strategies* (Boulder, CO: Westview, 1981). For an advanced treatment of how the structures of NGOs affect their agenda-setting powers, see W. Wong, *Internal Affairs: How the Structure of NGOs Transforms Human Rights* (Cornell University Press, 2012).

54. See P. Shenon, "Mobile Phones Primed, Affluent Thais Join Fray," *The New York Times*, May 20, 1992, A10.

55. See S. Shreir, ed., *Women's Movements of the World: An International Directory and Reference Guide* (Essex, UK: Longman, 1988). See also Women, Law, and Development International's website, http://www.wld.org.

56. Bailey and Daws, *United Nations*, 90.

57. The United Nations Fourth World Conference on Women Platform for Action, Beijing, China, September 1995, http://www.un.org/womenwatch/daw/beijing/platform/plat1.htm#statement (accessed June 18, 2013).

58. Both courts have websites: see www.icty.org and http://www.ictr.org; for the ICC, see http://www.icc-cpi.int. For slightly outdated but comprehensive treatments of the state of international criminal law, see S. Ratner and J. Abrams, *Accountability for Human Rights Atrocities in International Law: Beyond the Nuremburg Legacy*, 2nd ed. (Oxford: Oxford University Press, 2001); A. Cassese, *International Criminal Law* (Oxford: Oxford University Press, 2003), and Y. Beigbeder, *Judging War Criminals: The Politics of International Justice* (New York: St. Martin's Press, 1999).

59. For critical discussions on the ICC, see H. Carey and S. Mitchell, eds., Trials and Tribulations of International Prosecution (Lanham, MD: Lexington Books, 2012).

60. See "The ICC Indictment of Bashir: A Turning Point for Sudan?" International Crisis Group website, www.crisisgroup.org (accessed July 2, 2013); and N. MacFarquhar and M. Simons, "Bashir Defies War Crime Arrest Order," *The New York Times*, March 5, 2009, http://www.nytimes.com/2009/03/06/world/africa/06sudan.html?_r=1 (accessed June 18, 2013). For a critical take on the ICC's predilection to issue arrest warrants while conflicts are still taking place, see P. Stoett, "Justice, Peace, and Windmills: An Analysis of 'Live Indictments' by the International Criminal Court," in H. Carey and S. Mitchell, eds., *Trials and Tribulations of International Prosecution* (Lanham, MD: Lexington Books, 2012), 117–31.

61. For an analysis, see C. Moon, *Narrating Political Reconciliation: South Africa's Truth and Reconciliation Commission* (Lanham, MD: Lexington Books, 2007).

PART THREE

DIRECTIONS

In this final section, we look forward and examine some of the big issues likely to dominate the study of global politics in the 21st century. These are burning issues already, and all these challenges are familiar ones: environmental degradation and climate change; population growth, migration, dislocation, and health; and the impact of information technology on global politics. However, we contend that these issues will loom larger than most on the canvas of global politics in the near future. Climate change and natural resource depletion will pose serious threats to human security and international justice. Population growth and movement will place tremendous burdens on the world's food supply and other natural resources, exacerbating social friction, and the threat of pandemics of infectious diseases will continue to dominate global public health efforts. Advanced information technology will continue to provide opportunities for human and social well-being, as well as aggravating existing economic and social problems. Although the prognostications can at times be bleak, the fact that the human race has survived so many centuries of war, plague, and hardship offers some comfort! As we discussed in preceding chapters, societies and governments have proved capable of cooperating and addressing political problems. Of course, the prospects for conflict and failure exist as well. The pivotal question will be whether humanity can respond collectively, and effectively, to the global challenges we face.

Global Ecopolitics: Crises and Change

The whole point of being a doomsayer is to agitate the world into proving you wrong or into doing something about it if you are right.

—Les Kaufman, 1993[1]

It is time to understand "the environment" for what it is: the national security issue of the twenty-first century.

—Morton Kaplan, 1994[2]

Human society has been built using the planet as an endless debit account.

—Clive Doucet, 2007[3]

INTRODUCTION: OUR HABITAT IN PERIL

The earth has endured centuries of human population growth, agricultural development, resource extraction, landscape-ravaging wars, and industrial pollution, but we are clearly moving into a new era. As we watch the **polar ice caps** melt with unprecedented speed, the Amazon jungle continue to burn, and the oceans emptied of fish by industrial harvesting, it is difficult to escape the impression that human society is committing collective suicide. Major UN–sponsored reports, such as the Millennium Ecosystem Assessment (2005) and the Global Environmental Outlook (2012), highlight a broad range of serious environmental challenges, including the following:[4]

- *Biodiversity loss and habitat destruction.* Sixty percent of our ecosystems have been degraded, and resource exploitation has caused irreversible damage to the earth's natural processes. About 35 percent of the world's **mangrove forests** have been lost since 1980. The species extinction rate is now 100 to 1000 times above the background (or natural) rate, and will only increase as the impacts of climate change intensify.

- *Land stress and degradation.* The conversion of land to agriculture and the widespread use of pesticides and fertilizers are altering the land surface of the earth more rapidly than at any time in human history, and climate change is altering both polar and arid regions. One of the most severe and prolonged droughts in recorded North American history occurred in 2012.

- *Ocean stress.* Fisheries resources are being overexploited, with all major commercial fisheries now fully harvested or overharvested. In the past 20 years, 20 percent of the world's biodiverse coral reefs have been destroyed, and climate change is accelerating this process, as well as raising sea levels to dangerous heights.

- *Freshwater stress.* The quality of aquatic ecosystems continues to decline, a function of increased demand for fresh water as well as the increased threat to safe supplies from pollution and invasive species. In 2013 it was reported that the North American Great Lakes water levels were reaching record lows, and invasive species continue to threaten native fish and crustacean populations.

This chapter can only present a partial description of the tremendous challenges posed by contemporary and future global ecopolitics. However, we should note that—as both liberal institutionalists and critical theorists stress—crises present opportunities for cooperation: environmental diplomacy, transnational activism, and corporate activity are often aligned with public concern to combat these problems. The question we face is whether, given intransigence, competitiveness, and the sheer reliance on a fossil fuel–based economy in countries such as Canada—where tar sands oil production has further increased **greenhouse gas** (GHG) emissions —we will collectively overcome these problems, or continue along the path of inequity described in Chapter 8.

Industrialization and environmental destruction: Till death do they part? A spectacular column of smoke and fire rises beside the derrick as the first oil and gas is flared at Imperial Oil's Leduc No. 1 on February 13, 1947, in Alberta, Canada. The initial daily production was about 1000 barrels; by 2011, daily production of oil from the Albertan tar sands operations exceeded 1.7 million barrels. (CP PHOTO)

While it was once possible to relegate environmental issues to a second tier of priorities in the IR discipline, today even structural realists acknowledge that the environment is pertinent to national security, geopolitical thinking, and international political economy. For example, due to climate change the Arctic will soon become navigable on a year-round basis, provoking new political tension among circumpolar states over territorial and resource claims (Canada assumed the chair of the Arctic Council in 2013). The development of the numerous international environmental regimes discussed in this chapter pushed analysts to think harder about cooperative solutions to problems of the **global commons**, and the maintenance and effectiveness of related institutions. Many other theorists, especially ecofeminists, began their analytical assumptions with concern over the **biosphere** foremost in mind, but even those who did not, such as most neo-Marxists, have had to incorporate ecology into their thinking about the evolution of the world system. And constructivists of all stripes would agree that one of the most important social conventions in any community, be it a small village or the global one, is the set of dominant assumptions and attitudes we have constructed to rationalize our approach to nature.[5]

Global ecopolitics is where ecological concerns meet international political theory and action. We address the more specific issue of overpopulation and the movement of peoples, as well as the spread of infectious diseases, in Chapter 11. Here, we will focus on how environmental problems are a source of both convergence and divergence in global politics, moving from a discussion of the main actors and governance structures involved, to problems of the commons and climate change, the oceans, land degradation, and species impoverishment. We then discuss transboundary issues, before visiting the ongoing debate over the linkages between environmental degradation and violent conflict. What emerges is a complex political landscape full of challenges and opportunities that simply must be faced if human society is to survive its own onslaught on the earth.

GLOBAL ECOPOLITICS: ACTORS AND STRUCTURES

One of global ecopolitics' distinctions is the sheer level of complexity involved, which can be demonstrated with reference to the many actors in the field. Obviously, the state remains a central player. Most of the environmental diplomacy we discuss below was conducted by state agents, often representing the executive branch of government but also departments and agencies. In Canada (see Profile 10.1), these include the departments of Environment, Foreign Affairs and International Trade, and Natural Resources, as well as the Public Health Agency. To confuse matters somewhat, we often see other levels of government (for example, the premiers of Canadian provinces, or governors of American states) taking decisive action on international agreements. Indeed, national government leaders from federal states often find themselves playing two-level games at international talks, dealing with other state officials in negotiations while faced with the daunting prospect of going home and actually implementing agreements that may challenge the jurisdictional authority of other levels of government in their own country. For example, in 1997 the Canadian government negotiated and signed the Kyoto Protocol on climate change, committing Canada to reducing its greenhouse gas emissions (GHGE) by 6 percent from its 1990 levels. This was met with open disdain by several provincial governments, who under the Canadian constitution have authority over many of the areas that need to be changed in order to achieve such goals. Representatives from the supranational European Union face a similar dilemma.

At the international level, state cooperation and civil society engagement has given rise to *global environmental governance.* In 1972, the UN sponsored the Conference on the Human Environment (UNCHE) in Stockholm, where the **UN Environment Programme (UNEP)** was created. Its secretariat, based in Nairobi, attempts to coordinate all the UN bodies involved in environmental areas. One of UNEP's most important tasks was to aid in the setup of the UN Conference on Environment and Development (UNCED), held in Rio de Janeiro, Brazil, in June 1992, under the leadership of Canadian Maurice Strong. UNCED was the largest diplomatic summit ever, and it generated a great deal of press coverage around the world. It established the UN Commission on Sustainable Development (CSD), the "Rio Declaration," a framework for action labelled Agenda 21, as well as several landmark agreements discussed in this chapter. A "Rio+10" summit was held in 2002, and a "Rio+20" summit was held in 2012. But none of these initiatives have even come close to solving the ecological crises we are watching unfold today; and most of them have yet to receive the necessary funding for full implementation.

When it comes to the environmental impact of the role played by the major development players in the UN system, many analysts are highly critical. In particular, the International Bank for Reconstruction and Development (IBRD or World Bank) and the International Monetary Fund (IMF) have come under fire for promoting large-scale industrialization and

PROFILE 10.1 Selected Canadian International Environmental Commitments—and Withdrawals

1909	Treaty between the United States and Great Britain Relating to Boundary Waters	1989	Basel Convention on the Control of Transboundary Movements of Hazardous Wastes and Their Disposal
1916	Convention between the United States and United Kingdom for the Protection of Migratory Birds in Canada and the United States	1991	Canada–U.S. Air Quality Agreement
			NOx Protocol to the 1979 LRTAP Convention/Declaration on the Protection of the Arctic Environment
1946	International Convention for the Regulation of Whaling (Canada withdrew in 1982)	1992	UN Framework Convention on Climate Change
			Convention on Biological Diversity
1963	Treaty Banning Nuclear Weapons Tests in the Atmosphere, in Outer Space, and Under Water		Agenda 21
			"Rio Declaration" Statement of Guiding Principles on Forests
1971	Convention on Wetlands of International Importance	1993	North American Agreement on Environmental Co-operation (NAFTA)
1972	Canada–U.S. Great Lakes Water Quality Agreement (renewed in 2012)		Convention for the Prevention of Pollution from Ships (some annexes)
	Stockholm Declaration on the Environment	1994	International Tropical Timber Agreement (revised in 2006; Canada withdraws in 2013)
	London Convention on the Prevention of Marine Pollution by Dumping of Wastes and Other Matter		Protocol to LRTAP on Sulphur Emission Reductions
	Convention Concerning the Protection of World Cultural and Natural Heritage	1995	UN Agreement on Straddling Fish Stocks and Highly Migratory Fish Stocks
1973	Convention on International Trade in Endangered Species of Wild Fauna and Flora		United Nations Convention to Combat Desertification (Canada withdrew in 2013) in Those Countries Experiencing Serious Drought and Desertification, Particularly in Africa
1978	Protocol on the International Convention for the Prevention of Pollution from Ships		
1979	Convention on Long-Range Transboundary Air Pollution (LRTAP)	1996	Comprehensive Nuclear Test Ban Treaty
1981	Convention on the Prohibition of Military or Any Other Hostile Use of Environmental Modification Techniques	1997	Kyoto Protocol on Climate Change (ratified 2002; withdrew 2012)
			Canada–Chile Agreement on Environmental Co-operation
1982	UN Convention on the Law of the Sea (ratified 2003)	2000	Biosafety Protocol for Biodiversity Convention (signed but not ratified)
1985	Vienna Convention on the Protection of the Ozone Layer	2004	Stockholm Convention on Persistent Organic Pollutants
	Canada–U.S. Agreement Concerning Pacific Salmon	2004	Rotterdam Convention on the Prior Informed Consent Procedure for Certain Hazardous Chemicals and Pesticides
1986	Canada–U.S. Agreement on the Transboundary Movement of Hazardous Waste		
1987	Montreal Protocol on Substances That Deplete the Ozone Layer	2013	Minamata Convention on Mercury

structural adjustment programs that encourage the depletion of natural resources for export. We should note, however, that initiatives such as the Global Environmental Facility are contributing to the advancement of less harmful environmental technologies. Meanwhile, suggestions to establish a World Environmental Organization, which would supersede the UNEP and be placed on an equal footing with the WTO (World Trade Organization) or IMF, have not been realized.

Perhaps just as importantly, however, the private sector plays a large role in any form of environmental policymaking, be it a supportive or oppositional one. The extractive industries (those that take natural resources from the earth for redistribution at a profit elsewhere) are self-evidently major actors; this includes the energy industry (oil and natural gas, coal, and uranium) and mining, forestry, and fishing. As our previous discussions of MNCs have made clear, these are extraordinarily powerful industries, though they are not free from the vagaries of the marketplace or **geopolitics**. Increasingly, they are being forced to adapt to the environmental agenda, but they are often accused of engaging in public relations campaigns that "greenwash" their actual negative contribution or "ecological footprint." Private-sector actors are also playing a major role in funding research and implementing renewable energy sources (such as wind, geothermal, and solar power) and advancing recycling technology, to name but a few areas. Efforts to **privatize** water and other elements of the commons are more controversial. While there is often a wide divide between the pro-globalization, market liberal approach to environmental challenges (which suggests that the solution lays in further economic growth and market-based decisions) and those who believe either a strong state (a "green leviathan") or a socialist one is necessary, most analysis today accepts the significance of private-sector participation in locating achievable solutions.[6]

Many observers would claim that NGOs have been the principal instigators all along, since they played a large role in forcing states to take environmental concerns seriously in the first place. NGOs have often assumed a watchdog role, reporting on the activities of MNCs and governments for the general public; they can also influence policy formulation at the national level. For example, in the past, Greenpeace members have been included in the official American delegation to the International Whaling Commission, where the United States has consistently opposed lifting the global moratorium on commercial whaling now in place (controversially, it insists Alaskan Inuit and First Nations peples should have the right to whale, but not Japanese or Norwegian coastal fishermen). NGOs also influence the operations of multilateral forums, contributing to World Conservation Union meetings and their outcomes. At times, they are criticized for insisting on a Western environmentalist ethic, even in local situations where people are more attuned to living on the land than most NGO members have ever been, and for focusing on a few key issues, including ones that can aid in fundraising appeals. No doubt, this is a cause of some friction, as the debate over the Canadian seal hunt suggests. Groups such as the International Fund for Animal Welfare (IFAW) strongly oppose the hunt, which in 2013 was allocated a quota of 400,000 harp seals. Sealers argue they are engaging in a vital aspect of their livelihood in economically depressed regions, and that urban environmentalists neither understand nor care about them. (Though taking baby whitecoat seals is banned, harp seals over two weeks old can be killed, which enrages those who campaign tirelessly against this hunt.) With some exemptions, seal products remain banned in the United States and were banned in the European Union in May of 2009, and in Belarus, Kazakhstan, and Russia in 2011, though markets persist in Asia. The Canadian government adamantly opposes the bans, and has appealed to the WTO.

We should add a few words here as well about the vital role played by science in global eco-politics, in issues ranging from the debates over the impact of genetically modified organisms (see Profile 10.2), to concerns with the implementation of nanotechnology, to discrepancies over the remaining populations of endangered species. However, nowhere is the relationship between science and politics more evident than on the issue of climate change. From a political perspective, the series of assessment reports published by the Intergovernmental Panel on Climate Change (IPCC) could be a vital step toward achieving the type of collective action such global problems demand, confirming what many political analysts have suggested: science is playing an increasingly large role in galvanizing political action, even at the international level. Scientific consensus was certainly integral to the process of negotiating an international regime to curb the destruction of the ozone layer. However, there is a fine line between the necessary use of science to protect human and ecological health, and the adoption of a techno-cratic approach to governance that would put inordinate power in the hands of "scientific experts," many of them employed by large corporations with their own commercial interests.

Finally, there is the individual—as consumer, as voter, as taxpayer, as political animal. This is one subfield of global politics where we can without equivocation say that the actions of each of us make a difference, and that our own thinking about the environment and change will impact our broader local and ultimately global communities. As David Suzuki and Holly Dressel have argued, a growing environmental consciousness is emerging at the local and community level, exerting pressure for positive change on governments, corporations, and

PROFILE 10.2 Genetically Modified Organisms (GMOs)

Genetic engineering refers to a variety of techniques aimed at deliberately changing the genetic makeup of a cell or organism. Scientists have been able to modify the genes of many crops, including tobacco, tomatoes, corn, soybeans, canola, squash, potatoes, and cotton. Some crops, such as the Flavr Savr tomato (which is designed to prolong freshness) have been available in North American markets for many years. The tomato (along with a wide range of other GM crops) is FDA–approved, but critics have argued that the long-term effects on health and cross-pollination and contamination scenarios are unknown. Many plants have been modified to increase their resistance to weed killers, insects, viruses, or fungi. Researchers can also genetically engineer many food animals, including fish, cows, goats, sheep, and pigs. This can be combined with cloning techniques to produce identical animals, which can be used for research into human health issues and even for organ transplants. Critics are concerned about the ethical implications of modifying nature and

possible accidents. The powerful biotechnology industry, much of it located in the United States and Japan, wants the EU and others to open their markets to GMOs, while the EU—reflecting European public opinion—is reluctant to do so. The industry and GMO advocates argue that such technology improves crop yields and holds the promise of eliminating or reducing world hunger and nutritional deficiencies. However, concerns remain about the tendency of large firms to force farmers to use their products (especially in the southern hemisphere) and the lack of labelling identifying GMO products in supermarkets. NGOs such as Greenpeace have made GMOs part of their campaign platform. While the Biosafety Protocol of the Convention on Biological Diversity dealt with the issue to some degree, it remains a contested trade, public health, and ethical issue.

SOURCE: FOR A CANADIAN PERSPECTIVE, SEE S. MULLIGAN, "CANADA AND THE GENE REVOLUTION IN AGRICULTURAL BIOTECHNOLOGY," IN C. GORE AND P. STOETT, EDS., *ENVIRONMENTAL CHALLENGES AND OPPORTUNITIES: LOCAL-GLOBAL PERSPECTIVES ON CANADIAN ISSUES* (TORONTO: EMOND MONTGOMERY, 2009), 43–70.

societies.[7] Though the ecological and political problems we discuss below seem insurmountable, in ecopolitics positive action often begins at the kitchen table.

PROBLEMS OF THE COMMONS

Global environmental issues are often characterized as problems of the commons, public goods management, or, more technically, international common pool resources. According to Wilfred Beckerman, this "refers to situations in which nobody can be excluded from the use of an asset—such as common grazing land, or fishing grounds, or the atmosphere [but] one person's use of the asset reduces the amount available to other potential users' unrestricted use of the asset and can easily lead to over-use, so that only if some voluntary or enforcement mechanism is introduced can the supply be matched to the demand."[8] One example of an international common pool resource is the moon, though most resources are rather more accessible! The essential problem is that everyone has an incentive to conserve the commons together but also has an individual incentive to exploit them: cooperation is necessary to balance these counterincentives. Or, as Stephen Krasner puts it, "the basic challenge for states is to overcome market failure, the situation in which individual rational self-interested policies produce outcomes that leave each state worse off than it might otherwise have been."[9] The added dimension of environmental degradation demands we move beyond asking simply how states can share resources to asking how they can simultaneously conserve, preserve, or avoid polluting them.

Solutions to typical problems of the commons are rather elusive. Many have argued that the privatization of land or other resources will increase the sense of environmental responsibility or stewardship by rights holders. This proposition is debatable enough in a domestic context, but is even less clear when it comes to the international arena, where privatization is akin to territorialization. For example, the 1982 UN Convention on the Law of the Sea (UNCLOS) designated new 200-nautical-mile (approximately 370-kilometre) **exclusive economic zones (EEZs)** in which coastal states would have not only resource rights but also inherent environmental responsibilities. The hope was that inside the 200-mile limit, increased coastal authority by individual states would lead to better management. Instead, "coastal countries such as Canada and the United States displaced overseas fleets from Europe and Japan with new programs and subsidies to build up their domestic fleets [then] scooped up cod and salmon on both coasts with alarming speed, and disastrous results."[10] Relying on the responsibility or stewardship of rights holders (be they individuals or states) may not be the best approach to protecting the environment. Furthermore, the entire principle of private property and legal ownership of resources is far from universal, and some peoples, such as indigenous groups, would reject this concept as a colonial imposition. Finally, the creation of strong global governance structures to reduce or prevent unsustainable exploitation of the environment is viewed with concern by states and corporations concerned with economic growth and profit.

Indeed, one of the central ecopolitical questions that concerns scholars is how dealing with the commons affects national sovereignty, the core principle of the UN Charter. Does the rise of transboundary pollution problems justify infringements on the sovereignty of states, as do cases of extreme international security concerns and genocide? Is there a "responsibility to protect" the environment? Has the creation of institutions designed to mitigate environmental damage threatened the long-term future of the nation-state as predicted by the older functionalist school (see Chapter 5)? It is quite clear, in the legal sense, that the principle of sovereignty remains sacrosanct. In 1962, the UN General Assembly adopted a resolution that referred to the "inalienable right" of all states to freely "dispose of their natural wealth and resources."[11] Malaysia made particular reference to this precept during the forestry negotiations leading up to UNCED in 1992. This is a common north–south sticking point as southern state elites claim that any global environmental agenda infringes on their national sovereignty. Principle 2 of the Rio Declaration asserts that "states have the sovereign right to exploit their own resources pursuant to their own environmental and developmental policies."

There is also the question of cost distribution, or who should pay for international efforts to save the commons. On issues such as ozone-layer depletion and global warming, there is a large divide between the North and the South on burden sharing. The collective decision to protect the ozone layer (which shields us from the sun's ultraviolet radiation) from volatile chemicals known as **chlorofluorocarbons (CFCs)** used in refrigeration, industrial production, and aerosol cans set an important precedent. CFC molecules destroy ozone molecules in the earth's atmosphere, resulting in higher levels of exposure to ultraviolet radiation from the sun, especially in northern and southern latitudes. The result is increased rates of skin cancer, eye problems, and adverse impacts on animals, plants, and agriculture. But the vast majority of states affected by this potential crisis did not even use CFCs in their industries. The Montreal Protocol to the 1985 Vienna Convention on the Protection of the Ozone Layer established a cost-sharing agreement to help less-industrialized states develop alternatives to CFC production; by mid-2012, the Fund had supported the transfer of technology and capacity building through over 6850 projects and activities in 145 low-income countries. Environmental diplomat R.E. Benedick concludes, "As a consequence of the ozone issue, the richer nations for the first time acknowledged a responsibility to help developing countries to implement needed environmental policies without sacrificing aspirations for improved standards of living."[12] However, one might argue that the Montreal Protocol, a fairly demanding document reached in a relatively short time, was successful because the scientific consensus on the causes of ozone depletion was widely accepted, there was genuine international fear of the consequences, and CFCs were relatively easy to replace in products and industrial processes at low cost. This formula for success has been difficult to replicate in many other areas related to the environment.

Another example of relative success in managing the commons is Antarctica, which is in essence the world's largest wildlife sanctuary, home to some 100 million birds, including the famous penguin, six species of seals, fifteen species of whales, and ice sheets that offer unique windows on geophysical history. The Antarctic Treaty, in many ways a landmark, was signed in 1959.[13] Though several nations have laid (and maintain) claim to specific parts of Antarctica, they all agreed to adhere to a common management scheme. Both of the Cold War superpowers signed, and Antarctica became the world's first nuclear-free zone. Antarctica has maintained its non-militarized status since. The treaty provides onsite verification measures on research conducted in the region, and it opened the door for non-claimant nations to establish research facilities on the continent. Canada participates in the **Antarctic Treaty System (ATS)** as a non-consultative party (i.e., it has no voting rights in ATS meetings but can attend as an observer). The ATS involves other management regimes, such as the **Convention on the Conservation of Antarctic Marine Living Resources (CCAMLR)**, well known for its ecosystem approach to resource management. But this example of success must be tempered by several facts. Many would rather see a global, UN–based approach to managing this common area. Realists point out the lack of access to resources or military value of Antarctica, suggesting it is an anomaly. And the Antarctic ice sheet, which contains close to 90 percent of the world's ice, is beginning to collapse due to climate change, especially in the West Antarctic. It is to that much more stubborn and complex issue that we turn next.

CLIMATE CHANGE

The logic of the greenhouse effect is well understood: human activity is causing an increasing accumulation of greenhouse gases (GHGs) in the earth's atmosphere, preventing more and more solar heat from escaping back into space. The naturally occurring greenhouse effect is essential to life on Earth as we know it; we would not survive on what would otherwise be a cold barren planet. But human activity has increased the levels of carbon dioxide, methane, nitrous oxide, and other greenhouse gases in the atmosphere, increasing global temperatures. This has led to increased calls from the scientific community and environmental groups (and increasingly governments and publics) for mitigation strategies to reduce GHG emissions to hold global temperature increases to safe levels. Meanwhile, current climate change impacts such as the increased frequency and intensity of extreme weather events, such as hurricanes (including Hurricane Katrina, which devastated New Orleans in 2005, and Sandy, which hit the U.S. East Coast in 2012), melting ice sheets and thawing permafrost, droughts in Africa, disastrous wildfires across Australia in early 2013, and the movement of environmental refugees from Pacific islands such as Vanuatu due to rising sea levels, force us to think about the potential damage climate change could cause in the future, and what adaptation measures can be taken to adjust to the climate change that is already occurring.

Our heavy reliance on the burning of fossil fuels (coal, oil, and natural gas) for energy generation and transportation releases billions of tonnes of GHGs into the atmosphere every year, and deforestation, livestock farming, cement production, and other activities add millions more. Unusual warming has also shifted the distribution and seasonal appearance of vector-borne diseases such as malaria, dengue fever, and schistosomiasis; and invasive species, such as the zebra mussel and pine beetle in Canada, are encouraged by warmer temperatures to spread their assault on local ecosystems. Circumpolar states such as Canada and Russia will face special challenges and opportunities as the Arctic passages become ice-free on a year-round basis, encouraging shipping and oil drilling. Drought has become more common in many regions, flooding more common in others. Indeed, climate uncertainty is the new normal.

In the face of growing climate change effects, awareness and calls for action have increased. The 2007 Human Development Report focused on the pressing issue of how low-income states can adapt to climate change. In 2007, Al Gore and the IPCC won the Nobel Peace Prize for their work on raising awareness and understanding of the issue (and Gore's documentary film, *An Inconvenient Truth*, won an Oscar). An estimated two billion people watched some part

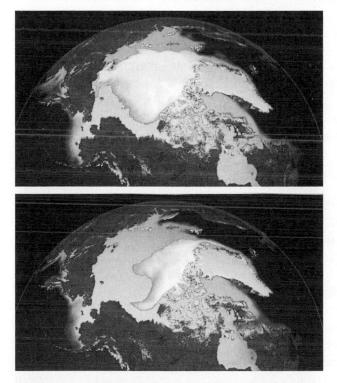

Global environmental change. The change in the amount of Arctic sea ice from 1980 (top) to 2012 (bottom) as observed by passive microwave sensors on NASA's Nimbus-7 satellite and by the Special Sensor Microwave Imager/Sounder (SSMIS) from the Defense Meteorological Satellite Program (DMSP). The data shows the ice cover for the period of November 1 through January 31 in their respective years. (Jessica Wilson/NASA/Science Source)

Threatened by climate change. A polar bear mother and her cubs walk along the shore of Hudson Bay near Churchill, Manitoba. In 2007 the United States government decided to place the polar bear on the threatened species list due to the impact of climate change on the arctic environment. Canada has refused to do so, leading to diplomatic tensions. (THE CANADIAN PRESS/Jonathan Hayward)

of the Live Earth concert televised worldwide on July 7, 2007. Increasingly, large corporations (including Alcoa, Caterpillar, Duke Energy, Du Pont, and General Electric) are calling for laws mandating greenhouse cuts. "Going green" has become fashionable, and national and local governments are passing emissions reductions regulations and incentives. This concern and action is both a validation of earlier scientific claims and environmentalists' concerns and a central challenge to conventional approaches to economic activity, though climate change denial has also become a cottage public relations industry in Washington, D.C., and elsewhere.

In 1992, a Framework Convention on Climate Change (UNFCCC) was signed at the UNCED in Rio, committing the signatory states of the industrialized world to reduce their GHG emissions to 1990 levels by the year 2000. However, emissions continued virtually unabated, as countries failed to take concrete action in domestic regulations or laws. It was not until a conference of the Rio signatories in Kyoto, Japan, took place in December 1997 that states committed themselves to more strict emissions controls in the Kyoto Protocol to the UNFCCC. Under the Kyoto Protocol, industrialized countries agreed to reduce their GHG emissions to an average of 5 percent below 1990 levels by the years 2008 to 2012. The exact formula was different for each state: Canada, for example, pledged to reduce emissions to 6 percent below 1990 levels by 2010, though it did not ratify the Kyoto Protocol until 2002. However, Canada has been unwilling to meet its obligations to the Kyoto Protocol; its emissions have increased by as much as 30 percent since 1990. The implementation of the Protocol was complicated by the objections of several provincial governments and a change in federal government. Canada withdrew from its Kyoto obligations in 2012. The Kyoto Protocol called for more than cuts to GHG emissions: it permitted industrialized states to gain credit for investing, either as donors or as partners, in conservation measures through the Clean Development Mechanism (CDM) and Joint Implementation; it called for the establishment of an international carbon trading system, which would price carbon then allow states that exceed their targeted cuts to sell quotas to overproducing states; and it called for an Adaptation Fund, to help assist those hardest hit by climate change who can least afford to adapt or pay. Unfortunately, none of these measures have been implemented to the extent necessary to meet the challenges of climate change.

The Kyoto Protocol came into force on February 16, 2005, following the long-awaited ratification by Russia. As of May 2011, 191 countries had ratified it, although one of the key greenhouse gas producers, the United States, remains a non-signatory, and several large emitter states such as China and India are presently exempt from targets as they were not considered industrialized countries when the UNFCCC was signed in 1992 (see Profile 10.3). While some states did succeed in reaching their Kyoto greenhouse gas reduction goals by the target date of 2012 and others have achieved notable reductions, this accomplishment must be tempered by the fact that the global economic recession has been an important factor in some of these reductions, and overall global emissions of GHG continue to rise. In December of 2012, at

Doha, Qatar, the Kyoto Protocol was extended, with further pledges toward an average 18 percent reduction from 1990 levels by 2020. However, not all parties to the Kyoto Protocol agreed to this extension, and few observers are optimistic that the largest GHG emitters (especially the U.S. and China) will significantly reduce their emissions. As diplomatic efforts to develop a new global climate change treaty continue, there are hopeful signs of progress as local government policies and regional agreements establish controls on GHG reductions and alternative and renewable energy sources gain support from publics around the world.

PROFILE 10.3 Carbon Dioxide and National Responsibility

The growth rate of carbon emissions worldwide tripled in the first four years of this decade as compared with the rate in the 1990s, surpassing even the most significant increases suggested in recent United Nation's climate reports.

China has surpassed the United States as the largest emitter, though we should bear in mind that from a per capita perspective it is far behind most states.

CARBON DIOXIDE EMISSION RATES FOR 2009

	COUNTRY	TOTAL EMISSIONS (MILLIONS OF METRIC TONNES)	PER CAPITA EMISSIONS (METRIC TONNES PER PERSON)
1.	China	7707	5.82
2.	United States	5425	17.67
3.	India	1591	1.38
4.	Russia	1557	11.12
5.	Japan	1098	8.64
6.	Germany	766	9.3
7.	**Canada**	**541**	**16.15**
8.	Iran	529	6.96
9.	South Korea	528	10.89
10.	United Kingdom	520	8.35
11.	South Africa	451	9.2
12.	Mexico	444	3.99
13.	Saudi Arabia	438	17.3
14.	Brazil	425	2.14
15.	Australia	418	19.64
16.	Indonesia	415	1.73
17.	Italy	408	7.01
18.	France	397	6.3
19.	Spain	330	7.13
20.	Poland	286	7.43

SOURCE: US ENERGY INFORMATION ADMINISTRATION. FOUND AT: HTTP://WWW.EIA.GOV/CFAPPS/IPDBPROJECT/IEDINDEX3 .CFM?TID=90&PID=44&AID=8 (ACCESSED JUNE 2012).

In 2007 the IPCC released its Fourth Synthesis Report, which contained the direst warnings yet of the impact of human activity on the climate (the Fifth Report is due in early 2014). The report concluded that "warming of the climate system is unequivocal, as is now evident from observations of increases in global average air and ocean temperatures, widespread melting of snow and ice and rising average global sea level."[14] The report clearly attributes the increased concentrations of the four principal GHGs (carbon dioxide, methane, nitrous oxide, and halocarbons) to human activity. Energy supply accounted for 25.9 percent of global greenhouse gas emissions, with industry (19.4 percent), forestry (17.4 percent), agriculture (13.5 percent), and transport (13.1 percent) making up the other major sources of emissions. While some industries (such as the automobile industry) are moving rapidly toward technological adjustments to reduce carbon footprints, others (such as aviation and cement) are having a much harder time.

A wide number of issues related to global warming are now at the forefront of the global politics agenda. For example, the impact of the Asian Brown Cloud (see Profile 10.4) may be even more profound than previously thought. Scientists are now claiming that in combination with greenhouse gas emissions, the haze is accountable for the rapid retreat of the Himalayan glaciers. This loss of ice will have severe consequences for the hundreds of millions of people in Asia who live near the mountain range, since it will induce flooding in the short term and will result in drought in the long term.[15] As mentioned above, scientists have also warned that the ice sheets in Antarctica and Greenland, and other Arctic ice sheets at the North Pole, are beginning to collapse. Combined with warmer, expanding water, this might lead to increases in sea levels sufficient to force hundreds of millions of evacuations from coastal areas and small islands around the world. Such catastrophic predictions are not alarmist, but based on sound science.

PROFILE 10.4 The Asian Brown Cloud

In early 1999 scientists were startled to discover a brown haze covering most of the South and Southeast Asian regions, as well as large swaths of the Indian Ocean—a haze covering approximately 10 million square kilometres. This was at first attributed to forest fires (most deliberately set to clear brush for agriculture), but it is now believed to be the consequence of a mixture of pollutants, including fossil fuel combustion. According to the UNEP, "Simulations with global climate models indicate that the haze could have major impacts on the monsoon circulation, regional rainfall patterns and vertical temperature profile of the atmosphere." Combined with greenhouse gases the cloud is thought to account for the retreat of the Himalayan glaciers.

One of the most interesting things about the haze, which since 2004 has been identified as drifting into the Middle East as well, is that it is probably misnamed. One atmospheric scientist at the Scripps Institution of Oceanography at the University of California, Veerabhadran Ramanathan, said the major contributors to this worldwide circle of pollution were Los Angeles, Delhi, Bombay, Beijing, and Cairo: "Pollution in the eastern United States can go in four or five days to Europe and in a week it goes from Europe to South Asia. This is fast transport which converts a local problem into a regional and global problem," the Indian scientist said. The brown cloud demonstrates both the problems of scientific inquiry into such large-scale problems and the urgent need to protect the commons.

SOURCE: UNEP/EARTHSCAN, *GLOBAL ENVIRONMENTAL OUTLOOK 3: PAST, PRESENT AND FUTURE PERSPECTIVES* (LONDON, 2002), PG. 222; A. HAMMOND, "SCIENTIST SAYS 'ASIAN BROWN CLOUD' THREATENS GULF," ENVIRONMENTAL NEWS NETWORK, FEB. 25, 2004. FOUND AT: HTTP://WWW.ENN.COM/NEWS/2004-02-25/S_13447.ASP.

Indeed, as sea levels increase the very existence of some states will be threatened. Some low-lying countries (such as the Netherlands) have the resources to adapt and protect their populations, while others (such as Bangladesh) do not. The coastal dwellers of one South Pacific island, Vanuatu, have had to be moved inland, giving them the title of the world's first climate change refugees. The melting of Arctic ice intensifies the global warming process, since ice normally reflects ultraviolet rays back into space: the less ice there is to reflect the sun's radiation, the more ultraviolet is absorbed and trapped in the atmosphere. Furthermore, the melting of permafrost will release unknown quantities of methane, a more intense greenhouse gas than carbon dioxide. In another example of linkage, the overfishing crisis will only be magnified as sea warming causes acidification and the destruction of coral reefs, which in turn threatens to cause accelerated marine mammal extinction. Threats to global food security are also linked to climate change: food prices are rising because of a number of factors, including the price of oil (a reflection of continued turmoil in the Middle East and rising demand in China, India, and elsewhere), speculation on futures markets for food, the use of arable land for biofuel production, and the land degradation related to agricultural overproduction and climate change.

There is widespread recognition that international cooperation will be required to meet the challenges of climate change in the area of mitigation (reducing emissions) and adaptation (adjusting to a warmer world), including the famous "Stern Report" written by a British economist who makes dire warnings about the potential economic costs of not taking strong action.[16] While some states participate in the CDM, which grants carbon credits for contributions to energy conservation measures in less-industrialized states and accepted its six thousandth project in early 2013, others are reluctant to commit to what they see as a redistribution of wealth on an international scale. Similarly, the carbon trading system strikes some as a mechanism to permit polluting as usual, while rewarding states that have defunct economies for reasons other than pollution abatement.

Why has it proven so difficult to secure a binding international treaty on climate change, and even harder to achieve compliance? First, governments are concerned that rigorous emissions regulations or taxes will damage economic growth and competitiveness. This has been a major reason why the U.S. and now Canadian governments have been reluctant to agree to any climate change mitigation process that does not involve China and India. Second, it is difficult to secure a climate change treaty among many states with divergent interests. Any negotiated agreement will be the product of the lowest common denominator among the participants, and is therefore likely to be watered down to meet a minimally acceptable standard. The UNFCCC negotiations at Bali failed to achieve agreement on binding cuts because some states (especially the U.S.) refused to agree to such a policy. Climate change is often seen through the lenses of the broader north–south debate about responsibility and the need to ensure that human rights and development are not compromised in any mitigation efforts. Third, there is the familiar problem of compliance and enforcement. Governments may sign treaties binding them to emissions cuts (such as Kyoto) but then fail to live up to their commitments with little or no international repercussions. Finally, domestic politics can drive government negotiation positions. For example, in Canada the Conservative majority government has a strong constituency base in Alberta, and its obvious reluctance to seriously pursue carbon reduction commitments is often attributed to this domestic political reality. Furthermore, the priorities of governments at home (economic growth, employment) and political vulnerability (electoral politics, coalition governments) also influence their positions in climate change negotiations. For these reasons, securing an international agreement on climate change that supersedes the limited Kyoto Protocol framework will be a daunting challenge.

The Secretary-General's weather report. UN Secretary-General Ban Ki-moon referred to extreme weather events, such as droughts, floods, and hurricanes, as the "new normal" as he appealed to participants at the 18th session of the Conference of Parties of the UN Framework Convention on Climate Change (UNFCCC) in Doha, Qatar, December 4, 2012. (Reuters/Fadi Al-Assaad)

Given the media exposure and diplomatic activity surrounding this issue area, it is tempting to focus entirely on climate change as the main ecopolitical debate of our time. But we should remember that many other issue areas, all of which are linked in one way or another to climate change, demand similar attention. Organizations of states and non-state actors have developed around these issues, many of them located in Montreal (see Profile 10.5). We turn now to brief discussions of several of these issues, beginning with what might well be the most dramatic: the fate of the oceans.

THE OCEANS IN CRISIS

June 8, 2009, was the first UN-declared World Oceans Day, and the resulting publicity about the plight of the oceans could not have come soon enough. In retrospect, it may be understandable that the oceans, which cover two-thirds of the earth's surface, have been viewed as an inexhaustible commons throughout much of human history. Yet the oceans have endured a relentless assault in recent centuries, one that threatens our own existence. As Sylvia Earle wrote in 1995, the "living ocean drives planetary chemistry, governs climate and weather, and otherwise provides the cornerstone of the life-support system for all creatures on our planet, from deep-sea starfish to desert sagebrush. … Our future and the state of the oceans are one."[17] But just as we are all connected to the oceans, their fate is inextricably linked to global politics.

Historically, the seas have been viewed as a commons, and in fact "freedom of the seas" has long been an accepted legal term. This freedom involved the right not just to travel but also to harvest resources and pollute. Restrictions on all of these rights have been slowly developing with the establishment of related international regimes. The UNCLOS took nine years to negotiate (1973

PROFILE 10.5 The Montreal Connection

Montreal is renowned for its old world charm, cosmopolitanism, and summer jazz festival. But given its location next to the once-heavily-polluted St. Lawrence River, few would expect Montreal to also become a magnet for international organizations dealing with environmental problems; yet, with the support of the federal government (no doubt influenced by continued fears over separatism), Montreal has attracted a great deal of expertise and officialdom to the area. In fact, one can take a cursory glance at the extent of multilateral action on environmental issues with a survey of the bodies that have located there. The following organizations are already located in Montreal:

- The Secretariat of the Multilateral Fund of the Montreal Ozone Protocol

- The North American Commission for Environmental Cooperation (a North American Free Trade Agreement institution)

- The Secretariat of the United Nations Convention on Biological Diversity

- The Montreal office of the World Conservation Union

- The Network of Expertise for the Global Environment

- The International Secretariat for Water

- The Secretariat of the International Civil Aviation Organization

Note: the ICAO is a major (and recently contested) prize for Montreal and it is working on efforts to curb greenhouse gas emissions from aviation (currently exempt from Kyoto)

Montreal lost a bid for the Desertification Secretariat, which was located in Bonn, Germany.

---

to 1982), and 159 states and other entities initially signed the Convention. In November 1993, Guyana became the 60th state to deposit its instrument of ratification with the UN, and the Law of the Sea officially became effective in November 1994. It established an International Seabed Authority that would facilitate the sharing of deep-sea resources, particularly any derived from deep-sea mining, among all states. This notion of sharing proceeds from resource extraction was opposed in the United States (and some other Western states), which argued that such revenue sharing would undermine the profitability of deep-sea mining. As a result, many Western states have signed the Law of the Sea but have not ratified it. Canada did not ratify the Law of the Sea until November 2003; there were 165 ratifications as of early 2013. Nonetheless it has become largely accepted as the most authoritative international legal instrument on ocean issues, and firmly establishes the norm that coastal states have EEZs extending from their shorelines.

Yet UNCLOS has had very limited impact on curtailing what has become known as the global oceans crisis. There are many interlinked threats facing the oceans today, and we have space to address only a few of them here.[18] Overfishing is perhaps the most visible, as ever-greater numbers of people compete to catch dwindling supplies of edible species. There are limits to sustainable yield harvests, and we have surpassed them in most popular fish stocks. Previously, the world witnessed the near-extinction of many species of whales due to an under-regulated regime, advanced technology that gave whalers a decisive edge, and the urge to capitalize on investments before stocks ran out completely. This galvanized the NGO and scientific community to protest whaling practices, and in 1982 the International Whaling Commission adopted a zero-quota commercial catch limit on all species of whales, a prohibition still in place today (limited Aboriginal and so-called scientific whaling still takes place, and whale meat is still sold in some Asian markets). This was and remains a highly controversial story in ecopolitical history, pitting different conceptions of human–nature relations and animal rights against each other and raising sharp diplomatic conflicts between former whaling states such as the U.S. and Australia against contemporary whalers such as Japan and Norway.[19] The important point, however, is that many of the great whale populations have made recoveries, even if they now face different, climate-oriented threats, and the pressure to resume commercial whaling remains.

There has been no such success with fish, which have less charismatic appeal, and are of course widely eaten across the earth. By 2000, it had become apparent that global fish catches had been declining for over a decade, and the Food and Agriculture Organization (FAO) declared that three-quarters of major species stocks were either fully exploited or nearing collapse. In 2007, the FAO estimated that over 80 percent of global fish stocks were fully exploited or overexploited, and required "effective and precautionary management."[20] The sheer size of discarded bycatch (i.e., the non-targeted fish species, as well as marine mammals, that are killed in the process and then simply dumped back into the sea) is also a tremendous problem, as is bottom trawling and the use of lengthy driftnets that collect everything in their kilometres-long path (these are banned in most cases but are still used; some become detached from fishing vessels and roam the sea as indiscriminate "ghostnets"). Most ocean fishing is governed by sovereign states with exclusive rights to coastal waters, but many states sell the right to fish in their marine territory; and illegal fishing is very common in areas where coastal states have limited enforcement capacities.

While there are numerous regional agreements to regulate certain fisheries in specific areas (see Profile 10.6), and a series of UNCLOS-related agreements on overfishing and the use of driftnets as well as a soft-law FAO Code of Conduct for Responsible Fisheries, there is no effective enforcement of such provisions.[21] An FAO International Plan of Action to Deter, Prevent and Eliminate Illegal, Unreported, and Unregulated Fishing has had some success in Asia and elsewhere, but it is of course impossible to ascertain its impact.[22] Optimism persists that aquaculture—for example, the farming of fish such as Atlantic salmon, and the

Plastic nightmare. A boy collects plastic materials near a polluted coastline to sell in Manila on April 9, 2008. The oceans are filling with plastic particles due to human negligence, threatening wildlife. (Reuters/Cheryl Ravelo)

PROFILE 10.6 Canada Gets Aggressive: Defending Migratory Fish Stocks

Managing international fisheries has often proven to be one of the more complex diplomatic tasks. The so-called cod wars between Iceland and Britain in the 1960s and 1970s provide a historical example of potential conflict over dwindling resources, but Canadians have a more recent example on which to reflect. The case involved the Spanish fishing fleet and an uncharacteristically assertive Canadian government. The Spanish Basques were fishing off the coast of Newfoundland as early as 1530, and by the 1580s, French Basque ships were returning from the area loaded with cod and, eventually, whale oil. In 1994, the multilateral Northwest Atlantic Fisheries Organization (NAFO) had set limits on the total allowable catch of Greenland halibut (or turbot), allocating national quotas

for this resource. The European Union, pressured by Spain and Portugal, rejected the quotas as unfair.

Canada imposed a unilateral moratorium, concerned with the depleting turbot stocks, and eventually seized the Spanish fishing vessel *Estai*, claiming that the trawler was not only violating the quota rules but also using illegal fish nets in the process. Since the vessel was on the high seas, Canada was, in effect, breaking international law. Canada's seizure of the Spanish trawler led to international tension, because Canada's international legal jurisdiction stops after the 200-nautical-mile (1 nautical mile = 1852 metres) EEZ provision of UNCLOS. Thus, the fishery dilemma quickly became a foreign policy problem. Eventually, Canada passed legislation that would make it legal (in the domestic context, if not in the international) to physically stop ships from fishing near the exclusive economic zone. A subsequent international agreement on straddling stocks was hammered out in New York, giving coastal states the right to inspect ships fishing near such areas. Is the lesson here that Canada had to break international law to make it? Or that realists are right, that states will only take serious international environmental action if their national interest is directly at stake?

Seized ship: A victory for conservation, or piracy?
Onlookers watch the Spanish trawler *Estai* arrive at St. John's on March 12, 1995. A Canadian fisheries patrol vessel fired the first salvo in what became the Great Turbot War between Canada and the European Union. (CP Picture Archive/Fred Chartrand)

For a succinct analysis of the Canada–Spain "Fish War," see Andrew Cooper, *Canadian Foreign Policy: Old Habits, New Directions* (Scarborough, ON: Prentice Hall Allyn and Bacon, 1997), 142–72.

huge shrimp industry in southeast Asia—will provide some relief, but environmentalists are concerned with the ecological impact of introducing new fish species to ecosystems and the salinization of marshlands and other vulnerable ecosystems.[23] Put simply, we would be extremely hard pressed to support over eight billion people without the protein supplied by fish stocks. The collapse of the world's fisheries present an unprecedented challenge to global food security, and the ethical and legal obligations that follow from this premise make it clear than we must act quickly and responsibly.[24]

The second most visible threats are the numerous sources of pollution affecting our oceans. Spectacular accidents, such as the Exxon Valdez oil spill off Alaska in 1989 and the Deepwater

Horizon/BP oil spill in the Gulf of Mexico in 2010, are dramatic and highly publicized events. Yet far more pernicious is the daily legal and illegal dumping of discharged oil and other wastes at sea by ships. Though the International Maritime Organization (IMO) negotiated a Convention on the Prevention of Pollution from Ships (MARPOL) as early as 1973, its implementation remains a serious problem. Pollution from persistent organic pollutants (POPs), which are transported through the atmosphere, also affects ocean health, and these pollutants are extremely difficult to source; a convention is in place to limit the production and use of certain POPs, but has had limited effect, especially in the more fragile Arctic and Antarctic Ocean ecosystems. Coastal pollution remains a grave threat to the health of fish and marine mammals as well. Despite decades of progress in human sanitation systems, raw sewage and agricultural runoff are still primary sources of pollution, and sewage-borne invasive pathogens such as cholera are serious threats to human security in many southern coastal regions. The dumping of excessive nutrients through nitrogen fixation (fertilizers entering the oceans through sewage and agricultural runoff) and industrial and vehicle emissions is exacerbated by the destruction of "natural interceptors" such as coastal wetlands, coral reefs, and mangrove forests; these fall victim to coastal development, but as a result leave shorelines more vulnerable to extreme storm surges. This in turn adds to the natural process of eutrophication (excessive plant growth and decay) and toxic blooms, which kill fish and drive away birds and mammals. Further, the human alteration of river systems and estuaries has increased the level of sedimentation entering the oceans, depriving ocean species of needed sunlight. Invasive alien species are dumped from the ballast water of cargo ships. And non-biodegradable litter is scattered throughout the seas, killing countless marine mammals and birds. While the existence of large concentrations of plastic debris in the oceans is well-documented—including a floating "island of plastic" or "garbage patch" in the Pacific Ocean roughly the size of the state of Texas—the full impact of this pollution is even more insidious: when the plastics begin to break down, they form barely observable pollution particles in the water, ingested by birds, fish, and other wildlife. Aided by ocean currents, certain areas are being turned into an uninhabitable plastic soup.

All of this occurs in the context of climate change, and the oceans play a key role in maintaining atmospheric balance; the concern is that polar warming and ice cap melting, which has been accelerating in recent years, will slow down the global atmosphere/ocean "heat engine," which could alter the flow of major ocean currents and affect atmospheric temperatures, and perhaps over the long term even cause an ice age. While this sounds more like the stuff of science fiction (and has been the source of inspiration for several such films), it is a serious long-term concern, along with the sea-level rise and extreme weather events discussed in the preceding section. But the impact of climate change is not limited to changing weather patterns. For example, the exotic, biodiverse coastal reefs are particularly vulnerable ecosystems, and not only is the acidification of the oceans bleaching them to death, but also higher concentrations of carbon dioxide in the oceans impair the growth of their limestone skeletons. Compounded with the effects of sedimentation, irresponsible tourism, and overfishing, the reefs are in danger of extinction, despite the vital role they play in regulating the ocean ecosystems in the Indian Ocean, Southeast Asia, and the far-western Pacific.[25] There is no international agreement designed specifically to protect the coral reefs, though such protection is arguably enshrined in the UNCLOS and other conventions. Coral reefs generally fall within the EEZs of states, so they are not in the strict sense considered part of the global commons; yet their key natural role prompts many to argue they should be treated as such. Climate change is also affecting the eating, reproductive, and migratory patterns of marine mammals, birds, fish stocks, and plankton, and it facilitates the spread of dangerous invasive species that are transported across oceans by commercial shipping lines.

The oceans crisis is one of the most urgent issues we face: here we have a true problem of the commons, and the complex patchwork of governance efforts has thus far failed to reduce the severity of the problem.

DEFORESTATION AND LAND DEGRADATION

Another serious global problem is the impact of human activity on land surface, in particular the removal of the world's forests and the decreasing availability of arable land. Deforestation has become an increasingly popular and public issue in the past three decades, not least because of its link to climate change. For example, a program known as REDD—Reducing Emissions Caused by Deforestation and Degradation—figured prominently at the Copenhagen conference in 2009 and again at Doha in 2012. While tropical rainforest depletion has gathered the most attention, it is important to remember that wetlands, boreal forests, and temperate rainforest depletion are all serious problems. According to the FAO, between 2000 and 2010, over 13 million hectares of forest cover was destroyed or lost worldwide each year. When the loss of forest cover from deforestation and natural disasters is measured against reforestation and natural forest growth, between 2000 and 2010 the total net loss of forest cover each year was 5.2 million hectares, an area roughly equivalent to the size of Costa Rica.[26]

International efforts to curb deforestation have, predictably enough, generated sustained political friction. Low-income countries see these efforts as inimical to their own economic development, arguing that industrialized countries, having exploited much of their own forests, are now trying to prevent them from exploiting their own. These development-driven motives have led to high rates of forest cover loss in most parts of the world. For example, in South America, 64 million hectares of forest cover (about 7 percent of total forest cover in the two regions) was destroyed between 1990 and 2005. While the rate of net forest cover loss has slowed in recent years, between 2005 and 2010 the average annual loss of forest cover in South America was still 3.6 million hectares.[27] Much of this occurred in Brazil, which between 2000 and 2010 experienced an average net loss of forest cover of 2.6 million hectares every year. Between 2000 and 2010 the countries experiencing the greatest average annual net losses in forest cover were Brazil, Australia, Indonesia, Nigeria, Tanzania, Zimbabwe, Congo, Myanmar, Bolivia, and Venezuela.[28] In Haiti, more than 90 percent of the country's rainforest has disappeared. Forest destruction occurs for many economically driven reasons, including a local desire for pastureland, export crops, fuel, and lucrative foreign markets for hardwood.

Another tragedy of forest depletion is the impossibility of full regeneration. Old-growth timber areas (in both tropical and temperate zones) possess ecosystems and **biodiversity** developed over thousands of years. Although they cover less than 10 percent of the earth's surface, it is estimated that tropical forest ecosystems may contain up to 90 percent of all species. Replanted or second-growth regions never achieve this level of biodiversity.[29] In addition, because in many cases forests are cleared for pastureland or cropland, the delicate soil is often exhausted after a few years. As a result, the forest cannot regenerate because the land cannot support it. The subsequent loss of trees reduces the capacity of the earth to produce oxygen and absorb carbon dioxide, which in turn contributes to climate change (as does the carbon released when felled trees are burnt or converted to charcoal). Rainfall patterns are affected, and soil erosion increases because of a lack of root structures, contributing to deadly floods in states such as Bangladesh.

Cemetery for biodiversity. Amazon deforested rainforest near the river Jurua, which flows from Peru into Brazil, and local Kulina inhabitants. Though deforestation has slowed in recent decades, it remains a principal threat to biodiversity and a source of carbon emissions. (© Joerg Boethling/Alamy)

In addition to loss of forest cover, land and soil degradation is a serious environmental problem. Land and soil degradation comes in many forms, including soil erosion, nutrient depletion, water scarcity, salinity, and disruption of biological processes. In 2011, the FAO estimated that 25 percent of the world's land was highly degraded.[30] Much of this degradation is once again caused by human activity: deforestation, overgrazing, nutrient depletion, and agricultural mismanagement. In severe cases, soil degradation can result in desertification and complete loss of land productivity. Because it takes thousands of years to form a few centimetres of topsoil, this problem has severe implications for the world's food supply. Further, poorly designed irrigation systems and aquaculture (described in the preceding section) can cause salinization and other problems, and the use of pesticides and herbicides, a major interest of MNCs involved in agribusiness, can cause many long-term problems for both ecology and human health. Others worry that the introduction of GMOs and new biotechnology will further homogenize crops, lowering food security in the long run and harming poor farmers who are forced to buy biotech products (see Profile 10.2); and that any substantive shift toward using biofuels such as ethanol to power vehicles will put even more pressure on limited land and further increase food prices.[31]

Taken together, deforestation and land degradation represent a serious assault on the earth's land mass. A UN Convention to Combat Desertification was signed after the Rio Summit of 1992, and there are two complex major international initiatives to govern world forestry, the International Tropical Timber Organization (ITTO) and the Tropical Forestry Action Plan launched in 1985 (later renamed the Tropical Forestry Action Programme, and largely considered a failure). Unquestionably, forestry practices in countries such as Canada and the United States have improved in recent decades, and public concern over the fate of forest ecosystems remains a strong stimulant. (In an apparent cost-saving measure, Canada withdrew from the ITTO in 2013.) But overall, global deforestation, as well as the desertification of arable land and wildlife habitat destruction, continues at an unsustainable pace. In the meantime, as our next section indicates, we are fundamentally changing the evolutionary path of the world's species, altering some, and finishing others altogether.

SPECIES IMPOVERISHMENT

The physical division of the earth into nation-states is contrary to the flow of nature, and this becomes most apparent when we consider the fate of migratory mammals that do not recognize borders and have their paths disrupted by such constructions. This issue raises a broader question: are the many species of animals and plants that are currently endangered part of the commons, regardless of where they live? From an ecological viewpoint, the crisis presented by dwindling shark and tiger populations and current attempts to save them is really one of biodiversity, or, put more emphatically, what M. Brock Fenton and others call *species impoverishment*.[32] Though there is nothing unnatural and certainly nothing new about extinction, the 20th century in particular saw more extinctions in the wild world than ever before. Scientists are still debating the causes of the late Cretaceous extinction, in which the large dinosaurs were rendered extinct, about 65 million years ago. This is a question partly of effect, for as David Jablonski notes in a fascinating essay on the topic, the late Cretaceous extinction is a very complex phenomenon: "Tropical marine groups were more severely affected than temperate or polar ones; open-ocean plankton and larger swimmers, such as the mosasaurs, were affected more than bottom dwellers; and large land dwellers more affected than small ones, even though some larger forms survived as well."[33] Whatever caused this extinction, it did not kill off all the species on earth at the time, nor did it even come close to doing so. And the key difference: it was, by any account, not preventable with human effort (humans weren't around, according to most scientists!). Humans are believed to be at least partially responsible for the large extinction of land animals in the Pleistocene period, but the development of agriculture so fundamentally changed the human–nature relationship that we have been able to affect a myriad of ecosystems, even the biosphere, with our economic activities.

The human tendency to overhunt constitutes a principal threat to biodiversity today. Columbus discovered the Caribbean monk seal, the single tropical pinniped, in what was called the New World. It has not been seen since 1922. The Steller's sea cow was spotted by a Russian hunting expedition in 1741 in the Aleutians; it was regarded as extinct by the late 18th century. More recently, we have witnessed massive fish extinctions—more than 200 species—from Lake Victoria in Africa. These extinctions had many causes, including overfishing, pollution, and the introduction of alien species, such as the Nile perch. Les Kaufman has referred to Lake Victoria as the "Hiroshima of the biological apocalypse."[34] The reduction of species populations will, of course, have a severe impact on their reproductive health. While this may increase the chances of survival for some, since there is less competition for limited resources, it may lessen the chances of survival for the group as a whole. An important element here is the gene pool, which itself must be sufficiently diverse for healthy populations to thrive: "Gene pools are being converted into gene puddles vulnerable to evaporation in an ecological and evolutionary sense."[35] Other crises will have direct impacts on human survivability; for example, tropical deforestation or coral reef bleaching may deny future generations medical remedies, and the recent, puzzling decline of pollinating global honeybee populations reduces our food security.

The loss of genetic diversity may well be the most serious long-term threat to our environment. As James Scarff notes,

> The elimination of a species reduces the genetic capacity of the ecosystem to respond to perturbations or long-term changes in the environment. Such a loss may also initiate irreversible ecological adjustments which destabilize the ecosystem leading to further extinctions. Economically, the extinction of a species represents the permanent loss of a renewable resource of unknown value [as well as] potential uses for medicine, scientific research, human food, education, and recreation.[36]

The international community has taken steps to limit the degradation of wildlife species. There are numerous fisheries agreements and institutions in place, such as the previously mentioned Northwest Atlantic Fisheries Organization and the International Whaling Commission. Early organizations included the International Council for Bird Preservation

(1909) and the International Congress for the Protection of Nature (1913). As early as 1886 a Treaty Concerning the Regulation of Salmon Fishing in the Rhine River Basin was signed by Germany, Luxembourg, the Netherlands, and Switzerland. The first international agreement to conserve a marine mammal was in all likelihood the Fur Seal Convention of 1911, signed by Japan, Russia, Great Britain (for pre-independence Canada), and the United States. Another groundbreaking agreement was the U.S.–Great Britain Migratory Birds Convention, signed in 1916, which was a precursor to a range of contemporary transborder agreements.[37]

What Robert Boardman has called the "linchpin of the system"[38] was originally formed in 1948 as the International Union for the Protection of Nature, now known as the **International Union for Conservation of Nature (IUCN)**. The IUCN is a unique umbrella organization that covers intergovernmental and transnational conservation activity, often working laterally with a plethora of other organizations—both state multilateral and non-governmental in composition—that have achieved global significance. The IUCN World Congress (held in Jeju, South Korea, in 2012) attracts thousands of experts and advocates involved in conservation efforts from around the world every four years. The 1973 **Convention on International Trade in Endangered Species of Wild Fauna and Flora (CITES)** is often heralded as one of the IUCN's diplomatic successes. Included among the 30 000 species of animals and plants covered under the convention's provisions are elephants and, by extension, their cherished ivory; in 1989 CITES instituted a controversial international ivory trade ban (periodically lifted to allow sales of stockpiled ivory from three southern African states to Japan). But CITES is often torn between northern states demanding complete protection of species and southern and Asian states wanting to trade in animal parts as part of a broader conservation strategy. The role of opposing NGOs lobbying CITES delegations is interesting as well, as they compete to have their worldviews accepted by state delegates. The Convention on Biological Diversity (CBD), signed in Rio de Janeiro in 1992, further committed states to preserving biodiversity and committed the North to paying the South for use of genetic material found in the latter. The treaty, signed by more than 160 countries in 1992 (the United States signed after Bill Clinton's election later that year, but has not ratified the treaty), went into effect in 1993. Delegates from all the signatories form a Conference of the Parties (COP), which meets every other year to review progress made toward the three central thrusts of the treaty: the conservation of biodiversity, the sustainable use of biological resources, and the equitable sharing of the benefits arising from such use (the twelfth COP will take place in South Korea in 2014). An additional Biosafety Protocol for the Convention on Biological Diversity (CBD) was negotiated in 2000, and the Nagoya Protocol on sharing genetic resources was passed in Japan in 2010 but as of 2013 has yet to enter into force.[39] Another new development was the first meeting, in Bonn, Germany, in early 2013, of the Intergovernmental Panel on Biodiversity and Ecosystem Services (IPBES), which aims to bring policy and science to a closer understanding of the crisis (in a manner similar to that of the IPCC).

Facing an uncertain future. A Silverback mountain gorilla in Virunga National Park in the eastern Congo. Although the number of gorillas has slowly increased from 140 in 1980 to approximately 420 in 2009, deforestation, war, disease, and poaching continue to threaten the gorilla population in the reserve. (AP Photo/Jerome Delay)

Another major threat to biodiversity is Invasive Alien Species (IAS), which excel at surviving in new environments because of the lack of natural predators and/or climate change. Though bio-invasion is nothing new, IAS today pose severe challenges to ecological integrity, economic security, environmental philosophy, and international modes of governance. Both unintentional and purposive introductions of alien species have often proven disastrous to local ecologies, and the incidental spread of IAS as a result of international trade is a pervasive problem; one author refers to them as "pathogens of globalization."[40] In addition, the symbioses between globalization and global warming are increasing the likelihood of bio-invasions at both the microbial and species levels, causing shifts in pathogenic virulence, as discussed in the section on climate change earlier in this chaper.[41] Beyond the question of climate change, however, IAS are a conceptual challenge, because the mode of their introduction varies considerably, from intentional to incidental, and they are to some extent a normal natural phenomenon. They are a governance challenge because they cross borders, and often result from trade and other factors, such as the introduction of genetically modified organisms that rely on other governance mechanisms. They also raise ethical challenges, because the costs of dealing with them are not always shared among those who cause this risk, and environmental ethicists struggle with the idea of killing large numbers of one species to protect others.

Various bilateral, and often voluntary, measures have been instituted, for example, to deal with Great Lakes ballast water and the fear of the voracious Asian carp; and there are numerous multilateral agreements that touch upon IAS, such as the CBD. In 1997, the Global Invasive Species Programme (GISP) was founded, but unfortunately it was disbanded in 2011. Indeed, this is an area where global governance is just beginning to take shape, and it will face large obstacles, not the least of which is the political economy of trade and the apparent supremacy of the WTO in relation to environmental matters. Yet without hard work in this area, species such as the black jellyfish, the Asian tiger mosquito, the yellow crazy ant, the European shore crab, and many other varieties of aggressive shrubs, trees, insects, seaweed, and other species will choke local ecosystems and diminish biodiversity in their wake. In North America the movement of voracious Asian carp up the Mississippi, threatening the Great Lakes with yet another major invasion, has drawn much public interest and cost millions of dollars in preventive measures.

However, global governance efforts to preserve biodiversity are meaningless if the broader problem, the preservation of habitat, is not addressed. This task requires much more than the regulation of fishing fleets or the ban on alligator-skin purses or the confiscation of exotic plants at borders. It requires creating the conditions in which humankind no longer has the perceived need to destroy natural habitat. Despite encouraging conservation programs around the world, we are a long way from environmental sustainability, and many scientists are already resigned to the need to begin cloning endangered species to ensure the continuation of their gene pools. Scientific understanding of the fundamental interconnectivity of all things natural, long a fundamental principal of indigenous knowledge, means that we have no excuse.[42]

TRANSBORDER ENVIRONMENTAL ISSUES

Transborder pollution flows from one country into another, through rivers, streams, lakes, air, and even underground. Since power differentials usually exist between neighbouring states—one is often more industrialized or has a geographic advantage, such as being upstream—realists argue that transborder pollution will be the cause of future violent conflict. However, many states—Canada and the United States with their **International Joint Commission (IJC)** are often used as an example—co-manage their mutual frontiers on an ongoing basis. Even so, the potential for conflict exists: Canada and the United States argued for years over the effects of **acid rain** that came to Canada from southern industrial regions and continue to dispute the co-management of the Pacific salmon stock, the prospects of drilling for oil in the Arctic Wildlife Refuge in Alaska, the diversion of water from Devil's Lake outlet in North Dakota, and other points of contention.

Perhaps the most famous case of transborder pollution resulted from an accident at the Chernobyl nuclear reactor in Ukraine in April 1986 (at the time, Ukraine was still part of the Soviet Union). A meltdown in a reactor unit caused an explosion and fire that spread airborne radioactivity as far away as Italy and Sweden. Soviet leaders made matters worse by initially shrouding the event in secrecy, not even informing neighbouring states of incoming radio-activity. In Scandinavia, nomadic Laplanders were severely affected as their reindeer herds ate toxic grass. Leaks of radioactive inert gases and iodine from a reactor near St. Petersburg in the 1990s have accentuated the fear that more Chernobyls are waiting to happen. Throughout the Cold War, Eastern Europe had served as a captive market for the Soviet nuclear industry, and Soviet-designed reactors (located in Czechoslovakia, Hungary, Bulgaria, and Eastern Germany) did not always include sufficient emergency core cooling systems or containment vessels. Since the unprecedented nuclear disaster at Chernobyl, a new customary norm has emerged in international law: states have an obligation to inform bordering states if a disaster with such far-reaching consequences has occurred.

Aftermath of ecological calamity. Workers who constructed the cement sarcophagus covering Chernobyl's deadly reactor in 1986 pose with a banner reading: "We will fulfill the government's order!" Thousands of workers who took part in the cleanup of Chernobyl have died from the after-effects suffered during the work, according to information from the Union-Chernobyl-Ukraine, and their children have suffered severe health problems, including thyroid cancer, congenital birth deformities, and leukemia. The area remains cordoned today. (AP Photo/Volodymyr Repik/CP Images)

Other transborder pollution problems have resulted from industrialization. Several regional agreements aim at reducing acid precipitation (acid rain), which damages forests and lakes. For example, in 1988, 24 European states signed a treaty to limit nitrogen oxide emissions to 1988 levels by 1995, and Canada and the United States have a bilateral agreement that was the result of many years of protracted bargaining.[43] However, without effective scrubbers for smokestacks burning lignite (a highly sulphurous coal), acid rain will continue to be a major problem, particularly in Eastern Europe.

Yet another transborder problem is the circulation of pesticides, an issue that illustrates the complexity of both modern science and the world economy. For example, in 1990 U.S. manufacturers exported more than 24 million kilograms of pesticides such as DDT, dieldrin, toxaphene, endrin, ethyl parathion, and other compounds that were banned, restricted, or unregistered for use in the United States. Most of these were shipped to southern states, such as Argentina, Colombia, Ecuador, and the Philippines, though a significant amount went to Belgium, Japan, and the Netherlands. The Stockholm Convention on **Persistent Organic Pollutants** (**POPs**), which went into force in 2004, has limited this trade. Nevertheless, in his excellent study of pesticide regulation, John Wargo draws attention to the difficulty of regulating such international commerce in products that are highly hazardous to both human and ecosystem health:

> An active ingredient produced in the United States may be shipped to Switzerland where it is combined with other ingredients and shipped to Egypt. In Egypt, it might be applied as an insecticide to cotton. Cottonseeds may then be harvested and sold to a commodity broker in Israel, who then sells them to a manufacturer of cottonseed oil in Italy. The Italian firm may then sell the oil, perhaps mixed with other oil from seeds grown in Guatemala with the help of another pesticide, to an American food processing company.[44]

Another local and regional environmental issue is access to fresh water. Though recent events, such as flooding in India, Bangladesh, and Mozambique, suggest that the problem of water is one of overabundance, water scarcity is also a growing concern. Only about 3 percent of the world's water is fresh, and much of that is frozen in the polar ice caps. In effect, less than 1 percent of the world's water is easily accessible fresh water. Heated debates have ensued over whether the privatization of water is a violation of basic human rights, since it is generally considered a common public good. About 600 million people lack access to safe drinking water, and 2.5 billion are without proper sanitation. Approximately 3.4 billion people live in areas with high water security threats.[45]

Aquifers (underground water supplies) in many of the world's regions are running dry or becoming contaminated with seawater, arsenic, and other dangerous chemicals. Many major rivers are mere streams when they reach the coast due to diversion of water for irrigation. In some regions, the increased rate of water use has had dramatic consequences. A stark example can be found in the Aral Sea region of Central Asia. During Soviet rule, massive quantities of water were diverted from the river systems feeding the Aral Sea to irrigate a huge agricultural project. The flow of water to the Aral Sea slowed to a trickle, and as a result the Sea has now shrunk to just 10 percent of its former size. Not only has this devastated the local fishing industry but also the dry sea salt is swept up by winds into dust storms, which deposit salt over a wide area, poisoning land and people.[46] Within a geopolitically contested region, the reduced flow of water in the tributary rivers of the shrinking Sea has been a major cause of concern for the states of the former Soviet Union, though they have established an intergovernmental commission for water coordination.

In fact, a new term has been coined to refer to conflicts over water resources: *hydropolitics.*[47] Water conflict has been an acute problem in areas with arid climates, such as northern Africa and the Middle East (see Profile 10.8 on page 399). As water consumption increases alongside population and economic growth, the quest for sources of fresh water becomes more dramatic and has already been the cause of conflict between several states. There are 261 river basins shared by two or more states, including the Nile, Jordan, Euphrates, Amazon, Mekong, Rhine, Ganges, Indu, and Colorado. They are all potential sources of both conflict and cooperation. As we discussed at the beginning of this chapter, water scarcity will not automatically lead to protracted and perhaps violent future conflict. Some argue that shared resources can bring out the best in states, promoting their ability to cooperate when they must to achieve mutual benefits. Thomas Homer-Dixon argues that, though there are historical examples of wars caused

PROFILE 10.7 Canada's Freshwater Supply

Canada has a large supply of fresh water, and this is expected to be a growing issue in its relations with the United States. In both countries, water demand continues to increase, making successful management all the more important in the future. According to a 2011 Environment Canada report, Canadian per capita water consumption is the second highest in the world, exceeded only by the U.S. The average Canadian uses 328 litres of water a day, with 35 percent consumed for bathing, 30 percent for toilet flushing, 25 percent for laundry and cleaning, and 10 percent for cooking and drinking.

Other factors to consider:

- Canada has about 7 percent of the world's renewable fresh water, making it the third largest water supply in the world.

- Approximately 60 percent of Canada's fresh water drains north, while 85 percent of the population lives within 300 kilometres of the Canada–U.S. border.

- Between 1972 and 1991, Canada's water usage increased from 24 billion cubic metres per year to over 45 billion cubic metres per year. By 2006, Canada's water usage exceeded 60 billion cubic metres per year, though it has declined slightly since.

- The Great Lakes constitute one of the largest systems of freshwater reservoirs on earth, with 18 percent of the world's fresh surface water; however, water levels are reaching record lows as of 2013, and invasive species, such as the notorious Asian carp, continue to threaten native fish populations.

- About 7.6 percent of Canada is covered by fresh water in lakes and rivers—755 165 square kilometres. To this can be added 195 059 square kilometres of perennial snow and ice. Canada is a water superpower: one day this may be the most valuable resource of all, far outweighing the significance of oil and natural gas deposits.

- In 2009, over 100 First Nations communities lived under permanent boil water advisories.

There is mounting pressure on provincial governments to begin bulk water exports to the increasingly dry United States, but this is a highly sensitive subject to Canadians, and legislation actually prevents this. One can reasonably expect this pressure to continue to increase, however.

SOURCES: ENVIRONMENT CANADA, *EVERYBODY'S TALKING ABOUT WATER: IT'S TIME FOR ACTION!* FOUND AT: HTTP://WWW.EC.GC.CA/PUBLICATIONS/DEFAULT .ASP?LANG=EN&XML=B0D70C82-3263-4C05-9A76-AC005C913750 (ACCESSED FEB. 22, 2013.); E. NORMAN, ET. AL., *WATER SECURITY: A PRIMER 2010* (VANCOUVER: PROGRAM ON WATER GOVERNANCE, 2010), CANADIAN WATER NETWORK. FOUND AT: HTTP://WWW.CWN-RCE.CA/RESOURCES/ CATEGORY/23-REPORTS (ACCESSED FEB. 22, 2013); D. BOYD, *CANADA VS. THE OECD: AN ENVIRONMENTAL COMPARISON* (VICTORIA: UNIVERSITY OF VICTORIA, 2001); ENVIRONMENT CANADA, *WATER.* FOUND AT: HTTP://WWW.EC.GC.CA/ EAU-WATER/DEFAULT.ASP?LANG=EN&N=65EAA3F5-1 (ACCESSED FEB. 22, 2013)

by the quest for non-renewable resources (such as oil and minerals), "the story is different for renewables like cropland, forests, fish and fresh water. It is hard to find clear historical or contemporary examples of major wars motivated mainly by scarcities of renewables."[48] This analytic caution is certainly warranted, but it does not really contradict the claim that conflicts over resources are potential causes of international and civil warfare, as well as factors in long-range geostrategic thinking and trade policy, as water-rich states such as Canada (see Profile 10.7) contemplate bulk water exports.

Water is not the only resource that might spark future conflicts, but given the increasing consumption and decreasing availability of this vital resource, water may become as much a factor in war between states as oil and strategic minerals have been in the past. In the longer term, these stresses are expected to worsen. According to one estimate, by 2075 the number of people living in regions with chronic water shortages could be as high as three to seven billion, while the number of people living in regions with high water stress could be as high as four to

PROFILE 10.8 Water and Interstate Conflict in North Africa and the Middle East?

THE NILE

The Nile River is one of the most famous and historic rivers of the world. It is also a river of tremendous regional economic importance. The Nile is the primary source of water for both human consumption and agriculture in northeast Africa, in particular Egypt and the Sudan. In fact, almost all of Egypt's water is drawn from the Nile. However, almost all of the source water of the Nile originates outside Egypt, in the seven countries that straddle the Nile River Basin: Sudan, Ethiopia, Kenya, Rwanda, Burundi, Tanzania, and Zaire. The exploitation of water resources in these countries would reduce the flow of water to the Nile and to Egypt. To the Egyptian government, this is a major security concern, prompting former Egyptian president Anwar Sadat and former foreign minister Boutros Boutros-Ghali to warn that conflict over water might result in Egypt going to war. In 1999, the Nile Basin Initiative was signed, and there are hopes that this can help manage the situation as well as promote development in the region.

THE JORDAN RIVER BASIN

The Jordan River Basin is a valley in the central Middle East that collects most of the rainwater that falls on the region. Syria, Lebanon, Israel, Jordan, and the West Bank are heavily dependent on the Jordan Basin for their water supplies, and since the creation of Israel in 1948, access to this water supply has been a factor in the Arab–Israeli conflict. In fact, approximately 40 percent of Israel's groundwater originates in the territories occupied by Israel in 1967. Water demands in Israel are rising as the population increases, and this has resulted in an increased dependence on water drawn from the Jordan Basin. Israel has also drawn water from groundwater aquifers, which are becoming saline from overuse. Israel runs a water deficit, drawing out more water than nature replaces. Water has become a crucial point of discussion and dispute between Israel and the Palestinian people (who have had their access to water restricted by the Israeli government), as well as between Israel and neighbouring Arab states. Conflict over water could easily spark a wider conflagration in a region already beset with conflicts and high levels of tension, and resource sharing must be part of any future peace negotiations.

SOURCE: M. LOWI, *WATER AND POWER: THE POLITICS OF A SCARCE RESOURCE IN THE JORDAN RIVER BASIN* (CAMBRIDGE, UK: CAMBRIDGE UNIVERSITY PRESS, 1993) AND C. LIPCHIN, D. SANDLER, AND E. CUSHMAN, EDS., *THE JORDAN AND DEAD SEA BASIN: A REGIONAL AND INTERNATIONAL ENVIRONMENTAL CHALLENGE,* NATO SCIENCE FOR PEACE AND SECURITY PROGRAMME (DORDRECHT: SPRINGER, 2007).

nine billion, depending on the scenario. As a result, the danger of conflict over water scarcity, especially in combination with population growth and climate change, cannot be ignored.[49]

ENVIRONMENTAL DEGRADATION AND MILITARY CONFLICT: AN ONGOING CIRCLE

The link between military preparation and environmental degradation has been increasingly regarded as a security issue in the study of international relations. However, the conceptualization of the environment as a security problem is not without its detractors. Skeptics argue that it is inappropriate to characterize environmental issues as security issues because the environment is not an enemy and environmental issues cannot be addressed through traditional military means. Others argue that little hard evidence exists to support the link between environmental degradation and conflict and war.[50] However, there is often a vicious circle at play when it comes to military conflict and the environment. War can cause severe environmental destruction, which contributes to resource scarcity, which in turn contributes to structural conditions conducive to conflict and more war. We will deal with each turn of the circle in this section.

On November 5, 2003, the UN declared that each November 6 would be recognized as the International Day for Preventing the Exploitation of the Environment in War and Conflict. While it may seem self-evident, the fact that war is bad for the environment is often over-looked. The environment can be harmed incidentally, a function of strategic necessity or negligence; it can be harmed deliberately, a strategy often referred to as *ecocide*; and it can be harmed in the course of military preparation, not only in terms of munitions/weapons testing, but also in terms of the atmospheric pollution, chemical spills, and radioactive waste emitted by the military–industrial complex.[51] Invariably, military strategy and tactics, offensive and defensive, involve a good deal of environmental assault and modification. As early as 2400 BCE, Entemenar—the ruler of Sumer—modified the land by constructing a canal that diverted water from the Tigris to the Euphrates watershed, which ceased Sumer's dependence on the Kingdom of Umma. As Fred Roots has pointed out, the groundwater rose with this construction, which caused a rapid increase in salinity, impoverishing Umma. Eventually, however, Sumer suffered as well, as its own over-irrigated desert soils were leached. Roots concludes that by 2200 BCE, "mighty Sumer was easy prey for upstart Babylon, which had less wealth and poorer technology but a clean environmental base." On a further note, Roots cites the most famous Biblical example of environmental modification for military purposes, the parting of the Red Sea by Moses: "The mechanism by which Moses accomplished this rapid environmental modification is not clear to ordinary mortals today, but presumably he did it all by triggering tectonic movements. Certainly the geological structure and accumulated crustal stress in the Red Sea graben makes this a good potential location … if God is on your side."[52]

An incomplete list of major ecologically disruptive wars stretches back to the Persian–Scythian War of 512 BCE (as the Scythians retreated they hindered Persian pursuit with a scorched-earth policy, a theme found frequently over the long years of military history). The Peloponnesian War (431 to 404 BCE), made famous by Thucydides, saw the annually repeated destruction of Athenian grain crops by the Spartans. At the end of the Third Punic War, the Roman victors polluted the farmland around Carthage with salt. Genghis Khan, leading the Mongols through Asia and Eastern Europe, destroyed irrigation works located along the Tigris River in Mesopotamia. The Dutch flooded their own land to keep away French troops in the Franco–Dutch War of 1672 to 1678. Destruction of agricultural land, intended to starve rebellious states into the Union, was routine policy during the last years of the American Civil War. The Chinese used scorched-earth tactics to put down the Taiping Rebellion (1850 to 1864). The Portuguese used herbicides to destroy crops during the Angolan War of Independence (1961 to 1975). Water and water-related facilities have often been targeted in times of war. In the ancient period, wells were poisoned to deny water to the enemy, a practice that continued for centuries. In the 20th century, hydroelectric dams were targets during World War II and the Korean War. Irrigation systems in North Vietnam were bombed by the United States during the Vietnam War, and Syria and Israel had violent clashes over water in the mid-1960s. In the Gulf War, Kuwaiti desalination plants were destroyed by Iraq, while coalition bombing largely destroyed Iraq's water supply system, both in 1991 and in 2003.

In North America and Europe, concerns with the environmental impact of war first became pronounced in the 1960s. It became apparent that, with the advent of nuclear weapons, it was now possible for military conflict to destroy most of the biosphere. Perhaps the most widely read account of such Armageddon-like forecasting was Carl Sagan's discussion in the widely read journal *Foreign Affairs* of the possible climatic catastrophe—nuclear winter—that would follow even small-scale nuclear war. Atmospheric nuclear tests in the 1950s created radioactive fallout that travelled thousands of kilometres, raising public concern over the discovery of cesium-137, strontium 90, carbon 14, and various isotopes of plutonium in the environment. An earlier book by Jonathan Schell received a popular reaction, and public awareness of the ill effects of nuclear testing (including the discovery of iodine in breast milk) was partly responsible for the eventual acceptance of the Partial Test Ban Treaty in 1963.[53]

The end of the Cold War and the deliberate burning of an estimated 500 million barrels of oil in Kuwait after the Gulf War of 1990 to 1991 provoked a shift from an understandable nuclear preoccupation to concerns over how conventional warfare has harmed ecosystems and caused related population displacements in various regions of the world. However, the U.S. military probably inflicted the largest single wartime assault on an ecosystem during the Vietnam War. The destruction of large areas of Indochina's forests using herbicides was intended to remove the forest cover concealing the location and movement of enemy forces and to deprive them of their food supply. Many chemical herbicides were used, especially the infamous Agent Orange (2,4-D and 2,4,5-T), Agent White (2,4-D and Picloram), and Agent Blue (Cucodylic Acid). In addition to the landscape alteration wrought by the infamous Rome plough (which tore up entire fields to destroy farming capability), more than 17 000 square kilometres of South Vietnam were damaged by herbicides, and over 1500 square kilometres of ecologically sensitive mangrove forest were completely destroyed. This campaign generated understandable moral outrage in the United States itself, and while some 10 000 affected U.S. veterans won $180 million in damages in a civil suit against Dow, Monsanto, and other manufacturers, the Vietnamese have never been compensated.[54] The Vietnam War coincided with a growing domestic environmentalist movement in the U.S., and was probably the first military campaign that was heavily criticized in some quarters for its environmental impact. Richard Falk wrote in 1973: "Surely it is no exaggeration to consider the forests and plantations treated by Agent Orange as an Auschwitz for environmental values, certainly not from the perspective of such a distinct environmental species as the mangrove tree or nipa palm."[55] In the 1999 military intervention in Serbia, NATO bombing "destroyed fertilizer plants and oil refineries located on the tributary of the Danube river, resulting in fires and the release of petroleum byproducts and other carcinogens into the water. Additional bombs … released large amounts of PCBs and liquid mercury into other Danube tributaries, posing severe danger to human life."[56]

Despite a treaty designed to curb the deliberate damage of the environment during warfare in 1977 (the Convention on the Prohibition of Military or Any Other Hostile Use of Environmental Modification Techniques, or ENMOD), it is clear that ecocide continues to be employed in war. In Colombia, the so-called war on drugs has seen widespread spraying of "broad spectrum herbicides in ecologically fragile areas. In a single two-week period in 2000, approximately 25 000 hectares were fumigated from the air with a

Toxic conflict. A U.S. soldier from the 1st Marine Expeditionary Force stands guard at a burning oil well at the Rumeila oil fields in Iraq, March 23, 2003. Several oil wells were set ablaze by retreating Iraqi troops in the Rumeila area, the second-largest offshore oil field in the country, near the Kuwaiti border. (AP Photo/Ian Waldie)

glyphosate-based chemical agent." Is this spraying meant simply to stop narcotics production, or is it an instrument of war against FARC rebels? In Mexico, Zapatista rebels have "denounced what they consider to be hostile environmental modification aimed at stopping their insurgency. According to villagers in Zapatista regions, the government's massive spraying of pesticides to control the Mediterranean fruit fly has deliberately hit food crops, ruining them. The villagers say the spraying is a thinly disguised attempt to destroy the food security of farming communities suspected of harbouring rebel sympathizers."[57] The same communities suspect local forest fires could be deliberately set as well, a theme repeated by the Yanomami in the Brazilian Amazon, and indigenous peoples in Kalimantan, Indonesia.

The use of such techniques has long-term consequences. The German Army first used liquid chlorine (which inflames the lungs, causing those exposed to drown in their own exudation) near Ypres, Belgium, in April 1915. In June 1916, the allies first used the even deadlier phosgene during the famous Battle of the Somme. According to Robert Harris and Jeremy Paxman, "Long after the initial bombardment had occurred, an area which had been contaminated by mustard gas was liable to remain dangerous. The liquid formed pools in shell craters. ... It polluted water. In cold weather it froze like water and stayed in the soil: mustard used in the winter of 1917 poisoned men in the spring of 1918 when the ground thawed."[58] Land mines destroy arable land long after they are planted as well. Similarly, areas near many of the nuclear weapons production plants in the United States and Russia are contaminated by various chemical hazards and radiation, and Canada continues to lament the chemical residue left by the long-abandoned Cold War Distant Early Warning System in the North. Today, we are more likely to worry about whether there will be a long-lasting health impact from depleted uranium (DU) projectiles fired by U.S. tanks and planes to penetrate Iraqi and Serbian armour. We can safely predict that there will be similar instances and long-term problems in the future so long as states do not take the ENMOD convention seriously. Military research projects involving even more ambitious environmental modification techniques, such as cloud seeding and other forms of weather modification, have been ongoing. Research in even more exotic fields, such as nanotechnology and the ionosphere, will also have military applications.

However, our circle does not end here. Military violence and political instability can lead to increased environmental scarcity and, thus, enhance the prospects for more military conflict. The hypothesis that environmental degradation is a cause of conflict in the international system is built on the logic of scarcity. As the population of the planet increases, and as industrialization and consumption continue to grow and spread, the scarcity of resources will become increasingly acute for three main reasons:

1. Human activity will increasingly consume more resources, degrading the quality and availability of resources.

2. Population growth will increase the number of people making demands on a shrinking resource pie.

3. Resources will not be distributed equally, and the concentration of resources in a small segment of the population will decrease the availability of that resource to the rest of the population.

As available resources deteriorate or are depleted, competition for access to these resources will increase, and spontaneous conflict and organized war over resources might result. Indeed, some would argue that this process has already begun. Michael T. Klare argues that we are currently witnessing a "concerted drive by governments and resource firms to gain control over whatever remains of the world's raw materials base."[59] A major Canadian-led international research project on environmental scarcity and violent conflict reached a similar conclusion:

> Scarcities of renewable resources will increase sharply. The total area of high quality agricultural land will drop, as will the extent of forests and the number of species they sustain. Coming generations will also see the widespread depletion and degradation of aquifers, rivers, and other water resources; the decline of many fisheries; and perhaps significant climate change … environmental scarcities are already contributing to violent conflicts in many areas of the world. These conflicts are probably the early signs of an upsurge of violence in the coming decades that will be induced or aggravated by scarcity.[60]

A number of different environmental issues have been cited as causes of existing or future conflicts:

- The degradation and loss of arable land, with consequent implications for crop and livestock production
- The destruction of forests and consequent loss of forestry-related employment, revenue, topsoil, and species diversity
- The depletion and degradation of freshwater supplies
- The depletion of strategic minerals, including oil
- The overexploitation and consequent depletion of fisheries resources

An illustration of the link between environmental degradation, resource scarcity, and political upheaval and violence can be found in the plight of Haiti. A combination of population growth, land shortages, and corrupt leadership bent on expropriating available wealth has left Haiti the poorest country in the western Hemisphere. Haiti's forests have virtually disappeared, cut down to create more land for cultivation. Poor Haitians move up the mountainsides, clearing more forests and exhausting the land. The loss of the forest contributes to soil erosion, which has rendered almost half of the countryside unsuitable for farming. This, coupled with population growth, has led to a fall in per capita incomes. People have migrated to the cities, especially Port-au-Prince, a teeming city dominated by enormous slums. Many others have fled Haiti as refugees. Political instability and civil strife have characterized recent Haitian politics as the rich political classes use increasing levels of force and repression to maintain their control over the country. In 1986 the "Baby Doc" Duvalier regime collapsed, and international intervention restored civilian rule. Political instability in Haiti in the early 1990s resulted in the creation of a UN peacekeeping mission that helped to restore order, but the environmental and economic problems of the country were never resolved. In 2004 violence erupted as President Aristide was pushed from power. The UN has returned to Haiti again, and order is always a tentative prospect in this troubled state. A devastating earthquake in early 2010, killing over 300 000 and leaving over one million homeless, compounded the problem. Indeed, the severity of environmental degradation in the country raises doubts about the prospects for long-term economic and political stability.

In Brazil, fears persist that the unequal distribution of land and wealth could create domestic instability and increasingly violent conflict in the future. Although Brazil ranked sixth in the world in gross domestic product in 2011, the distribution of wealth in Brazil is highly unequal. In fact, the poorest 40 percent of the Brazilian population receives only 7 percent of total income. Land distribution is even more unequal, with less than 1 percent of all landowners controlling almost half of Brazil's privately held land. As a result, Brazil has some 12 million landless peasants while more than 180 million hectares of farmable land lie unused. Many of these peasants have migrated to the cities, feeding Brazil's expanding urban slums. Lack of housing, jobs, and access to government services, as well as extreme poverty, have contributed to a soaring crime rate. Recently, there has been a move to return to the land, in the form of squatting and occupying unused tracts of land. This has brought the landless peasants and the Landless Workers' Movement, the organization that represents them, into conflict with local landowners and the police. This confrontation has not always been peaceful: more than 1700 people have been killed in the past decade. More radical organizations committed to armed struggle have grown rapidly. Unless meaningful land reform is enacted over the opposition of the politically powerful land-owning class, a violent conflict over land distribution may be in Brazil's near future.

As was discussed in Chapters 6 and 8, many would argue that access to oil was a major factor in the 2003 invasion of Iraq. But there are many other, less-well-known examples. The dispute over the Spratly and Paracel Islands in the South China Sea carries the potential for interstate conflict over the right to exploit oil and mineral deposits on the seabed. The Spratly Islands are a group of 500 small islands situated in the South China Sea. Six states lay claim to some or all of the Spratly Islands or their territorial waters: Brunei, China, Malaysia, the Philippines, Taiwan, and Vietnam (see Chapter 6). Although most of the islands are mere outcroppings of rock or coral, they possess strategic value for three reasons: they are located in the middle of an important international sea lane, their territorial waters are rich in fish stocks, and their seabeds contain oil and mineral deposits. The Spratly Islands dispute has had a violent dimension, particularly between Vietnam and China. These two countries have clashed over some of the islands in 1974, 1982, 1988, and 1992. Most countries that lay claim to some or all of the islands maintain military garrisons on selected islands, and all maintain an air force and naval presence in and around the islands. Despite calls for a regional conference on the future of the islands, and the opening of talks between China and Vietnam, the Spratly Islands remain a subject of intense interstate dispute. There are concerns that this dispute, and many others with similar profiles, could result in armed conflict at any time.

Perhaps the greatest challenge to those who wish to avoid future resource wars relates to the impact of climate change. A body of research suggests a relationship exists between war and climate change-induced mechanisms such as changes in rainfall and temperature, natural disasters, and economic hardship. James Lee suggests that two kinds of climate change–induced wars will occur: "cold" wars involving states in northern and southern latitudes drawn into conflict over resources and territory, and "hot" wars involving countries in equatorial regions experiencing increased scarcity.[61] Another study found strong historical linkages between temperature and armed conflict in Africa.[62] However, other studies have found that the link between climate change-related factors and armed conflict is weak or nonexistent.[63] Nevertheless, as Jurgen Scheffan and Antonella Battaglini suggest, even if there is currently no clear evidence of the environment–conflict hypothesis, "the magnitude of climate change has the potential to undermine human security and overwhelm the adaptive capacities of societies in many world regions."[64] We may, therefore, not witness the full impact of climate change on war frequency or intensity until some time in the future.

CONCLUSIONS

In this chapter, we have discussed the main agents and structures in global ecopolitics; problems of the commons, including climate change, the crisis of the oceans, land degradation and deforestation, and species impoverishment; transborder pollution; military activity; and resource conflicts. All these problems are interrelated and require concerted international action to meet the challenges they pose. It may be the case that we are on the verge of civilizational collapse, and that this crisis (or, rather, this set of interlinked crises) will spur unprecedented innovations as various political communities struggle to adapt.[65] As Thomas Friedman warns us, "The world … is getting hot, flat, and crowded. That is, global warming, the stunning rise of middle classes all over the world, and rapid population growth have converged in a way that could make our planet dangerously unstable."[66]

This should impose an obligation on states and individuals to seek climate change mitigation and adaptation norms that embrace global environmental justice. Indeed, as Michael Mason suggests, it is the "intersection of individual rights and responsibilities with (inter)state obligations that offers concrete possibilities for citizen participation in global decisionmaking."[67]

The steps taken from here, such as a serious effort to reduce greenhouse gas emissions, the provision of adequate funding for global climate change adaptation, and the sound management of the world's land, oceans, fresh water, and atmospheric resources, will play a significant role in shaping the lives of future generations. It is clear that a momentous effort lies before us all, in our capacities as researchers, teachers, policymakers, global citizens, consumers, family members, and individuals. Though controversies abound, what emerges from the scientific and legal community is an emphasis on adopting the precautionary principle in environmental management. The principle, which is endorsed in the Rio Declaration of 1992, Agenda 21, the UNFCC, the CBD, and a plethora of other international agreements, insists that, in the absence of scientific certainty regarding the future impact of human activity, we should err on the side of caution.[68] Today, the precautionary principle is a very logical self-imposed restraint.

Endnotes

1. "Why the Ark Is Sinking," in L. Kaufman and K. Mallory, eds., *The Last Extinction*, 2nd ed. (Cambridge, MA: MIT Press, 1993), 1–46, 12.

2. M. Kaplan, "The Coming Anarchy," *Atlantic Monthly*, February 1994, 58.

3. C. Doucet, *Urban Meltdown: Cities, Climate Change and Politics as Usual* (Gabriola Island, BC: New Society Publishers, 2007), xvii.

4. See *The Millennium Ecosystem Assessment* (Washington, DC: Island Press, 2005) and *Global Environmental Outlook GEO5: Environment for the Future We Want* (New York: UNEP, 2012).

5. The relationship between understandings of IR and ecology is explored in much greater depth in E. Laferrière and P. Stoett, *International Relations Theory and Ecological Thought: Towards a Synthesis* (London: Routledge, 1999). See also M. Mies and V. Shiva, *Ecofeminism* (Halifax: Fernwood Publications, 1993); N. Choucri, ed., *Global Accord: Environmental Challenges and International Responses* (Cambridge, MA: MIT Press, 1993); R. Eckersley, *The Green State: Rethinking Democracy and Sovereignty* (Cambridge: MIT Press, 2004); M. Paterson, *Understanding Global Environmental Politics: Domination, Accumulation, Resistance* (Basingstoke: Macmillan, 2000); S. Dalby, *Environmental Security* (Minneapolis: University of Minnesota Press, 2002); P. Dauvergne, ed., *Handbook of Global Environmental Politics* (Cheltenham, UK: Edward Elgar, 2005); and E. Laferrière and P. Stoett, eds., *International Ecopolitical Theory: Critical Approaches* (Vancouver: University of British Columbia Press, 2006).

6. See J. Clapp, "Global Environmental Governance for Corporate Responsibility and Accountability," *Global Environmental Politics* 5, no. 3 (2005), 23–34; and J. Clapp and P. Dauvergne, eds., *Paths to a Green World: The Political Economy of the Global Environment* (Cambridge: MIT Press, 2005).

7. D. Suzuki and H. Dressel, *Good News For a Change: How Everyday People Are Helping the Planet* (Vancouver: Greystone Books, 2003). See also P. Wapner, *Environmental Activism and World Civic Politics* (Albany, NY: SUNY Press, 1996).

8. W. Beckerman, "Global Warming and International Action: An Economic Perspective," in A. Hurrell and B. Kingsbury, eds., *The International Politics of the Environment* (Oxford: Clarendon Press, 1992), 253–89.

9. S. Krasner, "Sovereignty, Regimes, and Human Rights," in V. Rittberger, ed., *Regime Theory and International Relations* (Oxford: Clarendon Press, 1993), 139–67. See also P.M. Wijkman, "Managing the Global Commons," *International Organization* 36, no. 3 (1982), 511–36; S. Buck, *The Global Commons: An Introduction* (Washington, DC: Island Press, 1998); E. Ostrom, *Governing the Commons: The Evolution of Institutions for Collective Action* (Cambridge, UK: Cambridge University Press, 1990); and E. DeSombre, *Global Environmental Institutions* (New York: Routledge, 2006).

10. M. M'Gonigle and D. Babicki, "The Turbot's Last Stand?" *The Globe and Mail,* July 21, 1995, A19.

11. General Assembly Resolution 1803 (XVII), December 14, 1962. See N. Schrijver, *Sovereignty over Natural Resources: Balancing Rights and Duties* (Cambridge, UK: Cambridge University Press, 1997).

12. R.E. Benedick, *Ozone Diplomacy: New Directions in Safeguarding the Planet* (Cambridge MA: Harvard University Press, 1991), 207. See also K. Litfin, *Ozone Discourses: Science and Politics in Global Environmental Cooperation* (New York: Columbia University Press, 1994).

13. For the complete text, see *Antarctic Journal of the United States* (Natural Science Foundation) 26, no. 4 (December 1991). See also O.S. Stokke and D. Vidas, eds., *Governing the Antarctic: The Effectiveness and Legitimacy of the Antarctic Treaty System* (Cambridge, UK: Cambridge University Press, 1996); and S. Blumenfeld, "For Science and Peace: The Creation and Evolution of the Antarctic Treaty System: A Model for International Cooperation and Governance," *Yale Economic Review* Winter/Spring 2010, 28.

14. IPCC, *Climate Change 2007: Synthesis Report—An Assessment of the Intergovernmental Panel on Climate Change,* 30.

15. See "Asian Brown Clouds Intensify Global Warming," *Environmental News Service,* August 1, 2007, http://www.ens-newswire.com/ens/aug2007/2007-08-01-02.asp (accessed June 18, 2013).

16. N. Stern, *The Economics of Climate Change: The Stern Review* (Cambridge: Cambridge University Press, 2007); T. Flannery, *The Weather Makers: Our Changing Climate and What It Means for Life on Earth* (New York: Penguin, 2006); G. Monbiot, *Heat: How to Stop the Planet from Burning* (Toronto: Doubleday Canada, 2006); and W. Burroughs, *Climate Change: A Multidisciplinary Approach* (New York: Cambridge University Press, 2007).

17. S. Earle, *Sea Change: a Message of the Oceans* (New York: Fawcett Columbine, 1995), xii. See also A. Mitchell, *Sea Sick: The Global Ocean in Crisis* (Toronto: McClelland and Stewart, 2009).

18. Much of the following information is taken from the UNEP's *Global Environmental Outlook 3* (New York: UNEP and Earthscan, 2002), 180–209.

19. See P. Stoett, *The International Politics of Whaling* (Vancouver: University of British Columbia Press, 1997). On the impact of whaling on the oceans, see J. Estes, ed., *Whales, Whaling, and Ocean Ecosystems* (Santa Cruz: University of California Press, 2006) and D. Burnett, *The Sounding of the Whale: Science and Cetaceans in the Twentieth Century* (Chicago: University of Chicago Press, 2012).

20. See *The State of World Fisheries and Aquaculture 2000* (Rome: Food and Agriculture Organization, 2001); and *The State of World Fisheries and Aquaculture, 2008* (Rome: Food and Agriculture Organization, 2009), 7.

21. See E. Allison, "Big Laws, Small Catches: Global Ocean Governance and the Fisheries Crisis," *Journal of International Development* 13 (2001), 933–50; and L. Juda, "Rio Plus Ten: The Evolution of International Marine Fisheries Governance," *Ocean Development and International Law* 33 (2002), 109–144.

22. See K. Riddle, "Illegal, Unreported, and Unregulated Fishing: Is International Cooperation Contagious?," *Ocean Development and International Law* 37 (2006), 265–97.

23. For a Canadian perspective, see J. Volpe and K. Shaw, "Fish Farms and Neoliberalism: Salmon Aquaculture in British Columbia," in C. Gore and P. Stoett, eds., *Environmental Challenges and Opportunities: Local–Global Perspectives on Canadian Issues* (Toronto: Emond Montgomery, 2009), 131–58.

24. See R. Rayfuse, "The Challenge of Sustainable High Seas Fisheries," in N. Schrijver and F. Weiss, eds., *International Law and Sustainable Development: Principles and Practice* (Netherlands: Martinus Nijhoff, 2004), 467–99.

25. See C. Wilkinson, ed., *Status of Coral Reefs of the World* (Townsville: Australian Institute of Marine Science, 2000).

26. Data from *Global Forest Resources Assessment 2010* (Rome: Food and Agriculture Organization of the United Nations, 2010), 16–17; *State of the World's Forests, 2011* (Rome: Food and Agriculture Organization of the United Nations, 2011); and *State of the World's Forests, 2009* (Rome: Food and Agriculture Organization of the United Nations, 2008), http://www.fao.org/docrep/013/i1757e/i1757e.pdf (accessed June 2012).

27. *State of the World's Forests 2009,* 35, and *Global Forest Resources Assessment 2010,* 17.

28. *Global Forest Resources Assessment 2010* (Rome: Food and Agriculture Organization of the United Nations, 2010), 21.

29. See United Nations Department of Public Information, "Press Release of the Secretary-General's Report on Implementing Agenda 21," Johannesburg Summit 2002, http://www.johannesburgsummit.org/html/media_info/pressreleases_factsheets/press_summary_sg_report2801.pdf (accessed May 27, 2004).

30. *The State of the World's Land and Water Resources for Food and Agriculture: Managing Systems at Risk* (Rome: FAO, 2011), 113.

31. On GMOs, see R. Falkner, ed., *The International Politics of Genetically Modified Food: Diplomacy, Trade and Law* (Houndmills, UK: Palgrave, 2007), 138–54; for Canadian perspectives, see P. Andrée, *Genetically Modified Diplomacy: The Global Politics of Agricultural Biotechnology and the Environment* (Vancouver: UBC Press, 2006); and S. Mulligan, as in Profile 10.1. On biofuels, see C.F. Runge and B. Senauer, "How Biofuels Could Starve the Poor," *Foreign Affairs* 86, no. 3 (May/June 2007).

32. M.B. Fenton, "Species Impoverishment," in J. Leith, R. Price, and J. Spencer, eds., *Planet Earth: Problems and Prospects* (Montreal/Kingston: McGill-Queen's University Press, 1995), 83–110. See also P. Ehrlich and A. Ehrlich, *Extinction* (New York: Wiley, 1986); N. Eldredge, *The Miner's Canary: Unravelling the Mysteries of Extinction* (New York: Prentice Hall, 1991); and P. Colinvaux, *Why Big Fierce Animals Are Rare: An Ecologist's Perspective* (Princeton: Princeton University Press, 1978). For an excellent Canadian text, see S. Bocking, *Biodiversity in Canada: Ecology, Ideas, and Action* (Peterborough, ON: Broadview Press, 2000).

33. D. Jablonski, "Mass Extinctions: New Answers, New Questions," in L. Kaufman and K. Mallory, eds., *The Last Extinction,* 2nd ed. (Cambridge, MA: MIT Press, 1993), 47–68, 52.

34. "Why the Ark Is Sinking," in L. Kaufman and K. Mallory, eds., *The Last Extinction,* 2nd ed. (Cambridge, MA: MIT Press, 1993), 1–46, 43. See also Kaufman's "Catastrophic Change in Species-Rich Freshwater Ecosystems: The Lessons of Lake Victoria," *Bioscience* 42, no. 11 (1992), 846–58; Y. Baskin, "Africa's Troubled Waters: Fish Introductions and a Changing Physical Profile Muddy Lake Victoria's Future," *Bioscience* 42, no. 7 (1992), 476–81; and the controversial Hubert Sauper 2004 film *Darwin's Nightmare.*

35. T. Foose, "Riders of the Last Ark: The Role of Captive Breeding in Conservation Strategies," in L. Kaufman and K. Mallory, eds., *The Last Extinction,* 149–78.

36. J. Scarff, "Ethical Issues in Whale and Small Cetacean Management," *Environmental Ethics* 2, no. 3 (1980), 241–80, 244n., 14.

37. See R. Boardman, *The International Politics of Bird Conservation: Biodiversity, Regionalism and Global Governance* (Northampton, MA: Edward Elgar, 2006).

38. R. Boardman, *International Organization and the Conservation of Nature* (Bloomington: Indiana University Press, 1981).

39. See P. Stoett, "Wildlife Conservation: Institutional and Normative Considerations," in N. Schrijver and F. Weiss, eds., *International Law and Sustainable Development: Principles and Practice* (Leiden, NL: Martinus Nijhoff, 2004), 501–18; and P. Stoett and P. Le Prestre, "International Initiatives, Commitments, and Disappointments: Canada, CITES, and the CBD," in K. Beazley and R. Boardman, eds., *Politics of the Wild: Canada and Endangered Species* (Toronto: Oxford University Press, 2001), 120–1; and G. Rosendal, "Impact of Overlapping International Regimes: The Case of Biodiversity," *Global Governance* 7, no. 2 (2001), 95–117.

40. C. Bright, "Invasive Species: Pathogens of Globalization," *Foreign Policy,* Fall 1999: 50–8; see also P. Stoett, "Counter-Bioinvasion: Conceptual and Governance Challenges," *Environmental Politics* 16, no. 3 (2007), 433–52.

41. See A. Price-Smith, *The Health of Nations: Infectious Disease, Environmental Change, and Their Effects on National Security and Development* (Cambridge: MIT Press, 2002).

42. An important contribution to this awareness was the famous text by R. Carson, *Silent Spring* (Boston: Houghton Mifflin, 1962).

43. See D. Munton and G. Castle, "Reducing Acid Rain, 1980s," in D. Munton and J. Kirton, eds., *Canadian Foreign Policy: Selected Cases* (Scarborough: Prentice Hall, 1992), 367–80. Critics charge that the G.W. Bush

administration (2001–2009) slowly dismantled the Clean Air Act of 1972, thus harming this bilateral agreement as well.

44. J. Wargo, *Our Children's Toxic Legacy: How Science and Law Fail to Protect Us from Pesticides* (New Haven: Yale University Press, 1996), 281. Note that there is an energetic debate between those who wish to ban DDT outright and those who claim the pesticide is still necessary to kill disease-spreading mosquitoes in Africa.

45. *Global Environmental Outlook 5: Environment for the Future We Want* (New York: United Nations Environment Programme, 2012), 98, 115.

46. See W. Ellis, "A Soviet Sea Lies Dying," *National Geographic*, February 1990, 73–93.

47. See L. Ohlsson, ed., *Hydropolitics: Conflicts over Water as a Development Constraint* (London: Zed, 1995). See also M. Lowi, *Water and Power: The Politics of a Scarce Resource in the Jordan River Basin* (Cambridge: Cambridge University Press, 1993); and the award-winning book by K. Conca, *Governing Water: Contentious Transnational Politics and Global Institution Building* (Cambridge, MA: MIT Press, 2006).

48. T. Homer-Dixon, "The Myth of Global Water Wars," *The Globe and Mail*, November 9, 1995, A23. He adds that the alarmist concern with inevitable water wars "distracts the public's attention from the real results of water scarcity. Shortages reduce food production, aggravate poverty and disease, spur large migrations, and undermine a state's moral authority and capacity to govern. Over time, these stresses can tear apart a poor society's social fabric, causing chronic popular unrest and violence."

49. M. Falkenmark, A. Berntell, A. Jägerskog, J. Lundqvist, M. Matz, and H. Tropp, *On the Verge of a New Water Scarcity: A Call for Good Governance and Human Ingenuity*, SIWI Policy Brief (Stockholm: Stockholm International Water Institute, 2007), 6.

50. See, for example, M. Levy, "Is the Environment a National Security Issue?" *International Security* 20 (Fall 1995), 35–62; S. Dalby, *Environmental Security*; and Astri Suhrke, "Environmental Change, Migration, and Conflict: A Lethal Feedback Dynamic?" in C. Crocker, F. Osler Hampson, and P. Aall, eds., *Managing Global Chaos: Sources of and Responses to International Conflict* (Washington, DC: United States Institute of Peace Press, 1996), 113–27.

51. See W. Thomas, *Scorched Earth: The Military's Assault on the Environment* (Philadelphia: New Society Publishers, 1995); N. Gleditsch, "Armed Conflict and the Environment," in P. Diehl and N.P. Gleditsch, eds., *Environmental Conflict* (Boulder, CO: Westview Press, 2001), 251–72; S. Lanier-Graham, *The Ecology of War: Environmental Impacts of Weaponry and Warfare* (New York: Walker and Company, 1993); and N. Brown, "Climate, Ecology and International Security," *Survival* 31 (1989), 519–32.

52. E.F. Roots, "International Agreements to Prohibit or Control Modification of the Environment for Military Purposes: An Historical Overview and Comments on Current Issues," in Bruno Schiefer, ed., *Verifying Obligations Respecting Arms Control and the Environment: A Post Gulf War Assessment* (Saskatchewan: University of Saskatchewan, 1992), 13–34, 13.

53. C. Sagan, "Nuclear War and Climatic Catastrophe: Some Policy Implications," *Foreign Affairs* 62 (Winter 1983/84), 257–92; J. Schell, *The Fate of the Earth* (New York: Knopf, 1982). See also C. Caufield, *Multiple Exposures: Chronicles of the Radiation Age* (London: Secker and Warburg, 1989).

54. See P. Robinson, *The Effects of Weapons on Ecosystems* (Toronto: Pergamon for UNEP, 1979), 15; and A. Westing, ed., *Herbicides in War* (London: Taylor and Francis, 1984). For a fascinating legal and sociological discussion of the reactions of American Vietnam veterans to Agent Orange, see J. Jacobs and D. McNamara, "Vietnam Veterans and the Agent Orange Controversy," *Armed Forces and Society* 13, no. 1 (1986), 57–80; and F. Wilcox, *Waiting for an Army to Die: The Tragedy of Agent Orange* (New York: Random House, 1983).

55. R. Falk, "Environmental Warfare and Ecocide: Facts, Appraisal, and Proposals," *Bulletin of Peace Proposals* 4, no. 1 (1973), 84.

56. E. DeSombre, *The Global Environment and World Politics: International Relations for the 21st Century* (London: Continuum, 2002), 46.

57. All quotes in this paragraph are from S. Pimiento Chamorro and E. Hammond, "Addressing Environmental Modification in Post–Cold War Conflict," paper presented to the Civil Society Conference to Review ENMOD and Related Agreements on Hostile Modification of the Environment, Amsterdam, May 2001. The paper was written for a discontinued NGO named The Sunshine Project. See http://pogoblog.typepad.com/pogo/2008/02/the-sun-sets-on.html (accessed June 28, 2013).

58. R. Harris and J. Paxman, *A Higher Form of Killing: The Secret Story of Gas and Germ Warfare* (London, UK: Chatto and Windus, 1982), 27. This is a fascinating book for anyone interested in the evolution of chemical and biological weapons.

59. M.T. Klare, *The Race for What's Left: The Global Scramble for the World's Last Resources* (New York: Picador, 2012), 12.

60. T. Homer-Dixon, "Environmental Scarcities and Violent Conflict: Evidence from Cases," *International Security* 19 (Summer 1994); see also his *Environment, Scarcity, and Violence* (Princeton: Princeton University Press, 1999).

61. See J.R. Lee, *Climate Change and Armed Conflict: Hot and Cold Wars* (New York: Routledge, 2009).

62. M.B. Burke, et al., "Warming Increases the Risk of Civil War in Africa," *Proceedings of the National Academy of Arts and Sciences of the United States of America*, 106, no. 49 (December 2009), 20670-674.

63. See, for example, N.P. Gleditsch, "Whither the Weather? Climate Change and Conflict," *Journal of Peace Research* 49, no. 1 (January 2012), 3–9; and O.M. Theisen, H. Holtermann, and H. Buhaug, "Climate Wars? Assessing the Claim That Drought Breeds Conflict," *International Security* 36, no. 3 (Winter 2011/2012), 79–106.

64. J. Scheffran and A. Battaglini, "Climate and Conflicts: The Security Risks of Global Warming," *Regional Environmental Change* 11, no. 1 (Supplement, March 2011), 27–39.

65. For an engaging read on this theme, see T. Homer-Dixon, *The Upside of Down: Catastrophe, Creativity, and the Renewal of Civilization* (Toronto: Alfred Knopf, 2006).

66. Thomas L. Friedman, *Hot, Flat, and Crowded: Why We Need a Green Revolution—and How It Can Renew America* (New York: Farrar, Straus and Giroux, 2008), 5.

67. M. Mason, "Citizenship Entitlements Beyond Borders? Identifying Mechanisms of Access and Redress for Affected Publics in International Environmental Laws," *Global Governance* 12, no. 3 (2006), 283–304, 285.

68. D. Freestone, "The Precautionary Principle," in R. Churchill and D. Freestone, eds., *International Law and Global Climate Change* (London: Graham and Trotham, 1991), 21–39. The discourse on GMOs is especially indicative of the debates that can ensue over the implementation of this principle, as proponents argue the benefits of genetic manipulation outweigh the contested risks feared by opponents.

Population Growth, Movements, and Global Health

To couple the concept of freedom to breed with the belief that everyone born has an equal right to the commons is to lock the world into a tragic course of action.

—*Garrett Hardin, 1968*[1]

The existence of refugees is a symptom of the disappearance of economic and political liberalism. The basic real solution of the refugee problem, real or potential, is necessarily therefore related to the solution of the great problems of economic and political adjustment in the contemporary world.

—*Sir John Hope Simpson, 1938*[2]

INTRODUCTION

The preceding chapters on human rights, human security, and global ecopolitics are linked by shared concerns with the impact of population growth and population movements and the quest to provide for human health needs. While the spectre of an overcrowded world is unsettling, the image of hundreds of millions of migrants and desperate refugees provokes even more anxiety. Some analysts insist these problems are exaggerated, and that overconsumption is a bigger problem than overpopulation; others argue that population growth remains the gravest threat to the future of humanity. While this debate rages, refugee movements continue to challenge national sovereignty and human rights laws, and international surveillance of infectious disease is one of the key challenges for global governance today.

Liberal institutionalists argue that governments should create regimes and strengthen international organizations and law to help us cope with these issues. In contrast, realists predict that states will respond to population movements and related problems by strengthening their laws to restrict immigration and increasing border security. Neo-Marxists have argued that both international organizations and state security are in effect further entrenching a global **apartheid** system whereby the poor and sick are neglected, marginalized, and perhaps even quarantined, to protect the relatively wealthy from potential harm. Feminists have long argued that the debate over population control has been a masculine moral construction that ignores women's reproductive health and rights, and that migration's dark side—global trafficking, largely for the sex trade—needs more serious treatment. Other critical theorists stress the reflexive **securitization** of these issues; they are seen as security problems to be addressed by using instruments such as the police, border guards, electronic surveillance, and the army. Instead, the focus should be on the socio-economic factors that actually drive population-related issues.

This chapter begins by asking whether overpopulation itself is the main problem we face. While population growth remains a serious global challenge, we are as concerned today with consumption patterns per capita as we are with sheer numbers of people. Furthermore, many states are more preoccupied with the effects of an aging population than a growing one. Next, we examine one of the more visible manifestations of population growth and movement, the increasing **urbanization** of our world, which (along with the climate change issue) is enhancing the political importance of the governance of cities in world affairs. We then discuss immediate concerns with population control measures, most notably their potential impact on women's reproductive health and rights.

From population issues themselves we turn to populations on the move. We begin by discussing the causes and consequences of international migration, including efforts to protect migratory workers, and the myriad human security threats associated with refugee movements. These include political persecution, the link between environmental degradation and population movements, the often invisible plight of the internally displaced, and the global sex trade. Finally, we close with a discussion of a topic that is intrinsically linked to all of these factors, namely the spread of infectious diseases, such as **HIV/AIDS**, SARS, the swine flu, and the avian flu.

THE OVERPOPULATION DEBATE

Overpopulation is a fairly recent concept: historically, the leaders of most political units (from villages to city-states to modern nation-states) have viewed population growth as a factor in military and economic power. At the end of the last Ice Age, when migrations to the area we now know as the Americas began, the entire Earth probably supported fewer than 10 million people. By 1930, the population of the planet had reached 2 billion, and by 1972, 3.85 billion. According to the UN Population Division, global population reached 6.9 billion in 2010, and is projected to reach 9.3 billion by 2050, an increase of 2.4 billion people (roughly equivalent to the entire population of the planet in 1950) in just 40 years (see Profile 11.1).[3]

Demographers liken population growth rates to large cargo ships: one can stop the engines, but it will be some time before the ship itself comes to a halt. Because so many women in the world today are of childbearing age, even if fertility rates fall from the 2006 to 2010 global average of 2.5 children per woman, world population will still increase. This growth comes at a time when a major food crisis may be looming on the horizon. During the 1960s and 1970s, the so-called green revolution increased crop yields through the use of irrigation, pesticides, and fertilizer. This is a less viable option today, when almost all prime arable land has been put to use, the excessive use of pesticides has often caused more problems than it has solved, and the conversion of food crops to biofuel continues in many areas. The promise of GMOs (genetically modified organisms; see Chapter 10) remains politically and scientifically contentious. Though enough food is available to feed everyone now, and malnutrition and

PROFILE 11.1 The 20 Most Populous States, 2009

Note: As with all statistics, we must be cautious about accepting population figures; they are at best crude estimates, based on government census data that often exclude the homeless and those living in remote rural areas, and that are subject to sudden changes due to war, pandemics, and natural disasters.

1. China 1 341 335 000
2. India 1 224 614 000
3. United States 310 384 000
4. Indonesia 239 871 000
5. Brazil 194 946 000
6. Pakistan 173 593 000
7. Nigeria 158 423 000
8. Bangladesh 148 692 000
9. Russian Federation 142 958 000
10. Japan 126 536 000
11. Mexico 113 423 000
12. Philippines 93 261 000
13. Vietnam 87 848 000
14. Ethiopia 82 950 000
15. Germany 82 302 000
16. Egypt 81 121 000
17. Iran (Islamic Republic of) 73 974 000
18. Turkey 72 752 000
19. Thailand 69 122 000
20. Democratic Republic of the Congo 65 966 000

Canada (2011): 33 477 000

SOURCE: UNITED NATIONS, DEPARTMENT OF ECONOMIC AND SOCIAL AFFAIRS, POPULATION DIVISION, UN WORLD POPULATION PROSPECTS. FOUND AT: HTTP://ESA.UN.ORG/UNPD/WPP/SORTING-TABLES/TAB-SORTING_POPULATION.HTM (ACCESSED JUNE 2012).

undernourishment are largely a consequence of inadequate distribution, this may not be the case when we have nine billion people to feed and climate change wreaks havoc on agricultural production. A sudden increase in food and commodity prices in 2008 made even basic foodstuffs unaffordable for millions of people worldwide, providing a warning of how fragile food security can be in a world of increasing demand, high energy costs, and growing reliance on non-local food sources.

Population growth is also distributed unevenly across the world's regions. The so-called **demographic transition** experienced by the industrialized countries involved the decline of both death and birth rates as medical technology reduced infant mortality and extended life spans. People also became less likely to raise large families due to a combination of birth control and advances in the economic and social status of women. As a result, many developed countries have birth rates below population replacement levels, raising a set of issues related to the "greying" of societies and debates over immigration. However, in many regions this demographic transition has not taken place. High infant mortality rates encourage parents to have more children since infant survival is less certain. With more limited economic or social opportunities, women tend to have more children at an earlier age. Larger families provide parents with at least some prospect for care in old age in the absence of government social safety nets. Therefore, most of the population growth in the future will take place in lower-income states, with serious consequences for food security, environmental sustainability, employment opportunities, and provision of health care, education, and other social services.

In China and India, each with well over one billion citizens, it is doubtful any sort of transition can stem massive population increases. Many argue that China's **one-child policy**, while a threat to individual liberty (and to the lives of consequently unwanted children—usually female), was a necessary step that should be followed elsewhere to avoid a global "population bomb," a phrase popularized in the 1970s by writers such as Paul and Anne Ehrlich, who argued that massive increases in population threatened not just the standard of living of people around the globe but also human life itself.[4] In what has become a classic piece of **neo-Malthusian** literature, "The Tragedy of the Commons," professor of human ecology Garrett Hardin argued that in order to ensure our future collective survival the freedom to reproduce must be limited.[5]

Of course, many dismiss this as an extreme position. Some argue that the demographic transition is imminent. State control of reproduction is certainly viewed as an infringement on civil liberties in most countries, and contradicts the conventions espoused by most religions. Others suggest that high populations themselves are not to blame for global environmental problems: rather, the high consumption patterns and large ecological footprints of people in the high-income world are the real culprits. According to a classic formula developed in the 1960s, the environmental impacts of population size, affluence (i.e., consumption), and technology are interrelated.[6] However, while the industrialized countries have clearly contributed more to global warming and other environmental problems than lower-income countries, one cannot ignore the substantial environmental and consumption impact that millions more people have on the planet each year. It should be clear, then, that both the North and the South have an important role to play in decreasing the negative effects of population growth.

China's one-child policy, which began in the early 1990s, has been the most controversial with respect to the ethics of government-imposed birth control. Renamed the Population and Family Planning Law in 2002, the policy limits reproduction to one child for each couple in the cities, and two for those who live in rural areas and whose first child is a girl. Families of ethnic minorities are allowed to have two or three children. This demonstrates some sensitivity to the problems of gendercide and ethnocide the original policy entailed. The Chinese government claims that the policy has led to 300 million fewer births, and it has vowed to maintain the policy in order to achieve its goal of controlling the population at the 1.6 billion level by 2050. Inducements to comply include charging fees for services for second children that were free for the first and rewarding single-child couples with promotions at work and free university education for the child. Abortions are strongly "encouraged" in the advent of a second pregnancy. In some cases, this policy has resulted in **infanticide**: since baby boys are more highly valued than girls, couples intent on having a son may resort to murder should a girl be produced. Similarly, some families in India, China, and elsewhere have used prenatal amniocentesis and ultrasound scanning to discover the sex of fetuses, and then aborted the females.[7] During the 1970s, China's fertility rate fell from 6 children per woman to about 2.5; despite this drop, most people would agree that China still has a tremendous overpopulation problem. However, the ethical questions remain and will become only more pronounced as governments and international aid agencies struggle with continued population growth.

The UN Conference on Population and Development in Cairo in 1994 did produce several concrete goals and an action plan for the UN Population Fund (UNFPA), subsequently linked to the MDGs. Yet it is clear that the UN has little direct control over population policies. Some states, such as Canada and Japan, are more concerned with aging populations and actually seek to raise birth rates in the short term. Two of the more visible outcomes of the population explosion are urbanization and the demand for family-planning policies in crowded states.

URBANIZATION

One of the most pronounced effects of population growth and movement is urbanization.[8] Earth passed a demographic milestone in 2008, when it was estimated that half of the world's population (or approximately 3.3 billion people) lived in urban areas.[9] In recent years, increased attention has been devoted to the challenges of urbanization, especially with respect to governance, poverty and slums, the provision of services, and environmental sustainability. With the number of people living in cities expected to reach six billion (two-thirds of the world's population) in 2050, this is likely to be one of the growing areas of study in global politics. The city has often been viewed as a primary indicator of "modernity"; urbanization followed industrialization, which meant that **gross national product (GNP)** was increasing and society was advancing toward the Western ideal. Cities came to symbolize a certain notion of progress, but do the steel and glass high-rise buildings of Bangkok and Shanghai offer positive proof of the development of Thailand and China? Or do they merely put a glittering face on the detrimental effects of rapid economic growth? Is the quality of life in burgeoning but highly polluted Mexico City an improvement over life in rural Mexico?

The pure logic behind the quest for the city is clear. Big cities with high population densities reduce the unit costs of infrastructure: it becomes cheaper to supply essential services (such as water, electricity, and education) to people if they live closer together. Companies are more likely to invest in cities, where both labour pools and urban middle-class markets are more easily accessible than they are in remote areas. Employment opportunities, and the image of a better life, attract migratory labour. And since all this activity is highly concentrated, it can be regulated by government and, to the extent possible under a market economy, urban planning can facilitate a more humane, less alienating centre of human life. For example, some cities favour an "eco-density" approach to urban planning and public transport that is considered more environmentally sustainable than sprawling suburbs served by highways, and many cities have joined climate change initiatives and made other efforts to reduce their ecological footprint. However, if cities produce more pollution than can be safely managed, if traffic congestion not only creates smog but also actually impedes transportation, if neighbouring land is degraded because of waste disposal needs and excessive demands on natural resources, and if most rural–urban migrants end up in unsanitary and politically marginalized shantytowns, is urbanization really a step in the right developmental direction? Increasingly, analysts of sustainable development cast rapid urbanization in a negative light. This view is tied, of course, to population growth. Most dramatically, the spectre of rising and politically influential **megacities**, great centres of sprawl, chaos, and pollution, looms (see Profiles 11.2 and 11.3). The air quality at the summer 2008 Olympics in Beijing was perhaps a startling revelation for viewers of the games, but experts have long lamented the impact of rapid urbanization on human and environmental health.

It is clear that the combination of urbanization, poverty, poor services, and lax regulations can have disastrous environmental effects.

Desperation among plenty. A man holding a sign panhandles for money during the evening rush hour at the corner of Bay and Front Streets in the financial district of downtown Toronto. (The Canadian Press/Michael Hudson)

PROFILE 11.2 Megacities

Generally, *megacities* or *urban agglomerations* are defined as those with more than 10 million inhabitants. Below we list the world's megacities in 1975 and 2007, and the projected populations of these megacities in 2025. Think about this: the city of Tokyo has more inhabitants than the massive country of Canada! Of course, by 2025 many new urban areas will be counted as megacities.

Note: It is very difficult to compare estimates of city size, since different surveys include different areas as part of city centres. For example, if we exclude the suburban areas around New York, Los Angeles, or Tokyo, their populations would be considerably reduced. In addition, the homeless often go uncounted. Finally, cities often have an incentive to exaggerate their population numbers for purposes of obtaining funding.

All numbers below are in millions.

MEGACITIES, 1975	MEGACITIES, 2010	PROJECTED POPULATIONS, 2025
Tokyo, Japan 26.6	Tokyo 36.9	Tokyo 38.7
New York–Newark, U.S. 15.9	New York 20.1	New York 23.6
Mexico City, Mexico 10.7	Mexico City 20.15	Mexico City 32.9
	Mumbai (Bombay), India 19.4	Mumbai 26.55
	São Paulo, Brazil 19.65	São Paulo 23.2
	Delhi, India 21.9	Delhi 32.9
	Shanghai, China 19.55	Shanghai 28.4
	Kolkata (Calcutta), India 14.3	Kolkata (Calcutta), 18.7
	Dhaka, Bangladesh 14.9	Dhaka, 22.9
	Buenos Aires, Argentina 13.4	Buenos Aires, 15.5
	Los Angeles, USA 13.2	Los Angeles, 15.7
	Karachi, Pakistan 13.5	Karachi, 20.2
	Al-Qahirah (Cairo), Egypt 11.1	Al-Qahirah (Cairo), 14.75
	Rio de Janeiro, Brazil 11.9	Rio de Janeiro, 13.6
	Osaka/Kobe, Japan 11.9	Osaka/Kobe, 14.4
	Beijing, China 15	Beijing, 22.6
	Manila, Philippines 11.65	Manila, 14.3
	Moskva (Moscow), Russia 11.5	Moskva (Moscow) 12.6
	Istanbul, Turkey 10.95	Istanbul 14.5

SOURCES: UNITED NATIONS DEPARTMENT OF ECONOMIC AND SOCIAL AFFAIRS, POPULATION DIVISION, EXECSUM_WEB.PDF (ACCESSED AUG. 5, 2012); WORLD URBANIZATION PROSPECTS, THE 2011 REVISION. UNITED NATIONS DEPARTMENT OF ECONOMIC AND SOCIAL AFFAIRS. FOUND AT: HTTP://ESA.UN.ORG/UNPD/WUP/CD-ROM/URBAN-AGGLOMERATIONS.HTM (ACCESSED FEB. 22, 2013).

Katmandu, Nepal, a city designed for some 40 000 occupants, now has more than 800 000, and the famous Katmandu Valley is covered by a blue haze of pollution from cars, wood fires, kilns, and construction, which forces pedestrians and cyclists to wear cloth masks (a scene common in Mexico City, Tokyo, Beijing, and many other urban centres). The rapid urbanization of Bhopal, India, was what made the 1984 industrial accident in that city so disastrous

PROFILE 11.3 An Emerging Global Megacity System?

Here is an interesting scenario: what if the megacity replaces national governments as the primary means of expressing political power and conducting global interactions? The trend toward the megacity is evident in Ontario, where the provincial government amalgamated the different districts of Toronto into one big administration, and in Montreal, where the same thing happened in 2003 (neither effort proceeded without controversy). Business today is conducted largely between cities, not countries. Likewise, travel is from metropolis to metropolis. As cities increase in size and wealth, devouring more of the countryside around them, the megacity may become the most important political unit. This is not without historical precedent: in the period 800 to 322 BCE, a Greek city-state system flourished. The population varied: larger cities such as Syracuse, Acragas, and Athens had around 50 000 citizens, while smaller settlements, such as Siris and Thourioi in Sicily, had but several thousand. Eventually, Athens formed a far-reaching empire that kept other cities under domination; this move was opposed by Sparta and other cities in the Peloponnesian League. War between the two alliances broke out in 431 BCE, and the entire system fell to Philip of Macedonia later that century. Might we see a world where dominant cities such as New York, Beijing, London, and Tokyo battle it out for commercial and cultural supremacy? While this is an interesting scenario, most states retain tight control over borders in the post-September 11 era, and large cities are especially vulnerable to terrorist attack. This suggests that if megacities are to rise as the new centres of autonomous political power, they will have to usurp the traditional, jealously guarded security role played by the national state apparatus first.

SOURCE: K. HOLSTI, *INTERNATIONAL POLITICS: A FRAMEWORK FOR ANALYSIS*, 7TH ED. (ENGLEWOOD CLIFFS, NJ: PRENTICE HALL, 1995), PG. 36; K. FREEMAN, *GREEK CITY STATES* (LONDON: METHUEN, 1948); G. MODELSKI, *WORLD CITIES: -3000 TO 2000* (WASHINGTON, DC: FAROS, 2003); P. KING & P. TAYLOR, EDS., *WORLD CITIES IN A WORLD-SYSTEM* (CAMBRIDGE, UK: CAMBRIDGE UNIVERSITY PRESS, 1995).

in terms of human casualties, as leaked gas from a Union Carbide pesticide plant descended on the sleeping occupants of a nearby shantytown, killing thousands. Violence is common in many urban centres throughout the world, as are illicit forms of economic activity; inner-city schooling is often relatively inadequate, and there are fewer social opportunities for restless youth. The sorry list goes on and on: infrastructure unable to meet city demands; unequal access to the available infrastructure; and lack of precautions against the environmental risks, both natural and industrial, that face certain segments of city populations.[10] Rural populations, meanwhile, play the role of provider to the large city, not only servicing it with food, wood, textile resources, and other commodities, but also absorbing urban pollution and waste.

However, none of this guarantees that megacities must become violent, overcrowded dystopias in the future. Many cities are coping well with growth, adopting cleaner environmental standards and recycling programs that lower the total waste burden, pursuing urban agriculture, attracting tourists with their historical importance while protecting cherished monuments, and diversifying their economic activities to avoid the traps inherent in dependent development. Large cities are centres of commerce and culture, and they continue to play a leading role in defining the nation-state while revealing the reach of globalization. (Most major retail and entertainment outlets can be found in cities as diverse as Paris, Shanghai, and Mexico City.) The dangers are that urban growth will spiral out of control, marginalized urban populations will continue to suffer, and **urban bias** will lead to the further neglect and exploitation of the rural countryside. Yet this tide will not be stemmed, and—as we will now see—efforts to control population growth are inherently controversial and often quite dangerous.

WOMEN'S RIGHTS AND BIRTH CONTROL

If we do accept the proposition that overpopulation is a real and urgent problem, we must explore the practical and ethical implications of controlling it. Birth control has been the technological cause of reduced fertility in the industrialized North, combining with higher education levels and higher standards of living to reduce reproductive rates. As mentioned earlier, China's highly controversial "one-child" policy has been credited with lowering birth rates, but critics charge it has made unfair demands of parents, especially mothers, and has even resulted in the infanticide of girls and forced abortions. In the South, irreversible female sterilization is popular, but concerns have been raised about health impacts. For example, the drug quinacrine is in fact an antimalarial that causes scar tissue if placed directly in the womb, permanently blocking the fallopian tubes. But Quinacrine also damages DNA in bacteria, so experts worry it might cause cancer; it was banned in India in 1998, but remained in use in Chile, the Philippines, Venezuela, Vietnam, and elsewhere.[11]

Beyond immediate health concerns, many raise questions regarding the ethics of encouraging women—largely rural, uneducated women in developing countries—to submit themselves to birth control measures (men are also encouraged to pursue vasectomies). A common complaint is that the population issue, when it gets into the hands of government leaders and international bureaucrats at the UN and elsewhere, becomes a faceless numbers game. Groups such as the International Planned Parenthood Federation promote birth control as a means toward greater societal stability but thus deflect attention from women's sexuality and reproductive freedom.[12] The abortion issue is even more divisive, since many religious representatives refuse to deal with policies that they think legitimize abortion-on-demand. During the Reagan and both Bush administrations, the United States refused to fund Planned Parenthood programs because of their acceptance of abortion and contraception; the Obama administration has once again reversed this policy. Yet the health impacts of unsafe abortion practices pose a major threat to women in many regions today.

Others argue that instead of focusing on reducing sheer numbers, policies designed to limit population increases should concentrate on reducing infant mortality and improving women's reproductive health. The lack of access to health care is a primary factor here. A 2008 study released by the **World Health Organization (WHO)** estimated that 358 000 women died from pregnancy-related causes each year, and almost all these deaths (99 percent) occurred in low-income states; this is an improvement over the past two decades, but is still unacceptable if we are to take the **Millennium Development Goals** seriously.[13] In 2005, maternal mortality rates in low-income states averaged 450 in 100 000 births. In contrast, maternal mortality rates in higher-income states averaged just 9 in 100 000. The maternal mortality rate was highest in sub-Saharan Africa at 900 deaths per 100 000 births. Many families are further burdened with the growing transference of diseases such as HIV/AIDS to newborns.

We should also consider the words of Mahbub ul Haq, a famous Pakistani economist and former special advisor to the administrator of the UN Development Programme (UNDP) who passed away in 1998. While he was the minister of planning and finance in Pakistan (1982 to 1988) he worked hard, aided by a **USAID** grant, to "saturate the villages with condoms." Nonetheless, "it was my greatest policy disaster. Despite the campaign, the population growth rate actually went up, from 3 to 3.1 percent. What went wrong? The answer is that female literacy in the villages was only 6 percent. Without investing in educating women, it was naïve to expect investment in condoms to yield any effective results. If I had to do it all over again, I would put almost all that money into boosting female literacy."[14] These are hard-learned lessons, and there simply is not enough development funding to afford repeating such mistakes. Of course, birth control is the responsibility of men as well. Millions of men have undergone vasectomies in the past two decades, and medical advances may make it possible for men to take a birth control pill themselves. Failing this, the good, old-fashioned condom is a safe and reliable way to avoid unwanted pregnancy and to protect partners from sexually transmitted diseases.

MIGRATION AND GLOBAL POLITICS

People are always on the move, for the purpose of escape, enrichment, or just plain adventure. As Sidney Klein has demonstrated, mass migrations "go back millions of years," long before the advent of the modern nation-state.[15] Early movements in Mesopotamia of Assyrians and Hittites, and of Indo-Europeans into India, date back to 2000 BCE. The people who developed Greek civilization filtered down through the Balkan peninsula to the shores of the Aegean Sea about 1900 BCE, undermining the older Cretan civilization, and around 1150 BCE other Greek-speaking tribes invaded from the North. The Greeks would go on to form the city-states, such as Athens and Sparta, which many historians view as the beginning of the international system (see Chapter 2).

Many generations later, the industrializing states of Europe used the emigration of tens of millions of Europeans to head off a looming overpopulation problem in the 19th and early 20th centuries; they encouraged immigration in the post–World War II period to provide the labourers needed for reconstruction. In fact, Europe's burgeoning cities would have suffered from unprecedented overpopulation between 1840 and 1940 were it not for the migration of almost 60 million people from Europe to countries such as the United States, Russia, Argentina, Canada, Brazil, and Australia. The great European exodus was caused by a combination of push-and-pull factors. The age of individual liberalism meant that people were, literally, free to move, and more likely to seek new opportunities; many fled political persecution. Europeans were pushed out of Europe by rising population density and scarcity of work; in an extreme case, millions fled the famine in Ireland in 1846. As usual, technological advances played a decisive role: the steamship made sea travel more accessible, and railroads were instrumental in distributing travellers to and from ports. On the pull side, many receiving states, such as Canada, actively campaigned to attract valuable migrant labourers and farmers (though Australia and New Zealand discouraged the importation of cheap labour).

Today, economists still consider migration (the crossing of borders for temporary or permanent stay) the result of push-and-pull factors. Unemployment, low wages, environmental deterioration, warfare, and other negatives push migrants (or, in more extreme cases, refugees); while the promise of employment, higher wages, education for children, and other positive expectations pull them across borders and into urban zones. The world's labour force is projected to grow by almost one billion during the next two decades, mostly in countries hard pressed to generate anywhere near an adequate number of jobs. Already, internal migration within countries like China is startling, and the global recession of 2008 to 2009 only exacerbated this phenomenon. International boundaries further complicate matters; despite the rhetoric of proponents of globalization, borders remain very relevant in immigration, refugee, and migrant worker policy, especially in a post–September 11 world (see Chapter 6).

The migration of peoples, in all its forms, has become much more prominent in global politics in the last few years. According to the website of the International Organization for Migration, there were over 214 million migrants worldwide in 2013, meaning that over 3 percent of the global population lives outside its country of birth.[16] Most migration remains stimulated by economic motives, and most of it is legal; only approximately 10 to 15 percent of the global migrant population is unauthorized or illegal (see Profile 11.4). The economic impact of migration is far from insignificant. Remittance money (sent home by migrants) is an important source of income for families and for developing countries. In fact, the annual amount of remittances (estimated at over US$530 billion in 2012) is three times more than the annual amount of foreign aid flows.[17] While the predominant image of an economic migrant is an individual who comes from a low-income country and settles in a high-income country, in fact about 40 percent of migrants move to another middle-income or lower-income country. Migration is generally beneficial to the recipient country (particularly those countries with aging populations), since some migrant workers have skills that may be in short supply in fast-changing economies, while others are willing to do jobs considered undesirable. On the other hand, while remittances can be economically valuable for developing countries, "brain drain" is a serious problem in many countries struggling to retain their skilled workers, professionals, health providers, and scientists.[18]

It is also important to understand that ethnicity and population movements are often closely connected, and are both linked to the broader politics of space.[19] Two terms frequently used to reflect this are *irredenta* and *diaspora*. Irredenta are minorities found outside but close to their ethnic homeland, who often call for the right to self-determination. Hitler used Germans living abroad to encourage acceptance of his expansionist foreign policy. Irredenta are created by shifts in political geography—the movement of borders induced by occupation or annexation, for example. Diasporas are groups of migrants who live outside their area of

---

PROFILE 11.4   Migrants and Refugees: What Is the Difference?

Generally speaking, the difference between *migrants* and *refugees* is that the former leave their country voluntarily, while the latter are forced to do so. Migrants are individuals who cross international borders with the aim of settling in another country (tourists and business travellers are not considered migrants). On the other hand, refugees have fled their country of origin due to persecution (or fear of persecution) based on race, religion, nationality, or political beliefs, and as a result are unwilling to return to their home country. However, the distinction between voluntary and involuntary movement of peoples is necessarily fuzzy. Many migrants and refugees are fleeing economic hardship or political instability. Verifying the accuracy of claims of persecution or fear of

persecution is difficult. Anthony Richmond prefers the terms *proactive* and *reactive* migration. We should note also the existence of another category of migrants who are usually labelled *unauthorized*, *illegal*, or *non-documented* migrants or aliens. According to the Program of Action of the International Conference on Population and Development (ICPD), *documented migrants* are "those who satisfy all the legal requirements to enter, stay and, if applicable, hold employment in the country of destination." By this definition, all others are "illegal."

See also Profile 11.6 on page 428 on Civil War refugees and Canada.

SOURCE: A. RICHMOND, *GLOBAL APARTHEID: REFUGEES, RACISM, AND THE NEW WORLD ORDER* (OXFORD: OXFORD UNIVERSITY PRESS, 1994).

ethnic origin. Many diasporas have been very influential because of their cosmopolitan orientation, diverse language skills, and commercial contacts. Examples include Jews and Greeks in the Ottoman Empire, Germans in Tsarist Russia, and Chinese in many Asian states, including Thailand and Malaysia. Other diasporas are linked more directly to population movements induced by the opportunity of working abroad, such as Algerians and Senegalese in France, Jamaicans and Pakistanis in Great Britain, and Mexicans and Filipinos in the United States. These groups often become permanent citizens, and, as in the case of the American Cuban community, they can be quite vocal in political terms.[20]

Despite the economic value of migration, there is a growing public backlash in many developed countries against illegal immigration, refugees, and asylum seekers. For example, the 2007 election campaign of French President Nicolas Sarkozy was openly hostile to foreigners. Italian politicians blamed migrants for the death of a woman in Rome in 2007, touching off a series of violent attacks against migrants. In much of Europe, there is concern that Muslim immigrants in particular have not integrated into society and hold values inconsistent with social norms. Violence against immigrants has become common in Europe, while protests against discrimination have taken place since 2005, with some turning violent. In the spring of 2008, nearly 50 migrant workers were killed in South Africa. In the United States, where 12 million illegal migrants live, opposition to immigration has grown steadily. An immigration-reform bill failed to pass Congress despite the support of then-President Bush and Republican and Democratic Party leaders, although political support for immigration reform gained momentum under the Obama administration in 2013. An increasing number of people worldwide are worried that migrant workers will take jobs or will change the character of a society. Governments are more likely to view migrants as an economic burden or a security threat (especially in the context of international terrorism). Even in Canada, a country built largely by immigrant labour, the trend is toward increased limitations.[21] As pressure grows for governments to adopt more stringent rules for immigrants, refugees, and asylum seekers, illegal immigration and forced expulsions might become even more frequent.

The migration and refugee issue area reinforces the concept of the state system based on territory and sovereignty, for much of the world lives behind relatively closed borders, and states are increasingly protecting their own citizens before admitting others. Realists would argue that increased population pressure and migration, far from encouraging convergence and cooperation, will be a source of divergence and conflict in the world system. As migration increases states will take ever more desperate measures to protect their borders from foreign intrusion. This fact is most evident in the **immigration** and border control policies of states. Trade liberalization encourages **capital mobility**, but there has not been a commensurate opening of borders to labour migration. If anything, the opposite has occurred as governments increase entry requirements and attempt to lure only those migrants who can clearly afford to pay their own way or possess the means to contribute to or invest in the economy. Nowhere is this as acute as in Europe, where the fall of the Soviet Union and Eastern bloc states led to one wave of **emigration** (see Profile 11.5), while in recent years a second wave of migrants from North Africa and the Middle East have caused growing concern in EU (European Union) countries. While labour mobility is famously fluid within the EU, it is another thing to get into the EU from the outside. As opposition to migration increases in Europe, governments have placed more emphasis on border controls. The EU has established a border security organization known as Frontex, which is responsible for (among other things) preventing illegal immigration into the EU using patrol boats, spotter aircraft, and radar. We need not stop at Europe, however, for a look at contemporary efforts to control migrant flows. America's

No port-of-entry. Would-be immigrants wait on a Frontex ship for Greek authorities to move them to a police station, at Piraeus port near Athens, June 12, 2011. Greece is one of the main conduits used by illegal African and Asian immigrants who wish to enter the EU. (Reuters/John Kolesidis)

border with Mexico is guarded by walls and fences and patrolled by 40 000 federal agents equipped with infrared cameras, motion detectors, spotter drones, helicopters, and all-terrain vehicles. India is completing construction of a 4100-kilometre fence along its border with Bangladesh. Physical border security is not the only mechanism used to prevent illegal migration. The United Kingdom is introducing identity cards for foreigners, and France is planning to use DNA tests to verify that migrant families are in fact related. The EU has a fingerprint database for asylum seekers, and in the United States and Canada every detained illegal immigrant is fingerprinted and entered into a database available to law enforcement agencies, while an electronic system called E-Verify allows employers to check whether workers are authorized to be in the country. **Biometric identification** systems, such as iris recognition technology, are common in airports today. These measures have drawn criticism from human rights and privacy advocates in Canada and elsewhere, and have even fuelled charges of institutional racism and **xenophobia**.

Will tighter border controls work? Interceptions of illegal migrants have fallen in recent years in Europe and the United States, and some claim this as evidence of the success of more heavily guarded borders. However, the sheer volume of migrants guarantees that some will always manage to pass even the most heavily guarded borders. Organized criminal groups benefit by charging huge sums to transport indebted migrants into the EU or the U.S. Increasingly desperate migrants are attempting more dangerous routes into Europe and America, crossing turbulent seas in flimsy craft, trekking through desert, or travelling in cargo containers; thousands die every year. Ironically, tight border controls discourage migrants from leaving: the tougher the border, the more likely a migrant is to stay permanently and have their family attempt to join them. Finally, there is the reality that rich economies need foreign labour, even as public attitudes toward migrants have become more negative.

PROFILE 11.5 Mass Migration and the Former Soviet Union

Few areas have experienced the type of turmoil brought on by the dissolution of the Soviet Union in the late 1980s. One of the more pronounced effects of this political transformation was a huge exodus of ethnic groups across the region. After 1989, more than nine million people left their homes because of ethnic tension or environmental disasters. This figure means that 1 out of every 30 residents of the former Soviet Union migrated! Many of them were Russians moving back into Russia from former republics such as Ukraine, Latvia, and Belarus. They had originally moved as part of Moscow's efforts to "Russify" outlying areas, but after the fall of the Soviet Union they felt relatively unsafe outside Russia. In other cases it is clear that people were forced to migrate: some 3.6 million refugees fled from the Armenia–Azerbaijan war and the fighting in Chechnya in the mid-1990s alone. Many of the migrants were trying to return to ancestral homelands after their previous forced evacuation during the Stalin era. Slavic peoples moved in large numbers from the five new states of Central Asia—Turkmenistan, Uzbekistan, Kazakhstan, Tajikistan, and Kyrgyzstan. Large numbers of people also fled the severe environmental decay of the Aral Sea in Central Asia, dangerous levels of radiation in the Semipalatinsk nuclear testing range, and the infamous Chernobyl meltdown (see Chapter 10). Given the economic crises Russia faced, many educated and highly skilled people sought employment elsewhere, leading to a severe "brain drain" crisis. In addition, a very disturbing trend has emerged involving the emigration of Russian women who are being trafficked into the global sex industry: tens of thousands of women have left the former Soviet Union under these circumstances since 1990. The economic crisis in the late 2000s only exacerbated the trend.

SOURCE: R. EVANS, "MASS INTERNAL MIGRATIONS UNSETTLE FORMER SOVIET STATES," *THE GLOBE AND MAIL*, MAY 23, 1996; T. HELENIAK, "MIGRATION DILEMMAS HAUNT POST-SOVIET RUSSIA," MIGRATION INFORMATION SOURCE OF THE MIGRATION POLICY INSTITUTE. FOUND AT: HTTP://WWW.MIGRATIONINFORMATION .ORG/PROFILES/DISPLAY.CFM?ID=62 (ACCESSED APRIL 28, 2004).

For these reasons, alternatives to fences and surveillance have been put forward. One idea is called *circular migration*: migrants are let into a country for a specific period of time and then are required to return after that time has expired. This has been attempted in Spain to accommodate seasonal labour demand in the agricultural and tourism sectors. Another alternative is the active recruitment of migrant workers by employers, with the assistance of governments. It is unclear if such measures, long practised in Canada, Germany, and elsewhere, have resolved the issue of migrants refusing to return home and disappearing into the local diaspora, or reduced the social hostility toward migrants that favours tight border controls. Finally, there is the question of citizenship, and establishing a legal basis by which unauthorized or illegal migrants can become legal residents. This has proved controversial in the United States. Ultimately, migration is a challenge to the concept of citizenship and nation, and an important reflection of the tension between a world of sovereign, territorial states and the eternal push-and-pull factors that drive population movements.

Migration has become an increasingly important subject for international diplomacy. Since 2001, the International Organization for Migration (IOM) has conducted a dialogue process designed to promote an exchange of views and cooperation on migration issues. In July 2007 the first Global Forum on Migration and Development was convened in Brussels to promote international dialogue and cooperation on migration. The forum, which consisted of 43 countries, the EU, and a large number of civil society actors and international organizations, emphasized the relationship between migration and development, and promoted legal migration as an opportunity for development in both origin and destination countries. Human rights and gender-sensitive policies were also recognized as key components of the migration dialogue.[22] The Forum has grown in popularity, and the 2012 Summit, held in Mauritius, focused on regional issues in Africa, where migrant labour is a major issue.

Indeed, one of the lesser-known human rights issues today concerns the plight of vulnerable migrant workers. The International Convention on the Protection of the Rights of All Migrant Workers and Members of Their Families entered into force in 2003 without the commitment of major labour-importing states such as Canada, Germany, the U.K., France, and the U.S. The Convention requests governments to pursue non-discriminatory practices regarding migrant employees, including undocumented migrants, and their families. It is, in essence, an attempt to guarantee migrant workers the same rights that are already enshrined in the Universal Declaration of Human Rights (1948) and the subsequent International Covenants on Human Rights. For example, Article 10 states, "No migrant worker or member of his or her family shall be held in slavery or servitude"; Article 12 calls for their right to "freedom of thought, conscience and religion," including the right to "ensure the religious and moral education of their children in conformity with their own convictions"; and Article 18 gives migrants "the right to equality with nationals of the State concerned before the courts and tribunals."

Another multilateral effort to aid migrants has been the work of the IOM, which has assisted in many efforts to help refugees but also helps migrants settle in new areas and acquire needed job skills. By 1976 the IOM had permanent offices in Indonesia, Malaysia, Singapore, and Thailand. In the 1980s the IOM became increasingly involved in migration and refugee assistance in Latin America, and in 1991 was entrusted by the UN Disaster Relief Coordinator to organize the **repatriation** of foreigners stranded in the Gulf region after Iraq's invasion of Kuwait; this amounted to some 200 000 repatriations.[23] The IOM was also involved extensively with the U.S.–Haitian refugee situation, helping with the interview process of migrants and refugees in Port-au-Prince (the in-country refugee processing system); Miami (facilitating domestic transportation for approved refugees); and Kingston, Guantanamo, and the Turks and Caicos Islands. The IOM prepares case files, coordinates interviews with American immigration officers, arranges for departure assistance, and aids resettlement in the United States for approved refugees. Since it is dependent on receiving states for funding, it is often accused of being an organization that merely fulfills the wishes of the United States and other donor countries; some critical theorists argue it is a mechanism designed to maintain global apartheid separating the rich from the poor states and managing related disturbances.

Many multilateral organizations and countries have put migration somewhere on their policy agendas, if not front and centre. For example, the G8 states hold annual summits and lesser-publicized ministerial-level meetings to discuss economic and political coordination, including migration issues. The OECD (Organisation for Economic Co-operation and Development) surveys migration trends as well, and as discussed earlier the EU has a variety of mechanisms designed to both facilitate labour movement within the Union and limit migration into it. Canada has been participating in the Intergovernmental Consultations on Asylum, Refugee, and Migration Policies in Europe, North America, and Australia (commonly referred to as either the IGC or the Informal Consultations) based, with its own small secretariat, in Geneva. At present, 17 governments take part in the consultations, which began in 1985, and generate documentation on issues such as temporary protection, asylum procedures, trafficking in illegal aliens, and unaccompanied minors. The **UN High Commissioner for Refugees (UNHCR)** and IOM both participate in the process, though it has a rather closed-door image. Since the consultations are among countries of destination only, they have been criticized for what one analyst believes is a self-protective focus on "removals, prevention of asylum-seeking, and individuals seeking asylum in order to avoid asylum shopping."[24] However, we should not exaggerate the IGC's ability to realize its goal, since most states—including Canada—remain reluctant to lose their ability to be flexible on asylum, refugee, or migration policies.

REFUGEES

According to the Universal Declaration of Human Rights, "Everyone has the right to seek and enjoy in other countries asylum from persecution."[25] Though we usually envision the individual asylum seeker when we think of refugees, we should also keep in mind that mass expulsions have been common forms of policy throughout history: some 15 million Africans were forced overseas into slavery before 1850, and massive forced movements were notable before, during, and after World War II.[26] During the Cold War, the West often considered some refugee movements (political defections involving individuals or small groups fleeing from the Soviet Union or other Eastern-bloc countries) to be political priorities. Today it is extremely difficult to measure the number of refugees worldwide, and we must rely on estimates. When G.J. van Heuven Goedhart was appointed the first UN High Commissioner for Refugees in 1951, there were around 1.25 million refugees; in 1976, there were 2.8 million; by 1980, almost 8.5 million; by 1992, almost 18 million; and there were over 10.5 million in 2011 (the crisis in Syria alone generated at least 600 000 in 2012).[27] The largest sources of refugees are, not surprisingly, states where prolonged and severe conflict has occurred. However, while armed conflict continues to be a primary cause of refugee flows and internal displacement, a range of push-and-pull factors induces refugee movements; the UN High Commissioner for Refugees now looks at "human displacement" as its main challenge instead of the historical, human rights violations orientation of refugee claims.[28] While political refugees were once regarded as "the tragic product of an incompatible juxtaposition, whether of faction, class, religion, ideology, or nationality,"[29] other factors such as the environment, lack of development, and overpopulation play major roles in migration patterns, necessitating even more complex models. It is no surprise, then, that there are legal and philosophical disputes about who should qualify for refugee status; we turn to one of those disputes now, but add that, no matter how well managed and liberal a refugee policy might be, there will always be a certain percentage of applicants who make false claims, and this further stigmatizes claimants with legitimate refugee status.

ENVIRONMENTAL REFUGEES AND ECOPOLITICAL VIOLENCE

Shoreline erosion, coastal flooding, deforestation, agricultural disruption, and extreme weather events: these and other manifestations of climate change are expected to be major migration triggers in the future. The term

Temporary homes, built by conflict. Syrian refugees fleeing the violence in their country walk between tents at the first Syrian refugee camp, in the area of Zaatari in Mafraq Governorate, July 31, 2012. By 2013 the civil war in Syria has generated the world's worst refugee crisis since the Rwandan genocide. (© epa european pressphoto agency b.v./Alamy)

environmental refugee is controversial, because under international law refugees must be fleeing persecution and must cross an international boundary. This is far from a matter of semantics, because governments have legal obligations to provide protection to political refugees, and there is resistance to extending those same rights to people fleeing environmental degradation who happen to cross territorial boundaries in the process. With some estimates placing the number of environmental "refugees" at 200 million by 2050, this debate is likely to intensify.[30]

Many analysts have drawn a disturbing connection between environmental degradation, failed states, armed conflict, and refugee flows. Environmental degradation and resource scarcity increase demands on government finances and services. For example, shortages of water require expensive dams or new irrigation systems. The loss of rural incomes from environmental degradation provokes migration to cities, increasing demands for transport, energy, water, sanitation, food, and health care. As economic activity is affected by environmental degradation, government revenues decline, reducing the ability of governments to maintain services and order. As Thomas Homer-Dixon argues, "A widening gap between state capacity and demands on the state, along with the misguided economic interventions such a gap often provokes, aggravates popular and elite grievances, increases rivalry between elite factions, and erodes a state's legitimacy."[31] As a result, conflict between communal groups or between governments and disaffected communal groups will intensify as competition to control resources and wealth grows. In many cases, political elites will hoard whatever surplus wealth is produced, and use it to maintain their power and their privileged lifestyles. The rest of the population will struggle for what share of the resource pie is left, or they will seek to overthrow the political elites. The overall result is the erosion and collapse of social order, and the disintegration of the state as different factions and groups do battle over a shrinking economic base, often destroying what little in the way of resources, facilities, or livelihoods remained to them. This condition of near anarchy exacerbates the "wild west" mentality of overexploitation of natural resources. Conservation and preservation become impossible. In the worst cases, these factors can converge into a horrific blend of violent conflict, crime, poverty, disease, and starvation and malnutrition, often in areas of the world least equipped to respond to such crises or to manage them effectively.

In the face of such conditions, a natural reaction of people is to flee to escape the violence of war or the hardships of economic deprivation. Environmentally induced social instability or armed conflicts can thus create large refugee movements. These movements in turn are identified as another source of potential conflict, for refugee movements create tensions and disputes in the regions or countries that receive them. As Nazli Choucri has argued, the "masses of forcefully uprooted persons … might become a key element in the lethal feedback dynamic between environmental degradation and violent conflict."[32] The influx of a large number of refugees can alter land availability and distribution patterns, disturb economic relations, alter the political and social climate, and upset the local ecological balance. In the Canadian study on environmental degradation and violent conflict discussed in Chapter 10, Homer-Dixon argued that "there is substantial evidence to support the hypothesis that environmental scarcity causes large population movements, which in turn causes group identity conflicts."[33] Nazli Choucri argues that "environmental degradation forces people to move, sometimes across borders, and most assuredly to impinge on and ultimately challenge [host] populations."[34]

However, because migrations and the effects they produce are influenced by a wide variety of factors, the link between mass refugee movements and the spread of conflict is not an automatic one. In fact, according to Astri Suhrke, conflict will occur "only under conditions of zero-sum interaction—whether actual or perceived. The alternative is a value-added model, where migrants are incorporated into the host society without collective strife, typically by providing needed labour and skills. Nor does ethnic differentiation between host population(s) and newcomers necessarily make the incorporation process conflictual."[35] Integration with local communities may indeed be a difficult process, but refugees are often isolated in remote encampments, and are not always viewed as a threat. Nonetheless, there are many examples of environmentally induced refugee movements provoking social upheaval and violence. Refugee flows from Bangladesh into northeast India (arising largely from population growth and land scarcity) have provoked communal conflict between migrant and indigenous peoples. In Assam, the Lalung peoples have reacted angrily and sometimes violently against the Muslim Bengali migrants, whom they accuse of appropriating scarce farmland. In Tripura, Tripuris conducted an insurgency over access to land, which was in short supply due to a massive influx of refugees from Bangladesh. Efforts by the Indian government to return dispossessed land and stop the flow of migration have met with mixed success in the face of continued environmental stresses on land resources and relentless flooding in the region. In Africa, refugees fleeing environmental degradation and armed conflict in Somalia and Darfur have created tensions in neighbouring countries, especially in Kenya, which has stated its intention to refuse further refugee claimants in 2013 due to the security threat posed by Somali terrorists. However, the campaign to drive Somali refugees out of major Kenyan cities such as Nairobi and into the internationally funded refugee camps closer to the border has raised serious human rights concerns.

More generally, it is quite logical to assume that increasing environmental degradation will lead to more people being forced to move for survival reasons; indeed, entire small island populations will be forced to move due to rising sea levels. At present, the Refugee Convention would not automatically qualify them as refugees, and many would argue this is unfair, since the ecological destruction forcing their departure is so often caused by elements beyond their control. Presently, however, one must be fleeing abject political persecution and cross a border to either qualify as a refugee or seek asylum. It is unlikely this will change in the future, as industrialized states fear it would open the doors to hundreds of thousands of asylum seekers to include categories such as economic migrants and environmental refugees in the official definition. We turn now to a brief discussion of the international refugee regime.

MULTILATERAL RESPONSES TO REFUGEE CRISES: EFFORTS AND DILEMMAS

Usually, asylum seekers will arrive at an airport, or cross a border, by themselves or with their family. They can apply for asylum with local authorities, and the process of refugee determination will begin. A lawyer, UNHCR representatives, or others who can support their claim will provide assistance, while the refugee determination board involved will face the difficult task of deciding whether or not the applicant would suffer unacceptable persecution if returned home. However, in many cases (especially where conflict has forced people to flee) refugee arrivals number in the tens of thousands, making the asylum process impossible to implement. At the international level, the UNHCR remains the principal organization whose mandate is to aid and assist refugees; it is constantly employed today in all the major regions of the globe. While its primary mandate relates to caring for those Convention refugees who cross borders, it is increasingly dealing with internally displaced persons as well—but can do so only when requested by the Security Council, General Assembly, or host country. The UNHCR budget, which is derived from voluntary contributions (largely from states but also from nongovernmental organizations and individuals), is divided into funding for general programs (basic projects for refugee aid and durable solutions, the most important of which is repatriation) and special programs, which include responses to sudden emergencies such as the outflow of more than one million Rwandans from that troubled state in 1994. As the UNHCR was designed to solve what was in 1945 considered a temporary problem—the relocation of people displaced by World War II in Europe—it was not created as a permanent agency. As such, it needs to have its mandate renewed every five years, and to solicit states and private donors for funding on a continual basis.

Several other UN bodies are involved in refugee protection and assistance. Most notably, the United Nations Relief Works Administration (UNRWA), another voluntary, contribution-based international organization, was established in 1949 to deal with the refugees generated by the first Arab–Israeli War, and its operations have expanded to include health care and education provision. It had more than 4.7 million people registered in 2013, located in Jordan, Syria, Lebanon, the West Bank, and the Gaza Strip.[36] The UNRWA, with more than 18 000 Palestinian employees, is the single largest operating program within the UN system. Despite the political uncertainty in the region, it "carries on a thankless task, criticized for not doing more while financial contributors grow restive in support of a relief operation that has no end in sight."[37] In the 1990s, a Canadian-led international committee, the Refugee Working Group, toured Jordanian refugee camps for Palestinians, with an aim toward incorporating the refugee question into the broader Middle East peace process. However, this initiative achieved little, as successive Israeli governments proved reluctant to include the right of Palestinian refugee return on the bargaining table (see Chapter 7). Although Canada continues to provide food aid support to UNRWA, the Harper Government has assumed a much more pro Israel diplomatic position in recent years, and has not played a significant role in efforts to resolve the Palestinian refugee issue or the larger Israeli–Palestinian conflict.

There is a long tradition of humanitarian aid organizations predating World War II, but most of the extant organizations can trace their roots directly to that epic confrontation. The UN Relief and Rehabilitation Administration (UNRRA) was established by the allies in 1943 to follow them into liberated areas at the close of World War II to provide immediate relief to victims of the war, including concentration camp survivors. The UN International Children's Emergency Fund (UNICEF) was established in 1946, and in 1953 moved into longer-term programs beyond Europe and Asia. UNICEF delivers aid to drought and war-stricken regions and works with the WHO to help meet the nutritional requirements of refugee children. The WHO is also involved with assessing the nutritional requirements of refugee populations. For example, in 1988 an international conference, Nutrition in Times of Disaster, was convened at WHO headquarters in Geneva. More broadly, the UNHCR works in conjunction with the World Food Programme in many cases of unexpected refugee flows.

The UNHCR also consults over 300 NGOs (non-governmental organizations) that play roles in relief operations. The most significant NGO partner is the International Committee of the Red Cross (ICRC), and, in Islamic countries, the International Committee of the Red Crescent. The first transnational humanitarian organization, the ICRC dates back to 1859, and it was charged in 1864 with overseeing the implementation of the first Geneva Convention. In 2013 the ICRC had offices in 80 countries and over 13 000 staff. A considerable portion of its operations involve refugee assistance: examples are El Salvador, Nicaragua, Sudan, Angola, Mozambique, Uganda, Rwanda, Somalia (and Somali refugees in Kenya), Afghanistan, Pakistan, the Thai/Cambodian border, and the territories occupied by Israel. The ICRC represents displaced civilians to governments and armed movements; actively protects them through its ability to achieve legal access (occasionally denied) to refugee and internment camps; provides medical, food, and material assistance; and runs the Tracing Agency, which seeks to reunite displaced and separated families.[38]

The ICRC and UNHCR have some overlap in their mandates, but a general division of labour has evolved: the ICRC assumes primary responsibility for persons displaced within a country during wartime, while the UNHCR has exclusive responsibility for refugees in countries of temporary or first asylum. This distinction, however, is not permanent, as was evidenced with the ill-fated Safe Haven plan in Bosnia-Herzegovina, when the UNHCR was mandated by the Security Council to protect and feed internally displaced persons. In an African case, a UN withdrawal left the ICRC to service genuine cross-border refugees as well.[39] Though it might appear as if these two agencies overlap considerably, it is essential that each exist independent of the other. The Red Cross is involved with warfare-related situations exclusively, while the UNHCR is not. The Red Cross operates independently from the UN system (although it has observer status in the General Assembly), while the UNHCR does not. The Red Cross is willing to go where the UNHCR is not, and the UNHCR does things the Red Cross cannot. Both are desperately needed today; unfortunately, both are entirely dependent on the voluntary contributions of states and individuals for funding, which is habitually meagre.

Meanwhile, humanitarian relief organizations can find themselves in terrible ethical and practical dilemmas. Should they accept the military protection of forces active in the area, including international intervention forces, and thus risk losing the perception that they are impartial? Without this protection they are potential targets for kidnapping and theft; with it they may be seen as enemies by at least one side of the conflict. Should they cooperate extensively with occupying powers, such as the coalition forces that operated in Iraq? Should they aid refugees who are clearly violent criminals? The latter question surfaced most markedly

---

PROFILE 11.6 Civil War Refugees and a Complicated Example

In 1996, Canada issued guidelines that reduce the confusion over who can be admitted as a refugee during a civil war. If they are members of a large, persecuted group, they are considered refugees under the United Nations refugee convention, which includes persecution based on race, religion, nationality, or membership in a social group. Civilians caught in indiscriminate shelling or looting are not considered refugees unless they are members of an ethnic or religious group that is a target. However, they must show that they cannot flee to another part of their home country or that another group cannot protect them. Of course, they also have to make it to Canada somehow, not an easy feat for someone with no income trapped in a war zone.

In early 2013 a particularly complicated situation arose due to the complex humanitarian emergency in Syria. Thousands of displaced Iraqi and Iranian refugees who had fled violence in their own countries were located in Syria when the civil war erupted there in 2012. Most of them subsequently went to Turkey to escape the violence. Meanwhile Canada had made a commitment to accept 20 000 Iraqi refugees from Syria, Jordan, and Lebanon back in 2009; 12 000 had been resettled by 2012. So the Canadian government will assist some 5000 Iraqi and Iranian refugees to leave Turkey since even their former place of asylum (Syria) is no longer acceptable, and these refugees faced harsh challenges adjusting to life in Turkey. This sort of convoluted movement of the stateless populations will probably become even more common in the future when civil wars cause population displacement.

SOURCE: LILA SARICK, "GUIDE ON CIVIL-WAR REFUGEES ISSUED," *THE GLOBE AND MAIL*, MAR. 8, 1996, PG. A7.

after hundreds of thousands of Hutus fled the Rwandan Patriotic Front after the genocide in Rwanda in 1994; many of them had participated in the genocide before crossing into Zaire, and even used the camps as recruitment grounds for raising a possible retaliatory force. This ultimately caused some groups, such as Médecins sans Frontières (Doctors without Borders), to withdraw, even though this entailed abandoning thousands of innocent women and children in dire need of food and medical assistance.[40] NGOs must prepare for these moral dilemmas in the future.

It might also be argued that aid agencies contribute to structural violence, merely by seeking a return to "normalcy" in crisis situations. For example, Mark Duffield argues that the problem with helping the displaced Sudanese is not the rush to cope with emergency situations, or complicity in perpetuating the civil war in Sudan, but rather the fact that efforts to obtain peace can result in the continuation of old patterns of exploitation and, by extension, genocidal policies not directly linked to the civil war effort. As he puts it,

> Goal-oriented humanitarianism in the transition zone can be argued to have reinforced those everyday relations that denote "peace." In other words, aid agencies have strengthened and tacitly supported those economic and political relations of desocialisation, subordination and exploitation that constitute normal life. In the transition zone, since the Dinka are enmeshed in such relations, aid policy has been complicit in their oppression.[41]

Similarly, the UNRWA might be accused of perpetuating the status quo in Israeli–Palestinian relations. However, these concerns must be weighed against the cost of non-intervention in immediate human suffering, lack of education for youth, chronic long-term malnutrition, and other problems.

Other NGOs play important roles in emergency humanitarian assistance as well. Notably, the Save the Children Fund has played a key role in many refugee relief situations (more than half the world's refugees are children) in places as diverse as Russia, Hungary, Korea, Algeria, Jordan, Gaza and the West Bank, Cambodia, Laos, Central America, Iraq, Rwanda, Zaire, Nepal, and Bangladesh. The Save the Children Fund was founded in 1919 by a British schoolteacher named Eglantyne Jebb, who would draft the Declaration of the Rights of the Child in 1923, adopted by the League of Nations in 1923 and, much later, redrafted as the 1989 UN Convention on the Rights of the Child. In 1979 various national units came together under the umbrella of the Geneva-based International Save the Children Alliance (ISCA, known today simply as Save the Children), which now has 30 member organizations.[42]

Every state contributes to refugee assistance in their own way, incurring related costs when it grants asylum on its own territory but also through multilateral funding mechanisms. For example, Canada currently funds overseas emergency refugee assistance through the International Humanitarian Assistance (IHA) budget of the **Canadian International Development Agency (CIDA)**; however, this traditionally amounts to a small percentage of the IHA budget. Most of the activities of the UN Office for the Coordination of Humanitarian Affairs and its Central Emergency Response Funds are devoted to responding to natural disasters, and this immediate need will only increase as extreme weather events accompany future climate change. Since it is fairly safe to predict that future armed conflicts will generate refugee flows, we need more reliable multilateral resources for emergency assistance. As for the idea that giving aid to refugees will foster dependence and corrupt the initiative of refugees themselves, this has been widely disputed by scholars such as David Keen.[43] What matters is the way in which emergency aid is delivered: agencies and governments must struggle to preserve human dignity and cultural uniqueness as far as possible. Of course, in times of severe crisis, it is difficult to prepare for the unexpected. Diligent observation of political developments, including the unfolding of complex humanitarian situations, government and rebel-group aggression and persecution, and environmental impact assessment are vital tools in the fight against harm.

THE INTERNALLY DISPLACED

Most displaced people do not cross national borders. There are millions of "involuntary migrants" who are victims of political violence and environmental degradation and natural disasters but are not officially considered refugees because they do not step, sail, drive, or fly over an imaginary line that distinguishes one state from another. With notable exceptions, their plight is still considered purely one of domestic policy. Rural–urban migration; extreme weather events; population displacement caused by large-scale development projects, deforestation, and soil degradation; and even forced expulsions are still considered the domestic affairs of sovereign states, and although outside funding agencies can certainly wield influence in directing governments away from these processes, stopping them altogether is not a distinct possibility under the present circumstances. It is important to stress that such movements are often quite orchestrated, and not always the byproduct of natural disasters beyond the control of governments. Whether the consequence of ethnic cleansing, industrialization, ecocide, or inadequate responses to disasters that marginalize certain sectors of society, such population movements are both human rights dilemmas for the international community and major sources of destabilization for governments. In 2011, there were an estimated 26.4 million **internally displaced persons (IDPs)** in at least 50 countries as a result of conflict and violence alone.[44] The largest number (between 3.9 and 5.3 million) were in Colombia, followed by Iraq, Sudan, the DRC, and Somalia (an astounding 16 percent of the population). Huge IDP populations rose in 2012 in Syria (around two million) and Mali.

Again, such population movements are not always the result of armed conflict, but often reflect government policies. For example, the government of Indonesia has orchestrated one of the largest internal movements of people in history. In an effort to reduce overcrowding on the main Indonesian island of Java, over six million people have been moved to outlying islands such as Sumatra, Kalimantan, Sulawesi, and Irian Jaya. Most of those resettled work in agriculture and many now actually own their own land. Lately, the migrants have found work in other areas, such as rubber and coffee plantations, fish ponds, and seaweed processing plants. However, despite reforestation projects in Eastern Kalimantan, there is widespread deforestation (especially for the burgeoning palm oil plantation industry), and many of the migrants are living in dire poverty in their new locations. Violence has frequently erupted between the newcomers and previous inhabitants (though this can be attributed to larger patterns of sectarian violence in the region). Nonetheless, the program continues, as Jakarta, the main city on Java, continues to grow, with almost 10 million inhabitants in 2012.[45]

In many ways, IDPs are the forgotten victims of war or development policies, and since sovereignty remains the cardinal principle of international law, their plight generally falls outside the attention of global governance efforts. It is still a matter of considerable debate whether the UNHCR or any other body should be permitted to interfere in the internal affairs of a state to help internally displaced people, though it does happen. When Russian forces caused people to flee the war zone in Chechnya, Russia asked the UNHCR to assist in the care of the internally displaced. However, this request was an exception to the rule. For example, even before the devastating cyclone of 2008, there were probably hundreds of thousands of internally displaced people in Burma. After the cyclone the number of displaced increased by tens of thousands, and the UNHCR had no ability to aid them without the permission of the military regime (see Chapter 9). The UN does have a Special Rapporteur on the Human Rights of IDPs (held since 2010 by Zambian Chaloka Beyani), and in 1998 the *Guiding Principles on Internal Displacement* were presented to the Commission on Human Rights.[46] However, these principles are not binding in international law and do not supersede sovereign jurisdiction, though it may be argued the "Responsibility to Protect" doctrine can be evoked in cases of extreme humanitarian emergencies, such as in Libya in 2011. However, it is unfortunately safe to assume that in the next few decades millions of IDPs will suffer, and this will in turn increase outward, cross-border migratory pressure as well.

GENDER, THE SEX TRADE, AND TRAFFICKING IN MIGRANTS

Women migrants and refugees face a unique set of obstacles as they resettle in new countries.[47] They are often the victims of systemic gender-based repression, and several states—Canada among them—have gone so far as to accept such women as legitimate Convention refugees.[48] This applies particularly to women who have fled states where they have legitimate fears of being coerced into traditions such as female genital mutilation (see Chapter 9). More generally, women migrants face special challenges when moving to countries such as obstacles obtaining employment to adequately support themselves and their children. In refugee camps, women (and single women in particular) and unaccompanied minors are especially vulnerable to harm, including sexual abuse.

Female migrants and refugees are especially at risk from sexual exploitation. Many become ensnared in the sex-trade industry as a result of economic destitution or physical coercion, or a combination of both. This represents a shameful failure to provide basic human rights to those affected, and increases the health risks to the women involved, especially in the form of exposure to HIV/AIDS and other sexually transmitted diseases. The sex-trade industry includes a global dimension in the form of sex tourism, complete with resorts and establishments designed to attract men visiting from around the world. There is an urgent need to respond to this global phenomenon by addressing systemic gender discrimination in general, and the circumstances of vulnerable groups such as migrant women and girls in particular. It is impossible to argue that issues of extreme exploitation and indentured servitude are too new to deal with. After all, even the long-defunct League of Nations had a Committee on the Abolition of White Slavery

Development or displacement? Laid out like row crops, cabins colonize a plot freshly cut from the rainforest. This settlement, designated SP 6, is the new home of hundreds of formerly landless peasants, volunteers in the national transmigration program. To ease crowding on the islands of Java and Bali, the Indonesian government offers five acres, a year's worth of rice, and a one-way air ticket to anyone who will move to an undeveloped region. (© George Steinmetz/Corbis)

(terminology largely discarded today), and before that there was an international Agreement for the Suppression of the White Slave Traffic and related conventions in 1904 and 1910, respectively. In 1995, the UN General Assembly passed a resolution on "traffic in women and girls," marking the beginning of the UN dialogue on this issue (see Profile 11.7). Yet we need more global attention to stop or at least limit sexual exploitation of female migrants, as well as more robust domestic legislation discouraging the practice.[49] One area where global attention is urgently needed is the problem of trafficking in human beings.

The illegal trafficking in migrants is of growing concern worldwide, although the precise scale of the problem is unknown. According to the UN Office of Drugs and Crime, human trafficking involves some 2.5 million people at any one time.[50] A major UN report published in 2012 argued that women and girls account for approximately 75 percent of all trafficking victims detected globally, and human trafficking for the purposes of sexual exploitation accounts for approximately 58 percent of all human trafficking activity, followed by forced labour at approximately 36 percent.[51] According to the Protocol to Prevent, Suppress, and Punish Trafficking in Persons, Especially Women and Children (part of the UN Convention against Transnational Organized Crime), trafficking in persons is defined as an act of recruiting, transporting, transferring, harbouring, or receiving a person through the use of force, coercion, or other means for the purpose of exploiting them. This Protocol came into force in 2003, and there has been a subsequent growth in national and international efforts to combat human trafficking. In 2010, the UN General Assembly adopted the Global Plan of Action to Combat Human Trafficking, in which signatories pledged to prevent trafficking, protect victims, prosecute criminals, and build partnerships to respond more effectively. By 2012, 134 countries and territories had criminalized human trafficking in domestic law. However, progress remains slow, as it has in the past. Despite measures such as the Convention on the Rights of the Child, which demands that "state parties … take measures to combat the illicit transfer and non-return of children abroad," trafficking in children remains rampant.[52] In the 1990s, a series of seminars and reports sponsored by the IOM concluded that trafficking was part of a much broader pattern of transnational criminal activity and could be dealt with only as an element of a coordinated strategy to eliminate that sector; however, the formation of such a coordinated strategy has proved elusive.[53] Today, convictions of individuals accused of human trafficking remain low, and significant obstacles to progress exist in the form of a lack of accurate information, suitable legislation, adequate enforcement capacity, and effective monitoring and assessment of national strategies. Government corruption, coercive techniques by traffickers, the stimulus of poverty, demand for cheap labour and prostitution, and many other factors

PROFILE 11.7 Transnational Prostitution: A Resolution

In 1995 the UN condemned the illicit and clandestine movement of persons across national and international borders, largely from the global South and former communist states in eastern Europe, and the forcing of women and children into sexually or economically oppressive and exploitative situations for the profit of recruiters, traffickers, and crime syndicates, as well as into other illegal activities related to trafficking, such as forced domestic labour, false marriages, clandestine employment, and false adoption. What is necessary, however, is a reduction in the demand side of this equation: without an eager market, sex traders would have no incentive to engage in their activities.

SOURCE: UN RESOLUTION A/RES/49/166, FEB. 24, 1995; UNESCO TRAFFICKING STATISTICS PROJECT. FOUND AT: HTTP://WWW.UNESCOBKK.ORG/INDEX.PHP?ID=1022.

continue to drive and facilitate human trafficking in general and trafficking in women and girls in particular.

One of the obstacles to progress on human trafficking is a widespread social prejudice against migrants. Discrimination against migrants, especially female migrants, takes many forms around the globe.[54] One of the greatest difficulties involves encouraging governments to accept the idea that all migrants, be they permanent (settlers), temporary contract workers, temporary professional transients, clandestine or illegal workers, asylum seekers, or genuine refugees as defined by the 1951 Convention, are entitled to the same rights. This implies that temporary workers and even illegal migrants would have the right to vote and receive the same social services as regular tax-paying citizens. Any proposition to this effect would likely be met with strong opposition, and yet the contributions to society made by migrants of all kinds certainly implies they deserve no less than the full protection of the law.

POPULATION MOVEMENT, THE SPREAD OF INFECTIOUS DISEASE, AND GLOBAL HEALTH

One of the most dangerous elements of population movement is that people can carry diseases with them when travelling. Epidemics are restricted to geographic and temporal boundaries; pandemics, on the other hand (such as malaria, tuberculosis, and HIV/AIDS) know no such boundaries. We may live in an age of pandemics, but it can be easily argued that human security has always faced its most prevalent and enduring threat from microorganisms. The bubonic plague, or Black Death, first struck Europe in 1348 and wiped out entire towns and villages: the rats that infested the overcrowded, unsanitary living conditions carried the plague bacillus. Between the hundreds of thousands of fatalities caused by the plague and those caused by the Hundred Years' War (England versus France, 1337 to 1453), the population of Europe did not recover until the 1500s. After the expansion of European civilization into colonized areas such as the Americas, indigenous peoples around the world suffered from the sudden introduction of foreign microbes; some of the diseases were deliberately spread. The Spanish flu of 1918 to 1919 was the most deadly of all, killing an estimated 20 to 30 million people (though some estimates are closer to 50 million). The historical record aside, some experts argue that the problem is getting worse, not better, despite the advancement of science. The rapid spread of the HIV/AIDS virus, and highly publicized events, such as the outbreak of the pneumonic plague in Surat, India, in 1994, the Ebola virus in Zaire in 1995, SARS in Canada and elsewhere in 2003, and the swine flu pandemic in 2009, have alerted governments and citizens to the importance of infectious disease, and the understandable panic they can cause among both local and distant populations.[55]

For example, in 2003 the discovery of "mad cow disease" (bovine spongiform encephalopathy, or BSE) in a single Canadian-born cow in the United States set off a national agricultural panic and a trade dispute with the U.S. BSE is a fatal disease that causes progressive neurological degeneration in cattle. In 1996, following outbreaks of BSE among British cattle, scientists found a possible link between BSE and a new variant of CJD (Creutzfeldt-Jakob disease), a rare disease similar to BSE that occurs in humans. Millions of cattle were slaughtered in Britain. The spread of the avian flu in 2002 to 2004, mostly in Asia but also in parts of North America including British Columbia, resulted in the slaughter of million of chickens. These pathogens have had relatively little impact on human populations due to precautionary measures such as slaughter and quarantine (they might prompt us to rethink our dependence on large-scale meat production, but that is another issue). However, there is widespread concern among epidemiologists that certain strains of avian flu (notably H5VN1, which killed some 250 people between 2003 and 2008, mostly in Asia) might at some point mutate and become transmissible from human to human. Given the impact of the so-called Spanish flu of 1918 to 1919 in an age without mass air travel, it is feared that such a massive pandemic today could kill hundreds of millions, if not billions, of people.

North Americans are familiar with **West Nile**, a mosquito-borne virus that can cause a range of illnesses, such as acute encephalitis (inflammation of the brain) or meningitis (inflammation of the membranes and fluid surrounding the brain and spinal cord). Birds are the main reservoir of the virus: when a mosquito bites an infected bird, the mosquito can spread the virus by biting another bird or another animal, such as a human. West Nile was first located in 1937 in Uganda. Later it was found in Asia, Europe, and the Middle East; it was not until 1999 that it was discovered in New York State. Preventive measures include using insect repellent and reporting dead birds to local health workers. Though it has had limited impact in terms of taking human life, West Nile is another indication of the perils of modern travel, since the pathogen was probably delivered by way of transported infected mammals or people.

Much more dramatic was the rise of **severe acute respiratory syndrome (SARS)**, a deadly form of pneumonia that emerged from China in November 2002, most likely linked to the practice of eating the masked palm civet and the raccoon dog in certain regions of that country. Much to the consternation of city officials, the WHO issued a global alert in March 2003, warning travellers to avoid certain regions, including Toronto, where SARS was most prevalent. SARS has all the characteristics of a pandemic disease: it is easily spread, transmitted by coughing or sneezing at close range, and it is lethal—though infected persons can survive if the disease is detected in time. The virus can also spread when a person touches a surface or object contaminated with infectious droplets and then touches his or her mouth, nose, or eyes; it is particularly dangerous for healthcare workers because of their increased likelihood of exposure. During the outbreak of 2003, at least 8098 people worldwide became sick, and some 774 died, 38 in Canada.[56] The outbreak provoked a closer look at how healthcare infrastructures can respond to sudden outbreaks. In contrast, the international response to the outbreak of what has been termed *Mexican swine flu* (H1N1) in winter 2009 has been much more efficient and coordinated. The WHO declared it a pandemic in June of 2009, although the overall numbers of deaths worldwide at that time were surprisingly low.

Worried about pandemics. Concern over the spread of infectious disease has grown as new strains of viruses and bacteria, many of them drug resistant, have become a major global health challenge. (© Peter Treanor / Alamy)

Though mosquitoes, food, drinking water, and other vectors transmit many infectious diseases, some are spread by direct human contact, and this is often exacerbated by international travel. For example, a major cause of HIV/ AIDS in sub-Saharan Africa is prostitution centred on the trucking routes of the region; another is the impact of military personnel having unprotected sex when stationed abroad. Similarly, many intravenous drug users who contract the disease do so when living as transients in large urban centres, such as Amsterdam and Vancouver. The fact that the earliest genetic traces of HIV proto-DNA was taken from a male who died in Zaire in 1954 is testament to how rapidly this pathogen has spread to almost all regions of the earth. Though it is impossible to give an accurate figure, between 31 and 35 million people were living with HIV/AIDS in 2011, and as many as 1.8 million died in 2010. Sub-Saharan Africa is the region most affected: over 22 million people, or 5 percent of the population, are infected with HIV. According to these estimates, 2.7 million new infections occurred in 2010, with over 1.8 million of them in sub-Saharan Africa.[57]

AIDS stands for **acquired immune deficiency syndrome** and it is caused by HIV, the *human immunodeficiency virus*. HIV and AIDS have no known cure or vaccine, though antiretroviral drugs are effective in mitigating its worst effects. Our immune systems fight off infections, and AIDS destroys this capacity. Thus, people with AIDS are highly susceptible to other sicknesses as well, such as the common cold. HIV-positive people will have antibodies to HIV, which can be discovered with a simple blood test. The most common prescription for avoiding HIV is to refrain from engaging in unprotected sex and from sharing intravenous needles. Intrauterine devices (IUDs), oral contraceptives, male and female sterilization, and natural family-planning methods such as rhythm and withdrawal provide no protection against sexually transmitted diseases (STDs). HIV/AIDS has reached epidemic proportions in areas of Africa (where two-thirds of all HIV/AIDS victims live) and Asia (where the sex industry has proliferated in the past few decades). International cooperation on HIV/AIDS continues: the 20th Annual International AIDS Conference will be held in Melbourne, Australia, in July 2014, and UN AIDS continues to work to reduce not only infections and deaths but also discrimination against AIDS patients.

There are a plethora of preventable diseases and avoidable health crises affecting low-income populations around the world: malaria, hepatitis B, micronutrient malnutrition, iodine and vitamin-A deficiency, syphilis, gonorrhea, genital herpes, and other sexually transmitted diseases, to name but a few. But HIV/AIDS is so prevalent, and so deadly, that it is actually transforming the social profile of entire societies, resulting in an unprecedented number of orphans, and a continuous crisis in the public sector. More broadly, it can be argued that such infectious diseases are threatening the state's capacity to govern in many countries. In a provocative and careful study, Andrew Price-Smith concludes that "since increasing disease prevalence destroys or debilitates national populations and compromises both productivity and governance, infectious disease may be correctly seen as both a direct and an indirect threat to the national security of seriously affected states," and it can also "compromise the ability of transitional states (e.g., Russia and South Africa) to consolidate democratic and effective systems of governance."[58] It also results in the social isolation of the infected, and entire states, such as Haiti, have become known for its prevalence. Though a great deal can be done with improved health care and education, we can be sure that HIV/AIDS and other pandemics will continue to spread as long as people are able to travel.

Dennis Pirages argues four major transformations are under way that "seem to be strengthening the microbes' hands." Rapid population growth and urbanization lead to situations conducive to the rapid spread of disease, especially in the teeming megacities of the South, where adequate health care is seemingly beyond reach for the majority of citizens, and in areas where overpopulation has led to mass movements. Many of the refugees fleeing violence in Rwanda in 1994 died from cholera in the resulting overcrowded refugee camps. Population pressure is forcing people to inhabit previously wild areas, and this has had two consequences: new inhabitants are bringing new diseases into these areas, harming the indigenous people and wildlife; and the newcomers themselves are exposed to new diseases, which are then spread into the general population. Pirages writes also of changes in human behaviour, such as the so-called sexual revolution of the late 1960s and 1970s in the United States and the global spread in the use of drugs, which facilitated the spread of disease. Cramped prison conditions, which help spread tuberculosis, result from policy shifts and increases in crime often linked to poverty. Third, the environment itself is changing in a way that makes it more difficult to control the spread of disease. Sudden or gradual climate change may give a temporary advantage to resident microbes. For example, Pirages suggests that a fatal outbreak of Hantavirus in the desert southwest of the United States may have been triggered by sudden rainstorms that increased population growth among the virus-carrying rodents. In each summer since 1999, the West Nile virus has surfaced in mosquitoes in New York, prompting massive pesticide sprays in the city; this may be related to climate change. Finally, Pirages refers to technological innovations that have increased, rather than decreased, the ability of microbes to travel, such as the invention of the airplane: "Aircraft cabins are an excellent place for a rendezvous with cosmopolitan world-traveling viruses and bacteria."[59] A virus that causes hemorrhagic fever is said to have found its way to Baltimore from Seoul by way of wharf rats that made the journey in cargo ships. These viruses seem to understand what many global politics analysts do as well: a truly interdependent and interconnected world economy presents as much opportunity as it does danger.

One of the major international initiatives underway to enhance global health and combat the spread of infectious disease of all kinds is the campaign to ensure access to essential medicines. The "right to health" was first established as a fundamental human right at the International Conference on Primary Health Care in Alma-Ata in 1978.[60] The right to health includes access to life-saving (or essential) medicines, which are "intended to be available at all times in adequate amounts ... at a price the individual and community can afford."[61] The issue of affordability has been the greatest obstacle to the availability of essential medicines in most parts of the world. In 1990, only about 5 percent of the world's resources for health research were being devoted to the health problems of low-income countries, where 93 percent of the world's preventable deaths occurred. This massive inequity (another reflection of the global disparities discussed in Chapter 8) subsequently became known as the "10/90 Gap" and was the basis for an international effort to address the disparity between need and investment in global health.[62] Despite significant improvements since the 1990s, it is still the case that one third of the world's population lacks access to modern drugs and vaccines. Even when available, the retail cost of these medicines in low-income countries is beyond the ability of most people living in poverty to pay, and amazingly the cost is often between 2.5 to 6.5 times the international market price, due to a combination of taxes and duties, supply scarcity, producer costs, and wholesale and retail markups.[63] Responding to this challenge requires the cooperation of many actors. Pharmaceutical companies invest large amounts of money in drug research and development, and to recoup these costs companies employ patent law to prevent third parties from producing or selling low-cost generic versions of drugs, typically for a period of 20 years. However, this practice keeps the costs of many essential medicines elevated beyond the ability of many poor people to pay.[64] Efforts to address the patent issue include partnering with pharmaceutical companies to grant voluntary licences for generic versions of patented drugs for specific markets in low-income countries. In this way, the patent is protected in high-income parts of the world but the medicines become more affordable in low-income areas. However, addressing patent-related costs is not sufficient to increase accessibility. Governments must also reduce or eliminate taxes and duties on essential medicines, and develop national drug policies and regulations to ensure adequate stocks and access. International efforts combining companies, governments, international organizations, and NGOs are required to develop subsidy programs to increase affordability and combat corruption and black market activity.

Canada's own experience with the effort to increase access to essential medicines is a cautionary tale of the frustrating process involved in responding to this need. In 2004, the Canadian Parliament passed a Bill called the Jean Chrétien Pledge to Africa, which among other measures created the Canadian Access to Medicines Regime (CAMR). The Regime was intended to reduce the costs of essential medicines by creating a system of compulsory licensing, in which generic drug companies would pay royalties to patent holders in return for producing drugs for a specific low-income country. However, the CAMR had lengthy procedural requirements and was incompatible with how many low-income countries purchased medicines, and it was rarely used. In an effort to streamline the CAMR process, Bill S-232 proposed to create a single-license arrangement that would apply to all low-income country markets, freeing the process from excessive bureaucratic hindrances. However, Bill S-232 was terminated when parliament was prorogued in 2009. The subsequent creation of Bill C-393 in 2010, which contained the same single-license provision as Bill S-232, received substantial national support due to a campaign driven by NGOs and prominent individuals such as Stephen Lewis, Margaret Atwood, James Orbinski, and K'naan. Against the opposition of pharmaceutical companies, Bill C-393 was passed in the House of Commons. However, debate on the Bill was delayed in Senate due to government pressure, and it died on the order paper when an election was called in 2011.[65] As this sobering example reveals, if access to essential medicines is to become a reality, more will have to be done to overcome obstacles at the corporate and governmental level, not only in Canada but also elsewhere.

Not surprisingly, analysts are divided on the conceptual implications of global health issues such as the spread of infectious disease, the rise in global cancer rates, and the effects of climate change on human health. Liberals tend to believe these common threats will contribute further to convergence as humanity struggles together to solve these problems and limit their impact. Realists will believe states will close their borders and take additional measures of self-protection; and critical theorists will emphasize the disproportionate suffering borne by the marginalized peoples we discussed at some length in Chapter 8. Scholars of all stripes are also concerned with the security implications of the possible deliberate spread of disease for military or terrorist purposes, as discussed in Chapter 6.[66] One thing is certain: international efforts to monitor these diseases are crucial, as are efforts to ensure we avoid new forms of biological apartheid by sharing medical technology, prevention programs, and treatment efforts. Beleaguered international institutions such as the WHO have key roles to play here, but so do national governments, multinational pharmaceutical firms, and NGOs. And another terrible affront to progress has risen as a major concern: the manufacture, sale, and use of counterfeit medicine by organized criminals. This is a more pronounced problem in some areas of Africa and Asia than elsewhere, but is becoming a universal threat. It is bad enough that people in dire need cannot access life-saving medicine; that people are dying from taking fake drugs sold for profit is simply morally reprehensible.

CONCLUSIONS

This chapter has covered many topics, and we must stress how interrelated they are, in theory and practice. While avoiding simplistic linear explanations, it can be plausibly argued that population growth can lead to increased population movement, massive urbanization, challenges to women's reproductive health and rights, drains on natural resources, political violence, increased opportunities for sexual exploitation, and increased opportunities for the spread of infectious disease. In both debates over population control measures and questions about the protection of refugees, economic inequities as well as gender issues are evident. This comes in the post–September 11 era, when migration policies among the industrialized states have, by and large, emphasized the closure, and not the liberalization, of borders.

However, it is safe to say that it is impossible to stop migratory pressure. Georges Tapinos notes this with regard to NAFTA: its initial success might absorb some of the surplus of Mexican labour resulting from industrialization and a decrease in agricultural subsidies, "but the majority will seek employment in the United States. It is a straightforward illustration of the fact that [trade and investment] liberalization between countries with significant differences in size, endowments, and production patterns cannot in the short run simultaneously achieve two objectives: an increase in the standard of living, and a decrease in the propensity to emigrate."[67] Globalization hardly seems the solution to the crises generated by population growth and movement; indeed, overconsumption of resources by citizens in industrialized states—those who have arguably benefited most from globalization—is part of the problem, not the solution. Realists would not be surprised that states have yet to develop an overarching ethos that permits responsive and systematic cooperation on these questions, while liberals suggest we are slowly on the way to creating institutions that may well do so in the future, providing individual rights are protected in the process. Neo-Marxists emphasize the links between exploitation, production, and migration, while feminists argue that a patriarchal world system is reflected by the problems we have discussed in this chapter. Constructivists suggest that the way we look at and think about these issues is the result of years of thinking within narrow boxes defined by nationalism, borders, and citizenship, and we need to forge a new understanding of human identities to escape these old patterns. The fear of global apartheid (or, if the potential of pandemics is realized, "global bio-apartheid") remains a central theme among critical theorists.

In this chapter we have examined issues related to the large population increases experienced in the 20th century, including the question of responsibility for promoting sustainable development, urbanization, birth control, and voluntary and involuntary population movements (including environmental refugees, victims of the global sex trade, and people fleeing disease). There can be little doubt that the increase in population puts additional strain on the natural ecosystems on which we all ultimately depend, and that overconsumption in both the North and the South exacerbates the environmental problems discussed in Chapter 10. If high populations are a reflection of poverty, so are large population movements. In this chapter, we discussed the push-and-pull factors involved in migration and then looked at the contemporary refugee crisis, with an emphasis on multilateral responses. It should be apparent that these interlinked themes, held together by our interest in security, political economy, and policy analysis, offer what is often contradictory evidence to those pursuing the convergence/divergence theme of this textbook. And we can be sure that the global population will continue to rise in the future, even as aging populations challenge the social structure and tax base of some countries. The realistic question is not whether things will be moving in this direction, but how we will cope with unprecedented numbers of people, millions of whom will be on the move, presenting the threats associated with population displacement and disease. In the midst of all this humanity, can compassion survive?

Endnotes

1. Garrett Hardin, "The Tragedy of the Commons," *Science* 162 (December 1968), 1243–8.
2. John Hope Simpson, *Refugees: Preliminary Report of a Survey* (London: Chatham House, 1938), 193.
3. Source: United Nations, Department of Economic and Social Affairs, Population Division, http://esa.un.org/unpd/wpp/.

4. See P. Ehrlich and A. Erlich, *The Population Explosion* (New York: Simon and Schuster, 1990).

5. Hardin, "The Tragedy of the Commons."

6. This formula is usually expressed as follows: $I = PAT$: impact is equal to population size, multiplied by per capita consumption (affluence), multiplied by a measure of the damage done by the technologies chosen to supply each unit of consumption.

7. Amniocentesis uses a sample of amniotic fluid from a pregnant woman's uterus to diagnose possible genetic defects and reveals the gender of the fetus in the process. See N. Kristof, "Peasants of China Discover New Way to Weed Out Girls," *The New York Times*, July 21, 1993, A1. It was the main cause, the critics alleged, of the high ratio of 117 boys born to every 100 girls in China, compared to the world average of 106 to 100.

8. Parts of this section are taken from P.J. Stoett, "Cities: To Love or to Loathe?" a review article based on J. Kasarda and A. Parnell, eds., *Third World Cities: Problems, Policies, and Prospects* (London: Sage, 1993); and J. Hardoy, D. Mitlin, and D. Satterthwaite, *Environmental Problems in Third World Cities* (London: Earthscan, 1992), which appeared in *Environmental Politics* 3, no. 2 (1994), 339–42.

9. *State of the World Population 2007: Unleashing the Potential of Urban Growth* (New York: United Nations Population Fund, 2007), 1.

10. See Kasarda and Parnell, *Third World Cities*; Hardoy, Mitlin, and Satterthwaite, *Environmental Problems*; and P. Gizewski and T. Homer-Dixon, "Urban Growth and Violence: Will the Future Resemble the Past?" *Project on Environment, Population and Security* (Toronto: AAAS and University College, University of Toronto, 1995); on Kibera, see J. Vasagar, "Residents Left Scrambling as Kenya Clears Shantytowns," *The Globe and Mail*, April 23, 2004, A12.

11. See R. Biswas, "Banned Drug Still Used on Women," *India Tribune*, January 25, 2004, http://www.tribuneindia.com/2004/20040125/herworld.htm#2 (accessed June 20, 2013).

12. See B. Hartmann, *Reproductive Rights and Wrongs: The Global Politics of Population Control and Contraceptive Choice* (New York: Harper and Row, 1987). For an excellent essay dealing with the transnational alliances and networks that have evolved related to population control issues, see B. Crane, "International Population Institutions: Adaptation to a Changing World Order," in P. Haas, R. Keohane, and M. Levy, eds., *Institutions for the Earth: Sources of Effective International Environmental Protection* (Cambridge, MA: MIT Press, 1994), 351–96.

13. This is an improvement over 2005, when approximately 536 000 women deaths were estimated by the WHO (see *Maternal Mortality in 2005: Estimates Developed by WHO, UNICEF, UNFPA, and the World Bank* [Geneva: World Health Organization, 2005], 1) and the 585 000 average deaths estimated by the UNFPA (United Nations Population Fund) in 1995. See "Maternity: Greater Peril?" *Populi: The UNFPA Magazine* 23, no. 1 (1996), 4–5. This suggests medical procedures and equipment may be improving at the global level. http://www.who.int/mediacentre/factsheets/fs348/en/index.html

14. "Hard Lessons in Population Planning," *Our Planet* 6, no. 3 (1994), 32.

15. *The Economics of Mass Migration in the Twentieth Century* (New York: Paragon House, 1987). See also Stephen Castles and Mark Miller, *The Age of Migration: International Population Movements in the Modern World* (New York: Guilford, 1993).

16. See: http://www.iom.int/cms/en/sites/iom/home/about-migration/facts--figures-1.html (accessed January 13, 2013). Taken as a whole, migrants would constitute the fourth-largest country on Earth today.

17. See C. Provost, "Migrant's billions put aid in the shade," *The Guardian*, January 30, 2013, http://www.guardian.co.uk/global-development/2013/jan/30/migrants-billions-overshadow-aid (accessed February 22, 2013).

18. In the most acute example, the "brain drain" exacerbates the AIDS crisis in Africa and elsewhere as trained doctors, nurses, and social workers leave areas where they are most needed for higher-paying jobs in northwestern countries.

19. For discussion see Y. Ferguson and B. Jones, *Political Space: Frontiers of Change and Governance in a Globalizing World* (Albany: SUNY Press, 2002).

20. See G. Shefer, *Modern Diasporas in International Politics* (New York: Taylor and Francis, 1986); and S. Dufoix, *Diasporas* (University of California Press, 2008).

21. See, for example, "Canadians Want Illegal Immigrants Deported: Poll," *National Post*, October 20, 2007, found at http://www.canada.com/nationalpost/news/story.html?id=f86690ed-a2ed-447c-8be8-21ba5a3dd922 (accessed January 13, 2013).

22. *Report of the First Meeting of the Global Forum on Migration and Development*, Belgium, July 9–11, 2007, http://www.gfmd.org/en/ (accessed July 1, 2013). The Global Migration Group links all the UN agencies dealing with some aspect of migration issues; see http://www.globalmigrationgroup.org/.

23. For a concise history of the IOM and discussion, see R. Appleyard, *International Migration: Challenge for the Nineties* (IOM: Geneva, 1991).

24. Nazare Albuguerque-Abell, "The Safe Third Country Concept: Deflection in Europe and Its Implications for Canada," *Refuge* 14, no. 9 (1995), 1–7, 5.

25. Universal Declaration of Human Rights, 1948, Article 14.

26. The postwar expulsion of millions of Germans from various regions following the Potsdam Treaty is particularly notable, though it is often ignored in popular histories of the war. See Alfred-Maurice de Zayas, "International Law and Mass Population Transfers," *Harvard International Law Journal* 16, no. 2 (1975), 207–58.

27. *Statistical Yearbook 2006: Trends in Displacement, Protection and Solutions* (New York: The United Nations High Commissioner for Refugees, 2007), 23–4.

28. See the UNHCR website: http://www.unhcr.org/pages/49c3646c11.html.

29. E. Buehrig, *The United Nations and the Palestinian Refugees: A Study in Nonterritorial Administration* (Bloomington: Indiana University Press, 1971), 3.

30. See Oli Brown, *Migration and Climate Change*, IOM Migration Research Series, no. 31 (Geneva: International Organization for Migration, 2008), 11.

31. T. Homer-Dixon, "Evidence from Cases," *International Security* 19, no. 1 (1994), 5–40. For a good case study, see C. Kahl, "Population Growth, Environmental Degradation, and State-Sponsored Violence: The Case of Kenya, 1991–93," *International Security* 23, no. 2 (1998), 80–119.

32. N. Choucri, "Environment, Development, and International Assistance: Crucial Linkages," in S.J. Brown and K.M. Schraub, eds., *Resolving Third World Conflict: Challenges for a New Era* (Washington, DC: United States Institute of Peace Press, 1992), 101.

33. Homer-Dixon, "Environmental Scarcities and Violent Conflict," 20.

34. Choucri, "Environment, Development, and International Assistance," 101. See also N. Myers, *Ultimate Security* (New York: Norton, 1993).

35. A. Suhrke, "Environmental Change, Migration, and Conflict: A Lethal Feedback Dynamic?" in C.A. Crocker, F.O. Hampson, and P. Aall, eds., *Managing Global Chaos: Sources of and Responses to International Conflict* (Washington, DC: United States Institute of Peace Press, 1996), 116. There is a voluminous literature on environmental refugees; see, for example, A. Nash, "Environmental Refugees: Consequences of Policies from a Western Perspective," *Discrete Dynamics in Nature and Society* 3 (1999), 227–38; and J. Morrissey, "Rethinking the Debate on Environmental Refugees," *Journal of Political Ecology* 19 (2012), 36–49.

36. Palestinian refugees in Israel were initially under the care of the UNRWA, but Israel assumed that responsibility in 1952. See A. Bligh, "From UNRWA to Israel: The 1952 Transfer of Responsibilities for Refugees in Israel," *Refuge* 14, no. 6 (1994), 7–10, 24; and UNRWA, "Switzerland and UNRWA to Host Major Conference on Humanitarian Assistance to Palestine Refugees," press release, http://unispal.un.org/UNISPAL.NSF/0/0648EDA975A9DE4285256E40005541DA (accessed June 30, 2013). For the latest statistics, see http://www.unrwa.org/userfiles/20120317152850.pdf.

37. R. Riggs and J. Plano, *The United Nations: International Organization and World Politics* (Belmont, CA: Wadsworth, 1994), 230.

38. F. Maurice and J. de Courten, "ICRC Activities for Refugees and Displaced Civilians," *International Review of the Red Cross* 280 (1991), 9–21.

39. This occurred in northwest Somalia, in 1990–91, where the ICRC extended its operations in aid of Ethiopian refugees after the World Food Programme and UNHCR suspended their activities for security reasons. The ICRC also found itself without proper military protection in Bosnia during the civil war there.

40. On this heart-wrenching decision, and others, see MSF staffer Fiona Terry's book, *Condemned to Repeat? The Paradox of Humanitarian Action* (Ithaca, NY: Cornell University Press, 2002); on the Rwandan genocide, see P. Gourevitch, *We Wish to Inform You That Tomorrow We Will Be Killed with Our Families: Stories from Rwanda* (New York: Farrar Straus and Giroux, 1998).

41. M. Duffield, *Global Governance and the New Wars: The Merging of Development and Security* (London: Zed Books, 2001), 205.

42. For an excellent essay on the Save the Children Fund in Britain and its constant interaction with the UNHCR, World Food Programme, and other UN bodies, see A. Penrose and J. Seaman, "The Save the Children Fund and Nutrition for Refugees," in P. Willetts, ed., "*The Conscience of the World": The Influence of Non-Governmental Organizations in the UN System* (Washington, DC: Brookings, 1996), 241–69. See also http://www.savethechildren.net/.

43. D. Keen, *Refugees: Rationing the Right to Life* (London: Zed Books, 1992), 55.

44. See the Norwegian Refugee Council's Internal Displacement Monitoring Centre report, Global Overview 2011: People Internally Displaced by Conflict and Violence (Geneva, 2012), available at http://www .internal-displacement.org/publications/global-overview-2011.pdf. For earlier reviews of the IDP challenge, see R. Cohen, *Human Rights Protection for Internally Displaced Persons* (Washington, DC: RPG, 1991); and F. Deng, *Protecting the Dispossessed: A Challenge for the International Community* (New York: Brookings, 1993).

45. S. Mydans, "Indonesia Resettles People to Relieve Crowding on Java," *The New York Times*, August 25, 1996, 4. For a report on a similar situation in Thailand, see D. Hubbel and N. Rajesh, "Not Seeing the People for the Forest: Thailand's Program of Reforestation by Forced Eviction," *Refuge* 12, no. 1 (1992), 20–1.

46. See R. Plender, "The Legal Basis of International Jurisdiction to Act with Regard to the Internally Displaced," *International Journal of Refugee Law* 6, no. 3 (1994), 345–61; the UN Guiding Principles on Internal Displacement can be found at http://www.unhcr.org/43ce1cff2.html.

47. See S. Martin, *Refugee Women* (Oxford: Lexington Books, 2004).

48. See N. Spencer-Nimmons, "Canada's Response to the Issue of Refugee Women: The Women at Risk Program," *Refuge* 14, no. 7 (1994), 13–18. We should note also the role played by the Canadian Working Group for Refugee Women, a subgroup of the NGO-based Canadian Council for Refugees.

49. In 1996 Canada joined Sweden, Norway, Denmark, France, Belgium, Germany, Australia, the United States, Finland, Iceland, and New Zealand in passing legislation making it possible to charge citizens abroad who purchase sex from minors. J. Sallot, "Canada Targets Overseas Child Sex," *The Globe and Mail*, April 4, 1996, A4.

50. See United Nations Office of Drugs and Crime, *Human Trafficking FAQs*, http://www.unodc.org/unodc/en/human-trafficking/faqs.html (accessed February 25, 2013).

51. See United Nations Office of Drugs and Crime, *Global Report on Trafficking in Humans, 2012* (New York: United Nations, 2012), 7, 25–6.

52. UN Resolution A/RES/44/25, November 20, 1989, Article 11.

53. "International Response to Trafficking in Migrants and the Safeguarding of Migrant Rights," *International Migration* 32, no. 4 (1994), 593–603. On the surge of this trade from the former Soviet bloc, see V. Malarek, *The Natashas: The New Global Sex Trade* (Toronto: Viking 2003); see also J. Vocks and J. Nijboer, "The Promised Land: a Study of Trafficking in Women from Central and Eastern Europe to the Netherlands," *European Journal on Criminal Policy and Research* 8 (2000), 379–88. For an interesting critical article, see J.O. Davidson, "Will the Real Sex Trade Please Stand Up?" *Feminist Review* 83 (2006), 4–22.

54. In the 1990s, the question of discrimination against migrants seeking employment was brought home to Canadians, as it was suggested that non-white Canadians were having a difficult time finding overseas jobs teaching English. "Asian Schools Avoid Non-white Canadians," *The Globe and Mail*, March 28, 1996, A1. For an interesting treatment of seasonal migrant workers in Canada, see T. Basok, *Tortillas and Tomatoes: Transmigrant Mexican Harvesters in Canada* (Montreal: McGill-Queen's University Press, 2002).

55. Two popular books were R. Preston, *The Hot Zone* (New York: Random House, 1994); and L. Garrett, *The Coming Plague: Newly Emerging Diseases in a World out of Balance* (New York: Farrar, Straus, and Giroux, 1994). See also F. Cartwright, *Disease and History* (New York: Thomas Crowell, 1972); and W. McNeill, *Plagues and Peoples* (London: Doubleday, 1976); and especially A. Cosby, *Ecological Imperialism* (Cambridge, UK: Cambridge University Press, 1994).

56. See "SARS Death Toll Rises to 38 in Toronto," CBCNews, http://www.cbc.ca/stories/2003/06/22/sars_030622 (accessed May 28, 2004). Though the disease was well contained after its initial period, there were reports that it resurfaced in China in April 2004.

57. Data from *UNAIDS Annual Report: Knowing Your Epidemic* (Geneva: Joint United Nations Programme on HIV/AIDS, 2008), 8; *AIDS 2008 Fact Sheet: HIV/AIDS*, http://www.aids2008.org/admin/images/upload/732.pdf (accessed June 20, 2013); and http://www.unaids.org/en/media/unaids/contentassets/documents/unaidspublication/2011/JC2225_UNAIDS_datatables_en.pdf (accessed September 5, 2012).

58. A. Price-Smith, *The Health of Nations: Infectious Disease, Environmental Change, and Their Effects on National Security and Development* (Cambridge, MA: MIT Press, 2002), 172. Price-Smith also presents an excellent chapter on how climate change can increase the range of pathogens (see Chapter 10).

59. D. Pirages, "Microsecurity: Disease Organism and Human Well-Being," *Environmental Change and Security Project Report* (Woodrow Wilson Center), 2 (1996), 9–14, 10; see also L. Garret, "The Return of Infectious Disease," *Foreign Affairs* 75, no. 1 (1996), 66–79.

60. Article 1, Declaration of Alma-Ata, *International Conference on Primary Health Care, USSR.* September 6–12, 1978.

61. H.V. Hogerzeil, "Essential Medicines and Human Rights: What Can They Learn from Each Other?" *Bulletin of the World Health Organization*, 84, no. 5 (May 2006), 371.

62. See "10/90 Gap," Global Forum for Health Research, http://www.globalforumhealth.org/about/1090-gap/ (accessed February 26, 2013).

63. "Ensuring Supplies of Drugs and Vaccines in Developing Countries: Without Medicines, Patients Die Needlessly," Disease Control Priorities Project (October 2008), http://www.dcp2.org/file/220/dcpp-drug-sandvaccines-web.pdf (accessed February 26, 2013).

64. "Prescription for Healthy Development: Increasing Access to Medicines," Task Force on HIV/AIDS, Malaria, TB, and Access to Essential Medicines (New York: UN Millennium Project, 2004), 66.

65. G. Galloway, "Tony Clement Urges Senators to Block Generic Drug Legislation," *The Globe and Mail,* March 24, 2011. http://www.theglobeandmail.com/news/politics/ottawa-notebook/tony-clement-urges-senators-to-block-generic-drug-legislation/article1955588/ (accessed February 26, 2013).

66. See M. Zacher and T. Keefe, *The Politics of Global Health Governance: United by Contagion* (New York: Palgrave Macmillan, 2008); R. Dodgson and K. Lee, "Global Health Governance: A Conceptual Review," in R. Wilkinson and S. Hughes, eds., *Global Governance: Critical Perspectives* (London: Routledge, 2002); D. Fidler, *SARS, Governance and the Globalization of Disease* (Basingstoke: Palgrave Macmillan, 2004); A. Kelle, "Securitization of International Public Health: Implications for Global Health Governance and the Biological Weapons Prohibition Regime," *Global Governance* 13 (2007), 217–35; and WHO (World Health Organization), *WHO Guidelines for the Global Surveillance of SARS: Updated Recommendations, October,* WHO/CDS/CSR/ARO/2004.1 (Geneva: WHO, 2004).

67. "International Migration and Development," *Population Bulletin of the UN* 36 (1994), 1–18, 12.

Technology and Information in Global Politics

Technology is now, for better or for worse, the principal driving force behind the ongoing rapid economic, social, and political change. Like any irrepressible force, the new technology can bestow on us undreamed of benefits but also inflict irreparable damage.

—Wassily Leontief, economist[1]

We, the representatives of the peoples of the world ... declare our common desire and commitment to build a people-centered, inclusive and development-oriented Information Society, where everyone can create, access, utilize and share information and knowledge, enabling individuals, communities and peoples to achieve their full potential in promoting their sustainable development and improving their quality of life.

—Declaration of Principles of the World Summit on the Information Society[2]

INTRODUCTION: GLOBAL POLITICS AND SOCIAL REVOLUTIONS

The history of human society is often conceptualized in terms of stages or revolutions representing significant leaps forward in human development. In each of these leaps, a close relationship exists between technological innovations and the evolution of political, economic, and social organizations. For example, the **Agricultural Revolution** greatly increased food production in 18th-century Europe through a combination of plow technology, cropping techniques, and changes in landholding practices. The **Industrial Revolution** represented a shift from agrarian-based economic activity to manufacturing, which profoundly altered the character of society and the nature of work. The **Green Revolution**, stimulated by the mechanization of agriculture and the development of new fertilizers, pesticides, and seeds, had a global impact in the form of increased food production as well as concerns over the safety of chemicals in the food supply. Today, we are in the midst of an **Information Revolution** driven by computers and communications technologies, which are having a profound impact on our societies and on global politics.

The impact of technology on human societies can also be seen in terms of economic waves stimulated by technical advances. In the 1920s, Russian economist Nikolai Kondratieff identified waves in the world economy approximately 50 to 60 years long, each characterized by a surge in economic growth and productivity. In 1939, economist Joseph Schumpeter explained these waves in terms of clusters of technical inventions, innovations (the development of new techniques and products from these inventions), and diffusion (the spread of these techniques and products around the world). Each wave of inventions, innovations, and diffusion stimulates a surge in economic activity, after which economic growth slows as the potential from new inventions is exhausted. Schumpeter characterized these waves as "creative gales of destruction" because they would sweep old industries aside and replace them with new ones. Following Schumpeter's reasoning, four such waves have been identified: the 1780s to 1840s, driven by the steam engine and innovations in textiles and iron; the 1840s to 1890s, and the era of the railway; the 1890s to 1930s, driven by electric power, chemical technologies, and improved steels; and the 1930s to 1980s, driven by the automobile and petroleum energy.[3]

The development of the computer began discussions of another potential revolution or wave in the evolution of human society. In 1980, Alvin Toffler's book *The Third Wave* argued that the transition from an agricultural society (the first wave) to an industrial society (the second wave) was being followed by a transition to an information society (the third wave).[4] In the same year, a study on the impact of computers argued that "the computer is not the only technological innovation of recent years, but it does constitute the common factor that speeds the development of all others. Above all ... it will alter the entire nervous system of social organization."[5] Today, we do not have to stretch our imaginations to argue that the computer and the information revolution constitute another wave in social development. This new information age is built on advances that have vastly increased the processing power of computers while reducing cost and bulk. Improvements in storage capacity and retrieval have led to an explosion in the gathering, storing, processing, and analysis of information, which has become increasingly vital to political and economic activity.

More importantly for the student of global politics, the development of improved communications technologies and the creation of many different international communications channels or "networks" have allowed computers and their users to transmit or disseminate information around the world. Information and data management is now the fastest-growing area of economic activity, prompting suggestions that the industrialized world is heading into a postindustrial and increasingly globalized society where new applications of information and communications technology (ICT) could actually transform social relations. As William J. Drake and Rikke Frank Jørgensen suggest, "The technologically enabled creation, distribution, and manipulation or application of information is becoming a key driving force and defining feature of social change worldwide."[6] As a result, global politics is increasingly characterized by the emergence of what the UN calls the "global information society." The UN has responded to the global implications of ICT by convening the World Summit on the Information Society (WSIS) in 2003 and 2005, followed up by annual WSIS Forum meetings and a series of ongoing projects.[7]

The development of ICT and the rise of the global information society have stimulated a lively theoretical debate. Realists accept that technological change is important because it has immediate implications for the economic and military power of states; but it will not transform the essential political realities of a self-help world of sovereign states. Liberals are more optimistic: the ICT and related networks promote global interdependence by facilitating trade, financial flows, and intercultural communication, strengthening the ability of neoliberal institutions to promote cooperation. Neo-Marxists charge that a global information society reflects and even exacerbates divergences in wealth and power, and promotes the economic liberalization theology underpinning globalization. However, most neo-Marxists would also advocate using the technology to rally for emancipatory change. Postmodernists warn that information is never neutral or autonomous from power, and is often manipulated in the interests of those who control it. At the same time, as constructivists would assert, ICT can change or challenge identities and belief systems and even create new cross-national constituencies. Feminists regard ICT as potentially liberating for women, enabling increased communication and networking. However, technology is embedded in male-dominated political and economic structures, reinforcing male power and dominance (the prevalence of pornography on the Internet raises many issues for feminists). Students of global ecopolitics raise concerns about the environmental impact of discarded computer hardware and the carbon emissions associated with running huge servers for "cloud" data storage, but are generally optimistic about the use of enhanced communication capacity to monitor environmental impact assessment and lobby for change.[8]

Dr. J.W. Mauchly with the electronic computing machine known as the ENIAC (top). (© Bettmann/CORBIS)
Computer chip developer Federico Faggin with Intel's 4004 at a 40 year anniversary event (bottom). (© Karsten Lemm/dpa/Corbis)

THE COMPUTER AND THE INFORMATION REVOLUTION

If any form of technological change has had a profound impact on the lives of millions of people in recent times, it is the advent of the personal computer (PC). The **ENIAC (electronic numerical integrator and calculator)** of 1946 is widely regarded as the first electronic computer. Initially designed to calculate the trajectories of artillery shells, ENIAC was a remarkable accomplishment for its time. It could execute 5000 arithmetic calculations per second. It was also 3 metres high, 30 metres long, and weighed more than 30 000 kilograms! ENIAC used 18 000 vacuum tubes and consumed 150 000 watts of power. With the invention of the transistor in 1947, computer design was liberated from the limitation of the vacuum tube. Through the 1950s and 1960s, large, centralized mainframe computers dominated the computer industry, and International Business Machines (IBM) became a dominant MNC (multinational corporation) in the 1970s. The combining of many miniature transistors on a single silicon chip (the integrated circuit) in 1959 and the development of the microprocessor (in essence a computer on a silicon chip) in 1971 profoundly altered the computer industry. Microchips rapidly became increasingly powerful. The 486 microprocessor, used in the early 1990s, could execute 54 million instructions per second, weighed only a few grams, and used less than two watts of electricity. By 2013, microprocessors were capable of executing over 100 000 million instructions per second. The speed of microprocessors now doubles every 18 months, in a formula known as Moore's Law.

These advances in miniaturization, processing power, and cost-effectiveness placed unprecedented technical capacity in the hands of individuals. The first PCs were introduced in 1975, and the number of computers began to grow rapidly. In 1971, there were approximately 50 000 computers of all kinds in the world; by 2006, that figure had skyrocketed to 885 million personal computers alone (up from 275 million just ten years earlier); and by 2008 one billion PCs were estimated to be in use worldwide, with that figure predicted to grow to 2 billion by 2015.[9] The computer industry has also become increasingly important to the global economy. Already by 1985, the output of the global electronics industry equalled the output of the world automobile industry and exceeded the output of the world steel industry.[10] Today, there are few industries or economic sectors that do not employ computers in some aspect of their operations. However, the development of computers was only one part of the information revolution: as the 2001 Human Development Report argued, "Today's technological transformations are intertwined with another transformation—globalization—and together they are creating a new paradigm: the network age."[11]

In one sense, the idea of networks is not new. In 1833 the innovation of Morse Code (coinvented by American Samuel Morse) ushered in the development of the telegraph in 1837, and telegraph lines soon extended across continents. In 1876, the telephone was invented by Alexander Graham Bell, and television demonstrators were being shown as early as the 1920s. Both inventions went on to become linked to vast networks of cables and transmission receivers around the globe. The networking of computers has had yet another profound impact, ushering in a new age of communications. Coupled with advances in communications technologies, computer networks facilitate business, entertainment, personal communication, financial transactions, and access to information. While the most famous of these networks is the Internet, a wide variety of other computer networks exist, which facilitate links between the computers of a specified group of people (such as corporate or government employees). As information and communication networks continue to grow in size and capacity, the issues associated with the global information society have become more important in global politics. These issues include the regulation of global communications networks; "e-governance" (the use of electronic media to develop and implement public policy); e-commerce and trade in information and communications services; freedom of speech, censorship, and privacy protection; cybercrime, hacking, and espionage; intellectual property and copyright protection; and the implications of ICT for lower-income states and marginalized people. As Jonathan Aronson has observed, "These technologically sophisticated networks are reshaping the landscape of politics and international relations, transforming global commerce, recasting societies and cultures, and altering policy formulation and implementation."[12]

THE INFORMATION AGE AND GLOBAL COMMUNICATIONS NETWORKS

Today, hundreds of millions of people have access to unprecedented communications links, including telephone, fax, email, text messaging, social networking websites, television, and international radio services. We live in what has been described as a "hyperconnected" world driven by mobile devices, big data, and social media, enabling us to communicate and exchange more information more frequently and at less cost than ever before.[13] In the past, the speed of communication was essentially equivalent to the speed of transportation. With the exception of very basic signalling using flags or smoke, messages could travel only as fast as the messenger carrying them. In practice, this meant the use of human, animal, or mechanical transport. While some of these communications methods were relatively swift and effective (such as the pony express system of Imperial China and the use of carrier pigeons), it might have taken days, weeks, months, or even years to transmit messages or news over long distances. In the 18th century, a trip around the world took several years by sailing ship. Today, jet aircraft can fly around the world in less than a day carrying large parcels and other mail items. Bulk cargo ships are far faster than the merchant sailing ships of just 200 years ago. Trucks can haul large amounts of freight over expansive road networks.

However, the most remarkable advances have been in the area of electronic communications. As recently as 100 years ago, the idea of virtually instantaneous global communication would have been dismissed as an unrealistic dream. Today, it is a commonplace for an increasing number of people around the world. From the development of copper wiring to fibre-optic fixed broadband cables to mobile broadband networks, technological advancements have enabled millions of people to communicate almost instantaneously using telephones or electronic messaging of various forms.[14] For example, international phone traffic increased from 38 billion minutes in 1991 to an estimated 438 billion minutes in 2011. And the use of Skype-to-Skype calls registered an astounding 145 billion minutes in 2011.[15] In 1960, a transatlantic telephone cable could carry 138 conversations; today's fibre-optic cables, a fraction of the original size, are capable of carrying 1.5 million conversations. In 1980, a copper wire phone line could transfer data at a rate of approximately one page per second. Today, an optical fibre the width of a human hair can carry the equivalent of 90 000 volumes of an encyclopedia per second.[16] The use of satellites and mobile broadband networks has freed global communications traffic from reliance on undersea or underground cables linking continents and cities. Electronic messaging has grown dramatically: approximately 144 billion emails and 8.6 trillion text messages were sent worldwide in 2012.[17] Moreover, the cost of this communication has decreased dramatically. The cost of a three-minute telephone call between New York and London fell from US$244.65 in 1930, to US$31.58 in 1970, to US$3.32 in 1990, to US$0.35 in 1998 (in 1990 dollars).[18] An email message from Calgary to Paris costs no more than an identical message from Calgary to Edmonton. Because of these developments, it is possible to speak of a communications revolution and the consequent "death of distance" made possible by the computer and the proliferation of networks around the world.

Another trend is clearly identifiable: the increasing use of wireless communications networks. Advances in wireless technology have been swift. The first-generation wireless phone was introduced in 1981 and was the size of a small suitcase! By the early 1990s, second-generation wireless phones were handheld and the first text message was sent in 1992. In 2001, third-generation wireless phones began to offer multimedia and networking capacities, and there has been a subsequent explosion in the use of mobile handheld devices. In 1991 there were 16 million mobile phone subscribers in the world, but by 2011 the number of subscriptions had ballooned to almost 6 billion, with more than double the number of mobile broadband subscriptions compared to fixed broadband subscriptions.[19] Wireless Internet access is now increasingly common worldwide: 80 percent of the 660 million new mobile cellular subscribers in 2011 were in the developing countries.[20] New generations of wireless technologies and devices are in continual development, promising faster access speeds and more information and social media services. We have only just entered the age of the "wireless" revolution.

You've come a long way, baby. Martin Cooper, chairman and CEO of ArrayComm, holds a Motorola DynaTAC, a 1973 prototype of the first handheld cellular telephone, in San Francisco in this April 2, 2003, photo. (AP Photo/Eric Risberg)

The most significant ICT network in global politics is the Internet, which has its origins in a U.S. military communications project known as the Advanced Research Projects Agency Network (ARPAnet). Developed in the 1960s, ARPAnet was established to ensure that communications between political and military leaders could be maintained even in the event of a nuclear attack. ARPAnet was transferred to the National Science Foundation, which renamed the network NSFnet. NSFnet was expanded to universities and government agencies in the 1980s and then turned over to private companies. The beginning of the explosion in Internet use occurred in the late 1980s, as more powerful computers emerged and the World Wide Web (WWW) was created. The WWW software, created by Tim Berners-Lee at the European Particle Physics Laboratory (CERN) in Switzerland in 1989, established the common user protocols for addresses, languages, file transfers, and browsers. The Web facilitated the use of the Internet through easier-to-use interface software (first introduced with Mosaic in 1993), enabling anyone with a computer, a modem, a browser, and the requisite interest to use the Internet. The growth of the Internet has been spectacular. The International Telecommunication Union estimates that Internet use increased from 4.4 million users in 1991 to approximately 2.3 billion in 2011, roughly one-third of the world's population.[21] In 1995, there were just 19 732 website hostnames online, a number that grew to over 630 million by early 2013.[22] Today, Internet users are just clicks away from abundant information, services, and entertainment, through email, e-banking, e-government, e-health, e-learning, and eBay.

Within the larger ICT revolution, something of a mini-revolution is occurring. The merger of the cellphone, handheld device, and Internet is creating the conditions for a very different kind of connectivity across people and places. The combination has brought the mobility of the cellphone together with the information and networking capacities of the Internet, creating a "nomadic" communications future.[23] This has begun to transform work, travel, and relationships between space and people. It has already had a practical impact on global politics. Elections monitoring by international observers now makes extensive use of text messaging. Large-scale international protests are now planned and coordinated worldwide through the use of the cellphone and the Internet, with images and digital video complementing traditional text. Human rights abuses have been exposed and publicized through general-traffic websites such as YouTube and dedicated sites such as Witness. Responses to local and international epidemics have been facilitated by mobile phone technology that greatly increases the ability to gather and disseminate data. Mobile devices and social media websites played a prominent role in the Arab Spring uprisings.

Another mini-revolution under way is the integration of ICT and the Internet with photographic or satellite imagery, in a fusion of physical geography and social science data. Google Earth provides virtually complete photographic images of the planet, overlaid with data provided by a combination of sources. Launched in 2005, Google Earth and similar "geobrowsers" are all made possible by high-resolution satellite imagery, powerful computers, cheap data storage, and broadband Internet connections. Geobrowsers have had an increasing impact on global politics in ways that were not anticipated by their designers. The human rights situation in Darfur has been highlighted by data overlays of destroyed villages over the geographic maps of the area, naturally without the consent of the Sudanese government. This has increased awareness of the violence in Darfur and has been an important tool for human rights activists. After Hurricane Katrina struck New Orleans in 2005, Google Earth was used by relief agencies to coordinate their efforts. An American charity equipped indigenous tribes in the Amazon rainforest to use Google Earth to assert their territorial rights against logging and mining operations.[24] Insurgents in Iraq have used Google Earth to plan attacks on U.S. and other coalition bases in the country, prompting concerns about the utility of geobrowsers for warfare or acts of terrorism. Other concerns are related to individual or organizational privacy in a world where places (homes, businesses, medical clinics) can be spotted and located with relative ease.

Some feel the long-term impact of transnational communications networks will be to bring humanity closer together, in a global village in which national borders become irrelevant and a transnational awareness of a shared human identity and destiny will take shape. In other words, the Internet might be one of the most important instruments of convergence in human history. However, this enthusiasm must be tempered with some sobering realities. While the Internet has realized its enormous potential for business, personal communication, and access to information, the quality and nature of the websites on the Internet vary widely. Some are reputable and of high quality, while others are virtually useless and contain false or misleading information. The Internet offers a forum to any individual or group that can construct a website (including hate groups and terrorist organizations), which demands vigilance and a careful critical perspective when viewing Web-based information. And one of the fastest-growing sectors on the Internet is pornography, a driving force behind the globalization of the sexual exploitation of women and children.

A particularly serious issue raised by ICT and the Internet is the relationship between the state and privacy and free speech. While Web advocates cite the Internet's capacity to promote democracy, diversity, and the free flow of information, all information can be manipulated and controlled. One survey of 40 countries found that 26 of them practised some form of **Internet filtering**, stopping their citizens from viewing certain general subjects or specific websites.[25] China operates the most rigorous Internet censorship effort in the world, which includes monitoring of individual Internet use and blocking access to a wide range of websites and subject matter, with the compliance of major search engines such as Google (see Profile 12.1). The tension between the state and the free flow of information has also been on display in the controversy over Wikileaks. Wikileaks is a nonprofit, online organization launched in 2007 that publishes anonymous submissions of classified documents, cables, videos, and other communications. Wikileaks has published a number of high-profile materials, including the so-called Collateral Murder video involving a U.S. Apache helicopter in Iraq, and the release of 251 287 U.S. diplomatic cables sent between 1996 and 2010. Wikileaks has provoked intense controversy, especially from government officials, who charge that its activities harm national security, compromise the vital confidentiality of diplomatic communications, and endanger individuals named in leaked materials. Wikileaks hopes the publication of such leaked materials will improve government transparency, reduce corruption, and strengthen democracy.[26] The founder of Wikileaks, Julian Assange, has also been the subject of controversy, as he was arrested on rape and sexual molestation charges in Sweden in 2010. Released on bail, Assange became a fugitive in the Ecuadorian Embassy in London in 2012.

PROFILE 12.1 China and the Internet

China is a good example of a country attempting to embrace communications technology while exercising political control over information content. As part of a government plan in place since the early 1990s, China has been developing its communications infrastructure, and by the end of 2011 there were over 500 million Internet users in China. However, the Chinese government continues to impose tight controls on the flow of information, fearing the consequences of an unshackled Internet for the country's political system. As the late Chinese leader Deng Xiaoping once said, "When you open the window, the flies come in." The Ministry of Information Industry controls Internet traffic entering the country, blocking Western news websites such as the BBC as well as the websites of human rights organizations and Chinese dissident groups. However, users in China can bypass government controls that block access to certain domain names by finding a proxy server that provides a link to Western news websites under a different domain name. The difficulty is finding such proxy servers. Email is one way of providing such information to Chinese Internet users, but the Chinese government employs 30 000 people to scan emails entering or leaving China for this kind of information. Prison sentences have been handed out to Chinese citizens who violate domestic laws on the dissemination of information and protest material over the Internet. In 2006, the search engine company Google was widely criticized for creating a special search site for users in China that met the censorship guidelines of the Chinese government. These practices included blocks on searches for subjects such as "Tibet" or specific websites such as the news site of the BBC. Google's response (that removing some Google search results was better than providing no Google services at all) was seen as self-serving, given the corporation's battle with other search engines for a share of the lucrative Chinese market. As China becomes more connected to the world economy, and as the economic importance of information flow increases, the interaction will become a fascinating case study in the clash between the power of the state and the forces of an electronic and supposedly borderless world.

SOURCE: CLARK BOYD, "BYPASSING CHINA'S NET FIREWALL," *BBC NEWS*, UK EDITION, MARCH 10, 2004. FOUND AT: HTTP://NEWS.BBC.CO.UK/1/HI/TECHNOLOGY/3548035.STM (ACCESSED MAY 31, 2004); RONALD DIEBERT, ET AL., EDS., *ACCESS DENIED: THE PRACTICE AND POLICY OF GLOBAL INTERNET FILTERING* (CAMBRIDGE, MA: MIT PRESS, 2008); STATISTICAL SURVEY REPORT ON THE INTERNET DEVELOPMENT IN CHINA (BEIJING: CHINA INTERNET NETWORK INFORMATION CENTER, JAN. 2008), 9. FOUND AT: HTTP://WWW.CNNIC.CN/UPLOADFILES/PDF/2008/2/29104126.PDF (ACCESSED JUNE 9, 2008).

Beyond issues related to privacy and free speech, the Internet remains dominated by material and perspectives generated by certain actors. Websites hosted in the rich industrialized world account for a majority of online content, and English is the dominant language of the Internet. The fact that globally popular websites and Web-based services are themselves owned by large corporations raises questions of how their behaviour can be managed or regulated. The content of the Internet is heavily corporate, and money matters in terms of vying for viewers (a familiar phenomenon to advertising executives and political campaign managers). This leaves little space for political dissent or protest, as Gregory J. Walters points out: "The Internet has been almost completely incorporated into the corporate media and communications system, and the political left has been relegated to the margins of cyberspace."[27] The Internet also raises issues related to individual privacy (including the security of financial and medical information) and copyright (witness the debates over file-sharing websites and content on YouTube). Finally, computer piracy and hacking have raised concerns about the security of computer systems and the challenges of responding to this problem in a world of governments with different legal systems. Government agents themselves are increasingly engaged in electronic espionage and hacking. These and other issues serve as a reminder that the considerable promise of the global information society must be viewed with healthy caution about the implications for global inequality and human rights.

THE INFORMATION AGE AND THE WORLD ECONOMY

The global economy is being transformed by the technological developments of the information age. As John Zysman and Abraham Newman argue, "[ICT] does more than just change the costs of transportation and communication: it alters the manner in which economic value is created, changes how international production is organized, and reopens basic societal bargains struck around individual liberty and economic rights."[28] The work experience is changing in many societies as technology alters the nature of products, production, and productivity. High-income countries are in transition from industrial or manufacturing-based economies to information or knowledge-based economies. The global economy is characterized by the increased mobility of capital and production made possible by ICT networks. As Jonathan Aronson has observed, "These technologically sophisticated networks are reshaping the landscape of politics and international relations, transforming global commerce, recasting societies and cultures, and altering policy formulation and implementation."[29] This economic transition is provoking intense political debate over the relationship between workers and employers, citizens and the state, and markets and regulation.

In the workplace, the impact of the computer and information revolution has been dramatic. By 1991, companies were spending more money on computer and communications equipment than on industrial, mining, farming, and construction equipment combined.[30] Businesses use computers for communications, data storage and retrieval, administration, payroll, record keeping, and budgeting. Banking and financial industries are almost entirely dependent on computers and communications links. Manufacturing industries use computers to design new products, operate their production facilities, manage inventories, track shipments, and distribute raw materials, supplies, and parts. The architecture, fashion, and graphic design fields make wide use of computers. Wireless broadband networks are eroding the traditional divisions between home, leisure, and workplace: work is increasingly something we do rather than a place we go.[31] The ICT revolution has also affected the very nature of work in modern industrialized societies as a whole. In the 1950s the majority of workers in the industrialized world were involved in manufacturing or transporting material goods.[32] By 1996 the OECD concluded that there was a clear trend in affluent countries toward an economy in which more than half of the labour force was engaged in the production, distribution, and use of information.[33]

In many ways, the information age has transformed national and international economic activity, blurring the distinction between the two. Most money is stored and exchanged in electronic form. Physical cash now makes up a small portion of most countries' money supplies, and increasingly direct deposit and credit and debit cards dominate commercial transactions. Major credit cards such as Visa, MasterCard, and American Express are accepted worldwide (as well as for online purchases), and it is possible to withdraw local currency from an ATM connected to a global network such as Plus or Interac. The direct deposit of paycheques and electronic bill payments are the norm. As we saw in Chapters 4 and 8, international trade and financial agreements paved the way for huge sums of money to cross borders, change hands, and be exchanged from one currency to another, often instantaneously. This was done within a growing international financial system of institutions and banks, all linked by communications networks and common information protocols. This has had a profound impact on government policy: with so much money in motion, rigid currency controls became increasingly irrelevant, and most governments have abandoned them. Central banks struggle to defend currencies under pressure, so great is the volume of international currency flows. Individual or corporate investors and fund managers can move money in and out of markets with great speed, complicating governmental responses to domestic and international economic crises. This was certainly the case during the onset of the financial crisis of 2007 to 2008 and subsequent crises in Europe and elsewhere. Technology facilitated the spread of toxic assets to banks and investment funds around the world, and in turn facilitated a market response characterized by mass panic as investors pulled their money out of banks, funds, and countries in an effort to preserve their assets. However, we should not blame the technology in isolation from political and ideological factors. Neoliberal economic views had dominated the financial sector for decades and contributed to a political consensus that the financial sector should be as free from regulation as possible. The global recession was brought about primarily because of extraordinary greed on the part of many financiers and bankers, unrealistic expectations of investment returns and debt servicing by large numbers of consumers, and poor regulatory oversight of large financial institutions in the United States and elsewhere.

Business has also been affected by the ICT revolution. In his book *The World Is Flat*, Thomas Friedman describes how businesses are redistributing various components of work around the world to where it can be done most efficiently and at the lowest cost.[34] ICT plays a crucial role in the offshore production of goods and outsourcing of services. Multinational corporations increasingly conduct business according to the principles of collaborative planning, forecasting, and replenishment. Suppliers and retailers cooperate to determine anticipated customer demand, which in turn informs production, shipping, and stockpiling of products. ICT enables businesses at all points of the product cycle—development, production, transportation, and sales—to instantly share data to optimize the flow of goods and services. Furthermore, the Internet and the Web have precipitated an enormous increase in electronic commerce (or e-commerce). In effect, the Internet has removed personal travel from the process of purchasing goods and services. E-commerce also widens the range of choice for consumers, who can now roam across the world in search of products, including those that are restricted or banned in their own countries. While still dependent on traditional mail and courier services for the physical delivery of the product, consumers need not go to the local shopping mall: the global shopping mall has come to them.

The ICT revolution is intimately connected to increasing economic interdependence. Together, ICT and globalization are having a mutually reinforcing impact on global politics, accelerating the pace of change, the spread of information, and the forging of relationship networks, and presenting new challenges to cultural identity and political authority. As Michael J. Mazaar notes, "The Internet would have had a substantial effect on world politics under any circumstance. In the context of globalization, that effect is magnified many times."[35] The impact of ICT on the global economy has been the subject of an intense and emotional debate. Advocates of ICT have stressed the beneficial effects of the technology. As ICT lowers the costs of information and travel and increases access to diverse supplies of resources, capital, and labour, economic activity is stimulated. In the liberal perspective, these are positive developments, which promote comparative advantage and increasing wealth and prosperity. The editors of one supportive report have argued, "There is growing evidence that ICT is driving innovation by allowing creative thinking and responsive problem-solving to provide the promise of never-before-seen opportunities for all."[36] Another study argued that a "hyperconnected" world in which ICT is always on, readily accessible, information rich, interactive, and always recording promises significant positive transformations in education, healthcare, government, business, and the workforce.[37]

However, many argue that this postindustrial society will be one not of promise but of increased dislocation, unemployment, and economic hardship for many, if not most, people. Unemployment and stagnant or falling wages and household incomes are growing concerns worldwide. While these problems are now attributed to global recession and financial crises, many allege that the underlying cause is the ICT revolution, coupled with the growing globalization of the world economy. Increases in telecommunications, trade, and financial flows have increased international competition, prompting firms to "downsize" (the technical term for firing employees) and facilitating their efforts to shift production to low-wage countries. Unemployment (and the social problems associated with it) is the inevitable result. In addition, those jobs that are created will be insufficient in number to replace the jobs lost, and many of them will be low-paying service-sector jobs with poor benefits and low job security (sometimes called "McJobs"). Globalization and technological change have driven employers and workers farther apart in many sectors of the economy: as profits rise and wages fall, the bulk of income and revenues will go to a few individuals, widening the gap between rich and poor. These conditions have led Ethan B. Kapstein to argue as follows:

The global economy is leaving millions of disaffected workers in its train. Inequality, unemployment, and endemic poverty have become its handmaidens. Rapid technological change and heightening international competition are fraying the job markets of the major industrialized countries. At the same time, systemic pressures are curtailing every government's ability to respond with new spending. Just when working people most need the nation-state as a buffer from the world economy, it is abandoning them.[38]

Christopher May has contended that the axiomatic divisions in society have remained despite the allegedly transformed nature of the knowledge-based economy. Basic questions, such as who knows what, who possesses value, and who works for whom, continue to define the workplace and the economy. Employment policies are still controlled by managers, and intellectual property rights have extended ownership into the realms of information and knowledge.[39]

Critics also argue that ICT and globalization are undermining the capacity of states to manage and intervene in their own economies, to the detriment of the wider social good. The decentralized and globalized character of communication, finance, and production in the networked information-age economy makes it difficult for governments to exercise regulatory and legal oversight. Governments are finding it increasingly difficult to respond to the tax implications of evolving business practices, as well as maintain effective fraud, privacy, labour rights, property rights, and financial transparency legislation. Government laws and regulations on financial activity are increasingly difficult to enforce in a world of global electronic commerce. The ability to move production and financial operations around the world enables businesses to find favourable regulatory environments abroad, avoid or minimize taxes, and escape government oversight. Corporations can also use the threat of relocation to leverage governments to change regulatory policies and laws on environmental protection and labour rights, creating a "race to the bottom" as governments compete to retain and attract business activities and investment by weakening social, environmental, and labour laws.[40]

Alternatively, many argue that these fears are alarmist and that protestors are the equivalent of modern-day Luddites, a reference to the British workers of the early 19th century who smashed the machines that threatened their jobs. Advocates of the computer and information revolution argue predictions that new technologies will cause unemployment and social dislocation have been common. In the 1930s, **automation** of manufacturing was blamed for increases in unemployment. In the 1940s, others predicted that computers would throw massive numbers of individuals into enforced idleness. Today, ICT is blamed for job losses and social dislocation, while its defenders argue that society benefits from technological innovation. Despite the increasing pace of technological change, and indeed because of it, employment, incomes, and living standards have risen steadily. Because computers and information systems enhance productivity, advocates maintain, they will increase real incomes, from either higher wages or lower prices. This increases the purchasing power of the average consumer, which stimulates other sectors of the economy. With respect to unemployment, innovation does not mean painful labour market adjustments will not occur, especially in the short term. The key is that these positions are in new sectors promising greater growth and social benefits, rather than in traditional employment sectors.

Others argue that the impact of ICT on societies and global economics has not been as significant as some predicted, due to the fact that many goods and services cannot be exchanged electronically.[41] It is also the case that states are far from irrelevant in the emergence of the information age. Governments create the rules and regulations that govern information flows. Governments promote or directly develop the infrastructure (such as satellites and communications facilities) that ICT requires. Governments pass laws protecting intellectual property rights and privacy. Governments have also taken an active role (along with corporations and citizens groups) in the social debate over ICT. Therefore, the state is very much alive and well in the information age. This debate is likely to continue, for it is an inescapable fact that many people in various economic sectors around the world felt less secure in their jobs even before the onset of the latest global recession. Furthermore, there is a general dissatisfaction with economic performance in the industrialized countries and concern over social problems caused at least in part by divisions between rich and poor. Whether the computer and information revolution is blamed (justly or unjustly) for these problems, responding to these conditions presents a major challenge to the economic and fiscal policies of governments, which could continue to pursue the opportunities of the information age while seeking to protect their societies against the worst of the economic dislocation that ICT, globalization, and recession might bring.

THE DIGITAL DIVIDE

The ICT revolution has serious implications for the problem of inequality in the global economy. On the one hand, information technology has the potential to make a significant contribution to economic development and the human condition of poor peoples around the world.[42] On the other hand, it also has the potential to widen the gap between rich and poor as wealthy societies stand to benefit most from new innovations. Information-age technologies and capacities are unevenly distributed: a digital divide has evolved within as well as among states.[43] Some countries, regions, and peoples remain marginalized and even excluded from the full economic benefits of the information age. These persons are disconnected from the communications networks that most citizens in the relatively affluent states take for granted. In 2011, two-thirds of the world's population was not yet online, and while over 70 percent of the population in high-income countries enjoyed Internet access, just over 24 percent of the population of low-income countries had access. Furthermore, while the majority of users in high-income countries had access to high-speed connections of 10 million bits per second

(10 Mbit/s), most connections in the low-income countries were limited to 2 Mbit/s, restricting the availability of many Internet services and functions.[44] Bridging this divide is a priority in national and international development strategies.

The promise and the limitations of ICT as an instrument of development can be illustrated by mobile telephone use in Africa. The mobile phone revolution has greatly expanded telephone use on the African continent. With a very low ratio of telephone landlines to population (1.4 fixed lines for every 100 Africans), the mobile phone has proven particularly valuable. Cellular phone subscribers in Africa have increased from over 37 million in 2002 to over 434 million in 2011, or 53 subscriptions for every 100 Africans.[45] This is an impressive development, because mobile technology has enabled many Africans to circumvent the infrastructure requirements of traditional telephones. However, the problem of inequality remains: despite the enormous increase in mobile phone use in Africa, the continent lags behind in the adoption of this technology. For example, in the Americas in 2011 there were over 105 cellular subscriptions for every 100 inhabitants. In 2007, the Connect Africa Summit established a set of goals to improve connectivity, access, and ICT skill development across the continent. Regarded as an integral part of the larger World Summit on the Information Society targets and the Millennium Development Goals, the Connect Africa Summit succeeded in raising pledges of US$55 billion to fund the effort.[46]

Critics suggest that real development will not come from the increased use of mobile devices; that heavy demand for the minerals used in cellphones, such as cobalt, have contributed to resource wars in the Congo and elsewhere; and that we are still uncertain as to whether the long-term use of mobile devices actually creates health problems, especially for children. Nonetheless, there is no escaping the importance of technology in development efforts, since information is now a "basic resource needed for technico-economic activity, on a par with matter and energy."[47] However, there is a danger that too much emphasis might be placed on ICT as a panacea for economic development problems. As Anthony P. D'Costa observes, "Past radical technological developments such as railways, telephone and television have not fundamentally transformed the economic structures of developing countries."[48] In a three-volume work on the information age, economics, and society, Manuel Castells argues that the world economy is now in an informational rather than an industrial mode of development. Castells observes that a new international division of labour has formed, and is "constructed around four different positions in the information/global economy: the producers of high value, based on information labour; the producers of high volume, based on low cost labour; the producers of raw materials, based on natural endowments; and the redundant producers, reduced to devalued labour."[49] The ICT revolution might help or hinder efforts to achieve greater global equality, but it will not be the only determinant of economic development. The digital divide is only one of many factors in the complex structure of the global economy.

If low-income countries hope to capitalize on the potential of ICT to escape from their disadvantageous positions in the international division of labour, they will have to make a major effort on a number of levels. They will have to improve their national communication and energy infrastructures to enable the adoption and effective use of computers and mobile devices. Taking advantage of the potential of the Internet and e-commerce depends on the availability, accessibility, and affordability of this infrastructure.[50] Furthermore, appropriate and effective legal and financial frameworks must be in place for knowledge-based economic activity to operate.[51] Most importantly, developing countries will need the human capital required of information-age activity, in the form of knowledge workers and information literacy. Educational disparities are a critical variable when development emphasizes technology.

Networked in North Kenya. A Masai person talks on his cellphone from the grasslands of the Lewa Wildlife Conservancy in North Kenya, Africa. There are now billions of cellphones in use around the world. (UIG via Getty Images)

Certainly, the technology aspects of development are inseparable from the human: the next generation of complex technology will increase wealth and opportunity for those with access to education. Can the digital divide be bridged? Technology and innovative methods may promise an answer: in Bangladesh, a bank issued microloans for the purchase of mobile phones to women, who then charged a cost for its shared use. This gave inexpensive phone access to millions of people.[52] The International Telecommunications Union launched an effort to "connect the unconnected" by 2015, a recognition of the need for international cooperation if ICT is to fulfill its development potential for poor countries. If properly managed at both the local and international level, ICT might prove to be a potential source of liberation from poverty and hardship. If improperly managed, or not managed at all, ICT will almost certainly contribute to increased economic disparity.

THE DISSEMINATION OF TECHNOLOGY, INFORMATION, AND IDEAS

The computer revolution and the creation of expanding communications channels have led to an explosion in the availability of information. Technology facilitates the creation, processing, accumulation, storage, and management of information on an unprecedented scale. Equally important is the decline in the cost of transmitting information. In 1970, the cost of transmitting a trillion bits of information across North America was US$150 000; by 2001, the cost had fallen to US$0.12.[53] Computers and mobile devices can now access and process vast amounts of Web-based information and data. Modern libraries are increasingly electronic, storing a growing amount of their information holdings in digital form and offering computerized access to their databases and to the databases of other libraries. Traditional media sources such as newspapers, magazines, and television programming all have online resources and archives that allow us to access a wide variety of news items, technical information, images, and music. Governments can receive information on domestic and international political events within minutes.

The availability and dissemination of ideas and information is having a dramatic effect on scientific discovery and innovation. Science can be a lonely enterprise; the image of the lone scientist toiling in a lab into the late hours of the night is an accurate one. However, scientific discovery is also a collaborative enterprise, as well as a competitive one. Scientists often seek out colleagues for assistance or advice. The process of scientific verification and review demands that experiments and discoveries be replicated and evaluated by scientific peer groups. The collaborative aspects of scientific discovery can thus be facilitated and accelerated by communications technology and the dissemination of information within **epistemic communities** of individuals dedicated to the common pursuit of ideas and objectives, regardless of their location or country of residence. In the past, innovations disseminated slowly, spreading only as fast as messages and people could travel. As a result, news of discoveries or innovations took a long time to come to the attention of those who could make use of them. In the television series *Connections*, host James Burke suggested that technological change was largely the result of inventors taking older discoveries, adding an innovation of their own, and applying it to the problem with which they were concerned. The result was a new way of doing things, inspired by the borrowing and adaptation of ideas. Today, the availability and dissemination of information allows would-be innovators to access a vast reservoir of information and ideas from around the world. New ideas and innovations appear almost daily, and those who are interested in certain scientific or technical pursuits can easily access the information they need.

However, the dissemination of scientific discovery and innovation is not always regarded as a good thing. In fact, many scientific discoveries and innovations are kept secret. The belief that national security may be put at risk is one rationale for preventing the spread of information. Another may be the commercial potential of the discovery and the desire to profit from it. Of course, there is an increasing trend toward using information networks for **industrial espionage** to steal information and data. This type of theft raises a number of questions about the security of personal information in an information age. Information about our financial situation, medical history, family records, and backgrounds increasingly resides in computers in electronic form. This is a growing problem for the privacy of the individual. There are similar concerns over the controversial introduction of "electronic voting" in the United States and elsewhere. In short, the dissemination of technology and ideas will continue to affect the global economy and the workplace. As James Rosenau argues, technology has "profoundly altered the scale on which human affairs take place, allowing people to do more things in less time and with wider repercussions than could have been imagined in earlier eras."[54] At the same time, technological advances and their economic implications will be jealously guarded in a world still full of competitive states, corporations, groups, and individuals.

THE MEDIA AND GLOBAL POLITICS

In the late 1980s, someone living in Canada interested in news and information from India, Brazil, or China would have to make do with limited television or radio, reports supplemented by week-old newspapers and back issues of magazines purchased at specialty news stores. Letters written to friends or relatives took days or weeks to deliver and long-distance telephone calls were expensive. Today, that same person now has access to satellite television stations and online newspapers, magazines, and radio stations. Electronic messaging, social media, and telephone calls are relatively inexpensive. The ICT revolution has greatly increased the availability of information and news from a wide range of sources around the world. In turn, this information is crucial to the impressions and opinions of events, peoples, and societies held by political and economic elites and a growing public audience throughout the world. How this information and news is gathered, packaged, and distributed is a matter of growing concern. As a result, the media (especially radio, television, and Internet news services) are rightfully accorded special significance in the study of global politics.

The term *media* refers to three related aspects of information dissemination: the technological means of communication, the production and distribution of information, and the content received by audiences.[55] In the 1990s, satellite news services began to expand dramatically, and forged links with virtually all satellite and cable service providers around the world. The televised 24-hour coverage of the fall of communism in Eastern Europe, the collapse of the Soviet Union, and the 1990 to 1991 Gulf War ushered in a new media age. German social theorist Jürgen Habermas suggested that "through the electronic media, these events were brought instantaneously before a ubiquitous public sphere. In the context of the French Revolution, Kant made reference to the reactions of a participatory public. At that time, he identified the phenomenon of a world public sphere, which today is becoming political reality for the first time in a cosmopolitan matrix of communication."[56] We are now accustomed to receiving news and information about events around the world virtually as they occur. As a result, we increasingly refer to a global media that delivers information, sounds, and images from political events (such as terrorist attacks), wars (such as Afghanistan and Syria), natural disasters (such as earthquakes and hurricanes), and a wide variety of cultural and sporting events to a global audience. Because of this, global media have had a notable impact on the knowledge and attitudes of individuals, as well as on the policies of governments.

The power of the media and related industries is potentially enormous, for they are the source of much of the information that people receive about the world in which they live. What is reported and what is excluded is crucially important in how people perceive events and ideas. In the past, newspapers, magazines, radio, and "newsreels" (short news presentations shown before feature films) were the dominant forms of media. Joseph Goebbels and the Nazi Party of Germany pioneered radio as a mass propaganda device in the 1930s, and it remains a powerful medium largely because it is easily accessible. There are more than two billion radios in the world, and in countries where illiteracy rates are high, the radio is the primary source of information about national or international events. International shortwave radio broadcasts, such as the Voice of America (VOA) and the British Broadcasting Corporation (BBC) World Service, reach into the remotest regions of the world to bring news items, political perspectives, and entertainment to those with shortwave receivers. Radio was also used extensively to deliver hate speeches in preparation for the genocide committed against the Tutsis in Rwanda in 1994. In conflicts such as Afghanistan and Iraq, as well as in many UN peacekeeping missions, establishing a "friendly" radio service is considered a priority.

Television is even more politically powerful, largely because of the impact images can have on human emotions and reactions. It brings a sense of immediacy, or presence, that other media do not possess. Globally, there are over 1.4 billion television sets, with those sets appearing in 98 percent of households in high-income countries and 73 percent of households in the rest of the world.[57] As James Rosenau has argued, "Access to television has become sufficiently global in scope that it must be regarded as a change of [fundamental] proportions."[58] Cable channels and satellite television channels continue to proliferate, and, like radio, many television networks are devoted to international broadcasting. The U.S.–based Cable News Network (CNN), the BBC, and the British-based International Television Network (ITN) are among the most prominent examples. CNN ushered in the age of the 24-hour news station in 1980, as a component of Turner Broadcasting System Inc.[59] Today, there has been a notable increase in international broadcasting aimed at projecting a national perspective into the global media arena, often in the language of the target audience. Many of these stations were established to counter the presence and presumed influence of CNN, the BBC, and ITN. This was a major motive for the creation of Fox News in the U.S. and France 24. Stations such as Russia Today are in English, while the German network Deutsche Welle and the U.S. TV channel Al-Hurra broadcast in Arabic.

In the Arab world, the media environment has been turned upside down by a private satellite news channel, Al-Jazeera (which roughly translates as "the Peninsula"). Al-Jazeera began broadcasting in 1996 and operates out of Qatar.[60] The station has established itself in the Arab world as an alternative to highly censored state-owned television networks. Al-Jazeera gained attention in the West for its broadcast of videotapes by al-Qaeda and Osama Bin Laden, but in the Arab world it is better known for its critical coverage of many Arab governments, as well as its coverage of the Israeli–Palestinian conflict, the wars in the region (particularly in Afghanistan, Iraq, and Syria), and the Arab Spring uprisings. Much of this coverage is unabashedly critical of Israel and the United States, drawing criticism from both countries. For example, while U.S. media coverage of the invasion and occupation of Iraq was criticized for its failure to present a range of opinion and show the bloody consequences of the conflict, the U.S. government accused Al-Jazeera of showing little other than civilian casualties, while providing scant information on the stated U.S. reasons for fighting. Nevertheless, the popularity of Al-Jazeera rests with its credibility in the region for broadcasting "news gathered independently by Arabs for Arabs and that sees events through *their* eyes."[61] In 2001, Al-Jazeera launched an Internet version of its news service, first in Arabic and then in English in 2006, which has brought the network and its perspective into the global arena.

The arrival of global media sources to the Middle East and the creation of Al-Jazeera have stimulated a debate about the transformative power of the media. Some argue the region is changing because of growing access to information delivered by global media sources, and Al-Jazeera is a reaction to this new reality. For example, Mohammed Jassim Al Ali (former managing director of Al-Jazeera) has argued, "Democracy is coming to the Middle East because of the communication revolution. You can no longer hide information and must now tell people the truth. If you don't the people won't follow you, they won't support you, they won't obey you."[62] Other observers are not so sanguine, arguing that media in the Arab world remain highly controlled by governments and rulers. As Mamoun Fandy argues, "The ownership of a given media outlet determines its coverage and the type of commentaries it airs.... The reality is that the Arab media's impact on transforming Middle Eastern societies is at best minimal."[63] Naomi Sakr agrees, arguing that editorial content in Arab media reflects the agendas of political and economic elites: political change causes change in editorial content, not the other way around.[64] It is notable that Al-Jazeera's editorial independence from the government of Qatar has been questioned.[65] This debate raises an interesting point about the global media. Certainly, there is very little critical coverage of Islamic Jihad, Hamas, or the Sudanese Islamic government in the Arab media. However, the same might be said when it comes to coverage of certain issues in U.S. or Western media. American news networks were notably uncritical of the war in Iraq and seldom make references to the reasons for the popularity of organizations like Hamas. Perhaps Al-Jazeera and other stations like it represent a new age in global media diversity, competition, and political debate.

However, we must be cautious when we proclaim that an age of global media is upon us. Perhaps it is more accurate to say that the potential for a global media is upon us, because the reality is that most programming in any given spot in the world is overwhelmingly local or national in its coverage. As Ted Magder suggests, "We may live in a world of globalization, but we do not yet live in the age of global news *per se*, either in the sense that audiences the world over pay attention to the same international stories on an everyday basis or even in the sense that audiences get more global (or foreign) news than in the past."[66] For the most part, citizens are interested in local news that directly impacts their lives, communities, and daily decisions. The economics of the media industry also play a role: local stories sell and are cheaper to produce, while international stories generally do not sell and are expensive to produce. When major events happen, media industries can mobilize rapidly, even sending their anchors to cover dramatic events—such as the fall of the Berlin Wall or the beginning of war against Iraq—from the scene. However, once the drama ends, and intensive or "special extended coverage" packages are no longer securing viewers, the old pattern of emphasis on local or national news returns. Furthermore, it is unclear just how much influence the media has on its audiences. Lived experiences and social frames of reference are difficult to challenge or alter. The volume of information available makes it difficult to assimilate complicated or contradictory messages. Media is also voluntary to the extent that a viewer can switch channels or websites (or even read a book!).

There is also a growing critical reflection on the role of the media that calls into question the existence of a new global media age. Some suggest that during the fall of the Berlin Wall, the collapse of the U.S.S.R., and the 1990 to 1991 Gulf War, the media (and the public who watched it) were mere spectators, not actors or agents or participants in the events. Concerns that the media are manipulated by economic or political elites have also grown. The Vietnam War was a watershed for the news media: one of the turning points of the war was CBS news anchor Walter Cronkite's televised statements declaring the war a bloody stalemate in which victory was impossible. Coverage of the war brought the brutalities of the conflict to televisions in the United States, and this coverage was a major reason for the change in American public opinion. This first "living room war" prompted a change in the relationship between the military and the media; in the 1989 to 1990 invasion of Panama and the 1990 to 1991 Gulf War, the media were tightly grouped into reporter "pools" and provided information in a controlled environment by way of daily news briefings from the U.S. military. Gone were the violent images, dead bodies, and expressions of disgust and discouragement by soldiers: instead, coverage was sanitized, almost bloodless, and homogenous. In the 2003 invasion of Iraq, the media were permitted to use so-called embedded reporters, who were assigned to U.S. units and whose coverage was heavily censored. The relationship between the military and news media has become so proximate that Daya Kishan Thussu and Des Freedman observe that "military and media networks have converged to the point where they are now virtually indistinguishable ... media constitute the spaces in which wars are fought and are the main ways through which populations (or audiences) experience war."[67] In this media age, then, the trend may not be toward greater understanding and participation, but toward passive, uncritical absorption of managed information.

Another concern is the concentration of international media in a shrinking number of large corporations. In the 1980s, the global media was concentrated in perhaps 50 corporations. Today, only a few companies dominate the global gathering, processing, and

Making Al-Jazeera famous. In this television image broadcast on April 15, 2002, by Arab satellite station Al-Jazeera, Osama Bin Laden, right, listens as his top deputy, Ayman al-Zawahiri, speaks at an undisclosed location. (AP Photo/Al-Jazeera/APTN)

dissemination of news programming, including The Walt Disney Company, Time Warner, CBS Corporation, Bertelsmann AG, Viacom, and News Corporation. Time Warner Inc. is an example of the extraordinary concentration of media services in large corporations. In 2013, Time Warner Inc. owned New Line Cinema, Time Inc., HBO, Turner Broadcasting System, Warner Bros., CNN, DC Comics, and Castle Rock Entertainment, among others. Companies owned by The Walt Disney Company include the American Broadcasting Company (ABC), ESPN, Hyperion Books, Touchstone Pictures, Marvel Studios, Pixar Animation Studios, Disney Channels Worldwide, and many others. Critics charge that major corporations essentially control the global media, a consequence of the neoliberal economic model, which promotes deregulation, privatization, and commercialization. The dominance of this model (in the U.S. and the global economy) has facilitated the creation of corporate media monoliths that in turn are promoting the spread of market-oriented values in news, advertising, and entertainment.[68] However, it is also the case that media-sector markets are intensely competitive in the global and national arena, and new sources of news and information are constantly emerging. The presence of transnational media giants does not necessarily translate into influence or dominance in societies that often have trusted local and national media outlets. And to be successful, even the largest media companies have to adjust to local tastes and interests. This debate shows no sign of abating, even as the size of some media corporations continues to grow and new ones rise to prominence.

The global media is of particular concern to developing countries. The rich industrialized world's domination of the global media and information content on the airwaves and the Internet raises concerns about the ability of the developing world to have its voice heard, its concerns expressed, and its cultures and values protected. Many developing countries see the rich world's domination of the information age and the global media as another factor promoting modernization, imperialism, and globalization, thereby perpetuating the dependence of poor countries.[69] Of course, some of these concerns are shared by certain industrialized countries (such as France and Canada) worried about the intrusion of American cultural products into their own societies. In the 1980s, several leaders from the southern hemisphere called for the adoption of a New World Information and Communication Order (NWICO) that would establish limits on the domination of the media and information networks and create space for the voices of the South. This effort never overcame opposition from rich countries, but the struggle continues in the form of disputes over cultural protection and control of local independent media establishments around the world.

THE GLOBAL MEDIA AND POLITICAL DECISION MAKING

There is growing interest in the influence the media might have on the foreign policy decisions of governments. The predominant view is that the media must play an important and in some cases decisive role in foreign policy decision making. The leaders of governments and their key advisors may be personally influenced by current news coverage or have their views framed by previous media portrayals of the issue in question. The media can also influence public opinion, which can then exert pressure on governments through elected representatives, opinion polls, and protest. This connection between the media and governments is sometimes described as a cause-and-effect relationship: the media pressures government. However, this is a very simplistic formula. International events can compel governments to react for reasons that have little to do with media exposure, while governments may have particular foreign policy goals they want to achieve. Therefore, caution must be exercised when attributing government action in global affairs to the media. Another interpretation of the relationship between the media and foreign policy decision making involves the use or manipulation of the media by governments to gain public support for foreign policy decisions. From this perspective, the media is a propaganda tool of government or the dominant economic elites (which may be inextricably linked from a Marxist viewpoint). This manipulation can be direct (in cases when state-operated media is essentially an arm of the government) or indirect (when media coverage reflects a larger elite consensus or a misplaced sense of national loyalty or patriotism). The causal relationship is therefore reversed: government manipulates the media. A third perspective suggests that the relationship between the media and foreign policy decision making is mutually influential. Media–government relations consist of an ongoing "conversation" in which each influences the other.[70] Despite this debate, there is general agreement that the media can exert some influence over foreign policy decision making in the following ways:

Agenda Setting. The items on any government's foreign policy agenda are those that are considered important enough to demand government attention. The global media (and the domestic national media) play a role in this process by bringing issues to the attention of the public. In the process of reporting on certain issues (and not reporting on others) the media influence the agenda confronting decision makers, and in so doing create a dilemma. As Stig Hjarvard argues, "Under special circumstances, the power of such globalized public opinion poses a severe problem for even the mightiest of nations, because public opinion demands political action that either contradicts national policies or outstrips the diplomatic, economic, or military power of the nations involved."[71] Hjarvard cites the example of the massacre of pro-democracy protestors in China at Tiananmen Square in 1989: the world expressed outrage, but what could be done beyond the sanctions levelled against China? The media may also structure agendas by influencing perceptions of which issues should have a higher priority than others. If an issue is a public issue, then it becomes an issue for elected officials, who must be sensitive to the concerns of their constituents. In Canada and in other parliamentary democratic systems, an issue can be raised in the legislature, at a press conference, or at a public meeting. Elected officials are required to respond in an informed manner, with some explanation of the government's response. As a result, issues brought to the foreign policy agenda by the media become relevant to unelected officials as well. Bureaucracies and bureaucrats pay close attention to media reports, for they know that members of the legislature and the executive have to respond to these issues, and will turn to the bureaucracy for advice and assistance in preparing responses.

Influencing Decision Makers. In addition to exerting pressure on government through public opinion, the media can often have a direct impact on decision makers themselves. Elected and unelected government officials (including prime ministers and presidents) watch television, listen to the radio, and read newspapers. As a result, they can be directly affected by media stories and media portrayals of the issues. For world leaders, as for publics, news items from global television networks such as CNN or ITN are often the first indication that an event has occurred, and the first source of information on breaking events. Government officials will also monitor media coverage of their own actions and responses to see how their own policies are played out in the media and what reactions those policies are receiving from the public.

Shaping Perceptions. Just as the media can bring issues to public attention, the media can also influence public perceptions of these issues. Media (especially television) can transmit sounds, images, or narratives that engender a strong emotional reaction in the public. Pictures of famine victims, human rights abuses, brutality, and human suffering can put strong pressure on governments to do something to alleviate or stop these injustices. In many cases, the media story may blame certain individuals or groups for these injustices and highlight a possible course of action or target for government policy. As a result, not only is the public made aware of the issue but also the media story may influence public perceptions of what ought to be done. This can create policymaking problems, for if governments and those advising them feel that this public perception of what ought to be done is not feasible or even dangerous, they will be reluctant to act. Alternatively, governments may find another course of action more appropriate and face the task of selling this policy to a public that may have different perceptions of the issue. The media can also provide the public with a sense of how their own individual feelings about an issue are shared (or not shared) by society. Media coverage of mass protests, rallies, and marches can provide a perception of what the rest of society feels is important. And because many people, from news commentators to protestors to foreign policy experts, have their opinions on what ought to be done solicited and broadcast to the public, the government must respond to the various proposals for action put forward from a wide variety of individuals.

*Embarrassing Government*s. The ability of the media to discover and reveal events around the world often forces governments to face the consequences of their actions in the international realm. It is increasingly difficult for governments to hide or ignore unfavourable news or politically problematic issues. If governments make mistakes, or make what in retrospect are poor decisions, they will quite likely have to respond to critical reports and investigations in the media. On other occasions, current government policies may be subject to criticism. As a result, governments and politicians often find themselves faced with embarrassing (and potentially politically damaging) inquiries into why the government is pursuing its course of action. For example, the efforts of the Liberal government under Jean Chrétien to expand Canadian trade in Asia through the "Team Canada" missions met with criticism from human rights organizations that the government was not doing enough to promote human rights in Asia. This criticism was accompanied by media stories and images of poorly paid workers toiling for long hours under terrible working conditions.

Together, the ability of the media to pressure governments through agenda setting, influencing decision makers, shaping perceptions, and embarrassing governments has been described as the "CNN Effect" (see Profile 12.2). Some might conclude that the power of the media is decisive as a determinant in foreign policy decision making, but this is inaccurate. After all, even if the agenda is at least in part set by media reports, in practice governments have a lot of flexibility over how they might actually respond to an issue. When public pressure encourages governments to do something, it does not always specify what that something should be. Agenda setting is not policy setting. Although media stories may influence the public's perceptions of what their government ought to do, only rarely is public opinion unified on an issue. The fact that public opinion is often split or undecided allows governments considerable room to manoeuvre when making decisions. As for the media affecting government leaders and key officials directly, while this can happen, they are also surrounded by advisors and experts armed with secret intelligence or information, wider historical perspectives, and policy experience. This group enables decision makers to draw on more sources of information and ideas than those presented on television. And while it is harder for governments to escape the consequences of poor decisions, the unintended consequences of their decisions, or even criminal or unethical decisions, the media also provide governments with an unprecedented capacity to explain and defend their actions or even to apologize and acknowledge mistakes.

THE INFORMATION AGE AND THE FUTURE OF THE STATE

Will the information age deliver the final blow to the supremacy of the state in international relations? According to liberals, the power of the state has been eroding due to increased economic interdependence and globalization. Now, the information age has ushered in an era of relatively unfettered flows of ideas, transactions, and communications across the world, virtually unaffected by states and governments. The state is now losing its capacity to control or influence the flow of information within and across its borders, and over what its citizens

---

PROFILE 12.2 **The "CNN Effect" and Global Politics**

In 1992 the U.S. government led a coalition of countries (which included Canada) in a UN Security Council–authorized intervention in Somalia, which had collapsed into communal warfare between rival clan factions. The objective of the operation was to establish order in the country and to facilitate the delivery of humanitarian relief to a population suffering from war and starvation. The prevailing explanation for this intervention was the extensive media coverage of human suffering in the weeks leading up to the intervention. As news reports and media images of starving and abused Somalis reached publics around the world, pressure built up on governments to respond. In the U.S. the coverage of the humanitarian crisis on CNN is said to have exerted a decisive influence on President Bush and the American public to intervene in Somalia. In Canada and other coalition governments, similar pressures were exerted through the media on government decision makers. In a *New York Times* editorial the famous American foreign policy elder statesman George Kennan argued that U.S. foreign policy was being led by the media, especially television. The link between media coverage and U.S. foreign policy was reinforced a few months later, when 18 U.S. soldiers were killed and their bodies dragged through the streets of the Somali capital of Mogadishu. The images of this act precipitated outrage in the U.S. public, and America withdrew from Somalia shortly thereafter. The phrase "CNN Effect" has since been used to describe a theory that policy making can be driven by media coverage rather than national interests. However,

the accuracy of the "CNN Effect" has been challenged by the argument that the U.S. decision to intervene in Somalia was driven primarily by diplomatic and bureaucratic debates in the government about what to do in Somalia. These debates predated media coverage of the crisis, and when reporters became aware of these internal government debates they dutifully reported on them in the news. This phenomenon is referred to as "news indexing," which theorizes that the media tend to follow and report on what political elites are discussing and thinking of doing. As a result, some critics of the "CNN Effect" concept charge that the media did not influence the U.S. government to intervene in Somalia, but rather the U.S. government influenced the media to focus on Somalia. Others suggest that the government and the media influenced each other, driving the Somalia issue further up on the U.S. government's agenda. Nevertheless, the "CNN Effect" remains a compelling explanation of some government actions.

In 2006, the news network Al-Jazeera provided graphic coverage of the July War in Lebanon. This coverage is said to have influenced political elites and publics in Saudi Arabia and Jordan to adopt more pro-Hezbullah positions than they might have otherwise. This link between coverage and foreign policy decision making was described as the "Al-Jazeera Effect."

SOURCE: PIERS ROBINSON, *THE CNN EFFECT: THE MYTH OF NEWS, FOREIGN POLICY AND INTERVENTION* (LONDON: ROUTLEDGE, 2002); PHILIP SEIB, ED, *NEW MEDIA AND THE NEW MIDDLE EAST* (NEW YORK: PALGRAVE, 2007); DEREK B. MILLER, *MEDIA PRESSURE ON FOREIGN POLICY: THE EVOLVING THEORETICAL FRAMEWORK* (NEW YORK: PALGRAVE MACMILLAN, 2007).

see, hear, and think. Individuals, groups, and organizations are in increasing contact across state borders, creating new communications networks, channels for ideas and debate, business and financial links, and international civil society organizations. Some observers suggest that information and communication technologies are "reformatting politics" by enabling NGOs and civil society organizations to link local issues with global issues and in the process become more effective and influential actors in world affairs.[72]

Many governments, including the government of Canada, now make little or no effort to directly control this flow of information (though they will make efforts to manipulate it, and political parties use it extensively to sell their policy platforms). This is particularly true of those governments in politically open societies. The struggle over the interpretation and portrayal of ideas and events goes on daily. Governments must continually grapple with issues related to the material content of information flows, as citizens' groups call for the ban or regulation of material they consider immoral or misleading. Domestic critics of government use their unprecedented access to information to criticize the government and its policies in the media. The most open of governments still keep much of their foreign and defence policy affairs (and many other areas as well) behind a veil of secrecy, which the media and citizens' groups often try to penetrate.

A fascinating case of the tension between government secrecy and freedom of information emerged in 2013 when Edward Snowden, a former Central Intelligence Agency (CIA) and National Security Agency (NSA) employee leaked classified information on the existence of PRISM, a classified U.S. surveillance operation. PRISM allegedly accessed the servers of major Internet firms, including Google, Facebook, Microsoft, and Yahoo, to track the online communications of foreign nationals and tens of millions of Americans. President Obama defended the program, arguing that access to information was acquired in a manner consistent with the Constitution and requirements for legal oversight. Snowden also revealed the existence of large-scale U.S. government hacking efforts, which targeted the embassies of China and EU (European Union) countries, among many others. The U.S. government charged Snowden with theft of government property and the unauthorized release of classified defence and intelligence information. Snowden fled to Hong Kong and then to Moscow, while an international legal battle ensued over his extradition and return to the U.S.

For many governments, the free flow of information represents a threat to the power, and even the survival, of the regime. Ideas and information, particularly if they expose lies, abuses, or the controversial nature of ideological claims, can be politically powerful. During the Cold War, the Soviet Union and Eastern Europe jammed foreign radio broadcasts (especially Radio Free Europe, the Voice of America, the BBC World Service, and Radio Liberty) and foreign television broadcasts. Telephone links to the outside world were tightly controlled and monitored; as late as 1987, the Soviet Union possessed only 16 international long-distance telephone circuits.[73] Newspapers were heavily controlled and censored. Photocopy machines were not available to the public. Underground literature (called *Samizdat*) was replicated by hand, on typewriter, and passed from person to person. Today, countries such as North Korea, Sudan, and Iran, impose draconian restrictions on information flows within and across their borders. And as we have seen in our discussion of the global media, Western governments have not escaped criticism about the control of the media either.[74] Despite such efforts, information and communications technologies can be powerful instruments of dissent, even in countries with highly authoritarian political systems. Audio and videotapes have played instrumental roles in the toppling of governments. In the years before the Iranian revolution, audiotapes recorded by the Ayatollah Khomeini in France and smuggled into Iran played a decisive role in the undermining of the Shah's regime and the enormous popularity of Khomeini on his return from exile. In the Philippines, the dictatorship of Ferdinand Marcos fell in part due to the circulation of videotapes showing the assassination of the Philippine opposition leader, Benigno Aquino. Telephone, fax, and computer networks have also played a role in political dissent. During and after the Tiananmen Square protests of 1989, protestors and sympathizers abroad made extensive use of fax machines and email to gather and disseminate information on events at Tiananmen. In Thailand, protestors against the military government used telephone and fax lines to communicate and coordinate their efforts. When the government employed force to suppress the protests, cutting phone lines and shooting at the demonstrators, the opposition remained in communication using cellular telephones. In Serbia, street demonstrations broke out in protest of the government's cancellation of local election results in 1997. The protestors employed a radio station to combat government domination of the media. When this was shut down, the protestors communicated with each other and the outside world using the Internet. Antiglobalization organizations and anti–Iraq War protests have used ICT to plan their campaigns and disseminate their messages. As Isabel Vincent observes, "It used to be that guerrilla fighters lugged AK-47s and sent battlefield news in rolled-up scraps of paper, faithfully carried by couriers through treacherous jungles and mountain passes. Today's revolutionary carries a laptop, and plugs into the Net."[75] The Internet has also been used as an instrument of communication and activism by human rights advocates (see Profile 12.3).

More recently, considerable attention has been devoted to the role of social media as a catalyst and enabler of the protests and revolutions of the Arab Spring. The influence of social media in the Middle East is not new: in 2009 the "Twitter Revolution" in Iran featured the use of Twitter and Facebook to mobilize supporters of the Iranian opposition after the highly questionable election victory of President Mahmoud Ahmadinejad.[76] Pictures and videos of subsequent protests, including a video of a protestor being shot, were posted on YouTube. As protests and revolutions began to spread across the Arab world beginning in late 2010, it became clear that social media had an important influence on the unfolding events.[77] In Egypt, the famous Tahrir Square protests were organized on a Facebook group, "We are all Khalid Said," named after a protestor beaten to death by police.[78] Social media continued to play a role in mobilizing and organizing protests, even when the Egyptian government attempted to deny access to social media sites by severing access to the Internet: Google and Twitter responded by creating a "speak-to-tweet" service that enabled voicemail messages left at designated telephone numbers to be sent out as Twitter messages.[79] In Libya, the government blocked access to YouTube and social media sites as protests began, but thousands of videos intended for YouTube and Al-Jazeera were uploaded nonetheless, through the use of "mirrored sites" and the smuggling of memory cards and USB devices across the country's borders.[80] In Syria, protestors made extensive use of Facebook pages as bulletin boards to organize, and used YouTube to post videos of government violence against peaceful protests. As the violence increased and the government shut off Internet access in some parts of the country, more use was made of smuggled satellite phones and mobile devices, and Skype messages (Twitter does not seem to have been used as extensively in Syria as it has in other countries).[81] The impact of social media on the Arab Spring has been hotly contested. Malcolm Gladwell has argued that social media is not useful or beneficial to protestors because social media ties are characterized by "weak-tie" personal connections between individuals, while high risk activism requires "strong-tie" personal connections. Furthermore, social media makes it easier for protestors to express themselves, but harder for their protest to have any

PROFILE 12.3 Hacktivism at the University of Toronto

In the Munk Centre for International Studies at the University of Toronto is a facility known as The Citizen Lab. Established in 2001 through the efforts of Professor Ron Diebert, the Lab engages in what Dr. Diebert calls "hacktivism," a combination of traditional computer hacking and social and political activism. Dr. Diebert believes that understanding how technology works and what is behind it is essential to a liberal, democratic society: "Citizens can't just accept technology at face value. They need to open the lid, so to speak, understand how it works, beneath the surface." By bringing together a diverse group of faculty and students from computer science through political science, Dr. Diebert wanted to encourage the creation of a group of technically adept activists. The heart of Citizen Lab activities is the OpenNet Initiative, targeted at countries that attempt to block access to the World Wide Web.

"Hacktivists" at the lab attempt to identify what methods governments use to block access to certain websites. The Lab then develops techniques and software to help citizens in these countries circumvent the controls. The Citizen Lab also operates the Information Warfare Monitor in cooperation with the SecDev Group, an international security think tank based in Ottawa. The Monitor is a research program exploring the use of cyberspace as an environment for the exercise of state power. In March 2009 it exposed a large Chinese-government cyber-espionage effort directed against the Tibetan community worldwide. The spying campaign, called GhostNet by the authors of the report, involved the infection of at least 1295 computers in 103 countries with malware designed to provide full access to secret files and personal information, including those in the offices of the Dalai Lama.

How do target countries feel about the activities of the Citizen Lab? "Some authoritarian regimes obviously don't like what we're doing," says Diebert. "But I feel we're working in support of broader principles of human rights, so I don't mind the controversy. Sometimes it helps."

SOURCE: CLARK BOYD, "'NET NINJAS' TAKE ON WEB CENSORSHIP," BBC NEWS, WORLD EDITION, APRIL 18, 2004. FOUND AT: HTTP://NEWS.BBC.CO.UK/GO/PR/FR=/=/2/HI/ TECHNOLOGY/3632757.STM (ACCESSED APRIL 18, 2004); INFORMATION WARFARE MONITOR, TRACKING GHOSTNET: INVESTIGATING A CYBER ESPIONAGE NETWORK, MARCH 29, 2009. FOUND AT: HTTP://WWW.SCRIBD.COM/DOC/13731776/ TRACKING-GHOSTNET-INVESTIGATING-A-CYBER-ESPIONAGE-NETWORK; THE CITIZEN LAB WEBSITE, WWW.CITIZENLAB.ORG.

impact.[82] Others, such as Larry Diamond, believe that the Internet's decentralized character and ability to quickly reach large groups of people greatly enhances the organizational capacity of activists.[83] Clay Shirky agrees, arguing that the Internet can reduce the costs of coordination among citizens in authoritarian countries.[84]

Despite the association of ICT with political freedom, governments can also harness the power offered by the information age. Does this new era of technology-induced freedom from state controls exist primarily in the minds of those who foresee a technological, transboundary world? Is the computer, information, and communications revolution overrated as an agent of change in global politics? After all, information has always been an important element of state power, and computers and communications technologies permit states to access, store, and use information as never before. States employ this information to their advantage in a number of ways. In their interactions with one another and with non-state actors, information (or "intelligence") has always been a vital dimension of diplomacy and war. Negotiation, bargaining, and conflict management efforts are facilitated by virtually instantaneous communication and the increasing capability of states to gather information independently. The telephone has become a central tool of contemporary diplomacy, and leaders and officials of

Sending a message. Egyptians use their mobile phones to record celebrations in Cairo's Tahrir Square, the epicentre of the popular revolt that drove veteran strongman Hosni Mubarak from power, on February 12, 2011. (AFP/Getty Images)

states often communicate with each other simply by picking up the phone. States also employ information as an instrument of state power, by disseminating information into the international system in the form of radio broadcasts, information services, and statements in the media. Governments may also spread **disinformation** in a deliberate attempt to mislead other governments (or their own populations). The ability of computers to store and retrieve information offers governments an unprecedented capability to watch over the lives of citizens and keep files on suspected subversive elements. For example, during the "Twitter Revolution" in Iran in 2009, Twitter was also used as a tool of repression, as vigilante Twitter accounts were established to lure protestors to locations where they could be arrested.[85] In Syria, regime supporters (known as the Syrian Electronic Army) pursued dissidents by tracking their Facebook activities—one reason the regime actually lifted an early ban on Facebook.[86] ICT technologies may therefore increase, rather than decrease, the power of the state with respect to the individual.

This raises the issue of information power. In the future, the states that are world leaders in computer development, information production, and communications technology will likely be the most powerful states in the international system. Just as past technical innovations increased the power of certain societies or states, the information age will increase the power of those states best able to develop and harness the potential of these new technologies. Many observers argue that the country best placed to increase its power and exert leadership in the information age remains the United States:

> Knowledge, more than ever before, is power. The one country that can best lead the information revolution will be more powerful than any other. For the foreseeable future, that country is the United States. America has apparent strength in

military power and economic production. Yet its most subtle comparative advantage is its ability to collect, process, act upon, and disseminate information, an edge that will almost certainly grow over the next decade.[87]

State power in the information age will not be dependent on natural endowments of population or resources or geographic position, although these will still have relevance. Instead, power will depend on technological leadership, on political, economic, and social flexibility, and on education.

A GLOBAL CULTURE?

The relationship between transnational communications networks and culture is a growing topic in the study of global politics. Dramatic statements have been made on the impact of the information age in the industrialized world. Bill Gates, for example, argues that a "global interactive network will transform our culture as dramatically as Gutenberg's press did in the middle ages."[88] Of course, it is not so much the network that will have this impact but the content it is carrying. Today, the global impact of such networks on cultures worldwide is beginning to be understood, and there are both encouraging and discouraging dimensions to this issue. Transnational communications technologies and the global media are shrinking the planet. Individuals around the world can watch the same news reports, listen to the same music, watch the same sporting events, see the same movies, eat the same food, and be exposed to advertising for the same consumer products. As a result, a global culture may be taking shape. To be sure, it exists only in very embryonic form today, if at all. And even if it does develop, most of the planet will not share in this experience. However, we may be witnessing the beginning of a form of cultural integration or homogenization, borne on the pathways opened up by transnational communications technologies and the information revolution.

Sociologists interested in technology have introduced a convergence theory that is not unlike the idea of convergence as we have used it in this book. According to this theory, "the opportunities and demands presented by modern technology promote the convergence of all societies toward a single set of social patterns and individual behaviours."[89] In other words, the adoption of Western technology will lead to the establishment of political institutions and cultural environments similar to those in the advanced European and American worlds. Thus, globalization will inevitably be realized through technological standardization. As a theory, however, this leaves some room for healthy speculation. One might point to the spread of capitalism as the source of this convergence instead of to the technology employed. Obvious cases exist where distaste for Western society has led to an assertion of anti-Western political change, such as the Iranian revolution that ushered into power the late Ayatollah Khomeini. Indeed, recent research indicates that there is a "contra-flow" of communication and cultural influences in much of the world that is a reaction to U.S. and Western cultural influences.[90] In a more general sense, one might argue that culture does not necessarily converge simply because of technological similarities. There are distinct patterns of social interaction within different societies despite a high rate of **technological convergence**. Japan, the United States, and Germany all have adopted industrial technology yet remain quite different in terms of cultural attributes. Though many would argue with this, we can even point out significant cultural differences between countries as similar in technological circumstances as the United States and Canada.

Television programming, movies, and music have become increasingly globalized. Audiences around the world can watch television programming from a wide variety of other countries. These programs can reveal the nature of life in other societies, and as a result television can be a powerful educational tool. However, television can also distort the perception of life in other countries. For example, exported Western soap operas have created the impression among many people in other societies that all North Americans and Europeans are wealthy. For several years, one of the most watched series around the world was *Baywatch*, and it features swimsuit models working on sunny Californian beaches. Another is *American Idol*, which has been replicated in many other states and depicts average citizens pursuing the American Dream of fame and monetary success. Children and family programming is also increasingly globalized, as suggested by the international success of the *Mighty Morphin Power Rangers* (dubbed into English from the original Japanese), the Canadian television series *Degrassi Junior High*, and the success of Japanese anime. Movies are also distributed internationally, as are music recordings. Quality cinema is shown at international film festivals (such as the famous Cannes and Sundance festivals), and the international success of "Bollywood" films produced in India demonstrates the cross-fertilization of cultural influences. Classical musicians and conductors move routinely across national borders. In the genres of rock, jazz, and blues, tours are often international in scope. Some varieties of music are explicitly international in inspiration, and are sometimes referred to as "world music."

Sporting events have also become internationalized. The Olympic Games and the World Cup (to name only two) are major international events, watched by hundreds of millions of people. Most athletic and sporting pursuits have some version of a world championship, whether it is in figure skating, ice hockey, or car racing. Many prominent sports teams, such as the Montreal Canadiens, New York Yankees, Dallas Cowboys, and Manchester United, have international followings. Frequently, sporting figures will become international celebrities, famous throughout the world and connected to the global advertising capacities of major multinationals such as Nike or Adidas. Sports can create a sense of human community, and some suggest that sporting events can be a force for peace, unifying peoples in a shared activity. Of course, sports can bring out intense state or even ethnic nationalism, as people cheer for their national team or competitor. Sporting events can also take on a political dimension. For example, witness the intense rivalry of the Canada–Soviet Union hockey confrontations, and the undertones of some football (soccer) matches during the World Cup. However, sports bring people (both participants and spectators) together, and the increasing trend toward international competitions, visiting tours of sport teams, and exchanges and trips in youth sports is another example of the blurring of national boundaries.

The wide availability of food and consumer items from other countries (made possible by global trade) also has contributed to the globalization of culture. Many food and consumer products are indistinguishable from the culture that produced them: when one thinks of sushi, one thinks of Japan; when one thinks of Mercedes, one thinks of Germany; when one thinks of Marlboro, one thinks of the United States; when one thinks of Roots, one thinks of Canada. In addition, advertising has a powerful cultural dimension, as advertising increasingly links products and the multinational corporations that produce them with music, images, and international celebrities.

However, considerable concern remains that this global culture may in fact be less of a fusion, or integration, of cultures from around the world than the spread—or, worse, imposition—of Western (and especially American) culture; some would argue we are witnessing cultural imperialism. The global culture is dominated by the English language, the U.S. film and

The ubiquitous franchise. McDonald's restaurants appear in over 100 countries around the world. Is this the face of an emerging global culture? (© Greg Balfour Evans / Alamy)

television industries, American and Western media networks, and advertising for Western-style consumption. For example, Hollywood dominates global cinema and the television programming industry; it supplies 80 percent of the world's demand for films and 70 percent of the world's demand for television shows. By the mid-1990s, Hollywood was making more than half its money abroad.[91] Icons of Western culture have spread dramatically, and some are approaching the status of global icons, such as the Golden Arches and Ronald McDonald of the American fast-food chain, or the omnipresent Coca-Cola sign. However, advertising also carries certain cultural values and messages, and can encourage Western-style consumerism and materialism, to the detriment of local businesses and traditions, and sometimes the very health of the local population. The dominance of Western cultural influences on the Internet is another reflection of this phenomenon. As a result, we are also witnessing a global cultural backlash, with populations increasingly suspicious and even hostile to foreign influences, although this rejection is likely to be selective: even as some influences are opposed others will be accepted.

WAR IN THE INFORMATION AGE: A REVOLUTION IN MILITARY AFFAIRS?

So far in this chapter we have explored how the rapid pace of technological change has affected (and perhaps even transformed) the global political economy, information flows, financial markets, global cultural politics, the media, and the state. This rapid technological change has also dramatically increased the capacities of modern weapons and the efficiency of military communications and information systems. Indeed, many observers of military affairs argue that we are witnessing a profound transformation in the effectiveness of military forces. This argument is based on a particular interpretation of military history, which argues that the development of military capabilities has not progressed in a steady, evolutionary fashion. Instead, increases in military capabilities have been characterized by sudden surges, or revolutions, in the effectiveness of weapons and military technique. These surges originate from technological, organizational, and larger social and economic innovations in certain countries. It can hardly be surprising that against the backdrop of the computer and information revolution, declarations have been made that we are experiencing a parallel military revolution. For example, Alvin and Heidi Toffler argue that "as we transition from brute-force to brain-force economies, we also necessarily invent what can only be called 'brain-force-war.'"[92] This transition is often referred to as the **Revolution in Military Affairs (RMA).**

An RMA is the relatively swift onset of a qualitative transformation in the effectiveness of military technologies that fundamentally alters the conduct of military operations and the nature of the strategic environment. One key concept that distinguishes changes in military technologies, doctrines, and organizations (which are not rare) from revolutionary developments (which are rare) is discontinuity. That is, revolutions are characterized by transformations in the nature of the conduct of military operations such that previous technologies and techniques are rendered obsolete. Early RMAs have been associated with gunpowder, the rise of the national citizen armies of the Napoleonic period, and the Blitzkrieg warfare of World War II (see Chapter 2). It is worth emphasizing that technological developments are not sufficient indicators of military revolutions, although weapons developments are almost always central to any revolution that has ever been identified. Military revolutions are also based on organizational innovation and are grounded in larger economic, social, and political changes that impact on military capabilities.

What are the components of the current RMA? Advocates of this concept point to the following:

- A decrease in the relationship between distance and accuracy, made possible by modern electronics. Precision-guided munitions are now capable of hitting targets over long distances with a high probability of success (though not as high as is often advertised by weapons manufacturers and governments);

- The increased use of remotely operated weapons systems, such as unpiloted aerial vehicles (UAVs, often called **drones**), and increased research into military **robotics** and artificial intelligence;

- The development of stealth technology, which renders some weapons systems extremely hard to detect by conventional radars;

- An increase in the capability to conduct surveillance and reconnaissance over the battlefield through the employment of remotely piloted vehicles, satellites, and signal-intelligence equipment;

- An increase in the capacity to store, analyze, and disseminate information in real time (no time delay) through communications and battle management systems, reducing the "fog of war";

- An increased capacity to fight at night and in all weather conditions with minimal degradation of effectiveness;

- An increased ability to engage in offensive information warfare to disrupt the opponent's military and civilian communications and thus influence the political and psychological dimensions of the conflict;

- The increased use of space-based surveillance, navigation, and communications systems;

- The development of doctrine and training and leadership skills assisted by realistic simulations;

- The potential to reduce civilian casualties and *collateral damage* associated with the use of military force.

Developing technologies also promise new methods of conducting information warfare, and managing the public relations and imagery of wars and interventions. In this sense, future wars will take place not only between combatants and their weapons systems, but also in the arena of public perception and opinion, the media, and in information and disinformation efforts mounted by governments, groups, and individuals.[93]

Not surprisingly, the leading proponents of the RMA concept work in the United States.[94] The objective is to ensure that the U.S. armed forces remain pre-eminent on the battlefield in the 21st century—a key element, realists would say, of maintaining U.S. hegemony.[95] Some U.S. allies (including Canada) are expected to try to remain as interoperable as possible with the U.S. military to ensure that their forces can cooperate effectively on the battlefield (a major issue in allied or coalition operations). However, few if any countries have the resources to implement RMA techniques and weapons with the enthusiasm displayed by America. Still, as we discussed in Chapter 6, as weapons technologies continue to diffuse through the international system, more countries are acquiring more modern weapons. They may not always be the most modern ones, but they are far more capable and destructive than previous generations of hardware and software. As a result, we can expect future interstate wars involving industrialized, information-age states to be fought with progressively more sophisticated technologies.

Considerable controversy is associated with the RMA.[96] Some security studies experts doubt that RMAs even exist, disputing the notion of historical discontinuities in the development of warfare.[97] Others point out that it is essentially an American enterprise and is, therefore, motivated more by the U.S. military and its corporate suppliers than by any sense of security requirements. Still others argue that the United States will move so far ahead of the rest of the world (including its key allies) in military capabilities that it will be more disposed toward unilateralism. Why would the U.S. invite other countries to participate in multilateral military efforts when only a few countries can provide significant military contributions? The short answer is that America will still value its allies because coalitions can impart a moral weight, or legitimacy, to U.S. actions. However, if most countries are contributing forces to U.S.–led efforts for purely symbolic purposes, what political influence or voice can these countries expect to have on U.S. policy? There is also controversy over the effectiveness and ethics of many new technologies. For every measure there is a countermeasure, and even the most sophisticated weapons can be defeated using relatively simple techniques. Doubts exist as to whether RMA capabilities will be effective in forest or jungle terrain. During the bombing of Serbia, the Serbian military made wide use of decoys, which proved effective against many high-technology weapons. In other cases, controversies may erupt concerning the use of certain weapons. This has occurred with respect to the alleged health effects of depleted uranium munitions in the Gulf War and in the former Yugoslavia, and in the use of area-denial munitions and cluster bombs, some of which fail to explode and thus represent a threat to civilians.

The extensive use of aerial drone strikes by the Obama administration in its campaign against terrorism has become a point of intense public controversy. The use of drones (alongside conventional airstrikes and cruise missile attacks) to target terrorist operatives began in 2002. Originally designed for reconnaissance roles, many drone variants are now equipped with missiles, and are being used by the U.S. Air Force and CIA as a preferred method of attack against targets in Afghanistan, Pakistan, Yemen, and Somalia. Drones are a quintessential RMA technology, incorporating the latest ICT revolution developments in networked communications, aerial and space-based surveillance, intelligence, and precision-guided munitions, enabling human operators at U.S. military bases around the world to conduct attacks against targets in distant countries.[98] While approximately 30 countries possess drone technology, the U.S. is by far the most frequent user: between 2002 and early 2013, the U.S.

Another revolution in military affairs? U.S. Air Force MQ-9 Reaper unmanned hunter killer weapon system. The ethical implications of using drones are being hotly debated. (© US Air Force Photo/Alamy)

conducted approximately 425 drone strikes in Pakistan, Yemen, and Somalia alone.[99] The use of drones, as well as conventional airstrikes, in these countries has attracted widespread international criticism and condemnation. Despite the ability of drones to launch missiles at specific targets such as buildings and vehicles, drone strikes have killed a large number of civilians. While precise data on deaths is notoriously difficult to gather and verify, the Bureau of Investigative Journalism estimates that by early 2013, U.S. drone strikes had killed between 473 and 893 civilians in Pakistan, 72 to178 in Yemen, and 11 to 57 in Somalia.[100] These deaths have provoked intense anti-American sentiment, especially in Pakistan, where 74 percent of Pakistanis surveyed to the U.S. as an "enemy" in 2012.[101] Drone strikes have also been used in the territories of countries with which the U.S. is not at war, raising questions about the violation of state sovereignty. The killing of terrorist suspects using drone strikes has also drawn criticism for being a campaign of targeted assassinations or extrajudicial executions disconnected from any due process of law. The Obama administration defends the use of drones, citing the legality of using force in self-defence against al-Qaeda and related organizations as a last resort. Nevertheless, in 2013 a debate was underway in the U.S. over the appropriate level of legal or Congressional oversight in drone strike decisions made by the White House or the Pentagon. In February 2013, the UN announced a formal investigation into the legality and casualties of drone strikes, although the investigation will be limited to a specific set of strike incidents.[102]

Ultimately, some question the relevance of the RMA in an era where major war may be increasingly rare or even obsolete.[103] RMA capabilities will not enhance the ability of military forces to conduct peacekeeping missions or low-intensity conflicts, which are precisely the kind of operations militaries have been most frequently asked to perform. As Nigel Aylwin-Foster observed, "The US Army has developed over time a singular focus on conventional warfare, of a particularly swift and violent style, which left it ill-suited to the kind of operation it encountered as soon as conventional warfare ceased to be the primary focus in [Iraq]."[104] In Iraq and Afghanistan, "theory has clashed with reality" and forced the U.S. military to focus more on counterinsurgency, stability, and peace support operations.[105]

This last point raises the question of whether the RMA is an effort to prepare for the wrong kind of war, and therefore we should not pay an undue amount of attention to it. The vast majority of recent and current wars are fought not with the high-technology weapons and techniques of the 21st century but with the low-technology weapons and techniques of the 20th. As we discussed in Chapter 6, almost all these wars have been fought between communal groups at the substate level. The character of war in the future is therefore likely to be bifurcated between two styles. First, wars or interventions involving advanced industrialized states will feature modern weapons systems, highly trained professional personnel, and the organizational techniques characteristic of information-age societies. Second, other wars (likely far more numerous) will feature armed groups using light weapons and the techniques of 20th-century warfare or insurgency conflicts. The war in the former Yugoslavia and the civil war in Syria are examples of this kind of warfare. Interventions to stop such wars, or efforts to use peacekeeping forces to control them, will demand a capacity to meet this kind of combatant when the high-technology innovations of the RMA will be of little, or marginal, utility.

CONCLUSIONS

Where will the information age and developments in ICT take us? Innovation is very difficult to predict. New discoveries may open up completely new areas of human endeavour, much as the development of the computer has. The question for observers of global politics is how these innovations will affect the interaction of states, international organizations, MNCs, transnational political and cultural groups, and individuals. As we have seen, the impact up to now has been profound. The majority consensus is probably that the information age will accelerate the erosion of the state and enhance global interdependence. Perhaps a new era of global communication promises improved international understanding and the establishment of new patterns of human interaction across state boundaries. However, the information age may also enhance the power of some states (and corporations) in the international system and serve to make us all more vulnerable in varying ways. The pervasiveness of certain cultures and perspectives on computer networks and in the global media may lead to a cultural backlash against transnational communication. We must not forget that many of the people on this planet are essentially untouched by the information age. What does it promise these people? The information age may be a force of convergence for many in the international system, but it is also a force of divergence, not unlike many past revolutions in human history.

Endnotes

1. Quoted in C.W. Kegley Jr. and E.R. Wittkopf, *World Politics: Trend and Transformation*, 5th ed. (New York: St. Martin's Press, 1995), 554.
2. Geneva Declaration of Principles, World Summit on the Information Society, WSIS-03/GENEVA/DOC/4-E (December 12, 2003), 1.
3. See J. Goldstein, *Long Cycles: Prosperity and War in the Modern Age* (New Haven: Yale University Press, 1988); and C. Freeman, "Diffusion, the Spread of New Technology to Firms, Sectors, and Nations," in A. Heertje, ed., *Innovation, Technology, and Finance* (New York: Basil Blackwell, 1988), 38–70.
4. A. Toffler, *The Third Wave* (New York: Morrow, 1980).
5. S. Nora and A. Minc, *The Computerization of Society* (Cambridge, MA: MIT Press, 1980), 3.

6. W.J. Drake and R.F. Jørgensen, *Human Rights in the Global Information Society* (Cambridge, MA: The MIT Press, 2006), 1. See also C. May, *The Information Society: A Skeptical View* (Malden, MA: Blackwell, 2002).

7. See *Report on the World Summit on the Information Society: Stocktaking 2012* (Geneva: International Telecommunications Union, 2012), http://www.itu.int/wsis/stocktaking/docs/reports/S-POL-WSIS.REP-2012-PDF-E.pdf (accessed February 5, 2013).

8. For a good discussion on the different interpretations of the information age, and how this relates to environmental reform, see A. Mol, *Environmental Reform in the Information Age: The Contours of Informational Governance* (Cambridge University Press, 2008).

9. International Telecommunications Union, "Key Global Telecom Indicators for the World Telecommunications Service Sector," http://www.itu.int/ITU-D/ict/statistics/at_glance/KeyTelecom99.html (accessed May 19, 2008). The ITU stopped publishing data on PC use in 2005. Subsequent estimates are drawn from private research firm reports and summarized by the Worldometers website at http://www.worldometers.info/computers/ (accessed February 5, 2013).

10. M. Castels and L. D'Andrea Tyson, "High Technology Choices Ahead: Restructuring Interdependence," in J. Sewell and S. Tucker, eds., *Growth, Exports, and Jobs in a Changing World* (New Brunswick, NJ: Transaction Press, 1988), 57.

11. United Nations Development Programme, *Human Development Report 2001* (Oxford: Oxford University Press, 2001), 27.

12. J. Aronson, "Global Networks and Their Impact," in J.N. Rosenau and J.P. Singh, eds., *Information Technologies and Global Politics: The Changing Scope of Power and Governance* (Albany, NY: State University of New York Press, 2002), 39.

13. See S. Doutta and B. Bilbao-Osorio, eds., *The Global Information Technology Report 2012: Living in a Hyperconnected World* (Geneva: World Economic Forum, 2012).

14. See I. de Sola Pool, in E.M. Noam, ed., *Technologies without Boundaries: On Telecommunications in a Global Age* (Cambridge, MA: Harvard University Press, 1990).

15. International Telecommunications Union, "Key Global Telecom Indicators for the World Telecommunications Service Sector," http://www.itu.int/ITU-D/ict/statistics/at_glance/KeyTelecom99.html (accessed May 19, 2008); and "International Call Traffic Growth Slows as Skype's Volumes Soar," TeleGeography press release, January 9, 2012, http://www.telegeography.com/press/press-releases/2012/01/09/international-call-traffic-growth-slows-as-skypes-volumes-soar/index.html (accessed February 5, 2013).

16. A. Lightman and W. Rojas, *Brave New Unwired World: The Digital Big Bang and the Infinite Internet* (New York, John Wiley and Sons, 2002), 9.

17. See "Internet 2012 in Numbers," *Royal Pingdom Tech Blog*, January 16, 2013, http://royal.pingdom.com/2013/01/16/internet-2012-in-numbers/ (accessed February 5, 2013); S. Radicati and Q. Hoang, "E-mail Statistics Report, 2012–2016" (Palo Alto: The Radicati Group, 2012), http://www.radicati.com/wp/wp-content/uploads/2012/04/Email-Statistics-Report-2012-2016-Executive-Summary.pdf (accessed February 5, 2013); and H. Kelly, "OMG, the Text Message Turns 20. But Has SMS Peaked?" CNN Tech, December 3, 2012, http://www.cnn.com/2012/12/03/tech/mobile/sms-text-message-20 (accessed February 5, 2013).

18. See *Global Economic Prospects and the Developing Countries* (Washington, DC: World Bank, 1992); and *Human Development Report 1999* (New York: United Nations, 2000).

19. International Telecommunications Union, *Measuring the Information Society 2012: Executive Summary.* (Geneva: ITU, 2012), 1.

20. See "Key Statistical Highlights: ITU Data Release June 2012," ITU World Telecommunications/ICT indicators Database (Geneva: ITU, 2012).

21. International Telecommunications Union, *Measuring the Information Society 2012.* (Geneva: ITU, 2012), 3

22. See Netcraft Ltd. "February 2013 Web Server Survey," http://news.netcraft.com/archives/2013/02/01/february-2013-web-server-survey.html (accessed February 5, 2013).

23. A. Kluth, "Nomads at Last," *The Economist* 387, no. 8575 (April 12, 2008), 3–5.

24. See "The World on Your Desktop," *The Economist* 384, no. 8545 (September 8, 2007), 19.

25. See R. Faris and N. Villeneuve, "Measuring Global Internet Filtering," in R. Diebert, et al., eds., *Access Denied: The Practice and Policy of Global Internet Filtering* (Cambridge, MA: The MIT Press, 2008), 5. See also R. Diebert, J. Palfrey, R. Rohozinski, and J. Zittrain, eds., *Access Controlled: The Shaping of Power, Rights, and Rule in Cyberspace* (Cambridge, MA: MIT Press, 2010).

26. See "About," *Wikileaks*, http://www.wikileaks.ch/About.html (accessed February 7, 2013).

27. G.J. Walters, *Human Rights in an Information Age: A Philosophical Analysis* (Toronto: University of Toronto Press, 2001), 5.

28. J. Zysman and A. Newman, "Frameworks for Understanding the Political Economy of the Digital Era," in J. Zysman and A. Newman, eds., *How Revolutionary Was the Digital Revolution?* (Stanford, CA: Stanford University Press, 2006), 4.

29. J. Aronson, "Global Networks and Their Impact," in J.N. Rosenau and J.P. Singh, eds., *Information Technologies and Global Politics: The Changing Scope of Power and Governance* (Albany, NY: State University of New York Press, 2002), 39.

30. See P. Pritchett, *The Employee Handbook of New Work Habits for a Radically Changing World* (Dallas: Pritchett and Associates, 1996), 4.

31. Farnsworth et al., 27.

32. P. Drucker, *Post-Capitalist Society* (New York: Harper Business, 1993), 40.

33. Dominique Foray and Bengt-Ålce Lundvall, "The Knowledge-Based Economy: From the Economics of Knowledge to the Learning Economy," *Employment and Growth in the Knowledge-Based Economy*, OECD Documents (Paris: Organization for Economic Cooperation and Development, 1996), 16.

34. T. Friedman, *The World Is Flat* (New York: Farrar, Straus and Giroux, 2006).

35. M.J. Mazaar, "Introduction: Information Technology and World Politics: The Growing Connection," in M J. Mazaar, ed., *Information Technology in World Politics* (New York: Palgrave MacMillan, 2002), 2.

36. See S. Dutta and I. Mia, eds., *The Global Information Technology Report 2006–2007*, ix.

37. See J. Fredette, et al., "The Promise and Peril of a Hyperconnectivity for Organizations and Societies," in S. Doutta and B. Bilbao-Osorio, eds., *The Global Information Technology Report 2012*, 113–14.

38. E.B. Kapstein, "Workers and the World Economy," *Foreign Affairs* 75 (May/June 1996), 16.

39. C. May, *The Information Society: A Skeptical View* (Malden, MA: Blackwell, 2002).

40. See A. Tonnelson, *The Race to the Bottom* (Boulder, CO: Westview Press, 2000).

41. See E. Brousseau and N. Curien, "Internet Economics, Digital Economics," in E. Brousseau and N. Curien, eds., *Internet and Digital Economics: Principles, Methods and Applications* (Cambridge: Cambridge University Press, 2007), 1–56.

42. E.G. Carayannis and C.M. Sipp, *E-Development toward the Knowledge Economy: Leveraging Technology, Innovation and Entrepreneurship for "Smart" Development* (New York: Palgrave MacMillan, 2007), 4.

43. See J. James, *Bridging the Global Digital Divide* (Chattenham, UK: Edward Elgar, 2003), x.

44. International Telecommunications Union, *Measuring the Information Society 2012: Executive Summary* (Geneva: ITU, 2012), 3.

45. See International Telecommunications Union, "Key Global Telecom Indicators for the World Telecommunication Service Sector," http://www.itu.int/ITU-D/ict/statistics/at_glance/KeyTelecom.html (accessed February 9, 2013).

46. "Connect Africa Summit Outcomes Report," http://www.itu.int/ITU-D/connect/africa/2007/summit/pdf/finalreport.pdf (accessed July 1, 2013), 3.

47. J. Salomon and A. Lebeau, *Mirages of Development: Science and Technology for the Third Worlds* (Boulder CO; London: Lynne Rienner, 1993), 86. See also Paul Kennedy's *Preparing for the Twentieth Century* (New York: Random House, 1993).

48. A.P. D'Costa, "Introduction: Charting a New Development Trajectory?" in A.P. D'Costa, ed., *The New Economy in Development: ICT Challenges and Opportunities* (New York: Palgrave Macmillan, 2006), 10.

49. M. Castells, *The Information Age, Volume 1: The Rise of the Network Society* (Oxford: Blackwell, 1996), 147.

50. See M. Kagami, M. Tsuji, and E. Giovannetti, eds., *Information Technology Policy and the Digital Divide: Lessons for Developing Countries* (Cheltenham, UK: Edward Elgar, 2004).

51. See S. Roy, *Globalisation, ICT and Developing Nations: Challenges in the Information Age* (New Delhi: Sage Publications, 2005).

52. A. Lightman and W. Rojas, *Brave New Unwired World*, xii.

53. United Nations Development Programme, *Human Development Report*, 30.

54. J. Rosenau, *Turbulence in World Politics* (Princeton: Princeton University Press, 1990), 17.

55. T. Flew, *Understanding Global Media* (New York: Palgrave Macmillan, 2007), 1–3.

56. Global Initiative for Inclusive Information and Communication Technologies, *Making Television Accessible* (Geneva: ITU, 2011), I, http://www.itu.int/ITU-D/sis/PwDs/Documents/ITU-G3ict%20Making_TV_Accessible_Report_November_2011.pdf (accessed February 9, 2013).

57. J. Habermas, *Between Facts and Norms: Contributions to a Discourse Theory of Law and Democracy* (Cambridge, UK: Polity Press and Blackwell Publishers, 1996), 514.

58. J. Rosenau, *Turbulence in World Politics: A Theory of Change and Continuity* (Princeton, NJ: Princeton University Press, 1990), 339–43.

59. For a discussion of CNN's development, see D. Flournoy, "Coverage, Competition, and Credibility: The CNN International Standard," in T. Silvia, ed., *Global News: Perspectives on the Information Age* (Ames, IA: Iowa State University Press, 2001), 15–44.

60. See N. Miladi, "Mapping the Al-Jazeera Phenomenon," in D.K. Thussu and D. Freedman, eds., *War and the Media: Reporting Conflict 24/7* (London: Sage Publications, 2003), 149–60.

61. P. Seib, ed., *New Media and the New Middle East* (New York: Palgrave, 2007), xiii.

62. Quoted in M. Zayani, "Introduction: Al-Jazeera and the Vicissitudes of the New Arab Mediascape," in M. Zayani, ed., *The Al-Jazeera Phenomenon: Critical Perspectives on the New Arab Media* (Boulder, CO: Paradigm, 2005), 33.

63. M. Fandy, *(Un)Civil War of Words: Media and Politics in the Arab World* (Westport, CT: Praeger, 2007), 139, 142.

64. D. Sabbagh, "Al-Jazeera's Political Independence Questioned amid Qatar Intervention," *The Guardian*, September 39, 2012, http://www.guardian.co.uk/media/2012/sep/30/al-jazeera-independence-questioned-qatar (accessed February 10, 2013).

65. N. Sakr, *Arab Media and Political Renewal: Community, Legitimacy and Public Life* (London: I.B. Tauris, 2007), 6.

66. T. Magder, "Watching What We Say: Global Communication in a Time of Fear," in Thissu and Freedman, "War and the Media," 33.

67. See D.K. Thissu and D. Freedman, "Introduction," in Thissu and Freedman, "War and the Media," 7.

68. See L. Artz, "The Corporate Model from National to Transnational," in L. Artz and Y.R. Kamalipour, eds., *The Media Globe: Trends in International Mass Media* (Lanham, MD: Rowman and Littlefield, 2007), 141–61.

69. C. Sparks, *Globalization, Development, and the Mass Media* (London: Sage Publications, 2007), 189.

70. D.B. Miller, *Media Pressure on Foreign Policy: The Evolving Theoretical Framework* (New York: Palgrave Macmillan, 2007), 9.

71. S. Hjarvard, "News Media and the Globalization of the Public Sphere," in S. Hjarvard, ed., *News in a Globalized Society* (Gothenburg, SE: Nordicom, 2001), 18.

72. See J. Dean, J.W. Anderson, and G. Lovink, eds., *Reformatting Politics: Information Technology and Global Civil Society* (New York: Routledge, 2006).

73. A. Ramirez, "Dial Direct to Moscow and Beyond," *The New York Times*, May 20, 1992, D1.

74. Some argue that the media in advanced capitalist states are just as manipulative and that there is a connection between the owners of the media and pro–status quo forces in government. The most famous proponent of this view is Noam Chomsky; see, for example, *Media Control: The Spectacular Achievements of Propaganda* (New York: Seven Stories Press, 1997).

75. L. Diamond, "Liberation Technology," *Journal of Democracy* 213 (July 2010), 69–83.

76. D. Khoury, et al., "People's Power: The Arab World in Revolt," *Perspectives*, Special Issue 2 (May 2011), 83.

77. D.D. Kirkpatrick and D.E. Sanger, "A Tunisian-Egyptian Link That Shook Arab History," *The New York Times*, February 13, 2011, http://www.nytimes.com/2011/02/14/world/middleeast/14egypt-tunisia-protests.html (accessed February 10, 2013).

78. C. Arthur, "Google and Twitter Launch Service Enabling Egyptians to Tweet by Phone," *The Guardian*, February 1, 2011, http://www.guardian.co.uk/technology/2011/feb/01/google-twitter-egypt/print. (accessed February 10, 2013).

79. See E. Mekay, "One Libyan Battle is Fought in Social Media and News Media," *The New York Times*, February 1, 2011, http://www.nytimes.com/2011/02/24/world/middleeast/24iht-m24libya.html (accessed February 10, 2013); and M. O'Neill, "How YouTube is Aiding the Libyan Revolution," *Social Times*, February 26, 2011, http://socialtimes.com/youtube-libyan-revolution_b39678 (accessed February 10, 2013).

80. D. Rosenberg, "Syria Adopts Two-Faced Strategy with Social Media," *The Jerusalem Post*, May 23, 2011, http://www.jpost.com/MiddleEast/Article.aspx?id=221847 (accessed February 10, 2013).

81. M. Gladwell, "Small Change: Why the Revolution Will Not Be Tweeted," *The New Yorker*, October 4, 2010, http://www.newyorker.com/reporting/2010/10/04/101004fa_fact_gladwell (accessed February 10, 2013).

82. Diamond, "Liberation Technology," 70.

83. C. Shirky, "The Political Power of Social Media," *Foreign Affairs* 90, 1 (January/February 2011), 2.

84. E. Morozov, "Iran: Downside to the 'Twitter Revolution,'" *Dissent* 56, 4 (Fall 2009), 10–14.

85. J. Preston, "Seeking to Disrupt Protestors, Syria Cracks Down on Social Media," *The New York Times*, May 22, 2011, http://www.nytimes.com/2011/05/23/world/middleeast/23facebook.html?_r=3&. (accessed February 10, 2011).

86. I. Vincent, "Rebel Dispatches Find Home on Net," *The Globe and Mail*, June 11, 1996, A1.

87. J. Nye Jr. and W. Owens, "America's Information Edge," *Foreign Affairs* 75 (March/April 1996), 20.

88. B. Gates, *The Road Ahead*, 2nd ed. (London: Penguin Books, 1995), 9.

89. R. Volti, *Society and Technological Change*, 2nd ed. (New York: St. Martin's Press, 1992), 235.

90. See D.K. Thussu, "Mapping Global Media Flow and Contra-Flow," in D.K. Thussu, ed., *Media on the Move: Global Flow and Contra-Flow* (London: Routledge, 2007), 11–32.

91. "Star Wars," *The Economist*, March 22, 1997, 15.

92. A. Toffler and H. Toffler, *War and Anti-War: Survival at the Dawn of the 21st Century* (Boston: Little, Brown and Company, 1993), 10–11. See also R. Preston and S. Wise, *Men in Arms: A History of Warfare and Its Interrelationships with Western Society*, 4th ed. (New York: Holt, Rinehart, and Winston, 1979).

93. See Y.R. Kamalipour and N. Snow, eds., *War, Media, and Propaganda: A Global Perspective* (Lanham, MD: Rowman and Littlefield, 2004); D. Miller, ed., *Tell Me Lies: Propaganda and Media Distortion in the Attack on Iraq* (London: Pluto, 2004); and M. Ignatieff, *Virtual War* (Toronto: Penguin Books of Canada, 2000).

94. See R.O. Hundley, *Past Revolutions, Future Transformations: What Can the History of Revolutions in Military Affairs Tell Us about Transforming the U.S. Military?* (Santa Monica, CA: Rand, 1999).

95. For a cautious note, see B.R. Posen, "Command of the Commons: The Military Foundations of U.S. Hegemony," *International Security* 28 (Summer 2003), 5–47.

96. For a discussion of the many issues surrounding the RMA, see B. Schreer and E. Whitlock, eds., *Divergent Perspectives on Military Transformation* (Berlin: Stiftung Wissenschaft und Politik, 2005), 30–36; C.S. Gray, *Strategy for Chaos* (London: Frank Cass, 2002); and T. Gongora and H. von Riekhoff, eds., *Toward a Revolution in Military Affairs? Defence and Security at the Dawn of the Twenty-First Century* (Westport, CT: Greenwood Press, 2000).

97. See "United States' Drone Wars: Strategic Geography 2012," in *Strategic Survey 2012: The Annual Review of World Affairs* (London: Routledge and IISS, 2012), vii.

98. See "Covert Drone War," The Bureau of Investigative Journalism, http://www.thebureauinvestigates.com/category/projects/drone-data/ (accessed February 11, 2013).

99. See "Covert Drone War," Bureau of Investigative Journalism, http://www.thebureauinvestigates.com/category/projects/drone-data/ (accessed February 11, 2013).

100. P.J. Crowley, "The Cost of Obama's Secret Drone War," *BBC World Service*, February 8, 2013, http://www.bbc.co.uk/news/world-us-canada-21389200 (accessed February 11, 2013).

101. O. Bowcott, "UN to Examine UK and US Drone Strikes," *The Guardian*, January 24, 2013, http://www.guardian.co.uk/world/2013/jan/24/un-examine-uk-afghanistan-drone-strikes (accessed February 11, 2013).

102. See P.L. Ritcheson, "The Future of Military Affairs: Revolution or Evolution?" *Strategic Review* 24 (Spring 1996), 31–40.

103. M. Mandelbaum, "Is Major War Obsolete?" *Survival* (Winter 1998/99), 20–38.

104. N. Aylwin-Foster, "Changing the Army for Counterinsurgency Operations," *Military Review*, November/December 2005), 9.

105. *The Military Balance 2007* (London: International Institute for Strategic Studies, 2007), 15.

New Directions in Theory and Practice

Pessimism over the future of the world comes from a confusion between civilization and security. In the immediate future there will be less security than in the immediate past, less stability. But, on the whole, the great ages have been unstable ages.

—A. North Whitehead[1]

Society wills and acts collectively, as the output of systems (including law-making systems) which aggregate the willing and acting of individual human beings. But the intervention of those systems creates a new mind-world, a new form of human reality, a new form of human world. The public mind is society's private mind. The public mind of international society is the private mind of the human species.

—Philip Allott[2]

To all other peoples and governments who are watching today, from the grandest capitals to the small village where my father was born: know that America is a friend of each nation and every man, woman and child who seeks a future of peace and dignity, and we are ready to lead once more.

—Barack Hussein Obama[3]

INTRODUCTION: THE FUTURE OF GLOBAL POLITICS

Predicting the future is a perilous enterprise. As Nicholas Rescher has argued, "The three most salient facts about the future are that it does not (yet) exist, that it unavoidably will, and that we do—and can—have only very incomplete information about its nature, let alone achieve control of it."[4] Nevertheless, prediction is a vitally important element of global politics. For example, climate change is already one of the dominant issues of the early 21st century, and the debate over appropriate mitigation and adaptation strategies is based on scientific predictions of the future impact of increasing greenhouse gas emissions and projections of trends in observable phenomena such as melting ice sheets, rising sea levels, and migrating tree species.

Efforts to prevent armed conflict through early intervention depend on predictions of the imminent outbreak of violence, based on the observation of key indicators such as arms races, propaganda campaigns and inflammatory rhetoric, and lower-level violence. Major economic decisions are made by states, corporations, and investors based on predictions of key indicators such as inflation, interest rates, and commodity prices. Naturally, being able to anticipate future events or conditions allows us to prepare for those eventualities, reduce risks, or take steps to prevent certain events from happening. As a result, despite the difficulties inherent in prediction, huge investments are made by governments, armed forces, corporations, investors, and scholars to devise the analytical equivalent of a crystal ball that will enable them to see into the future, even if the vision is a bit cloudy.

When predictions are made about the future of global politics, they are most often based on trends or identifiable patterns in the behaviour of actors or phenomena. While identifying such trends and projecting them into the future is the most important tool of prediction, identifiable trends can change. In the 1980s, economic trends led some analysts to suggest that Japan would supplant the United States as the world's largest economy, with political and military conflict between the two a distinct possibility.[5] However, Japanese economic growth rates stagnated in the 1990s, undercutting the basis for both predictions. In addition, unanticipated events (such as the fall of the Soviet Union, the September 11, 2001, terrorist attacks on the U.S., or the Arab Spring uprisings) can alter the course of world affairs and confound predictions made under a very different set of circumstances. Our ability to predict must therefore be constantly questioned, and our predictions must be made with commensurate humility. David Staley suggests we should view the future in the same way we view the past, not through the prism of scientific prediction and certainty but through the historical lens of interpretation and context.[6]

We begin this chapter by exploring the future relevance of the issues raised in Part One of the book. How will IR (international relations) theory evolve in the future, and what will be the forces driving theoretical innovation? What new ideas might emerge that will help us understand the world in which we live? We then turn to the power politics theme that was so central to our overview of major events and transitions in history. Though we are clearly in a new era, old questions remain: What distribution of power is emerging in our world? What is the significance of the rise of China? Is a new Cold War developing between the West and a resurgent Russia? And what will be the future of American power in the world, and the consequences for its allies, such as Canada? In Part Two of the book, we examined the challenges of international security, conflict management, globalization, and human rights. While we explored the possible origins of future wars throughout the text, is it possible that future wars will occur between "civilizations" rather than between states? In the age of globalization, what are the key issues facing the future of the global economy? In the realm of international organizations and international law, as we shall see, the future will present many new challenges to these instruments of global governance, dialogue, and cooperation. In Part Three, we examined the environment, population and health issues, and the information age. Can multilateralism succeed in meeting these challenges?

Three things seem certain at this point. First, these issues are not new. They have always been with us in some form and always will be, barring a cataclysmic event such as a global epidemic, a large-scale nuclear war, or a catastrophic meteor impact. Even if the state system as we know it were to crumble, we would still debate the distribution of power, the merits of trade, the risks and benefits of cooperation, the causes of friction between peoples and societies, the prospects for equality and sustainable development, and other ageless themes. Second, we tend to interpret these issues through our embedded belief systems, lived experiences, and intellectual theories and frameworks (whether that entails a structural realist, liberalist, critical theory, or other perspective). Denying this is futile, but being imprisoned by it is not necessary either. Students should strive to apply other ways of thinking about global issues, even those that evoke intellectual discomfort, some of which we hope you have acquired through this textbook. Third, although there will be many developments in global politics that are successfully anticipated and many others that we fail to predict, we can be certain that the dynamic relationship between these events and our responses will continue, as long as people are genuinely interested in not only understanding the world but also forging a new one.

THE FUTURE OF THEORY

As this text has illustrated, meta-theoretical discourse—debate about theory—is important. Theory provides us with a framework for looking at the world, with structures for organizing and prioritizing the bewildering array of issues and events that constitute global politics. Although a claim could be made that certain perspectives (such as realism and liberalism) have had their moments of dominance in the field, there has never been a universally accepted theoretical framework describing the nature and dynamics of global politics. This is why so much disagreement exists on the issues covered in this book. We have introduced several contending perspectives, such as idealism, realism, liberalism, Marxism, feminism, and constructivism, among others. However, while these theories offer very different ways of looking at the world, there is considerable overlap between many of these theories on many issues. For example, one can be a realist with Marxist leanings; in fact, some interpretations of the foundational work of E.H. Carr suggest this was his persuasion.[7] One can be a structural realist based in a world systems theory of global politics, as the Argentinean author Carlos Escude's idea of peripheral realist foreign policy suggests.[8] While most feminists would reject a realist interpretation of events, many are quite willing to accept a liberal or Marxist one.[9] Regime theory is fairly strongly rooted in liberal suppositions about cooperation under conditions of self-interest, but there have been efforts to critically analyze the normative and socially constructed aspects of regimes.[10] Geopolitical theory can be analyzed from an environmentalist perspective.[11] Practical foreign policy questions, such as the wisdom of humanitarian intervention, are being revisited by philosophers of different persuasions.[12] Distinctions between theoretical perspectives are not hard boundaries, and theoretical innovation and flexibility is, arguably, much more common today than ever.

It may make more sense to speak of an epistemological division in the discipline, predicated on thinking about the nature of knowledge itself, rather than a division based on essentialist ideologies or theoretical perspectives. In other words, debates between positivists and postpositivists might have as much to tell us as disputes between the realists, liberals, and critical theorists.[13] Methodological issues are still very much part of the study of global politics. The discipline has been through several periods of self-examination in the past, pushing methodology in new directions. The study of global politics has moved from a historical discipline based on the analysis of leaders and military strategy to one fixated on the Cold War and game theory constructions. It has moved from a behaviouralist period, where quantification of data and rational choice assumptions regarding human nature led to efforts to model human behaviour at the international level, to a discipline concerned with the validity of its own prevalent assumptions and their impact upon the real world. Social constructivism, as developed by Alexander Wendt and others, is often seen as an effort to bridge the divide between rationalist approaches (neorealism, neoliberalism) and "reflectivist" approaches (postmodernism, some feminist theory, normative theory, and historical sociology).[14] While social constructivism certainly rose in prominence during the 1990s and 2000s, we suggest that the growing urgency around issues such as terrorism, climate change, social injustice, and unrest and revolution will enhance the theoretical attention paid to the role of human agency and belief systems in global politics.

While the split between positivists and postpositivists is still defining the work of many scholars in the field, it can be argued that both sides of this divide are more willing to listen to the other, and this is a good thing. On the one hand, the need for empirical data gathering is undeniable, and testing various hypotheses in the laboratory of distant and recent history gives us clues about patterns of behaviour, though we should always be cautious about using this to predict the future. On the other hand, the values and aspirations that guide the actors in global politics did not emerge from a vacuum; they are the product of social-norm construction and the ebb and flow of events, which are interpreted according to the intellectual prisms (some might say "prisons") from which we see the world. Finally, there is a place for **normative theory** in global politics, defined by Chris Brown as "that body of work which addresses the moral dimensions of international relations and the wider questions of meaning and interpretation generated by the discipline ... the ethical nature of the relations between communities/states, whether [it is] focused on violence and war, or the new(er) agenda, which mixes these traditional concerns with the modern demand for international distributive justice."[15] Ethics are the topic of legitimate study in global politics, even among those who favour Machiavelli over Kant. It is our hope that future scholars in the discipline will approach global politics with a favourable attitude toward the many possibilities of synthesis and cross-pollination this vast field has undergone over the past 100 years.

In the future we can expect even greater diversity among students and scholars of global politics, as the interdisciplinary nature of the field continues to expand and sophisticated contributions increase from analysts around the world. Of course, to some degree this is already the case. Global politics as a discipline is itself globalizing. Some might argue that we have no right to call global politics a discipline, because of the breadth and scope of the subject matter, but we respectfully disagree. The study of the big issues facing us all cannot be properly achieved without an interdisciplinary approach that offers a large forum for the voices and concerns that must be heard. Theories of IR are richer because of past examples of such dialogue: dependency theory originated in Latin America, many alternative development models were conceptualized in Asia and Africa, and political economy and ecofeminist contributions from India reflected experiences in South Asia. In the future, we can expect more ideas and theoretical innovations to spread through the discipline, as exposure to different traditions and experiences from previously unheard sources generate new debates and new understandings. New explorations of IR theory drawing on Asian perspectives are underway.[16] The increased dialogue between postcolonial theory and IR promises a reshaping of our understanding of many enduring concepts.[17] It is our hope that the decline in what Turan Kayaoglu called the *Westphalian Eurocentrism* of the discipline will not only permit other intellectual traditions to become part of traditional dialogues and debates but also expose Western scholarship to alternative views.[18] Conferences in the southern hemisphere, Internet communications, and a wider audience of the curious and dedicated intellects from around the Earth will further enrich the discipline in the years to come, unless we revert to fixed ideological lines and the suppression of alternative views, as was seen on both sides at various times during the Cold War.

Another reason we expect IR theory to become more dynamic is because more people than ever are aware of its importance. While there will always be limitations on the number of specialists in the discipline—for example, there are only so many jobs at universities and think tanks for professionals to pursue such questions as part of their occupations— interest is widespread, and many people engaged in other academic disciplines and professions now realize that global politics is a vital component of self- and collective identification, global governance, public health, economic prosperity and marginalization, environmental management, social policy, and migration. There is a growing connection between legal scholarship and international relations theory, exploring the nexus between international norms, laws, and institutions.[19] Scholarship in IR has reconnected with the study of philosophy and religion, inspiring a new examination of old influences on the discipline.[20] The relationship between global politics and geography is under re-examination, with Robert Kaplan suggesting that geography still matters, and we all must "recover a sensibility about time and space that has been lost in the jet and information age."[21] Furthermore, continued concern with environmental degradation will engender more theoretical construction on issues of the commons, regime building, and the links between ecology, gender, violence, and cooperation.[22] In short, global politics cannot be ignored. It has become a tired cliché to suggest that for many North Americans September 11 and the Iraq War brought world politics home, but it is certainly the case. Europeans, engaged in their ambitious and controversial project of political integration, are also forging new self-identities in the process. Protest movements and revolutions around the globe, many in areas that we would never have heard of a few decades ago, are spawning fresh insights with their strategies to seek solidarity elsewhere with other transnational actors. Diasporas continue their struggles in their adopted societies, spreading awareness of different cultures and distant conflicts. Indigenous peoples around the world cooperate with each other and their supporters in the ongoing struggle against centuries-old patterns of exclusion, marginalization, and genocide. And, finally, while globalization can be viewed as a force for division and conflict as well as a force for interdependence and cooperation, it remains a subject of dialogue that engages peoples around the world.

While all of this diversification and widespread interest is a positive thing for IR theory, we would also suggest that the traditional questions raised by IR theory are alive and well. There are reliable continuities in global politics, age-old debates to which, it would seem, we are destined to repeatedly return. This text has suggested that we live in a world characterized by two forces: convergence and divergence. The simplistic question is, which is the stronger? The answer, it seems, is neither: the two phenomena seem to exist side by side in the international system. We see convergence in the increasing interdependence between states, in the growth of IGOs (intergovernmental organizations) and NGOs (non-governmental organizations), in the awareness and action devoted to transnational issues such as the environment, and in the increase in contact, travel, and transactions between the peoples of the world. However, we see divergence in conflict between states, in the disintegration of some states, in intrastate wars and separation movements, in the increasing gap between rich and poor, and in the split between the technological haves and have-nots. At this point, identifying a dominant trend is impossible, although it is clear that for some convergence is the reality in their lives, while for others divergence is the more powerful influence. In Canada, we are very privileged in many ways, but we are not immune from these forces. Even as globalization links us to the world of trade, travel, and telecommunications, it stimulates national debates about our economic future, our culture, and public health. The enduring national unity debate is a reminder that we are not immune from the forces of divergence. Nor are we immune from broader conflicts between the United States and its proclaimed enemies. Indeed, the question of American dominance in world affairs is necessarily of primary importance to all states today, but this is nothing new: states were often forced to make a choice of allegiance during the Cold War as well.

The central questions asked by IR theory will continue to frame the debate to come: Is it still reasonable to view the world from a state-centric perspective? Are theories of grand evolutionary changes valid when explaining history, and if so where do they suggest we are heading? What types of subconscious learning processes are at work in the perpetuation of conflict, domination, and resistance? Is the spread of liberal democracy of inherent value, not only in terms of human development and freedom, but also in terms of the promotion of peace? Or is this simply another face on an old process, the structural growth of capital accumulation, accompanied by cultural imperialism? Can we respond effectively to climate change? When will we overcome the historically demonstrable urge toward organized violence? These, and many more, theoretical questions will remain salient to the people of this century.

THE FUTURE DISTRIBUTION OF POWER

In Chapters 2 and 3, we observed that changes in what realists call the distribution of power are an eternal feature of global politics. Historically, the rise and decline of civilizations, societies, states, and empires are accompanied by shifts in the patterns of interaction between these actors. These shifts in patterns of interaction can take a number of forms: threat perceptions might change as some states increase in power and others decline, balances in power will be destabilized, new alliances may form and old ones will weaken or disintegrate, patterns of diplomacy and trade will reflect new markets and new centres of growth and innovation, and some political units will fragment (like the Austro-Hungarian Empire) and others will amalgamate (the 13 American colonies) or be absorbed (Bavaria). Because shifts in the distribution of power can so profoundly alter the shape of global politics and the security and foreign policy strategies of states, trends in relative power distribution are watched very closely. As Richard Little observes in his excellent historical account of the balance-of-power idea, the concept is one of the most enduring theories in international relations literature, and certainly the most widely cited.[23]

However, the balance-of-power concept is far from a historical artifact. The concern over global and regional power balances is a prime example of how an idea grounded in historical observation can have an impact on how contemporary global politics is described and how states should conduct themselves. The balance of power is a central feature of contemporary debates on the future of global politics in general and U.S. foreign policy in particular. At the core of the general debate is whether global politics will retain its unipolar quality (with or without America acting as the hegemon) or whether a multipolar or other form of system is evolving as other countries (such as China) or other regions (such as Europe) rise in both absolute and relative power. At the core of the U.S. foreign policy debate is how American policy might—or might not—have an impact on America's hegemonic status and affect the future of the global balance of power. It is sobering to consider that the debate on the future of U.S. foreign policy is so heavily influenced by a concept that has been in use for over 500 years. The balance-of-power concept is also relevant for the role it plays as a theory of regional power politics in Asia, while the consequences of the Iraq War (which include the weakening of the power of Iraq and domestic political instability) and the civil war in Syria have raised concerns about the future balance of power in the Persian Gulf and the Middle East.[24]

Many observers of global politics have argued that a multipolar system is already emerging. In a striking observation, in 2004 the U.S. government's own National Intelligence Council noted, "The likely emergence of China and India as major new global players—similar to the rise of Germany in the 19th century and the United States in the early 20th century—will transform the geopolitical landscape, with impacts potentially as dramatic as those of the previous two centuries."[25] In a provocative book, Parag Khanna makes the observation that the world is now dominated by three empires: a declining United States, a rising but struggling China, and an increasingly powerful European Union. Khanna argues that "Big is back" in the study of global politics: it is inter-imperial relations that drive global politics, not international or inter-civilizational relations.[26] Fareed Zakaria has argued that global politics is increasingly characterized not by the presumed decline of the West but the "rise of the rest," meaning the non-Western countries. This "post-American world" will usher in not an Asian century but a complex blend of Eastern and Western powers. For Zakaria, U.S. foreign policy in this transformed world must avoid hegemonic pretension and instead work to establish an inclusive multipolar global system.[27] Kishore Mahbubani agrees, arguing, "The West will not lose power. It will have to share power."[28] Meanwhile, Robert Kagan argues that the post–Cold War delusions about the end of ideological conflict and the triumph of liberal democracy have been dashed. We now live in a world more analogous to the 19th century, a world divided between democratic states and autocratic states, with a single power (the United States) that is most influential but not dominant.[29] Michael Mazarr predicts a world of intensifying "entangled rivalry" and competition, driven by "hundreds of powerful agents, each with goals, interests, missions, and values they are aiming to promote, preserve and protect."[30] While all of these views speak to the existence of a multipolar world, some analysts have argued that we live in neither a unipolar nor a multipolar system: for example, Richard Haas suggests that contemporary global politics is characterized by so many centres of power (Haas identifies six major state powers as well as numerous regional powers, organizations, companies, media outlets, and NGOs) that it is functionally "nonpolar."[31]

A common theme in the contemporary literature on the balance of power is the rise of China. The Chinese economy is now the second largest in the world, having surpassed Italy in 2000, France in 2002, the United Kingdom in 2006, Germany in 2007, and Japan in 2010. Since 1978, China's economy has grown by an average of 10 percent per year, prompting the U.S. National Intelligence Council to predict that China will become the world's largest economy "a few years before 2030."[32] China is a major financial and manufacturing centre, has massive foreign reserves (exceeding three trillion U.S. dollars in 2012), and is a growing diplomatic and economic presence in Africa, Latin America, and the Middle East. China's emergence has enormous significance for global politics. The famous classical realist author Hans Morgenthau argued that the "policy of the status quo aims at the maintenance of the distribution of power as it exists at a particular moment in history."[33] The rise of China certainly threatens the status quo and the maintenance of the international balance of power and U.S. pre-eminence that has existed since the end of World War Two. How will America react? The Obama administration announced a "pivot to Asia" in 2012, combining a reorientation of U.S. military resources with an increased attentiveness to allies and strategic issues in the region. James Dobbins suggested that China has become America's "default adversary" and the possibility of a future war between the two countries should neither be ignored nor exaggerated.[34]

The rise of China has stimulated a lively debate in America. Some American analysts argue that China is a rising revisionist state seeking to remake the international system. Economic power is the basis of military power, and a stronger China will exert itself regionally and globally to protect and promote its interests. As Richard K. Betts argued, "Should we want China to get rich or not? For realists, the answer should be no, since a rich China would overturn any balance of power."[35] However, other analysts dispute the notion that China represents this kind of threat, characterizing the objectives of the Chinese government as primarily defensive. For example, Andrew Nathan and Andrew Scobell suggest that Chinese foreign policy objectives have not changed much since the end of the Cold War and are driven by a desire to blunt destabilizing influences from abroad, avoid territorial losses, reduce neighbour suspicions, and sustain economic growth.[36] China also faces serious domestic social and environmental problems, and has joined a large number of international institutions and become further integrated into the global trade regime by joining the WTO (World Trade Organization). As Alastair Iain Johnston concludes, "It is not clear that describing China as a revisionist or non–status-quo state is accurate at this moment in history."[37] Others agree, pointing out that viewing China through the prism of balance-of-power theory might lead to erroneous assumptions, dangerous policies, and self-fulfilling prophecies.[38] This has sparked a debate on whether U.S. policy should engage or contain China.[39] Others suggest that confrontation is not inevitable. Mark Brawley has argued that the Chinese leadership fears U.S. preventive action against a rising China, and therefore will be cautious in rhetoric and action until Chinese economic and military power is more fully developed.[40] Furthermore, much of the world's behaviour toward China has sought to avoid isolating and alienating the country.[41] Challenging the current international order would not be easy: it is deeply entrenched and supported by states other than America. As a result, G. John Ikenberry argues it is more likely that China will join the Western international order rather than oppose it.[42]

The rise of China is not the only point of debate in discussions about the future distribution of power in global politics. Countries such as Brazil, Russia, and India are also increasingly prominent, with growing economies and a growing presence in international politics and trade. Together with China, these countries are often referred to collectively as the "BRICs." However, India has significant challenges with respect to poverty, resources, and internal stability. It also faces growing regional tensions with Pakistan and China, as well as the ongoing troubles of Sri Lanka and Central Asia. Some speculate that the EU may become a counterbalance to the United States. The combined economies of EU members exceed the size of the American economy, and as European integration deepens and the EU takes on more of a foreign policy role, Europe could well become the new centre of power in world affairs. The problem with this projection is the high level of disagreement on foreign and security policy matters among EU members despite recent efforts to increase coordination and cooperation, as well as a series of economic crises that have strained relations between many countries in the EU and weakened support for European institutions.[43] Furthermore, despite recent tensions between Europe and America on a wide range of issues from trade to the environment to the Iraq War, the political and security relationship between Europe and America remains strong. The two continents are thus likely to remain friendly even as the relationship is redefined.[44] Japan is frequently mentioned in discussions of the contemporary balance of power, as its economy remains large and technologically advanced. However, Japanese economic growth has stagnated and Japan lacks the global diplomatic and military reach associated with hegemonic ambitions. Other non-European countries that consistently rank in the top 15 in GDP—South Korea, Australia, Canada, and Mexico—are not expected to increase in power to the point that they become new entrants to the great power order. The power politics of the future are thus likely to be relatively stable, characterized by a dominant United States, a rising but cautious and internally challenged China, a declining Japan, a prosperous but still divided Europe, and rising regional powers such as India and Brazil. However, the resurgence of Russia has added a new element to deliberations about the future of power politics, and we turn now to this topic.

A NEW COLD WAR?

The end of the Cold War was a world-changing event. However, there is growing concern over a possible new Cold War between a resurgent Russia and America and Europe. As Eugene B. Rumer has observed: "In Europe and the United States, the Russian resurgence in the international arena has been a matter of considerable and growing discomfort partly because Russia's newly confident voice has resonated with Cold War–like echoes.... The question of whether the West and Russia are heading into a new Cold War–style confrontation is being asked with increasing frequency on both sides of the Atlantic."[45] This concern has renewed interest in the origins and characteristics of the Cold War, in an effort to avoid repeating the mistakes of the past. As we discussed in Chapter 3, after the Cold War Russia faced enormous political, economic, and social problems. While many of these problems persist, under President Vladimir Putin (who moved into the position of prime minister in 2008 and returned as president in 2012) Russia has returned to prominence in global politics. Putin enjoys widespread support in Russia, although there is growing opposition to his authoritarian and oligarchic rule and fraudulent electoral tactics. During his tenure, the overall economy grew rapidly (largely due to surging oil and gas revenues), the quality of life improved for many Russians (though it declined for many as well), relative security and stability replaced the uncertainties of the 1990s, and Russia was once again an actor on the world stage. Putin's leadership and the resurgence of Russia have raised serious concerns about the domestic political direction of the country as well as a debate over the intentions and ambitions behind Russian foreign policy.

Observers of Russian domestic politics are now deeply concerned about the state of Russian democracy. The Russian leadership is dominated by ex-secret police and security services associates of Putin and Russia's new economic elites. These two constituencies have collaborated to centralize political and economic power by dominating the state bureaucracy and regional governments and controlling Russia's natural resource wealth (particularly the energy sector). Some estimates suggest that as many as 70 percent of senior Russian civil servants had links to the Russian secret police and secret service at some point in their careers.[46] Much of the media is heavily influenced (some critics would say controlled) by the state, and has become increasingly nationalistic. The actions of the West are heavily criticized and framed as part of a larger plan to isolate and marginalize Russia and interfere in the domestic affairs of the country. The activities of opposition parties are constrained, citizen groups are carefully monitored, and protests are often restricted or banned. Russia today is sometimes compared to the **Weimar Republic** in interwar Germany, when economic hardship, political humiliation, and a sense of national persecution created fertile ground for the emergence of authoritarian rule. The implications for the future of global politics are stark: an authoritarian, nationalistic Russia driven to restore its pride and place in the world is an uncomfortable thought. Some observers, such as Edward Lucas, suggest that a new Cold War is already under way between Russia and the West, driven by Russia's slide into authoritarianism.[47] However, others are not so willing to put the blame on Russia. For example, Stephen F. Cohen puts much of the blame for a new Cold War on Western (and especially U.S.) policy, which he argues has ignored Russia's legitimate security interests.[48]

The relationship between Russia and most Western industrialized states has deteriorated due to a number of ongoing disputes, despite the attempt by the Obama administration to "reset" relations in 2009. First, while the continued expansion of the North Atlantic Treaty Organization (NATO) was regarded by the alliance as an effort to build a wider post-Cold War security framework in Europe, in Russia the expansion was interpreted as a threat and an attempt at strategic encirclement. Second, the geopolitics of oil and natural gas resources and pipeline routes in Eastern Europe, Central Asia, and the Caucasus has caused considerable friction. Russia has used the interruption of oil supplies to exert pressure on the Ukraine and Georgia, and there are concerns that Europe, heavily dependent on oil and natural gas from Russia, might suffer a similar form of coercion. Third, the issue of the independence of Kosovo (discussed in Chapter 7) has pitted Russia against the United States and most of Europe since 1999. While Washington, Ottawa, and most European capitals have supported Kosovo's independence, the Russian government has opposed it on the grounds that Kosovo's independence is illegal and a violation of Serbian sovereignty. Fourth, Russia has pursued practices toward some of its neighbours that most Western governments find aggressive and provocative. Prominent examples include the cyber attacks against Estonia in 2007 and the military invasion of Georgia in 2008. In 2012, efforts by Russia to increase economic integration with neighbours such as Belarus and Kazakhstan were criticized as a "re-Sovietization" by then U.S. Secretary of State Hilary Clinton: Putin subsequently dismissed such concerns as "utter nonsense."[49] Fifth, the planned installation of a U.S. missile defence system in Europe has caused consternation in Russia, despite assurances from the Obama administration that the system was aimed at defending Europe from possible missile attack from the Middle East. Sixth, tensions over Russia's support for the Assad government in the Syrian Civil War and refusal to agree to a UN Security Council Resolution on some form of intervention in the conflict frustrated and angered many Western governments. Finally, there has been considerable friction over Western democracy promotion in Russia and the countries of the former Soviet Union. The Russian government views democracy promotion as meddling in the internal affairs of Russia and the countries in which Russia has a direct security interest. In particular, Russian officials have been critical of Western support for NGOs operating in Russia, and in 2012 a new law was passed compelling NGOs receiving funding from abroad to register as foreign agents. The Russian government has also been critical of Western support for democratic opposition movements in Serbia, Georgia, Ukraine, and (unsuccessfully) Belarus, and all these efforts were actively resisted by Moscow.[50]

Does this mean that a new Cold War is under way or is inevitable? The answer is no, for it is quite clear that there are significant differences between the situation today and the Cold War standoff. The ideological dimension of the Cold War does not exist today, and there is no arms race between Russia and the U.S. of the kind that horrified previous generations. Instead, as described in Chapter 7, the two governments have signed a series of new nuclear arms control agreements. Russia became a member of the WTO in 2012. On many issues, such as nuclear proliferation, terrorism, and climate change, Russia and most other industrialized states have many common interests. Despite some inflammatory rhetoric and bellicose statements and actions, Russian resurgence may mean no more than the return of Russia to great-power status after the hiatus caused by the end of the Cold War.[51] Finally, there is the practical matter of the limits to Russian power. The gross domestic product (GDP) of Russia was an estimated US$1.95 trillion in 2012, in contrast to U.S. GDP at US$15.6 trillion and China at US$8.2 trillion, suggesting Russia does not possess the economic capacities required to carry out a new Cold War.[52] Russia needs good relations with the world even as it reasserts its great-power status and will have a choice of which path to follow.[53] Leaders in other countries will have choices as well, and as constructivists would remind us, it is these choices and not some inevitable fate that will determine whether a new Cold War emerges between countries that ought to know better.

THE FUTURE OF THE AMERICAN EMPIRE

In Chapter 4 we explored the concept of hegemony, hegemonic decline, and the debate over the decline of U.S. power. In many ways, these issues are more salient today than ever before, and we can expect debates about the role of America in the world to be a persistent theme in global politics in the future, because the implications of these debates are so enormous. A growing number of people of varying ideological persuasions now feel comfortable referring to the "American Empire" as a fact of our time. However, the fate of that empire will be decisive in determining the character of global politics in the future. Are the days of American Empire numbered? There is certainly inconclusive evidence of U.S. hegemonic decline. First, the wars in Afghanistan and Iraq, and the massive economic stimulus packages and bailouts of financial institutions initiated in the wake of the financial crisis in 2008 to 2009, plunged the United States deep into debt. Obviously, there are only two ways to make up the difference between spending and revenues while avoiding high inflation rates, and that is through borrowing or raising taxes (a politically difficult task in the U.S.). However, at some point the debts will have to be paid, and budgets balanced. All the while, the money spent on defence and military adventure abroad is money not being invested in infrastructure upgrades, health care, education, and scientific innovation at home. Even though the U.S. economy is large and its private scientific and research base is enormous, the diversion of some government funds away from long-term economic development is worrisome to many U.S. analysts. The Obama administration is attempting to use generous economic stimulus spending to achieve some of these broader social objectives, but ultimately the economic health of the country depends on a recovery from recession.

Second, America's global legitimacy and credibility have been weakened. This is significant because according to hegemonic stability theory, a hegemon's status depends on some loyalty from willing followers. If a hegemon provides public goods and establishes norms and rules for the governance of the system, much of the power derived from such privilege rests on the willingness of most states to accept these norms and rules. This willingness to follow is in essence the test of legitimacy in global politics (one faced by international institutions and law as well). However, some commentators suggest that the U.S. invasion of Iraq has damaged this vital aspect of American power. For example, G. John Ikenberry has argued that

> it is hard to think of another instance in American diplomatic history where a strategic wrong turn has done so much damage to the country's international position—its prestige, credibility, security partnerships and goodwill of other countries—in so short a time, with so little to show for it. A single-minded American campaign against terrorism and rogue states in which countries are either "with us or against us" and bullied into support is not leadership but a geostrategic wrecking ball that will destroy America's own half-century old international architecture.[54]

However, the invasion of Iraq was not the only reason for the decline in America's international credibility. U.S. government opposition to the Kyoto Protocol, objection to the ICC (International Criminal Court) among other U.S. government positions, and the often-bellicose rhetoric of the Bush administration all contributed to a growing skepticism of American leadership. Even erstwhile defenders of American power and righteousness became concerned about the implications of the anti-American backlash on U.S. power. In particular, the divide between America and Europe is troubling for those who have long regarded the strategic and political partnership of America and Europe as a bulwark of global peace and stability. In his reflection on the transatlantic divide, Robert Kagan observed: "It is precisely the question of legitimacy that divides Americans and Europeans today—not the legitimacy of each other's political institutions, perhaps, but the legitimacy of their respective visions of world order. More to the point, for the first time since World War II, a majority of Europeans has come to doubt the legitimacy of U.S. global leadership."[55] Others, like George Soros, were far more biting in their criticism of the Bush administration, not out of anti-American spite or a rejection of America's core values, but because they feel those very values are being betrayed.[56] The Obama administration recognized this challenge, but it remains to be seen if America's legitimacy and credibility can be fully restored, especially in fiscally challenging times when austerity is an important constraint.[57]

Third, others have suggested that U.S. foreign policy has overemphasized hard power, at the expense of an underappreciated American resource: soft power. Joseph Nye is the leading proponent of this view. For Nye, "This soft power—getting others to want the outcomes you want—co-opts people rather than coerces them. Soft power rests on the ability to shape the preferences of others."[58] Nye goes on to argue that "winning the peace is harder than winning a war, and soft power is essential to winning the peace. Yet the way we went to war in Iraq proved to be as costly for our soft power as it was a stunning victory for our hard power."[59] In the future, will American governments be more aware of the relationship between power, economics, and legitimacy? Will they recognize the significance of soft power and the importance of balancing the use of the military instrument within a larger political and diplomatic context? Will they recognize the value of multilateral action, and the fact that the United States has been uniquely fortunate since the end of World War II to face an environment in which most of the great powers of the world are its allies? These have been overt goals of the Obama administration, which entered its second term in 2012.

Of course, it will take more than American initiative to restore its legitimacy among its allies and its soft power around the world. America's allies must be willing to accept U.S. leadership to some extent. However, this may not be the reaction of other key states. States might form a grand alliance to counterbalance American power. Alternatively, states might form or strengthen regional trade and political organizations to undermine or reduce the influence of global institutions such as the WTO and the IMF. Transatlantic relations between Europe and the United States might break down over trade and political and security issues. If this happens, U.S. power will have to exert itself in a less favourable international environment than it has in the past. On the other hand, it is likely that the United States and its allies will reach accommodation more often than not. Shared interests and shared values will bring America and other countries together in cooperative efforts that may rebuild trust and confidence. As for U.S. decline, a note of caution is warranted. The decline of the Roman Empire is sometimes recorded as beginning with the end of the Antonine Emperors in 180 CE; the Vandals sacked Rome 275 years later. Decline, it would seem, is a slow process.

For other analysts, the reality of U.S. global dominance is unlikely to change and will continue to characterize the global distribution of military, economic, and diplomatic power. In their influential book *World Out of Balance: International Relations and the Challenge of American Primacy*, William Wohlforth and Stephen Brooks argued that U.S. preponderance would endure and result in a more stable world order.[60] However, this "primacist" view seldom comes without the qualification that the U.S. government must act appropriately to preserve its dominant position. For example, while Barry Posen asserts that "unipolarity and U.S. hegemony will likely be around for some time," this does not mean that the United States can sustain its position indefinitely.[61] Posen argues that the United States can maintain its pre-eminence, but only if it maintains a disciplined approach to foreign policy. Niall Fergusson argues that the existence of an American "liberal empire" is evident by all economic, military, and diplomatic measures. Fergusson believes that the threat to this empire comes not from rising rivals but from a failure of Americans to recognize the reality of their imperial status and exert the necessary leadership to maintain it. Americans, Fergusson notes, would rather "consume than conquer."[62]

Not all primacists arrive at the same conclusions. Nuno Monteiro cautions that while unipolarity may endure, it will not lead to an era of peace as the U.S. may not be willing to act as a guarantor of peace in the world's regions, or will find itself engaged in wars against revisionist regional powers.[63] Joseph Nye has argued that U.S. military power, economic power, and ideological/cultural "soft" power will endure into the future, despite the neglect of soft power, which Nye finds troubling. Nye suggests that the United States must combine its hard power and its soft power into a "smart power" strategy.[64] In a similar vein, Amy Chua has observed that successful empires maintain their longevity through co-optation or toleration. Political, religious, and cultural understanding and accommodation can encourage cooperation and a willing (though sometimes grudging) loyalty that helps preserve the power of the empire. Chua argues that the United States can maintain its power by following such policies in the future.[65] However, many analysts that accept U.S. hegemony as fact argue there are limits to what American policy can do to influence or counteract balance of power behaviour. Joseph Joffe and Julia Sweig have argued that America is unpopular and resented because it looks, acts, and talks like a hegemon and is therefore a natural magnet for resentment and hostility.[66] Others have suggested that the U.S. must avoid hegemonic pretensions and alter its foreign policy strategy to accommodate balance of power behaviour. For example, Christopher Layne argues that U.S. grand strategy since the 1940s has been driven by the desire to achieve security through expanding its power and pursuing hegemony, particularly in Western Europe, East Asia, and the Persian Gulf. Layne argues that this approach cannot be successful because it will provoke balancing behaviour by other states (particularly China) and overstretch U.S. resources. Instead, Layne suggests the United States should pursue an "offshore balancing strategy" as the only alternative to seeking hegemony.[67]

A CLASH OF CIVILIZATIONS?

In a famous and controversial article published in the influential journal *Foreign Affairs* in 1993, the late Harvard professor Samuel Huntington argued that the primary source of conflict in the future would not be ideology, economics, or nationalism. Rather, future wars would occur between the world's civilizations: "Nation states will remain the most powerful actors in world affairs, but the principal conflicts of global politics will occur between nations and groups of different civilizations. The clash of civilizations will dominate world politics. The fault lines between civilizations will be the battle lines of the future."[68] Huntington defined a civilization in the following manner:

> A civilization is a cultural entity. Villages, regions, ethnic groups, nationalities, religious groups, all have distinct cultures at different levels of cultural heterogeneity ... Arabs, Chinese, and Westerners, however, are not part of any broader cultural entity. They constitute civilizations. A civilization is thus the highest cultural grouping of people and the broadest level of cultural identity people have short of that which distinguishes humans from other species.[69]

According to Huntington, there are eight major civilizations in the world: Western, Confucian, Japanese, Islamic, Hindu, Slavic-Orthodox, Latin American, and African. Many recent and current conflicts in the contemporary international system are taking place along these fault lines, in places such as the former Yugoslavia, Azerbaijan, Armenia and Georgia, the Horn of Africa, Russia and Chechnya, India and Pakistan, and India and China. He predicted that the conflicts of the future will increasingly take place along the fault lines where civilizations meet.

Huntington offered several explanations as to why inter-civilization disputes are growing and will become the basis for most future conflicts. First, civilizations are more fundamental than the state, for our self-identities owe less to the state than to the civilization to which we belong. Civilizations are differentiated by history, religion, language, culture, and tradition; as a result, differences among civilizations have generated the longest and most violent conflicts and will do so increasingly in the future. Second, increasing global interdependence, interaction, and contact between peoples of different civilizations are not contributing to understanding and accommodation but, rather, is making more people aware of the differences between them. Interdependence and globalization are contributing to civilization-consciousness among the peoples of the world. Third, economic and social change around the world is altering the relationship between individuals and traditional social institutions. In particular, the state is in decline and religion is replacing it. The revival of religion around the world means a world increasingly united around the religious heritages of civilizations rather than the nationalist heritage of nation-states. Fourth, the spread and power of Western civilization is provoking a counter-reaction in other civilizations. Civilization-consciousness is in part a reaction to the encroachment of Western culture and values on traditional belief systems, and an anti-Western return to civilization roots is underway around the world. Fifth, Huntington suggested that civilizational differences are less subject to change or flexible adaptation. Negotiations, compromises, and resolution of disputes are more difficult to achieve between civilizations than between states. Finally, Huntington argued that economic patterns are assuming civilizational forms and shapes. Civilization links will become more important factors in the creation of economic zones of activity, with peoples of shared heritage more disposed toward doing business with each other than they are with peoples of other civilizations.

Ultimately, Huntington warned that civilization identity is becoming increasingly important as an influence on the perceptions of peoples around the world. This influence will create an "us versus them" mentality, which will drive inter-civilization differences on a whole range of international issues, including human rights, immigration, trade, the environment, and the spread of Western culture (which has already provoked a backlash against the West in many countries). The future may be one of "the West against the rest." This argument (as Huntington himself pointed out) is not an original one. Kishore Mahbubani has argued that the central axis of conflict in the world in the future will be between Western civilization and the non-Western civilizations of the world.[70] This conflict will take two forms: on the one hand there will be a struggle for military, economic, and institutional power. On the other hand, there will be a struggle over culture. The response of the non-Western world in this struggle will continue to be varied. Some non-Western states will adopt a policy of isolation, in effect sealing off their societies and economies from the West. Other states will join the West and adopt Western values and institutions, including democracy, law, and human rights. The difficulty with this course of action is that it involves the import of value systems that are very different from those shared by the majority (or a significant portion) of the population. This may create social and political unrest between those who want to Westernize and those who want to protect the history and culture of the society. A final option is to acquire military and economic power to resist the West and to make common cause with other non-Western peoples in this effort. The reaction of the West will also be crucial. In the long term, Huntington argued that the West must recognize that the dominance of Western civilization around the world is ending and that other civilizations will begin to re-exert their place and influence on global politics. The West, along with all of the world's civilizations, will have to develop an increased understanding of the philosophical and religious differences between them. There will be no universal civilization but a world of civilizations.

Huntington's thesis has stirred considerable debate, and the attacks of September 11, 2001, and the subsequent "war on terror" and the invasion of Iraq launched by the Bush administration added fuel to the controversy over the clash of civilizations thesis. In the United States and some other countries, the September 11 attacks and subsequent response have been cast as a civilization clash: the attacks were carried out by militant Islamic fundamentalists preaching hatred against the West in general and the United States in particular. Walter Laqueur argued that the motive of Islamic fundamentalist terrorism does not originate with poverty or repression but the desire to destroy Western civilization.[71] Norman Podhoretz, one of the leading figures of the neoconservative movement in the United States, argues that America is fighting World War IV against "Islamofascism."[72] Meanwhile, in the Islamic world the wars in Afghanistan and Iraq are widely regarded as a Western crusade against Islam, part of a long history of Western oppression of Muslims. Anthony Pagden has argued that the history of the East and the West is a history of 2500 years of struggle and conflict. In this context, Pagden suggests that "the 'clash of civilizations'—a crude but useful phrase—is the enduring reality of Islamic life, as it has always been a central feature of Islamic history."[73] These sentiments have been strengthened by strident rhetoric emanating from political and religious extremists in the West and the Islamic world.

However, there are serious limitations to the clash of civilizations thesis. Huntington's critics argue that the boundary between civilizations is far from distinct and that conflict within civilizations (intra-civilization conflict) may be more common than clashes between civilizations. For example, the future will thus be characterized as much by conflict within the Muslim world (between Muslim states or between Shia and Sunni Muslims) than wars between the Muslim and Christian civilizations. Others stress that states are a far more decisive force than Huntington suggests. Instead of civilizations motivating the actions of states, it is more accurate to say that states dominate civilizations and cultures. Huntington has also been criticized for overestimating the role played by culture in the world. Most peoples and governments are motivated not by cultural concerns but by concerns over economic growth. The world is characterized not by the triumph of religious and culturally oriented governments but by the failure of such governments. The West remains a source of attraction for non-Western peoples, in particular the young, the poor, and the oppressed. Many people today would identify themselves with neither state nor culture, reflecting cosmopolitan values revolving around universal concerns such as ecology or human rights. Huntington's thesis is based on such broad generalizations that it is often decried as inaccurate and poor social science, closer to rhetorical incitement than serious historical and political analysis. In his far-ranging book *A Metahistory of the Clash of Civilizations: Us and Them beyond Orientalism*, Arshin Adib-Moghaddam argues that current cultural dialogues emphasizing the differences between Muslims and Europeans, Americans and Arabs, and the Orient and the Occident have been exaggerated and the idea of a clash of civilizations is largely a myth.[74] Chiara Bottici and Benoit Challand reach a similar conclusion, suggesting the clash of civilizations has become a cognitive scheme or practical image—a political myth—through which people understand the world. Nevertheless, the clash of civilizations thesis remains a serious point of discussion in the debate about the origins of the conflicts and wars of the future.

THE FUTURE OF GLOBALIZATION

Our discussion of the global economy suggests that economic issues have increased in importance in global politics. It is clear that this trend will continue into the future, with the dominant concerns revolving around the relationship between markets and regulation, the stability of the global trade and financial system, and the persistent inequities in wealth distribution. In the coming years the theoretical debate underpinning economic policy is likely to become more intense and antagonistic. We live in a world in which news and debates on economics, business, government fiscal policy (taxing and spending), government monetary policy (interest rates and money supply), and the decisions of international financial institutions such as the International Monetary Fund and the World Bank are dominated by liberal economic principles. In fact, if there is one foundation to the modern world economy, it is liberal economic theory translated into practice by decades of government policy and international negotiations. In recent decades, a variant of liberal economic thinking has emerged known as neoliberalism. The neoliberal agenda emphasizes the global freedom of capital and reduction of state intervention. Neoliberals argue that such policies are essential to foster economic growth and the improvement of living standards worldwide, and this view is reflected in the formula of the Washington Consensus and the operations of large financial institutions and corporations. Will the neoliberal agenda triumph? Some scholars, such as the neo-Marxist Stephen Gill, see the agents of the global economy representing an emerging system of global economic governance (a "disciplinary neoliberalism") based on a quasi-constitutional framework for the reconstitution of the legal rights, prerogatives, and freedom of movement for capital on a world scale (a "new constitutionalism").[75] Gill envisions a global system designed to promote the interests of capital first and foremost. Given how entrenched neoliberal thinking is in many of the world's leading financial institutions, it is not hard to envision the kind of future Gill suggests.

However, the neoliberal agenda has come under growing pressure from critical economists and a variety of domestic and international groups and organizations as the drawbacks and failures of the neoliberal approach have become more evident in the wake of frequent financial crises and economic recessions. Keynesian or interventionist liberals are skeptical of the neoliberal ideology, arguing that markets require management and regulation if equitable distributions of wealth and social development are to be achieved. As George Soros has suggested,

"To stabilize and regulate a truly global economy, we need some global system of political decision making. In short, we need a global society to support our global economy."[76] Soros envisions a global system of regulatory measures exerting control over the worst effects and excesses of the hidden hand of the market. Soros is far from alone in this vision, as the concern about the implications of globalization grows. There are those who feel their entire cultural identity is threatened by Westernization, and feel the need to defend their way of life. Labour and worker's rights organizations are concerned about the exploitation of labour. Environmentalists point to the link between globalization and damage to the ecology. Fair trade advocates make the case for increased balance in profit sharing. Anti-poverty organizations highlight the need for greater justice in the distribution of wealth, water and food, health care, and services. It is also the case that most governments do not subscribe to the neoliberal agenda, at least not in the form it takes in the United States. The question of whether neoliberal economic theory or more interventionist liberal economic theory becomes the guiding framework for the policies and practices of the world economy is one of the biggest questions of our time. Of course, the debate over globalization is largely an intra-liberal debate. Realists remind us that states act in their own narrow self-interest to promote their own economic power. For Edward Luttwak, the ability of states to meet the challenges of privatization, deregulation, and globalization—what he refers to as "turbo-capitalism"—will determine whether they will be winners or losers in the new global economy.[77] Meanwhile, neo-Marxists remind us that economic elites act to promote their own privilege over the marginalized and exploited. Evidence supporting these theoretical perspectives is visible in international economic affairs today. And so, while liberal economics is the orthodoxy and dominates economic debate and policy decisions, it does not have a monopoly on theory or practice and is not beyond criticism (or in some cases, outright opposition).

The magnitude of economic globalization is striking when aggregate statistics on economic growth and trade and financial flows are used as measures. According to the World Bank, the world's economic output totalled US$63 trillion in 2010.[78] Trade continues to be an important force in global economic growth; the value of merchandise trade alone was over US$15 trillion in 2010.[79] Investment flows have also increased steadily: the value of all foreign direct investment (FDI) inflows was over US$1.4 trillion in 2010.[80] Global financial flows are facilitated by big currency markets in New York, London, Zurich, Tokyo, and Hong Kong, among others. In 2010, the value of trade in global currency reached US$4 trillion per day, an increase of 20 percent since 2007.[81] The sheer volume of global trade and financial transactions raises questions about how (or if) these flows can be managed and regulated effectively. The history of the world economy discussed in Chapter 4 is far from irrelevant in contemporary debates about the future of global economic relations. The prevailing view today is that national boundaries will continue to erode in the face of an irresistible tide of globalization and the unstoppable expansion of trade, financial, and other economic activity. However, in the early 1900s people felt much the same way about the global economy: unprecedented levels of economic integration had developed over decades along with an international financial system. Nevertheless, it all came to a disastrous end in World War I. As Jeffry A. Frieden observes in his excellent history of the global economy, "The bases on which global capitalism rests today are not much different from what they were in 1900, and the potential for their disruption is as present today as then. Globalization is still a choice, not a fact."[82] Frieden's caution is especially pertinent in light of the global recession that began in 2008, and the accompanying concern that states might turn to protectionism and economic nationalism in response.

One trend in particular animates both proponents and opponents of globalization, and will continue to be a central point of ideological divergence: the privatization of the commons and the deregulation of public control over private commercial and industrial activity. This represents the continuation of a trend that began when capitalism took over as the dominant mode of production in Europe and eventually spread around the world. The acceptance of a culturally significant definition of private property was in direct conflict with many social norms in Asia, Africa, and North and South America, for most of the past millennium. The process of appropriation of the commons for the pursuit of private and corporate gain remains the defining feature of global capitalism; it permeates every area of life, from resources, land, water, and the provision of previously public services to less tangible aspects of modern life, such as intellectual property rights, gene patents, and even the right to pollute. Water, in particular, will be the focus of great debate, as neoliberals argue that privatization will lead to more efficiency, while critics charge that this amounts to an appropriation of what was once considered one of the most basic human rights: access to water as a precondition for survival.[83] The biopolitics of the future will involve furious debates, in both national and multilateral forums, about the intersection between the ethics of genetic manipulation and genetically modified organisms and the profit factor in their development and dissemination.

The debate over development will continue as well. As Jeffrey Sachs points out, globalization can be a force for good, but it is simply not true that a rising tide lifts all boats.[84] Most scholars and activists engaged in the development issues of our time have largely forsaken "modernization" theory as a form of cultural imperialism, and dismissed the once-hegemonic belief that large-scale infrastructure development (dams, pipelines, highways, railroads) was the precondition for economic and political development. However, this model of development remains popular with key decision makers in donor states and most recipient states. This is due to a persistent belief in some circles that modernization through infrastructure development is the best path to development, and because this model of development creates opportunities for donor state corporations to secure large contracts with developing countries. Many recipient states also pursue the industrial and infrastructure model of development because industrialization is seen as synonymous with growth and economic power. Neo-Marxists remind us of another explanation: elites in developing countries are looking after their interests above all else, and large industrial and infrastructure projects promise wealth and power for those that control them. It is likely that the infrastructure model of development will persist, and it would be inaccurate to dismiss it entirely: a very real problem in many developing countries is a lack of serviceable infrastructure. However, in the future we can expect development projects to take more of a local and community-based focus. This will place a greater emphasis on environmental sustainability, women in development, and microcredit arrangements consisting of small loans to individuals to start their own businesses.[85] Nevertheless, we will still witness a cultural divide between those societies that have largely accepted privatization and capitalism as the dominant mode of development, and those that either reject this model or are determined to fashion it in their own way. The latter approach (local adaptation and development) would seem to hold the most promise. Ultimately, the stark dichotomy between market and socialized life is a false one. Societies around the world have thrived on marketplace interactions. As William J. Bernstein observes, "Trade is an irreducible and intrinsic human impulse, as primal as the needs for food, shelter, sexual intimacy, and companionship."[86] It is also the case that even the most industrialized and free market states provide a wide range of public goods for their citizens, from health care to education to pensions. The broader question is what type of synthesis between public and private property rights will emerge in the long term.

Finally, the future of economic globalization itself is in question. The collapse of the Doha Round of the WTO talks, the persistence of trade disputes, the rising tide of opposition to economic integration in most parts of the world, and the most recent global recession raise doubts as to whether increased progress on world trade liberalization is possible. Have globalization, economic interdependence, and the implementation of liberal economic principles in the structure of the world economy and the institutions that govern it reached the pinnacle of what is politically possible? For most liberal observers, protectionism is likely to be the key issue in the management of the world economy in the future. The concern is that rising protectionist sentiment in governments and populations around the world will precipitate a new era of economic nationalism, reducing trade and stifling the international flow of capital. This in turn will worsen the global recession and precipitate a world economic downturn that will lead to greater economic hardship for people around the world. Faced with the inability to make progress in the WTO, states will turn instead to regional multilateral agreements to secure markets and access to resources, or to networks of bilateral trade agreements with select partners. The result will be an increasingly fragmented world economy, with little or no capacity for the global governance Soros and many others suggest is necessary if the global economy is to be managed effectively. Global economic diplomacy, in the form of G8 and G20 Summits, among many other mechanisms, is dedicated to avoiding such a scenario, but while agreements are often reached on general principles and objectives, participating governments are not always willing or capable of following through on these commitments. For liberals, the stakes are high: the fragmentation of world economic patterns and the rise in protectionism will lead to a world that is less prosperous, less respectful of individual liberties, and less peaceful in the future. As Robert Skidelsky has argued, "The sole question is whether the retreat from the wilder shores of globalization will be orderly or disorderly: whether we will return to the bloc economics of the 1930s or whether we have the wisdom to build a managed and modified form of globalization, free from the illusion that everything can be left safely to the markets."[87]

FUTURE CRISES IN THE GLOBAL ECONOMY

The global economy has suffered through numerous economic crises. The Wall Street Crash in 1929 and the ensuing Great Depression still resonates today. The oil shock of the 1970s caused economic turmoil worldwide. In the 1980s, the U.S. savings and loan crisis, the Japanese property crash, and the Latin American debt default crisis spread fear about the global financial system. The 1997 Asian financial crisis and the Russian financial crisis of 1998 shook confidence in globalization. The collapse of the "dot-com" companies' stock values in 2000 and 2001 revealed the influence of unfettered speculation in global stock markets. The frequency and severity of these crises has led to growing fears that the global economic system is unstable, prone to sudden shocks that can spread through an integrated world economy. Another example of this instability occurred in 2007 to 2008 in the form of the U.S. mortgage crisis, which destabilized financial markets worldwide. The roots of the crisis go back to 2005, when large numbers of low-income borrowers with poor credit histories took out long-term house mortgages (called "subprime" mortgages) with low initial interest rates. That is, to the borrowers the costs of purchasing a home looked affordable because initial interest rates payments (for the first two years or so) were quite modest. By 2006, 20 percent of all new mortgages in the U.S. were subprime.[88] However, through the neglect of the homebuyer or the deliberate manipulation of the lenders, what was forgotten or concealed was that interest rates on the mortgage loan would jump dramatically after the initial two- or three-year period of low rates. When the interest payments on the subprime mortgages went up, it had devastating consequences for the homebuyers' personal finances. In dramatically increasing numbers through 2007 and early 2008, people began to default on their loans and were forced out of their homes.

In the past, clients defaulting on their loans would mean that the lenders (banks, for the most part) would be saddled with the loss. However, most of these mortgages were financed by packaging them into financial products and selling them to other U.S. and foreign banks and investment funds. Why would anyone buy a package of debt? These mortgage products had value because of the promise of the repayment of the loan in full (the principal) along with the interest on that loan. If the loan was repaid in full along with the interest, the buyer of the loan package (a bank or investment fund) would make a considerable profit. Anticipating these profits, American and foreign banks and investment funds invested heavily in these mortgage financial products, often without a clear understanding of the risk. This is how the global financial system became involved in the crisis. When American homebuyers were forced to default in large numbers, the value of the mortgage packages crumbled almost overnight, and banks and investment funds around the world lost billions of dollars. Banks alone announced losses of over US$60 billion in 2008, and by early 2009 some predictions of total global losses from the financial crisis exceeded US$2.2 trillion.[89] The shock reverberated through the global financial system. The financial losses from defaults on mortgage loans in Cleveland and Phoenix have impacted on the finances of investors in Asia and Europe. Some major banks and mortgage lenders (such as Bear Sterns, Fannie Mae, and Freddie Mac in the U.S., and Northern Rock in the United Kingdom) went bankrupt and had to be bailed out by governments using taxpayers' money and borrowed funds. The result was an enormous transfer of private sector debt to public sector debt, especially in America. In summarizing the cause of the disaster, *The Economist* made the following observation:

> For the critics of modern finance [the crisis] ... was the inevitable consequence of the laissez-faire philosophy that allowed financial services to innovate and spread almost unchecked. This has created a complex, interdependent system prone to conflicts of interest. Fraud has been rampant in the sale of subprime mortgages. Spurred by pay that was geared to short-term gains, bankers and fund managers stand accused of pocketing bonuses with no thought for the longer-term consequences of what they were doing. Their gambling has been fed by the knowledge that, if disaster struck, someone else—borrowers, investors, taxpayers—would end up bearing at least some of the losses.[90]

By the end of 2008, the crisis had spread beyond the U.S. economy and beyond the global financial sector. How did the crisis spread? First, financial institutions worldwide became much more careful about lending and raised their interest rates. The result was a global capital shortage (often called a "credit crunch") that slowed economic growth because businesses and investors now longer had access to cheap capital through low-interest loans. Banks became reluctant to lend to each other because they no longer trusted each other's finances. Second, the housing market began to deflate in other countries when interest rates rose, credit dried up, and property values fell. Third, as a result of the crisis, the U.S. housing market was hit hard by a drop in home values and a slump in construction, dealing another blow to a U.S. economy already hit by a declining dollar, famously high levels of household debt, and higher fuel prices. U.S. business expansion slowed due to a lack of affordable credit. Unemployment began to climb as businesses downsized their workforces. As the U.S. economy slowed, American consumers bought less of the world's exported products, reducing global demand for goods, services, and raw materials. American consumer spending before the crisis totalled US$9 trillion per year, as against US$1 trillion in China and US$600,000 in India. This served as a reminder of the crucial importance of the U.S. economy (25 percent of the global total) and the familiar refrain that when the U.S. sneezes the world catches a cold. By 2013, the consequences of the transfer of private debt to public debt from the mortgage crisis (piled on top of the debt incurred by the wars fought in Iraq and Afghanistan) were still being felt in the U.S., endangering economic recovery from the recession and sparking political budgetary battles between the Obama administration and Congress. The worldwide impact of the U.S. mortgage crisis, and the subsequent economic crisis in Europe that began in 2009 and was still ongoing in 2013, has reinforced concerns over the continued vulnerability of the global economy to unexpected shocks and has provided more fuel to critics of the global financial system and even capitalism itself.

HUMAN RIGHTS AND INTERNATIONAL LAW

We have yet to establish a universal international human rights order. Establishing such an order is a priority for many human rights activists. However, others caution that any universal order would only be the result of coercion or cultural imperialism. What is more disturbing is the unseemly level of hypocrisy evident in the realm of human rights. The grand pronouncements of state representatives and international legal conventions seem meaningless as human rights abuses continue on a daily basis. Often, human rights abuses in one country attract a great deal of attention, while similar abuses in other countries are ignored. It is also the case that most governments are critical of human rights abuses in other countries while paying less attention to abuses at home. Whether it is the treatment of indigenous peoples in Canada and Australia, the incarceration without due process of thousands of Muslim men after September 11 in the United States, the denial of the right to education of women in many states, the passive acceptance of the international trade in human beings, or hundreds of other controversial practices, no states are immune from questions about their domestic and foreign policies on human rights. In the future, we can expect human rights violations (and erratic and inconsistent responses to them) to remain a prominent feature of global politics.

Can we expect a reasonable improvement in the global human rights situation? For all the lofty talk about the primacy of international law, the need to establish some sort of universal set of guidelines for the interaction between states, and the need to promote adherence to the founding principles of the United Nations, a world governed by law remains a hope, not a reality. While many states obey most international laws at least some of the time, they break those laws when decision makers feel it is in their interests to do so. Imagine, for example, telling a police officer that you were speeding down the highway because you had decided that following the law was not in your best interests that day! Imagine if most drivers on the road with you felt the same way and drove accordingly! There is no global culture of implicit acceptance of international law as the arbiter in disputes, and of course there is no police officer to enforce the law. Yet a world governed by law would promise much. For example, the American response to September 11 has been a heavily militarized one. While it quickly became apparent that the United States interpreted the attacks as an assault not only on America but also on the free world and civilization itself, others such as Mary Robinson, then the UN High Commissioner for Human Rights, suggested that it would be better to view the September 11 attacks as a crime against humanity. This would encourage a response to terrorism based not on statist reflexes and outright military power, but on a more liberal international effort to establish the rule of international law, strengthen the UN, coordinate law enforcement and intelligence-gathering institutions, increase financial regulation, use international courts, and lower the disparity between rich and poor. The turn to an excessively militarized strategy in the war on terror may be viewed as a significant lost opportunity to strengthen international stability and order.[91] Whether or not this would have been politically palatable in the United States is, however, another matter. Recall also, from Chapter 10, that Canada once broke international law to enforce a fisheries conservation measure that would later become codified law, proving you sometimes need to break law to make it.

However, there is some cause for optimism. We have seen several developments that might well give rise to a new stage in the evolution of human rights and humanitarian law. South Africa's Truth and Reconciliation Commission represented a bold, if troubled, effort to permit a traumatized society to come to terms with its past. The establishment of the International Criminal Court, based loosely on the ad hoc tribunals for the former Yugoslavia and Rwanda, puts unprecedented emphasis on the accountability of individuals under international criminal law. The fact that court has tried individuals and indicted others shows that the court is taken seriously by at least some states. Given the historical record, it is likely that the court will be used only to prosecute individuals who have committed crimes against humanity in peripheral states and members of defeated military regimes. But the potential is there for a much more robust and lasting effort to take such criminals to task, including such often-ignored crimes as rape as an instrument of war, ethnic cleansing, and genocide. Various ad hoc courts in places such as Sierra Leone, Cambodia, and Iraq, beset with their own unique difficulties, will further contribute to ending the culture of impunity. However, the ICC will have to determine its proper political role, as the controversial indictment of the Sudanese president has made clear.

For international law in general, the prospects are as exciting as they are daunting. Globalization is accompanied by the legal property rights regime that reflects Western institutions and corporate law, so there will no doubt be great opportunities for private international lawyers. International public law is also attracting increasing numbers of bright and ambitious students. The International Court of Justice will be used for its dual purpose: to hear cases based on disputes between states, in its role as arbitrator, and to pass judgment on questions of advisory opinion, such as the construction of the so-called security fence by Israel. These judgments do not always change the behaviour of states, but they do focus attention on the issues, and suggest that the real role for international law is not as an ordering device with definitive powers, but as an instrument of legitimacy and moral suasion with limited but real influence in global politics.[92]

HUMAN HEALTH, THE ENVIRONMENT, AND MULTILATERALISM

We have some major choices ahead of us regarding the future health of the planet. Our dependence on fossil fuels for energy is affecting the climate, contributing to conflict, and limiting the options for future generations. The immense by-product of industrialization and urban concentration, and the sheer waste involved in the productive and consumptive processes of this era, is difficult to fathom. Overfishing and pollution threaten the oceans and marine life, and fresh water is becoming increasingly precious. The availability of land for cultivation is decreasing. The widespread use of chemical fertilizers has increased crop yields but also increased pollution. Mono-crop agriculture has marginalized traditional farmers. Deforestation is a consequence of population pressure and expanding agricultural, forestry, and mining industries, and is accompanied by the loss of global biodiversity and the threat to the livelihood and rights of indigenous peoples. In short, the price that has been paid for economic development, modernization, and globalization has been very high. Increased calls for the adoption of sustainable economic and environmental practices are likely to increase in the future.

The need for multilateral coordination to mitigate and adapt to these consequences is obvious. All liberals, and even many realists, would agree. However, whether adequate multilateral responses can be forged is still uncertain. Can a world still organized into sovereign territorial states organize itself to respond to truly global issues? Critical theorists remind us that the very multilateral institutions being constructed to "manage" such issues are products of the very states, companies, and household habits that have encouraged this type of development for many decades. Thus they argue transnational solidarity with those most affected is also necessary. We can expect the marginalized and disadvantaged to join in alliances in order to fight what they perceive as their unjust treatment by the international community. Despite the seemingly insurmountable obstacles to change, there is hope for the future. More and more people are becoming aware of environmental degradation, pollution, and climate change. As a result, environmentally friendly practices, products, and industries are gaining in size and popularity. Most societies and cultural traditions have some sort of stewardship principle, which suggests present generations have an ethical obligation to look ahead and consider the impact of their actions on the yet unborn. Taken together, this may manifest itself in a slow but steady movement toward the adoption of more sustainable practices.

Beyond the ecological harm caused by industrialization, militarization, agribusiness, and consumption, there are many threats to human health related to the human population itself. Though the worst predictions of a "population bomb" expected a few decades ago have not come to pass, we are nonetheless living in a world with over seven billion people, and the figure continues to rise, adding to environmental and migratory pressures and the negative aspects of mass, rapid urbanization. Again, there is a need for multilateral assistance, market access, and freedom from repression and corruption in order to improve the conditions of life for the millions of undernourished and marginalized people. A key factor moving forward will be effective state governance around the world. Daron Acemoglu and James A. Robinson argue that poor countries are poor because they have "extractive institutions" ruled by narrow elites that have organized society for their own benefit at the expense of the rest of the population.[93] In the absence of improvements in government institutions, we can foresee an even larger role for the informal sector in the future as people are forced to rely less on the state and legal economic activity and more on their own survival strategies. At the same time, we can also foresee increased tensions within many countries in both the developing and developed worlds over the privatization and deregulation of everything from public space to water rights to health care. States intent on pursuing this course will face growing opposition and increasingly fractious domestic politics, while others will resort to oppressive measures, which will in turn threaten their own fragile legitimacy. And yet, this scenario too can be avoided if governments and international institutions turn away from an ideological fixation on market liberalization and boundless privatization toward a more balanced approach. There are signs this may already be happening: the Washington Consensus formula itself is under revision, and the IMF and the World Bank, among others, are increasingly cognizant of the social and environmental impact of economic policies. Perhaps the future will be characterized by a new consensus on achieving a harmony between the market and social and environmental sustainability. Constructivist and feminist theorists would contend that part of the problem has been the tendency to resort to blueprints, ready-made models that are supposed to apply everywhere, regardless of circumstances. This needs to change, not only because of large differences in culture, history, structural power, and other variables, but also because development and environmental management and population issues are not static, but fluid: priorities often change over even short periods of time.

Another threat to human security that has made numerous appearances in this text is the modern pandemic. HIV/AIDS has killed over 25 million people in the past three decades. Infectious diseases such as SARS can spread rapidly throughout the world. Drug-resistant variants of diseases such as tuberculosis are a possible new threat to global public health. As is the case with the uncountable deaths the world has witnessed due to malnutrition and easily preventable diseases, most victims of future pandemics will be in the poor parts of the world because the medical services required to help them are absent or in short supply. While there has been some progress made toward achieving the Millennium Goals (see Chapter 8), there is an urgent need to accelerate such action, and once again the costs of delay are as debilitating as they are heart-wrenching. All the wireless networks we create, and renewable energy advances we pursue, and peace negotiations we conduct will be in vain if the international community does not address these fundamental threats to human security. Every year billions of dollars are spent on militaries and on the production of goods and services that are simply not needed. Can the will and a way be found to devote the mere fraction of these resources that would be necessary to mitigate the intolerable harm done by disease and marginalization around the world?

The population of the planet will continue to increase. However, population growth rates have slowed in many areas, in some cases due to tragic circumstances, but in most due to active family-planning measures and changing perspectives on the utility and challenges of having several children. But we will face new demographic challenges in the future. In areas devastated with pandemics, especially in the HIV/AIDS context, states will have to cope with an unprecedented number of orphans and single-parent families. Areas affected with rampant violence will struggle with accompanying physical and psychological health problems, as well as the legacy of environmental destruction, land mines, and the need to overcome the past. And other health crises are quickly looming. These include the increase in global rates of obesity, heart disease, and cancer, and the economic impact of aging populations in both high-income Western states and many poorer non-Western states.[94]

CANADA AND THE FUTURE OF GLOBAL POLITICS

In many ways, Canadians are extraordinarily fortunate. Canada is largely insulated from the full effects of war and instability abroad, and faces no direct military threat to its territory or society. Canada possesses the second-largest territory in the world (after Russia) with a population of approximately 35 million people. The country is rich in fresh water, arable land, and mineral resources. The Canadian economy is the eleventh-largest in the world, with a highly educated workforce and an advanced communications, transportation, and energy infrastructure. Canada ranks in the top 15 countries in the world in wealth per capita. The country is among the world leaders in key social health indicators such as infant mortality, adult literacy, and life expectancy. Canada consistently ranks among the top six countries in the world on the UN Human Development Index. By most accounts, Canada is one of the best places to live in the world. In some ways, this makes Canada strong, even though most Canadians do not tend to see the country this way. As Michael Byers has argued, "We are, believe it or not, the envy of the world. We are—take a deep breath and don't laugh—a powerful country."[95]

However, Canada's place and role in the world has been a subject of criticism and debate in recent years. A common theme is Canada's declining profile in global politics, and how Canada can capture, or recapture, a more influential role in world affairs. For example, Andrew Cohen has argued that "our vision is less broad today than it was in the past, especially in the decade or so after the Second World War. We are no longer as strong a soldier, as generous a donor, and as effective a diplomat, and it has diminished us as a people."[96] To recapture a worthy role in world affairs, Cohen suggests Canada increase the size and capacity of its military, increase foreign aid, diversify its trade, and reinvigorate the foreign service. In another popular book, Jennifer Welsh observed that Canadians are "at a significant crossroads. Either we make the choices that will allow us to thrive on the North American continent and contribute actively in creating a better world, or we will cease to exist—in anything but name—as a sovereign country."[97] Welsh believes that Canada must choose what kind of society it wants to be in the future, and it must contribute leadership, money, ideas, and people to create a working world. The message is consistent: because it can, Canada must exert itself in the realm of global politics.

But what are Canada's international priorities? There is much less agreement on this question among observers of Canada and Canadians themselves. Byers suggests that "Canada should, as a country, be asserting itself as a 'global citizen,' shaping the international agenda and using its influence to secure positive, progressive change."[98] Drawing on liberal and constructivist themes, he supports the idea of Canada as a source of new ideas and an agent of change. Others suggest that Canada's role should be defined by its national interests, which according to Steven Kendall Holloway can be identified as national security (including territorial sovereignty), political autonomy, national unity, economic prosperity, and principled self-image (identity).[99] This perspective, more akin with realism, is based on a self-professed sober reflection on Canada's capacities and power in the international system. On the other hand, feminist scholars point out the marginalization of women's voices in much of this debate, and call for a more inclusive approach to thinking about Canadian foreign policy and a broader vision of policy options.[100] The lack of consensus on Canada's role in the world ensures that the debate over Canadian foreign policy will continue.

What challenges does Canada face in the global politics of the future? Climate change will have a growing impact on Canada in the form of warming temperatures, thawing permafrost, soil and coastal erosion, water shortages in the Great Lakes, invasive alien species, extreme weather events, and many other adaptation challenges. The Northwest Passage is expected to be clear of ice for longer periods in the future, raising the possibility that it will become an increasingly important, year-round sea lane. This in turn raises questions about Canadian sovereignty and the economic development of the North, and the place and role of Canada's northern First Nations and Inuit peoples. Arctic security is likely to become increasingly important, with possible disputes over territory and natural resource rights between Canada and Russia and other northern countries. Climate change will also impact on Canadian agriculture and fisheries. Canada's extensive energy sector, especially the tar sands of Alberta, will also come under increasing pressure from rising world energy demand on the one hand and calls for greenhouse gas emission reductions on the other, creating tension between those wishing to take advantage of the economic boom of high energy prices and those wanting to reduce the use of fossil fuels. The recent rise of natural gas production in the United States will challenge the conventional belief that Canada can profit endlessly from exporting crude oil southwards, with or without new and controversial continental pipelines.

We can also expect globalization to continue to have both positive and negative impacts upon Canadian society and the Canadian economy. While international trade and financial flows have been beneficial to many Canadians and have served to increase Canadian exports and facilitate foreign investment, many workers and lower-income Canadians have not seen these benefits in their own lives. Tensions between the obligation to establish laws and regulations consistent with international trade and financial agreements and calls to protect workers, the environment and natural resources, culture, and social programs are likely to continue and even intensify as global economic conditions take a turn for the worse. Canadians have been hit by credit and stock market shocks in the international financial system, and although the fundamentals of the Canadian banking system remain sound, Canada has not been immune to the effects of the global recession. The collapse of the Doha Round of WTO negotiations may prove to be a temporary stumbling block in the path of continued international trade liberalization, but there is a chance that Doha could be a turning point and we will see the rise of protectionism worldwide. This would lower Canada's access to global markets, hurting the Canadian economy and Canadian firms and workers.

Canada's relationship with the United States will continue to be a priority for Canadian governments. With the Obama administration elected to a second term, Canada will as always seek a positive relationship with America, trying to preserve access to U.S. markets and cooperate with the United States on North American security, while at the same time preserving Canadian autonomy and sovereignty. U.S. concerns over border security and the threat of terrorism will continue to place pressure on Canada to cooperate even more closely on North American security. In this respect, the attacks of September 11 are an enduring influence on Canada–U.S. relations. Successive Canadian governments have faced the challenge of how to engage in political, economic, and security cooperation with the United States while still maintaining Canadian sovereignty and foreign policy independence. Even prior to September 11, U.S. officials were looking with unease at the famously undefended Canada–U.S. border as a possible route for terrorists to enter the United States. After September 11, they began looking at border security with much greater concern, and sought policy changes by the Canadian government to strengthen controls over airport security, immigration, and border management. The Canadian government was in a difficult position. On the one hand, there were legitimate security concerns shared by both countries that required increased security cooperation. On the other hand, talk in the United States of "harmonizing" national regulations and building a "perimeter" around the border of North America made many Canadians very nervous. Fearing unilateral U.S. action that could have damaged Canada's access to U.S. markets, the Canadian government did increase the resources spent on a variety of security measures and entered into a new set of security and border management agreements with the United States. This fundamental tension between security and sovereignty in Canada's relations with the U.S. will continue to be a feature of Canadian foreign policy in the future, though a border agreement reached in 2012 is promising.

The Canada–U.S. relationship will also be characterized by conflict and cooperation over issues such as energy policy, climate change and pollution, immigration and refugee policy reform, and trade disputes. The future of Canada's distinctiveness in the face of U.S. cultural influences—especially in the film, television, and Internet mediums—is likely to remain an ongoing concern. Internationally, Canada will also continue to balance its commitments as an ally of the United States with a desire to chart an independent course on many topics, as it has in the past over land mines, the ICC, and the Iraq War. In short, the Obama administration and the Harper government will have to address a familiar agenda and manage their foreign policy differences.

CONCLUSION: ON THE THEME OF INEVITABILITY

Many of the topics we have covered in this book elicit despair. As we warned in the introduction, the complexity of global politics is overwhelming, and the challenges we face seem insurmountable. Forces beyond our individual control drive global structures and processes. Much of the ideological fixations of the past and present, from the recourse to violent conflict throughout history to the tide of globalization, seem as inevitable as changes in the weather. Yet change is the result of human actions, decisions, fears, courage, and other inherently intangible factors. We are all actors on the global stage, and we cannot absent ourselves from the judgments of history. In this light, we all have an obligation to be as informed as possible, and to think beyond our immediate self-interests and desires.

This would, we think, include the need to reflect upon history itself. To even attempt to understand the global politics of the present and future, we need a firm grounding in the past. This grounding will of necessity be formed within our own perspectives on the world, shaped by our experiences and what we have learned through socialization and intellectual inquiry. Yet sensitivity to the past is vital. For example, the word *crusade* has a strong connotation for many people because it evokes an era when Christian forces strove to force their worldview on others, including Muslims and Jews. George W. Bush's initial use of the term after September 11 was quickly rescinded, but it spoke volumes about the general historical ignorance that threatens to make the "clash of civilizations" thesis become an all-consuming reality. This does not in any way justify the use of terrorism, but implies that responses to terrorism, and all of the challenges we will face in the future, need to be cautious and grounded in a sound knowledge and sensitivity to the contemporary implications of history.

The changing nature of global politics suggests that the stability of the global economy, the future of the state, climate change and environmental degradation, global equity and justice, and armed conflict will be the principal issues before students in the 21st century. Further, theoretical debates about how best to study and understand our world will continue to drive the discipline toward new and exciting ideas and normative questions about the ethical implications of our actions. It is our hope that this textbook has provided you with a foundation for understanding the world in which we live, and that your interest in global politics will not end here. This is only the beginning of a lifelong attentiveness to the challenges we will all face in the future. Again, it is tempting to look back at the collective experience of global politics with resignation, and capitulate to the depressing state of human relations and the immense problems involved in achieving international cooperation on the vital issues we face today and in the near future. Yet our perspective must change in spite of (and indeed because of) what appears to be the increasing parochialism of humanity. Given the continuing threats we collectively face—from poverty to terrorism, from war to planetary environmental degradation—it is clear that decision makers and citizens alike must think as globally as possible. The construction of the international equivalent of gated communities, built on ultimately unsustainable foundations, is no long-term answer. States and peoples cannot deal with the increasingly transnational global agenda in a unilateral or isolationist fashion. Our very survival will depend on our capacity for innovation and cooperation. States with extensive multilateral ties, such as Canada, have a vital role to play. But more to the point, we all do. The first step toward solving such problems is learning about them, and we hope this text has provided a challenging introduction to, as well as encouraged further exploration of, the complex world of global politics.

Endnotes

1. A.N. Whitehead, *Science and the Modern World* (New York: New American Library, 1953), 208.
2. P. Allott, "The Concept of International Law," in M. Byers, ed., *The Role of Law in International Politics* (Oxford: Oxford University Press, 2001), 69–89, 70.
3. "Transcript: Inaugural Address of Barack Obama," *The Washington Post*, January 20, 2009, http://media .washingtonpost.com/wp-srv/politics/documents/Obama_Inaugural_Address_012009.html (accessed June 28, 2013).
4. N. Rescher, *Predicting the Future: An Introduction to the Theory of Forecasting* (New York: SUNY Press, 1998), 2. See also the well-regarded journal, *Futures: The Journal of Policy, Planning, and Futures Studies.*
5. G. Friedman and M. Lebard, *The Coming War with Japan* (New York: St. Martin's Press, 1991).
6. D.J. Staley, *History and Future: Using Historical Thinking to Imagine the Future* (Lanham, MD: Lexington Books, 2007).
7. See the excellent introduction by M. Cox to a reprint of Carr's classic, *The Twenty Years' Crisis 1919 to 1939: An Introduction to the Study of International Relations* (London: Palgrave, 2001). See also M. Cox, ed., *E H. Carr: A Critical Reappraisal* (London: Palgrave Macmillan, 2000); and R. Falk, "The Critical Realist Tradition and the Demystification of Power," in S. Gill and J. Mittleman, eds., *Innovation and Transformation in International Studies* (Cambridge, UK: Cambridge University Press, 1997).
8. See C. Escude, *Foreign Policy Theory in Menem's Argentina* (Gainesville: University of Florida Press, 1997); on neoclassical realism, see S. Lobell, N. Ripsman, and J. Taliaferro, *Neoclassical Realism, the State, and Foreign Policy* (Cambridge: Cambridge University Press, 2009).
9. See J. Ann Tickner, "Identity in International Relations Theory: Feminist Perspectives," in Y. Lapid and F. Kratochwil, eds., *The Return of Culture and Identity in IR Theory* (Boulder, CO: Lynne Rienner, 1997), 147–62; and C. Enloe, *The Morning After: Sexual Politics at the End of the Cold War* (Berkeley: California University Press, 1993).
10. See O. Young, "Rights, Rules, and Resources in World Affairs," in O. Young, ed., *Global Governance: Drawing Insights from the Environmental Experience* (Cambridge, MA: MIT Press, 1997), 1–23; and A. Hasenclever, P. Mayer, and V. Rittbeuger, "Integrating Theories of International Regimes," *Review of International Studies* 26, no. 1 (2000), 3–33.
11. See D. Deudney, "Bringing Nature Back In: Geopolitical Theory from the Greeks to the Global Era," in D. Deudney and R. Matthew, eds., *Contested Grounds: Security and Conflict in the New Environmental Politics* (Albany: SUNY Press, 1999), 25–57. See also E. Laferrière and P. Stoett, *IR Theory and Ecological Thought: Toward a Synthesis* (London: Routledge, 1999).
12. See A. Jokic, ed., *Humanitarian Intervention: Moral and Philosophical Issues* (Toronto: Broadview Press, 2003).
13. This is not to argue, however, that the familiar trichotomy is not inherently useful, or cannot be used to great effect. See, for example, M. Doyle, *Ways of War and Peace: Realism, Liberalism, and Socialism* (New York: W.W. Norton, 1997).
14. This explanation is offered by Steve Smith, "Reflectivist and Constructivist Approaches to International Theory," in S. Smith and J. Baylis, eds., *The Globalization of World Politics: An Introduction to International Relations*, 2nd ed. (Oxford: Oxford University Press, 2001), 224–49. Ken Booth offers a fascinating critical survey of theoretical linkages in his *Theory of World Security* (Cambridge: Cambridge University Press, 2007).

15. C. Brown, *International Relations Theory: New Normative Approaches* (Hemel Hempstead, Hertfordshire, UK: Harvester Wheatsheaf, 1992), 3–4. For an example of normative analysis, see R. Irwin, ed., *Ethics and Security in Canadian Foreign Policy* (Vancouver: UBC Press, 2001). Environmental issues have raised the further question of intergenerational ethics: see E.B. Weiss, "Intergenerational Equity: Toward an International Legal Framework," in N. Choucri, ed., *Global Accord: Environmental Challenges and International Responses* (Cambridge, MA: MIT Press, 1993).

16. For example, see A. Acharya and B. Buzan, eds., *Non-Western International Relations Theory: Perspectives on and beyond Asia* (New York: Routledge, 2010); and E. Sridharan, *International Relations and South Asia: Security, Political Economy, Domestic Politics, Identities, and Images* (London: Oxford University Press, 2011).

17. For example, see S. Seth, ed., *Postcolonial Theory and International Relations: A Critical Introduction* (New York: Routledge, 2013).

18. T. Kayaoglu, "Westphalian Eurocentrism in International Relations Theory," *International Studies Review* 12, 2 (June 2010), 193–217. This is also important for understanding the past and could be a key contribution of the constructivist approach. As N. Inayatullah and D. Blaney write, a "commitment to a constructivist IR theory requires … a comparative and historical analysis of how cultures conceptualize others"; see "Knowing Encounters: Beyond Parochialism in IR Theory," in Y. Lapid and F. Kratochwil, eds., *The Return of Culture and Identity in IR Theory* (Boulder, CO: Lynne Rienner, 1997), 65–84, 82.

19. For example, see A. Sinclair, *International Relations Theory and International Law: A Critical Approach* (New York: Cambridge University Press, 2010.

20. See J.L. Snyder, ed., *Religion and International Relations Theory* (New York: Columbia University Press, 2010); and C. Moore and C. Ferrands, eds., *International Relations Theory and Philosophy: Interpretive Dialogues* (New York: Routledge, 2010).

21. R.D. Kaplan, *The Revenge of Geography: What the Map Tells Us about Coming Conflicts and the Battle against Fate* (New York: Random House, 2012), xix.

22. See, for example, M. Schnurr and L. Swatuk, eds., *Natural Resources and Conflict: Towards Critical Environmental Security* (London: Palgrave Macmillan, 2012).

23. R. Little, *The Balance of Power in International Relations: Metaphors, Myths, and Models* (Cambridge: Cambridge University Press, 2007), 3.

24. T. Dodge, *Iraq: From War to a New Authoritarianism* (London: International Institute of Strategic Studies, 2012).

25. National Intelligence Council, *Mapping the Global Future: Report of the National Intelligence Council's 2020 Project* (Washington, DC: US Government Printing Office, 2004), 47.

26. P. Khanna, *The Second World: Empires and Influence in the New World Order* (New York: Random House, 2008), xiv.

27. F. Zakaria, *The Post-American World* (New York: W.W. Norton and Company, Inc., 2008); and F. Zakaria, *The Post-American World: Release 2.0* (New York: W.W. Norton and Company, Inc., 2011).

28. Kishore Mahbubani, *The Great Convergence: Asia, the West, and the Logic of One World* (New York: Public Affairs, 2013), 11.

29. R. Kagan, *The Return of History and the End of Dreams* (New York: Alfred A. Knopf, 2008).

30. M.J. Mazarr, "Rivalry's New Face," *Survival* 54 (August/September 2012), 94.

31. R. Haas, "The Age of Nonpolarity," *Foreign Affairs* 87, no. 3 (May/June 2008), 44–56.

32. See "China Overview," The World Bank, http://www.worldbank.org/en/country/china/overview (accessed February 18, 2013); and *Global Trends 2030: Alternative Worlds* (U.S. National Intelligence Council, 2012), iv.

33. H.J. Morgenthau, *Politics among Nations: The Struggle for Power and Peace*, 5th ed. (New York: Alfred A. Knopf, 1978), 46.

34. J. Dobbins, "War with China," *Survival* 54, 4 (August/September 2012), 7.

35. R.K. Betts, "Wealth, Power, and Instability: East Asia and the United States after the Cold War," *International Security* 18 (Winter 1993/94), 55.

36. A.J. Nathan and A. Scobell, "How China Sees America: The Sum of Beijing's Fears," *Foreign Affairs* 91, 5 (September/October 2012), 32.

37. A.I. Johnston, "Is China a Status Quo Power?" *International Security* 27 (Spring 2003), 6.

38. See C. Constantin and B. Job, "China's Strategic Vision," in B. MacDonald, ed., *Canadians and Asia-Pacific Security*, Vimy Paper 2008 (Ottawa: Conference of Defence Associations Institute, 2008), 28–41.

39. C. Layne, "China's Challenge to US Hegemony," *Current History* 107, no. 705 (January 2008), 13–18.
40. M. Brawley, "The Political Economy of Balance of Power Theory," in T.V. Paul, J.J. Wirtz, and M. Fortman, *Balance of Power: Theory and Practice in the Twenty-First Century* (Stanford, CA: Stanford University Press, 2004), 110–11.
41. See "Angry China," *The Economist* 387, no. 8578 (May 2008), 13.
42. G. John Ikenberry, "The Rise of China and the Future of the West," *Foreign Affairs* 87, no. 1 (January/February 2008), 23–37.
43. See S. Gänzle and A.G. Sens, eds., *The Changing Politics of European Security: Europe Alone?* (New York: Palgrave Macmillan, 2007).
44. S. Serfaty, ed., *A Recast Partnership? Institutional Dimensions of Transatlantic Relations* (Washington, DC: Center for Strategic and International Studies, 2008).
45. See E.B. Rumer, *Russian Foreign Policy Beyond Putin*, Adelphi Paper 390 (London: Routledge and the International Institute of Strategic Studies, 2007), 8; and R. Sakwa, "'New Cold War' or Twenty Years' Crisis? Russia and International Politics," *International Affairs* 84, no. 2 (March 2008), 241–67.
46. See International Institute for Strategic Studies, "Russia/Eurasia," *Strategic Survey 2007* (New York: Routledge, 2007), 188.
47. E. Lucas, *The New Cold War: Putin's Russia and the Threat to the West* (New York: Palgrave Macmillan, 2008).
48. See S.F. Cohen, "The New American Cold War," *The Nation*, July 10, 2006.
49. "Post-Soviet Integration is Unstoppable—Putin," *RiaNovosti* (February 14, 2013), http://en.ria.ru/russia/20130214/179465611.html (accessed February 15, 2013).
50. See M. MacKinnon, *The New Cold War: Revolutions, Rigged Elections, and Pipeline Politics in the Former Soviet Union* (Toronto: Random House Canada, 2008).
51. See "Russia Resurgent," *The Economist*, August 16, 2008, 11.51
52. GDP data from the International Monetary Fund World Economic Outlook Database, http://www.imf.org/external/pubs/ft/weo/2012/02/weodata/index.aspx (accessed February 15, 2013).
53. O. Antonenko, "Medvedev's Choice," *Survival* 50, no. 2 (April/May 2008), 25–31.
54. G. John Ikenberry, "The End of the Neo-Conservative Moment," *Survival* 46 (Spring 2004), 7.
55. R. Kagan, "America's Crisis of Legitimacy," *Foreign Affairs* 83 (March/April 2004), 65.
56. G. Soros, *The Bubble of American Supremacy: Correcting the Misuse of American Power* (New York: Public Affairs, 2004).
57. See D.H. Allin and E. Jones, *Weary Policeman: American Power in an Age of Austerity* (London: International Institute of Strategic Studies, 2012).
58. J.S. Nye Jr., *Soft Power: The Means to Success in World Politics* (New York: Public Affairs, 2004), 5.
59. W. Wohlforth and S. Brooks, *World Out of Balance: International Relations and the Challenge of American Primacy* (Princeton, NJ: Princeton University Press, 2008).
60. Ibid., xii. Of course, even the hard-power victory was a short-lived one as the harsh realities of occupying a country amid fierce resistance took hold.
61. B. Posen, "Command of the Commons: The Military Foundations of U.S. Hegemony," *International Security* 28 (Summer 2003), 6.
62. N.P. Monteiro, "Unrest Assured," *International Security* 36, 3 (Winter 2011/12), 9-40.
63. N. Fergusson, *Colossus: The Price of America's Empire* (New York: The Penguin Press, 2004), 29.
64. J.S. Nye Jr., "Recovering American Leadership," *Survival* 50, no. 1 (February/March 2008), 55–68.
65. A. Chua, *Day of Empire: How Hyperpowers Rise to Global Dominance—and Why They Fail* (New York: Doubleday, 2007).
66. See J. Joffe, *The Imperial Temptation of America* (New York: W.W. Norton and Company Inc., 2006); and J. Sweig, *Friendly Fire: Losing Friends and Making Enemies in the Anti-American Century* (New York: Public Affairs, 2006).
67. C. Layne, *The Peace of Illusions: American Grand Strategy from 1940 to the Present* (Ithaca, NY: Cornell University Press, 2006), 6. See also C. Layne, "The Unipolar Illusion Revisited: The Coming End of the United States' Unipolar Moment," *International Security* 31, no. 2 (Fall 2006), 37.
68. S.P. Huntington, "The Clash of Civilizations?" *Foreign Affairs* 72, no. 3 (Summer 1993), 22.
69. Ibid., 23–4.
70. K. Mahbubani, "The West and the Rest," *The National Interest*, Summer 1992, 3–13.

71. W. Laqueur, *No End to War: Terrorism in the 21st Century* (New York: Continuum, 2003).

72. N. Podhoretz, *World War IV: The Long Struggle against Islamofascism* (New York: Doubleday, 2007).

73. A. Pagden, *Worlds at War: The 2,500-year Struggle Between East and West* (New York: Random House, 2008), 538.

74. A. Adib-Moghaddam, *A Metahistory of the Clash of Civilizations: Us and Them beyond Orientalism* (London: C. Hurst, 2011).

75. S. Gill, "New Constitutionalism, Democratisation and Global Political Economy," in *Pacifica Review* 10, no. 1 (February 1998), 23–38.

76. G. Soros, *The Crisis of Global Capitalism: Open Society Endangered* (New York: Public Affairs, 1998), xxix.

77. E. Luttwak, *Turbo-Capitalism: Winners and Losers in the Global Economy* (New York: HarperCollins, 1999); see also his "Power Relations in the New Economy," *Survival* 44 (Summer 2002), 7–17.

78. *2012 World Development Indicators* (Washington, DC: The World Bank, 2012), 209.

79. Ibid., 228.

80. Ibid., 367.

81. See *Triennial Central Bank Survey: Report on Global Foreign Exchange Market Activity in 2010* (Basel: Bank for International Settlements, 2010), 6.

82. J.A. Frieden, *Global Capitalism: Its Fall and Rise in the Twentieth Century* (New York: W.W. Norton and Company, 2006), xvi.

83. See in particular M. de Villiers, *Water* (Toronto: Stoddart, 2000); and M. Barlow and T. Clarke, *Blue Gold: The Battle against Corporate Theft of the World's Water* (Toronto: Stoddart, 2002), from whom we steal this lovely quote by Michael Parfit (p. xi): "Watersheds come in families; nested levels of intimacy. On the grandest scale the hydrologic web is like all humanity—Serbs, Russians, Koyukon Indians, Amish, the billion lives in the People's Republic of China—it's broadly troubled, but it's hard to know how to help. As you work upstream toward home, you're more closely related. The big river is like your nation, a little out of hand. The lake is your cousin. The creek is your sister. The pond is her child. And, for better or worse, in sickness and in health, you're married to your kitchen sink."

84. J. Sachs, "Disruptions and Potential in the Global Economy," *Current History* 107, no. 705 (January 2008), 21.

85. See H. Weber, *The Politics of Microcredit: Global Governance and Poverty Reduction* (London: Pluto, 2001).

86. W.J. Bernstein, *A Splendid Exchange: How Trade Shaped the World* (New York: Atlantic Monthly Press, 2008), 18.

87. R. Skidelsky, "After the Crash: The Future of Globalization," *Survival* 54, 3 (June/July 2012), 26.

88. "CSI: Credit Crunch: A Special Report on the World Economy," *The Economist*, October 20, 2007, 4.

89. See International Monetary Fund, *Global Financial Stability Report Market Update*, January 28, 2009, 1, http://www.imf.org/external/pubs/ft/fmu/eng/2009/01/index.htm (accessed June 28, 2013).

90. "What Went Wrong: Wall Street's Crisis," *The Economist*, March 22, 2008, 79.

91. See D. Archibugi and I. Young, "Envisioning a Global Rule of Law," in J. Sterba, ed., *Terrorism and International Justice* (Oxford: Oxford University Press, 2003), 158–70.

92. For a collection of sophisticated discussions on international law, see M. Byers, ed., *The Role of Law in International Politics* (Oxford: Oxford University Press, 2001).

93. D. Acemoglu and J.A. Robinson, *Why Nations Fail: the Origins of Power, Prosperity, and Poverty* (New York: Crown Business, 2012), 3, 368–9.

94. See S. Raymond, "Foreign Assistance in an Aging World," *Foreign Affairs*, (March/April 2003), 91–105.

95. M. Byers, *Intent for Nation: What Is Canada For?* (Vancouver: Douglas and McIntyre, 2007), 4. For an analysis asserting Canada's strengths within the context of its close ties with the United States, see M. Hart, *From Pride to Influence: Toward a New Canadian Foreign Policy* (Vancouver: UBC Press, 2008).

96. A. Cohen, *While Canada Slept: How We Lost Our Place in the World* (Toronto: McClelland and Stewart Ltd., 2003), 2.

97. J. Welsh, *At Home in the World: Canada's Global Vision for the 21st Century* (Toronto: Harper Collins, 2004), 23.

98. Byers, *Intent for Nation*, 5.

99. S.K. Holloway, *Canadian Foreign Policy: Defining the National Interest* (Peterborough, ON: Broadview Press, 2006), 2.

100. See C.T. Sjolander, H.A. Smith, and D. Stienstra, eds., *Feminist Perspectives on Canadian Foreign Policy* (Don Mills, ON: Oxford University Press, 2003).

Glossary

ABM See *anti-ballistic missile.* (p.90)

absolute advantage Adam Smith's principle that free trade will benefit all states because they will specialize in those goods they produce most efficiently and trade with other states for those goods they do not produce efficiently. The result is a more efficient use of resources, more goods for consumption, and the political benefits of increased cooperation. (p.129)

absolute gains A theoretical approach suggesting that states judge their self-interest on a wide range of military, political, economic, and cultural considerations, and then act based on this broad judgment. Contrasts with relative gains. (p.125)

absolute poverty The condition of being unable to meet basic human subsistence needs, defined by the United Nations as food, safe drinking water, sanitation facilities, health, education, information, and shelter. In monetary terms, absolute poverty is sometimes measured as an income of US$1.25 a day. Often contrasted with "relative" or comparative poverty. (p.122)

acid rain Sulphur dioxide and nitrogen oxide combined with precipitation. Caused by atmospheric emissions of industry, automobiles, and power plants; harms and in some cases destroys the ecosystems of forests and lakes. (p.396)

ACP See *African, Caribbean and Pacific States.* (p.308)

Acquired Immune Deficiency Syndrome (AIDS) A fatal disease that destroys the body's immune system; spread mainly through sexual contact or injection with infected blood. Often viewed as the plague of the late 20th century. (p.435)

adjudication Deciding a legal issue through the courts or some other third party that can make a binding decision. (p.286)

advisory opinion An ICJ (International Court of Justice) non-binding legal opinion provided by request from the United Nations, a specialized agency, or member states. (p.183)

African, Caribbean and Pacific (ACP) States An organization of 79 states established in 1975 to promote development and trade cooperation between its members and the European Union. (p.308)

African National Congress (ANC) A South African political party, founded in 1912, that for years opposed apartheid and is now the governing party. Its former leader, Nelson Mandela, was released from prison in 1990 and served as South Africa's first president. (p.284)

African Union (AU) A regional international organization founded in July 1999 (formerly the Organization for African Unity or OAU) to promote development, sovereignty, and cooperation among independent African states; is often involved in regional peacekeeping efforts as well. (p.266)

Agricultural Revolution Large-scale shifts in prevailing food production methods that have an impact on the whole of society. (p.443)

AIDS See *Acquired Immune Deficiency Syndrome.* (p.435)

Alexander the Great (Alexander III) (356–323 BCE) King of Macedon, 336–323 B.C.E. Conquered Thrace, Illyria, and Egypt; invaded Persia and northern India; virtual leader of Mediterranean centre of civilization. (p.41)

Alexander III See *Alexander the Great.* (p.41)

alliance A group of actors who pool their resources for a common cause, usually in relation to national defence against a specific external threat. (p.73)

alliance cohesion The degree to which the members of an alliance hold common goals and coordinate policy. (p.74)

Allied powers Most commonly used in reference to the alliance of countries that fought the Axis Powers led by Nazi Germany and Imperial Japan in World War II. Included the U.S., the United Kingdom, the Soviet Union, Canada, Australia, and many others. (p.68)

American Civil War (1861–65) War between the United States of America (Union) and the secessionist Southern Confederate States of America (Confederacy). The war destroyed the Confederacy and ended the institution of slavery in the United States. (p.56)

anarchy In its most basic form, the absence of central government in a society. In global politics it is often used to refer to the absence of a world government, which remains a prominent part of the realist perspective's ontology. More generally, it refers to lawlessness, and the collective action dilemmas this presents to political actors. (p.17)

ANC See *African National Congress.* (p.284)

Angell, Norman (1874–1967) Famous British pacifist who wrote *The Great Illusion*, 1910. In international relations theory, he was somewhere between an idealist and a liberal. (p.13)

Antarctic Treaty System (ATS) A set of negotiated agreements based on the Antarctic Treaty, signed in 1959 by 12 so-called consultative parties with claims on and able to demonstrate a substantial scientific interest in Antarctica. Established the area as a demilitarized zone; various subsequent agreements have been added on conservation and environmental protection. (p.380)

anti-ballistic missile (ABM) A missile designed to intercept and destroy incoming ballistic missiles. The development and deployment of ABMs had been restricted for 30 years by the 1972 ABM Treaty, which was abrogated by the United States in 2002. (p.90)

anticipatory compliance A phenomenon in governmental or non-governmental organizations in which junior officials, trying to anticipate what their superiors want to hear, will omit or de-emphasize information that contrasts with the views of senior officials and leaders; this has profound implications for foreign policy decisions. (p.114)

anti-Semitism Prejudice, discrimination, or persecution against Jewish people. (p.66)

apartheid Racial separation policy in South Africa until the early 1990s; is sometimes used to refer to the treatment of Palestinians by the Israeli government. (p.337)

appeasement Efforts to satisfy a potential aggressor by making territorial or other concessions. Most famously, this largely maligned policy failed to satisfy Adolf Hitler and prevent World War II, though it is impossible to argue that other approaches would have produced other outcomes. (p.67)

Arab League (or League of Arab States) An organization of 22 Arab states in the Middle East and North and Northeast Africa, founded March 1945. (p.161)

Arab Spring Term used in reference to a series of uprisings and revolutions in the Middle East and North Africa that began in late 2010. The term alludes to the Revolutions of 1848 (the "springtime of the people") and the uprising against communist rule in Czechoslovakia in 1968 (the "Prague Spring"). (p.213)

armistice In the general sense, a negotiated peace; most often used to describe the end of World War I. (p.63)

arms control Any diplomatic effort designed to regulate levels or types of arms (bilaterally or multilaterally, with conventional or nuclear arms). (p.14)

ASEAN See *Association of Southeast Asian Nations.* (p.317)

Asian Development Bank A multilateral bank similar to the World Bank with a regional focus; headquarters established in 1966 in Manila, Philippines. (p.161)

Association of Southeast Asian Nations (ASEAN) International organization formed by the Bangkok Declaration in 1967, by Indonesia, Malaysia, the Philippines, Singapore, and Thailand. Membership has expanded and now also includes Brunei, Burma (Myanmar), Cambodia, Laos, and Vietnam. (p.317)

Atlantic Charter Statement of general principles, signed by Roosevelt and Churchill in August 1941, related to postwar order, including principles of national self-determination, opposition to aggression, disarmament, and equal access to trade and raw materials. (p.164)

atomic bomb A weapon based on the rapid splitting of fissionable materials, inducing an explosion with deadly blast, heat, and radiation impact; more commonly referred to as a *nuclear weapon.* (p.69)

ATS See *Antarctic Treaty System.* (p.380)

AU See *African Union.* (p.266)

authoritarianism A political system in which individual freedom is subordinate to the power of the state, which is concentrated in one leader or group not accountable to the people; often referred to as *totalitarianism.* (p.103)

automation The replacement of human workers with machines. See *robotics.* (p.454)

Axis powers Alliance of countries led by Nazi Germany and Imperial Japan in World War II. Also included Italy and some smaller countries conquered by Germany and led by collaborator governments. (p.68)

balance of payments The net flow of money into, and out of, a state. Encompasses trade, tourist expenditures, sales of services, foreign aid, debt payments, profits, etc. (p.126)

balance of power The condition that exists within a contemporary or historical system (regional or global) in which no one state has the power to dominate all the others. (p.16)

balance of trade The relationship between exports and imports. (p.125)

ballistic missile A missile using a ballistic guidance system influenced by gravity and friction and employing no thrust after its initial boost phase. Some such missiles travel 300 metres; others can travel halfway around the world. (p.259)

basic human needs Adequate food intake (calories, vitamins, protein, minerals, etc.), disease-free and toxin-free drinking water, minimum clothing and shelter, literacy, sanitation, health care, employment, and dignity. (p.306)

Bay of Pigs A part of the Cuban coastline where in 1961 a group of Cuban refugees staged a failed invasion under American auspices. (p.95)

beggar-thy-neighbour An economic policy of states that attempts to alter their balance of trade by devaluing currency and raising barriers to imports. This strategy is associated with mercantilism. (p.126)

Berlin Wall A wall erected in 1961 by East Germany to prevent people from fleeing East Germany into the West. It encircled West Berlin, which was controlled by the Western allies during the Cold War, and became a symbol of the East–West division until it was dismantled in 1989 as the Cold War ended. (p.93)

biodiversity According to the Convention on Biological Diversity, the variability among living organisms from all sources including, inter alia, terrestrial, marine, and other aquatic ecosystems and the ecological complexes of which they are part; this includes diversity within species, between species, and of ecosystems. (p.391)

biometric identification The identification of individuals through the acquisition, storage, and retrieval of information about their physical or behavioural traits. Biometric data can include voice, fingerprint, gait, DNA, retinal, fingerprint, and many other traits. (p.421)

biosphere Life and living processes at or near the earth's surface, extending from the oceans' floors and the lithosphere to about 75 kilometres into the atmosphere. (p.374)

bipolar/bipolarity Global political system with two competing poles of great power, such as during the U.S.–U.S.S.R. Cold War era. (p.74)

bipolycentrism A distribution of power in which there are two main poles of power as well as a number of other less powerful, but still significant, power centres. (p.75)

Bolsheviks Members of the radical minority in the Russian Social Democratic Party (1903–17), led by Vladimir Lenin. Carried out the Communist revolution of 1917. (p.63)

bounded rationality The argument that rational actor decisions are seldom made under ideal conditions due to time constraints, incomplete information, and limited individual capacity. (p.108)

bourgeoisie An originally French term for the middle or merchant class. It became a derogatory term with its adoption by Karl Marx and Friedrich Engels to represent the owners of the means of production and the class enemy of the proletariat (workers). (p.23)

boycott The refusal of a country to import goods and services from another country; done for punitive reasons; also a strategy employed by NGOs and other civil society groups to ostracize MNCs and other companies for labour, environmental, and other human rights issues. (p.97)

Bretton Woods system The post–World War II international monetary order, named after the 1944 conference held at Bretton Woods, New Hampshire; the main institutions in the system were the IMF, IBRD, and GATT. (p.145)

bureaucratic politics model An approach to the study of foreign policy that focuses on bargaining and compromises among governmental organizations and agencies pursuing their own interests. (p.107)

Camp David A mountain retreat for the U.S. president in Maryland, and site of the famous

Camp David accords signed in 1978 by President Anwar el-Sadat of Egypt and Prime Minister Menachem Begin of Israel. (p.245)

Canadian International Development Agency (CIDA) Agency of the Canadian government responsible for planning and implementing Canada's development programs. (p.429)

capitalism An economic system based on the private ownership of property and commercial enterprise, competition for profits, and limited government interference in the marketplace. (p.142)

capital mobility Ability of international investors to invest in foreign countries with minimal constraints. (p.420)

cartel An international agreement among producers of a commodity that attempts to control the production and pricing of that commodity. See *Organization of the Petroleum Exporting Countries*. (p.151)

Catherine the Great (Catherine II) (1729–96) Tsarina of Russia, 1762–96. Expanded and strengthened the Russian Empire, chiefly at the expense of Turkey. (p.54)

CCAMLR See *Convention on the Conservation of Antarctic Marine Living Resources*. (p.380)

CFCs See *chlorofluorocarbons*. (p.380)

chlorofluorocarbons (CFCs) Gaseous compounds largely used in refrigeration and air conditioning sectors, as well as in aerosols and in the manufacture of plastics and other products; thought to be largely responsible for ozone-layer depletion; broadly phased out by the Montreal Protocol. The most widely used CFC was CFC-12. (p.380)

Churchill, Winston (1874–1965) British prime minister (1940–45, 1951–55), naval officer, and author; known as one of the greatest wartime leaders and orators in history. (p.73)

CIDA See *Canadian International Development Agency*. (p.429)

CIS See *Commonwealth of Independent States*. (p.101)

CITES See *Convention on International Trade in Endangered Species of Wild Fauna and Flora*. (p.394)

classical liberals Liberals such as Adam Smith and David Ricardo who established the principles of modern liberal economic theory, based on free trade and minimal government interference in the operation of the market. (p.129)

client states States highly dependent on great powers for military or economic aid. (p.80)

climate change Long-term changes in weather patterns. In global politics, most often used to refer to anthropomorphic climate change, the warming of the earth due to the buildup of carbon dioxide and other greenhouse gasses in the atmosphere from human activity, especially the burning of fossil fuels. (p.3)

Cold War The ideological, economic, and geopolitical hostility between the United States and the U.S.S.R. in the bipolar era (roughly 1947–90). (p.4)

collective defence An effort by two or more states to defend their territory or their interests against a common threat or enemy. Collective defence arrangements are generally called *alliances*. (p.73)

collective security Mutual multilateral consent to an agreement that declares that aggression by one state on any other is an attack on the whole; the primary security mechanism created by the UN Charter in Chapter VII. (p.14)

commodity speculation The purchase of a commodity with an aim to sell it when, and if, its value increases. Commodity speculation can drive up prices and can distort government efforts to manage the economy. (p.300)

Commonwealth Voluntary association of former dominions, colonies, and other overseas territories of Britain. By 2013, there were 54 state members; the annual meeting of heads of state generates some attention. (p.6)

Commonwealth of Independent States (CIS) Arrangement among many of the former republics of the U.S.S.R., formed in December 1991. Includes Armenia, Azerbaijan, Byelorussia (Belarus), Kazakhstan, Kirghizia (Kyrgyzstan), Moldavia (Moldova), Russia, Tadzhikistan (Tajikistan), Turkmenistan, Ukraine, Uzbekistan, and Georgia. (p.101)

communal conflicts Conflicts between communal groups, primarily racial and ethnic groups. The roots of communal conflicts are local, including competing claims to power, autonomy, or independence based upon asserted differences of ethnicity, nationality, religion, language, or social class. (p.207)

comparative advantage David Ricardo's concept that states will still benefit from free trade even if they do not have an absolute advantage in any good. Such states will still have a comparative advantage with respect to trading partners if they produce some goods more efficiently than others do. That comparative advantage is enough for them to benefit from trade. (p.129)

complex interdependence Developed by Robert Keohane and Joseph Nye, a framework that refers to the complex transnational connections between states and societies. The main argument is that the decline of military force as a policy tool and the increased importance of economic and other actors should increase the probability of cooperation among states. It is considered as a synthesis of elements of realist and liberal thought. (p.21)

compradore A native and/or citizen of a colonized country who acts as the agent of the colonizer. In postcolonial Central and South America, the comprador class refers to the local elites whose interests are intertwined with the wealthy classes in the United States. (p.134)

Concert of Europe A system of consultation established among the European powers after the defeat of Napoleon (1815). The aim of the concert was to maintain the peace and manage the balance of power in Europe, which it did with considerable success until the outbreak of the Crimean War (1854–56). (p.55)

Congress of Vienna (1814–15) Peace conference following the Napoleonic Wars at which the great powers—Austria, Russia, Prussia, Great Britain, and France—agreed on territorial and political terms of settlement. (p.55)

conscription A policy requiring all men of a certain age to serve in the military, during peace or war. Also referred to as the *draft*. (p.60)

constructive engagement The attempt to influence a state's domestic policies by maintaining trade and diplomatic ties, as opposed to the use of sanctions. (p.339)

constructivism One of the dominant paradigms/critical theories of international relations discipline, suggesting that the social construction of dominant ideas, including anarchy and conflict, has a decisive role in the outcome of events. Often associated with a liberal or a radical/critical perspective. (p.30)

containment The United States' grand strategy during the Cold War, designed to contain the perceived military, political, and ideological threat of the U.S.S.R. (p.91)

Convention on International Trade in Endangered Species of Wild Fauna and Flora (CITES) Multilateral accord (1973) that regulates export, transit, and importation of endangered animal and plant species. Meets biannually to determine species' status. The Convention has 177 member states as of 2013. (p.394)

Convention on the Conservation of Antarctic Marine Living Resources (CCAMLR) Promulgated in 1980 by consultative parties to the Antarctic Treaty System to protect the environment and resources of the Antarctic seas region. (p.380)

corporate social responsibilities Perceived ethical obligations of the private sector toward the people and ecology affected by its operations, often expressed in voluntary behavioural codes. (p.304)

Council of Europe International body created in 1949 by representatives of Great Britain, France, Belgium, the Netherlands, Luxembourg, Norway, Sweden, Denmark, Ireland, and Italy; joined by Greece and Turkey in 1950; aimed toward a European federation. (p.341)

counterinsurgency Efforts by governments and armed forces to defeat guerrilla or insurgency movements seeking to overthrow the government. Sometimes referred to by its acronym, COIN, such operations are considered a challenge for conventional militaries and are frequently associated with human rights abuses and repression. (p.275)

Crimean War (1854–56) France, Great Britain, and Turkey allied against Russia and fought a bitter war on the Crimean peninsula. (p.55)

crimes against humanity Genocide, enslavement, rape, deportation, imprisonment, murder, torture, or persecutions on political, racial, or religious grounds committed against any civilian population. (p.344)

crimes against peace Generally, planning, preparing, initiating, or waging a war of aggression and participating in a common plan or conspiracy for the accomplishment of war crimes. (p.344)

cruise missile A missile, guided remotely (from satellites in some cases), that can fly low enough to escape radar detection, and can deliver conventional or nuclear warheads. (p.11)

cultural imperialism Imposition of values on one society by another by direct administrative means (such as education) or more subtle means (such as television commercials); some critics charge it is also inherent in any universalizing project related to global governance and international law. (p.304)

currency speculation Purchasing of foreign currency with an aim to sell it when, and if, its value increases. Currency speculation can drive up the value of currencies and can distort government efforts to manage the economy. (p.152)

customary law Law derived from customary behaviour and a long acceptance of that behaviour by actors in the social setting. In international law, customary law can be codified or made into formal law through treaties between states or through the creation of domestic law within states. (p.180)

customs union An agreement among a group of states establishing a common external tariff applicable to all imports from outside the member states. As a complementary measure, internal barriers to trade are removed. Different from a free trade area, in which internal barriers are removed but external tariff barriers remain set by individual states. (p.315)

Defence Industrial Base Term used in reference to the capacity of a state to design, produce, and maintain military equipment. Critics of the political influence of defence industries often use the term *military–industrial complex* instead. (p.221)

Defensive Realism Approach in the realist school of international relations theory that suggests states seek survival and self-help in an anarchic system primarily through defensive, rather than offensive, policies to protect their territory and sovereignty. (p.19)

deficit The amount by which a government's spending exceeds its revenues in any fiscal year; there is great controversy in policy circles regarding the impact of deficit spending. (p.126)

democraticization Efforts to introduce or increase participatory and responsible government in states, primarily through elections and the development of institutions, law, and police and judicial system reform. Democratization is often assisted by outside governments and NGOs. (p.99)

demographic transition A theory that argues that the decline in the industrialized states' birth rates is a direct consequence of social and economic development, and that with time other states will follow. (p.412)

Dependency Theory Contends that advanced capitalist states have created a neo-colonial relationship with postcolonial countries, which are dependent on capital, technology, and the market demands of rich states; originated in Central and South America in the work of critical theorists, especially neo-Marxists. (p.26)

desertification Process in which potentially productive land is transformed into arid, desert-like territory. A severe form of land erosion. (p.301)

détente A relaxation of tensions or a decrease in the level of hostility between the superpowers during the Cold War. (p.81)

deterrence Persuading an opponent not to attack by making sure it is aware that a counterattack would follow. Pertains especially to the nuclear strategy of the superpowers during the Cold War. (p.87)

disinformation Spreading of false propaganda or forged documents to confuse counterintelligence or create political confusion, unrest, and scandal. Some would argue that governments do this with their own citizens as well. (p.468)

doves Informal term used to describe political figures or commentators who advocate less hardline or confrontational approaches to their countries' enemies. (p.83)

drone A pilotless aircraft technology used by militaries and intelligence agencies for reconnaissance, targeting, and missile strikes. The U.S. government's use of drones to attack terrorist suspects has created considerable international controversy. (p.472)

dumping The practice of exporting a good to another country and selling that good at a price below the cost of production, gaining a large market share for the seller and at the same time putting competing producers out of business. The price of the product will then be raised to achieve a profit. Dumping is illegal in most international trade agreements, although accusations of dumping remain common. (p.148)

ecocide Deliberate destruction of the environment for military purposes. Can also refer to other forms of environmental destruction. (p.28)

ecofeminists Feminists who regard gender discrimination and environmental degradation as parts of a social structure that simultaneously devalues both women and nature. They suggest that gender equality may influence the environmental behaviour of states. In other words, states with greater gender equality are more likely to protect the environment. (p.27)

Economic and Social Council (ECOSOC)
Established under the UN Charter as the principal organ to coordinate economic, social, and related work of the 14 UN specialized agencies, UN functional commissions, and 5 UN regional commissions. (p.166)

Economic Community of West African States (ECOWAS) Founded in 1975 to promote cooperation in West Africa; often involved in regional peacekeeping efforts. ECOWAS currently has 15 members. (p.266)

ECOSOC See *Economic and Social Council.* (p.166)

ECOWAS See *Economic Community of West African States.* (p.266)

EEZ See *exclusive economic zone.* (p.379)

electronic numerical integrator and computer (ENIAC) One of the first operational computers. It was so large that it filled a 9-by-17-metre room. (p.445)

embargo The refusal of one country or a group of countries to export goods to another, for punitive reasons. One famous example is the American embargo on Cuba. (p.66)

emigration Leaving one's home country to live in another. (p.420)

English School realists A group of realist scholars (mainly Charles Manning, Martin Wight, and Hedley Bull) who had a common academic understanding of global politics, and contributed the idea of an "international society" or a "society of states." Also referred to as *liberal realists.* (p.19)

enhanced interrogation A term used by the George W. Bush administration to describe interrogation techniques that included hypothermia, stress positions, and waterboarding. These techniques were used at secret CIA detention centres and secret prisons around the world. The legality of these techniques has been repeatedly challenged; they are generally considered torture by legal experts. (p.231)

ENIAC See *electronic numerical integrator and computer.* (p.445)

epistemic community A global network of knowledge-based professionals in scientific and technological areas that share essential professional values and often have an impact on policy decisions. (p.457)

EPZs See *export processing zones.* (p.296)

ethnic cleansing The forced removal of an ethnic group from their area of residence using tactics that include executions, the destruction of homes, and rape to instill fear in the target population. In its ultimate form, ethnic cleansing constitutes genocide. (p.210)

ethnic conflicts Conflicts between ethnic groups, often as a result of intergroup differences, ancient hatreds and century-old feuds, collective fear of the future, ethnic security dilemmas, and/or ethnic nationalism. (p.207)

EU See *European Union.* (p.124)

euro The common currency of European Union states, introduced gradually in the late 1990s and now in use in 17 out of 27 EU states in the "eurozone." Following the global recession, the eurozone has faced an economic crisis, which has had its deepest impact on the southern states: Greece, Spain, Italy, and Portugal. (p.315)

European Union (EU) Previously the European Economic Community, established by the Treaty of Rome, signed on March 25, 1957, and further cemented by the Maastricht Treaty (though it was rejected by some members) of 1991. After a series of enlargements, now includes 27 states that have coordinated policies in a number of areas, such as migration and currency, but have fallen short of a common security and foreign policy. (p.124)

exchange rate The values of two currencies relative to each other. For example, one Canadian dollar may be worth 90 cents of an American dollar. (p.127)

exclusive economic zone (EEZ) The 200-nautical-mile or 370-kilometre area in which coastal states have jurisdiction over the resources of the sea and the seabed (that is, beyond their 12-mile or 19-kilometre territory) but not territorial rights. Accepted as customary law. (p.379)

export processing zones (EPZs) Industrial zones within a state in which imported materials undergo some degree of processing before being re-exported. EPZs have special regulations and other incentives established by governments to attract foreign investors; free trade zones, special economic zones, bonded warehouses, free ports, and customs zones are also considered export processing zones. (p.296)

exports Products shipped or otherwise transferred to foreign states. (p.6)

extradition The process by which one country will apprehend and transfer an individual to another country. Typically, extradition follows a process agreed to in an extradition treaty between two countries, and usually involves individuals charged or convicted of crimes in one country who have fled to another. Not all countries have extradition treaties with each other, complicating extradition in some cases. (p.234)

extraordinary rendition The process by which an individual is transferred from one country to another in secret and without legal oversight. The U.S. government has used extraordinary rendition to move suspected terrorists to detention facilities in other countries around the world, often for enhanced interrogation or torture. (p.231)

extraterritoriality In diplomatic practice, the tradition that visiting diplomats are exempt from local legal jurisdiction. (p.245)

FAO See *Food and Agriculture Organization of the UN.* (p.161)

fascism An authoritarian ideology that subsumes individuals before the state; popular in Italy, Spain, and Germany in the period leading up to World War II. (p.63)

FDI See *foreign direct investment.* (p.309)

feminism In IR theory, perspectives emphasizing the role of gender in global politics; feminists are most often liberal or critical theorists, while some are Marxists or ecofeminists. (p.26)

first strike The opening attack in a hypothetical nuclear war, launched by an aggressor state in hopes that it will destroy the attacked nation's capacity to retaliate. (p.88)

Food and Agriculture Organization of the UN (FAO) Formed in 1945 as a UN specialized agency to deal with food production; based in Rome. (p.161)

foreign direct investment (FDI) Buying stock, real estate, industry, mines, or other assets in a foreign country with the aim of gaining a controlling interest (usually over 50 percent) in that asset. Differs from portfolio investment, which involves investment solely to gain capital appreciation through market fluctuations. (p.309)

Fourteen Points U.S. President Woodrow Wilson's formulation of allied war aims and of a general peace program, delivered to Congress on January 8, 1918. (p.14)

Fourth World An expression referring to peoples living nomadic or pastoral lifestyles outside the industrialized norm and/or stateless and marginalized peoples (especially indigenous peoples). (p.305)

free trade International movement of goods completely or relatively unrestricted by tariffs or non-tariff barriers. (p.9)

functionalism International cooperation in largely technical areas (communications, travel, trade, environmental protection) and related theories about possibly resultant political integration. (p.185)

G7 See *Group of Seven.* (p.154)

G8 See *Group of Eight.* (p.6)

G77 See *Group of 77.* (p.308)

game theory A mathematical approach to modelling political behaviour. It is used by international relations scholars to evaluate decision-making patterns among two or more actors under certain prescribed conditions. (p.115)

GATS See *General Agreement on Trade in Services.* (p.149)

GATT See *General Agreement on Tariffs and Trade.* (p.127)

GDP See *gross domestic product.* (p.16)

General Agreement on Tariffs and Trade (GATT) Concluded in 1948, followed by successive rounds of negotiations culminating in the establishment of the World Trade Organization in 1995. General aim is to facilitate expanded international trade with the reduction of trade barriers. (p.127)

General Agreement on Trade in Services (GATS) An agreement first reached in GATT (and which now is part of the WTO) that seeks trade liberalization in the service sector. (p.149)

General Assembly The democratic core of the UN, in which all 193 member states are equally represented. Meets at the UN headquarters in New York City. (p.165)

Generalized System of Preferences (GSP) A system approved by GATT in 1971 that authorizes developed countries to give preferential tariff treatment to less-developed countries. (p.308)

genetically modified organisms (GMOs) Plants and animals genetically altered by adding, subtracting, or otherwise changing their genetic code; also referred to as *living modified organisms* in the Cartegena Protocol of the CBD. (p.293)

genetic engineering Biotechnological process by which the natural genetic code of an organism is altered, producing genetically modified organisms. A contentious ethical and trade issue today. (p.378)

geopolitics A form of foreign policy analysis that emphasizes the link between geographic variables (such as location, resources, and topography) and political behaviour. Political action is seen as largely determined by geography. (p.377)

glasnost The Soviet policy of increased openness, developed and implemented under the leadership of Mikhail Gorbachev in the late 1980s. (p.99)

global civil society Voluntary associations, movements, parties, unions, and individuals that promote social change and resist institutions advancing the neoliberal economic policy agenda of privatization and deregulation and the elimination of social safety nets and economic borders. (p.177)

global commons Elements of the earth and atmosphere (oceans, seabed, atmosphere, outer space) that are the property of no one nation or individual but are deemed to be the property of all. (p.374)

global governance The regulation of interdependent relations between and among states, markets, citizens, organizations, and other non-state transnational actors through the development of institutions, law, and other formal or informal mechanisms of cooperation. (p.159)

globalization Term used to describe the increasing interconnection between states, economies, and societies through telecommunications technology, trade, and travel such that events in one part of the world have repercussions in other parts of the world. (p.3)

global prohibition regimes Norms established in international or domestic law that prohibit states and non-state actors from pursuing certain activities, such as piracy, slavery, hijacking, counterfeiting, and many other practices deemed unacceptable and illegal. (p.188)

GMOs See *genetically modified organisms.* (p.293)

GNP See *gross national product.* (p.414)

Golan Heights Contested territory adjacent to Israel, which has occupied it since the 1967 war. (p.207)

good offices Services, roles, and functions provided by a third party in an effort to resolve a dispute. (p.247)

Great Depression Severe unemployment and financial collapse of the early 1930s; international in scope. (p.66)

great powers The most powerful political units in a system (usually states). (p.76)

greenhouse gas Gases (typically carbon dioxide, nitrous oxide, and methane) that contribute to the greenhouse effect, or trapping of heat from the sun in the Earth's atmosphere. The natural greenhouse effect is a necessary condition of life on Earth, but the excessive buildup of greenhouse gases due to human activity is leading to dangerous increases in global temperatures. (p.374)

Green Revolution The increase in agricultural production in many developing countries in the 1950s and 1960s, made possible by genetically engineered grains, fertilizers, and more efficient use of land. (p.443)

gross domestic product (GDP) A measure of national income that excludes foreign earnings. (p.16)

gross national product (GNP) The sum of all the goods and services produced by a state's nationals, whether in that state or abroad. (p.414)

Group of Eight (G8) The eight largest economies (the United States, Japan, Germany, France, Russia, Italy, the United Kingdom, and Canada); government representatives meet often to coordinate political and economic policies. (p.6)

Group of Seven (G7) The seven economically largest free-market states: Canada, France, United Kingdom, Italy, Japan, the United States, and Germany. Russia is now a participant in what are now referred to as the G8. (p.154)

Group of 77 (G77) The 77 Third World states that co-sponsored the Joint Declaration of Developing Countries in 1963 calling for greater equity in North–South trade. Currently includes 130 members. (p.308)

groupthink The tendency of decision makers to develop, in groups, a common perception of an issue or problem and exclude those with different opinions or ideas. (p.114)

GSP See *Generalized System of Preferences.* (p.308)

Guantanamo Bay U.S. naval base on Cuba, controlled by and under the jurisdiction of the U.S. under the terms of a U.S.–Cuba treaty. The Cuban government disputes the right of the U.S. to control the base. The naval base is the location of the infamous Guantanamo Bay Detention Camp, used by the U.S. to hold prisoners seized in the war on terror. The camp has been the target of strong domestic and international criticism over its suspect legality and the use of torture/enhanced interrogation in the facility. (p.231)

gunrunning Informal term used to refer to illegal trafficking in small arms and light weapons. (p.221)

Hapsburg Ruling house of Austria, 1282–1918; provided the emperors of the Holy Roman Empire from 1438 to 1806. (p.43)

hard power A reference to traditional measures of power, such as economic capability, population, and especially military strength. (p.16)

hawks An informal term for political figures or commentators who advocate more uncompromising or confrontational policies toward their country's enemies. (p.83)

head of state An individual who represents the sovereignty of a state. In many cases, this individual is different from the head of government (for example, the British monarch and the British prime minister; the Queen of Canada, represented by the Governor-General, and the prime minister of Canada); in the United States, the president assumes both roles. (p.244)

hegemonic power/hegemon A dominant state that uses its military and economic power to establish global rules and institutions in accord with its interests. (p.138)

hegemonic stability Theory that a leading state can provide the public good of stability in the global political system, on the condition that it maintain its contested hegemonic status. (p.75)

hegemony Political dominance; either undisputed leadership in politics or dominance in the realm of ideas. (p.75)

HIV Human Immunodeficiency Virus, which can lead to AIDS. See *acquired immune deficiency syndrome.* (p.435)

Hobson, John (1858–1940) English economist who wrote on imperialism. (p.24)

Holy Roman Empire (962–1806 CE) Western European political entity claiming to be successor to the Roman Empire (suspended in 476 CE); a European commonwealth; lost importance after Thirty Years' War (1618–48). (p.54)

homogenization Any process in which different entities become increasingly similar; the diminishment of diversity. (p.300)

human security A framework that focuses on vulnerable individuals, rather than states, as the reference point for security policy. Freedom from want and freedom from fear are the cornerstones of the human security agenda. The governments of Canada and Norway were once the most vocal state advocates of human security. (p.4)

IAEA See *International Atomic Energy Agency.* (p.188)

IBRD See *International Bank for Reconstruction and Development.* (p.132)

ICBM See *intercontinental ballistic missile.* (p.90)

ICC See *International Criminal Court.* (p.181)

ICISS See *International Commission on Intervention and State Sovereignty.* (p.277)

ICJ See *International Court of Justice.* (p.171)

ICRC See *International Committee of the Red Cross.* (p.175)

IDA See *International Development Association.* (p.309)

idealism A post–World War I political theory based largely on liberal philosophies about the preservation of peace. U.S. president Woodrow Wilson's Fourteen Points and the League of Nations are often described as manifestations of idealism in global politics. Idealism is generally considered to have vanished as a distinct theory with the outbreak of World War II. (p.13)

IDPs See *internally displaced persons.* (p.430)

IFC See *International Finance Corporation.* (p.309)

IFIs See *international financial institutions.* (p.121)

IGOs See *intergovernmental organizations.* (p.160)

IJC See *International Joint Commission.* (p.395)

IMF See *International Monetary Fund.* (p.123)

immigration The arrival of foreigners in a country for the purpose of taking up residence; a vital source of economic production. (p.420)

imperialism A policy of establishing political and economic control over foreign territories and all the intellectual accompaniments; at times used to refer to the spread of Western capitalism and the current processes of globalization. See also *cultural imperialism.* (p.24)

incendiary weapons Bombs and munitions used to start fires. Typical incendiary munitions include napalm and white phosphorus. (p.264)

industrial espionage The use of human or electronic means to covertly acquire industrial secrets. (p.457)

Industrial Revolution The mechanization of industry and associated changes in social and economic patterns in Europe (and especially Great Britain) in the late 18th and early 19th centuries. (p.443)

infanticide The deliberate killing of infants. (p.413)

Information Revolution The social and economic changes caused by advances in computer and communications technology. (p.443)

insurgency A philosophical and operational approach to warfare most commonly used by resistance or revolutionary movements incapable of achieving victory through conventional military means. Often referred to as *guerrilla warfare,* insurgencies emphasize efforts to secure political loyalty among the population and utilize small-unit hit-and-run tactics, rather than achieve decisive victory in battle. (p.228)

Intellectual Property Rights (IPR) A legal framework establishing ownership over ideas, discoveries, designs, and artistic creations. Common examples of IPR include copyright, trademark, and patents. (p.148)

intercontinental ballistic missile (ICBM) A ballistic missile capable of flying from one continent to another. Ballistic missiles were a central feature of nuclear deterrence during the Cold War. (p.90)

interdependence A state of affairs in which states and societies are increasingly connected by trade, finance, travel, and communication to the point they become mutually sensitive and responsive to events and policy changes. Interdependence is considered (especially by liberals) a characteristic of contemporary relations between nation-states. (p.162)

intergovernmental organizations (IGOs) International organizations created by and composed of member states. (p.160)

internally displaced persons (IDPs) Individuals or groups fleeing war or human and/or natural disasters who have not crossed an internationally recognized state border. (p.430)

International Atomic Energy Agency (IAEA) A United Nations agency that inspects nuclear power plants (and carries out other periodic inspections) to ensure compliance with the Non-Proliferation Treaty; it also promotes the development of nuclear energy. (p.188)

International Bank for Reconstruction and Development (IBRD) Development-based lending agency affiliated with the UN; commonly referred to as the World Bank. (p.132)

International Commission on Intervention and State Sovereignty (ICISS) An international panel of experts convened to explore the issue of when intervention in a state was justifiable in order to protect human security. The commission's final report was titled *The Responsibility to Protect*. (p.277)

International Committee of the Red Cross (ICRC) A neutral humanitarian relief organization, founded in 1859 and based in Switzerland, that cares for the wounded during battle and observes the treatment of prisoners of war. Its counterpart in Muslim countries is the International Committee of the Red Crescent. (p.175)

International Court of Justice (ICJ) The World Court, which sits in The Hague, Netherlands, with 15 judges. (p.171)

International Criminal Court (ICC) Created in 1998 by the 120 signatories to the Rome Statute. The Rome Statute entered into force on July 1, 2002. The 18 judges of the ICC were elected in February 2003, and the ICC was formally inaugurated in March 2003; located in The Hague, Netherlands. (p.181)

International Development Association (IDA) An affiliate of the World Bank (IBRD) that provides interest-free, long-term loans to developing states. (p.309)

International Finance Corporation (IFC) Created in 1956 to finance overseas investments by private companies without necessarily requiring government guarantees; borrows from the World Bank. (p.309)

international financial institutions (IFIs) International organizations created to manage and establish rules for the conduct of international financial transactions and macro-level initiatives for development and crisis response. (p.121)

International Joint Commission (IJC) Canada–U.S. body established by the Boundary Waters Treaty of 1909 to deal mainly with transborder water resource questions. Consists of three Canadian and three American commissioners. Provides analysis and rulings related to transborder environmental issues, such as Great Lakes pollution. (p.395)

International Monetary Fund (IMF) Autonomous but affiliated with the UN since 1947; designed to facilitate international trade, reduce inequities in exchange, and stabilize currencies. (p.123)

International Office of Weights and Measures Intergovernmental organization established in 1875 to standardize weights and measures; affiliated with the UN since 1949. (p.162)

International Organization for Migration (IOM) International organization established in 1951 and dedicated to the promotion of orderly and humane human migration. (p.161)

International Telecommunication Union (ITU) An amalgamation of the International Telegraph Union (established 1865) and the International Radiotelegraph Union (established 1906). Established in 1932 under the title of International Telecommunication Convention; renamed the International Telecommunication Union in 1934. (p.162)

International Union for Conservation of Nature (IUCN) Promotes sustainable development and preservation of nature; involves governments, NGOs, and networks of scientists; based in Gland, Switzerland. (p.394)

Internet An information network of computers that enables users to communicate and access information from all linked computers and other communications devices. Originated in a U.S. military communications project. (p.301)

Internet filtering One of several strategies used to control or restrict certain content or traffic flows over the Internet. Internet filtering is most often employed by governments to restrict popular access to certain information or websites. (p.449)

Intifada A series of clashes between Palestinian youths and Israeli security forces in the occupied territories that escalated into a full-scale revolt in December 1987. The El-Aqsa Intifada began in 2000. (p.248)

IOM See *International Organization for Migration.* (p.161)

Iron Age The historical epoch characterized by the widespread use of iron in tools and weapons. (p.48)

isolationism A foreign-policy approach emphasizing self-reliance and limited economic or political interaction with the international system. (p.63)

ITU See *International Telecommunication Union.* (p.162)

IUCN See *International Union for Conservation of Nature.* (p.394)

jus ad bellum Principles used to decide whether a war is just. (p.342)

jus cogens A principle of international law that is accepted with such universality and commitment by states as to be considered a legally incontestable norm. Examples include prohibition of genocide, slavery, and piracy. Sometimes referred to as *compelling law* or *peremptory norms.* (p.332)

jus in bello Principles used to decide what types of violence are permissible in war. (p.342)

Kellogg–Briand Pact Pact signed in 1928 by 44 states, renouncing war and promoting peaceful dispute settlement; named after U.S. Secretary of State Frank Kellogg and French Foreign Minister Aristide Briand. (p.14)

Kennan, George (1904–2005) American diplomat and historian; ambassador to the U.S.S.R., 1952. (p.91)

Keynesian liberalism An approach to liberal economics that calls for higher levels of government intervention and regulation in the market than envisioned by classical liberals. Named after the influential liberal economist John Maynard Keynes. (p.130)

Khmer Rouge (Red Cambodians) Communist rulers of Kampuchea, 1975–79, under Pol Pot and Leng Saray. (p.365)

Korean War North Korea attacked South Korea in June 1950; UN forces under American command joined in late June; Chinese communists joined North Korea in November 1950; armistice concluded in July 1953. Korea remains what many would consider to be the last Cold War front. (p.38)

La Francophonie Group of French-speaking states that meets to coordinate development policies, with 56 member states in 2013. (p.6)

LDCs See *less-developed countries.* (p.124)

League of Nations The international organization that existed, without American membership, between the end of World War I and the end of World War II. (p.14)

Lenin, Vladimir I. (1870–1924) Russian revolutionist and statesman; founder of Bolshevism, the Third International, and the Soviet Union. (p.24)

less-developed countries (LDCs) Those states with the lowest levels of socioeconomic development as defined by the UN in terms of income (less that US$750 per capita GNP), human resource weakness, and economic vulnerability. (p.124)

liberal feminists Thinkers who argue that women have unequal opportunities to contribute to society, and that this form of discrimination holds back the development of society as a whole. They do not seek to eliminate institutions but to change them through women's participation. (p.27)

liberal institutionalism A branch of liberal theory that emphasizes the leading role played by international organizations and regimes in world politics, especially in economic affairs. (p.21)

Liberal International Economic Order (LIEO) The theoretical principles and institutional structures that managed the world economy after World War II. (p.145)

liberalism Political philosophy emphasizing liberty and equality. In international relations, liberal theory describes global politics as increasingly interdependent. Liberals typically support international trade, institutions, law, and democratic systems of governance as a path to a more peaceful world. (p.13)

liberal realists A branch of realism (also referred to as *English School realists*) that characterizes global politics as fundamentally anarchic but strongly influenced by a society of states that adhere to strong norms and rules of behaviour most of the time. (p.19)

LIEO See *Liberal International Economic Order.* (p.145)

Lomé Convention Agreement concluded between the EU and over 70 African, Caribbean, and Pacific (ACP) countries, allowing the latter preferential trade relations and greater economic and technical assistance. Superseded by the Cotonou Agreement of 2003. (p.308)

long cycles The theory that hegemons rise and decline in regular patterns, which in turn influence the international economy and the outbreak of hegemonic wars. (p.200)

Luxemburg, Rosa (1870–1919) German Marxist. Founded Spartacus Party during World War I; wrote on imperialism. (p.24)

Maastricht Treaty Signed by European Community on February 7, 1992, outlining steps toward further integration. See *European Union.* (p.315)

MAD See *mutual assured destruction.* (p.88)

MAI See *Multilateral Agreement on Investment.* (p.293)

malnutrition Results from inadequate or unbalanced diet, usually deficient in protein, vitamins, or minerals. (p.7)

mangrove forests Ecosystems consisting of various forms of trees and bushes that thrive in tropical and sub-tropical sedimentary coastline areas. Many of the world's mangrove forest areas are threatened by sea level rise and storm surges due to climate change. (p.373)

marketization Movement away from state-controlled economy toward private property rights, open competition, trade liberalization, open investment, and floating currency. (p.298)

Marshall Plan U.S. Secretary of State George Marshall's 1947 plan to aid the reconstruction of European industry after World War II. (p.93)

Marx, Karl (1818–83) German economist and historian. Founder of the ideology of communism; proponent of historical materialism. (p.23)

mediation Efforts by an individual, group, or state to facilitate a negotiated agreement between two parties to a dispute. Mediation is an important instrument in global politics, and is often referred to as *third party mediation.* (p.265)

megacities Generally this refers to cities (usually including their immediate municipalities) with over 10 million inhabitants. (p.414)

mercantilism The perspective holding that international trade should be regulated by the state to maximize national income. Also known as *economic nationalism* and *neomercantilism*. (p.125)

middle powers Countries that do not possess the power attributes of the great powers but that can have a significant impact on international politics in certain specific regions or in certain specific issue-areas. Canada is often described as a middle power, though some call it a satellite of the United States. (p.32)

Millennium Development Goals A series of eight international development goals established at the United Nations Development Summit in 2000. (p.417)

MNC See *multinational corporation.* (p.21)

modernization A special paradigm of development, largely discredited today, evoking a progressive accumulation of social changes with a developmental sequence of industrialization, urbanization, education, communication, mobilization, and political participation. (p.299)

money laundering The effort and process of concealing the source of money or other assets, typically used by criminal organizations to transfer the proceeds of illegal activity into money and assets that can bought and sold in the legal economy. (p.236)

Most Favoured Nation (MFN) Term used in international trade to identify favoured trading partners. A country granted MFN status by another country is given trade access and privileges (such as low tariff barriers and national treatment provisions) such that they are treated the same as any other country with MFN status. (p.148)

multilateral Involving three or more states; usually connotes cooperative action. (p.6)

Multilateral Agreement on Investment (MAI) Originally an OECD-coordinated effort to protect foreign investors from governmental intrusion; disbanded but still on the larger WTO agenda. (p.293)

multilateralism See *multilateral.* (p.6)

multinational corporation (MNC) A profit-seeking enterprise with operations in at least two states. Powerful actors in global politics today. (p.21)

multipolar/multipolarity A distribution of power in which there are a number of poles, or great powers, in the system. This was characteristic of the pre–World War I era, and some analysts believe it can lead to instability. (p.74)

mutual assured destruction (MAD) The underlying nature of the nuclear stalemate between the superpowers during the Cold War. Both the United States and the Soviet Union possessed such large and capable arsenals that each side knew that if it attempted to attack the other with nuclear weapons, it would receive a devastating nuclear blow in return. As a result, both sides were deterred from using nuclear weapons against each other. See also *deterrence.* (p.88)

NAFO See *Northwest Atlantic Fisheries Organization.* (p.161)

NAFTA See *North American Free Trade Agreement.* (p.6)

NAM See *Nonaligned Movement.* (p.82)

nanotechnology The application of advances in atomic and molecular engineering. (p.293)

Napoleon Bonaparte (Napoleon I) (1769–1821) Emperor of France, 1804–15. Famous military general and political leader. (p.55)

Napoleon I See *Napoleon Bonaparte.* (p.55)

Napoleonic Wars (1796–1815) Waged by France under the French Revolution and later under Napoleon against England, Austria, Prussia, Russia, and most of the other countries of Europe. Ended with France's defeat at Waterloo. (p.55)

nationalism A sense of shared identity among a group of people, especially with respect to an ideology of attachment to a nation and to its shared interests. (p.55)

nationalization A government's assumption of the ownership of property, often previously owned by citizens from another state. Famous cases include the nationalization of the Suez Canal, and

Cuban and Iranian appropriation of American commercial property. (p.95)

NATO See *North Atlantic Treaty Organization*. (p.6)

natural law A system of law binding on individuals by virtue of their nature as rational human beings. Natural law is considered universal across the human experience. (p.179)

neo-Gramscian A theoretical approach associated with the critical theory developed by Antonio Gramsci, emphasizing the importance of social forces and ideas in the construction of world order. (p.295)

neo-Malthusian perspective Argument that resources will be outstripped by population growth in the modern era; has led to calls for strict population control. (p.413)

neo-Marxist Scholar who amends and/or extends Marxist ideas in order to explain contemporary global politics and economic conditions. Neo-Marxists developed theories such as "dependency" and "the world system" to illustrate how neoliberal capitalism hindered development and brought increased inequality between states and peoples in the global economy. (p.25)

neorealist A realist scholar whose work emphasizes the importance of structural explanations like anarchy for power politics over the importance of human nature or domestic politics. (p.17)

New International Economic Order (NIEO) Statement of priorities adopted at the Sixth Special Session of the UN General Assembly in 1974, calling for equal participation of LDCs in the North–South dialogue. (p.308)

New START A bilateral arms treaty signed in 2010 by the U.S. and Russia, further reducing nuclear warheads and tightening verification measures. Expires in 2021. (p.89)

NGOs See *non-governmental organizations*. (p.5)

NIEO See *New International Economic Order*. (p.308)

Nonaligned Movement (NAM) An effort begun in 1955 by developing countries to cooperate on issues of joint interest, especially decolonization, neutrality in the Cold War, and a more favourable international economic environment for their products. The NAM is largely moribund today. (p.82)

non-discrimination A principle of free trade that requires any member of a trade organization or agreement (such as the WTO) to treat all imports entering the country in the same way. In other words, states cannot discriminate against some members of a trade agreement by imposing higher tariffs on a good coming from one country while lowering the tariff on the same good coming from another country. The tariff must be the same for both countries, provided both countries are members of the trade agreement. (p.148)

non-governmental organizations (NGOs) Groups of individuals that do not represent the views of governments; usually operating for the purpose of charity or value propagation. (p.5)

Non-Proliferation Treaty Treaty signed in 1968 and in force in 1970, aimed at preventing the spread of nuclear weapons to more states, while promoting the use of "peaceful nuclear power." (p.161)

non-specific compensation A conflict management technique in which one party to a dispute agrees to offer the other an incentive or payoff (that was not part of the original dispute) in an effort to reach an agreement. (p.247)

non-tariff barriers Erected by a government to discourage imports, usually consisting of formal and voluntary quotas, prohibitions of certain imports, discriminatory restrictions, and licensing requirements. Now the main way governments restrict international trade and engage in protectionism. (p.148)

NORAD See *North American Air Defence Agreement*. (p.84)

normative theory Normative theory focuses on values and value preferences. It is primarily concerned with explaining what ought to be, rather than what is. Propositions in normative theory typically do not require empirical testing as a means of establishing their validity. (p.483)

norms Collective or shared beliefs about appropriate and inappropriate behaviour. In international relations, norms are taken by liberals to be important influences over the actions of states and non-state actors. (p.19)

North American Air Defence Agreement (NORAD) Signed on May 12, 1958, by the United States and Canada, creating a continental air defence (and later ballistic missile defence) warning and surveillance system in response to Cold War fears of an airborne attack by the former Soviet Union. In 1981 it was renamed the North American Aerospace Defence Agreement. (p.84)

North American Free Trade Agreement (NAFTA) Trilateral economic agreement reducing barriers on trade between Canada, the United States, and Mexico; contains side agreements on labour rights and environmental protection. (p.6)

North Atlantic Treaty Organization (NATO) Collective defence alliance and international organization created in 1949 to prevent the U.S.S.R. from attaining political influence or territorial conquests in Europe. Composed of 28 states in 2013, the alliance has restructured itself after the Cold War and admitted many new members. NATO headquarters is in Brussels. (p.6)

Northwest Atlantic Fisheries Organization (NAFO) International organization of 14 members established to regulate fishing in the northwest Atlantic; the secretariat is in Dartmouth, Nova Scotia. (p.161)

Nuremberg war crimes trials (1945–49) Trials of Nazis for war crimes by an international military tribunal; several were subsequently executed. See *war crimes trials*. (p.70)

OAS See *Organization of American States.* (p.161)

OECD See *Organisation for Economic Co-operation and Development.* (p.155)

Offensive Realism Approach in the realist school of international relations theory that suggests states seek survival and self-help in an anarchic

system primarily through offensive policies such as conquest and expansion, rather than defensive policies. (p.19)

omnicide Literally, the killing of all life, as might result from a nuclear war. (p.88)

one-child policy The official population-control policy of the government of China introduced in 1978. Under the policy, urban Chinese households are restricted to one child. Exceptions are made for couples with twins, rural-area families, ethnic minorities, and couples who are only children themselves. (p.412)

OPEC See *Organization of the Petroleum Exporting Countries.* (p.124)

Organisation for Economic Co-operation and Development (OECD) An organization of 30 industrialized states organized around the principles of representative democracy and free market economics. (p.155)

Organization for Security and Co-operation in Europe (OSCE) A multilateral forum for discussing a wide range of political questions in Europe; includes Canada, the United States, Russia, and all of the European states. Established in 1995 to give permanent staff and headquarters to the Council on Security and Co-operation in Europe (CSCE). (p.265)

Organization of American States (OAS) Intergovernmental organization of 35 states of North and South America established in 1948 as a forum for political dialogue. Canada joined in 1990. (p.161)

Organization of the Petroleum Exporting Countries (OPEC) Producers' cartel setting price floors and production ceilings of crude petroleum; its members are the Arab oil producers (Saudi Arabia, Kuwait, the United Arab Emirates, Qatar, Iran, Iraq, Algeria, and Libya), Nigeria, Venezuela, and Indonesia. (p.124)

OSCE See *Organization for Security and Co-operation in Europe.* (p.265)

peace movement A social movement composed of various organizations and groups mobilized around the cause of peace, either in general terms or with respect to a certain war (for example, Vietnam or Iraq) or a possible war (Cold War). Peace movements advocate a number of strategies, including pacifism, non-violent resistance, boycotts, diplomacy, the support of antiwar political candidates, and peaceful demonstrations. (p.178)

per capita Per person; when aggregate statistical information, such as GNP, is put into per-person form, it is expressed as so many units per capita. (p.292)

perestroika Economic reform policies instituted by Mikhail Gorbachev in the Soviet Union in the late 1980s. (p.99)

Persistent Organic Pollutants (POPs) Waste product compounds resistant to environmental degradation. POPs can travel over large distances in the environment, accumulate in flora and fauna (including the human body), and cause long-term environmental and health effects. (p.396)

Peter I See *Peter the Great.* (p.54)

Peter the Great (Peter I) (1672–1725) Czar of Russia, 1682–1725. Founder of the modern Russian state. (p.54)

polar ice caps The ice-covered polar regions of planets, but in common usage the polar ice caps of the Earth. The extensive change in the thickness and extent of the polar ice caps in recent decades is one of the most prominent features of climate change. (p.373)

polarity The number of poles, or concentrations of power, in a region or in the international system. Systems with one dominant concentration of power are called *unipolar*; those with two, *bipolar*; and those with many, *multipolar*. (p.74)

Politburo The supreme decision-making body of the Soviet Union during the Cold War. (p.100)

pooled sovereignty The voluntary sharing or ceding of some sovereign decision-making powers by states to a cooperative, institutional framework. The European Union is often cited as an example of pooled sovereignty. (p.315)

postcolonial feminists Postcolonial feminists emphasize the experiences and perspectives of postcolonial women. Their philosophy is based on the experiences of racism and colonialism in postcolonial economic, political, and cultural contexts. (p.27)

Prisoner's Dilemma In game theory, a model that demonstrates how two actors can make self-interested decisions based on distrust and isolation from one another that leave them worse off than if they had trusted one another and cooperated instead. (p.115)

privatize The transfer of publicly operated and owned assets or organizations from government management and control to the private sector. (p.377)

proletariat The ancient Roman word for those so poor that they could only give birth to children for military service. Karl Marx and Friedrich Engels used the term to represent the working-class elements in society. (p.23)

protectionism Using tariffs and non-tariff barriers to control or restrict the flow of imports into a state in order to protect domestic industry; usually associated with neomercantilism. (p.127)

proxy wars Wars, usually in the South, in which the great powers are indirectly involved. (p.80)

public goods Publicly funded and regulated services or infrastructure, open to use by all members of a society; in the international sense, the provision of political, military, and economic stability by a hegemon. (p.138)

quota A quantitative limitation imposed by government, usually applied to inflows of goods or migrants. (p.309)

radical feminists Radical feminists emphasize the patriarchal roots of inequality between men and women, or more specifically the social dominance of women by men. They view patriarchy as dividing rights, privileges, and power primarily by gender, and as a result oppressing women and privileging men. They are skeptical of political action within the current system, and instead support broader and more transformational social changes to eliminate patriarchy. (p.27)

ratification Official state approval of an international treaty, achieved when a state legislature approves (ratifies) a treaty by passing the necessary laws to align domestic law and regulation with treaty obligations. International treaties enter into force (that is, are activated) only when a certain number of signatory states ratify the treaty. (p.259)

rational actor model A theory of decision making based on rational actors making decisions in a rational choice process, designed to maximize their desired outcomes. (p.107)

realpolitik A German word meaning practical politics, but generally employed as a synonym for power politics in the realist tradition. (p.15)

recession Rise in unemployment, decline of investment and growth; usually a period of less than a year. Recessions in important markets cause international concern. (p.291)

reciprocity The principle that a state should reciprocate when another state grants it trade concessions. This reciprocity should come in the form of trade concessions equivalent in value to the concessions granted to it by its trading partners. (p.148)

Red Cambodians See *Khmer Rouge.* (p.365)

refugee A person who has fled outside the borders of his or her country of origin because of fear of persecution, discrimination, or political oppression. (p.26)

regime Rules, principles, and decision-making procedures governing international behaviour in certain issue areas. (p.21)

regime theory A theory, grounded in the liberal tradition, that argues that international institutions or regimes affect the behaviour of states through rules, principles, and decision-making procedures. (p.185)

relative gains The difference between actors experiencing a different rate of increase in some measure of capacity (such as economic wealth). If one actor is gaining capacity relative to the other actors, it is experiencing a relative gain with respect to the others. (p.125)

repatriation The resettlement by a refugee in his or her home state. (p.423)

reprisal A hostile, illegal act rendered legal when carried out in response to a previous illegal act. (p.181)

resolution Formal decision of an international organization, usually either registering a widely held or consensus opinion and/or recommending some sort of action (for example, a UN Security Council Resolution). (p.95)

Responsibility to Protect (R2P) A principle established at the UN World Summit in 2005 with the aim to address the inability of the world community to protect populations from wars, genocides, and other violent events; if states are unable to protect their own citizens, then international intervention is warranted. Though some analysts claim this is a norm, others argue it is used as a justification for selective interventions. (p.262)

Revolution in Military Affairs (RMA) The idea that military history has developed in a series of dramatic shifts in military capability, based on technological and social developments. The current RMA is based on computers and the information age. (p.471)

robotics Use of highly complex machines to perform complicated manufacturing tasks. See *automation.* (p.472)

Rousseau, Jean Jacques (1712–78) French philosopher, author of *The Social Contract.* Influenced the concept of popular sovereignty. (p.18)

SALT See **Strategic Arms Limitation Treaties.** (p.90)

SAPs See *structural adjustment programs.* (p.309)

SARS See *severe acute respiratory syndrome.* (p.434)

satisficing Propensity of decision makers to select an alternative or option that meets minimally acceptable standards at that moment. (p.108)

Schlieffen Plan The German military strategy for the conquest of France, put into action in WWI. The plan called for German armies to sweep through neutral Belgium and envelop Paris. (p.61)

Secretariat The administrative organ of the UN, headed by the Secretary-General; more generally, the administrative branch of any international organization. (p.170)

Secretary-General Chief administrative officer of the UN who also plays an important, if often controversial, diplomatic role. (p.161)

securitization In international relations theory, a concept associated with constructivist approaches to international relations that explores the process of how and why an issue becomes identified as a security concern or threat to a state or a group, and how this process influences responses and policies. (p.411)

Security Council Fifteen states (five permanent members) sit on this chief collective security organ of the UN. The permanent members are the U.S., France, China, Russia, and the U.K. (p.165)

security dilemma A product of international anarchy in which states seek to rely on their own means to ensure their security by developing their military forces. In doing so, they inspire fear and distrust in their neighbours, who also arm. This reaction starts an arms race in which none of the participants is any more secure (and may in fact be less secure) than it was initially. (p.18)

self-determination The claim that people have the right to self-rule and (should they desire it) statehood. (p.196)

severe acute respiratory syndrome (SARS) Deadly form of pneumonia, which emerged from China in November 2002 and infected many people in other countries, including Canada. (p.434)

Shiite The smaller of the two major branches of Islam, consisting of those who regard Ali, son-in-law of Muhammad, as the prophet's legitimate successor. (p.44)

SLBM See *submarine-launched ballistic missile.* (p.90)

small states Term used to identify those states that are the weakest in terms of power in a regional or global context. (p.77)

socialist or Marxist feminists Focus on the links between capitalism and patriarchy as the fundamental cause of women's oppression and identify "class" rather than "sex" as the ultimate cause of women's oppression. (p.27)

soft power Elements of state power—such as ideological attractiveness, culture, information capacity, and education—that have traditionally been disregarded (especially by realists) in favour of military or economic strength. (p.20)

sovereignty A government's ability to manage internal affairs and independently represent itself externally. A principle securing non-interference from other states, the keystone of the Charter of the UN. (p.33)

START See *Strategic Arms Reduction Treaty.* Superseded by SORT and then New START. (p.90)

state A political entity possessing determined territory, permanent population, active government, and sovereign recognition by other states. Can also refer to the governing element of society with a monopoly on legitimate coercive violence or the instrument of the ruling economic classes. (p.9)

state-sponsored terrorism Government support for terrorist individuals or groups acting abroad. (p.224)

state terrorism The use of state power to terrorize civilians into compliance. (p.223)

Strategic Arms Limitation Treaties Treaties between United States and U.S.S.R., signed in 1972 and 1979. (p.90)

Strategic Arms Reduction Treaty (START) Two treaties, START I and START II, reached between the United States and the U.S.S.R./Russia that made deep cuts in the nuclear arsenals of both countries. (p.90)

structural adjustment programs (SAPs) Economic policies established as conditions for IMF or World Bank loans to developing countries, usually requiring such countries to limit their spending, eliminate subsidies, and promote trade liberalization. (p.309)

structural realists Structural realists consider anarchy (absence of global government) as the central organizing principle of the international system; this structure forces states to pursue power for their own survival. Contemporary structural realists such as Kenneth Waltz, John Mearsheimer, and Robert Jervis are also often known as *neorealists*. (p.17)

submarine-launched ballistic missile (SLBM) A ballistic missile launched from a nuclear-capable submarine. (p.90)

subsidies Government programs that extend direct financial support, tax exemptions, or low-interest credit to certain firms engaged in the research or production of goods with considerable economic potential. Subsidies are used by governments to assist certain economic sectors to ensure their growth or survival. (p.127)

summit diplomacy The diplomatic practice of engaging in negotiation or reaching agreement on international issues through the summit meetings of high-level officials or heads of state and government. (p.245)

Sunni The larger of the two major branches of Islam, consisting of those who regard the first four caliphs as the legitimate successors of Muhammad. (p.44)

superpowers The former U.S.S.R. and the United States during the Cold War era. (p.80)

synthesis An idea formed by a combination of other ideas. (p.9)

tariff A tax levied on imports. Free traders aim to eliminate them. (p.127)

technological convergence The idea that differing societies are using the same technologies and thus moving toward more common cultures. (p.469)

Thirty Years' War (1618–48) General European war fought mainly in Germany; petty German princes and foreign powers (France, Sweden, Denmark, England) against the Holy Roman Empire (Hapsburgs in Austria, Germany, Italy, the Netherlands, and Spain); also a religious war of Protestants against Catholics. Ended with the Treaty of Westphalia. (p.43)

tied aid Foreign aid extended to recipient countries on the condition that at least part of the aid

will be used to purchase goods and services from the donor country; most bilateral aid is in fact some form of tied aid. (p.310)

torture Deliberate inflicting of pain, physical or psychological, often state-directed. (p.332)

trade Exchanges of products, services, or money between states. (p.103)

trade-related intellectual property rights (TRIPs) An issue in international trade law and GATT/WTO negotiations concerning the protection of patent and copyright holders from piracy and copyright infringement. (p.149)

transnational Term commonly used to denote an actor, process, or event that has an impact across borders, such as transnational corporation, transnational organized crime, and transnational governance. (p.5)

Trans Pacific Partnership (TPP) Proposed free trade agreement under negotiation since 2010, with over 10 participating countries (including Canada). (p.317)

Trilateral Commission A commission, formed in 1973 by private citizens from the United States, Europe, and Japan, that produces advice for governments and others regarding the management of the global economy. (p.154)

TRIPs See *trade-related intellectual property rights.* (p.149)

Truman Doctrine Outlined to Congress by U.S. President Truman in March 1947 in support of the Greek–Turkish aid bill; calls for the containment of communism by giving aid to like-minded governments. (p.91)

Trusteeship Council Originally one of the main organs of the UN, authorized to examine and discuss the political, economic, social, and educational advancement of the peoples of Trust Territories, the Council is now defunct. (p.166)

unacceptable damage The prospective costs of fighting a war (number of casualties and/or level of destruction) considered sufficient to deter an aggressor from starting a war. In deterrence theory, the ability of a state to retaliate after a nuclear attack and inflict unacceptable damage on the attacking state will deter such an attack. During the Cold War there were various formulas as to what constituted unacceptable damage, including the ability of each side to kill 50 percent of the other's population. (p.87)

UN Children's Fund (UNICEF) UN agency established in 1946 to provide food and health care to children after World War II; now provides humanitarian and development assistance to millions of mothers and children worldwide. (p.296)

UN Conference on Trade and Development (UNCTAD) A coalition of Southern or developing states that began meeting in 1964. (p.161)

UN Development Programme (UNDP) Coordinates and supports UN development projects. (p.161)

UN Educational, Scientific, and Cultural Organization (UNESCO) Founded in 1945 as a specialized UN agency, located in Paris, France. It develops ideas and establishes standards on education, culture, and communication. (p.161)

UN Environment Program (UNEP) UN agency that leads international effort to protect the environment and promote sustainable growth. Many extant multilateral environmental agreements were created by or are associated with UNEP. (p.375)

UNCTAD See *UN Conference on Trade and Development.* (p.161)

UNDP See *UN Development Programme.* (p.161)

UNESCO See *UN Educational, Scientific, and Cultural Organization.* (p.161)

UNHCR See *UN High Commissioner for Refugees.* (p.423)

UN High Commissioner for Refugees (UNHCR) Established in 1950 by the UN General Assembly to safeguard the rights and well-being of refugees and to lead and coordinate international action to protect refugees and resolve refugee problems worldwide. (p.423)

UNICEF See *UN Children's Fund.* (p.296)

unilateral One-sided; said of the actions of a state taken without consultation or approval of others. (p.18)

unipolar/unipolarity A region or international system in which there is one dominant actor. Some argue that the current international system is a unipolar one, with the United States as the one remaining superpower. (p.75)

Universal Postal Union (UPU) Established in 1874 with headquarters in Bern, Switzerland; became a specialized agency of the UN in 1947. (p.162)

UPU See *Universal Postal Union.* (p.162)

urban bias A phenomenon wherein development policy tends to favour urban development as opposed to rural development, discussed in the 1970s by Michael Lipton. (p.416)

urbanization The process of growth, often rapid, of cities. (p.411)

USAID American foreign-aid department. (p.417)

verification Process of determining that all sides of an international agreement are in compliance. (p.258)

Versailles Treaty The principal treaty terminating World War I. (p.62)

veto The right to prohibit certain actions. The permanent members of the Security Council have a veto over the Council's substantive actions. (p.94)

war crimes Includes perpetrating mass murder; ill-treatment, deportation, or forced labour of prisoners; killing hostages; plunder; and wanton destruction with no military necessity. (p.344)

war crimes trials Prosecution of war criminals by an international tribunal, following World War II at Nuremberg and Tokyo, and presently at The Hague. May also take place within domestic jurisdiction of states. (p.344)

Warsaw Pact A treaty signed by the Soviet bloc states in 1955 pledging mutual military allegiance to the Soviet Union; dissolved in 1991. (p.81)

Washington Consensus Package of policies and practices championed by the U.S. government and private sector as a guide to development policy. The Washington Consensus advocates fiscal discipline, privatization, and deregulation as the best development options for poor states. The package was widely criticized as a recipe for social hardship and upheaval in developing countries. (p.300)

weapons of mass destruction (WMD) Most commonly refers to unconventional weapons, specifically nuclear, chemical, biological, and radiological weapons. (p.196)

weighted voting A system of voting, such as that used in the IBRD, where the value of a member's vote is determined by the contribution (usually financial) the member makes. (p.309)

Weimar Republic (1919–33) German state established under a democratic federal constitution passed by a constitutional assembly in the city of Weimar. (p.488)

West Nile A mosquito-borne virus common in temperate and tropical areas of the world. The virus has spread rapidly in recent decades and is now a prominent global health concern, with increasing death rates and no vaccine currently available. (p.434)

WHO See *World Health Organization.* **(p.417)**

Wilson, Woodrow (1856–1924) Twenty-seventh president of the United States, 1913–21; known for his internationalism. (p.13)

World Bank This institution, which was formally known as the International Bank for Reconstruction and Development and includes the International Development Agency, is a leading lender of money for development purposes. The World Bank Group includes the World Bank and three other agencies: the International Finance Corporation (IFC), the Multilateral Investment Guarantee Agency (MIGA), and the International Centre for Settlement of Investment Disputes (ICSID). (p.132)

World Health Organization (WHO) A specialized agency of the UN, headquartered in Geneva, founded in 1948 to promote and assist global health programs, including children's immunization and infectious disease surveillance. (p.417)

World System Theory A theoretical approach that emphasizes the global character of capitalism as the organizing principle of international politics. (p.135)

World Trade Organization (WTO) International organization established in 1995 as the successor to the GATT. Headquartered in Geneva, it has 153 member states and is the central forum for international negotiations on world trade. (p.128)

WTO See *World Trade Organization.* **(p.128)**

xenophobia A strong dislike, fear, or suspicion of other groups or nationalities. (p.421)

Yalta Conference A February 1945 summit meeting of Franklin Roosevelt, Josef Stalin, and Winston Churchill at which major postwar issues were discussed, such as the status of Central and Eastern Europe and voting arrangements in the UN. (p.164)

zero-sum game A relationship in which a gain for one actor entails a loss for another actor. Realists saw the Cold War as a zero-sum game. (p.75)

Index